SIMONE DE BEAUVOIR

The Second Sex

Simone de Beauvoir was born in Paris in 1908. In 1929 she became the youngest person ever to obtain the *agrégation* in philosophy at the Sorbonne, placing second to Jean-Paul Sartre. She taught in lycées in Marseille and Rouen from 1931 to 1937, and in Paris from 1938 to 1943. After the war, she emerged as one of the leaders of the existentialist movement, working with Sartre on *Les Temps Modernes*. The author of many books, including the novel *The Mandarins* (1957), which was awarded the Prix Goncourt, Beauvoir was one of the most influential thinkers of her generation. She died in 1986.

Constance Borde and Sheila Malovany-Chevallier have lived in Paris for more than forty years and are both graduates of Rutgers University, New Jersey. Borde and Malovany-Chevallier were faculty members at the Institut d'Études Politiques. They have been translating books and articles on social science, art, and feminist literature for many years and have jointly authored numerous books in English and in French on subjects ranging from grammar to politics to American cooking.

The Second Sex

SIMONE DE BEAUVOIR | *The Second Sex*

63

TRANSLATED BY CONSTANCE BORDE
AND SHEILA MALOVANY-CHEVALLIER

With an Introduction by Judith Thurman

VINTAGE BOOKS
A DIVISION OF RANDOM HOUSE, INC.
NEW YORK

FIRST VINTAGE BOOKS EDITION, MAY 2011

Le deuxième sexe copyright © *1949 by Éditions Gallimard, Paris*
Translation copyright © 2009 by Constance Borde and Sheila Malovany-Chevallier
Introduction copyright © 2010 by Judith Thurman

The Library of Congress has cataloged the Knopf edition as follows:
Beauvoir, Simone de, 1908–1986.
[Deuxième sexe. English]
The second sex / Simone de Beauvoir ; translated by Constance Borde and
Sheila Malovany Chevallier.
p. cm.
Includes bibliographical references and index.
1. Women. I. Borde, Constance. II. Malovany-Chevallier, Sheila. III. Title.
HQ1208.B352 2010
305.401—dc22
2009023164

Vintage ISBN: 978-0-307-27778-7

Book design by Pei Koay

www.vintagebooks.com

Printed in the United States of America
10 9 8 7

To Jacques Bost

There is a good principle that created
order, light, and man
and a bad principle that created
chaos, darkness, and woman.

—PYTHAGORAS

Everything that has been written by men
about women should be viewed with suspicion,
because they are both judge and party.

—POULAIN DE LA BARRE

Introduction

In 1946, Simone de Beauvoir began to outline what she thought would be an autobiographical essay explaining why, when she had tried to define herself, the first sentence that came to mind was "I am a woman." That October, my maiden aunt, Beauvoir's contemporary, came to visit me in the hospital nursery. I was a day old, and she found a little tag on my bassinet that announced, "It's a Girl!" In the next bassinet was another newborn ("a lot punier," she recalled), whose little tag announced, "I'm a Boy!" There we lay, innocent of a distinction—between a female object and a male subject—that would shape our destinies. It would also shape Beauvoir's great treatise on the subject.

Beauvoir was then a thirty-eight-year-old public intellectual who had been enfranchised for only a year. Legal birth control would be denied to French women until 1967, and legal abortion, until 1975. Not until the late 1960s was there an elected female head of state anywhere in the world. Girls of my generation searching for examples of exceptional women outside the ranks of queens and courtesans, and of a few artists and saints, found precious few. (The queens, as Beauvoir remarks, "were neither male nor female: they were sovereigns.") Opportunities for women have proliferated so broadly in the past six decades, at least in the Western world, that the distance between 2010 and 1949, when *The Second Sex* was published in France, seems like an eternity (until, that is, one opens a newspaper—the victims of misogyny and sexual abuse are still with us, everywhere). While no one individual or her work is responsible for that seismic shift in laws and attitudes, the millions of young women who now confidently assume that their entitlement to work, pleasure, and autonomy is equal to that of their brothers owe a measure of their freedom to Beauvoir. *The Second Sex* was an act of Promethean audacity—a theft of Olympian fire—from which there was no turning back. It is not the last word on "the problem of woman," which, Beauvoir wrote, "has always been a problem of men," but it marks the place in history where an enlightenment begins.

———

Simone-Ernestine-Lucie-Marie Bertrand de Beauvoir was born in 1908 into a reactionary Catholic family with pretensions to nobility. She had a Proustian childhood on the Boulevard Saint-Germain, in Paris. But after World War I, her father, Georges, lost most of his fortune, and without dowries Simone and her sister, Hélène, had dim prospects for a marriage within their class. Their mother, Françoise, a banker's daughter who had never lived without servants, did all the housework and sewing for the family. Her pious martyrdom indelibly impressed Simone, who would improve upon Virginia Woolf's famous advice and move to a room of her own—in a hotel, with maid service. Like Woolf, and a striking number of other great women writers,[1] Beauvoir was childless. And like Colette, who wasn't (she relegated her late-born, only daughter to the care of surrogates), she regarded motherhood as a threat to her integrity. Colette is a ubiquitous presence in *The Second Sex*, which gives a new perspective to her boast, in a memoir of 1946, that "my strain of virility saved me from the danger which threatens the writer, elevated to a happy and tender parent, of becoming a mediocre author . . . Beneath the still young woman that I was, an old boy of forty saw to the well-being of a possibly precious part of myself."

Mme de Beauvoir, intent on keeping up a facade of gentility, however shabby, sent her daughters to an elite convent school where Simone, for a while, ardently desired to become a nun, one of the few respectable vocations open to an ambitious girl. When she lost her faith as a teenager, her dreams of a transcendent union (dreams that proved remarkably tenacious) shifted from Christ to an enchanting classmate named ZaZa and to a rich, indolent first cousin and childhood playmate, Jacques, who took her slumming and gave her a taste for alcohol and for louche nightlife that she never outgrew. (Not many bookish virgins with a particle in their surname got drunk with the hookers and drug addicts at Le Styx.) Her mother hoped vainly that the worthless Jacques would propose. Her father, a

---

1. Jane Austen, George Eliot, Emily Brontë, Charlotte Brontë, Emily Dickinson, Louisa May Alcott, Christina Rossetti, Lou Andreas-Salomé, Gertrude Stein, Christina Stead, Isak Dinesen, Katherine Mansfield, Edith Wharton, Simone Weil, Willa Cather, Carson McCullers, Anna de Noailles, Djuna Barnes, Marianne Moore, Hilda Doolittle, Marguerite Yourcenar, Sigrid Undset, Else Lasker-Schüler, Eudora Welty, Lillian Hellman, Monique Wittig, to name a few.

ladies' man, knew better: he told his temperamental, ill-dressed, pimply genius of a daughter that she would never marry. But by then Simone de Beauvoir had seen what a woman of almost any quality—highborn or low, pure or impure, contented with her lot or alienated—could expect from a man's world.

Beauvoir's singular brilliance was apparent from a young age to her teachers, and to herself. An insatiable curiosity and a prodigious capacity for synthetic reading and analysis (a more inspired grind may never have existed) nourished her drive. One of her boyfriends dubbed her Castor (the Beaver), a nickname that stuck. She had a sense of inferiority, it would appear, only in relation to Jean-Paul Sartre. They met in 1929, as university students (she a star at the Sorbonne, he at the Ecole Normale Supérieure), cramming, as a team, for France's most brutal and competitive postgraduate examination, the *agrégation* in philosophy. (On their first study date, she explained Leibniz to him.) Success would qualify her for a lifetime sinecure teaching at a lycée, and liberate her from her family. When the results were posted, Sartre was first and Beauvoir second (she was the ninth woman who had ever passed), and that, forever, was the order of precedence—Adam before Eve—in their creation myth as a couple.

Even though their ideal was of a love without domination, it was part of the myth that Sartre was Beauvoir's first man. After Georges de Beauvoir confronted them (they had been living together more or less openly), Sartre, the more bourgeois, proposed marriage, and Beauvoir told him "not to be silly." She had emerged from her age of awkwardness as a severe beauty with high cheekbones and a regal forehead who wore her dark hair plaited and rolled—an old-fashioned duenna's coif rather piquantly at odds with her appetites and behavior. Both sexes attracted her, and Sartre was never the most compelling of her lovers, but they recognized that each possessed something uniquely necessary to the other. As he put it one afternoon, walking in the Tuileries, "You and I together are as one" (*on ne fait qu'un*). He categorized their union as an "essential" love that only death could sunder, although in time, he said, they would naturally both have "contingent" loves—freely enjoyed and fraternally confessed in a spirit of "authenticity." (She often recruited, and shared, his girls, some of whom were her students, and her first novel, *She Came to Stay*, in 1943, was based on one of their ménages à trois.) "At every level," Beauvoir reflected, years later, of the pain she had suffered and inflicted, "we failed to face the weight of reality, priding ourselves on what we called our 'radical freedom.'" But they also failed to fault themselves for the contingent casualties—the inessential others—who were sacrificed to their experiment. And the burden of free love, Beauvoir would discover, was grossly unequal for a woman and for a man.

If Beauvoir has proved to be an irresistible subject for biographers, it is, in part, because she and Sartre, as a pharaonic couple of incestuous deities, reigned over twentieth-century French intellectual life in the decades of its greatest ferment. But the most fascinating subjects tend to be those richest in contradictions, and *The Second Sex,* no less than Beauvoir's prolific and important fiction, memoirs, and correspondence, seethes with them. Deirdre Bair, Beauvoir's biographer, touches upon a fundamental paradox in the introduction to her admirable life. She and Sartre's biographer Annie Cohen-Solal had been lecturing together at Harvard. At the conclusion of their talk, she writes, "I could not help but comment to my distinguished audience that every question asked about Sartre concerned his work, while all those asked about Beauvoir concerned her personal life." Yet Sartre's work, and specifically the existentialist notion of an opposition between a sovereign self—a subject—and an objectified Other, gave Beauvoir the conceptual scaffold for *The Second Sex,*[2] while her life as a woman (indeed, as Sartre's woman) impelled her to write it. He had once told her that she had "a man's intelligence," and there is no evidence that he changed his mind about a patronizing slight that she, too, accepted as a compliment until she began to consider what it implied. It implied, she would write, that "humanity is male, and man defines woman, not in herself, but in relation to himself," and by all the qualities (Colette's strain of "virility") she is presumed to lack. Her "twinship" with Sartre was an illusion.

The Second Sex has been called a "feminist bible," an epithet bound to discourage impious readers wary of a sacred text and a personality cult. Beauvoir herself was as devout an atheist as she had once been a Catholic, and she dismisses religions—even when they worship a goddess—as the inventions of men to perpetuate their dominion. The analogy is fitting, though, and not only to the grandeur of a book that was the first of its kind but also to its structure. Beauvoir begins her narrative, like the author of

---

2. It has been credited by Beauvoir and others for having given her the scaffold, although a journal from her university years, which was discovered after her death by her companion and adopted daughter, Sylvie Le Bon de Beauvoir, suggests that Beauvoir had arrived at the notion of a fundamental conflict between self and Other before she met Sartre, partly through her reading of Henri Bergson, but partly through her own struggle—an explicit and implicit subtext of *The Second Sex*—with an imperious need for love that she experienced as a temptation to self-abnegation.

Genesis, with a fall into knowledge. The two volumes that elaborate on the consequences of that fall are the Old and New Testaments of an unchosen people with a history of enslavement. ("Facts and Myths" is a chronicle of womankind from prehistory to the 1940s; "Lived Experience" is a minutely detailed case study of contemporary womanhood and its stations of the cross from girlhood through puberty and sexual initiation to maturity and old age, with detours from the well-trodden road to Calvary taken by mystics and lesbians.) The epic concludes, like Revelation, with an eloquent, if utopian, vision of redemption:

> The same drama of flesh and spirit, and of finitude and transcendence, plays itself out in both sexes; both are eaten away by time, stalked by death, they have the same essential need of the other; and they can take the same glory from their freedom; if they knew how to savor it, they would no longer be tempted to contend for false privileges; and fraternity could then be born between them.

The first English edition of *The Second Sex* was published in 1953. Blanche Knopf, the wife of Alfred Knopf, Beauvoir's American publisher, had heard of the book on a scouting trip to Paris. Thinking that this sensational literary property was a highbrow sex manual, she had asked an academic who knew about the birds and the bees, H. M. Parshley, a retired professor of zoology at Smith College, for a reader's report. His enthusiasm for the work ("intelligent, learned, and well-balanced . . . not feminist in any doctrinaire sense") won him the commission to translate it. But Alfred Knopf asked Parshley to condense the text, noting, without undue masculine gallantry, that Beauvoir "certainly suffers from verbal diarrhea." Parshley appealed to the author for advice on the "minor cuts and abridgments" that Knopf felt were essential for the American market. She was either too busy or unwilling to reply, because he heard nothing until he received an indignant letter protesting that "so much of what seems important to me will have been omitted." But she signed off graciously on the edition.

While the translation was a labor of love from which Parshley nearly expired, he lacked a background in philosophy, or in French literature. He also lacked a credential more pertinent, perhaps, to the audience for a foundational work of modern feminism, a second X chromosome. This eagerly awaited new translation, by Constance Borde and Sheila Malovany-Chevallier—the first since Parshley's—is a magisterial exercise in fidelity. The cuts have been restored, and the English is as lucid and elegant as

Beauvoir's ambition to be exhaustive permits it to be. She is a bold, saga-
cious, often dazzling writer and a master aphorist,[3] but no one would
accuse her of being a lapidary stylist. It is hard to find a description for the
prose that does justice both to its incisive power and to its manic garrulity.
Elizabeth Hardwick came closest, perhaps, when she called *The Second Sex*
"madly sensible and brilliantly confused."

The stamina that it takes to read *The Second Sex* in its entirety pales
before the feat of writing it. (Sartre was happy when his beaver was busy,
Beauvoir told Bair, because "I was no bother to him.") One is humbled to
learn that this eight-hundred-page encyclopedia of the folklore, customs,
laws, history, religion, philosophy, anthropology, literature, economic systems, and received ideas that have, since time began, objectified women
was researched and composed in about fourteen months,[4] between 1946
and 1949, while Beauvoir was also engaged with other literary projects,
traveling widely, editing and contributing to *Les Temps Modernes*, Sartre's
leftist political review, and juggling her commitments to him and "the
Family" (their entourage of friends, groupies, disciples, and lovers) with a
wild, transatlantic love affair. On a trip to America in 1947, she had met the
novelist Nelson Algren, the most significant of her male others, and it was
he who advised her to expand the essay on women into a book. He had
shown her the "underside" of his native Chicago, and that year and the
next they explored the United States and Mexico together. Her encounter
with a racism that she had never witnessed firsthand, and her friendship
with Richard Wright, the author of *Native Son*, helped to clarify her understanding of sexism, and its relation to the anti-Semitism that she certainly
had witnessed firsthand before and during the war, but, with Sartre, had
never openly challenged. The black, the Jew, and the woman, she concluded, were objectified as the Other in ways that were both overtly
despotic and insidious, but with the same result: their particularity as
human beings was reduced to a lazy, abstract cliché ("the eternal feminine"; "the black soul"; "the Jewish character") that served as a rationale
for their subjugation.

---

3. The cult of the Virgin is "the rehabilitation of woman by the achievement of her defeat";
"The average Western male's ideal is a woman who . . . intelligently resists but yields in the
end"; "The traditional woman . . . tries to conceal her dependence from herself, which is a
way of consenting to it." Examples are numerous.
4. In reference libraries and in lecture halls—Beauvoir audited classes by Lacan and Lévi-
Strauss, among others—and in interviews with women of all backgrounds on two continents.

Not all of Beauvoir's staggering erudition and mandarin authority in *The Second Sex* is reliable (she would repudiate a number of her more contentious or blinkered generalities, though not all of them). Her single most famous assertion—"One is not born, but rather becomes, woman"—has been disputed by more recent feminist scholars, and a substantial body of research in biology and the social sciences supports their argument that some sexual differences (besides the obvious ones) are innate rather than "situational." Instead of rejecting "otherness" as an imposed cultural construct, women, in their opinion, should cultivate it as a source of self-knowledge and expression, and use it as the basis to critique patriarchal institutions. Many readers have also been alienated by Beauvoir's visceral horror of fertility—the "curse" of reproduction—and her desire, as they see it, to homogenize the human race.

Yet a revolution cannot begin until the diffuse, private indignation of individuals coalesces into a common cause. Beauvoir not only marshaled a vast arsenal of fact and theory; she galvanized a critical mass of consciousness—a collective identity—that was indispensable to the women's movement. Her insights have breached the solitude of countless readers around the world who thought that the fears, transgressions, fantasies, and desires that fed their ambivalence about being female were aberrant or unique. No woman before her had written publicly, with greater candor and less euphemism, about the most intimate secrets of her sex.

One of those secrets—the hardest, perhaps, for Beauvoir to avow—is that a free woman may refuse to be owned without wanting to renounce, or being able to transcend, her yearning to be possessed.[5] "As long as the temptations of facility remain," she wrote, by which she meant the temptations of romantic love, financial security, and a sense of purpose or status derived from a man, all of which Sartre had, at one time or another, provided for her, a woman "needs to expend a greater moral effort than the male to choose the path of independence." Colette, who would have smiled, and not kindly, at the phrase, "moral effort," states the problem less cerebrally: "How to liberate my true hope? Everything is against me. The first obstacle to my escape is this woman's body barring my way, a voluptuous body with closed eyes, voluntarily blind, stretched out full, ready to perish."

---

5. It was a source of her bad faith in fictionalizing the affair with Algren in her finest novel, *The Mandarins*.

To a reader of this new translation—a young feminist perhaps, for whom the very title may seem as quaint as a pair of bloomers—I would suggest that the best way to appreciate *The Second Sex* is to read it in the spirit it was written: as a deep and urgent personal meditation on a true hope that, as she will probably discover, is still elusive for many of us: to become, in every sense, one's own woman.

—Judith Thurman

Translators' Note

We have spent the past three years researching *Le deuxième sexe* and translating it into English—into *The Second Sex*. It has been a daunting task and a splendid learning experience during which this monumental work entered our personal lives and changed the way we see the world. Questions naturally arose about the act of translating itself, about ourselves and our roles, and about our responsibilities to both Simone de Beauvoir and her readers.

Translation has always been fraught with such questions, and different times have produced different conceptions of translating. Perhaps this is why, while great works of art seldom age, translations do. The job of the translator is not to simplify or readapt the text for a modern or foreign audience but to find the true voice of the original work, as it was written for its time and with its original intent. Seeking signification in another's words transports the translator into the mind of the writer. When the text is an opus like *The Second Sex*, whose impact on society was so decisive, the task of bringing into English the closest version possible of Simone de Beauvoir's voice, expression, and mind is greater still.

This is not the first translation of *Le deuxième sexe* into English, but it is the first complete one. H. M. Parshley translated it in 1953, but he abridged and edited passages and simplified some of the complex philosophical language. We have translated *Le deuxième sexe* as it was written, unabridged and unsimplified, maintaining Beauvoir's philosophical language. The long and dense paragraphs that were changed in the 1953 translation to conform to more traditional styles of punctuation—or even eliminated—have now been translated as she wrote them, all within the confines of English. Long paragraphs (sometimes going on for pages) are a stylistic aspect of her writing that is essential, integral to the development of her arguments. Cutting her sentences, cutting her paragraphs, and using a more traditional and conventional punctuation do not render Simone de

Beauvoir's voice. Beauvoir's style expresses her reasoning. Her prose has its own consistent grammar, and that grammar follows a logic.

We did not modernize the language Beauvoir used and had access to in 1949. This decision precluded the use of the word "gender," for example, as applied today. We also stayed close to Beauvoir's complicated syntax and punctuation as well as to certain usages of language that to us felt a bit awkward at first. One of the difficulties was her extensive use of the semi-colon, a punctuation mark that has suffered setbacks over the past decades in English and French and has somewhat fallen into disuse.

Nor did we modernize structures such as "If the subject attempts to assert himself, the other is nonetheless necessary for him." Today we would say, "If the subject attempts to assert her or himself . . ." There are examples where the word "individual" clearly refers to a woman, but Beauvoir, because of French rules of grammar, uses the masculine pronoun. We therefore do the same in English.

The reader will see some inconsistent punctuation and style, most evident in quotations. Indeed, while we were tempted to standardize it, we carried Beauvoir's style and formatting into English as much as possible. In addition, we used the same chapter headings and numbers that she did in the original two-volume Gallimard edition. We also made the decision to keep close to Beauvoir's tense usage, most noticeably regarding the French use of the present tense for the historical past.

One particularly complex and compelling issue was how to translate *la femme*. In *Le deuxième sexe*, the term has at least two meanings: "the woman" and "woman." At times it can also mean "women," depending on the context. "Woman" in English used alone without an article captures woman as an institution, a concept, femininity as determined and defined by society, culture, history. Thus in a French sentence such as *Le problème de la femme a toujours été un problème d'hommes*, we have used "woman" without an article: "The problem of woman has always been a problem of men."

Beauvoir occasionally—but rarely—uses *femme* without an article to signify woman as determined by society as just described. In such cases, of course, we do the same. The famous sentence, *On ne naît pas femme: on le devient*, reads, in our translation: "One is not born, but rather becomes, woman." The original translation by H. M. Parshley read, "One is not born, but rather becomes a woman."

Another notable change we made was in the translation of *la jeune fille*. This is the title of an important chapter in Volume II dealing with the period in a female's life between childhood and adulthood. While it is often translated as "the young girl" (by Parshley and other translators of French works), we think it clearly means "girl."

| PART ONE |

FORMATIVE YEARS

CHAPTER 1

Childhood

One is not born, but rather becomes, woman. No biological, psychic, or economic destiny defines the figure that the human female takes on in society; it is civilization as a whole that elaborates this intermediary product between the male and the eunuch that is called feminine. Only the mediation of another can constitute an individual as an *Other*. Inasmuch as he exists for himself, the child would not grasp himself as sexually differentiated. For girls and boys, the body is first the radiation of a subjectivity, the instrument that brings about the comprehension of the world: they apprehend the universe through their eyes and hands, and not through their sexual parts. The drama of birth and weaning takes place in the same way for infants of both sexes; they have the same interests and pleasures; sucking is the first source of their most pleasurable sensations; they then go through an anal phase in which they get their greatest satisfactions from excretory functions common to both; their genital development is similar; they explore their bodies with the same curiosity and the same indifference; they derive the same uncertain pleasure from the clitoris and the penis; insofar as their sensibility already needs an object, it turns toward the mother: it is the soft, smooth, supple feminine flesh that arouses sexual desires, and these desires are prehensile; the girl like the boy kisses, touches, and caresses her mother in an aggressive manner; they feel the same jealousy at the birth of a new child; they show it with the same behavior: anger, sulking, urinary problems; they have recourse to the same coquetry to gain the love of adults. Up to twelve, the girl is just as sturdy as her brothers; she shows the same intellectual aptitudes; she is not barred from competing with them in any area. If well before puberty and sometimes even starting from early childhood she already appears sexually specified, it is not because mysterious instincts immediately destine her to passivity, coquetry, or motherhood but because the intervention of others in the infant's life is almost originary, and her vocation is imperiously breathed into her from the first years of her life.

The world is first present to the newborn only in the form of immanent sensations; he is still immersed within the Whole as he was when he was living in the darkness of a womb; whether raised on the breast or on a bottle, he is invested with the warmth of maternal flesh. Little by little he learns to perceive objects as distinct from himself: he separates himself from them; at the same time, more or less suddenly, he is removed from the nourishing body; sometimes he reacts to this separation with a violent fit;[1] in any case, when it is consummated—around six months—he begins to manifest the desire to seduce others by mimicking, which then turns into a real display. Of course, this attitude is not defined by a reflective choice; but it is not necessary to *think* a situation to *exist* it. In an immediate way the newborn lives the primeval drama of every existent—that is, the drama of one's relation to the Other. Man experiences his abandonment in anguish. Fleeing his freedom and subjectivity, he would like to lose himself within the Whole: here is the origin of his cosmic and pantheistic reveries, of his desire for oblivion, sleep, ecstasy, and death. He never manages to abolish his separated self: at the least he wishes to achieve the solidity of the in-itself, to be petrified in thing; it is uniquely when he is fixed by the gaze of others that he appears to himself as a being. It is in this vein that the child's behavior has to be interpreted: in a bodily form he discovers finitude, solitude, and abandonment in an alien world; he tries to compensate for this catastrophe by alienating his existence in an image whose reality and value will be established by others. It would seem that from the time he recognizes his reflection in a mirror—a time that coincides with weaning—he begins to affirm his identity:[2] his self merges with this reflection in such a way that it is formed only by alienating itself. Whether the mirror as such plays a more or less considerable role, what is sure is that the child at about six months of age begins to understand his parents' miming and to grasp himself under their gaze as an object. He is already an autonomous subject transcending himself toward the world: but it is only in an alienated form that he will encounter himself.

When the child grows up, he fights against his original abandonment in two ways. He tries to deny the separation: he crushes himself in his mother's arms, he seeks her loving warmth, he wants her caresses. And he

---

1. Judith Gautier says in her accounts of her memories that she cried and wasted away so terribly when she was pulled away from her wet nurse that she had to be reunited with her. She was weaned much later.

2. This is Dr. Lacan's theory in *Les complexes familiaux dans la formation de l'individu* (*Family Complexes in the Formation of the Individual*). This fundamental fact would explain that during its development "the self keeps the ambiguous form of spectacle."

tries to win the approbation of others in order to justify himself. Adults are to him as gods: they have the power to confer being on him. He experiences the magic of the gaze that metamorphoses him now into a delicious little angel and now into a monster. These two modes of defense are not mutually exclusive: on the contrary, they complete and infuse each other. When seduction is successful, the feeling of justification finds physical confirmation in the kisses and caresses received: it is the same contented passivity that the child experiences in his mother's lap and under her benevolent eyes. During the first three or four years of life, there is no difference between girls' and boys' attitudes; they all try to perpetuate the happy state preceding weaning; both boys and girls show the same behavior of seduction and display. Boys are just as desirous as their sisters to please, to be smiled at, to be admired.

It is more satisfying to deny brutal separation than to overcome it, more radical to be lost in the heart of the Whole than to be petrified by the consciousness of others: carnal fusion creates a deeper alienation than any abdication under the gaze of another. Seduction and display represent a more complex and less easy stage than the simple abandonment in maternal arms. The magic of the adult gaze is capricious; the child pretends to be invisible, his parents play the game, grope around for him, they laugh, and then suddenly they declare: "You are bothersome, you are not invisible at all." A child's phrase amuses, then he repeats it: this time, they shrug their shoulders. In this world as unsure and unpredictable as Kafka's universe, one stumbles at every step.[3] That is why so many children are afraid of growing up; they desperately want their parents to continue taking them on their laps, taking them into their bed: through physical frustration they experience ever more cruelly that abandonment of which the human being never becomes aware without anguish.

It is here that little girls first appear privileged. A second weaning, slower and less brutal than the first one, withdraws the mother's body from the child's embraces; but little by little boys are the ones who are denied

---

3. In *L'orange bleue* (*The Blue Orange*), Yassu Gauclère says about her father: "His good mood seemed as fearsome as his impatiences because nothing explained to me what could bring it about . . . As uncertain of the changes in his mood as I would have been of a god's whims, I revered him with anxiety . . . I threw out my words as I might have played heads or tails, wondering how they would be received." And further on, she tells the following anecdote: "For example, one day, after being scolded, I began my litany: old table, floor brush, stove, large bowl, milk bottle, casserole, and so on. My mother heard me and burst out laughing . . . A few days later, I tried to use my litany to soften my grandmother, who once again had scolded me: I should have known better this time. Instead of making her laugh, I made her angrier and got an extra punishment. I told myself that adults' behavior was truly incomprehensible."

kisses and caresses; the little girl continues to be doted upon, she is allowed to hide behind her mother's skirts, her father takes her on his knees and pats her hair; she is dressed in dresses as lovely as kisses, her tears and whims are treated indulgently, her hair is done carefully, her expressions and affectations amuse: physical contact and complaisant looks protect her against the anxiety of solitude. For the little boy, on the other hand, even affectations are forbidden; his attempts at seduction, his games irritate. "A man doesn't ask for kisses . . . A man doesn't look at himself in the mirror . . . A man doesn't cry," he is told. He has to be "a little man"; he obtains adults' approbation by freeing himself from them. He will please by not seeming to seek to please.

Many boys, frightened by the harsh independence they are condemned to, thus desire to be girls; in times when they were first dressed as girls, they cried when they had to give dresses up for long pants and had to have their curls cut. Some obstinately would choose femininity, which is one of the ways of gravitating toward homosexuality: "I wanted passionately to be a girl, and I was unconscious of the grandeur of being a man to the point of trying to urinate sitting down," Maurice Sachs recounts.[4] However, if the boy at first seems less favored than his sisters, it is because there are greater designs for him. The requirements he is subjected to immediately imply a higher estimation. In his memoirs, Maurras recounts that he was jealous of a cadet his mother and grandmother doted upon; his father took him by the hand and out of the room. "We are men; let's leave these women," he told him. The child is persuaded that more is demanded of boys because of their superiority; the pride of his virility is breathed into him in order to encourage him in this difficult path; this abstract notion takes on a concrete form for him: it is embodied in the penis; he does not experience pride spontaneously in his little indolent sex organ; but he feels it through the attitude of those around him. Mothers and wet nurses perpetuate the tradition that assimilates phallus and maleness; whether they recognize its prestige in amorous gratitude or in submission, or that they gain revenge by seeing it in the baby in a reduced form, they treat the child's penis with a singular deference. Rabelais reports on Gargantua's wet nurses' games and words;[5] history has recorded those of Louis XIII's wet nurses. Less daring

---

4. *Le sabbath* (*Witches' Sabbath*).

5. "And already beginning to exercise his codpiece, which each and every day his nurses would adorn with lovely bouquets, fine ribbons, beautiful flowers, pretty tufts, and they spent their time bringing it back and forth between their hands like a cylinder of salve, then they laughed their heads off when it raised its ears, as if they liked the game. One would call it my little spigot, another my ninepin, another my coral branch, another my stopper, my cork, my gimlet, my ramrod, my awl, my pendant."

women, however, give a friendly name to the little boy's sex organ, they speak to him about it as of a little person who is both himself and other than himself; they make of it, according to the words already cited, "an alter ego usually craftier, more intelligent, and more clever than the individual."[6] Anatomically, the penis is totally apt to play this role; considered apart from the body, it looks like a little natural plaything, a kind of doll. The child is esteemed by esteeming his double. A father told me that one of his sons at the age of three was still urinating sitting down; surrounded by sisters and girl cousins, he was a shy and sad child; one day his father took him with him to the toilet and said: "I will show you how men do it." From then on, the child, proud to be urinating standing up, scorned the girls "who urinated through a hole"; his scorn came originally not from the fact that they were lacking an organ but that they had not like him been singled out and initiated by the father. So, far from the penis being discovered as an immediate privilege from which the boy would draw a feeling of superiority, its value seems, on the contrary, like a compensation—invented by adults and fervently accepted by the child—for the hardships of the last weaning: in that way he is protected against regret that he is no longer a breast-feeding baby or a girl. From then on, he will embody his transcendence and his arrogant sovereignty in his sex.[7]

The girl's lot is very different. Mothers and wet nurses have neither reverence nor tenderness for her genital parts; they do not focus attention on this secret organ of which only the outside envelope can be seen and that cannot be taken hold of; in one sense, she does not have a sex. She does not experience this absence as a lack; her body is evidently a plenitude for her; but she finds herself in the world differently from the boy; and a group of factors can transform this difference into inferiority in her eyes.

Few questions are as much discussed by psychoanalysts as the famous "female castration complex." Most accept today that penis envy manifests itself in very different ways depending on the individual case.[8] First, many girls are ignorant of male anatomy until an advanced age. The child accepts naturally that there are men and women as there are a sun and a moon: she believes in essences contained in words, and his curiosity is at

---

6. Cited by A. Bálint, *The Psychoanalysis of the Nursery.*

7. See Volume I, Chapter 2, p. 57.

8. Besides Freud's and Adler's works, there is today an abundant literature on the subject. Abraham was the first one to put forward the idea that the girl considered her sex a wound resulting from a mutilation. Karen Horney, Jones, Jeanne Lampl-de Groot, H. Deutsch, and A. Bálint studied the question from a psychoanalytical point of view. Saussure tries to reconcile psychoanalysis with Piaget's and Luquet's ideas. See also Pollack, *Children's Ideas on Sex Differences.*

first not analytical. For many others, this little piece of flesh hanging between boys' legs is insignificant or even derisory; it is a particularity like that of clothes and hairstyle; often the female child discovers it at a younger brother's birth, and "when the little girl is very young," says Helene Deutsch, "she is not impressed by her younger brother's penis"; she cites the example of an eighteen-month-old girl who remained absolutely indifferent to the discovery of the penis and did not give it any value until much later, in connection with her personal preoccupations. The penis can even be considered an anomaly: it is a growth, a vague hanging thing like nodules, teats, and warts; it can inspire disgust. Lastly, the fact is that there are many cases of the little girl being interested in a brother's or a friend's penis; but that does not mean she experiences a specifically sexual jealousy and even less that she feels deeply moved by the absence of this organ; she desires to appropriate it for herself as she desires to appropriate any object; but this desire may remain superficial.

It is certain that the excretory function and particularly the urinary one interest children passionately: wetting the bed is often a protest against the parents' marked preference for another child. There are countries where men urinate sitting down, and there are women who urinate standing up: this is the way among many women peasants; but in contemporary Western society, custom generally has it that they squat, while the standing position is reserved to males. This is the most striking sexual difference for the little girl. To urinate she has to squat down, remove some clothes, and above all hide, a shameful and uncomfortable servitude. Shame increases in the frequent cases in which she suffers from involuntary urinary emissions, when bursting out laughing, for example; control is worse than for boys. For them, the urinary function is like a free game with the attraction of all games in which freedom is exercised; the penis can be handled, through it one can act, which is one of the child's deep interests. A little girl seeing a boy urinate declared admiringly: "How practical!"[9] The stream can be aimed at will, the urine directed far away: the boy draws a feeling of omnipotence from it. Freud spoke of "the burning ambition of early diuretics"; Stekel discussed this formula sensibly, but it is true that, as Karen Horney says, "fantasies of omnipotence, especially of a sadistic character, are as a matter of fact more easily associated with the jet of urine passed by the male";[10] there are many such fantasies in children, and they

9. Cited by A. Bálint.
10. "On the Genesis of the Castration Complex in Women," *International Journal of Psychoanalysis* (1923–24).

survive in some men.[11] Abraham speaks of "the great pleasure women experience watering the garden with a hose"; I think, in agreement with Sartre's and Bachelard's theories,[12] that it is not necessarily the assimilation of the hose with the penis that is the source of pleasure;[13] every stream of water seems like a miracle, a defiance of gravity: directing or governing it means carrying off a little victory over natural laws; in any case, for the little boy there is a daily amusement that is impossible for his sisters. He is also able to establish many relations with things through the urinary stream, especially in the countryside: water, earth, moss, snow. There are little girls who lie on their backs and try to practice urinating "in the air" or who try to urinate standing up in order to have these experiences. According to Karen Horney, they also envy the opportunity to exhibit that the boy is granted. A sick woman suddenly exclaimed, after seeing a man urinating in the street: "If I might ask a gift of Providence, it would be to be able just for once to urinate like a man," Karen Horney reports. It seems to girls that the boy, having the right to touch his penis, can use it as a plaything, while their organs are taboo. That these factors make the possession of a male sex organ desirable for many of them is a fact confirmed by many studies and confidences gathered by psychiatrists. Havelock Ellis quotes the words of a patient he calls Zenia: "The noise of a jet of water, especially coming out of a long hose, has always been very stimulating for me, recalling the noise of the stream of urine observed in childhood in my brother and even in other people."[14] Another woman, Mrs. R.S., recounts that as a child she absolutely loved holding a little friend's penis in her hands; one day she was given a hose: "It seemed delicious to hold that as if I was holding a penis." She emphasized that the penis had no sexual meaning for her; she only knew its urinary usage. The most interesting case, that of Florrie, is reported by Havelock Ellis and later analyzed by Stekel.[15] Here is a detailed account from it.

> The woman concerned is very intelligent, artistic, active, biologically normal, and not homosexual. She says that the urinary function played a great role in her childhood; she played urinary games with

---

11. Montherlant's "The caterpillars," *June Solstice*.
12. See Volume I, Part One, Chapter 2.
13. It is clear, though, in some cases.
14. Cf. Ellis [discussion of "undinism" in *Studies in the Psychology of Sex*.—TRANS.].
15. H. Ellis, *Studies in the Psychology of Sex*, Volume 13.

her brothers, and they wet their hands without feeling disgust. "My earliest ideas of the superiority of the male were connected with urination. I felt aggrieved with nature because I lacked so useful and ornamental an organ. No teapot without a spout felt so forlorn. It required no one to instill into me the theory of male predominance and superiority. Constant proof was before me." She took great pleasure in urinating in the country. "Nothing could come up to the entrancing sound as the stream descended on crackling leaves in the depth of a wood and she watched its absorption. Most of all she was fascinated by the idea of doing it into water" [as are many little boys]. There is a quantity of childish and vulgar imagery showing little boys urinating in ponds and brooks. Florrie complains that the style of her knickers prevented her from trying various desired experiments, but often during country walks she would hold back as long as she could and then suddenly relieve herself standing. "I can distinctly remember the strange and delicious sensation of this forbidden delight, and also my puzzled feeling that it came stand-ing." In her opinion, the style of children's clothing has great importance for feminine psychology in general. "It was not only a source of annoyance to me that I had to unfasten my drawers and then squat down for fear of wetting them in front, but the flap at the back, which must be removed to uncover the posterior parts during the act, accounts for my early impression that in girls this function is connected with those parts. The first distinction in sex that impressed me—the one great difference in sex—was that boys urinated standing and that girls had to sit down . . . The fact that my earliest feelings of shyness were more associated with the back than the front may have thus originated." All these impressions were of great importance in Florrie's case because her father often whipped her until the blood came and also a governess had once spanked her to make her urinate; she was obsessed by masochistic dreams and fancies in which she saw herself whipped by a school mistress under the eyes of all and having to urinate against her will, "an idea that gives one a curious sense of gratification." At the age of fifteen it happened that under urgent need she urinated standing in a deserted street. "In trying to analyze my sensations, I think the most promi-nent lay in the shame that came from standing, and the consequently greater distance the stream had to descend. It seemed to make the affair important and conspicuous, even though clothing hid it. In the ordinary attitude there is a kind of privacy. As a small child, too, the stream had not far to go, but at the age of fifteen I was tall and it seemed to give one a glow of shame to think of this stream falling unchecked such a distance. (I am sure that the ladies who fled in horror from the urinette at Portsmouth thought it most indecent for a woman to stand, legs apart, and to pull up her clothes and make a stream which descended unabashed all that way.)"[16] She renewed this experience at twenty and frequently thereafter. She felt a mixture of shame and pleasure at the idea that she might be surprised and that she would be incapable of stopping. "The stream seemed to be drawn from me without my consent, and *yet with even more pleasure than if I were doing it freely.*[17] This curious feeling—that it is being drawn away by some unseen power which is determined that one shall do it—is an entirely feminine pleasure and a subtle charm . . . There is a fierce charm in the torrent that binds one to its will by a mighty force." Later Florrie developed a flagellatory eroticism always combined with urinary obsessions.

This case is very interesting because it throws light on several elements of the child's experience. But of course there are particular circumstances that confer such a great importance upon them. For normally raised little girls, the boy's urinary privilege is too secondary a thing to engender a feeling of inferiority directly. Psychoanalysts following Freud who think that the mere discovery of the penis would be sufficient to produce a trauma seriously misunderstand the child's mentality; it is much less rational than they seem to think, it does not establish clear-cut categories and is not bothered by contradictions. When the little girl seeing a penis declares, "I had one too" or "I'll have one too," or even "I have one too," this is not a defense in bad faith; presence and absence are not mutually exclusive; the child—as his drawings prove—believes much less in what he *sees* with his eyes than in the signifying *types* that he has determined once and for all: he often draws without looking, and in any case he finds in his perceptions only what he puts there. Saussure, who emphasizes this point, quotes this very important observation of Luquet's: "Once a line is considered wrong, it is as if inexistent, *the child literally no longer sees it,* hypnotized in a way by the new line that replaces it, nor does he take into account lines that can

16. In an allusion to an episode she related previously: at Portsmouth a modern urinette for ladies was opened that called for the standing position; all the clients were seen to depart hastily as soon as they entered.
17. Florrie's italics.

be accidentally found on his paper."[18] Male anatomy constitutes a strong form that is often imposed on the little girl; and *literally she no longer sees* her own body. Saussure brings up the example of a four-year-old girl who, trying to urinate like a boy between the bars of a fence, said she wanted "a little long thing that runs." She affirmed at the same time that she had a penis and that she did not have one, which goes along with the thinking by "participation" that Piaget described in children. The little girl takes it for granted that all children are born with a penis but that the parents then cut some of them off to make girls; this idea satisfies the artificialism of the child who glorifies his parents and "conceives of them as the cause of everything he possesses," says Piaget; he does not see punishment in castration right away. For it to become a frustration, the little girl has to be unhappy with her situation for some reason; as Deutsch justly points out, an exterior event like the sight of a penis could not lead to an internal development. "The sight of the male organ can have a traumatic effect," she says, "but only if a chain of prior experiences that would create that effect had preceded it." If the little girl feels powerless to satisfy her desires of masturbation or exhibition, if her parents repress her onanism, if she feels less loved or less valued than her brothers, then she will project her dissatisfaction onto the male organ. "The little girl's discovery of the anatomical difference with the boy confirms a previously felt need; it is her rationalization, so to speak."[19] And Adler also insisted on the fact that it is the validation by the parents and others that gives the boy prestige, and that the penis becomes the explanation and symbol in the little girl's eyes. Her brother is considered superior; he himself takes pride in his maleness; so she envies him and feels frustrated. Sometimes she resents her mother and less often her father; either she accuses herself of being mutilated, or she consoles herself by thinking that the penis is hidden in her body and that one day it will come out.

It is sure that the absence of a penis will play an important role in the little girl's destiny, even if she does not really envy those who possess one. The great privilege that the boy gets from it is that as he is bestowed with an organ that can be seen and held, he can at least partially alienate himself in it. He projects the mystery of his body and its dangers outside himself, which permits him to keep them at a distance: of course, he feels endan-

---

18. "Psychologie génétique et psychanalyse" ("Genetic Psychology and Psychoanalysis"), *Revue Française de Psychanalyse* (1933).

19. H. Deutsch, *Psychology of Women*. She also cites the authority of K. Abraham and J.H.W. van Ophuijsen.

gered through his penis, he fears castration, but this fear is easier to dominate than the pervasive overall fear the girl feels concerning her "insides," a fear that will often be perpetuated throughout her whole life as a woman. She has a deep concern about everything happening inside her; from the start, she is far more opaque to herself and more profoundly inhabited by the worrying mystery of life than the male. Because he recognizes himself in an alter ego, the little boy can boldly assume his subjectivity; the very object in which he alienates himself becomes a symbol of autonomy, transcendence, and power: he measures the size of his penis; he compares his urinary stream with that of his friends; later, erection and ejaculation will be sources of satisfaction and challenge. But a little girl cannot incarnate herself in any part of her own body. As compensation, and to fill the role of alter ego for her, she is handed a foreign object: a doll. Note that the bandage wrapped on an injured finger is also called a *poupée* ("doll" in French): a finger dressed and separate from the others is looked on with amusement and a kind of pride with which the child initiates the process of its alienation. But it is a figurine with a human face—or a corn husk or even a piece of wood—that will most satisfyingly replace this double, this natural toy, this penis.

The great difference is that, on the one hand, the doll represents the whole body and, on the other hand, it is a passive thing. As such, the little girl will be encouraged to alienate herself in her person as a whole and to consider it an inert given. While the boy seeks himself in his penis as an autonomous subject, the little girl pampers her doll and dresses her as she dreams of being dressed and pampered; inversely, she thinks of herself as a marvelous doll.[20] Through compliments and admonishments, through images and words, she discovers the meaning of the words "pretty" and "ugly"; she soon knows that to please, she has to be "pretty as a picture"; she tries to resemble an image, she disguises herself, she looks at herself in the mirror, she compares herself to princesses and fairies from tales. Marie Bashkirtseff gives a striking example of this infantile coquetry.* It is certainly not by chance that, weaned late—she was three and a half—she fervently felt the need at the age of four or five to be admired and to exist for others: the shock must have been violent in a more mature child, and she had to struggle even harder to overcome the inflicted separation. "At five years old," she writes in her diary, "I would dress in Mummy's lace, with

---

20. The analogy between the woman and the doll remains until the adult age; in French, a woman is vulgarly called a doll; in English, a dressed-up woman is said to be "dolled up."

* Bashkirtseff, *I Am the Most Interesting Book of All.*—TRANS.

flowers in my hair, and I would go and dance in the living room. I was Petipa, the great dancer, and the whole house was there to *look at me*."

This narcissism appears so precociously for the little girl and will play so fundamental a part in her life that it is readily considered as emanating from a mysterious feminine instinct. But we have just seen that in reality it is not an anatomical destiny that dictates her attitude. The difference that distinguishes her from boys is a fact that she could assume in many ways. Having a penis is certainly a privilege, but one whose value naturally diminishes when the child loses interest in his excretory functions and becomes socialized: if he retains interest in it past the age of eight or nine years, it is because the penis has become the symbol of a socially valorized virility. The fact is that the influence of education and society is enormous here. All children try to compensate for the separation of weaning by seductive and attention-seeking behavior; the boy is forced to go beyond this stage, he is saved from his narcissism by turning his attention to his penis, whereas the girl is reinforced in this tendency to make herself object, which is common to all children. The doll helps her, but it does not have a determining role; the boy can also treasure a teddy bear or a rag doll on whom he can project himself; it is in their life's overall form that each factor—penis, doll—takes on its importance.

Thus, the passivity that essentially characterizes the "feminine" woman is a trait that develops in her from her earliest years. But it is false to claim that therein lies a biological given; in fact, it is a destiny imposed on her by her teachers and by society. The great advantage for the boy is that his way of existing for others leads him to posit himself for himself. He carries out the apprenticeship of his existence as free movement toward the world; he rivals other boys in toughness and independence; he looks down on girls. Climbing trees, fighting with his companions, confronting them in violent games, he grasps his body as a means to dominate nature and as a fighting tool; he is proud of his muscles, as he is of his sex organ; through games, sports, fights, challenges, and exploits, he finds a balanced use of his strength; at the same time, he learns the severe lessons of violence; he learns to take blows, to deride pain, to hold back tears from the earliest age. He undertakes, he invents, he dares. Granted, he also experiences himself as if "for others"; he tests his own virility, and consequently, trouble ensues with adults and friends. But what is very important is that there is no fundamental opposition between this objective figure that is his and his will for self-affirmation in concrete projects. It is by doing that he makes himself be, in one single movement. On the contrary, for the woman there is, from the start, a conflict between her autonomous existence and her "being-other"; she is taught that to please, she must try to please, must make herself object; she must therefore renounce her autonomy. She is treated like a living doll, and freedom is denied her; thus a vicious circle is closed; for the less she exercises her freedom to understand, grasp, and discover the world around her, the less she will find its resources, and the less she will dare to affirm herself as subject; if she were encouraged, she could show the same vibrant exuberance, the same curiosity, the same spirit of initiative, and the same intrepidness as the boy. Sometimes this does happen when she is given a male upbringing; she is thus spared many problems.[21] Interestingly, this is the kind of education that a father habitually gives his daughter; women brought up by a man escape many of the defects of femininity. But customs oppose treating girls exactly like boys. I knew a village where girls of three and four years old were persecuted because their father made them wear trousers: "Are they girls or boys?" And the other children tried to find out; the result was their pleading to wear dresses. Unless she leads a very solitary life, even if parents allow her to have boyish manners, the girl's companions, her friends, and her teachers will be shocked. There will always be aunts, grandmothers, and girl cousins to counterbalance the father's influence. Normally, his role regarding his daughters is secondary. One of the woman's curses—as Michelet has justly pointed out—is that in her childhood she is left in the hands of women. The boy is also brought up by his mother in the beginning; but she respects his maleness and he escapes from her relatively quickly, whereas the mother wants to integrate the girl into the feminine world.[22]

We will see later how complex the relation is between the mother and the daughter: for the mother, the daughter is both her double and an other, the mother cherishes her and at the same time is hostile to her; she imposes her own destiny on her child: it is a way to proudly claim her own femininity and also to take revenge on it. The same process is found with pederasts, gamblers, drug addicts, and all those who are flattered to belong to a certain community, and are also humiliated by it: they try through ardent proselytism to win over converts. Thus, women given the care of a little girl are bent on transforming her into women like themselves with zeal and arrogance mixed with resentment. And even a generous mother who sincerely wants the best for her child will, as a rule, think it wiser to make a "true

21. At least in her early childhood. In today's society, adolescent conflicts could, on the contrary, be exacerbated.
22. There are, of course, many exceptions: but the mother's role in bringing up a boy cannot be studied here.

woman" of her, as that is the way she will be best accepted by society. So she is given other little girls as friends, she is entrusted to female teachers, she lives among matrons as in the days of the gynaeceum, books and games are chosen for her that introduce her to her destiny, her ears are filled with the treasures of feminine wisdom, feminine virtues are presented to her, she is taught cooking, sewing, and housework as well as how to dress, how to take care of her personal appearance, charm, and modesty; she is dressed in uncomfortable and fancy clothes that she has to take care of, her hair is done in complicated styles, posture is imposed on her: stand up straight, don't walk like a duck; to be graceful, she has to repress spontaneous movements, she is told not to look like a tomboy, strenuous exercise is banned, she is forbidden to fight; in short, she is committed to becoming, like her elders, a servant and an idol. Today, thanks to feminism's breakthroughs, it is becoming more and more normal to encourage her to pursue her education, to devote herself to sports; but she is more easily excused for not succeeding; success is made more difficult for her as another kind of accomplishment is demanded of her: she must at least *also* be a woman; she must not *lose* her femininity.

In her early years she resigns herself to this lot without much difficulty. The child inhabits the level of play and dream, he plays at being, he plays at doing; doing and being are not clearly distinguishable when it is a question of imaginary accomplishments. The little girl can compensate for boys' superiority of the moment by those promises inherent in her woman's destiny, which she already achieves in her play. Because she still only knows her childhood universe, her mother seems endowed with more authority than her father; she imagines the world as a sort of matriarchy; she imitates her mother, she identifies with her; often she even inverses the roles: "When I am big and you are little . . . ," she often says. The doll is not only her double: it is also her child, functions that are not mutually exclusive insofar as the real child is also an alter ego for the mother; when she scolds, punishes, and then consoles her doll, she is defending herself against her mother, and she assumes a mother's dignity: she sums up both elements of the couple as she entrusts herself to her doll, educates her, asserts her sovereign authority over her, and sometimes even tears off her arms, beats her, tortures her; that is to say, through her she accomplishes the experience of subjective affirmation and alienation. Often the mother is associated with this imaginary life: in playing with the doll and the mother, the child plays both the father and the mother, a couple where the man is excluded. No "maternal instinct," innate and mysterious, lies therein either. The little girl observes that child care falls to the mother, that is what she is taught; stories told, books read, all her little experience confirms it; she is encouraged to feel delight for these future riches, she is given dolls so she will already feel the tangible aspect of those riches. Her "vocation" is determined imperiously. Because her lot seems to be the child, and also because she is more interested in her "insides" than the boy, the little girl is particularly curious about the mystery of procreation; she quickly ceases to believe that babies are born in cabbages or delivered by the stork; especially in cases where the mother gives her brothers or sisters, she soon learns that babies are formed in their mother's body. Besides, parents today make less of a mystery of it than before; she is generally more amazed than frightened because the phenomenon seems like magic to her; she does not yet grasp all of the physiological implications. First of all, she is unaware of the father's role and supposes that the woman gets pregnant by eating certain foods, a legendary theme (queens in fairy tales give birth to a little girl or a handsome boy after eating this fruit, that fish) and one that later leads some women to link the idea of gestation and the digestive system. Together these problems and these discoveries absorb a great part of the little girl's interests and feed her imagination. I will cite a typical example from Jung,[23] which bears remarkable analogies with that of little Hans, analyzed by Freud around the same time:

> When Anna was about three years old she began to question her parents about where babies come from; Anna had heard that children are "little angels." She first seemed to think that when people die, they go to heaven and are reincarnated as babies. At age four she had a little brother; she hadn't seemed to notice her mother's pregnancy but when she saw her the day after the birth, she looked at her "with something like a mixture of embarrassment and suspicion" and finally asked her, "Aren't you going to die now?" She was sent to her grandmother's for some time; when she came back, a nurse had arrived and was installed near the bed; she at first hated her but then she amused herself playing nurse; she was jealous of her brother: she sniggered, made up stories, disobeyed and threatened to go back to her grandmother's; she often accused her mother of not telling the truth, because she suspected her of lying about the infant's birth; feeling obscurely that there was a difference between "having" a child as a nurse and having one as a mother, she asked

---

23. Jung, "Pyschic Conflicts of a Child."

her mother: "Shall I be a different woman from you?" She got into the habit of yelling for her parents during the night; and as the earthquake of Messina was much talked about she made it the pretext of her anxieties; she constantly asked questions about it. One day, she asked outright: "Why is Sophie younger than I? Where was Freddie before? Was he in heaven and what was he doing there?" Her mother decided she ought to explain that the little brother grew inside her stomach like plants in the earth. Anna was enchanted with this idea. Then she asked: "But did he come all by himself?" "Yes." "But he can't walk yet!" "He crawled out." "Did he come out here (pointing to her chest), or did he come out of your mouth?" Without waiting for an answer, she said she knew it was the stork that had brought it; but in the evening she suddenly said: "My brother is in Italy;[24] he has a house made of cloth and glass and it doesn't fall down"; and she was no longer interested in the earthquake and asked to see photos of the eruption. She spoke again of the stork to her dolls but without much conviction. Soon however, she had new curiosities. Seeing her father in bed: "Why are you in bed? Have you got a plant in your inside too?" She had a dream; she dreamed of Noah's Ark: "And underneath, there was a lid which opened and all the little animals fell out"; in fact, her Noah's Ark opened by the roof: At this time, she again had nightmares: one could guess that she was wondering about the father's role. A pregnant woman having visited her mother, the next day her mother saw Anna put a doll under her skirts and take it out slowly, saying: "Look, the baby is coming out, now it is all out." Some time later, eating an orange, she said: "I'll swallow it all down into my stomach, and then I shall get a baby." One morning, her father was in the bathroom, she jumped on his bed, lay flat on her face, and flailed with her legs, crying out, "Look, is that what Papa does?" For five months she seemed to forget her preoccupations and then she began to mistrust her father: she thought he wanted to drown her, etc. One day she was happily sowing seeds in the earth with the gardener, and she asked her father: "How did the eyes grow into the head? And the hair?" The father explained that they were already there from the beginning and grew with the head. Then, she asked: "But how did Fritz get into Mama? Who stuck him in? And who stuck you into

24. This was a made-up older brother who played a big role in her games.

your mama? Where did he come out?" Her father said, smiling, "What do you think?" So she pointed to his sexual organs: "Did he come out from there?" "Well, yes." "But how did he get into Mama? Did someone sow the seed?" So the father explained that it is the father who gives the seed. She seemed totally satisfied and the next day she teased her mother: "Papa told me that Fritz was a little angel and was brought down from heaven by the stork." She was much calmer than before; she had, though, a dream in which she saw gardeners urinating, her father among them; she also dreamed, after seeing the gardener plane a drawer, that he was planing her genitals; she was obviously preoccupied with knowing the father's exact role. It seems that, almost completely enlightened at the age of five, she did not experience any other disturbance.*

This story is characteristic, although very often the little girl is less precisely inquisitive about the role played by the father, or the parents are much more evasive on this point. Many little girls hide cushions under their pinafores to play at being pregnant, or else they walk around with their doll in the folds of their skirts and let it fall into the cradle, or they give it their breast. Boys, like girls, admire the mystery of motherhood; all children have an "in depth" imagination that makes them sense secret riches inside things; they are all sensitive to the miracle of "nesting," dolls that contain other, smaller dolls, boxes containing other boxes, vignettes identically reproduced in reduced form; they are all enchanted when a bud is unfolded before their eyes, when they are shown a chick in its shell or the surprise of "Japanese flowers" in a bowl of water. One little boy, upon opening an Easter egg full of little sugar eggs, exclaimed with delight: "Oh! A mummy!" Having a child emerge from a woman's stomach is beautiful, like a magic trick. The mother seems endowed with wonderful fairy powers. Many boys bemoan that such a privilege is denied them; if, later, they take eggs from nests, stamp on young plants, if they destroy life around them with a kind of rage, it is out of revenge at not being able to hatch life, while the little girl is enchanted with the thought of creating it one day.

In addition to this hope made concrete by playing with dolls, a housewife's life also provides the little girl with possibilities of affirming herself. A great part of housework can be accomplished by a very young child; a boy is usually exempted from it; but his sister is allowed, even asked, to

---

* In Jung, *Development of Personality.*—TRANS.

sweep, dust, peel vegetables, wash a newborn, watch the stew. In particular, the older sister often participates in maternal chores; either for convenience or because of hostility and sadism, the mother unloads many of her functions onto her; she is then prematurely integrated into the universe of the serious; feeling her importance will help her assume her femininity; but she is deprived of the happy gratuitousness, the carefree childhood; a woman before her time, she understands too soon what limits this specificity imposes on a human being; she enters adolescence as an adult, which gives her story a unique character. The overburdened child can prematurely be a slave, condemned to a joyless existence. But, if no more than an effort equal to her is demanded, she experiences the pride of feeling efficient like a grown person and is delighted to feel solidarity with adults. This solidarity is possible for the child because there is not much distance between the child and the housewife. A man specialized in his profession is separated from the infant stage by years of training; paternal activities are profoundly mysterious for the little boy; the man he will be later is barely sketched in him. On the contrary, the mother's activities are accessible to the little girl. "She's already a little woman," say her parents, and often she is considered more precocious than the boy: in fact, if she is closer to the adult stage, it is because this stage traditionally remains more infantile for the majority of women. The fact is that she feels precocious, she is flattered to play the role of "little mother" to the younger ones; she easily becomes important, she speaks reason, she gives orders, she takes on superior airs with her brothers, who are still closed in the baby circle, she talks to her mother on an equal footing.

In spite of these compensations, she does not accept her assigned destiny without regret; growing up, she envies boys their virility. Sometimes parents and grandparents poorly hide the fact that they would have preferred a male offspring to a female; or else they show more affection to the brother than to the sister: research shows that the majority of parents wish to have sons rather than daughters. Boys are spoken to with more seriousness and more esteem, and more rights are granted them; they themselves treat girls with contempt, they play among themselves and exclude girls from their group, they insult them: they call them names like "piss pots," thus evoking girls' secret childhood humiliations. In France, in coeducational schools, the boys' caste deliberately oppresses and persecutes the girls'. But girls are reprimanded if they want to compete or fight with them. They doubly envy singularly boyish activities: they have a spontaneous desire to affirm their power over the world, and they protest against the inferior situation they are condemned to. They suffer in being forbidden to climb trees, ladders, and roofs, among other activities. Adler observes that the notions of high and low have great importance, the idea of spatial elevation implying a spiritual superiority, as can be seen in numerous heroic myths; to attain a peak or a summit is to emerge beyond the given world as sovereign subject; between boys, it is frequently a pretext for challenge. The little girl, to whom exploits are forbidden and who sits under a tree or by a cliff and sees the triumphant boys above her, feels herself, body and soul, inferior. And the same is true if she is left *behind* in a race or a jumping competition, or if she is thrown *to the ground* in a fight or simply pushed to the side.

The more the child matures, the more his universe expands and masculine superiority asserts itself. Very often, identification with the mother no longer seems a satisfactory solution. If the little girl at first accepts her feminine vocation, it is not that she means to abdicate: on the contrary, it is to rule; she wants to be a matron because matrons' society seems privileged to her; but when her acquaintances, studies, amusements, and reading material tear her away from the maternal circle, she realizes that it is not women but men who are the masters of the world. It is this revelation—far more than the discovery of the penis—that imperiously modifies her consciousness of herself.

She first discovers the hierarchy of the sexes in the family experience; little by little she understands that the father's authority is not the one felt most in daily life, but it is the sovereign one; it has all the more impact for not being wasted on trifling matters; even though the mother reigns over the household, she is clever enough to put the father's will first; at important moments, she makes demands, rewards, and punishes in his name. The father's life is surrounded by mysterious prestige: the hours he spends in the home, the room where he works, the objects around him, his occupations, his habits, have a sacred character. It is he who feeds the family, is the one in charge and the head. Usually he works outside the home, and it is through him that the household communicates with the rest of the world: he is the embodiment of this adventurous, immense, difficult, and marvelous world; he is transcendence, he is God.[25] This is what the child feels physically in the power of his arms that lift her, in the strength of his body that she huddles against. The mother loses her place of honor to him just as

---

25. "His generous person inspired in me a great love and an extreme fear," says Mme de Noailles, speaking of her father. "First of all, he astounded me. The first man astounds a little girl. I well understood that everything depended on him."

Isis once did to Ra and the earth to the sun. But for the child, her situation is deeply altered: she was intended one day to become a woman like her all-powerful mother; she will never be the sovereign father; the bond that attached her to her mother was an active emulation; from her father she can only passively expect esteem. The boy grasps paternal superiority through a feeling of rivalry, whereas the girl endures it with impotent admiration. I have already stated that what Freud called the "Electra complex" is not, as he maintains, a sexual desire; it is a deep abdication of the subject who consents to be object in submission and adoration. If the father shows tenderness for his daughter, she feels her existence magnificently justified; she is endowed with all the merits that others have to acquire the hard way; she is fulfilled and deified. It may be that she nostalgically searches for this plenitude and peace her whole life. If she is refused love, she can feel guilty and condemned forever; or else she can seek self-esteem elsewhere and become indifferent—even hostile—to her father. Besides, the father is not the only one to hold the keys to the world: all men normally share virile prestige; there is no reason to consider them father "substitutes." It is implicitly as men that grandfathers, older brothers, uncles, girlfriends' fathers, friends of the family, professors, priests, or doctors fascinate a little girl. The emotional consideration that adult women show the Man would be enough to perch him on a pedestal.[26]

Everything helps to confirm this hierarchy in the little girl's eyes. Her historical and literary culture, the songs and legends she is raised on, are an exaltation of the man. Men made Greece, the Roman Empire, France, and all countries, they discovered the earth and invented the tools to develop it, they governed it, peopled it with statues, paintings, and books. Children's literature, mythology, tales, and stories reflect the myths created by men's pride and desires: the little girl discovers the world and reads her destiny through the eyes of men. Male superiority is overwhelming: Perseus, Her-

---

26. It is worth noting that the cult of the father is most prevalent with the oldest child: the man is more involved in his first paternal experience; it is often he who consoles his daughter, as he consoles his son, when the mother is occupied with newborns, and the daughter becomes ardently attached to him. On the contrary, the younger child never has her father to herself; she is ordinarily jealous of both him and her older sister; she attaches herself to that same sister whom the devoted father invests with great prestige, or she turns to her mother, or she revolts against her family and looks for relief somewhere else. In large families, the youngest girl child finds other ways to have a special place. Of course, many circumstances can motivate the father to have special preferences. But almost all of the cases I know confirm this observation on the contrasting attitudes of the oldest and the youngest sisters.

cules, David, Achilles, Lancelot, Duguesclin, Bayard, Napoleon—so many men for one Joan of Arc; and behind her stands the great male figure of Saint Michael the archangel! Nothing is more boring than books retracing the lives of famous women: they are very pale figures next to those of the great men; and most are immersed in the shadows of some male hero. Eve was not created for herself but as Adam's companion and drawn from his side; in the Bible few women are noteworthy for their actions: Ruth merely found herself a husband. Esther gained the Jews' grace by kneeling before Ahasuerus, and even then she was only a docile instrument in Mordecai's hands; Judith was bolder, but she too obeyed the priests and her exploit has a dubious aftertaste: it could not be compared to the pure and shining triumph of young David. Mythology's goddesses are frivolous or capricious, and they all tremble before Jupiter; while Prometheus magnificently steals the fire from the sky, Pandora opens the box of catastrophes. There are a few sorceresses, some old women who wield formidable power in stories. Among them is "The Garden of Paradise" by Andersen, in which the figure of the mother of the winds recalls that of the primitive Great Goddess: her four enormous sons fearfully obey her; she beats and encloses them in bags when they behave badly. But they are not attractive characters. More seductive are the fairies, mermaids, and nymphs who escape male domination; but their existence is dubious and barely individualized; they are involved in the human world without having their own destiny: the day Andersen's little mermaid becomes a woman, she experiences the yoke of love and suffering that is her lot. In contemporary accounts as in ancient legends, the man is the privileged hero. Mme de Ségur's books are a curious exception: they describe a matriarchal society where the husband plays a ridiculous character when he is not absent; but usually the image of the father is, as in the real world, surrounded by glory. It is under the aegis of the father sanctified by his absence that the feminine dramas of *Little Women* take place. In adventure stories it is boys who go around the world, travel as sailors on boats, subsist on breadfruit in the jungle. All important events happen because of men. Reality confirms these novels and legends. If the little girl reads the newspapers, if she listens to adult conversation, she notices that today, as in the past, men lead the world. The heads of state, generals, explorers, musicians, and painters she admires are men; it is men who make her heart beat with enthusiasm.

That prestige is reflected in the supernatural world. Generally, as a result of the role religion plays in women's lives, the little girl, more dominated by the mother than the boy, is also more subjected to religious influences. And in Western religions, God the Father is a man, an old man endowed with a specifically virile attribute, luxuriant white beard.[27] For Christians, Christ is even more concretely a man of flesh and blood with a long blond beard. Angels have no sex, according to theologians; but they have masculine names and are shown as handsome young men. God's emissaries on earth—the pope, the bishop whose ring is kissed, the priest who says Mass, the preacher, the person one kneels before in the secrecy of the confessional—these are men. For a pious little girl, relations with the eternal Father are analogous to those she maintains with her earthly father; as they take place on an imaginary level, she experiences an even more total surrender. The Catholic religion, among others, exercises on her the most troubling of influences.[28] The Virgin welcomes the angel's words on her knees. "I am the *handmaiden* of the Lord," she answers. Mary Magdalene is prostrate at Christ's feet, and she washes them with her long womanly hair. Women saints declare their love to a radiant Christ on their knees. On his knees, surrounded by the odor of incense, the child gives himself up to God's and the angels' gaze: a man's gaze. There are many analogies between erotic and mystical language as spoken by women; for example, Saint Thérèse writes of the child Jesus:

> Oh my beloved, by your love I accept not to see on earth the sweetness of your gaze, not to feel the inexpressible kiss from your mouth, but I beg of you to embrace me with your love . . .

> *My beloved, of your first smile*
> *Let me soon glimpse the sweetness.*
> *Ah! Leave me in my burning deliriousness,*
> *Yes, let me hide myself in your heart!*

> I want to be mesmerized by your divine gaze; I want to become prey to your love. One day, I have hope, you will melt on me

---

27. "Moreover, I was no longer suffering from my inability to *see* God, because I had recently managed to imagine him in the form of my dead grandfather; this image in truth was rather human; but I had quickly glorified it by separating my grandfather's head from his bust and mentally putting it on a sky blue background where white clouds made him a collar," Yassu Gauclère says in *The Blue Orange*.

28. There is no doubt that women are infinitely more passive, given to man, servile, and humiliated in Catholic countries, Italy, Spain, and France, than in the Protestant Scandinavian and Anglo-Saxon ones. And this comes in great part from their own attitude: the cult of the Virgin, confession, and so on invites them to masochism.

carrying me to love's hearth; you will put me into this burning
chasm to make me become, once and for all, the lucky victim.

But it must not be concluded from this that these effusions are always
sexual; rather, when female sexuality develops, it is penetrated with the
religious feeling that woman has devoted to man since childhood. It is true
that the little girl experiences a thrill in the confessional and even at the foot
of the altar close to what she will later feel in her lover's arms: woman's
love is one of the forms of experience in which a consciousness makes itself
an object for a being that transcends it; and these are also the passive
delights that the young pious girl tastes in the shadows of the church.

Prostrate, her face buried in her hands, she experiences the miracle of
renunciation: on her knees she climbs to heaven; her abandon in God's
arms assures her an assumption lined with clouds and angels. She models
her earthly future on this marvelous experience. The child can also discover it in other ways: everything encourages her to abandon herself in
dreams to the arms of men to be transported to a sky of glory. She learns
that to be happy, she has to be loved; to be loved, she has to await love.
Woman is Sleeping Beauty, Donkey Skin, Cinderella, Snow White, the one
who receives and endures. In songs and tales, the young man sets off to
seek the woman; he fights against dragons, he combats giants; she is locked
up in a tower, a palace, a garden, a cave, chained to a rock, captive, put to
sleep: she is waiting. *One day my prince will come . . . Someday he'll come
along, the man I love . . .* the popular refrains breathe dreams of patience
and hope in her. The supreme necessity for woman is to charm a masculine
heart; this is the recompense all heroines aspire to, even if they are intrepid,
adventuresome; and only their beauty is asked of them in most cases. It is
thus understandable that attention to her physical appearance can become a
real obsession for the little girl; princesses or shepherds, one must always
be pretty to conquer love and happiness; ugliness is cruelly associated with
meanness, and when one sees the misfortunes that befall ugly girls, one
does not know if it is their crimes or their disgrace that destiny punishes.
Young beauties promised a glorious future often start out in the role of victim; the story of Geneviève de Brabant or of Griselda are not as innocent
as it would seem; love and suffering are intertwined in a troubling way;
woman is assured of the most delicious triumphs when falling to the bottom of abjection; whether it be a question of God or a man, the little girl
learns that by consenting to the most serious renunciations, she will
become all-powerful: she takes pleasure in a masochism that promises her
supreme conquests. Saint Blandine, white and bloody in the paws of lions,

Snow White lying as if dead in a glass coffin, Sleeping Beauty, Atala fainting, a whole cohort of tender heroines beaten, passive, wounded, on their
knees, humiliated, teach their younger sisters the fascinating prestige of
martyred, abandoned, and resigned beauty. It is not surprising that while
her brother plays at the hero, the little girl plays so easily at the martyr: the
pagans throw her to the lions, Bluebeard drags her by her hair, the king, her
husband, exiles her to the depth of the forests; she resigns herself, she suffers, she dies, and her brow is haloed with glory. "While still a little girl, I
wanted to draw men's attention, trouble them, be saved by them, die in
their arms," Mme de Noailles writes. A remarkable example of these
masochistic musings is found in *La voile noire* (The Black Sail) by Maria Le
Hardouin.

> At seven, from I don't know which rib, I made my first man. He
> was tall, thin, very young, dressed in a suit of black satin with long
> · sleeves touching the ground. His beautiful blond hair cascaded in
> heavy curls onto his shoulders . . . I called him Edmond . . . Then a
> day came when I gave him two brothers . . . These three brothers:
> Edmond, Charles, and Cedric, all three dressed in black satin, all
> three blond and slim, procured for me strange blessings. Their feet
> shod in silk were so beautiful and their hands so fragile that I felt
> all sorts of movements in my soul . . . I became their sister
> Marguerite . . . I loved to represent myself as subjected to the whims
> of my brothers and totally at their mercy. I dreamed that my oldest
> brother, Edmond, had the right of life and death over me. I never
> had permission to raise my eyes to his face. He had me whipped
> under the slightest pretext. When he addressed himself to me, I
> was so overwhelmed by fear and respect that I found nothing else
> to answer him and mumbled constantly "Yes, my lordship," "No,
> my lordship," and I savored the strange delight of feeling like an
> idiot . . . When the suffering he imposed on me was too great, I
> murmured "Thank you, my lordship," and there came a moment
> when, almost faltering from suffering, I placed, so as not to shout,
> my lips on his hand, while, some movement finally breaking my
> heart, I reached one of these states in which one desires to die from
> too much happiness.

At an early age, the little girl already dreams she has reached the age of
love; at nine or ten, she loves to make herself up, she pads her blouse, she
disguises herself as a lady. She does not, however, look for any erotic expe-

rience with little boys: if she does go with them into the corner to play "doctor," it is only out of sexual curiosity. But the partner of her amorous dreaming is an adult, either purely imaginary or based on real individuals: in the latter case, the child is satisfied to love him from afar. In Colette Audry's memoirs there is a very good example of a child's dreaming;[29] she recounts that she discovered love at five years of age:

This naturally had nothing to do with the little sexual pleasures of childhood, the satisfaction I felt, for example, straddling a certain chair in the dining room or caressing myself before falling asleep . . . The only common characteristic between the feeling and the pleasure is that I carefully hid them both from those around me . . . My love for this young man consisted in thinking of him before falling asleep and imagining marvelous stories . . . In Privas, I was in love with all the department heads of my father's office . . . I was never very deeply hurt by their departure, because they were barely more than a pretext for my amorous musings . . . In the evening in bed I got my revenge for too much youth and shyness. I prepared everything very carefully, I did not have any trouble making him present to me, but it was a question of transforming myself, me, so that I could see myself from the interior because I became her, and stopped being I. First, I was pretty and eighteen years old. A tin of sweets helped me a lot: a long tin of rectangular and flat sweets that depicted two girls surrounded by doves. I was the dark, curly-headed one, dressed in a long muslin dress. A ten-year absence had separated us. He returned scarcely aged, and the sight of this marvelous creature overwhelmed him. She seemed to barely remember him, she was unaffected, indifferent, and witty. I composed truly brilliant conversations for this first meeting. They were followed by misunderstandings, a whole difficult conquest, cruel hours of discouragement and jealousy for him. Finally, pushed to the limit, he admitted his love. She listened to him in silence, and just at the moment he thought all was lost, she told him she had never stopped loving him, and they embraced a little. The scene normally took place on a park bench, in the evening. I saw the two forms close together, I heard the murmur of voices, I felt at the same time the warm body contact. But then everything came

---

29. *Aux yeux du souvenir* (In the Eyes of Memory).

loose . . . never did I broach marriage[30] . . . The next day I thought of it a little while washing. I don't know why the soapy face I was looking at in the mirror delighted me (the rest of the time I didn't find myself beautiful) and filled me with hope. I would have considered for hours this misty, tilted face that seemed to be waiting for me from afar on the road to the future. But I had to hurry; once I dried my face, everything was over, and I got back my banal child's face, which no longer interested me.

Games and dreams orient the girl toward passivity; but she is a human being before becoming a woman; and she already knows that accepting herself as woman means resigning and mutilating herself; while renunciation might be tempting, mutilation is abhorrent. Man and Love are still far away in the mist of the future; in the present, the little girl seeks activity, autonomy, like her brothers. The burden of freedom is not heavy for children, because it does not involve responsibility; they know they are safe in the shelter of adults: they are not tempted to flee from themselves. The girl's spontaneous zest for life, her taste for games, laughter, and adventure, make her consider the maternal circle narrow and stultifying. She wants to escape her mother's authority, an authority that is wielded in a more routine and intimate manner than the one that boys have to accept. Rare are the cases in which she is as understanding and discreet as in this Sido that Colette painted with love. Not to mention the almost pathological cases—there are many[31]—where the mother is a kind of executioner, satisfying her domineering and sadistic instincts on the child; her daughter is the privileged object opposite whom she attempts to affirm herself as sovereign subject; this attempt makes the child balk in revolt. Colette Audry described this rebellion of a normal girl against a normal mother:

I wouldn't have known how to answer the truth, however innocent it was, because I never felt innocent in front of Mama. She was the essential adult, and I resented her for it as long as I was not yet cured. There was deep inside me a kind of tumultuous and fierce

---

30. Unlike Le Hardouin's masochistic imagination, Audry's is sadistic. She wants the beloved to be wounded, in danger, for her to save him heroically, not without humiliating him. This is a personal note, characteristic of a woman who will never accept passivity and will attempt to conquer her autonomy as a human being.

31. Cf. V. Leduc, *L'asphyxie* (*In the Prison of Her Skin*); S. de Tervagne, *La haine maternelle* (Maternal Hatred); H. Bazin, *Vipère au poing* (*Viper in the Fist*).

sore that I was sure of always finding raw . . . I didn't think she was too strict; nor that she hadn't the right. I thought: no, no, no with all my strength. I didn't even blame her for her authority or for her orders or arbitrary defenses but for *wanting to subjugate me.* She said it sometimes: when she didn't say it, her eyes and voice did. Or else she told ladies that children are much more docile after a punishment. These words stuck in my throat, unforgettable: I couldn't vomit them; I couldn't swallow them. This anger was my guilt in front of her and also my shame in front of me (because in reality she frightened me, and all I had on my side in the form of retaliation were a few violent words or acts of insolence) but also my glory, nevertheless: as long as the sore was there, and living the silent madness that made me only repeat, "Subjugate, docile, punishment, humiliation," I wouldn't be subjugated.

Rebellion is even more violent in the frequent cases when the mother has lost her prestige. She appears as the one who waits, endures, complains, cries, and makes scenes: and in daily reality this thankless role does not lead to any apotheosis; victim, she is scorned; shrew, she is detested; her destiny appears to be the prototype of bland *repetition:* with her, life only repeats itself stupidly without going anywhere; blocked in her housewifely role, she stops the expansion of her existence, she is obstacle and negation. Her daughter wants *not* to take after her. She dedicates a cult to women who have escaped feminine servitude: actresses, writers, and professors; she gives herself enthusiastically to sports and to studies, she climbs trees, tears her clothes, tries to compete with boys. Very often she has a best friend in whom she confides; it is an exclusive friendship like a love affair that usually includes sharing sexual secrets: the little girls exchange information they have succeeded in getting and talk about it. Often there is a triangle, one of the girls falling in love with her girlfriend's brother: thus Sonya in *War and Peace* is in love with her best friend Natasha's brother. In any case, this friendship is shrouded in mystery, and in general at this period the child loves to have secrets; she makes a secret of the most insignificant thing: thus does she react against the secrecies that thwart her curiosity; it is also a way of giving herself importance; she tries by all means to acquire it; she tries to be part of adults' lives, she makes up stories about them that she only half believes and in which she plays a major role. With her friends, she feigns returning boys' scorn with scorn; they form a closed group, they sneer and mock them. But in fact, she is flattered when they treat her as an equal; she seeks their approbation. She would like to belong to the privileged caste. The same movement that in primitive hordes subjects woman to male supremacy is manifested in each new "arrival" by a refusal of her lot: in her, transcendence condemns the absurdity of immanence. She is annoyed at being oppressed by rules of decency, bothered by her clothes, enslaved to cleaning tasks, held back in all her enthusiasms; on this point there have been many studies that have almost all given the same result:[32] all the boys—like Plato in the past—say they would have hated to be girls; almost all the girls are sorry not to be boys. According to Havelock Ellis's statistics, one boy out of a hundred wanted to be a girl; more than 75 percent of the girls would have preferred to change sex. According to a study by Karl Pipal (cited by Baudouin in his work *L'âme enfantine* [*The Mind of the Child*]), out of twenty boys of twelve to fourteen years of age, eighteen said they would rather be anything in the whole world than a girl; out of twenty-two girls, ten wished to be boys and gave the following reasons: "Boys are better: they do not have to suffer like women . . . My mother would love me more . . . A boy does more interesting work . . . A boy has more aptitude for school . . . I would have fun frightening girls . . . I would not fear boys anymore . . . They are freer . . . Boys' games are more fun . . . They are not held back by their clothes." This last observation is recurrent: almost all the girls complain of being bothered by their clothes, of not being free in their movements, of having to watch their skirts or light-colored outfits that get dirty so easily. At about ten or twelve years of age, most little girls are really tomboys, that is, children who lack the license to be boys. Not only do they suffer from it as a privation and an injustice, but the regime they are condemned to is unhealthy. The exuberance of life is prohibited to them, their stunted vigor turns into nervousness; their goody-goody occupations do not exhaust their brimming energy; they are bored: out of boredom and to compensate for the inferiority from which they suffer, they indulge in morose and romantic daydreams; they begin to have a taste for these facile escapes and lose the sense of reality; they succumb to their emotions with a confused exaltation; since they cannot act, they talk, readily mixing up serious words with totally meaningless ones; abandoned, "misunderstood," they go looking for consolation in narcissistic sentiments: they look on themselves as heroines in novels, admire themselves, and complain; it is natural for them to become

---

32. There is an exception, for example, in a Swiss school where boys and girls participating in the same coeducation, in privileged conditions of comfort and freedom, all declared themselves satisfied; but such circumstances are exceptional. Obviously, the girls *could be* as happy as the boys, but in present society the fact is that they are not.

keen on their appearance and to playact: these defects will grow during puberty. Their malaise expresses itself in impatience, tantrums, tears; they indulge in tears—an indulgence many women keep later—largely because they love to play the victim: it is both a protest against the harshness of their destiny and a way of endearing themselves to others. "Little girls love to cry so much that I have known them to cry in front of a mirror in order to double the pleasure," says Monsignor Dupanloup. Most of their dramas concern relations with their family; they try to break their bonds with their mothers: either they are hostile to them, or they continue to feel a profound need for protection; they would like to monopolize their fathers' love for themselves; they are jealous, touchy, demanding. They often make up stories; they imagine they are adopted, that their parents are not really theirs; they attribute a secret life to them; they dream about their sexual relations; they love to imagine that their father is misunderstood, unhappy, that he is not finding in his wife the ideal companion that his daughter would be for him; or, on the contrary, that the mother rightly finds him rough and brutal, that she is appalled by any physical relations with him. Fantasies, acting out, childish tragedies, false enthusiasms, strange things: the reason must be sought not in a mysterious feminine soul but in the child's situation.

It is a strange experience for an individual recognizing himself as subject, autonomy, and transcendence, as an absolute, to discover inferiority—as a given essence—in his self: it is a strange experience for one who posits himself for himself as One to be revealed to himself as alterity. That is what happens to the little girl when, learning about the world, she grasps herself as a woman in it. The sphere she belongs to is closed everywhere, limited, dominated by the male universe: as high as she climbs, as far as she dares go, there will always be a ceiling over her head, walls that block her path. Man's gods are in such a faraway heaven that in truth, for him, there are no gods: the little girl lives among gods with a human face.

This is not a unique situation. American blacks, partially integrated into a civilization that nevertheless considers them an inferior caste, live it; what Bigger Thomas experiences with so much bitterness at the dawn of his life is this definitive inferiority, this cursed alterity inscribed in the color of his skin: he watches planes pass and knows that because he is black the sky is out of bounds for him.[33] Because she is woman, the girl knows that the sea and the poles, a thousand adventures, a thousand joys, are forbidden to her: she is born on the wrong side. The great difference is that the blacks

---

33. Richard Wright, *Native Son*.

endure their lot in revolt—no privilege compensates for its severity—while for the woman her complicity is invited. Earlier I recalled that in addition to the authentic claim of the subject who claims sovereign freedom, there is an inauthentic desire for renunciation and escape in the existent;[34] these are the delights of passivity that parents and educators, books and myths, women and men dangle before the little girl's eyes; in early childhood she is already taught to taste them; temptation becomes more and more insidious; and she yields to it even more fatally as the thrust of her transcendence comes up against harsher and harsher resistance. But in accepting her passivity, she also accepts without resistance enduring a destiny that is going to be imposed on her from the exterior, and this fatality frightens her. Whether ambitious, scatterbrained, or shy, the young boy leaps toward an open future; he will be a sailor or an engineer, he will stay in the fields or will leave for the city, he will see the world, he will become rich; he feels free faced with a future where unexpected opportunities await him. The girl will be wife, mother, grandmother; she will take care of her house exactly as her mother does, she will take care of her children as she was taken care of: she is twelve years old, and her story is already written in the heavens; she will discover it day after day without shaping it; she is curious but frightened when she thinks about this life whose every step is planned in advance and toward which each day irrevocably moves her.

This is why the little girl, even more so than her brothers, is preoccupied with sexual mysteries; of course boys are interested as well, just as passionately; but in their future, their role of husband and father is not what concerns them the most; marriage and motherhood put in question the little girl's whole destiny; and as soon as she begins to perceive their secrets, her body seems odiously threatened to her. The magic of motherhood has faded: whether she has been informed early or not, she knows, in a more or less coherent manner, that a baby does not appear by chance in the mother's belly and does not come out at the wave of a magic wand; she questions herself anxiously. Often it seems not extraordinary at all but rather horrible that a parasitic body should proliferate inside her body; the idea of this monstrous swelling frightens her. And how will the baby get out? Even if she was never told about the cries and suffering of childbirth, she has overheard things, she has read the words in the Bible: "In sorrow thou shalt bring forth children"; she has the presentiment of tortures she cannot even imagine; she invents strange operations around her navel; she

---

34. See Introduction to Volume I.

is no less reassured if she supposes that the fetus will be expelled by her anus: little girls have been seen to have nervous constipation attacks when they thought they had discovered the birthing process. Accurate explanations will not bring much relief: images of swelling, tearing, and hemorrhaging will haunt her. The more imaginative she is, the more sensitive the little girl will be to these visions; but no girl could look at them without shuddering. Colette relates how her mother found her in a faint after reading Zola's description of a birth:

> [The author depicted the birth] with a rough-and-ready, crude wealth of detail, an anatomical precision, and a lingering over colours, postures and cries, in which I recognized none of the tranquil, knowing experience on which I as a country girl could draw. I felt credulous, startled and vulnerable in my nascent femininity . . . Other words, right in front of my eyes, depicted flesh splitting open, excrement and sullied blood . . . The lawn rose to welcome me . . . like one of those little hares that poachers sometimes brought, freshly killed, into the kitchen.*

The reassurance offered by grown-ups leaves the child worried; growing up, she learns not to trust the word of adults; often it is on the very mysteries of her conception that she has caught them in lies; and she also knows that they consider the most frightening things normal; if she has ever experienced a violent physical shock—tonsils removed, tooth pulled, whitlow lanced—she will project the remembered anxiety onto childbirth.

The physical nature of pregnancy and childbirth suggests as well that "something physical" takes place between the spouses. The often-encountered word "blood" in expressions like "same-blood children," "pure blood," and "mixed blood" sometimes orients the childish imagination; it is supposed that marriage is accompanied by some solemn transfusion. But more often the "physical thing" seems to be linked to the urinary and excremental systems; in particular, children think that the man urinates into the woman. This sexual operation is thought of as *dirty*. This is what overwhelms the child for whom "dirty" things have been rife with the strictest taboos: How, then, can it be that they are integrated into adults' lives? The child is first of all protected from scandal by the very absurdity he discovers: he finds there is no sense to what he hears around him, what

---

* *Claudine's House.*—TRANS.

he reads, what he writes; everything seems unreal to him. In Carson McCullers's charming book *The Member of the Wedding*, the young heroine surprises two neighbors in bed nude; the very anomaly of the story keeps her from giving it too much importance:

It was a summer Sunday and the hall door of the Marlowes' room was open. She could see only a portion of the room, part of the dresser and only the footpiece of the bed with Mrs. Marlowe's corset on it. But there was a sound in the quiet room she could not place, and when she stepped over the threshold she was startled by a sight that, after a single glance, sent her running to the kitchen, crying: Mr. Marlowe is having a fit! Berenice had hurried through the hall, but when she looked into the front room, she merely bunched her lips and banged the door . . . Frankie had tried to question Berenice and find out what was the matter. But Berenice had only said that they were common people and added that with a certain party in the house they ought at least to know enough to shut a door. Though Frankie knew she was the certain party, still she did not understand. What kind of a fit was it? she asked. But Berenice would only answer: Baby, just a common fit. And Frankie knew from the voice's tones that there was more to it than she was told. Later she only remembered the Marlowes as common people.

When children are warned against strangers, when a sexual incident is described to them, it is often explained in terms of sickness, maniacs, or madmen; it is a convenient explanation; the little girl fondled by her neighbor at the cinema or the girl who sees a man expose himself thinks that she is dealing with a crazy man; of course, encountering madness is unpleasant: an epileptic attack, hysteria, or a violent quarrel upsets the adult world order, and the child who witnesses it feels in danger; but after all, just as there are homeless, beggars, and injured people with hideous sores in harmonious society, there can also be some abnormal ones without its base disintegrating. It is when parents, friends, and teachers are suspected of celebrating black masses that the child really becomes afraid.

When I was first told about sexual relations between man and woman, I declared that such things were impossible since my parents would have had to do likewise, and I thought too highly of them to believe it. I said that it was much too disgusting for me ever to do it.

Unfortunately, I was to be disabused shortly after when I heard what my parents were doing . . . that was a fearful moment; I hid my face under the bedcovers, stopped my ears, and wished I were a thousand miles from there.[35]

How to go from the image of dressed and dignified people, these people who teach decency, reserve, and reason, to that of naked beasts confronting each other? Here is a contradiction that shakes their pedestal, darkens the sky. Often the child stubbornly refuses the odious revelation. "My parents don't do that," he declares. Or he tries to give coitus a decent image. "When you want a child," said a little girl, "you go to the doctor; you undress, you cover your eyes, because you mustn't watch; the doctor ties the parents together and helps them so that it works right"; she had changed the act of love into a surgical operation, rather unpleasant at that, but as honorable as going to the dentist. But despite denial and escape, embarrassment and doubt creep into the child's heart; a phenomenon as painful as weaning occurs: it is no longer separating the child from the maternal flesh, but the protective universe that surrounds him falls apart; he finds himself without a roof over his head, abandoned, absolutely alone before a future as dark as night. What adds to the little girl's anxiety is that she cannot discern the exact shape of the equivocal curse that weighs on her. The information she gets is inconsistent, books are contradictory; even technical explanations do not dissipate the heavy shadow; a hundred questions arise: Is the sexual act painful? Or delicious? How long does it last? Five minutes or all night? Sometimes you read that a woman became a mother with one embrace, and sometimes you remain sterile after hours of sexual activity. Do people "do that" every day? Or rarely? The child tries to learn more by reading the Bible, consulting dictionaries, asking friends, and he gropes in darkness and disgust. An interesting document on this point is the study made by Dr. Liepmann; here are a few responses given to him by young girls about their sexual initiation:

I continued to stray among my nebulous and twisted ideas. No one broached the subject, neither my mother nor my schoolteacher; no book treated the subject fully. Little by little a sort of perilous and ugly mystery was woven around the act, which at first had seemed so natural to me. The older girls of twelve used crude jokes to bridge

---

35. Cited by Dr. W. Liepmann, *Youth and Sexuality*.

the gap between themselves and our classmates. All that was still so vague and disgusting; we argued about where the baby was formed, if perhaps the thing only took place once for the man since marriage was the occasion for so much fuss. My period at fifteen was another new surprise. It was my turn to be caught up, in a way, in the round.

. . . Sexual initiation! An expression never to be mentioned in our parents' house! . . . I searched in books, but I agonized and wore myself out looking for the road to follow . . . I went to a boys' school: for my schoolteacher the question did not even seem to exist . . . Horlam's work, *Little Boy and Little Girl,* finally brought me the truth. My tense state and unbearable overexcitement disappeared, although I was very unhappy and took a long time to recognize and understand that eroticism and sexuality alone constitute real love.

Stages of my initiation: (1) First questions and a few vague notions (totally unsatisfactory). From three and a half to eleven years old . . . No answers to the questions I had in the following years. When I was seven, right there feeding my rabbit, I suddenly saw little naked ones underneath her . . . My mother told me that in animals and people little ones grow in their mother's belly and come out through the loins. This birth through the loins seemed unreasonable to me . . . a nursemaid told me about pregnancy, birth, and menstruation . . . Finally, my father replied to my last question about his true function with obscure stories about pollen and pistil. (2) Some attempts at personal experimentation (eleven to thirteen years old). I dug out an encyclopedia and a medical book . . . It was only theoretical information in strange gigantic words. (3) Testing of acquired knowledge (thirteen to twenty): (*a*) in daily life, (*b*) in scientific works.

At eight, I often played with a boy my age. One day we broached the subject. I already knew, because my mother had already told me, that a woman has many eggs inside her . . . and that a child was born from one of these eggs whenever the mother strongly desired it . . . Giving this same answer to my friend, I received this reply: "You are completely stupid! When our butcher and his wife want a baby, they go to bed and do dirty things." I was indignant . . . We had then (around twelve and a half) a maid who told me all sorts of scandalous tales. I never said a word to Mama, as I was ashamed; but

I asked her if sitting on a man's knees could give you a baby. She explained everything as best she could.

At school I learned where babies emerged, and I had the feeling that it was something horrible. But how did they come into the world? We both formed a rather monstrous idea about the thing, especially since one winter morning on the way to school together in the darkness we met a certain man who showed us his sexual parts and asked us, "Don't they seem good enough to eat?" Our disgust was inconceivable, and we were literally nauseated. Until I was twenty-one, I thought babies were born through the navel.

A little girl took me aside and asked me: "Do you know where babies come from?" Finally she decided to speak out: "Goodness! How foolish you are! Kids come out of women's stomachs, and for them to be born, women have to do completely disgusting things with men!" Then she went into details about how disgusting. But I had become totally transformed, absolutely unable to believe that such things could be possible. We slept in the same room as our parents . . . One night later I heard take place what I had thought was impossible, and, yes, I was ashamed, I was ashamed of my parents. All of this made of me another being. I went through horrible moral suffering. I considered myself a deeply depraved creature because I was now aware of these things.

It should be said that even coherent instruction would not resolve the problem; in spite of the best will of parents and teachers, the sexual experience could not be put into words and concepts; it could only be understood by living it; all analysis, however serious, will have a comic side and will fail to deliver the truth. When, from the poetic loves of flowers to the nuptials of fish, by way of the chick, the cat, or the kid, one reaches the human species, the mystery of conception can be theoretically elucidated: that of voluptuousness and sexual love remains total. How would one explain the pleasure of a caress or a kiss to a dispassionate child? Kisses are given and received in a family way, sometimes even on the lips: Why do these mucus exchanges in certain encounters provoke dizziness? It is like describing colors to the blind. As long as there is no intuition of the excitement and desire that give the sexual function its meaning and unity, the different elements seem shocking and monstrous. In particular, the little girl is revolted when she understands that she is virgin and sealed, and that to change into a woman a man's sex must penetrate her. Since exhibitionism is a widespread perversion, many little girls have seen the penis in an erection; in any case, they have observed the sexual organs of animals, and it is unfortunate that the horse's so often draws their attention; one imagines that they would be frightened by it. Fear of childbirth, fear of the male sex organ, fear of the "crises" that threaten married couples, disgust for dirty practices, derision for actions devoid of signification, all of this often leads a young girl to declare: "I will never marry."[36] Therein lies the surest defense against pain, folly, and obscenity. It is useless to try to explain that when the day comes, neither deflowering nor childbirth would seem so terrible, that millions of women resign themselves to it and are none the worse for it. When a child fears an outside occurrence, he is relieved of the fear, but not by predicting that, later, he will accept it naturally: it is himself he fears meeting in the far-off future, alienated and lost. The metamorphosis of the caterpillar, through chrysalis and into butterfly, brings about a deep uneasiness: Is it still the same caterpillar after this long sleep? Does she recognize herself beneath these brilliant wings? I knew little girls who were plunged into an alarming reverie at the sight of a chrysalis.

And yet the metamorphosis takes place. The little girl herself does not understand the meaning, but she realizes that in her relations with the world and her own body something is changing subtly: she is sensitive to contacts, tastes, and odors that previously left her indifferent; baroque images pass through her head; she barely recognizes herself in mirrors; she feels "funny," and things seem "funny"; such is the case of little Emily, described by Richard Hughes in *A High Wind in Jamaica*:

> Emily, for coolness, sat up to her chin in water, and hundreds of
> infant fish were tickling with their inquisitive mouths every inch
> of her body, a sort of expressionless light kissing. Anyhow she had
> lately come to hate being touched—but this was abominable. At last,
> when she could stand it no longer, she clambered out and dressed.

36. "Filled with repugnance, I implored God to grant me a religious vocation that would allow me to escape the laws of maternity. And after having long reflected on the repugnant mysteries that I hid in spite of myself, reinforced by such repulsion as by a divine sign, I concluded: chastity is certainly my vocation," writes Yassu Gauclère in *The Blue Orange*. Among others, the idea of perforation horrified her. "Here, then, is what makes the wedding night so terrible! This discovery overwhelmed me, adding the physical terror of this operation that I imagined to be extremely painful to the disgust I previously felt. My terror would have been all the worse if I had supposed that birth came about through the same channel; but having known for a long time that children were born from their mother's belly, I believed that they were detached by segmentation."

Even Margaret Kennedy's serene Tessa feels this strange disturbance:

> Suddenly she had become intensely miserable. She stared down into the darkness of the hall, cut in two by the moonlight which streamed in through the open door. She could not bear it. She jumped up with a little cry of exasperation. "Oh!" she exclaimed. "How I hate it all!" . . . She ran out to hide herself in the mountains, frightened and furious, pursued by a desolate foreboding which seemed to fill the quiet house. As she stumbled up towards the pass she kept murmuring to herself: "I wish I could die! I wish I was dead!"
>
> She knew that she did not mean this; she was not in the least anxious to die. But the violence of such a statement seemed to satisfy her.*

This disturbing moment is described at length in Carson McCullers's previously mentioned book, *The Member of the Wedding:*

> This was the summer when Frankie was sick and tired of being Frankie. She hated herself, and had become a loafer and a big no-good who hung around the summer kitchen: dirty and greedy and mean and sad. Besides being too mean to live, she was a criminal . . . Then the spring of that year had been a long queer season. Things began to change . . . There was something about the green trees and the flowers of April that made Frankie sad. She did not know why she was sad, but because of this peculiar sadness, she began to realize that she ought to leave the town . . . She ought to leave the town and go to some place far away. For the late spring, that year, was lazy and too sweet. The long afternoons flowered and lasted and the green sweetness sickened her . . . Many things made Frankie suddenly wish to cry. Very early in the morning she would sometimes go out into the yard and stand for a long time looking at the sunrise sky. And it was as though a question came into her heart, and the sky did not answer. Things she had never noticed much before began to hurt her: home lights watched from the evening sidewalks, an unknown voice from an alley. She would stare at the lights and listen to the voice, and something inside her stiffened and waited. But the lights would darken, the voice fall silent, and though

---

* *The Constant Nymph.*—TRANS.

she waited, that was all. She was afraid of these things that made her suddenly wonder who she was, and what she was going to be in the world, and why she was standing at that minute, seeing a light, or listening, or staring up into the sky: alone. She was afraid, and there was a queer tightness in her chest . . .

She went around town, and the things she saw and heard seemed to be left somehow unfinished, and there was the tightness in her that would not break. She would hurry to do something, but what she did was always wrong . . . After the long twilights of this season, when Frankie had walked around the sidewalks of the town, a jazz sadness quivered her nerves and her heart stiffened and almost stopped.

What is happening in this troubled period is that the child's body is becoming a woman's body and being made flesh. Except in the case of glandular deficiency where the subject remains fixed in the infantile stage, the puberty crisis begins around the age of twelve or thirteen.[37] This crisis begins much earlier for girls than for boys, and it brings about far greater changes. The little girl approaches it with worry and displeasure. As her breasts and body hair develop, a feeling is born that sometimes changes into pride, but begins as shame; suddenly the child displays modesty, she refuses to show herself nude, even to her sisters or her mother, she inspects herself with surprise mixed with horror, and she observes with anxiety the swelling of this hard core, somewhat painful, appearing under nipples that until recently were as inoffensive as a navel. She is worried to discover a vulnerable spot in herself: undoubtedly this pain is slight compared with a burn or a toothache; but in an accident or illness, pain was always abnormal, while the youthful breast is normally the center of who knows what indefinable resentment. Something is happening, something that is not an illness, but that involves the very law of existence and is yet struggle and suffering. Of course, from birth to puberty the little girl grew up, but she never felt growth; day after day, her body was present like an exact finished thing; now she is "developing": the very word horrifies her; vital phenomena are only reassuring when they have found a balance and taken on the stable aspect of a fresh flower, a polished animal; but in the blossoming of her breasts, the little girl feels the ambiguity of the word "living." She is neither gold nor diamond, but a strange matter, moving and uncertain, inside of which impure chemistries develop. She is used to a free-flowing

---

37. These purely physiological processes have already been described in Volume I, Chapter 1. [In Part One, "Destiny."—Trans.]

head of hair that falls like a silken skein; but this new growth under her arms, beneath her belly, metamorphoses her into an animal or alga. Whether she is more or less prepared for it, she foresees in these changes a finality that rips her from her self; thus hurled into a vital cycle that goes beyond the moment of her own existence, she senses a dependence that dooms her to man, child, and tomb. In themselves, her breasts seem to be a useless and indiscreet proliferation. Arms, legs, skin, muscles, and even the round buttocks she sits on, all have had until now a clear usefulness; only the sex organ defined as urinary was a bit dubious, though secret and invisible to others. Her breasts show through her sweater or blouse, and this body that the little girl identified with self appears to her as flesh; it is an object that others look at and see. "For two years I wore capes to hide my chest, I was so ashamed of it," a woman told me. And another: "I still remember the strange confusion I felt when a friend of my age, but more developed than I was, stooped to pick up a ball, I noticed by the opening in her blouse two already heavy breasts: this body so similar to mine, on which my body would be modeled, made me blush for myself." "At thirteen, I walked around bare legged, in a short dress," another woman told me. "A man, sniggering, made a comment about my fat calves. The next day, my mother made me wear stockings and lengthen my skirt, but I will never forget the shock I suddenly felt in seeing myself *seen*." The little girl feels that her body is escaping her, that it is no longer the clear expression of her individuality; it becomes foreign to her; and at the same moment, she is grasped by others as a thing: on the street, eyes follow her, her body is subject to comments; she would like to become invisible; she is afraid of becoming flesh and afraid to show her flesh.

This disgust is expressed in many young girls by the desire to lose weight: they do not want to eat anymore; if they are forced, they vomit; they watch their weight incessantly. Others become pathologically shy; entering a room or going out on the street becomes a torture. From these experiences, psychoses sometimes develop. A typical example is Nadia, the patient from *Les obsessions et la psychasthénie* (Obsessions and Psychasthenia), described by Janet:

Nadia, a young girl from a wealthy and remarkably intelligent family, was stylish, artistic, and above all an excellent musician; but from infancy she was obstinate and irritable . . . : "She demanded excessive affection from everyone, her parents, sisters, and servants, but she was so demanding and dominating that she soon alienated people; horribly susceptible, when her cousins used mockery to try to change her character, she acquired a sense of shame fixed on her body." Then, too, her need for affection made her wish to remain a child, to remain a little girl to be petted, one whose every whim is indulged, and in short made her fear growing up . . . A precocious puberty worsened her troubles, mixing fears of modesty with fears of growing up: "Since men like plump women, I want to remain extremely thin." Pubic hair and growing breasts added to her fears. From the age of eleven, as she wore short skirts, it seemed to her that everyone eyed her; she was given long skirts and was then ashamed of her feet, her hips, and so on. The appearance of menstruation drove her half-mad; believing that she was the only one in the world having the monstrosity of pubic hair, she labored up to the age of twenty "to rid herself of this savage decoration by depilation." The development of breasts exacerbated these obsessions because she had always had a horror of obesity; she did not detest it in others; but for herself she considered it a defect. "I don't care about being pretty, but I would be too *ashamed* if I became bloated, that would horrify me; if by bad luck I became fat, I wouldn't dare let anyone see me." So she tried every means, all kinds of prayers and conjurations, to prevent normal growth: she swore to repeat prayers five or ten times, to hop five times on one foot. "If I touch one piano note four times in the same piece, I accept growing and not being loved by anyone." Finally she decided not to eat. "I did not want to get fat, nor to grow up, nor resemble a woman because I always wanted to remain a little girl." She solemnly promised to accept no food at all; when she yielded to her mother's pleas to take some food and broke her vow, she knelt for hours writing out vows and tearing them up. Her mother died when she was eighteen, and she then imposed a strict regime on herself: two clear bouillon soups, an egg yolk, a spoonful of vinegar, a cup of tea with the juice of a whole lemon, was all she would take in a day. Hunger devoured her. "Sometimes I spent hours thinking of food, I was so hungry: I swallowed my saliva, gnawed on my handkerchief, and rolled on the floor from wanting to eat." But she resisted temptations. She was pretty, but believed that her face was puffy and covered with pimples; if her doctor stated that he did not see them, she said he didn't understand anything, that he couldn't see the pimples between the skin and the flesh. She left her family in the end and hid in a small apartment, seeing only a guardian and the doctor; she never went out; she accepted her father's visit, but only with difficulty; he brought about a serious relapse by telling her that she looked well; she dreaded having a fat face, healthy complexion, big muscles. She lived most of the time in darkness, so intolerable it was for her to be seen or even *visible*.

Very often the parents' attitude contributes to inculcating shame in the little girl for her physical appearance. A woman's testimony:

> I suffered from a very keen sense of physical inferiority, which was accentuated by continual nagging at home . . . Mother, in her excessive pride, wanted me to appear at my best, and she always found many faults that required "covering up" to point out to the dressmaker; for instance, drooping shoulders! Heavy hips! Too flat in the back! Bust too prominent! Having had a swollen neck for years, it was not possible for me to have an open neck. And so on. I was particularly worried on account of the appearance of my feet . . . and I was nagged on account of my gait . . . There was some truth in every criticism . . . but sometimes I was so embarrassed, particularly during my "backfisch" stage, that at times I was at a loss to know how to move about. If I met someone, my first thought was: "If I could only hide my feet!"[38]

This shame makes the girl act awkwardly, blush at the drop of a hat; this blushing increases her timidity, and itself becomes the object of a phobia. Stekel recounts, among others, a woman who "as a young girl blushed so pathologically and violently that for a year she wore bandages around her face with the excuse of toothaches."[39]

Sometimes, in prepuberty preceding the arrival of her period, the girl does not yet feel disgust for her body; she is proud of becoming a woman, she eagerly awaits her maturing breasts, she pads her blouse with handkerchiefs and brags around her older sisters; she does not yet grasp the meaning of the phenomena taking place in her. Her first period exposes this meaning, and feelings of shame appear. If they existed already, they are confirmed and magnified from this moment on. All the accounts agree: whether or not the child has been warned, the event always appears repugnant and humiliating. The mother very often neglected to warn her; it has been noted that mothers explain the mysteries of pregnancy, childbirth,

---

38. Stekel, *Frigidity in Woman*.
39. Ibid.

and even sexual relations to their daughters more easily than that of menstruation;[40] they themselves hate this feminine servitude, a hatred that reflects men's old mystical terrors and one that they transmit to their offspring. When the girl finds suspicious stains on her underwear, she thinks she has diarrhea, a fatal hemorrhage, a venereal disease. According to a survey that Havelock Ellis cited in 1896, out of 125 American high school students 36 at the time of their first period knew absolutely nothing on the question, 39 had vague ideas; that is, more than half of the girls were unaware. And according to Helene Deutsch, things had not changed much by 1946. Ellis cites the case of a young girl who threw herself into the Seine in Saint-Ouen because she thought she had an "unknown disease." Stekel, in *Letters to a Mother*, tells the story of a little girl who tried to commit suicide, seeing in the menstrual flow the sign of and punishment for the impurities that sullied her soul. It is natural for the young girl to be afraid: it seems to her that her life is seeping out of her. According to Klein and the English psychoanalytic school, blood is for the young girl the manifestation of a wound of the internal organs. Even if cautious advice saves her from excessive anxiety, she is ashamed, she feels dirty: she rushes to the sink, she tries to wash or hide her dirtied underwear. There is a typical account of the experience in Colette Audry's book *In the Eyes of Memory*:

At the heart of this exaltation, the brutal and finished drama. One evening while getting undressed, I thought I was sick; it did not frighten me, and I kept myself from saying anything in the hope that it would disappear the next day . . . Four weeks later, the illness occurred again, but more violently. I was quietly going to throw my knickers into the hamper behind the bathroom door. It was so hot that the diamond-shaped tiles of the hallway were warm under my naked feet. When I then got into bed, Mama opened my bedroom door: she came to explain things to me. I am unable to remember the effect her words had on me at that time, but while she was whispering, Kaki poked her head in. The sight of this round and curious face drove me crazy. I screamed at her to get out of there and she disappeared in fright. I begged Mama to go and beat her because she hadn't knocked before entering. My mother's calmness, her knowing and quietly happy air, were all it took to make me lose my head. When she left, I dug myself in for a stormy night.

---

40. Cf. The works of Daly and Chadwick, cited by Deutsch, in *Psychology of Women* (1946).

Two memories all of a sudden come back: a few months earlier, coming back from a walk with Kaki, Mama and I had met the old doctor from Privas, built like a logger with a full white beard. "Your daughter is growing up, madam," he said while looking at me; and I hated him right then and there without understanding anything. A little later, coming back from Paris, Mama put away some new little towels in the chest of drawers. "What is that?" Kaki asked. Mama had this natural air of adults who reveal one part of the truth while omitting the other three: "It's for Colette soon." Speechless, unable to utter one question, I hated my mother.

That whole night I tossed and turned in my bed. It was not possible. I was going to wake up. Mama was mistaken, it would go away and not come back again . . . The next day, secretly changed and stained, I had to confront the others. I looked at my sister with hatred because she did not yet know, because all of a sudden she found herself, unknown to her, endowed with an overwhelming superiority over me. Then I began to hate men, who would never experience this, and who knew. And then I also hated women who accepted it so calmly. I was sure that if they had been warned of what was happening to me, they would all be overjoyed. "So it's your turn now," they would have thought. That one too, I said to myself when I saw one. And this one too. I was had by the world. I had trouble walking and didn't dare run. The earth, the sun-hot greenery, even the food, seemed to give off a suspicious smell . . . The crisis passed and I began to hope against hope that it would not come back again. One month later, I had to face the facts and accept the evil definitively, in a heavy stupor this time. There was now in my memory a "before." All the rest of my existence would no longer be anything but an "after."

Things happen in a similar way for most little girls. Many of them are horrified at the idea of sharing their secret with those around them. A friend told me that, motherless, she lived between her father and a primary school teacher and spent three months in fear and shame, hiding her stained underwear before it was discovered that she had begun menstruating. Even peasant women who might be expected to be hardened by their knowledge of the harshest sides of animal life are horrified by this malediction, which in the countryside is still taboo: I knew a young woman farmer who washed her underwear in secret in the frozen brook, putting her soaking garment directly back on her naked skin to hide her unspeakable secret. I could cite a hundred similar facts. Even admitting this astonishing misfortune offers no relief. Undoubtedly, the mother who slapped her daughter brutally, saying, "Stupid! You're much too young," is exceptional. But this is not only about being in a bad mood; most mothers fail to give the child the necessary explanations, and so she is full of anxiety before this new state brought about by the first menstruation crisis: she wonders if the future does not hold other painful surprises for her; or else she imagines that from now on she could become pregnant by the simple presence or contact with a man, and she feels real terror of males. Even if she is spared these anxieties by intelligent explanations, she is not so easily granted peace of mind. Prior to this, the girl could, with a little bad faith, still think herself an asexual being, she could just not think herself; she even dreams of waking up one morning changed into a man; these days, mothers and aunts flatter and whisper to each other: "She's a big girl now"; the brotherhood of matrons has won: she belongs to them. Here she takes her place on the women's side without recourse. Sometimes, she is proud of it; she thinks she has now become an adult and an upheaval will occur in her existence. As Thyde Monnier recounts:

> Some of us had become "big girls" during vacation; others would while at school, and then, one after the other in the toilets in the courtyard, where they were sitting on their "thrones" like queens receiving their subjects, we would go and "see the blood."[41]

But the girl is soon disappointed because she sees that she has not gained any privilege and that life follows its normal course. The only novelty is the disgusting event repeated monthly; there are children that cry for hours when they learn they are condemned to this destiny; what adds to their revolt is that this shameful defect is known by men as well: what they would like is that the humiliating feminine condition at least be shrouded in mystery for them. But no, father, brothers, cousins, men know and even joke about it sometimes. This is when the shame of her too carnal body is born or exacerbated. And once the first surprise has passed, the monthly unpleasantness does not fade away at all: each time, the girl finds the same disgust when faced by this unappetizing and stagnant odor that comes from herself—a smell of swamps and wilted violets—this less red and more suspicious blood than that flowing from children's cuts and scratches. Day and

---

41. *Moi* (Me).

night she has to think of changing her protection, watching her underwear, her sheets, and solving a thousand little practical and repugnant problems; in thrifty families sanitary napkins are washed each month and take their place among the piles of handkerchiefs; this waste coming out of oneself has to be delivered to those handling the laundry: the laundress, servant, mother, or older sister. The types of bandages pharmacies sell in boxes named after flowers, Camellia or Edelweiss, are thrown out after use; but while traveling, on vacation, or on a trip it is not so easy to get rid of them, the toilet bowl being specifically prohibited. The young heroine of the *Psychoanalytical Journal* described her horror of the sanitary napkin;[42] she did not even consent to undress in front of her sister except in the dark during these times. This bothersome, annoying object can come loose during violent exercise; it is a worse humiliation than losing one's knickers in the middle of the street: this horrid possibility sometimes brings about fits of psychasthenia. By a kind of ill will of nature, indisposition and pain often do not begin until the initial bleeding—often hardly noticed—has passed; young girls are often irregular: they might be surprised during a walk, in the street, at friends'; they risk—like Mme de Chevreuse—dirtying their clothes or their seat; such a possibility makes one live in constant anxiety.[43] The greater the young girl's feeling of revulsion toward this feminine defect, the greater her obligation to pay careful attention to it so as not to expose herself to the awful humiliation of an accident or a little word of warning.

Here is the series of answers that Dr. Liepmann obtained during his study of juvenile sexuality:[44]

At sixteen years of age, when I was indisposed for the first time, I was very frightened in seeing it one morning. In truth, I knew it was going to happen, but I was so ashamed of it that I remained in bed for a whole half day and had one answer to all questions: I cannot get up.

I was speechless in astonishment when, not yet twelve, I was indisposed for the first time. I was struck by horror, and as my mother limited herself to telling me drily that this would happen every

---

42. Translated by Clara Malraux.

43. Disguised as a man during the Fronde, Mme de Chevreuse, after a long excursion on horseback, was unmasked because of bloodstains seen on the saddle.

44. Dr. W. Liepmann, *Youth and Sexuality.*

month, I considered it something disgusting and refused to accept that this did not also happen to men.

This adventure made my mother decide to initiate me, without forgetting menstruation at the same time. I then had my second disappointment because as soon as I was indisposed, I ran joyfully to my mother, who was still sleeping, and I woke her up, shouting "Mother, I have it!" "And that is why you woke me up?" she managed to say in response. In spite of everything, I considered this thing a real upheaval in my existence.

And so I felt the most intense horror when I was indisposed for the first time seeing that the bleeding did not stop after a few minutes. Nevertheless, I did not whisper a word to anyone, not to my mother either. I had just reached the age of fifteen. In addition I suffered very little. Only one time was I taken with such terrifying pain that I fainted and stayed on the floor in my room for almost three hours. But I still did not say anything to anyone.

When for the first time this indisposition occurred, I was about thirteen. My school friends and I had already talked about it, and I was proud to finally become one of the big girls. With great importance I explained to the gym teacher that it was impossible today for me to take part in the lesson because I was indisposed.

It was not my mother who initiated me. It was not until the age of nineteen that she had her period, and for fear of being scolded for dirtying her underwear, she buried it in a field.

I reached the age of eighteen, and I then had my period for the first time.[45] I was totally unprepared for what was happening . . . At night, I had violent bleeding accompanied by heavy diarrhea, and I could not rest for one second. In the morning, my heart racing, I ran to my mother and, weeping constantly, asked her advice. But I only obtained this harsh reprimand: "You should have been aware of it sooner and not have dirtied the sheets and bed." That was all as far as explanation was concerned. Naturally, I tried very hard to know what crime I might have committed, and I suffered terrible anguish.

I already knew what it was. I was waiting for it impatiently because I was hoping my mother would reveal to me how children were made.

---

45. She was a girl from a very poor Berlin family.

The celebrated day arrived, but my mother remained silent. Nevertheless, I was joyous. "From now on," I said to myself, "you can make children: you are a lady."

This crisis takes place at a still tender age; the boy only reaches adolescence at about fifteen or sixteen; the girl changes into a woman at thirteen or fourteen. But the essential difference in their experience does not stem from there; nor does it lie in the physiological manifestations that give it its awful shock in the case of the girl: puberty has a radically different meaning for the two sexes because it does not announce the same future to them.

Granted, boys too at puberty feel their body as an embarrassing presence, but because they have been proud of their virility from childhood, it is toward that virility that they proudly transcend the moment of their development; they proudly exhibit the hair growing between their legs, and that makes men of them; more than ever, their sex is an object of comparison and challenge. Becoming adults is an intimidating metamorphosis: many adolescents react with anxiety to a demanding freedom; but they accede to the dignified status of male with joy. On the contrary, to become a grown-up, the girl must confine herself within the limits that her femininity imposes on her. The boy admires undefined promises in the growing hair: she remains confused before the "brutal and finished drama" that limits her destiny. Just as the penis gets its privileged value from the social context, the social context makes menstruation a malediction. One symbolizes virility and the other femininity: it is because femininity means alterity and inferiority that its revelation is met with shame. The girl's life has always appeared to her to be determined by this impalpable essence to which the absence of the penis has not managed to give a positive image: it is this essence that is revealed in the red flow that escapes from between her thighs. If she has already assumed her condition, she welcomes the event with joy: "Now you are a lady." If she has always refused it, the bloody verdict strikes her like lightning; most often, she hesitates: the menstrual stain inclines her toward disgust and fear. "So this is what these words mean: being a woman!" The fate that until now has weighed on her ambivalently and from the outside is lodged in her belly; there is no escape; she feels trapped. In a sexually egalitarian society, she would envisage menstruation only as her unique way of acceding to an adult life; the human body has many other more repugnant servitudes in men and women: they easily make the best of them because as they are common to all they do not represent a flaw for anyone; menstrual periods inspire horror in adolescent girls because they thrust them into an inferior and damaged category. This feeling of degradation will weigh heavily on the girl. She would retain the pride of her bleeding body if she did not lose her self-respect as a human being. And if she succeeds in preserving her self-respect, she will feel the humiliation of her flesh much less vividly: the girl who opens paths of transcendence in sports, social, intellectual, and mystical activities will not see a mutilation in her specificity, and she will overcome it easily. If the young girl often develops psychoses in this period, it is because she feels defenseless in front of a deaf fate that condemns her to unimaginable trials; her femininity signifies illness, suffering, and death in her eyes, and she is transfixed by this destiny.

One example that vividly illustrates these anxieties is that of the patient called Molly described by Helene Deutsch:

Molly was fourteen when she began to suffer from psychic disorders; she was the fourth child in a family of five siblings. Her father is described as extremely strict and narrow-minded. He criticized the appearance and behavior of his children at every meal. The mother was worried and unhappy; and every so often the parents were not on speaking terms; one brother ran away from home. The patient was a gifted youngster, a good tap dancer; but she was shy, took the family troubles seriously, and was afraid of boys. Her older sister got married against her mother's wishes and Molly was very inter-ested in her pregnancy: she had a difficult delivery and forceps were necessary and she heard that women often die in childbirth. She took care of the baby for two months; when the sister left the house, there was a terrible scene and the mother fainted. Molly fainted too. She had seen classmates faint in class and her thoughts were much concerned with death and fainting. When she got her period, she told her mother with an embarrassed air: "That thing is here." She went with her sister to buy some menstrual pads; on meeting a man in the street, she hung her head. In general she acted "disgusted with herself." She never had pain during her periods, but tried to hide them from her mother, even when the latter saw stains on the sheets. She told her sister: "Anything might happen to me now. I might have a baby." When told: "You have to live with a man for that to hap-pen," she replied: "Well, I am living with two men—my father and your husband."

The father did not permit his daughters to go out . . . because one heard stories of rape: these fears helped to give Molly the idea of men being redoubtable creatures. From her first menstruation her anxiety about becoming pregnant and dying in childbirth became so severe that after a time she refused to leave her room, and now she sometimes stays in bed all day; if she has to go out of the house, she has an attack and faints. She is afraid of cars and taxis and she cannot sleep, she fears that someone is trying to enter the house at night, she screams and cries. She has eating spells; sometimes she eats too much to keep herself from fainting; she is also afraid when she feels closed in. She cannot go to school anymore or lead a normal life.

A similar story not linked to the crisis of menstruation but which shows the girl's anxiety about her insides is Nancy's:[46]

Toward the age of thirteen the little girl was on intimate terms with her older sister, and she had been proud to be in her confidence when the sister was secretly engaged and then married: to share the secret of a grown-up was to be accepted among the adults. She lived for a time with her sister; but when the latter told her that she was going "to buy" a baby, Nancy got jealous of her brother-in-law and of the coming child: to be treated again as a child to whom one made little mysteries of things was unbearable. She began to experience internal troubles and wanted to be operated on for appendicitis. The operation was a success, but during her stay at the hospital Nancy lived in a state of severe agitation; she made violent scenes with a nurse she disliked; she tried to seduce the doctor, making dates with him, being provocative and demanding throughout her crises to be treated as a woman. She accused herself of being to blame for the death of a little brother some years before. And in particular she felt sure that they had not removed her appendix or had left a part of it inside her; her claim that she had swallowed a penny was probably intended to make sure an X-ray would be taken.

This desire for an operation—and in particular for the removal of the appendix—is often seen at this age; girls thus express their fear of rape, pregnancy, or having a baby. They feel in their womb obscure perils and hope that the surgeon will save them from this unknown and threatening danger.

It is not only the arrival of her period that signals to the girl her destiny

---

46. Cited also by H. Deutsch, *Psychology of Women.*

as a woman. Other dubious phenomena occur in her. Until then, her eroticism was clitoral. It is difficult to know if solitary sexual practices are less widespread in girls than in boys; the girl indulges in them in her first two years, and perhaps even in the first months of her life; it seems that she stops at about two before taking them up again later; because of his anatomical makeup, this stem planted in the male flesh asks to be touched more than a secret mucous membrane: but the chances of rubbing—the child climbing on a gym apparatus or on trees or onto a bicycle—of contact with clothes, or in a game or even initiation by friends, older friends, or adults, frequently make the girl discover sensations she tries to renew. In any case, pleasure, when reached, is an autonomous sensation: it has the lightness and innocence of all childish amusements.[47] As a child, she hardly established a relation between these intimate delights and her destiny as a woman; her sexual relations with boys, if there were any, were essentially based on curiosity. And all of a sudden she experiences emotional confusion in which she does not recognize herself. Sensitivity of the erogenous zones is developing, and they are so numerous in the woman that her whole body can be considered erogenous: this is what comes across from familial caresses, innocent kisses, the casual touching of a dressmaker, a doctor, a hairdresser, or a friendly hand on her hair or neck; she learns and often deliberately seeks a deeper excitement in her relations of play and fighting with boys or girls: thus Gilberte fighting on the Champs Elysées with Proust; in the arms of her dancing partners, under her mother's naive eyes, she experiences a strange lassitude. And then, even a well-protected young woman is exposed to more specific experiences; in conventional circles regrettable incidents are hushed up by common agreement; but it often happens that some of the caresses of friends of the household, uncles, cousins, not to mention grandfathers and fathers, are much less inoffensive than the mother thinks; a professor, a priest, or a doctor was bold, indiscreet. Such experiences are found in *In the Prison of Her Skin* by Violette Leduc, in *Maternal Hatred* by Simone de Tervagne, and in *The Blue Orange* by Yassu Gauclère. Stekel thinks that grandfathers in particular are often very dangerous:

> I was fifteen. The night before the funeral, my grandfather came
> to sleep at our house. The next day, my mother was already up, he

---

47. Except, of course, in numerous cases where the direct or indirect intervention of the parents, or religious scruples, make a sin of it. Little girls have sometimes been subjected to abominable persecutions, under the pretext of saving them from "bad habits."

asked me if he could get into bed with me to play; I got up immediately without answering him . . . I began to be afraid of men, a woman recounted.

Another girl recalled receiving a serious shock at eight or ten years of age when her grandfather, an old man of sixty, had groped her genitals. He had taken her on his lap while sliding his finger into her vagina. The child had felt an immense anxiety but yet did not dare talk about it. Since that time she has been very afraid of everything sexual.[48]

Such incidents are usually endured in silence by the little girl because of the shame they cause. Moreover, if she does reveal them to her parents, their reaction is often to reprimand her. "Don't say such stupid things . . . you've got an evil mind." She is also silent about bizarre activities of some strangers. A little girl told Dr. Liepmann:

We had rented a room from the shoemaker in the basement. Often when our landlord was alone, he came to get me, took me in his arms, and kissed me for a long time all the while wiggling back and forth. His kiss wasn't superficial besides, since he stuck his tongue into my mouth. I detested him because of his ways. But I never whispered a word, as I was very fearful.[49]

In addition to enterprising companions and perverse girlfriends, there is this knee in the cinema pressed against the girl's, this hand at night in the train, sliding along her leg, these boys who sniggered when she passed, these men who followed her in the street, these embraces, these furtive touches. She does not really understand the meaning of these adventures. In the fifteen-year-old head, there is often a strange confusion because theoretical knowledge and concrete experiences do not match. She has already felt all the burnings of excitement and desire, but she imagines—like Clara d'Ellébeuse invented by Francis Jammes—that a male kiss is enough to make her a mother; she has a clear idea of the genital anatomy, but when her dancing partner embraces her, she thinks the agitation she feels is a migraine. It is certain that girls are better informed today than in the past. However, some psychiatrists affirm that there is more than one adolescent

---

48. *Frigidity in Woman.*
49. Liepmann, *Youth and Sexuality.*

girl who does not know that sexual organs have a use other than urinary.[50] In any case, girls do not draw much connection between their sexual agitation and the existence of their genital organs, since there is no sign as precise as the male erection indicating this correlation. There is such a gap between their romantic musings concerning man and love and the crudeness of certain facts that are revealed to them that they do not create any link between them. Thyde Monnier relates that she had made the pledge with a few girlfriends to see how a man was made and to tell it to the others:

> Having entered my father's room on purpose without knocking, I described it: "It looks like a leg of lamb; that is, it is like a rolling pin, and then there is a round thing." It was difficult to explain. I drew it. I even did it three times, and each one took hers away hidden in her blouse, and from time to time she burst out laughing while looking at it and then went all dreamy . . . How could innocent girls like us set up a connection between these objects and sentimental songs, pretty little romantic stories where love as a whole—respect, shyness, sighs, and kissing of the hand—is sublimated to the point of making a eunuch?[51]

Nevertheless, through reading, conversations, theater, and words she has overheard, the girl gives meaning to the disturbances of her flesh; she becomes appeal and desire. In her fevers, shivers, dampness, and uncertain states, her body takes on a new and unsettling dimension. The young man is proud of his sexual propensities because he assumes his virility joyfully; sexual desire is aggressive and prehensile for him; there is an affirmation of his subjectivity and transcendence in it; he boasts of it to his friends; his sex organ is for him a disturbance he takes pride in; the drive that sends him toward the female is of the same nature as that which throws him toward the world, and so he recognizes himself in it. On the contrary, the girl's sexual life has always been hidden; when her eroticism is transformed and invades her whole flesh, the mystery becomes agonizing: she undergoes the disturbance as a shameful illness; it is not active: it is a state, and even in imagination she cannot get rid of it by any autonomous decision; she does not dream of taking, pressing, violating: she is wait and appeal; she feels dependent; she feels herself at risk in her alienated flesh.

Her diffuse hope and her dream of happy passivity clearly reveal her

---

50. Cf. H. Deutsch, *Psychology of Women.*
51. *Me.*

body as an object destined for another; she seeks to know sexual experience only in its immanence; it is the contact of the hand, mouth, or another flesh that she desires; the image of her partner is left in the shadows, or she drowns it in an idealized haze; however, she cannot prevent his presence from haunting her. Her terrors and juvenile revulsions regarding man have assumed a more equivocal character than before, and because of that they are more agonizing. Before, they stemmed from a profound divorce between the child's organism and her future as an adult; now they come from this very complexity that the girl feels in her flesh. She understands that she is destined for possession because she wants it: and she revolts against her desires. She at once wishes for and fears the shameful passivity of the consenting prey. She is overwhelmed with confusion at the idea of baring herself before a man; but she also senses that she will then be given over to his gaze without recourse. The hand that takes and that touches has an even more imperious presence than do eyes: it is more frightening. But the most obvious and detestable symbol of physical possession is penetration by the male's sex organ. The girl hates the idea that this body she identifies with may be perforated as one perforates leather, that it can be torn as one tears a piece of fabric. But the girl refuses more than the wound and the accompanying pain; she refuses that these be *inflicted*. "The idea of being *pierced* by a man is horrible," a girl told me one day. It is not fear of the virile member that engenders horror of the man, but this fear is the confirmation and symbol; the idea of penetration acquires its obscene and humiliating meaning within a more generalized form, of which it is in turn an essential element.

The girl's anxiety shows itself in nightmares that torment her and fantasies that haunt her: just when she feels an insidious complaisance in herself, the idea of rape becomes obsessive in many cases. It manifests itself in dreams and behavior in the form of many more or less obvious symbols. The girl explores her room before going to bed for fear of finding some robber with shady intentions; she thinks she hears thieves in the house; an aggressor comes in through the window armed with a knife and he stabs her. In a more or less acute way, men inspire terror in her. She begins to feel a certain disgust for her father; she can no longer stand the smell of his tobacco, she detests going into the bathroom after him; even if she continues to cherish him, this physical revulsion is frequent; it takes on an intensified form if the child was already hostile to her father, as often happens in the youngest children. A dream often encountered by psychiatrists in their young female patients is that they imagine being raped by a man in front of an older woman and with her consent. It is clear that they are symbolically asking their mother for permission to give in to their desires. That is because one of the most detestable constraints weighing on them is that of hypocrisy. The girl is dedicated to "purity," to innocence, at precisely the moment she discovers in and around her the mysterious disturbances of life and sex. She has to be white like an ermine, transparent like crystal, she is dressed in vaporous organdy, her room is decorated with candy-colored hangings, people lower their voices when she approaches, she is prohibited from seeing indecent books; yet there is not one child on earth who does not relish "abominable" images and desires. She tries to hide them from her best friend, even from herself; she only wants to live or to think by the rules; her self-defiance gives her a devious, unhappy, and sickly look; and later, nothing will be harder than combating these inhibitions. But in spite of all these repressions, she feels oppressed by the weight of unspeakable faults. Her metamorphosis into a woman takes place not only in shame but in remorse for suffering that shame.

We understand that the awkward age is a period of painful distress for the girl. She does not want to remain a child. But the adult world seems frightening or boring to her. Colette Audry says:

> So I wanted to grow up, but never did I seriously dream of leading the life I saw adults lead . . . And thus the desire to grow up without ever assuming an adult state, without ever feeling solidarity with parents, mistresses of the house, housewives, or heads of family, was forming in me.

She would like to free herself from her mother's yoke; but she also has an ardent need for her protection. The faults that weigh on her consciousness—solitary sexual practices, dubious friendships, improper books—make this refuge necessary. The following letter, written to a girl-friend by a fifteen-year-old girl, is typical:

> Mother wants me to wear a long dress at the big dance party at W.'s—my first long dress. She is surprised that I do not want to. I begged her to let me wear my short pink dress for the last time . . . I am so afraid. This long dress makes me feel as if Mummy were going on a long trip and I did not know when she would. Isn't that silly? And sometimes she looks at me as though I were still a little girl. Ah, if she knew! She would tie my hands to the bed and despise me.[52]

---

52. Quoted by H. Deutsch, *Psychology of Women*.

Stekel's book *Frigidity in Woman* is a remarkable document on female childhood. In it a Viennese *süsse Mädel* wrote a detailed confession at about the age of twenty-one.* It is a concrete synthesis of all the moments we have studied separately:

"At the age of five I chose for my playmate Richard, a boy of six or seven . . . For a long time I had wanted to know how one can tell whether a child is a girl or a boy. I was told: by the earrings . . . or by the nose. This seemed to satisfy me, though I had a feeling that they were keeping something from me. Suddenly Richard expressed a desire to urinate . . . Then the thought came to me of lending him my chamber pot . . . When I saw his organ, which was something entirely new to me, I went into highest raptures: 'What have you there? My, isn't that nice! I'd like to have something like that, too.' Whereupon I took hold of the membrum and held it enthusiastically . . . My great-aunt's cough awoke us . . . and from that day on our doings and games were carefully watched."

At nine she played "marriage" and "doctor" with two other boys of eight and ten; they touched her parts and one day one of the boys touched her with his organ, saying that her parents had done just the same thing when they got married. "This aroused my indignation: 'Oh, no! They never did such a nasty thing!' " She kept up these games for a long time in a strong sexual friendship with the two boys. One day her aunt caught her and there was a frightful scene with threats to put her in the reformatory. She was prevented from seeing Arthur, whom she preferred, and she suffered a good deal from it; her work went badly, her writing was deformed, and she became cross-eyed. She started another intimacy with Walter and Franz. "Walter became the goal of all thoughts and feeling. I permitted him very submissively to reach under my dress while I sat or stood in front of him at the table, pretending to be busy with a writing exercise; whenever my mother . . . opened the door, he withdrew his hand on the instant; I, of course, was busy writing . . . In the course of time, we also behaved as husband and wife; but I never allowed him to stay long; whenever he thought he was inside me, I tore myself away saying that somebody was coming . . . I did not reflect that this was 'sinful' . . .

* *Süsse Mädel:* "sweet girl."—Trans.

"My childhood boy friendships were now over. All I had left were girl friends. I attached myself to Emmy, a highly refined, well-educated girl. One Christmas we exchanged gilded heart-shaped lockets with our initials engraved on them—we were, I believe, about twelve years of age at the time—and we looked upon this as a token of 'engagement'; we swore eternal faithfulness 'until death do us part.' I owe to Emmy a goodly part of my training. She taught me also a few things regarding sexual matters. As far back as during my fifth grade at school I began seriously to doubt the veracity of the stork story. I thought that children developed within the body and that the abdomen must be cut open before a child can be brought out. She filled me with particular horror of self-abuse. In school the Gospels contributed a share towards opening our eyes with regard to certain sexual matters. For instance, when Mary came to Elizabeth, the child is said to have 'leaped in her womb'; and we read other similarly remarkable Bible passages. We underscored these words; and when this was discovered the whole class barely escaped a 'black mark' in deportment. My girl friend told me also about the 'ninth month reminder' to which there is a reference in Schiller's *The Robbers* . . . Emmy's father moved from our locality and I was again alone. We corresponded, using for the purpose a cryptic alphabet which we had devised between ourselves; but I was lonesome and finally I attached myself to Hedl, a Jewish girl. Once Emmy caught me leaving school in Hedl's company; she created a scene on account of her jealousy . . . I kept up my friendship with Hedl until I entered the commercial school. We became close friends. We both dreamed of becoming sisters-in-law sometimes, because I was fond of one of her brothers. He was a student. Whenever he spoke to me I became so confused that I gave him an irrelevant answer. At dusk we sat in the music room, huddled together on the little divan, and often tears rolled down my cheek for no particular reason as he played the piano.

"Before I befriended Hedl, I went to school for a number of weeks with a certain girl, Ella, the daughter of poor people. Once she caught her parents in a 'tête-à-tête.' The creaking of the bed had awakened her . . . She came and told me that her father had crawled on top of her mother, and that the mother had cried out terribly; and then the father said to her mother: 'Go quickly and wash so that nothing will happen!' After this I was angry at her father and avoided him on the street, while for her mother I felt the greatest sympathy. (He must have hurt her terribly if she cried out so!)

"Again with another girl I discussed the possible length of the male membrum; I had heard that it was 12 to 15 cm long. During the fancy-work period (at school) we took the tape-measure and indicated the stated length on our stomachs, naturally reaching to the navel. This horrified us; if we should ever marry we would be literally impaled."

She saw a male dog excited by the proximity of a female, and felt strange stirrings inside herself. "If I saw a horse urinate in the street, my eyes were always glued to the wet spot in the road; I believe the length of time (urinating) is what always impressed me." She watched flies in copulation and in the country domesticated animals doing the same.

"At twelve I suffered a severe attack of tonsillitis. A friendly physician was called in. He seated himself on my bed and presently he stuck his hand under the covers, almost touching me on the genitalia. I exclaimed: 'Don't be so rude!' My mother hurried in; the doctor was much embarrassed. He declared I was a horrid monkey, saying he merely wanted to pinch me on the calf. I was compelled to ask his forgiveness . . . When I finally began to menstruate and my father came across the blood-stained cloths on one occasion, there was a terrible scene. How did it happen that he, so clean a man, had to live among such dirty females? . . . I felt the injustice of being put in the wrong on account of my menstruation." At fifteen she communicated with another girl in shorthand "so that no one else could decipher our missives. There was much to report about conquests. She copied for me a vast number of verses from the walls of lavatories; I took particular notice of one. It seemed to me that love, which ranged so high in my fantasy, was being dragged in the mud by it. The verse read: 'What is love's highest aim? Four buttocks on a stem.' I decided I would never get into that situation; a man who loves a young girl would be unable to ask such a thing of her.

"At fifteen and a half I had a new brother. I was tremendously jealous, for I had always been the only child in the family. My friend reminded me to observe 'how the baby boy was constructed,' but with the best intentions I was unable to give her the desired information . . . I could not look there. At about this time another girl described to me a bridal night scene . . . I think that then I made up my mind to marry after all, for I was very curious; only the 'panting like a horse,' as mentioned in the description, offended my aesthetic sense . . . Which one of us girls would not have gladly married then to undress before the beloved and be carried to bed in his arms? It seemed so thrilling!"

It will perhaps be said—even though this is a normal and not a pathological case—that this child was exceptionally "perverse"; she was only less watched over than others. If the curiosities and desires of "well-bred" girls do not manifest themselves in acts, they nonetheless exist in the form of fantasies and games. I once knew a very pious and disconcertingly innocent girl—who became an accomplished woman, devoted to maternity and religion—who one evening confided all trembling to an older woman, "How marvelous it must be to get undressed in front of a man! Let's suppose you are my husband"; and she began to undress, all trembling with emotion. No upbringing can prevent the girl from becoming aware of her body and dreaming of her destiny; the most one can do is to impose strict repression that will then weigh on her for her whole sexual life. What would be desirable is that she be taught, on the contrary, to accept herself without excuses and without shame.

One understands now the drama that rends the adolescent girl at puberty: she cannot become "a grown-up" without accepting her femininity; she already knew her sex condemned her to a mutilated and frozen existence; she now discovers it in the form of an impure illness and an obscure crime. Her inferiority was at first understood as a privation: the absence of a penis was converted to a stain and fault. She makes her way toward the future wounded, shamed, worried, and guilty.

CHAPTER 2

The Girl

Throughout her childhood, the little girl was bullied and mutilated; but she nonetheless grasped herself as an autonomous individual; in her relations with her family and friends, in her studies and games, she saw herself in the present as a transcendence: her future passivity was something she only imagined. Once she enters puberty, the future not only moves closer: it settles into her body; it becomes the most concrete reality. It retains the fateful quality it always had; while the adolescent boy is actively routed toward adulthood, the girl looks forward to the opening of this new and unforeseeable period where the plot is already hatched and toward which time is drawing her. As she is already detached from her childhood past, the present is for her only a transition; she sees no valid ends in it, only occupations. In a more or less disguised way, her youth is consumed by waiting. She is waiting for Man.

Surely the adolescent boy also dreams of woman, he desires her; but she will never be more than one element in his life: she does not encapsulate his destiny; from childhood, the little girl, whether wishing to realize herself as woman or overcome the limits of her femininity, has awaited the male for accomplishment and escape; he has the dazzling face of Perseus or Saint George; he is the liberator; he is also rich and powerful, he holds the keys to happiness, he is Prince Charming. She anticipates that in his caress she will feel carried away by the great current of life as when she rested in her mother's bosom; subjected to his gentle authority, she will find the same security as in her father's arms: the magic of embraces and gazes will petrify her back into an idol. She has always been convinced of male superiority; this male prestige is not a childish mirage; it has economic and social foundations; men are, without any question, the masters of the world; everything convinces the adolescent girl that it is in her interest to be their vassal; her parents prod her on; the father is proud of his daughter's success, the mother sees the promise of a prosperous future, friends envy and admire the one among them who gets the most masculine admiration; in American colleges, the student's status is based on the number of dates she has. Marriage is not only an honorable and less strenuous career than many others; it alone enables woman to attain her complete social dignity and also to realize herself sexually as lover and mother. This is the role her entourage thus envisages for her future, as she envisages it herself. Everyone unanimously agrees that catching a husband—or a protector in some cases—is for her the most important of undertakings. In her eyes, man embodies the Other, as she does for man; but for her this *Other* appears in the essential mode, and she grasps herself as the inessential opposite him. She will free herself from her parents' home, from her mother's hold; she will open up her future not by an active conquest but by passively and docilely delivering herself into the hands of a new master.

It has often been declared that if she resigns herself to this surrender, it is because physically and morally she has become inferior to boys and incapable of competing with them: forsaking hopeless competition, she entrusts the assurance of her happiness to a member of the superior caste. In fact, her humility does not stem from a given inferiority: on the contrary, her humility engenders all her failings; its source is in the adolescent girl's past, in the society around her, and precisely in this future that is proposed to her.

True, puberty transforms the girl's body. It is more fragile than before; female organs are vulnerable, their functioning delicate; strange and uncomfortable, breasts are a burden; they remind her of their presence during strenuous exercise, they quiver, they ache. From here on, woman's muscle force, endurance, and suppleness are inferior to man's. Hormonal imbalances create nervous and vasomotor instability. Menstrual periods are painful: headaches, stiffness, and abdominal cramps make normal activities painful and even impossible; added to these discomforts are psychic problems; nervous and irritable, the woman frequently undergoes a state of semi-alienation each month; central control of the nervous and sympathetic systems is no longer assured; circulation problems and some auto-intoxications turn the body into a screen between the woman and the world, a burning fog that weighs on her, stifling her and separating her: experienced through this suffering and passive flesh, the entire universe is a burden too heavy to bear. Oppressed and submerged, she becomes a stranger to herself because she is a stranger to the rest of the world. Syntheses disintegrate, instants are no longer connected, others are recognized but only abstractly; and if reasoning and logic do remain intact, as in melancholic delirium, they are subordinated to passions that surge out of organic disorder. These facts are extremely important; but the way the woman becomes conscious of them gives them their weight.

At about thirteen, boys serve a veritable apprenticeship in violence, developing their aggressiveness, their will for power, and their taste for competition; it is exactly at this moment that the little girl renounces rough games. Some sports remain accessible to her, but sport that is specialization, submission to artificial rules, does not offer the equivalent of a spontaneous and habitual recourse to force; it is marginal to life; it does not teach about the world and about one's self as intimately as does an unruly fight or an impulsive rock climb. The sportswoman never feels the conqueror's pride of the boy who pins down his comrade. In fact, in many countries, most girls have no athletic training; like fights, climbing is forbidden to them, they only submit to their bodies passively; far more clearly than in their early years, they must forgo *emerging* beyond the given world, affirming themselves *above* the rest of humanity: they are banned from exploring, daring, pushing back the limits of the possible. In particular, the attitude of defiance, so important for boys, is unknown to them; true, women compare themselves with each other, but defiance is something other than these passive confrontations: two freedoms confront each other as having a hold on the world whose limits they intend to push; climbing higher than a friend or getting the better in arm wrestling is affirming one's sovereignty over the world. These conquering actions are not permitted to the girl, and violence in particular is not permitted to her. Undoubtedly, in the adult world brute force plays no great role in normal times; but it nonetheless haunts the world; much of masculine behavior arises in a setting of potential violence: on every street corner skirmishes are waiting to happen; in most cases they are aborted; but it is enough for the man to feel in his fists his will for self-affirmation for him to feel confirmed in his sovereignty. The male has recourse to his fists and fighting when he encounters any affront or attempt to reduce him to an object: he does not let himself be transcended by others; he finds himself again in the heart of his subjectivity. Violence is the authentic test of every person's attachment to himself, his passions, and his own will; to radically reject it is to reject all objective truth, it is to isolate one's self in an abstract subjectivity; an anger or a revolt that does not exert itself in muscles remains imaginary. It is a terrible frustration not to be able to imprint the movements of one's heart on the face of the earth. In the South of the United States, it is strictly impossible for a black person to use violence against whites; this rule is the key to the mysterious "black soul"; the way the black experiences himself in the white world, his behavior in adjusting to it, the compensations he seeks, his whole way of feeling and acting, are explained on the basis of the passivity to which he is condemned. During the Occupation, the French who had decided not to let themselves resort to violent gestures against the occupants even in cases of provocation (whether out of egotistical prudence or because they had overriding duties) felt their situation in the world profoundly overturned: depending upon the whims of others, they could be changed into objects, their subjectivity no longer had the means to express itself concretely, it was merely a secondary phenomenon. In the same way, for the adolescent boy who is allowed to manifest himself imperiously, the universe has a totally different face from what it has for the adolescent girl whose feelings are deprived of immediate effectiveness; the former ceaselessly calls the world into question, he can at every instance revolt against the given and thus has the impression of actively confirming it when he accepts it; the latter only submits to it; the world is defined without her, and its face is immutable. This lack of physical power expresses itself as a more general timidity: she does not believe in a force she has not felt in her body, she does not dare to be enterprising, to revolt, to invent; doomed to docility, to resignation, she can only accept a place that society has already made for her. She accepts the order of things as a given. A woman told me that all through her youth, she denied her physical weakness with fierce bad faith; to accept it would have been to lose her taste and courage to undertake anything, even in intellectual or political fields. I knew a girl, brought up as a tomboy and exceptionally vigorous, who thought she was as strong as a man; though she was very pretty, though she had painful periods every month, she was completely unconscious of her femininity; she had a boy's toughness, exuberance of life, and initiative; she had a boy's boldness: on the street she would not hesitate to jump into a fistfight if she saw a child or a woman harassed. One or two bad experiences revealed to her that brute force is on the male's side. When she became aware of her weakness, a great part of her assurance crumbled; this was the beginning of an evolution that led her to feminize herself, to realize herself as passivity, to accept dependence. To lose confidence in one's body is to lose confidence in one's self. One needs only to see the importance that young men give to their muscles to understand that every subject grasps his body as his objective expression.

The young man's erotic drives only go to confirm the pride that he obtains from his body: he discovers in it the sign of transcendence and its power. The girl can succeed in accepting her desires: but most often they retain a shameful nature. Her whole body is experienced as embarrassment. The defiance she felt as a child regarding her "insides" contributes to giving the menstrual crisis the dubious nature that renders it loathsome. The psychic attitude evoked by menstrual servitude constitutes a heavy handicap. The threat that weighs on the girl during certain periods can seem so intolerable for her that she will give up expeditions and pleasures out of fear of her disgrace becoming known. The horror that this inspires has repercussions on her organism and increases her disorders and pains. It has been seen that one of the characteristics of female physiology is the tight link between endocrinal secretions and the nervous system: there is reciprocal action; a woman's body—and specifically the girl's—is a "hysterical" body in the sense that there is, so to speak, no distance between psychic life and its physiological realization. The turmoil brought about by the girl's discovery of the problems of puberty exacerbates them. Because her body is suspect to her, she scrutinizes it with anxiety and sees it as sick: it is sick. It has been seen that indeed this body is fragile and real organic disorders arise; but gynecologists concur that nine-tenths of their patients have imaginary illnesses; that is, either their illnesses have no physiological reality, or the organic disorder itself stems from a psychic attitude. To a great extent, the anguish of being a woman eats away at the female body.

It is clear that if woman's biological situation constitutes a handicap for her, it is because of the perspective from which it is grasped. Nervous frailty and vasomotor instability, when they do not become pathological, do not keep her from any profession: among males themselves, there is a great diversity of temperament. A one- or two-day indisposition per month, even painful, is not an obstacle either; in fact, many women accommodate themselves to it, particularly women for whom the monthly "curse" could be most bothersome: athletes, travelers, and women who do strenuous work. Most professions demand no more energy than women can provide. And in sports, the goal is not to succeed independently of physical aptitudes: it is the accomplishment of perfection proper to each organism; the lightweight champion is as worthy as the heavyweight; a female ski champion is no less a champion than the male who is more rapid than she: they belong to two different categories. It is precisely athletes who, positively concerned with their own accomplishments, feel the least handicapped in comparison to men. But nonetheless her physical weakness does not allow the woman to learn the lessons of violence: if it were possible to assert herself in her body and be part of the world in some other way, this deficiency would be easily compensated. If she could swim, scale rocks, pilot a plane, battle the elements, take risks, and venture out, she would not feel the timidity toward the world that I spoke about. It is within the whole context of a situation that leaves her few outlets that these singularities take on their importance, and not immediately but by confirming the inferiority complex that was developed in her by her childhood.

It is this complex as well that will weigh on her intellectual accomplishments. It has often been noted that from puberty, the girl loses ground in intellectual and artistic fields. There are many reasons for this. One of the most common is that the adolescent girl does not receive the same encouragement accorded to her brothers; on the contrary, she is expected to be a *woman as well*, and she must add to her professional work the duties that femininity implies. The headmistress of a professional school made these comments on the subject:

> The girl suddenly becomes a being who earns her living by working. She has new desires that have nothing to do with the family. It very often happens that she must make quite a considerable effort . . . she gets home at night exhausted, her head stuffed with the day's events . . . How will she be received? Her mother sends her right out to do an errand. There are home chores left unfinished to do, and she still has to take care of her own clothes. It is impossible to disconnect from the personal thoughts that continue to preoccupy her. She feels unhappy and compares her situation with that of her brother, who has no duties at home, and she revolts.[1]

Housework or everyday chores that the mother does not hesitate to impose on the girl student or trainee completely exhaust her. During the war I saw my students in Sèvres worn out by family tasks added on top of their schoolwork: one developed Pott's disease, the other meningitis. Mothers—we will see—are blindly hostile to freeing their daughters and, more or less deliberately, work at bullying them even more; for the adolescent boy, his effort to become a man is respected, and he is already granted great freedom. The girl is required to stay home; her outside activities are watched over: she is never encouraged to organize her own fun and pleasure. It is rare to see women organize a long hike on their own, a walking or biking trip, or take part in games such as billiards and bowling. Beyond a lack of initiative that comes from their education, customs make their independence difficult. If they wander the streets, they are stared at, accosted. I know some girls, far from shy, who get no enjoyment strolling through Paris alone because, incessantly bothered, they are incessantly on their

---

1. Cited by Liepmann, *Youth and Sexuality*.

guard: all their pleasure is ruined. If girl students run through the streets in happy groups as boys do, they attract attention; striding along, singing, talking, and laughing loudly or eating an apple are provocations, and they will be insulted or followed or approached. Lightheartedness immediately becomes a lack of decorum. This self-control imposed on the woman becomes second nature for "the well-bred girl" and kills spontaneity; lively exuberance is crushed. The result is tension and boredom. This boredom is contagious: girls tire of each other quickly; being in the same prison does not create solidarity among them, and this is one of the reasons the company of boys becomes so necessary. This inability to be self-sufficient brings on a shyness that extends over their whole lives and even marks their work. They think that brilliant triumphs are reserved for men; they do not dare aim too high. It has already been observed that fifteen-year-old girls, comparing themselves with boys, declare, "Boys are better." This conviction is debilitating. It encourages laziness and mediocrity. A girl—who had no particular deference for the stronger sex—reproached a man for his cowardice; when she was told that she herself was a coward, she complacently declared: "Oh! It's not the same thing for a woman."

The fundamental reason for this defeatism is that the adolescent girl does not consider herself responsible for her future; she judges it useless to demand much of herself since her lot in the end will not depend on her. Far from destining herself to man because she thinks she is inferior to him, it is because she is destined for him that, in accepting the idea of her inferiority, she constitutes it.

In fact, she will gain value in the eyes of males not by increasing her human worth but by modeling herself on their dreams. When she is inexperienced, she is not always aware of this. She sometimes acts as aggressively as boys; she tries to conquer them with a brusque authority, a proud frankness: this attitude is almost surely doomed to failure. From the most servile to the haughtiest, girls all learn that to please, they must give in to them. Their mothers urge them not to treat boys like companions, not to make advances to them, to assume a passive role. If they want to flirt or initiate a friendship, they should carefully avoid giving the impression they are taking the initiative; men do not like tomboys, nor bluestockings, nor thinking women; too much audacity, culture, intelligence, or character frightens them. In most novels, as George Eliot observes, it is the dumb, blond heroine who outshines the virile brunette; and in *The Mill on the Floss*, Maggie tries in vain to reverse the roles; in the end she dies and it is blond Lucy who marries Stephen. In *The Last of the Mohicans*, vapid Alice wins the hero's heart and not valiant Cora; in *Little Women* kindly Jo is only a childhood friend for Laurie; he vows his love to curly-haired and insipid Amy. To be feminine is to show oneself as weak, futile, passive, and docile. The girl is supposed not only to primp and dress herself up but also to repress her spontaneity and substitute for it the grace and charm she has been taught by her elder sisters. Any self-assertion will take away from her femininity and her seductiveness. A young man's venture into existence is relatively easy, as his vocations of human being and male are not contradictory; his childhood already predicted this happy fate. It is in accomplishing himself as independence and freedom that he acquires his social value and, concurrently, his manly prestige: the ambitious man, like Rastignac, targets money, glory, and women all at once; one of the stereotypes that stimulates him is that of the powerful and famous man adored by women. For the girl, on the contrary, there is a divorce between her properly human condition and her feminine vocation. This is why adolescence is such a difficult and decisive moment for woman. Until then, she was an autonomous individual: she now has to renounce her sovereignty. Not only is she torn like her brothers, and more acutely, between past and future, but in addition a conflict breaks out between her originary claim to be subject, activity, and freedom, on the one hand and, on the other, her erotic tendencies and the social pressure to assume herself as a passive object. She spontaneously grasps herself as the essential: How will she decide to become the inessential? If I can accomplish myself only as the *Other*, how will I renounce my *Self*? Such is the agonizing dilemma the woman-to-be must struggle with. Wavering from desire to disgust, from hope to fear, rebuffing what she invites, she is still suspended between the moment of childish independence and that of feminine submission: this is the incertitude that, as she grows out of the awkward age, gives her the bitter taste of unripe fruit.

The girl reacts to her situation differently depending on her earlier choices. The "little woman," the matron-to-be, can easily resign herself to her metamorphosis; but she may also have drawn a taste for authority from her condition as "little woman" that lets her rebel against the masculine yoke: she is ready to establish a matriarchy, not to become an erotic object and servant. This will often be the case of those older sisters who took on important responsibilities at a young age. The "tomboy," upon becoming a woman, often feels a burning disappointment that can drive her directly to homosexuality; but what she was looking for in independence and intensity was to possess the world: she may not want to renounce the power of her femininity, the experiences of maternity, a whole part of her destiny. Generally, with some resistance, the girl consents to her femininity: already at the stage of childish coquetry, in front of her father, in her erotic fantasies, she understood the charm of passivity; she discovers the power in it; vanity is soon mixed with the shame that her flesh inspires. That hand that moves her, that glance that excites her, they are an appeal, an invitation; her body seems endowed with magic virtues; it is a treasure, a weapon; she is proud of it. Her coquetry, which often has disappeared during her years of childhood autonomy, is revived. She tries makeup, hairstyles; instead of hiding her breasts, she massages them to make them bigger; she studies her smile in the mirror. The link is so tight between arousal and seduction that in all cases where erotic sensibility lies dormant, no desire to please is observed in the subject. Experiments have shown that patients suffering from a thyroid deficiency, and thus apathetic and sullen, can be transformed by an injection of glandular extracts: they begin to smile; they become gay and simpering. Psychologists imbued with materialistic metaphysics have boldly declared flirtatiousness an "instinct" secreted by the thyroid gland; but this obscure explanation is no more valid here than for early childhood. The fact is that in all cases of organic deficiency—lymphatism, anemia, and such—the body is endured as a burden; foreign, hostile, it neither hopes for nor promises anything; when it recovers its equilibrium and vitality, the subject at once recognizes it as his, and through it he transcends toward others.

For the girl, erotic transcendence consists in making herself prey in order to make a catch. She becomes an object; and she grasps herself as object; she is surprised to discover this new aspect of her being: it seems to her that she has been doubled; instead of coinciding exactly with her self, here she is existing *outside* of her self. Thus in Rosamond Lehmann's *Invitation to the Waltz*, Olivia discovers an unknown face in the mirror: it is she-object suddenly rising up opposite herself; she experiences a quickly fading but upsetting emotion:

Nowadays a peculiar emotion accompanied the moment of looking in the mirror: fitfully, rarely a stranger might emerge: a new self.

It had happened two or three times already . . . She looked in the glass and saw herself . . . Well, what was it? . . . But this was something else. This was a mysterious face; both dark and glowing; hair tumbling down, pushed back and upwards, as if in currents of fierce energy. Was it the frock that did it? Her body seemed to assemble itself harmoniously within it, to become centralized, to expand, both static and fluid; alive. It was the portrait of a young girl in pink. All the room's reflected objects seemed to frame, to present her, whispering: Here are You.

What astonishes Olivia are the promises she thinks she reads in this image in which she recognizes her childish dreams and which is herself; but the girl also cherishes in her carnal presence this body that fascinates her as if it were someone else's. She caresses herself, she embraces the curve of her shoulder, the bend of her elbow, she contemplates her bosom, her legs; solitary pleasure becomes a pretext for reverie, in it she seeks a tender self-possession. For the boy adolescent, there is an opposition between love of one's self and the erotic movement that thrusts him toward the object to be possessed: his narcissism generally disappears at the moment of sexual maturity. Instead of the woman being a passive object for the lover as for herself, there is a primitive blurring in her eroticism. In one complex step, she aims for her body's glorification through the homage of men for whom this body is intended; and it would be a simplification to say that she wants to be beautiful in order to charm, or that she seeks to charm to assure herself that she is beautiful: in the solitude of her room, in salons where she tries to attract the gaze of others, she does not separate man's desire from the love of her own self. This confusion is manifest in Marie Bashkirtseff.* It has already been seen that late weaning disposed her more deeply than any other child to wanting to be gazed at and valorized by others; from the age of five until the end of adolescence, she devotes all her love to her image; she madly admires her hands, her face, her grace, and she writes: "I am my own heroine." She wants to become an opera singer to be *gazed at* by a dazzled public so as to *look back* with a proud gaze; but this "autism" expresses itself through romantic dreams; from the age of twelve, she is in love: she wants to be loved, and the adoration that she seeks to inspire only confirms that which she devotes to herself. She dreams that the Duke of H., with whom she is in love without having ever spoken to him, prostrates himself at her feet: "You will be dazzled by my splendor and you will love me . . . You are worthy only of such a woman as I intend to be." The same ambivalence is found in Natasha in *War and Peace:*

> "Even mama doesn't understand. It's astonishing how intelligent
> I am and how . . . sweet she is," she went on, speaking of herself
> in the third person and imagining that it was some very intelligent
> man saying it about her, the most intelligent and best of men . . .
> "There's everything in her, everything," this man went on, "she's

---

* *I Am the Most Interesting Book of All.*—TRANS.

extraordinarily intelligent, sweet, and then, too, pretty, extraordinarily pretty, nimble—she swims, she's an excellent horsewoman, and the voice! One may say, an astonishing voice!" . . .

That morning she returned again to her favorite state of love and admiration for herself. "How lovely that Natasha is!" she said of herself again in the words of some collective male third person. "Pretty, a good voice, young, and doesn't bother anybody, only leave her in peace."

Katherine Mansfield (in "Prelude") has also described, in the character of Beryl, a case in which narcissism and the romantic desire for a woman's destiny are closely intermingled:

In the dining-room, by the flicker of a wood fire, Beryl sat on a hassock playing the guitar . . . She played and sang half to herself, for she was watching herself playing and singing. The firelight gleamed on her shoes, on the ruddy belly of the guitar, and on her white fingers . . .

"If I were outside the window and looked in and saw myself I really would be rather struck," thought she. Still more softly she played the accompaniment—not singing now but listening . . .

". . . The first time that I ever saw you, little girl—oh, you had no idea that you were not alone—you were sitting with your little feet upon a hassock, playing the guitar. God, I can never forget . . ." Beryl flung up her head and began to sing again:

> Even the moon is aweary . . .

But there came a loud bang at the door. The servant girl's crimson face popped through . . . But no, she could not stand that fool of a girl. She ran into the dark drawing-room and began walking up and down . . . Oh, she was restless, restless. There was a mirror over the mantel. She leaned her arms along and looked at her pale shadow in it. How beautiful she looked, but there was nobody to see, nobody . . .

Beryl smiled, and really her smile *was* so adorable that she smiled again.

This cult of the self is not only expressed by the girl as the adoration of her physical person; she wishes to possess and praise her entire self. This is the purpose of these diaries into which she freely pours her whole soul:

Marie Bashkirtseff's is famous, and it is a model of the genre. The girl speaks to her notebook the way she used to speak to her dolls, as a friend, a confidante, and addresses it as if it were a person. Recorded in its pages is a truth hidden from parents, friends, and teachers, and which enraptures the author when she is all alone. A twelve-year-old girl, who kept a diary until she was twenty, wrote the inscription:

> *I am the little notebook*
> *Nice, pretty, and discreet*
> *Tell me all your secrets*
> *I am the little notebook:*[2]

Others announce: "To be read after my death," or "To be burned when I die." The little girl's sense of secrecy that developed at prepuberty only grows in importance. She closes herself up in fierce solitude: she refuses to reveal to those around her the hidden self that she considers to be her real self and that is in fact an imaginary character: she plays at being a dancer like Tolstoy's Natasha, or a saint like Marie Lenéru, or simply that singular wonder that is herself. There is still an enormous difference between this heroine and the objective face that her parents and friends recognize in her. She is also convinced that she is misunderstood: her relationship with herself becomes even more passionate: she becomes intoxicated with her isolation, feels different, superior, exceptional: she promises that the future will take revenge on the mediocrity of her present life. From this narrow and petty existence she escapes by dreams. She has always loved to dream: she gives herself up to this penchant more than ever; she uses poetic clichés to mask a universe that intimidates her, she sanctifies the male sex with moonlight, rose-colored clouds, velvet nights; she turns her body into a marble, jasper, or mother-of-pearl temple; she tells herself foolish fairy tales. She sinks so often into such nonsense because she has no grasp on the world; if she had to *act*, she would be forced to see clearly, whereas she can *wait* in the fog. The young man dreams as well: he dreams especially of adventures where he plays an active role. The girl prefers wonderment to adventure; she spreads a vague magic light on things and people. The idea of magic is that of a passive force; because she is doomed to passivity and yet wants power, the adolescent girl must believe in magic: her body's magic that will bring men under her yoke, the magic of destiny in general that will

---

2. Cited by Debesse, *La crise d'originalité juvénile* (The Adolescent Identity Crisis).

fulfill her without her having *to do* anything. As for the real world, she tries to forget it:

"In school I sometimes escape, I know not how, the subject being explained and fly away to dreamland . . . ," writes a young girl. "I am thus so absorbed in delightful chimeras that I completely lose the notion of reality. I am nailed to my bench and, when I awake, I am amazed to find myself within four walls."

"I like to daydream much more than doing my verses," writes another, "to dream up nice, nonsensical stories or make up fairy tales when looking at mountains in the starlight. This is much more lovely because it is *more vague* and leaves the impression of repose, of refreshment."[3]

Daydreaming can take on a morbid form and invade the whole existence, as in the following case:

Marie B. . . . an intelligent and dreamy child, entering puberty at fourteen, had a psychic crisis with delusions of grandeur. "She suddenly announces to her parents that she is the queen of Spain, assumes haughty airs, wraps herself in a curtain, laughs, sings, commands, and orders." For two years, this state is repeated during her periods, then for eight years she leads a normal life but is dreamy, loves luxury, and often says bitterly, "I'm an employee's daughter." Toward twenty-three she grows apathetic, hateful of her surroundings, and manifests ambitious ideas; she gets worse to the point of being interned in Sainte-Anne asylum, where she spends eight months; she returns to her family, where, for three years she remains in bed, "disagreeable, mean, violent, capricious, unoccupied, and a burden to all those around her." She is taken back to Sainte-Anne for good and does not come out again. She remains in bed, interested in nothing. At certain periods—seeming to correspond to menstrual periods—she gets up, drapes herself in her bedcovers, strikes theatrical attitudes, poses, smiles at doctors, or looks at them ironically . . . Her comments often express a certain eroticism, and her regal attitude expresses megalomaniac concepts.

---

3. Cited by Marguerite Evard, *L'adolescente* (The Adolescent Girl).

She sinks further and further into her dreamworld, where smiles of satisfaction appear on her face; she is careless of her appearance and even dirties her bed. "She adorns herself with bizarre ornaments, shirtless, often naked, with a tinfoil diadem on her head and string or ribbon bracelets on her arms, her wrists, her shoulders, her ankles. Similar rings adorn her fingers." Yet at times she makes lucid comments on her condition. "I recall the crisis I had before. I knew deep down that it was not real. I was like a child who plays with dolls and who knows that her doll is not alive but wants to convince herself . . . I fixed my hair; I draped myself. I was having fun, and then little by little, as if in spite of myself, I became bewitched; it was like a dream I was living . . . I was like an actress who would play a role. I was in an imaginary world. I lived several lives at a time and *in each life, I was the principal player* . . . Ah! I had so many different lives; once I married a handsome American who wore golden glasses . . . We had a grand hotel and a room for each of us. What parties I gave! . . . I lived in the days of cavemen . . . I was wild in those days. I couldn't count how many men I slept with. Here people are a little backward. They don't understand why I go naked with a gold bracelet on my thigh. I used to have friends that I liked a lot. We had parties at my house. There were flowers, perfume, ermine fur. My friends gave me art objects, statues, cars . . . When I get into my sheets naked, it reminds me of old times. *I admired myself in mirrors,* as an artist . . . In my bewitched state, I was anything I wanted. I was even foolish. I took morphine, cocaine. I had lovers . . . They came to my house at night. They came two at a time. They brought hairdressers and we looked at postcards." She was also the mistress of two of her doctors. She says she had a three-year-old daughter. She has another six-year-old, very rich, who travels. Their father is a very chic man. "There are ten other similar stories. Every one is a feigned existence that she lives in her imagination."[4]

Clearly this morbid daydreaming was essentially to satiate the girl's narcissism, as she feels that her life was inadequate and is afraid to confront the

---

4. From Borel and Robin, *Les reveries morbides*. Cited by Minkowski in *La schizophrénie*. [Borel and Robin wrote *Les rêveurs éveillés* (Daydreamers). Minkowski wrote an article, "De la rêverie morbide au délire d'influence" ("From Morbid Reverie to Delusions of Grandeur"). —TRANS.]

reality of her existence. Marie B. merely carried to the extreme a compensation process common to many adolescents.

Nonetheless, this self-provided solitary cult is not enough for the girl. To fulfill herself, she needs to exist in another consciousness. She often turns to her friends for help. When she was younger, her best girlfriend provided support for her to escape the maternal circle, to explore the world and in particular the sexual world; now her friend is both an object wrenching her to the limits of her self and a witness who restores that self to her. Some young girls exhibit their nudity to each other, they compare their breasts: an example would be the scene in *Girls in Uniform* that shows the daring games of boarding-school girls;* they exchange random or particular caresses. As Colette recounts in *Claudine à l'école* (*Claudine at School*) and Rosamond Lehmann less frankly in *Dusty Answer*, nearly all girls have lesbian tendencies; these tendencies are barely distinguishable from narcissistic delights: in the other, it is the sweetness of her own skin, the form of her own curves, that each of them covets; and vice versa, implicit in her self-adoration is the cult of femininity in general. Sexually, man is subject; men are thus normally separated by the desire that drives them toward an object different from themselves; but woman is an absolute object of desire; this is why "special friendships" flourish in lycées, schools, boarding schools, and workshops; some are purely spiritual and others deeply carnal. In the first case, it is mainly a matter of friends opening their hearts to each other, exchanging confidences; the most passionate proof of confidence is to show one's intimate diary to the chosen one; short of sexual embraces, friends exchange extreme signs of tenderness and often give to each other, in indirect ways, a physical token of their feelings: thus Natasha burns her arm with a red-hot ruler to prove her love for Sonya; mostly they call each other thousands of affectionate names and exchange ardent letters. Here is an example of a letter written by Emily Dickinson, a young New England puritan, to a beloved female friend:

> I think of you all day, and dreamed of you last night . . . I was walking with you in the most wonderful garden, and helping you pick roses, and although we gathered with all our might, the basket was never full. And so all day I pray I may walk with you, and gather roses again, and as night draws on, it pleases me, and I count

---

* A reference to the 1931 German film *Mädchen in Uniform*.—TRANS.

impatiently the hours 'tween me and the darkness, and the dream of you and the roses, and the basket never full . . .

In his work on the adolescent girl's soul, Mendousse cites a great number of similar letters:

My Dear Suzanne . . . I would have liked to copy here a few verses from Song of Songs: how beautiful you are, my friend, how beautiful you are! Like the mystical bride, you were like the rose of Sharon, the lily of the valley, and like her, you have been for me more than an ordinary girl; you have been a symbol, the symbol of all things beautiful and lofty . . . and because of this, pure Suzanne, I love you with a pure and unselfish love that hints of the religious.

Another confesses less lofty emotions in her diary:

I was there, my waist encircled by this little white hand, my hand resting on her round shoulder, my arm on her bare, warm arm, pressed against the softness of her breast, with her lovely mouth before me, parted on her dainty teeth . . . I trembled and felt my face burning.[5]

In her book *The Adolescent Girl*, Mme Evard also collected a great number of these intimate effusions:

To my beloved fairy, my dearest darling. My lovely fairy. Oh! Tell me that you still love me, tell me that for you I am still the devoted friend. I am sad, I love you so, oh my L. . . . and I cannot speak to you, tell you enough of my affection for you; there are no words to describe my love. *Idolize* is a poor way to say what I feel; sometimes it seems that my heart will burst. To be loved by you is too beautiful, I cannot believe it. *Oh my dear,* tell, will you love me longer still?

It is easy to slip from these exalted affections into guilty juvenile crushes; sometimes one of the two girlfriends dominates and exercises her power sadistically over the other; but often, they are reciprocal loves without humiliation or struggle; the pleasure given and received remains as

5. Cited by Mendousse, *L'âme de l'adolescente* (The Adolescent Girl's Soul).

innocent as it was at the time when each one loved alone, without being doubled in a couple. But this very innocence is bland; when the adolescent girl decides to enter into life and becomes the Other, she hopes to rekindle the magic of the paternal gaze to her advantage; she demands the love and caresses of a divinity. She will turn to a woman less foreign and less fearsome than the male, but one who will possess male prestige: a woman who has a profession, who earns her living, who has a certain social base, will easily be as fascinating as a man: we know how many "flames" are lit in schoolgirls' hearts for professors and tutors. In *Regiment of Women*, Clemence Dane uses a chaste style to describe ardently burning passions. Sometimes the girl confides her great passion to her best friend; they even share it, adding spice to their experience. A schoolgirl writes to her best friend:

> I'm in bed with a cold, and can think only of Mlle X. . . . I never loved a teacher to this point. I already loved her a lot in my first year, but now it is real love. I think that I'm more passionate than you. I imagine kissing her; I half faint and thrill at the idea of seeing her when school begins.[6]

More often, she even dares admit her feeling to her idol herself:

> Dear Mademoiselle, I am in an indescribable state over you. When I do not see you, I would give the world to meet you; I think of you every moment. If I spot you, my eyes fill up with tears, I want to hide; I am so small, so ignorant in front of you. When you chat with me, I am embarrassed, moved, I seem to hear the sweet voice of a fairy and the humming of loving things, impossible to translate; I watch your slightest moves; I lose track of the conversation and mumble something stupid: you must admit, dear Mademoiselle, that this is all mixed up. I do see one thing clearly, that I love you from the depths of my soul.[7]

The headmistress of a professional school recounts:

> I recall that in my own youth, we fought over one of our young professors' lunch papers and paid up to twenty pfennigs to have it. Her used metro tickets were also objects of our collectors' rage.

---

6. Cited by Marguerite Evard, *The Adolescent Girl*.
7. Ibid.

Since she must play a masculine role, it is preferable for the loved woman not to be married; marriage does not always discourage the young admirer, but it interferes; she detests the idea that the object of her adoration could be under the control of a spouse or a lover. Her passions often unfold in secret, or at least on a purely platonic level; but the passage to a concrete eroticism is much easier here than if the loved object is masculine; even if she has had difficult experiences with friends her age, the feminine body does not frighten the girl; with her sisters or her mother, she has often experienced an intimacy where tenderness was subtly penetrated with sensuality, and when she is with the loved one she admires, slipping from tenderness to pleasure will take place just as subtly. When Dorothea Wieck kisses Herta Thiele on the lips in *Girls in Uniform*, this kiss is both maternal and sexual. Between women there is a complicity that disarms modesty; the excitement one arouses in the other is generally without violence; homosexual embraces involve neither defloration nor penetration: they satisfy infantile clitoral eroticism without demanding new and disquieting metamorphoses. The girl can realize her vocation as passive object without feeling deeply alienated. This is what Renée Vivien expresses in her verses, where she describes the relation of "damned women" and their lovers:

> *Our bodies to theirs are a kindred mirror . . .*
> *Our lunar kisses have a pallid softness,*
> *Our fingers do not ruffle the down on a cheek,*
> *And we are able, when the sash becomes untied,*
> *To be at the same time lovers and sisters.*[8]

And in these verses:

> *For we love gracefulness and delicacy,*
> *And my possession does not bruise your breasts . . .*
> *My mouth would not know how to bite your mouth roughly.*
>
> *My mouth will not bitterly bite your mouth.*[9]

Through the poetic impropriety of the words "breasts" and "mouth," she clearly promises her friend not to brutalize her. And it is in part out of

---

8. *A l'heure des mains jointes* (*At the Sweet Hour of Hand in Hand*). ["Psappha revit," trans. Gillian Spraggs.—TRANS.]

9. *Sillages* (Sea Wakes). ["Pareilles," trans. Gillian Spraggs.—TRANS.]

fear of violence and of rape that the adolescent girl often gives her first love to an older girl rather than to a man. The masculine woman reincarnates for her both the father and the mother: from the father she has authority and transcendence, she is the source and standard of values, she rises beyond the given world, she is divine; but she remains woman: whether she was too abruptly weaned from her mother's caresses or if, on the contrary, her mother pampered her too long, the adolescent girl, like her brothers, dreams of the warmth of the breast; in this flesh similar to hers she loses herself again in that immediate fusion with life that weaning destroyed; and through this foreign enveloping gaze, she overcomes the separation that individualizes her. Of course, all human relationships entail conflicts; all love entails jealousies. But many of the difficulties that arise between the virgin and her first male love are smoothed away here. The homosexual experience can take the shape of a true love; it can bring to the girl so happy a balance that she will want to continue it, repeat it, and will keep a nostalgic memory of it; it can awaken or give rise to a lesbian vocation.[10] But most often, it will only represent a stage: its very facility condemns it. In the love that she declares to a woman older than herself, the girl covets her own future: she is identifying with an idol; unless this idol is exceptionally superior, she loses her aura quickly; when she begins to assert herself, the younger one judges and compares: the other, who was chosen precisely because she was close and unintimidating, is not *other* enough to impose herself for very long; the male gods are more firmly in place because their heaven is more distant. Her curiosity and her sensuality incite the girl to desire more aggressive embraces. Very often, she has envisaged, from the start, a homosexual adventure just as a transition, an initiation, a temporary situation; she acts out jealousy, anger, pride, joy, and pain with the more or less admitted idea that she is imitating, without great risk, the adventures of which she dreams but that she does not yet dare, nor has had the occasion, to live. She is destined for man, she knows it, and she wants a normal and complete woman's destiny.

Man dazzles yet frightens her. To reconcile the contradictory feelings she has about him, she will dissociate in him the male that frightens her from the shining divinity whom she piously adores. Abrupt, awkward with her masculine acquaintances, she idolizes distant Prince Charmings: movie actors whose pictures she pastes over her bed, heroes, living or dead but inaccessible, an unknown glimpsed by chance and whom she knows she

---

10. See Chapter 4 of this volume.

will never meet again. Such loves raise no problems. Very often she approaches a socially prestigious or intellectual man who is physically unexciting: for example, an old, slightly ridiculous professor; these older men emerge from a world beyond the world where the adolescent girl is enclosed, and she can secretly devote herself to them, consecrate herself to them as one consecrates oneself to God: such a gift is in no way humiliating, it is freely given since the desire is not carnal. The romantic woman in love freely accepts that the chosen one be unassuming, ugly, a little foolish: she then feels all the more secure. She pretends to deplore the obstacles that separate her from him; but in reality she has chosen him precisely because no real rapport between them is possible. Thus she can make of love an abstract and purely subjective experience, unthreatening to her integrity; her heart beats, she feels the pain of absence, the pangs of presence, vexation, hope, bitterness, enthusiasm, but not authentically; no part of her is engaged. It is amusing to observe that the idol chosen is all the more dazzling the more distant it is: it is convenient for the everyday piano teacher to be ridiculous and ugly; but if one falls in love with a stranger who moves in inaccessible spheres, it is preferable that he be handsome and masculine. The important thing is that, in one way or another, the sexual issue not be raised. These make-believe loves prolong and confirm the narcissistic attitude where eroticism appears only in its immanence, without real presence of the Other. Finding a pretext that permits her to elude concrete experiences, the adolescent girl often develops an intense imaginary life. She chooses to confuse her fantasies with reality. Among other examples, Helene Deutsch describes a particularly significant one: a pretty and seductive girl, who could have easily been courted, refused all relations with young people around her; but at the age of thirteen, in her secret heart, she had chosen to idolize a rather ugly seventeen-year-old boy who had never spoken to her.[11] She got hold of a picture of him, wrote a dedication to herself on it, and for three years kept a diary recounting her imaginary experiences: they exchanged kisses and passionate embraces; there were sometimes crying scenes where she left with her eyes all red and swollen; then they were reconciled, and she sent herself flowers, and so on. When a move separated her from him, she wrote him letters she never sent him but that she answered herself. This story was most obviously a defense against real experiences that she feared.

This case is almost pathological. But it illustrates a normal process by

---

11. *Psychology of Women.*

magnifying it. Marie Bashkirtseff gives a gripping example of an imaginary sentimental existence. The Duke of H., with whom she claims to be in love, is someone to whom she has never spoken. What she really desires is to exalt herself; but being a woman, and especially in the period and class she belongs to, she had no chance of achieving success through an independent existence. At eighteen years of age, she lucidly notes: "I write to C. that I would like to be a man. I know that I could be someone; but where can one go in skirts? Marriage is women's only career; men have thirty-six chances, women have but one, zero, like in the bank." She thus needs a man's love; but to be able to confer a sovereign value on her, he must himself be a sovereign consciousness. "Never will a man beneath my position be able to please me," she writes. "A rich and independent man carries pride and a certain comfortable air with him. Self-assurance has a certain triumphant aura. I love H.'s capricious air, conceited and cruel: something of Nero in him." And further: "This annihilation of the woman before the superiority of the loved man must be the greatest thrill of self-love that the superior woman can experience." Thus narcissism leads to masochism: this liaison has already been seen in the child who dreams of Bluebeard, of Griselda, of the martyred saints. The self is constituted as for others, by others: the more powerful others are, the more riches and power the self has; captivating its master, it envelops in itself the virtues possessed by him; loved by Nero, Marie Bashkirtseff *would be* Nero; to annihilate oneself before others is to realize others at once in oneself and for oneself; in reality this dream of nothingness is an arrogant will to be. In fact, Bashkirtseff never met a man superb enough to alienate herself through him. It is one thing to kneel before a far-off god shaped by one's self and another thing to give one's self over to a flesh-and-blood man. Many girls long persist in stubbornly following their dream throughout the real world: they seek a male who seems superior to all others in his position, his merits, his intelligence; they want him to be older than themselves, already having carved out a place for himself in the world, enjoying authority and prestige; fortune and fame fascinate them: the chosen one appears as the absolute Subject who by his love will convey to them his splendor and his indispensability. His superiority idealizes the love that the girl brings to him: it is not only because he is a male that she wants to give herself to him, it is because he is *this* elite being. "I would like giants and all I find is men," a friend once said to me. In the name of these high standards, the girl disdains too-ordinary suitors and eludes the problem of sexuality. In her dreams and without risk, she cherishes an image of herself that enchants her as an image, though she has no intention of conforming to it. Thus,

Maria Le Hardouin explains that she gets pleasure from seeing herself as a victim, ever devoted to a man, when she is really authoritarian:

> Out of a kind of modesty, I could never in reality express my nature's hidden tendencies that I lived so deeply in my dreams. As I learned to know myself, I am in fact authoritarian, violent, and deeply incapable of flexibility.
>
> Always obeying a need to suppress myself, I sometimes imagined that I was an admirable woman, living only by duty, madly in love with a man whose every wish I endeavored to anticipate. We struggled within an ugly world of needs. He killed himself working and came home at night pale and undone. I lost my sight mending his clothes next to a lightless window. In a narrow smoky kitchen, I cooked some miserable meals. Sickness ceaselessly threatened our only child with death. Yet a sweet, crucified smile was always on my lips, and my eyes always showed that unbearable expression of silent courage that in reality I could never stand without disgust.[12]

Beyond these narcissistic gratifications, some girls do concretely find the need for a guide, a master. From the time they escape their parents' hold, they find themselves encumbered by an autonomy that they are not used to; they only know how to make negative use of it; they fall into caprice and extravagance; they want to give up their freedom. The story of the young and capricious girl, rebellious and spoiled, who is tamed by the love of a sensible man is a standard of cheap literature and cinema: it is a cliché that flatters both men and women. It is the story, among others, told by Mme de Ségur in *Quel amour d'enfant!* (*Such an Adorable Child!*). As a child, Gisèle, disappointed by her overly indulgent father, becomes attached to a severe old aunt; as a girl, she comes under the influence of an irritable young man, Julien, who judges her harshly, humiliates her, and tries to reform her; she marries a rich, characterless duke with whom she is extremely unhappy, and when, as a widow, she accepts the demanding love of her mentor, she finally finds joy and wisdom. In Louisa May Alcott's *Good Wives,* independent Jo begins to fall in love with her future husband because he seriously reproaches her for an imprudent act; he also scolds her, and she rushes to excuse herself and submit to him. In spite of the edgy pride of American women, Hollywood films have hundreds of times

---

12. *The Black Sail*.

presented *enfants terribles* tamed by the healthy brutality of a lover or husband: a couple of slaps, even a good spanking, seem to be a good means of seduction. But in reality, the passage from ideal love to sexual love is not so simple. Many women carefully avoid approaching the object of their passion through more or less admitted fear of disappointment. If the hero, the giant, or the demigod responds to the love he inspires and transforms it into a real-life experience, the girl panics; her idol becomes a male she shies away from, disgusted. There are flirtatious adolescents who do everything in their power to seduce a seemingly "interesting" or "fascinating" man, but paradoxically they recoil if he manifests too vivid an emotion in return; he was attractive because he seemed inaccessible: in love, he becomes commonplace. "He's just a man like the others." The young woman blames him for her disgrace; she uses this pretext to refuse physical contacts that shock her virgin sensibilities. If the girl gives in to her "Ideal one," she remains unmoved in his arms and "it happens," says Stekel, "that obsessed girls commit suicide after such scenes where the whole construction of amorous imagination collapses because the Ideal one is seen in the form of a 'brutal animal.' "[13] The taste for the impossible often leads the girl to fall in love with a man when he begins to court one of her friends, and very often she chooses a married man. She is readily fascinated by a Don Juan; she dreams of submitting and attaching herself to this seducer that no woman has ever held on to, and she kindles the hope of reforming him: but in fact, she knows she will fail in her undertaking, and this is the reason for her choice. Some girls end up forever incapable of knowing real and complete love. They will search all their lives for an ideal impossible to reach.

But there is a conflict between the girl's narcissism and the experiences for which her sexuality destines her. The woman only accepts herself as the inessential on the condition of finding herself the essential once again by abdicating. In making herself object, suddenly she has become an idol in which she proudly recognizes herself; but she refuses the implacable dialectic that makes her return to the inessential. She wants to be a fascinating treasure, not a thing to be taken. She loves to seem like a marvelous fetish, charged with magic emanations, not to see herself as flesh that lets herself be seen, touched, bruised: thus man prizes the woman prey, but flees the ogress Demeter.

Proud to capture masculine interest and to arouse admiration, woman is revolted by being captured in return. With puberty she learned shame:

13. *Frigidity in Woman.*

and shame is mixed with her coquetry and vanity, men's gazes flatter and hurt her at the same time; she would only like to be seen to the extent that she shows herself: eyes are always too penetrating. Hence the inconsistency disconcerting to men: she displays her décolletage and her legs, but she blushes and becomes vexed when someone looks at her. She enjoys provoking the male, but if she sees she has aroused his desire, she backs off in disgust: masculine desire is an offense as much as a tribute; insofar as she feels responsible for her charm, as she feels she is using it freely, she is enchanted with her victories: but while her features, her forms, her flesh, are given and endured, she wants to keep them from this foreign and indiscreet freedom that covets them. Here is the deep meaning of this primal modesty, which interferes in a disconcerting way with the boldest coquetry. A little girl can be surprisingly audacious because she does not realize that her initiatives reveal her in her passivity: as soon as she sees this, she becomes indignant and angry. Nothing is more ambiguous than a look; it exists at a distance, and that distance makes it seem respectable: but insidiously it takes hold of the perceived image. The unripe woman struggles with these traps. She begins to let herself go, but just as quickly she tenses up and kills the desire in herself. In her as yet uncertain body, the caress is felt at times as an unpleasant tickling, at times as a delicate pleasure; a kiss moves her first, and then abruptly makes her laugh; she follows each surrender with a revolt; she lets herself be kissed, but then she wipes her mouth noticeably; she is smiling and caring, then suddenly ironic and hostile; she makes promises and deliberately forgets them. In such a way, Mathilde de la Mole is seduced by Julien's beauty and rare qualities, desirous to reach an exceptional destiny through her love, but fiercely refusing the domination of her own senses and that of a foreign consciousness; she goes from servility to arrogance, from supplication to scorn; she demands an immediate payback for everything she gives. Such is also Monique, whose profile is drawn by Marcel Arland, who confuses excitement with sin, for whom love is a shameful abdication, whose blood is hot but who detests this ardor and who, while bridling, submits to it.

The "unripe fruit" defends herself against man by exhibiting a childish and perverse nature. This is often how the girl has been described: half-wild, half-dutiful. Colette, for one, depicted her in *Claudine at School* and also in *Le blé en herbe* (*Green Wheat*) in the guise of the seductive Vinca. She maintains an interest in the world around her, over which she reigns sovereign; but she is also curious and feels a sensual and romantic desire for man. Vinca gets scratched by brambles, fishes for shrimp, and climbs trees, and yet she quivers when her friend Phil touches her hand; she knows the agitation of the body becoming flesh, the first revelation of woman as woman; aroused, she begins to want to be pretty: at times she does her hair, she uses makeup, dresses in gauzy organdy, she takes pleasure in appearing attractive and seductive; she also wants to exist *for herself* and not only *for others*, at other times, she throws on old formless dresses, unbecoming trousers; there is a whole part of her that criticizes seduction and considers it as giving in: so she purposely lets herself be seen with ink-stained fingers, messy hair, dirty. This rebelliousness gives her a clumsiness she resents: she is annoyed by it, blushes, becomes even more awkward, and is horrified by these aborted attempts at seduction. At this point, the girl no longer wants to be a child, but she does not accept becoming an adult, and she blames herself for her childishness and then for her female resignation. She is in a state of constant denial.

This is the characteristic trait of the girl and gives the key to most of her behavior; she does not accept the destiny nature and society assign to her; and yet she does not actively repudiate it: she is too divided internally to enter into combat with the world; she confines herself to escaping reality or to contesting it symbolically. Each of her desires is matched by an anxiety: she is eager to take possession of her future, but she fears breaking with her past; she would like "to have" a man, she balks at being his prey. And behind each fear hides a desire: rape is abhorrent to her, but she aspires to passivity. Thus she is doomed to bad faith and all its ruses; she is predisposed to all sorts of negative obsessions that express the ambivalence of desire and anxiety.

One of the most common forms of adolescent contestation is giggling. High school girls and shopgirls burst into laughter while recounting love or risqué stories, while talking about their flirtations, meeting men, or seeing lovers kiss; I have known schoolgirls going to lovers' lane in the Luxembourg Gardens just to laugh; and others going to the Turkish baths to make fun of the fat women with sagging stomachs and hanging breasts they saw there; scoffing at the female body, ridiculing men, laughing at love, are ways of disavowing sexuality: this laughter that defies adults is a way of overcoming one's own embarrassment; one plays with images and words to kill the dangerous magic of them: for example, I saw twelve-year-old students burst out laughing when they saw a Latin text with the word *femur*. If in addition the girl lets herself be kissed and petted, she will get her revenge in laughing outright at her partner or with friends. I remember in a train compartment one night two girls being fondled one after the other by a traveling salesman overjoyed with his good luck: between each session they laughed hysterically, reverting to the behavior of the awkward age in a mixture of sexuality and shame. Girls giggle and they also resort to language to help them: some use words whose coarseness would make their brothers blush; half-ignorant, they are even less shocked by those expressions that do not evoke very precise images; the aim, of course, is to prevent these images from taking shape, at least to defuse them; the dirty stories high school girls tell each other are less to satisfy sexual instincts than to deny sexuality: they only want to consider the humorous side, like a mechanical or almost surgical operation. But like laughter, the use of obscene language is not only a protest: it is also a defiance of adults, a sort of sacrilege, a deliberately perverse kind of behavior. Rebuffing nature and society, the girl nettles and challenges them by many oddities. She often has food manias: she eats pencil lead, sealing wax, bits of wood, live shrimp, she swallows dozens of aspirins at a time, or she even ingests flies or spiders; I knew a girl—very obedient otherwise—who made horrible mixtures of coffee and white wine that she forced herself to swallow; other times she ate sugar soaked in vinegar; I saw another chewing determinedly into a white worm found in lettuce. All children endeavor to experience the world with their eyes, their hands, and more intimately their mouths and stomachs: but at the awkward age, the girl takes particular pleasure in exploring what is indigestible and repugnant. Very often, she is attracted by what is "disgusting." One of them, quite pretty and attractive when she wanted to be and carefully dressed, proved really fascinated by everything that seemed "dirty" to her: she touched insects, looked at dirty sanitary napkins, sucked the blood of her cuts. Playing with dirty things is obviously a way of overcoming disgust; this feeling becomes much more important at puberty: the girl is disgusted by her too-carnal body, by menstrual blood, by adults' sexual practices, by the male she is destined for; she denies it by indulging herself specifically in the familiarity of everything that disgusts her. "Since I have to bleed each month, I prove that my blood does not scare me by drinking that of my cuts. Since I will have to submit myself to a revolting test, why not eat a white worm?" This attitude is affirmed more clearly in self-mutilation, so frequent at this age. The girl gashes her thigh with a razor, burns herself with cigarettes, cuts and scratches herself; so as not to go to a boring garden party, a girl during my youth cut her foot with an ax and had to spend six weeks in bed. These sadomasochistic practices are both an anticipation of the sexual experience and a revolt against it; girls have to undergo these tests, hardening themselves to all possible ordeals and rendering them harmless, including the wedding night. When she puts a slug on her chest, when she swallows a bottle of aspirin, when she wounds herself, the girl is defying her future lover: you will never inflict on me anything more horrible than I inflict on myself. These are morose and haughty initiations in sexual adventure. Destined to be a passive prey, she claims her freedom right up to submitting to pain and disgust. When she inflicts the cut of the knife, the burning of a coal on herself, she is protesting against the penetration that deflowers her: she protests by nullifying it. Masochistic, since she welcomes the pain caused by her behavior, she is above all sadistic: as autonomous subject, she beats, scorns, and tortures this dependent flesh, this flesh condemned to submission that she detests but from which she does not want to separate herself. Because, in all these situations, she does not choose authentically to reject her destiny. Sadomasochistic crazes imply a fundamental bad faith: if the girl indulges in them, it means she accepts, through her rejections, her future as woman; she would not mutilate her flesh with hatred if first she did not recognize herself as flesh. Even her violent outbursts arise from a situation of resignation. When a boy revolts against his father or against the world, he engages in effective violence; he picks a quarrel with a friend, he fights, he affirms himself as subject with his fists: he imposes himself on the world; he goes beyond it. But affirming herself, imposing herself, are forbidden to the adolescent girl, and that is what fills her heart with revolt: she hopes neither to change the world nor to emerge from it; she knows or at least believes, and perhaps even wishes, herself tied up: she can only destroy; there is despair in her rage; during a frustrating evening, she breaks glasses, windows, vases: it is not to overcome her lot; it is only a symbolic protest. The girl rebels against her future enslavement through her present powerlessness; and her vain outbursts, far from freeing her from her bonds, often merely restrict her even more. Violence against herself or the universe around her always has a negative character: it is more spectacular than effective. The boy who climbs rocks or fights with his friends regards physical pain, the injuries and the bumps, as an insignificant consequence of the positive activities he indulges in; he neither seeks nor flees them for themselves (except if an inferiority complex puts him in a situation similar to women's). The girl watches herself suffer: she seeks in her own heart the taste of violence and revolt rather than being concerned with their results. Her perversity stems from the fact that she remains stuck in the childish universe from which she cannot or does not really want to escape; she struggles in her cage rather than seeking to get out of it; her attitudes are negative, reflexive, and symbolic. This perversity can take disturbing forms. Many young virgins are kleptomaniacs; kleptomania is a very ambiguous "sexual sublimation"; the desire to transgress laws, to violate a taboo, the giddiness of the dangerous and forbidden act, are certainly essential in the girl thief: but there is a double face. Taking objects without having the right is affirming one's autonomy arrogantly, it is putting oneself forward as subject facing the things stolen and the society that condemns stealing, and it is rejecting the established order as well as defying its guardians; but this defiance also has a masochistic side; the thief is fascinated by the risk she runs, by the abyss she will be thrown into if she is caught; it is the danger of being caught that gives such a voluptuous attraction to the act of taking; thus looked at with blame, or with a hand placed on her shoulder in shame, she can realize herself as object totally and without recourse. Taking without being taken in the anguish of becoming prey is the dangerous game of adolescent feminine sexuality. All perverse or illegal conduct found in girls has the same meaning. Some specialize in sending anonymous letters; others find pleasure in mystifying those around them: one fourteen-year-old persuaded a whole village that a house was haunted by spirits. They simultaneously enjoy the clandestine exercise of their power, disobedience, defiance of society, and the risk of being exposed; this is such an important element of their pleasure that they often unmask themselves, and they even sometimes accuse themselves of faults or crimes they have not committed. It is not surprising that the refusal to become object leads to constituting oneself as object: this process is common to all negative obsessions. It is in a single movement that in a hysterical paralysis the ill person fears paralysis, desires it, and brings it on: he is cured from it only by no longer thinking about it; likewise with psychasthenic tics. The depth of the girl's bad faith is what links her to these types of neuroses: manias, tics, conspiracies, perversities; many neurotic symptoms are found in her due to this ambivalence of desire and anxiety that has been pointed out. It is quite common, for example, for her to "run away"; she goes away at random, she wanders far from her father's house, and two or three days later she comes back by herself. It is not a real departure or a real act of rupture with the family; it is mere playacting, and the girl is often totally disconcerted if it is suggested that she leave her circle definitively: she wants to leave while not wanting to at the same time. Running away is sometimes linked to fantasies of prostitution: the girl dreams she is a prostitute, she plays this role more or less timidly; she wears excessive makeup, she leans out the window and winks at passersby; in some cases, she leaves the house and carries the drama so far that it becomes confused with reality. Such conduct often expresses a disgust with sexual desire, a feeling of guilt: since I have these thoughts, these appetites, I am no better than a prostitute, I am one, thinks a girl. Sometimes, she attempts to free herself: let's get it over with, let's go to the limit, she says to herself;

she wants to prove to herself that sexuality is of little importance by giving herself to the first one. At the same time, such an attitude is often a manifestation of hostility to the mother, either that the girl is horrified by her austere virtue or that she suspects her mother of being, herself, of easy morality; or she holds a grudge against her father who has shown himself too indifferent. In any case, in this obsession—as in the fantasies of pregnancy about which we have already spoken and that are often associated with it—there is the meeting of this inextricable confusion of revolt and complicity, characterized by psychasthenic dizziness. It is noteworthy that in all these behaviors the girl does not seek to go beyond the natural and social order, she does not attempt to push back the limits of the possible or to effectuate a transmutation of values; she settles for manifesting her revolt within an established world where boundaries and laws are preserved; this is the often-defined "devilish" attitude, implying a basic deception: the good is recognized so that it can be trampled upon, the rule is set so that it can be violated, the sacred is respected so that it is possible to perpetuate the sacrileges. The girl's attitude is defined essentially by the fact that in the agonizing shadows of bad faith, she refuses the world and her own destiny at the same time as she accepts them.

However, she does not confine herself to contesting negatively the situation imposed on her; she also tries to compensate for its insufficiencies. Although the future frightens her, the present dissatisfies her; she hesitates to become woman; she frets at still being only a child; she has already left her past; she is not yet committed to a new life. She is occupied, but she does not *do* anything; because she does not do anything, she *has* nothing, she *is nothing*. She tries to fill this void by playacting and mystifications. She is criticized for being devious, a liar, and troublesome. The truth is she is doomed to secrets and lies. At sixteen, a woman has already gone through disturbing experiences: puberty, menstrual periods, awakening of sexuality, first arousals, first passions, fears, disgust, and ambiguous experiences: she has hidden all these things in her heart; she has learned to guard her secrets preciously. The mere fact of having to hide her sanitary napkins and of concealing her periods inclines her to lies. In the short story "Old Mortality," Katherine Anne Porter recounts that young American women from the South, around 1900, made themselves ill by swallowing mixtures of salt and lemon to stop their periods when going to balls: they were afraid that the young men would recognize their state by the bags under their eyes, by contact with their hands, by a smell perhaps, and this idea upset them. It is difficult to play the idol, the fairy, or the remote princess when one feels a bloody piece of material between one's legs and, more generally, when one knows the primal misery of being a body. Modesty, a spontaneous refusal to let oneself be grasped as flesh, comes close to hypocrisy. But above all, the adolescent girl is condemned to the lie of pretending to be object, and a prestigious one, while she experiences herself as an uncertain, dispersed existence, knowing her failings. Makeup, false curls, corsets, padded bras, are lies; the face itself becomes a mask: spontaneous expressions are produced artfully, a wondrous passivity is imitated; there is nothing more surprising than suddenly discovering in the exercise of one's feminine functions a physiognomy with which one is familiar; its transcendence denies itself and imitates immanence; one's eyes no longer perceive, they reflect; one's body no longer lives: it waits; every gesture and smile becomes an appeal; disarmed, available, the girl is nothing but a flower offered, a fruit to be picked. Man encourages her in these lures by demanding to be lured: then he gets irritated, he accuses. But for the guileless girl, he has nothing but indifference and even hostility. He is only seduced by the one who sets traps for him; offered, she is still the one who stalks her prey; her passivity takes the form of an undertaking, she makes her weakness a tool of her strength; since she is forbidden to attack outright, she is reduced to maneuvers and calculations; and it is in her interest to appear freely given; therefore, she will be criticized for being perfidious and treacherous, and she is. But it is true that she is obliged to offer man the myth of her submission because he insists on dominating. And can one demand that she stifle her most essential claims? Her complaisance can only be perverted right from the outset. Besides, she cheats not only out of concerted, deliberate ruse. Because all roads are barred to her, because she cannot *do*, because she must *be*, a curse weighs on her. As a child, she played at being a dancer or a saint; later, she plays at being herself; what is really the truth? In the area in which she has been shut up, this is a word without sense. Truth is reality unveiled, and unveiling occurs through acts: but she does not act. The romances she tells herself about herself—and that she also often tells others—seem better ways of expressing the possibilities she feels in herself than the plain account of her daily life. She is unable to take stock of herself: so she consoles herself by playacting; she embodies a character she seeks to give importance to; she tries to stand out by extravagant behavior because she does not have the right to distinguish herself in specific activities. She knows she is without responsibilities, insignificant in this world of men: she makes trouble because she has nothing else important to do. Giraudoux's Electra is a woman who makes trouble, because it is up to Orestes alone to accomplish a real murder with a real sword. Like the child, the girl wears herself out in scenes and rages, she makes herself ill, she manifests signs of hysteria to try to attract attention and be someone who *counts*. She interferes in the destiny of others so that she can count; she uses any weapon she can; she tells secrets, she invents others, she betrays, she calumniates; she needs tragedy around her to feel alive since she finds no support in her own life. She is unpredictable for the same reason; the fantasies we form and the images by which we are lulled are contradictory: only action unifies the diversity of time. The girl does not have a real will but has desires, and she jumps from one to the other at random. What makes her flightiness sometimes dangerous is that at every moment, committing herself in dream only, she commits herself wholly. She puts herself on a level of intransigence and perfection; she has a taste for the definitive and absolute: if she cannot control the future, she wants to attain the eternal. "I will never give up. I want everything always. I need to prefer my life in order to accept it," writes Marie Lenéru. So echoes Anouilh's Antigone: "I want everything, immediately." This childish imperialism can only be found in an individual who dreams his destiny: dreams abolish time and obstacles, they need to be exaggerated to compensate for the small amount of reality; whoever has authentic projects knows a finitude that is the gauge of one's concrete power. The girl wants to receive *everything* because there is *nothing* that depends on her. That is where her character of *enfant terrible* comes from, faced with adults and man in particular. She does not accept the limitations an individual's insertion in the real world imposes; she defies him to go beyond them. Thus Hilda expects Solness to give her a kingdom: as she is not the one who has to conquer it, she wants it without limits; she demands that he build the highest tower ever built and that he "climb as high as he builds": he hesitates to climb, because he is afraid of heights; she who remains on the ground and looks on denies contingency and human weakness; she does not accept that reality imposes a limit on her dreams of grandeur.[14] Adults always seem mean and cautious to the girl who stops at nothing because she has nothing to lose; imagining herself taking the boldest risks, she dares them to match her in reality. Unable to put herself to the test, she invests herself with the most astonishing qualities without fear of being contradicted.

However, her uncertainty also stems from this lack of control; she dreams she is infinite; she is nevertheless alienated in the character she offers for the admiration of others; it depends on these foreign conscious-

---

14. See Ibsen, *The Master Builder*.

nesses: this double she identifies with herself but to whose presence she passively submits is dangerous for her. This explains why she is touchy and vain. The slightest criticism or gibe destabilizes her. Her worth does not derive from her own effort but from a fickle approbation. This is not defined by individual activities but by general reputation; it seems to be quantitatively measurable; the price of merchandise decreases when it becomes too common: thus the girl is only rare, exceptional, remarkable, or extraordinary if no other one is. Her female companions are rivals or enemies; she tries to denigrate, to deny them; she is jealous and hostile.

It is clear that all the faults for which the adolescent girl is reproached merely express her situation. It is a painful condition to know one is passive and dependent at the age of hope and ambition, at the age when the will to live and to take a place in the world intensifies; woman learns at this conquering age that no conquest is allowed her, that she must disavow herself, that her future depends on men's good offices. New social and sexual aspirations are awakened, but they are condemned to remain unsatisfied; all her vital or spiritual impulses are immediately barred. It is understandable that she should have trouble establishing her balance. Her erratic mood, her tears, and her nervous crises are less the result of a physiological fragility than the sign of her deep maladjustment.

However, this situation that the girl flees by a thousand inauthentic paths is also one that she sometimes assumes authentically. Her shortcomings make her irritating: but her unique virtues sometimes make her astonishing. Both have the same origin. From her rejection of the world, from her unsettled waiting, and from her nothingness, she can create a springboard for herself and emerge then in her solitude and her freedom.

The girl is secretive, tormented, in the throes of difficult conflicts. This complexity enriches her; her interior life develops more deeply than her brothers'; she is more attentive to her heart's desires that thus become more subtle, more varied; she has more psychological sense than boys turned toward external goals. She is able to give weight to these revolts that oppose her to the world. She avoids the traps of seriousness and conformism. The concerted lies of her circle meet with her irony and clearsightedness. She tests her situation's ambiguity on a daily basis: beyond sterile protest, she can have the courage to throw into question established optimism, preconceived values, and hypocritical and reassuring morality. Such is Maggie, the moving example given in *The Mill on the Floss*, in which George Eliot embodied the doubts and courageous rebellions of her youth against Victorian England; the heroes—particularly Tom, Maggie's brother—stubbornly affirm conventional wisdom, immobilizing morality in formal rules: Maggie tries to reintroduce a breath of life, she overturns them, she goes to the limits of her solitude and emerges as a pure freedom beyond the fossilized male universe.

The adolescent girl barely finds anything but a negative use of this freedom. But her openness can engender a precious faculty of receptivity; she will prove to be devoted, attentive, understanding, and loving. Rosamond Lehmann's heroines are marked by this docile generosity. In *Invitation to the Waltz*, Olivia, still shy and gauche, and barely interested in her appearance, is seen scrutinizing this world she will enter tomorrow with excited curiosity. She listens with all her heart to her succession of dancers, she endeavors to answer them according to their wishes, she is their echo, she vibrates, she accepts everything that is offered. Judy, the heroine of *Dusty Answer*, has the same endearing quality. She has not relinquished childhood joys; she likes to bathe naked at night in the park river; she loves nature, books, beauty, and life; she does not cultivate a narcissistic cult; without lies, without egotism, she does not look for an exaltation of self through men: her love is a gift. She bestows it on any being who seduces her, man or woman, Jennifer or Roddy. She gives herself without losing herself: she leads an independent student life; she has her own world, her own projects. But what distinguishes her from a boy is her attitude of expectation, her tender docility. In a subtle way, she is, in spite of everything, destined to the Other: the Other has a marvelous dimension in her eyes to the point that she is in love with all the young men of the neighboring family, their house, their sister, and their universe, all at the same time; it is not as a friend, it is as Other that Jennifer fascinates her. And she charms Roddy and his cousins by her capacity to yield to them, to shape herself to their desires; she is patience, sweetness, acceptance, and silent suffering.

Different but also captivating in the way she welcomes into her heart those she cherishes, Tessa, in Margaret Kennedy's *The Constant Nymph*, is simultaneously spontaneous, wild, and giving. She refuses to abdicate anything of herself: finery, makeup, disguises, hypocrisy, acquired charms, caution, and female submission are repugnant to her; she desires to be loved but not behind a mask; she yields to Lewis's moods, but without servility; she understands him, she vibrates in unison with him; but if they ever argue, Lewis knows that caresses will not subdue her: while authoritarian and vain Florence lets herself be conquered by kisses, Tessa succeeds in the extraordinary accomplishment of remaining free in her love, allowing her to love without either hostility or pride. Her nature has all the lures of artifice; to please, she never degrades herself, never lowers herself or locks herself in as object. Surrounded by artists who have committed their whole existence to musical creation, she does not feel this devouring demon within her; she wholly endeavors to love, understand, and help them: she does it effortlessly, out of a tender and spontaneous generosity, which is why she remains perfectly autonomous even in the instances in which she forgets herself in favor of others. Thanks to this pure authenticity, she is spared the conflicts of adolescence; she can suffer from the world's harshness, she is not divided within herself; she is harmonious both as a carefree child and as a very wise woman. The sensitive and generous girl, receptive and ardent, is very ready to become a great lover.

When not encountering love, she may encounter poetry. Because she does not act, she watches, she feels, she records; she responds deeply to a color or a smile; because her destiny is scattered outside her, in cities already built, on mature men's faces, she touches and tastes both passionately and more gratuitously than the young man. As she is poorly integrated into the human universe, and has trouble adapting to it, she is, like the child, able to see it; instead of being interested only in her grasp of things, she focuses on their meaning; she perceives particular profiles, unexpected metamorphoses. She rarely feels a creative urge, and all too often she lacks the techniques that would allow her to express herself; but in conversations, letters, literary essays, and rough drafts, she does show an original sensibility. The girl throws herself passionately into things, because she is not yet mutilated in her transcendence; and the fact that she does not accomplish anything, that she is nothing, will make her drive even more fervent: empty and unlimited, what she will seek to reach from within her nothingness is All. That is why she will devote a special love to Nature: more than the adolescent boy, she worships it. Untamed and inhuman, Nature encompasses most obviously the totality of what is. The adolescent girl has not yet annexed any part of the universe: thanks to this impoverishment, the whole universe is her kingdom; when she takes possession of it, she also proudly takes possession of herself. Colette often recounted these youthful orgies:

> For even then I so loved the dawn that my mother granted it to me
> as a reward. She used to agree to wake me at half-past three and off
> I would go, an empty basket on each arm, towards the kitchen-
> gardens that sheltered in the narrow bend of the river, in search
> of strawberries, black-currants, and hairy gooseberries.
> At half-past three everything slumbered still in a primal blue,
> blurred and dewy, and as I went down the sandy road the mist,

grounded by its own weight, bathed first my legs, then my well-built little body, reaching at last to my mouth and ears, and finally to that most sensitive part of all, my nostrils . . . It was on that road and at that hour that I first became aware of my own self, experienced an inexpressible state of grace, and felt one with the first breath of air that stirred, the first bird, and the sun so newly born that it still looked not quite round . . . I came back when the bell rang for the first Mass. But not before I had eaten my fill, not before I had described a great circle in the woods, like a dog out hunting on its own, and tasted the water of the two hidden springs which I wor-shipped.[15]

Mary Webb describes in *The House in Dormer Forest* the intense joys a girl can know in communion with a familiar landscape:

When the atmosphere of the house became too thunderous and Amber's nerves were strained to breaking-point, she crept away to the upper woods . . . It seemed to her that while Dormer lived by law, the forest lived by impulse. Through a gradual awakening to natural beauty, she reached a perception of beauty peculiar to herself. She began to perceive analogies. Nature became for her, not a fortuitous assemblage of pretty things, but a harmony, a poem solemn and austere . . . Beauty breathed there, light shone there that was not of the flower or the star. A tremor, mysterious and thrilling, seemed to run with the light . . . through the whispering forest . . . So her going out into the green world had in it something of a religious rite . . . On a still morning . . . she went up to the Birds' Orchard. She often did this before the day of petty irritation began . . . she found some comfort in the inconsequence of the bird people . . . she came at last to the upper wood, and was instantly at grips with beauty. There was for her literally something of wrestling, of the mood which says: "I will not let thee go until thou bless me" . . . Leaning against a wild pear tree, she was aware, by her inward hearing, of the tidal wave of sap that rose so full and strong that she could almost imagine it roaring like the sea. Then a tremor of wind shook the flowering tree-tops, and she awoke again to the senses, to the strangeness of these utterances of the

15. *Sido.*

leaves . . . Every petal, every leaf, seemed to be conning some
memory of profundities whence it had come. Every curving flower
seemed full of echoes too majestic for its fragility . . . A breath of
scented air came from the hilltops and stole among the branches.
That which had form, and knew the mortality which is in form,
trembled before that which passed, formless and immortal . . .
Because of it the place became no mere congregation of trees, but a
thing fierce as stellar space . . . For it possesses itself forever in a
vitality withheld, immutable. It was this that drew Amber with
breathless curiosity into the secret haunts of nature. It was this that
struck her now into a kind of ecstasy . . .

Women as different as Emily Brontë and Anna de Noailles experienced
similar fervor in their youth—and it continued throughout their lives.

The texts I have cited convincingly show the comfort the adolescent
girl finds in fields and woods. In the paternal house reign mother, laws, custom, and routine, and she wants to wrest herself from this past; she wants
to become a sovereign subject in her own turn: but socially she only
accedes to her adult life by becoming woman; she pays for her liberation
with an abdication; but in the midst of plants and animals she is a human
being; a subject, a freedom, she is freed both from her family and from
males. She finds an image of the solitude of her soul in the secrecy of
forests and the tangible figure of transcendence in the vast horizons of the
plains; she is herself this limitless land, this summit jutting toward the sky;
she can follow, she will follow, these roads that leave for an unknown
future; sitting on the hilltop, she dominates the riches of the world spread
out at her feet, given to her; through the water's palpitations, the shimmer-
ing of the light, she anticipates the joys, tears, and ecstasies that she does
not yet know; the adventures of her own heart are confusedly promised her
by ripples on the pond and patches of sun. Smells and colors speak a mysterious language, but one word stands out with triumphant clarity: "life."
Existence is not only an abstract destiny inscribed in town hall registers; it
is future and carnal richness. Having a body no longer seems like a shameful failing; in these desires that the adolescent girl repudiates under the
maternal gaze, she recognizes the sap mounting in the trees; she is no
longer cursed, she proudly claims her kinship with leaves and flowers; she
rumples a corolla, and she knows that a living prey will fill her empty hands
one day. Flesh is no longer filth: it is joy and beauty. Merged with sky and
heath, the girl is this vague breath that stirs up and kindles the universe, and
she is every sprig of heather; an individual rooted in the soil and infinite

consciousness, she is both spirit and life; her presence is imperious and triumphant like that of the earth itself.

Beyond Nature she sometimes seeks an even more remote and stunning reality; she is willing to lose herself in mystical ecstasies; in periods of faith many young female souls demanded that God fill the emptiness of their being; the vocations of Catherine of Siena and Teresa of Avila were revealed to them at a young age.[16] Joan of Arc was a girl. In other periods, humanity appears the supreme end; so the mystical impulse flows into defined projects; but it is also a youthful desire for the absolute that gave birth to the flame that nourished the life of Mme Roland or Rosa Luxemburg. From her subjugation, her impoverishment, and the depths of her refusal, the girl can extract the most daring courage. She finds poetry; she finds heroism too. One of the ways of assuming the fact that she is poorly integrated into society is to go beyond its restricting horizons.

The richness and strength of their nature and fortunate circumstances have enabled some women to continue in their adult lives their passionate projects from adolescence. But these are exceptions. George Eliot had Maggie Tulliver and Margaret Kennedy had Tessa die for good reason. It was a bitter destiny that the Brontë sisters had. The girl is touching because she rises up against the world, weak and alone; but the world is too powerful; she persists in refusing it, she is broken. Belle de Zuylen, who overwhelmed all of Europe with her mind's originality and caustic power, frightened all her suitors: her refusal to make concessions condemned her to long years of celibacy that weighed on her since she declared that the expression "virgin and martyr" was a pleonasm. This stubbornness is rare. In the immense majority of cases, the girl is aware that the fight is much too unequal, and she ends up yielding. "You will all die at fifteen," writes Diderot to Sophie Volland. When the fight has only been—as happens most often—a symbolic revolt, defeat is certain. Demanding in dreams, full of hope but passive, the girl makes adults smile with pity; they doom her to resignation. And in fact, the rebellious and eccentric girl that we left is found two years later, calmer, ready to consent to her woman's life. This is the future Colette predicted for Vinca; this is how the heroines of Mauriac's early novels appear. The adolescent crisis is a type of "work" similar to what Dr. Lagache calls "the work of mourning." The girl buries her childhood slowly—this autonomous and imperious individual she has been—and she enters adult existence submissively.

---

16. We will return to the specific characteristics of the feminine mystic.

Of course, it is not possible to establish defined categories based on age alone. Some women remain infantile their whole lives; the behaviors we have described are sometimes perpetuated to an advanced age. Nevertheless, on the whole, there is a big difference between the girlish fifteen-year-old and an older girl. The latter is adapted to reality; she scarcely advances on the imaginary level; she is less divided within herself than before. At about eighteen, Marie Bashkirtseff writes:

> The more I advance in age towards the end of my youth, the more I am covered with indifference. Little agitates me and everything used to agitate me.

Irène Reweliotty comments:

> To be accepted by men, you have to think and act like them; if you don't, they treat you like a black sheep, and solitude becomes your lot. And I, now, I'm fed up with solitude, and I want people not only around me but with me . . . Living now and no longer existing and waiting and dreaming and telling yourself everything within yourself, your mouth shut and your body motionless.

And further along:

> With so much flattery, wooing, and such, I become terribly ambitious. This is no longer the trembling, marvelous happiness of the fifteen-year-old. It is a kind of cold and hard intoxication to take my revenge on life, to climb. I flirt; I play at loving. I do not love . . . I gain in intelligence, in sangfroid, in ordinary lucidity. I lose my heart. It was as if it cracked . . . In two months, I left childhood behind.

Approximately the same sound comes from these secrets of a nineteen-year-old girl:

> In the old days Oh! What a conflict against a mentality that seemed incompatible with this century and the appeals of this century itself! I now have a peaceful feeling. Each new big idea that enters me, instead of provoking a painful upheaval, a destruction, and an incessant reconstruction, adapts marvelously to what is already in

me . . . Now I go seamlessly from theoretical thinking to daily life without attempting continuity.[17]

The girl—unless she is particularly graceless—accepts her femininity in the end; and she is often happy to enjoy gratuitously the pleasures and triumphs she gets from settling definitively into her destiny; as she is not yet bound to any duty, irresponsible, available, for her the present seems neither empty nor disappointing since it is just one step; dressing and flirting still have the lightness of a game, and her dreams of the future disguise their futility. This is how Virginia Woolf describes the impressions of a young coquette during a party:

> I feel myself shining in the dark. Silk is on my knee. My silk legs rub smoothly together. The stones of a necklace lie cold on my throat . . . I am arrayed, I am prepared . . . My hair is swept in one curve. My lips are precisely red. I am ready now to join men and women on the stairs, my peers. I pass them, exposed to their gaze, as they are to mine . . . I now begin to unfurl, in this scent, in this radiance, as a fern when its curled leaves unfurl . . . I feel a thousand capacities spring up in me. I am arch, gay, languid, melancholy by turns; I am rooted, but I flow. All gold, flowing that way, I say to this one, "Come" . . . He approaches. He makes towards me. This is the most exciting moment I have ever known. I flutter. I ripple . . . Are we not lovely sitting together here, I in my satin; he in black and white? My peers may look at me now. I look straight back at you, men and women. I am one of you. This is my world . . . The door opens. The door goes on opening. Now I think, next time it opens the whole of my life will be changed . . . The door opens. Come, I say to this one, rippling gold from head to heels. "Come," and he comes towards me.[18]

But the more the girl matures, the more maternal authority weighs on her. If she leads a housekeeper's life at home, she suffers from being only an assistant; she would like to devote her work to her own home, to her own children. Often the rivalry with her mother worsens: in particular, the older daughter is irritated if younger brothers and sisters are born; she

---

17. Cited by Debesse in *Adolescent Identity Crisis.*
18. *The Waves.*

feels her mother "has done her time," and it is up to her now to bear children, to reign. If she works outside the house, she suffers when she returns home from still being treated as a simple member of the family and not as an autonomous individual.

Less romantic than before, she begins to think much more of marriage than love. She no longer embellishes her future spouse with a prestigious halo: what she wishes for is to have a stable position in this world and to begin to lead her life as a woman. This is how Virginia Woolf describes the imaginings of a rich country girl:

> For soon in the hot midday when the bees hum round the hollyhocks my lover will come. He will stand under the cedar tree. To his one word I shall answer my one word. What has formed in me I shall give him. I shall have children; I shall have maids in aprons; men with pitchforks; a kitchen where they bring the ailing lambs to warm in baskets, where the hams hang and the onions glisten. I shall be like my mother, silent in a blue apron locking up the cupboards.

A similar dream dwells in poor Prue Sarn:

> It seemed such a terrible thing never to marry. All girls got married . . . And when girls got married, they had a cottage, and a lamp, maybe, to light when their man came home, or if it was only candles it was all one, for they could put them in the window, and he'd think "There's my missus now, lit the candles!" And then one day Mrs. Beguildy would be making a cot of rushes for 'em, and one day there'd be a babe in it, grand and solemn, and bidding letters sent round for the christening, and the neighbours coming round the babe's mother like bees round the queen. Often when things went wrong, I'd say to myself, "Ne'er mind, Prue Sarn! There'll come a day when you'll be queen in your own skep."[19]

For most older girls, whether they have a laborious or frivolous life, whether they be confined to the paternal household or partially get away from it, the conquest of a husband—or at the least a serious lover—turns into a more and more pressing enterprise. This concern is often harmful for feminine friendships. The "best friend" loses her privileged place. The

---

19. Mary Webb, *Precious Bane*.

girl sees rivals more than partners in her companions. I knew one such girl, intelligent and talented but who had chosen to think herself a "faraway princess": this is how she described herself in poems and literary essays; she sincerely admitted she did not remain attached to her childhood friends: if they were ugly and stupid, she did not like them; if seductive, she feared them. The impatient wait for a man, often involving maneuvers, ruses, and humiliations, blocks the girl's horizon; she becomes egotistical and hard. And if Prince Charming takes his time appearing, disgust and bitterness set in.

The girl's character and behavior express her situation: if it changes, the adolescent girl's attitude also changes. Today, it is becoming possible for her to take her future in her hands, instead of putting it in those of the man. If she is absorbed by studies, sports, a professional training, or a social and political activity, she frees herself from the male obsession; she is less preoccupied by love and sexual conflicts. However, she has a harder time than the young man in accomplishing herself as an autonomous individual. I have said that neither her family nor customs assist her attempts. Besides, even if she chooses independence, she still makes a place in her life for the man, for love. She will often be afraid of missing her destiny as a woman if she gives herself over entirely to any undertaking. She does not admit this feeling to herself: but it is there, it distorts all her best efforts, it sets up limits. In any case, the woman who works wants to reconcile her success with purely feminine successes; that not only requires devoting considerable time to her appearance and beauty but also, what is more serious, implies that her vital interests are divided. Outside of his regular studies, the male student amuses himself by freely exercising his mind, and from there emerge his best discoveries; the woman's daydreams are oriented in a different direction: she will think of her physical appearance, of man, of love, she will give the bare minimum to her studies to her career, whereas in these areas nothing is as necessary as the superfluous. It is not a question of mental weakness, of a lack of concentration, but of a split in her interests that do not coincide well. A vicious circle is knotted here: people are often surprised to see how easily a woman gives up music, studies, or a job as soon as she has found a husband; this is because she had committed too little of herself to her projects to derive benefit from their accomplishment. Everything converges to hold back her personal ambition while enormous social pressure encourages her to find a social position and justification in marriage. It is natural that she should not seek to create her place in this world by and for herself or that she should seek it timidly. As long as perfect economic equality is not realized in society and as long as customs allow the woman to profit as wife and mistress from the privileges held by certain men, the dream of passive success will be maintained in her and will hold back her own accomplishments.

However the girl approaches her existence as an adult, her apprenticeship is not yet over. By small increments or bluntly, she has to undergo her sexual initiation. There are girls who refuse. If sexually difficult incidents marked their childhood, if an awkward upbringing has gradually rooted a horror of sexuality in them, they carry over their adolescent repugnance of men. There are also circumstances that cause some women to have an extended virginity in spite of themselves. But in most cases, the girl accomplishes her sexual destiny at a more or less advanced age. How she braves it is obviously closely linked to her whole past. But this is also a novel experience that presents itself in unforeseen circumstances and to which she freely reacts. This is the new stage we must now consider.

CHAPTER 3

Sexual Initiation

In a sense, woman's sexual initiation, like man's, begins in infancy. There is a theoretical and practical initiation period that follows continuously from the oral, anal, and genital phases up to adulthood. But the young girl's erotic experiences are not a simple extension of her previous sexual activities; they are very often unexpected and brutal; they always constitute a new occurrence that creates a rupture with the past. While she is going through them, all the problems the young girl faces are concentrated in an urgent and acute form. In some cases, the crisis is easily resolved; there are tragic situations where the crisis can only be resolved through suicide or madness. In any case, the way woman reacts to the experiences strongly affects her destiny. All psychiatrists agree on the extreme importance her erotic beginnings have for her: their repercussions will be felt for the rest of her life.

The situation is profoundly different here for man and woman from the biological, social, and psychological points of view. For man, the passage from childhood sexuality to maturity is relatively simple: erotic pleasure is objectified; now, instead of being realized in his immanent presence, this erotic pleasure is intended for a transcendent being. The erection is the expression of this need; with penis, hands, mouth, with his whole body, the man reaches out to his partner, but he remains at the heart of this activity, as the subject generally does before the objects he perceives and the instruments he manipulates; he projects himself toward the other without losing his autonomy; feminine flesh is a prey for him, and he seizes in woman the attributes his sensuality requires of any object; of course he does not succeed in appropriating them: at least he holds them; the embrace and the kiss imply a partial failure: but this very failure is a stimulant and a joy. The act of love finds its unity in its natural culmination: orgasm. Coitus has a specific physiological aim; in ejaculation the male releases burdensome secretions; after orgasm, the male feels complete relief regularly accompanied by pleasure. And, of course, pleasure is not the only aim; it is often followed by disappointment: the need has disappeared rather than having been satisfied. In any case, a definite act is consummated, and the man's body remains intact: the service he has rendered to the species becomes one with his own pleasure. Woman's eroticism is far more complex and reflects the complexity of her situation. It has been seen that instead of integrating forces of the species into her individual life, the female is prey to the species, whose interests diverge from her own ends;[1] this antinomy reaches its height in woman; one of its manifestations is the opposition of two organs: the clitoris and the vagina. At the infant stage, the former is the center of feminine eroticism: some psychiatrists uphold the existence of vaginal sensitivity in little girls, but this is a very inaccurate opinion; at any rate, it would have only secondary importance. The clitoral system does not change with adulthood,[2] and woman preserves this erotic autonomy her whole life; like the male orgasm, the clitoral spasm is a kind of detumescence that occurs quasi-mechanically; but it is only indirectly linked to normal coitus, it plays no role whatsoever in procreation. The woman is penetrated and impregnated through the vagina; it becomes an erotic center uniquely through the intervention of the male, and this always constitutes a kind of rape. In the past, a woman was snatched from her childhood universe and thrown into her life as a wife by a real or simulated rape; this was an act of violence that changed the girl into a woman: it is also referred to as "ravishing" a girl's virginity or "taking" her flower. This deflowering is not the harmonious outcome of a continuous development; it is an abrupt rupture with the past, the beginning of a new cycle. Pleasure is then reached by contractions of the inside surface of the vagina; do these contractions result in a precise and definitive orgasm? This point is still being debated. The anatomical data are vague. "There is a great deal of anatomic and clinical evidence that most of the interior of the vagina is without nerves," states, among other things, the Kinsey Report. "A considerable amount of surgery may be performed inside the vagina without need for anesthetics. Nerves have been demonstrated inside the vagina only in an area in the anterior wall, proximate to the base of the clitoris." However, in addition to the stimulation of this innervated zone, "the female may be conscious of the intrusion of an object into the vagina, particularly if vaginal muscles are tightened; but the satisfaction so obtained is probably related more to muscle tonus than it is to erotic nerve

---

1. See Volume I, Chapter 1. [In Part One, "Destiny."—Trans.]
2. Unless excision is practiced, which is the rule in some primitive cultures.

stimulation."* Yet it is beyond doubt that vaginal pleasure exists; and even vaginal masturbation—for adult women—seems to be more widespread than Kinsey says.[3] But what is certain is that the vaginal reaction is very complex and can be qualified as psychophysiological because it not only concerns the entire nervous system but also depends on the whole situation lived by the subject: it requires profound consent of the individual as a whole; to establish itself, the new erotic cycle launched by the first coitus demands a kind of "preparation" of the nervous system, the elaboration of a totally new form that has to include the clitoral system as well; it takes a long time to be put in place, and sometimes it never succeeds in being created. It is striking that woman has the choice between two cycles, one of which perpetuates youthful independence, while the other destines her to man and children. The normal sexual act effectively makes woman dependent on the male and the species. It is he—as for most animals—who has the aggressive role and she who submits to his embrace. Ordinarily, she can be taken at any time by man, while he can take her only when he is in the state of erection; feminine refusal can be overcome except in the case of a rejection as profound as vaginismus, sealing woman more securely than the hymen; still vaginismus leaves the male means to relieve himself on a body that his muscular force permits him to reduce to his mercy. Since she is object, her inertia does not profoundly alter her natural role: to the extent that many men are not interested in whether the woman who shares their bed wants coitus or only submits to it. One can even go to bed with a dead woman. Coitus cannot take place without male consent, and male satisfaction is its natural end result. Fertilization can occur without the woman deriving any pleasure. On the other hand, fertilization is far from representing the completion of the sexual process for her; by contrast, it is at this

---

* The Kinsey Reports are two books on human sexual behavior: *Sexual Behavior in the Human Male* (1948) and *Sexual Behavior in the Human Female* (1953), by Alfred Kinsey, Wardell Pomeroy, and others.—TRANS.

3. "The use of an artificial penis in solitary sexual gratification may be traced down from classic times, and doubtless prevailed in the very earliest human civilization . . . In more recent years the following are a few of the objects found in the vagina or bladder whence they could only be removed by surgical interference: Pencils, sticks of sealing-wax, cotton-reels, hair-pins (and in Italy very commonly the bone-pins used in the hair), bodkins, knitting-needles, crochet-needles, needle-cases, compasses, glass stoppers, candles, corks, tumblers, forks, tooth-picks, toothbrushes, pomade-pots (in a case recorded by Schroeder with a cockchafer inside, a makeshift substitute for the Japanese *rin-no-tama*), while in one recent English case a full-sized hen's egg was removed from the vagina of a middle-aged married woman . . . the large objects, naturally, are found chiefly in the vagina, and in married women" (Havelock Ellis, *Studies in the Psychology of Sex*, Volume 1).

moment that the service demanded of her by the species begins: it takes place slowly and painfully in pregnancy, birth, and breast-feeding.

Man's "anatomical destiny" is profoundly different from woman's. Their moral and social situations are no less different. Patriarchal civilization condemned woman to chastity; the right of man to relieve his sexual desires is more or less openly recognized, whereas woman is confined within marriage: for her the act of the flesh, if not sanctified by the code, by a sacrament, is a fault, a fall, a defeat, a weakness; she is obliged to defend her virtue, her honor; if she "gives in" or if she "falls," she arouses disdain, whereas even the blame inflicted on her vanquisher brings him admiration. From primitive civilizations to our times, the bed has always been accepted as a "service" for a woman for which the male thanks her with gifts or guarantees her keep: but to serve is to give herself up to a master; there is no reciprocity at all in this relationship. The marriage structure, like the existence of prostitutes, proves it: the woman *gives herself;* the man remunerates her and takes her. Nothing forbids the male to act the master, to take inferior creatures: ancillary loves have always been tolerated, whereas the bourgeois woman who gives herself to a chauffeur or a gardener is socially degraded. Fiercely racist American men in the South have always been permitted by custom to sleep with black women, before the Civil War as today, and they exploit this right with a lordly arrogance; a white woman who had relations with a black man in the time of slavery would have been put to death, and today she would be lynched. To say he slept with a woman, a man says he "possessed" her, that he "had" her; on the contrary, "to have" someone is sometimes vulgarly expressed as "to fuck someone"; the Greeks called a woman who did not have sexual relations with the male *Parthenos adamatos,* an untaken virgin; the Romans called Messalina *invicta* because none of her lovers gave her satisfaction. So for the male lover, the love act is conquest and victory. While, in another man, the erection often seems like a ridiculous parody of voluntary action, each one nonetheless considers it in his own case with a certain pride. Males' erotic vocabulary is inspired by military vocabulary: the lover has the ardor of a soldier, his sexual organ stiffens like a bow, when he ejaculates, he "discharges," it is a machine gun, a cannon; he speaks of attack, assault, of victory. In his arousal there is a certain flavor of the heroic. "The generative act, consisting of the occupation of one being by another," writes Benda, "imposes, on the one hand, the idea of a conqueror, on the other of something conquered. Thus when they refer to their most civilized love relationships, they talk of conquest, attack, assault, siege and defense, defeat, and capitulation, clearly copying the idea of love from that of war. This act, involving the pollution of one being by another, imposes a certain pride on the polluter and some humiliation on the polluted, even when she is consenting."[4] This last phrase introduces a new myth: that man inflicts a stain on woman. In fact, sperm is not excrement; one speaks of "nocturnal pollution" because the sperm does not serve its natural purpose; while coffee can stain a light-colored dress, it is not said to be waste that defiles the stomach. Other men maintain, by contrast, that woman is impure because it is she who is "soiled by discharges" and that she pollutes the male. In any case, being the one who pollutes confers a dubious superiority. In fact, man's privileged situation comes from the integration of his biologically aggressive role into his social function of chief and master; it is through this function that physiological differences take on all their full meaning. Because man is sovereign in this world, he claims the violence of his desires as a sign of his sovereignty; it is said of a man endowed with great erotic capacities that he is strong and powerful: epithets that describe him as an activity and a transcendence; on the contrary, woman being only an object is considered *hot* or *cold;* that is, she will never manifest any qualities other than passive ones.

So the climate in which feminine sexuality awakens is nothing like the one surrounding the adolescent boy. Besides, when woman faces the male for the first time, her erotic attitude is very complex. It is not true, as has been held at times, that the virgin does not know desire and that the male awakens her sensuality; this legend once again betrays the male's taste for domination, never wanting his companion to be autonomous, even in the desire that she has for him; in fact, for man as well, desire is often aroused through contact with woman, and, on the contrary, most young girls feverishly long for caresses before a hand ever touches them. Isadora Duncan in *My Life* says,

> My hips, which had been like a boy's, took on another undulation, and through my whole being I felt one great surging, longing, unmistakable urge, so that I could no longer sleep at night, but tossed and turned in feverish, painful unrest.

In a long confession of her life to Stekel, a young woman recounts:

> I began vigorously to flirt. I had to have "my nerves tickler (*sic*)." I was a passionate dancer, and while dancing I always shut my eyes

---

4. *Uriel's Report.*

the better to enjoy it . . . During dancing, I was somewhat exhibitionistic; my sensuality seemed to overcome my feeling of shame. During the first year, I danced with avidity and great enjoyment. I slept many hours, masturbated daily, often keeping it up for an hour . . . I masturbated often until I was covered with sweat, too fatigued to continue, I fell asleep . . . I was burning and I would have taken anyone who would relieve me. I wasn't looking for a person, just a man.[5]

The issue here is rather that virginal agitation is not expressed as a precise need: the virgin does not know exactly what she wants. Aggressive childhood eroticism still survives in her; her first impulses were prehensile, and she still has the desire to embrace, to possess; she wants the prey that she covets to be endowed with the qualities which through taste, smell, and touch have been shown to her as values; for sexuality is not an isolated domain, it extends the dreams and joys of sensuality; children and adolescents of both sexes like what is smooth, creamy, satiny, soft, elastic: that which yields to pressure without collapsing or decomposing and slips under the gaze or the fingers; like man, woman is charmed by the warm softness of sand dunes, so often compared to breasts, or the light touch of silk, of the fluffy softness of an eiderdown, the velvet feeling of a flower or fruit; and the young girl especially cherishes the pale colors of pastels, froths of tulle and muslin. She has no taste for rough fabrics, gravel, rocks, bitter flavors, acrid odors; like her brothers, it was her mother's flesh that she first caressed and cherished; in her narcissism, in her diffuse or precise homosexual experiences, she posited herself as a subject and she sought the possession of a female body. When she faces the male, she has, in the palms of her hands and on her lips, the desire to actively caress a prey. But man, with his hard muscles, his scratchy and often hairy skin, his crude odor, and his coarse features, does not seem desirable to her, and he even stirs her repulsion. Renée Vivien expresses it this way:

> *I am a woman, I have no right to beauty*
> *They have condemned me to the ugliness of men . . .*
> *They have forbidden me your hair, your eyes*
> *Because your hair is long and scented with odors* *

---

5. *Frigidity in Woman.*
* *At the Sweet Hour of Hand in Hand*, trans. Gillian Spraggs.—TRANS.

If the prehensile, possessive tendency exists in woman more strongly, her orientation, like that of Renée Vivien, will be toward homosexuality. Or she will become attached only to males she can treat like women: thus the heroine of Rachilde's *Monsieur Vénus* buys herself a young lover whom she enjoys caressing passionately, but will not let herself be deflowered by him. There are women who love to caress young boys of thirteen or fourteen years old or even children, and who reject grown men. But we have seen that passive sexuality has also been developed since childhood in the majority of women: the woman loves to be hugged and caressed, and especially from puberty she wishes to be flesh in the arms of a man; the role of subject is normally his; she knows it; "A man does not need to be handsome," she has been told over and over; she should not look for the inert qualities of an object in him but for strength and virile force. She thus becomes divided within herself: she wants a strong embrace that will turn her into a trembling thing; but brutality and force are also hostile obstacles that wound her. Her sensuality is located both in her skin and in her hand: and their exigencies are in opposition to each other. Whenever possible, she chooses a compromise; she gives herself to a man who is virile but young and seductive enough to be an object of desire; she will be able to find all the traits she desires in a handsome adolescent; in the Song of Songs, there is a symmetry between the delights of the wife and those of the husband; she grasps in him what he seeks in her: earthly fauna and flora, precious stones, streams, stars. But she does not have the means to *take* these treasures; her anatomy condemns her to remaining awkward and impotent, like a eunuch: the desire for possession is thwarted for lack of an organ to incarnate it. And man refuses the passive role. Often, besides, circumstances lead the young girl to become the prey of a male whose caresses move her, but whom she has no pleasure to look at or caress in return. Not enough has been said not only about the fear of masculine aggressiveness but also about a deep feeling of frustration at the disgust that is mixed with her desires: sexual satisfaction must be achieved against the spontaneous thrust of her sensuality, while for the man the joy of touching and seeing merges with the sexual experience as such.

Even the elements of passive eroticism are ambiguous. Nothing is murkier than *contact*. Many men who triturate all sorts of material in their hands without disgust hate it when grass or animals touch them; women's flesh can tremble pleasantly or bristle at the touch of silk or velvet: I recall a childhood friend who had gooseflesh simply at the sight of a peach; the transition is easy from agitation to titillation, from irritation to pleasure; arms enlacing a body can be a refuge and protection, but they also imprison and suffocate. For the virgin, this ambiguity is perpetuated because of her paradoxical situation: the organ that will bring about her metamorphosis is sealed. Her flesh's uncertain and burning longing spreads through her whole body except in the very place where coitus should occur. No organ permits the virgin to satisfy her active eroticism; and she does not have the lived experience of he who dooms her to passivity.

However, this passivity is not pure inertia. For the woman to be aroused, positive phenomena must be produced in her organism: stimulation in erogenous zones, swelling of certain erectile tissue, secretions, temperature rise, pulse, and breathing acceleration. Desire and sexual pleasure demand a vital expenditure for her as for the male; receptive, the female need is in one sense active and is manifested in an increase of nervous and muscular energy. Apathetic and languid women are always cold; there is a question as to whether constitutional frigidity exists, and surely psychic factors play a preponderant role in the erotic capacities of woman; but it is certain that physiological insufficiencies and a depleted vitality are manifested in part by sexual indifference. If, on the other hand, vital energy is spent in voluntary activities—sports, for example—it is not invested in sex. Scandinavians are healthy, strong, and cold. "Fiery" women are those who combine their languor with "fire," like Italian or Spanish women, that is to say, women whose ardent vitality flows from their flesh. To *make* oneself object, to *make* oneself passive, is very different from *being* a passive object: a woman in love is neither asleep nor a corpse; there is a surge in her that ceaselessly falls and rises: it is this surge that creates the spell that perpetuates desire. But the balance between ardor and abandon is easy to destroy. Male desire is tension; it can invade a body where nerves and muscles are taut: positions and movements that demand a voluntary participation of the organism do not work against it, and instead often serve it. On the contrary, every voluntary effort keeps female flesh from being "taken"; this is why the woman spontaneously refuses forms of coitus that demand work and tension from her;[6] too many and too abrupt changes in position, the demands of consciously directed activities—actions or words—break the spell. The violence of uncontrolled tendencies can bring about tightening, contraction, or tension: some women scratch or bite, their bodies arching, infused with an unaccustomed force; but these phenomena are only produced when a certain paroxysm is attained, and it is attained only if first the absence of all inhibition—physical as well as moral—permits a

---

6. We will see further on that there can be psychological reasons that modify her immediate attitude.

concentration of all living energy into the sexual act. This means that it is not enough for the young girl to *let it happen;* if she is docile, languid, or removed, she satisfies neither her partner nor herself. She must participate actively in an adventure that neither her virgin body nor her consciousness—laden with taboos, prohibitions, prejudices, and exigencies—desires positively.

———

In the conditions just described, it is understandable that woman's erotic beginnings are not easy. Quite frequently, incidents that occur in childhood and youth provoke deep resistance in her, as has been seen; sometimes it is insurmountable; most often, the young girl tries to overcome it, but violent conflicts build up in her. Her strict education, the fear of sinning, and feelings of guilt toward her mother all create powerful blocks. Virginity is valued so highly in many circles that to lose it outside marriage seems a veritable disaster. The young girl who surrenders by coercion or by surprise thinks she dishonors herself. The "wedding night," which delivers the virgin to a man whom she has ordinarily not even chosen, and which attempts to condense into a few hours—or instants—the entire sexual initiation, is not a simple experience. In general, any "passage" is distressing because of its definitive and irreversible character: becoming a woman is breaking with the past, without recourse; but this particular passage is more dramatic than any other; it creates not only a hiatus between yesterday and tomorrow; it tears the young girl from the imaginary world where a great part of her existence took place and hurls her into the real world. By analogy with a bullfight, Michel Leiris calls the nuptial bed "a moment of truth"; for the virgin, this expression takes on its fullest and most fearsome meaning. During the engagement, dating, or courtship period, however basic it may have been, she continued to live in her familiar universe of ceremony and dreams; the suitor spoke a romantic, or at least courteous, language; it was still possible to make believe. And suddenly there she is, gazed upon by real eyes, handled by real hands: it is the implacable reality of this gazing and grasping that terrifies her.

Both anatomy and customs confer the role of initiator on the man. Without doubt, for the young male virgin, his first mistress also provides his initiation; but he possesses an erotic autonomy clearly manifested in the erection; his mistress only delivers to him the object in its reality that he already desires: a woman's body. The young girl needs a man to make her discover her own body: her dependence is much greater. From his very first experiences, man is ordinarily active and decisive, whether he pays his partner or courts and solicits her. By contrast, in most cases, the young girl *is* courted and solicited; even if it is she who first flirts with the man, he is the one who takes their relationship in hand; he is often older and more experienced, and it is accepted that he has the responsibility for this adventure that is new for her; his desire is more aggressive and imperious. Lover or husband, he is the one who leads her to the bed, where her only choice is to let go of herself and obey. Even if she had accepted this authority in her mind, she is panic-stricken the moment she must concretely submit to it. She first of all fears this gaze that engulfs her. Her modesty may have been taught her, but it has deep roots; men and women all know the shame of their flesh; in its pure, immobile presence, its unjustified immanence, the flesh exists in the gaze of another as the absurd contingence of facticity, and yet flesh is *oneself:* we want to prevent it from existing for others; we want to deny it. There are men who say they cannot stand to be naked in front of a woman, except in the state of erection; through the erection, the flesh becomes activity, force, the penis is no longer an inert object but, like the hand or the face, the imperious expression of a subjectivity. This is one reason why modesty paralyzes young men much less than young women; their aggressive role exposes them less to being gazed at; and if they are, they do not fear being judged, because it is not inert qualities that their mistresses demand of them: it is rather their amorous potency and their skill at giving pleasure that will give rise to complexes; at least they can defend themselves and try to win their match. Woman does not have the option of transforming her flesh into will: when she stops hiding it, she gives it up without defenses; even if she longs for caresses, she recoils from the idea of being seen and felt; all the more so as her breasts and buttocks are particularly fleshy; many adult women cannot bear to be seen from the rear even when they are dressed; imagine the resistance a naive girl in love has to overcome to consent to showing herself. A Phryne undoubtedly does not fear being gazed at; she bares herself, on the contrary, superbly. Her beauty clothes her. But even if she is the equal of Phryne, a young girl never feels it with certainty; she cannot have arrogant pride in her body as long as male approval has not confirmed her young vanity. And this is just what frightens her; the lover is even more terrifying than a gaze: he is a judge; he is going to reveal her to herself in her truth; even passionately taken with her own image, every young girl doubts herself at the moment of the masculine verdict; this is why she demands darkness, she hides in the sheets; when she admired herself in the mirror, she was only dreaming: she was dreaming through man's eyes; now the eyes are really there; impossible to cheat; impossible to fight: a mysterious freedom decides, and this decision is final. In the real ordeal of the erotic experience, the obsessions of childhood and adolescence will finally fade or be confirmed forever; many young girls suffer from muscular calves, breasts that are too little or too big, narrow hips, a wart; or else they fear some secret malformation. Stekel writes:

> Every young girl carries in her all sorts of ridiculous fears that she barely dares to admit to herself. One would not believe how many young girls suffer from the obsession of being physically abnormal and torment themselves secretly because they cannot be sure of being normally constructed. One young girl, for example, believed that her "lower opening" was not in the right place. She thought that sexual intercourse took place through the navel. She was unhappy because her navel was closed and she could not stick her finger in it. Another thought she was a hermaphrodite. And another thought she was crippled and would never be able to have sexual relations.[7]

Even if they are unfamiliar with these obsessions, they are terrified by the idea that certain regions of their bodies that did not exist for them or for anyone, that absolutely did not exist, will suddenly be seen. Will this unknown figure that the young girl must assume as her own provoke disgust? Indifference? Irony? She can only submit to male judgment: the die is cast. This is why man's attitude will have such deep resonance. His ardor and tenderness can give woman a confidence in herself that will stand up to every rejection: until she is eighty years old, she will believe she is this flower, this exotic bird that made man's desire bloom one night. On the contrary, if the lover or husband is clumsy, he will arouse an inferiority complex in her that is sometimes compounded by long-lasting neuroses; and she will hold a grudge that will be expressed in a stubborn frigidity. Stekel describes striking examples:

> A woman of 36 years of age suffers from such back pain across "the small of her back" for the past 14 years. These pains are so unbearable that she is forced to stay in bed for weeks . . . she felt the great pains for the first time during her wedding night. On that occasion, during the defloration, which caused her considerable pain, her husband exclaimed: "You have deceived me! You are not a virgin!" Her pains in the back represent the fixation of this painful episode. Her illness is her vengeance on the man. The various cures have cost

---

7. *Frigidity in Woman.*

him considerable money for her innumerable treatments . . . This woman was anaesthetic during her wedding night and she remained in this condition throughout her marital experience . . . The wedding night was for her a terrible mental shock that has influenced her whole life.

A woman consults me for various nervous troubles and particularly on account of her complete sexual frigidity . . . During her wedding night, her husband, after uncovering her, exclaimed: "Oh, how stubby and thick your limbs are!" Then he tried to carry out intercourse. She felt only pain and remained wholly frigid . . . She knows very well that the slightest remark he made about her during the wedding night was responsible for her sexual frigidity.

Another frigid woman says that "during her wedding night, her husband deeply insulted her" seeing her get undressed, he allegedly said: "My God, how thin you are!" Then he nevertheless decided to caress her. For her this moment was unforgettable and horrible. What brutality!

Mrs. Z.W. is also completely frigid. The great traumatism of her wedding night was that her husband supposedly said after the first intercourse: "You have a big hole, you tricked me."

The gaze is danger; hands are another threat. Woman does not usually have access to the universe of violence; she has never gone through the ordeal the young man overcame in childhood and adolescent fights: to be a thing of flesh on which others have a hold; and now that she is grasped, she is swept away in a body-to-body clasp where man is the stronger; she is no longer free to dream, to withdraw, to maneuver: she is given over to the male; he disposes of her. These wrestling-like embraces terrorize her, she who has never wrestled. She had let herself go to the caresses of a fiancé, a fellow student, a colleague, a civilized and courteous man: but he has assumed an unfamiliar, selfish, and stubborn attitude; she no longer has recourse against this stranger. It is not uncommon that the young girl's first experience is a real rape and that man's behavior is odiously brutal; particularly in the countryside, where customs are harsh, it often happens that a young peasant woman, half-consenting, half-outraged, in shame and fright, loses her virginity at the bottom of some ditch. What is in any case extremely frequent in all societies and classes is that the virgin is rushed by an egotistical lover seeking his own pleasure quickly, or by a husband convinced of his conjugal rights who takes his wife's resistance as an insult, to the point of becoming furious if the defloration is difficult.

In any case, however deferential and courteous a man might be, the first penetration is always a rape. While she desires caresses on her lips and breasts and perhaps yearns for a familiar or anticipated orgasm, here is a male sex organ tearing the young girl and introducing itself into regions where it was not invited. The painful surprise of a swooning virgin—who thinks she has finally reached the accomplishment of her voluptuous dreams and who feels in the secret of her sex an unexpected pain—in a husband's or lover's arms has often been described; the dreams faint away, the excitement dissipates, and love takes on the appearance of a surgical operation.

In the confessions gathered by Dr. Liepmann, there is the following and typical account. It concerns a very sexually unaware girl from a modest background:

"I often imagined that one could have a child just by the exchange of a kiss. During my eighteenth year, I made the acquaintance of a man with whom I really fell madly in love." She often went out with him, and during their conversations he explained to her that when a young girl loves a man, she must give herself to him because men cannot live without sexual relations and that as long as they cannot afford to get married, they have to have relations with young girls. She resisted. One day, he organized an excursion so that they could spend the night together. She wrote him a letter to repeat that "it would harm her too much." The morning of the arranged day, she gave him the letter, but he put it in his pocket without reading it and took her to the hotel; he dominated her morally, she loved him, she followed him. "I was as if hypnotized. As we were going along, I begged him to spare me . . . How I arrived at the hotel, I do not know at all. The only memory that remained is that my whole body trembled violently. My companion tried to calm me; but he succeeded only after much resistance. I was no longer mistress of my will, and in spite of myself I let myself go. When I found myself later in the street, it seemed to me that everything had only been a dream I had just awakened from." She refused to repeat the experience and for nine years did not have sexual relations with any other man. She then met one who asked her to marry him and she agreed.[8]

---

8. Published in French under the title *Jeunesse et sexualité* (Youth and Sexuality).

In this case, the defloration was a kind of rape. But even if it is consensual, it can be painful. Look at the fevers that tormented young Isadora Duncan. She met an admirably handsome actor with whom she fell in love at first sight and who courted her ardently:

> I myself felt ill and dizzy, while an irresistible longing to press him closer and closer surged in me, until, losing all control and falling into a fury, he carried me into the room. Frightened but ecstatic, the realisation was made clear to me. I confess my first impressions were a horrible fright, but a great pity for what he seemed to be suffering prevented me from running away from what was at first sheer torture . . . [The next day], what had been for me only a painful experience began again amid my martyr's sobs and cries.[9]

She was soon to know the paradise she lyrically described, first with this lover and then with others.

However, in actual experience, as previously in one's virginal imagination, it is not pain that plays the greatest role: the fact of penetration counts far more. In intercourse the man introduces only an exterior organ: woman is affected in her deepest interior. Undoubtedly, there are many young men who tread with anguish in the secret darkness of woman; their childhood terrors resurface at the threshold of caves and graves, and so does their fright in front of jaws, scythes, and wolf traps: they imagine that their swollen penis will be caught in the mucous sheath; the woman, once penetrated, does not have this feeling of danger; but she does feel carnally alienated. The property owner affirms his rights over his lands, the housewife over her house by proclaiming "no trespassing"; because of their frustrated transcendence, women, in particular, jealously defend their privacy: their room, their wardrobe, and their chests are sacred. Colette tells of an old prostitute who told her one day: "In my room, Madame, no man has ever set foot; for what I have to do with men, Paris is quite big enough." If not her body, at least she possessed a plot of land where entry was prohibited. The young girl, though, possesses little of her own except her body: it is her most precious treasure; the man who enters her *takes* it from her; the familiar word is confirmed by her lived experience. She experiences concretely the humiliation she had felt: she is dominated, subjugated, conquered. Like almost all females, she is *under* the man during inter-

---

9. *My Life.*

course.[10] Adler emphasized the feeling of inferiority resulting from this. Right from infancy, the notions of superior and inferior are extremely important; climbing trees is a prestigious act; heaven is above the earth; hell is underneath; to fall or to descend is to degrade oneself, and to climb is to exalt oneself; in wrestling, victory belongs to the one who pins his opponent down, whereas the woman lies on the bed in a position of defeat; it is even worse if the man straddles her like an animal subjugated by reins and a bit. In any case, she feels passive: she *is* caressed, penetrated; she undergoes intercourse, whereas the man spends himself actively. It is true that the male sex organ is not a striated muscle commanded by will; it is neither plowshare nor sword but merely flesh; but it is a voluntary movement that man imprints on her; he goes, he comes, stops, resumes, while the woman receives him submissively; it is the man—especially when the woman is a novice—who chooses the amorous positions, who decides the length and frequency of intercourse. She feels herself to be an instrument: all the freedom is in the other. This is what is poetically expressed by saying that woman is comparable to a violin and man to the bow that makes her vibrate. "In love," says Balzac, "leaving the soul out of consideration, woman is a lyre which only yields up its secrets to the man who can play upon it skilfully."[11] He *takes* his pleasure with her; he *gives* her pleasure; the words themselves do not imply reciprocity. Woman is imbued with collective images of the glorious aura of masculine sexual excitement that make feminine arousal a shameful abdication: her intimate experience confirms this asymmetry. It must not be forgotten that boy and girl adolescents experience their bodies differently: the former tranquilly takes his body for granted and proudly takes charge of his desires; for the latter, in spite of her narcissism, it is a strange and disturbing burden. Man's sex organ is neat and simple, like a finger; it can be innocently exhibited, and boys often show it off to their friends proudly and defiantly; the feminine sex organ is mysterious to the woman herself, hidden, tormented, mucous, and humid; it bleeds each month, it is sometimes soiled with bodily fluids, it has a secret and dangerous life. It is largely because woman does not recognize herself in it that she does not recognize her own desires. They are expressed in a

---

10. The position can undoubtedly be reversed. But in the first experiences, it is extremely rare for the man not to practice the so-called normal coitus.

11. *Physiology of Marriage*. In *Bréviaire de l'amour expérimental* (*A Ritual for Married Lovers*), Jules Guyot also says of the husband: "He is the minstrel who produces harmony or cacophony with his hand and bow. From this point of view woman is really a many-stringed instrument producing harmonious or discordant sounds depending on how she is tuned."

shameful manner. While the man has a "hard-on," the woman "gets wet"; there is in the very word infantile memories of the wet bed, of the guilty and involuntary desire to urinate; man has the same disgust for his nocturnal unconscious wet dreams; projecting a liquid, urine or sperm, is not humiliating: it is an active operation; but there is humiliation if the liquid escapes passively since the body then is no longer an organism, muscles, sphincters, and nerves, commanded by the brain and expressing the conscious subject, but a vase, a receptacle made of inert matter, and the plaything of mechanical caprices. If the flesh oozes—like an old wall or a dead body—it does not seem to be emitting liquid but deliquescing: a decomposition process that horrifies. Feminine heat is the flaccid palpitation of a shellfish; where man has impetuousness, woman merely has impatience; her desire can become ardent without ceasing to be passive; the man dives on his prey like the eagle and the hawk; she, like a carnivorous plant, waits for and watches the swamp where insects and children bog down; she is sucking, suction, sniffer, she is pitch and glue, immobile appeal, insinuating, and viscous: at least this is the way she indefinably feels. Thus, there is not only resistance against the male who attempts to subjugate her but also internal conflict. Superimposed on the taboos and inhibitions that arise from her education and society are disgust and refusals that stem from the erotic experience itself: they all reinforce each other to such an extent that often after the first coitus the woman is more in revolt against her sexual destiny than before.

Lastly, there is another factor that often gives man a hostile look and changes the sexual act into a grave danger: the danger of a child. An illegitimate child in most civilizations is such a social and economic handicap for the unmarried woman that one sees young girls committing suicide when they know they are pregnant and unwed mothers cutting the throats of their newborns; such a risk constitutes a quite powerful sexual brake, making many young girls observe the prenuptial chastity prescribed by customs. When the brake is insufficient, the young girl, while yielding to the lover, is horrified by the terrible danger he possesses in his loins. Stekel cites, among others, a young girl who for the entire duration of intercourse shouted: "Don't let anything happen! Don't let anything happen!" Even in marriage, the woman often does not want a child, her health is not good enough, or a child would be too great a burden on the young household. Whether he is lover or husband, if she does not have absolute confidence in her partner, her eroticism will be paralyzed by caution. Either she will anxiously watch the man's behavior, or else, once intercourse is over, she will run to the bathroom to chase the living germ from her belly, put there in spite of herself. This hygienic operation brutally contradicts the sensual magic of the caresses; she undergoes an absolute separation of the bodies that were merged in one single joy; thus the male sperm becomes a harmful germ, a soiling; she cleans herself as one cleans a dirty vase, while the man reclines on his bed in his superb wholeness. A young divorcée told me how horrified she was when—after a dubiously pleasurable wedding night—she had to shut herself in the bathroom and her husband nonchalantly lit a cigarette: it seems that the ruin of the couple was decided at that instant. The repugnance of the douche, the beaker, and the bidet is one of the frequent causes of feminine frigidity. The existence of surer and more convenient contraceptive devices is helping woman's sexual freedom a great deal; in a country like America where these practices are widespread, the number of young girls still virgins at marriage is much lower than in France; such practices make for far greater abandon during the love act. But there again, the young woman has to overcome her repugnance before treating her body as a thing: she can no more resign herself to being "corked" to satisfy a man's desires than she can to being "pierced" by him. Whether she has her uterus sealed or introduces some sperm-killing tampon, a woman who is conscious of the ambiguities of the body and sex will be bridled by cold premeditation; besides, many men consider the use of condoms repugnant. It is sexual behavior as a whole that justifies its various moments: conduct that when analyzed would seem repugnant seems natural when bodies are transfigured by the erotic virtues they possess; but inversely, when bodies and behaviors are decomposed into separate elements and deprived of meaning, these elements become disgusting and obscene. The surgical and dirty perception that penetration had in the eyes of the child returns if it is not carried out with the arousal, desire, and pleasure a woman in love will joyfully experience as union and fusion with the beloved: this is what happens with the concerted use of prophylactics. In any case, these precautions are not at the disposal of all women; many young girls do not know of any defense against the threats of pregnancy, and they feel great anguish that their lot depends on the goodwill of the man they give themselves up to.

It is understandable that an ordeal experienced through so much resistance, fraught with such weighty implications, often creates serious traumas. A latent precocious dementia has often been revealed by the first experience. Stekel gives several examples:

Miss M.G. . . . suddenly developed an acute delirium in her 19th year. I found her storming in her room, shouting repeatedly: "I won't! No! I won't!" She tore off her clothes and wanted to flee into the street naked . . . she had to be taken to the psychiatric clinic. There her delirium gradually abated and she passed into a catatonic state . . . This girl . . . was a clerk in an office, in love with the head clerk in the company . . . She had gone to the country with a girl friend . . . and a couple of young men who worked in the same office . . . she went to her room with one of the men [who] promised not to touch her and that "it was merely a prank." He roused her to slight tenderness for three nights without touching her virginity . . . She apparently remained "as cold as a dog's muzzle" and declared that it was disgraceful. For a few fleeting minutes her mind seemed confused and she exclaimed: "Alfred, Alfred." (Alfred was the head clerk's first name.) She was reproaching herself for what she had done (What would mother say about this if she knew?). Once she returned home, she took to her bed, complaining of a migraine.

Miss L.X.* . . . very depressed . . . She cried often and could not sleep; she had begun to have hallucinations and failed to recognize her environment. She had jumped to the windows and tried to throw herself out . . . She was taken to the sanitarium. I found this twenty-three-year-old girl sitting up in bed; she paid no attention to me when I entered . . . Her face depicted abject fear and horror; her limbs were crossed and they twitched vigorously. She was shouting. "No! No! No! You villain! Men such as you ought to be locked up! It hurts! Oh!" Then there followed some unintelligible mumbling. Suddenly her whole facial expression changed. Her eyes lit up, her lips pursed in the manner of kissing someone, her limbs ceased twitching and she gave forth outcries which suggested delight and rapture and love . . . Finally the attack ended in a subdued but persistent weeping . . . The patient kept pushing down her night-gown as if it were a dress, at the same time continually repeating the exclamation, "Don't!" It was known that a married colleague had often come to see her when she was ill, that she was first happy about it, but that later on she had had hallucinations and attempted suicide.† She got better but keeps all men at a distance and has rejected an earnest marriage offer.

---

* *Frigidity in Woman*. Discrepancy in initials: "K.L." in the English translation of Stekel's German text.—TRANS.
† Not in the English translation of Stekel's German text.—TRANS.

In other cases the illness triggered is less serious. Here is an example where regret for lost virginity plays the main role in the problems following the first coitus:

> A young twenty-three-year-old girl suffers from various phobias. The illness began at Franzensbad out of fear of catching a pregnancy by a kiss or a contact in a toilet . . . Perhaps a man had left some sperm in the water after masturbation; she insisted that the bathtub be cleaned three times in her presence and did not dare to move her bowels in the normal position. Some time afterwards she developed a phobia of tearing her hymen, she did not dare to dance, jump, cross a fence, or even walk except with very little steps; if she saw a post, she feared being deflowered by a clumsy movement and went around it, trembling all the way. Another of her phobias in a train or in the middle of a crowd was that a man could introduce his member from behind, deflower her, and provoke a pregnancy . . . During the last phase of the illness, she feared finding pins in her bed or on her shirt that could enter her vagina. Each evening the sick girl stayed naked in the middle of her room while her unfortunate mother was forced to go through a difficult examination of the bedclothes . . . She had always affirmed her love for her fiancé. An examination revealed that she was no longer a virgin and was putting off marriage because she feared her fiancé's disastrous observations. She admitted to him that she had been seduced by a tenor, married him, and was cured.[12]

In another case, remorse—uncompensated by voluptuous satisfaction—provoked psychic troubles:

> Miss H.B., twenty years old, after a trip to Italy with a girl friend, went into a serious depression. She refused to leave her room and did not utter one word. She was taken to a nursing home, where her situation got worse. She heard voices that were insulting her, everyone made fun of her, etc. She was brought back to her parents' where she stayed in a corner without moving. She asked the doctor: "Why didn't I come before the crime was committed?" She was dead. Everything was killed, destroyed. She was dirty. She could not

---

12. *Frigidity in Woman.*

sing one note, bridges with the world were burnt . . . The fiancé admitted having followed her to Rome where she gave herself to him after resisting a long time; she had crying fits . . . She admitted never having pleasure with her fiancé. She was cured when she found a lover who satisfied her and married her.

The "sweet Viennese girl" whose childish confessions I summarized also gave a detailed and gripping account of her first adult experiences. It will be noticed that—in spite of the very advanced nature of her previous adventures—her "initiation" still has an absolutely new character:

"At sixteen, I began working in an office. At seventeen and a half, I had my first holiday; it was a great period for me. I was courted on all sides . . . I was in love with a young office colleague . . . We went to the park. It was 15 April 1909. He made me sit next to him on a bench. He kissed me, begging me: open your lips; but I closed them convulsively. Then he began to unbutton my jacket. I would have let him when I remembered that I did not have any breasts; I gave up the voluptuous sensation I would have had if he had touched me . . . On 7 April a married colleague invited me to go to an exhibition with him. We drank wine at dinner. I lost some of my reserve and began telling him some ambiguous jokes. In spite of my begging, he hailed a cab, pushed me into it, and hardly had the horses started than he kissed me. He became more and more intimate, he pushed his hand farther and farther; I defended myself with all my strength and I do not remember if he got his way. The next day I went to the office rather flustered. He showed me his hands covered with the scratches I had given him . . . He asked me to come see him more often . . . I yielded, not very comfortable but still full of curiosity . . . As soon as he came near my sex I pulled away and returned to my place; but once, more clever than I, he overcame me and probably put his finger into my vagina. I cried with pain. It was June 1909 and I left on vacation. I took a trip with my girl friend. Two tourists arrived. They invited us to accompany them. My companion wanted to kiss my friend, she punched him. He came towards, grabbed me from behind, bent me to him, and kissed me. I did not resist . . . He invited me to come with him. I gave him my hand and we went into the middle of the forest. He kissed me . . . he kissed my sex, to my great indignation. I said to him: 'How can you do such a disgusting thing?' He put his penis in my hand . . . I

caressed it . . . all of a sudden he pulled away my hand and
threw a handkerchief over it to keep me from seeing what was
happening . . . Two days later we went to Liesing. All of a sudden
in a deserted field he took off his coat and put it on the grass . . . he
threw me down in such a way that one of his legs was placed
between mine. I still did not think how serious the situation was. I
begged him to kill me rather than deprive me of 'my most beautiful
finery.' He became very rough, swore at me, and threatened me with
the police. He covered my mouth with his hand and introduced his
penis. I thought my last hour had arrived. I had the feeling my
stomach was turning. When he was finally finished, I began to be
able to put up with him. He had to pick me up because I was still
stretched out. He covered my eyes and face with kisses. I did not see
or hear anything. If he had not held me back, I would have fallen
blindly in front of the traffic . . . We were alone in a second-class
compartment; he opened his trousers again to come towards me.
I screamed and ran quickly through the whole train until the last
running board . . . Finally he left me with a vulgar and strident
laugh that I will never forget, calling me a stupid goose who does not
know what is good. He let me return to Vienna alone. I went quickly
to the bathroom because I had felt something warm running along
my thigh. Frightened, I saw traces of blood. How could I hide this at
home? I went to bed as early as possible and cried for hours. I still
felt the pressure on my stomach caused by the pushing of his penis.
My strange attitude and lack of appetite told my mother something
had happened. I admitted everything to her. She did not see anything so terrible in it . . . My colleague did what he could to console
me. He took advantage of dark evenings to take walks with me in
the park and caress me under my skirts. I let him; but as soon as I felt
my vagina become wet I pulled myself away because I was terribly
ashamed."

She goes to a hotel with him sometimes but without sleeping with
him. She makes the acquaintance of a very rich young man that she
would like to marry. She sleeps with him but without feeling anything and with disgust. She resumes her relations with her colleague
but she misses the other one and begins to be cross-eyed and to lose
weight. She is sent to a sanitarium where she almost sleeps with a
young Russian, but she chases him from her bed at the last minute.
She begins affairs with a doctor and an officer but without consenting to complete sexual relations. Then she became mortally ill and

decided to go to a doctor. After her treatment she consented to give herself to a man who loved her and then married her. In marriage her frigidity disappeared.

In these few examples chosen from many similar ones, the partner's brutality or at least the abruptness of the event is the determining factor in the traumatism or disgust. The best situation for sexual initiation is one in which the girl learns to overcome her modesty, to get to know her partner, and to enjoy his caresses without violence or surprise, without fixed rules or a precise time frame. In this respect, the freedom of behavior appreciated by young American girls and more and more by French girls today can only be endorsed: they slip almost without noticing from necking and petting to complete sexual relations. The less tabooed it is, the smoother the initiation, and the freer the girl feels with her partner and the more the domination aspect of the male fades; if her lover is also young, a novice, shy, and an equal, the girl's defenses are not as strong; but her metamorphosis into a woman will also be less of a transformation. In *Green Wheat*, Colette's Vinca, the day after a rather brutal defloration, displays surprising placidity to her friend Phil: she did not feel "possessed"; on the contrary, she took pride in freeing herself of her virginity; she did not feel an overwhelming mental turmoil; in truth, Phil is wrong to be surprised as his girlfriend did not really know the male. Claudine was less unaffected after a turn on the dance floor in Renaud's arms. I was told of a French high school student still stuck in the "green fruit" stage who, having spent a night with a male school friend, ran to a girlfriend's the next morning to announce: "I slept with C. . . . it was a lot of fun." An American high school teacher told me his students stopped being virgins long before becoming women; their partners respect them too much to offend their modesty; the boys themselves are too young and too prudish to awaken any demon in the girls. There are girls who throw themselves into many erotic experiences in order to escape sexual anxiety; they hope to rid themselves of their curiosity and obsessions, but their acts often have a theoretical cast, rendering such behavior as unreal as the fantasies through which others anticipate the future. Giving oneself out of defiance, fear, or puritan rationalism is not achieving an authentic erotic experience: one merely reaches a pseudo-experience without danger and without much flavor; the sexual act is not accompanied by either anguish or shame, because arousal remains superficial and pleasure has not permeated the flesh. These deflowered virgins are still young girls; and it is likely that the day they find themselves in the grip of a sensual and imperious man, they will put up virginal resistance to him. Meanwhile, they remain in a kind of awkward age; caresses tickle them, kisses sometimes make them laugh: they look on physical love as a game, and if they are not in the mood to have fun, the lover's demands quickly seem importunate and abusive; they hold on to the disgusts, phobias, and prudishness of the adolescent girl. If they never go beyond this stage—which is, according to American males, the case with many American girls—they spend their lives in a state of semi-frigidity. Real sexual maturity for the woman who consents to becoming flesh can only occur in arousal and pleasure.

But it must not be thought that all difficulties subside in women with a passionate temperament. On the contrary, they sometimes worsen. Feminine arousal can reach an intensity unknown by man. Male desire is violent but localized, and he comes out of it—except perhaps in the instant of ejaculation—conscious of himself; woman, by contrast, undergoes a real alienation; for many, this metamorphosis is the most voluptuous and definitive moment of love; but it also has a magical and frightening side. The woman he is holding in his arms appears so absent from herself, so much in the throes of turmoil, that the man may feel afraid of her. The upheaval she feels is a far more radical transmutation than the male's aggressive frenzy. This fever frees her from shame; but when she awakes, it in turn makes her feel ashamed and horrified; for her to accept it happily—or even proudly—she has at least to be sexually and sensually fulfilled; she can admit to her desires if she has gloriously satisfied them: if not, she repudiates them angrily.

Here we reach the crucial problem of feminine eroticism: at the beginning of her erotic life, woman's abdication is not rewarded by a wild and confident sensual pleasure. She would readily sacrifice modesty and pride if it meant opening up the gates of paradise. But it has been seen that defloration is not a successful accomplishment of youthful eroticism; it is on the contrary an unusual phenomenon; vaginal pleasure is not attained immediately; according to Stekel's statistics—confirmed by many sexologists and psychologists—barely 4 percent of women experience pleasure at the first coitus; 50 percent do not reach vaginal pleasure for weeks, months, or even years. Psychic factors play an essential role in this. Woman's body is singularly "hysterical" in that there is often no distance between conscious facts and their organic expression; her moral inhibitions prevent the emergence of pleasure; as they are not counterbalanced by anything, they are often perpetuated and form a more and more powerful barrier. In many cases, a vicious circle is created: the lover's first clumsiness—a word, an awkward gesture, or an arrogant smile—will resonate throughout the whole honeymoon or even married life; disappointed by not experiencing pleasure immediately, the young woman feels a resentment that badly prepares her for a happier experience. It is true that if the man cannot give her normal satisfaction, he can always give her clitoral pleasure that, in spite of moralizing legends, can provide her with relaxation and contentment. But many women reject it because it seems to be *inflicted* even more than vaginal pleasure; because if women suffer from the egotism of men concerned only with their own satisfaction, they are also offended by too obvious a determination to give them pleasure. "Making the other come," says Stekel, "means dominating him; giving oneself to someone is abdicating one's will." Woman will accept pleasure more easily if it seems to flow naturally from man's own pleasure, as happens in normal and successful coitus. "Women submit themselves joyously as soon as they understand that the partner does not *want* to subjugate them," continues Stekel; inversely, if they feel this desire, they resist. Many shy away from being caressed by the hand because it is an instrument that does not participate in the pleasure it gives, it is activity and not flesh; and if sex itself does not come across as flesh penetrated with desire but as a cleverly used tool, woman will feel the same repulsion. Besides, anything else will seem to confirm the woman's failure to experience a normal woman's feelings. Stekel notes, after many, many observations, that all the desire of so-called frigid women aims at the norm. "They want to reach orgasm like a normal woman; no other process satisfies them morally."

Man's attitude is thus of extreme importance. If his desire is violent and brutal, his partner feels changed into a mere thing in his arms; but if he is too self-controlled, too detached, he does not constitute himself as flesh; he asks woman to make herself object without her being able to have a hold on him in return. In both cases, her pride rebels; to reconcile her metamorphosis into a carnal object with the demands of her subjectivity, she must make him her prey as she makes herself his. This is often why the woman obstinately remains frigid. If the lover lacks seductive techniques, if he is cold, negligent, or clumsy, he fails to awaken her sexuality, or he leaves her unsatisfied; but if he is virile and skillful, he can provoke reactions of rejection; woman fears his domination: some can find pleasure only with timid, inept, or even almost impotent men, ones who do not scare them away. It is easy for a man to awaken hostility and resentment in his mistress. Resentment is the most common source of feminine frigidity; in bed, the woman makes the male pay for all the affronts she considers she has been subjected to by an insulting coldness; her attitude is often one of an aggressive inferiority complex: since you do not love me, since I have flaws preventing me from being liked, and since I am despicable, I will not surrender to love, desire, and pleasure either. This is how she exacts vengeance both on him and on herself if he has humiliated her by his negligence, if he has aroused her jealousy, if he has declared himself too slowly, if he has made her his mistress when she desired marriage; the complaint can appear suddenly and set off this reaction even during a relationship that began happily. The man who caused this hostility can rarely succeed in undoing it: a persuasive testimony of love or appreciation may, however, sometimes modify the situation. It also happens that women who are defiant or stiff in their lovers' arms can be transformed by a ring on their finger: happy, flattered, their conscience at peace, they let all their defenses fall. But a newcomer, respectful, in love, and delicate, can best transform the disenchanted woman into a happy mistress or wife; if he frees her from her inferiority complex, she will give herself to him ardently.

Stekel's work *Frigidity in Woman* essentially focuses on demonstrating the role of psychic factors in feminine frigidity. The following examples clearly show that it is often an act of resentment of the husband or lover:

> Miss G.S. . . . had given herself to a man while waiting for him to marry her, while insisting on the fact "that she did not care about marriage," that she did not want "to be attached." She played the free woman. In truth, she was a slave to morality like her whole family. But her lover believed her and never spoke of marriage. Her stubbornness increased more and more until she became apathetic. When he finally did ask her to marry him, she took her revenge by admitting her numbness and no longer wanting to hear anything about a union. She no longer wanted to be happy. She had waited too long . . . She was consumed by jealousy and waited anxiously for the day he proposed so she could refuse it proudly. Then she wanted to commit suicide just to punish her lover in style.

> A very jealous woman who until then had found pleasure with her husband imagines that her husband is cheating on her while she was ill. Coming home, she decides to be cold to her husband. She would never be aroused by him again because he did not appreciate her and used her only when in need. Since her return she has been frigid. At first she used little tricks not to be aroused. She pictured to herself that her husband was flirting with her girl friend. But soon orgasm was replaced by pain.

> A young seventeen-year-old had an affair with a man and derived intense pleasure from it. Pregnant at nineteen, she asked her lover to marry her; he was ambivalent and advised her to get an abortion,

which she refused to do. Three weeks later, he declared he was ready to marry her and she became his wife. But she never forgave those three tormented weeks and became frigid. Later on, a talk with her husband overcame her frigidity.

Mrs. N.M. . . . learns that two days after the wedding, her husband went to see a former mistress. The orgasm she had had previously disappeared forever. She was obsessed by the thought that she no longer pleased her husband whom she thought she had disappointed; that is the cause of frigidity for her.

Even when a woman overcomes her resistance and eventually experiences vaginal pleasure, not all her problems are eliminated: the rhythm of her sexuality and that of the male do not coincide. She is much slower to reach orgasm than the man. The Kinsey Report states:

> For perhaps three-quarters of all males, orgasm is reached within two minutes after the initiation of the sexual relation . . . Considering the many upper level females who are so adversely conditioned to sexual situations that they may require ten to fifteen minutes of the most careful stimulation to bring them to climax, and considering the fair number of females who never come to climax in their whole lives, it is, of course, demanding that the male be quite abnormal in his ability to prolong sexual activity without ejaculation if he is required to match the female partner.

It is said that in India the husband, while fulfilling his conjugal duties, smokes his pipe to distract himself from his own pleasure and to make his wife's last; in the West, it is more the number of "times" that a Casanova boasts of; and his supreme pride is to have a woman beg for mercy: according to erotic tradition, this is not often a successful feat; men often complain of their partners' exacting demands: she is a wild uterus, an ogre, insatiable; she is never assuaged. Montaigne demonstrates this point of view in the third book of his *Essays:*

> They are incomparably more capable and ardent than we in the acts of love—and that priest of antiquity so testified, who had been once a man and then a woman . . . and besides, we have learned from their own mouth the proof that was once given in different centuries

by an emperor and an empress of Rome, master workmen and famous in this task: he indeed deflowered in one night ten captive Sarmatian virgins; but she actually in one night was good for twenty-five encounters, changing company according to her need and liking,

> *Adhuc ardens rigidae tentigine vulvo*
> *Et lassata viris, necdum satiata recessite.*[13]

We know about the dispute that occurred in Catalonia from a woman complaining of the over-assiduous efforts of her husband: not so much, in my opinion, that she was bothered by them (for I believe in miracles only in matters of faith) . . . There intervened that notable sentence of the Queen of Aragon, by which, after mature deliberation with her council, this good queen . . . ordained as the legitimate and necessary limit the number of six a day, relinquishing and giving up much of the need and desire of her sex, in order, she said, to establish an easy and consequently permanent and immutable formula.

It is true that sexual pleasure for woman is not at all the same as for man. I have already said that it is not known exactly if vaginal pleasure ever results in a definite orgasm: feminine confidences on this point are rare, and even when they try to be precise, they remain extremely vague; reactions seem to vary greatly according to the subject. What is certain is that coitus for man has a precise biological end: ejaculation. And certainly many other very complex intentions are involved in aiming at this end; but once obtained, it is seen as an achievement, and if not as the satisfaction of desire, at least as its suppression. On the other hand, the aim for woman is uncertain in the beginning and more psychic than physiological; she desires arousal and sexual pleasure in general, but her body does not project any clear conclusion of the love act: and thus for her coitus is never fully completed: it does not include any finality. Male pleasure soars; when it reaches a certain threshold, it fulfills itself and dies abruptly in the orgasm; the structure of the sexual act is finite and discontinuous. Feminine pleasure radiates through the whole body; it is not always centered in the genital

---

13. Juvenal. ["Her secret parts burning are tense with lust, / And, tired by men, but far from sated, she withdrew."—TRANS.]

system; vaginal contractions then even more than a true orgasm constitute a system of undulations that rhythmically arise, subside, re-form, reach for some instants a paroxysm, then blur and dissolve without ever completely dying. Because no fixed goal is assigned to it, pleasure aims at infinity: nervous or cardiac fatigue or psychic satiety often limits the woman's erotic possibilities rather than precise satisfaction; even fully fulfilled, even exhausted, she is never totally released: "*Lassata necdum satiata,*" according to Juvenal.

Man commits a grave error when he attempts to impose his own rhythm on his partner and when he is determined to give her an orgasm: often he only manages to destroy the form of pleasure she was experiencing in her own way.[14] This form is malleable enough to give itself a conclusion: spasms localized in the vagina or in the whole genital system or coming from the whole body can constitute a resolution; for certain women, they are produced fairly regularly and with sufficient violence to be likened to an orgasm; but a woman lover can also find a conclusion in the masculine orgasm that calms and satisfies her. And it is also possible that in a gradual and gentle way, the erotic phase dissolves calmly. Success requires not a mathematical synchronization of pleasure, whatever many meticulous but simplistic men believe, but the establishment of a complex erotic form. Many think that "making a woman come" is a question of time and technique, therefore of violence; they disregard the extent to which woman's sexuality is conditioned by the situation as a whole. Sexual pleasure for her, we have said, is a kind of spell; it demands total abandon; if words or gestures contest the magic of caresses, the spell vanishes. This is one of the reasons that the woman often closes her eyes: physiologically there is a reflex that compensates for the dilation of the pupil; but even in the dark she still lowers her eyelids; she wants to do away with the setting, the singularity of the moment, herself and her lover; she wants to lose herself within the carnal night as indistinct as the maternal breast. And even more particularly, she wants to abolish this separation that sets the male in front of her; she wants to merge with him. We have said already that she desires to remain a subject while making herself an object. More deeply alienated than man, as her whole body is desire and arousal, she remains a

---

14. Lawrence clearly saw the opposition of these two erotic forms. But it is arbitrary to declare as he does that the woman *must* not experience orgasm. It might be an error to try to provoke it at all costs, but it is also an error to reject it in all cases, as Don Cipriano does in *The Plumed Serpent*.

subject only through union with her partner; receiving and giving have to merge for both of them; if the man just takes without giving or if he gives pleasure without taking, she feels used; as soon as she realizes herself as Other, she is the inessential other; she has to invalidate alterity. Thus the moment of the separation of bodies is almost always painful for her. Man, after coitus, whether he feels sad or joyous, duped by nature or conqueror of woman, whatever the case, he repudiates the flesh; he becomes a whole body; he wants to sleep, take a bath, smoke a cigarette, get a breath of fresh air. She would like to prolong the bodily contact until the spell that made her flesh dissipates completely; separation is a painful wrenching like a new weaning; she resents the lover who pulls away from her too abruptly. But what wounds her even more are the words that contest the fusion in which she believed for a moment. The "wife of Gilles," whose story Madeleine Bourdouxhe told, pulls back when her husband asks her: "Did you come?" She puts her hand on his mouth; many women hate this word because it reduces the pleasure to an immanent and separated sensation. "Is it enough? Do you want more? Was it good?" The very fact of asking the question points out the separation and changes the love act into a mechanical operation assumed and controlled by the male. And this is precisely the reason he asks it. Much more than fusion and reciprocity, he seeks domination; when the unity of the couple is undone, he becomes the sole subject: a great deal of love or generosity is necessary to give up this privilege; he likes the woman to feel humiliated, possessed in spite of herself; he always wants to take her a little more than she gives herself. Woman would be spared many difficulties were man not to trail behind him so many complexes making him consider the love act a battle: then it would be possible for her not to consider the bed as an arena.

However, along with narcissism and pride, one observes in the young girl a desire to be dominated. According to some psychoanalysts, masochism is a characteristic of women, by means of which they can adapt to their erotic destiny. But the notion of masochism is very confused and has to be considered attentively.

Freudian psychoanalysts distinguish three forms of masochism: one is the link between pain and sexual pleasure, another is the feminine acceptance of erotic dependence, and the last resides in a mechanism of self-punishment. Woman is masochistic because pleasure and pain in her are linked through defloration and birth, and because she consents to her passive role.

It must first be pointed out that attributing erotic value to pain does not in any way constitute behavior of passive submission. Pain often serves to raise the tonus of the individual who experiences it, to awaken a sensitivity numbed by the very violence of arousal and pleasure; it is a sharp light bursting out in the carnal night, it removes the lover from the limbo where he is swooning so that he might once more be thrown into it. Pain is normally part of erotic frenzy; bodies that delight in being bodies for their reciprocal joy seek to find each other, unite with each other, and confront each other in every possible way. There is a wrenching from oneself in eroticism, a transport, an ecstasy: suffering also destroys the limits of the self, it is a going beyond and a paroxysm; pain has always played a big role in orgies; and it is well-known that the exquisite and the painful converge: a caress can become torture; torment gives pleasure. Embracing easily leads to biting, pinching, scratching; such behavior is not generally sadistic; it expresses a desire to merge and not to destroy; and the subject that submits to it does not seek to disavow and humiliate himself but to unite; besides, it is far from being specifically masculine. In fact, pain has a masochistic meaning only when it is grasped and desired as the manifestation of enslavement. As for the pain of defloration, it is specifically not accompanied by pleasure; and all women fear the suffering of giving birth, and they are happy that modern methods free them from it. Pain has neither more nor less place in their sexuality than in that of man.

Feminine docility is, moreover, a very equivocal notion. We have seen that most of the time the young girl accepts in her *imagination* the domination of a demigod, a hero, a male, but it is still only a narcissistic game. She is in no way disposed to submit to the carnal expression of this authority in reality. By contrast, she often refuses to give herself to a man she admires and respects, giving herself to an ordinary man instead. It is an error to seek the key to concrete behavior in fantasy, because fantasies are created and cherished as fantasies. The little girl who dreams of rape with a mixture of horror and complicity does not *desire* to be raped, and the event, if it occurred, would be a loathsome catastrophe. We have already seen in Maria Le Hardouin a typical example of this dissociation. She writes:

> But there remained an area on the path of abolition that I only
> entered with pinched nostrils and a beating heart. This was the path
> that beyond amorous sensuality led me to sensuality itself . . . there
> was no deceitful infamy that I did not commit in dreams. I suffered
> from the need to affirm myself in every possible way.[15]

---

15. *The Black Sail.*

The case of Marie Bashkirtseff should also be recalled:

All my life I have tried to place myself *voluntarily* under some kind of *illusory domination*, but all the people I tried were so ordinary in comparison with me that all I felt for them was disgust.

Moreover, it is true that the woman's sexual role is largely passive; but to live this passive situation in its immediacy is no more masochistic than the male's normal aggressiveness is sadistic; woman can transcend caresses, arousal, and penetration toward achieving her own pleasure, thus maintaining the affirmation of her subjectivity; she can also seek union with the lover and give herself to him, which signifies a surpassing of herself and not an abdication. Masochism exists when the individual chooses to constitute himself as a pure thing through the consciousness of the other, to represent oneself to oneself as a thing, to play at being a thing. "Masochism is an attempt not to fascinate the other by my objectivity but to make myself be fascinated by my objectivity for others."[16] Sade's Juliette or the young virgin from *La philosophie dans le boudoir* (*Philosophy in the Boudoir*), who both give themselves to the male in all possible ways, but for their own pleasure, are not in any way masochists. Lady Chatterley and Kate, in the total abandon they consent to, are not masochists. To speak of masochism, one has to posit the *self* and this alienated double has to be considered as founded on the other's freedom.

In this sense, true masochism can be found in some women. The young girl is susceptible to it since she is easily narcissistic and narcissism consists in alienating one's self in one's ego. If she experienced arousal and violent desire right from the beginning of her erotic initiation, she would live her experiences authentically and stop projecting them toward this ideal pole that she calls self; but in frigidity, the self continues to affirm itself; making it the thing of a male seems then like a fault. But "masochism, like sadism, is the assumption of guilt. I am guilty due to the very fact that I am an object." This idea of Sartre's fits in with the Freudian notion of self-punishment. The young girl considers herself guilty of delivering her self to another, and she punishes herself for it by willingly increasing humiliation and subjugation; we have seen that virgins defied their future lovers and punished themselves for their future submission by inflicting various tortures on themselves. When the lover is real and present, they persist in

---

16. J.-P. Sartre, *Being and Nothingness*.

this attitude. Frigidity itself can be seen as a punishment that woman imposes as much on herself as on her partner: wounded in her vanity, she resents him and herself, and she does not permit herself pleasure. In masochism, she will wildly enslave herself to the male, she will tell him words of adoration, she will wish to be humiliated, beaten; she will alienate herself more and more deeply out of fury for having agreed to the alienation. This is quite obviously Mathilde de la Mole's behavior, for example; she regrets having given herself to Julien, which is why she sometimes falls at his feet, bends over backward to indulge each of his whims, sacrifices her hair; but at the same time, she is in revolt against him as much as against herself; one imagines that she is icy in his arms. The fake abandon of the masochistic woman creates new barriers that keep her from pleasure; and at the same time, she is taking vengeance against herself for this inability to experience pleasure. The vicious circle from frigidity to masochism can establish itself forever, bringing sadistic behavior along with it as compensation. Becoming erotically mature can also deliver woman from her frigidity and her narcissism, and assuming her sexual passivity, she lives it immediately instead of playing the role. Because the paradox of masochism is that the subject reaffirms itself constantly even in its attempt to abdicate itself, it is in the gratuitous gift, in the spontaneous movement toward the other, that he succeeds in forgetting himself. It is thus true that woman will be more prone than man to masochistic temptation; her erotic situation as passive object commits her to playing passivity; this game is the self-punishment to which her narcissistic revolts and consequent frigidity lead her; the fact is that many women and in particular young girls are masochists. Colette, speaking of her first amorous experiences, confides to us in *Mes apprentissages* (*My Apprenticeships*):

> Ridden by youth and ignorance, I had known intoxication—a guilty rapture, an atrocious, impure, adolescent impulse. There are many scarcely nubile girls who dream of becoming the show, the plaything, the licentious masterpiece of some middle-aged man. It is an ugly dream that is punished by its fulfillment, a morbid thing, akin to the neuroses of puberty, the habit of eating chalk and coal, of drinking mouthwash, of reading dirty books and sticking pins into the palm of the hand.

This perfectly expresses the fact that masochism is part of juvenile perversions, that it is not an authentic solution of the conflict created by woman's sexual destiny, but a way of escaping it by wallowing in it. In no way does it represent the normal and happy blossoming of feminine eroticism.

This blossoming supposes that—in love, tenderness, and sensuality—woman succeeds in overcoming her passivity and establishing a relationship of reciprocity with her partner. The asymmetry of male and female eroticism creates insoluble problems as long as there is a battle of the sexes; they can easily be settled when a woman feels both desire and respect in a man; if he covets her in her flesh while recognizing her freedom, she recovers her essentialness at the moment she becomes object, she remains free in the submission to which she consents. Thus, the lovers can experience shared pleasure in their own way; each partner feels pleasure as being his own while at the same time having its source in the other. The words "receive" and "give" exchange meanings, joy is gratitude, pleasure is tenderness. In a concrete and sexual form the reciprocal recognition of the self and the other is accomplished in the keenest consciousness of the other and the self. Some women say they feel the masculine sex organ in themselves as a part of their own body; some men think they *are* the woman they penetrate; these expressions are obviously inaccurate; the dimension of the *other* remains; but the fact is that alterity no longer has a hostile character; this consciousness of the union of the bodies in their separation is what makes the sexual act moving; it is all the more overwhelming that the two beings who together passionately negate and affirm their limits are fellow creatures and yet are different. This difference that all too often isolates them becomes the source of their marveling when they join together; woman recognizes the virile passion in man's force as the reverse of the fever that burns within her, and this is the power she wields over him; this sex organ swollen with life belongs to her just as her smile belongs to the man who gives her pleasure. All the treasures of virility and femininity reflecting off and reappropriating each other make a moving and ecstatic unity. What is necessary for such harmony are not technical refinements but rather, on the basis of an immediate erotic attraction, a reciprocal generosity of body and soul.

This generosity is often hampered in man by his vanity and in woman by her timidity; if she does not overcome her inhibitions, she will not be able to make it thrive. This is why full sexual blossoming in woman arrives rather late: she reaches her erotic peak at about thirty-five. Unfortunately, if she is married, her husband is too used to her frigidity; she can still seduce new lovers, but she is beginning to fade: time is running out. At the very moment they cease to be desirable, many women finally decide to assume their desires.

The conditions under which woman's sexual life unfolds depend not only on these facts but also on her whole social and economic situation. It would be too vague to attempt to study this further without this context.

But several generally valid conclusions emerge from our examination. The erotic experience is one that most poignantly reveals to human beings their ambiguous condition; they experience it as flesh and as spirit, as the other and as subject. Woman experiences this conflict at its most dramatic because she assumes herself first as object and does not immediately find a confident autonomy in pleasure; she has to reconquer her dignity as transcendent and free subject while assuming her carnal condition: this is a delicate and risky enterprise that often fails. But the very difficulty of her situation protects her from the mystifications by which the male lets himself be duped; he is easily deceived by the fallacious privileges that his aggressive role and satisfied solitude of orgasm imply; he hesitates to recognize himself fully as flesh. Woman has a more authentic experience of herself.

Even if woman accommodates herself more or less exactly to her passive role, she is still frustrated as an active individual. She does not envy man his organ of possession: she envies in him his prey. It is a curious paradox that man lives in a sensual world of sweetness, tenderness, softness— a feminine world—while woman moves in the hard and harsh male universe; her hands still long for the embrace of smooth skin and soft flesh: adolescent boy, woman, flowers, furs, child; a whole part of herself remains available and wishes to possess a treasure similar to the one she gives the male. This explains why there subsists in many women, in a more or less latent form, a tendency toward homosexuality. For a set of complex reasons, there are those for whom this tendency asserts itself with particular authority. Not all women agree to give their sexual problems the one classic solution officially accepted by society. Thus must we envisage those who choose forbidden paths.

CHAPTER 4

The Lesbian

People are always ready to see the lesbian as wearing a felt hat, her hair short, and a necktie; her mannishness is seen as an abnormality indicating a hormonal imbalance. Nothing could be more erroneous than this confusion of the homosexual and the virago. There are many homosexual women among odalisques, courtesans, and the most deliberately "feminine" women; by contrast, a great number of "masculine" women are heterosexual. Sexologists and psychiatrists confirm what ordinary observation suggests: the immense majority of "cursed women" are constituted exactly like other women. Their sexuality is not determined by anatomical "destiny."

There are certainly cases where physiological givens create particular situations. There is no rigorous biological distinction between the two sexes; an identical soma is modified by hormonal activity whose orientation is genotypically defined, but can be diverted in the course of the fetus's development; this results in individuals halfway between male and female. Some men take on a feminine appearance because of late development of their male organs, and sometimes girls as well—athletic ones in particular—change into boys. Helene Deutsch tells of a young girl who ardently courted a married woman, wanted to run off and live with her: she realized one day that she was in fact a man, so she was able to marry her beloved and have children. But it must not be concluded that every homosexual woman is a "hidden man" in false guise. The hermaphrodite who has elements of two genital systems often has a female sexuality: I knew of one, exiled by the Nazis from Vienna, who greatly regretted her inability to appeal to either heterosexuals or homosexuals as she loved only men. Under the influence of male hormones, "viriloid" women present masculine secondary sexual characteristics; in infantile women, female hormones are deficient, and their development remains incomplete. These particularities can more or less directly trigger a lesbian orientation. A person with a vigorous, aggressive, and exuberant vitality wishes to exert himself actively and usually rejects passivity; an unattractive and malformed woman may try to compensate for her inferiority by acquiring virile attributes; if her erogenous sensitivity is undeveloped, she does not desire masculine caresses. But anatomy and hormones never define anything but a situation and do not posit the object toward which the situation will be transcended. Deutsch also cites the case of a wounded Polish legionnaire she treated during World War I who was, in fact, a young girl with marked viriloid characteristics; she had joined the army as a nurse, then succeeded in wearing the uniform; she nevertheless fell in love with a soldier—whom she later married—which caused her to be regarded as a male homosexual. Her masculine behavior did not contradict a feminine type of eroticism. Man himself does not exclusively desire woman; the fact that the male homosexual body can be perfectly virile implies that a woman's virility does not necessarily destine her to homosexuality.

Even in women physiologically normal themselves, it has sometimes been asserted that there is a distinction between "clitoral" and "vaginal" women, the former being destined to sapphic love; but it has been seen that all childhood eroticism is clitoral; whether it remains fixed at this stage or is transformed has nothing to do with anatomical facts; nor is it true, as has often been maintained, that infant masturbation explains the ulterior primacy of the clitoral system: a child's masturbation is recognized today by sexologists as an absolutely normal and generally widespread phenomenon. The development of feminine eroticism is—we have seen—a psychological situation in which physiological factors are included, but which depends on the subject's overall attitude to existence. Marañón considered sexuality to be "one-way," and that man attains a completed form of it, while for woman it remains "halfway"; only the lesbian could possess a libido as rich as a male's and would thus be a "superior" feminine type. In fact, feminine sexuality has its own structure, and the idea of a hierarchy in male and female libidos is absurd; the choice of sexual object in no way depends on the amount of energy woman might have.

Psychoanalysts have had the great merit of seeing a psychic phenomenon and not an organic one in inversion; to them, nonetheless, it still seems determined by external circumstances. But in fact they have not studied it very much. According to Freud, female erotic maturation requires the passage from the clitoral to the vaginal stage, symmetrical with the change transferring the love the little girl felt first for her mother to her father; various factors may hinder this development; the woman is not resigned to castration, hides the absence of the penis from herself, or remains fixated on her mother, for whom she seeks substitutes. For Adler, this fixation is not a passively endured accident: it is desired by the subject who, in her will for power, deliberately denies her mutilation and seeks to identify with the man whose domination she refuses. Whether from infantile fixation or masculine protest, homosexuality would appear in any case as unfinished development. In truth, the lesbian is no more a "failed" woman than a "superior" woman. The individual's history is not an inevitable progression: at every step, the past is grasped anew by a new choice, and the "normality" of the choice confers no privileged value on it: it must be judged by its authenticity. Homosexuality can be a way for woman to flee her condition or a way to assume it. Psychoanalysts' great error, through moralizing conformity, is that they never envisage it as anything but an inauthentic attitude.

Woman is an existent who is asked to make herself object; as subject she has an aggressive sensuality that does not find satisfaction in the masculine body: from this are born the conflicts her eroticism must overcome. The system is considered normal that, delivering her as prey to a male, restores her sovereignty by putting a baby in her arms: but this "naturalism" is determined by a more or less well understood social interest. Even heterosexuality permits other solutions. Homosexuality for woman is one attempt among others to reconcile her autonomy with the passivity of her flesh. And if nature is invoked, it could be said that every woman is naturally homosexual. The lesbian is characterized simply by her refusal of the male and her preference for feminine flesh; but every adolescent female fears penetration and masculine domination, and she feels a certain repulsion for the man's body; on the contrary, the feminine body is for her, as for man, an object of desire. As I have already said: men posit themselves as subjects, and at the same time they posit themselves as separate; to consider the other as a thing to take is to attack the virile ideal in the other and thus jointly in one's self as well; by contrast, the woman who regards herself as object sees herself and her fellow creatures as prey. The homosexual man inspires hostility from male and female heterosexuals as they both demand that man be a dominating subject;[1] by contrast, both sexes spontaneously view lesbians with indulgence. "I swear," says the comte de Tilly, "it is a rivalry that in no way bothers me; on the contrary, I find it amusing and I

---

1. A heterosexual woman can easily have a friendship with certain homosexual men, because she finds security and amusement in these asexual relations. But on the whole, she feels hostile toward these men who in themselves or in others degrade the sovereign male into a passive thing.

am immoral enough to laugh at it." Colette attributed this same amused indifference to Renaud faced with the couple Claudine and Rézi.[2] A man is more irritated by an active and autonomous heterosexual woman than by a nonaggressive homosexual one; only the former challenges masculine prerogatives; sapphic loves in no way contradict the traditional model of the division of the sexes: in most cases, they are an assumption of femininity and not a rejection of it. We have seen that they often appear in the adolescent girl as an ersatz form of heterosexual relations she has not yet had the opportunity or the audacity to experience: it is a stage, an apprenticeship, and the one who most ardently engages in such loves may tomorrow be the most ardent of wives, lovers, and mothers. What must be explained in the female homosexual is thus not the positive aspect of her choice but the negative side: she is not characterized by her preference for women but by the exclusiveness of this preference.

According to Jones and Hesnard, lesbians mostly fall into two categories: "masculine lesbians," who "try to act like men," and "feminine" ones, who "are afraid of men." It is a fact that one can, on the whole, observe two tendencies in homosexual women; some refuse passivity, while others choose to lose themselves passively in feminine arms; but these two attitudes react upon each other reciprocally; relations to the chosen object and to the rejected one are explained by each other reciprocally. For numerous reasons, as we shall see, the distinction given seems quite arbitrary.

To define the lesbian as "virile" because of her desire to "imitate man" is to doom her to inauthenticity. I have already said how psychoanalysts create ambiguities by accepting masculine-feminine categories as currently defined by society. Thus, man today represents the positive and the neuter—that is, the male and the human being—while woman represents the negative, the female. Every time she behaves like a human being, she is declared to be identifying with the male. Her sports, her political and intellectual activities, and her desire for other women are interpreted as "masculine protest"; there is a refusal to take into account the values toward which she is transcending, which inevitably leads to the belief that she is making the inauthentic choice of a subjective attitude. The great misunderstanding upon which this system of interpretation rests is to hold that it is *natural* for the human female to make a *feminine* woman of herself: being a heterosexual or even a mother is not enough to realize this ideal; the "real

---

2. It is noteworthy that English law punishes homosexuality in men while not considering it a crime for women.

woman" is an artificial product that civilization produces the way eunuchs were produced in the past; these supposed "instincts" of coquetry or docility are inculcated in her just as phallic pride is for man; he does not always accept his virile vocation; she has good reasons to accept even less docilely the vocation assigned to her. The notions of inferiority complex and masculinity complex remind me of the anecdote that Denis de Rougemont recounts in *La part du diable* (*The Devil's Share*): a woman imagined that birds were attacking her when she went walking in the country; after several months of psychoanalytical treatment that failed to cure her of her obsession, the doctor accompanied her to the clinic garden and realized that *the birds were attacking her*. Woman feels undermined because in fact the restrictions of femininity undermine her. She spontaneously chooses to be a complete individual, a subject, and a freedom before whom the world and future open: if this choice amounts to the choice of virility, it does so to the extent that femininity today means mutilation. Homosexuals' confessions collected by Havelock Ellis and Stekel—platonic in the first case and openly declared in the second—clearly show that feminine *specificity* is what outrages the two subjects:

> Ever since I can remember anything at all I could never think of myself as a girl and I was in perpetual trouble, with this as the real reason. When I was 5 or 6 years old I began to say to myself that, whatever anyone said, if I was not a boy at any rate I was not a girl . . . I regarded the conformation of my body as a mysterious accident . . . When I could only crawl my absorbing interest was hammers and carpet-nails. Before I could walk I begged to be put on horses' backs . . . By the time I was 7 it seemed to me that everything I liked was called wrong for a girl . . . I was not at all a happy little child and often cried and was made irritable; I was so confused by the talk about boys and girls . . . Every half-holiday I went out with the boys from my brothers' school . . . When I was about 11 my parents got more mortified at my behavior and perpetually threatened me with a boarding-school . . . My going was finally announced to me as a punishment to me for being what I was . . . In whatever direction my thoughts ran I always surveyed them from the point of view of a boy . . . A consideration of social matters led me to feel very sorry for women, whom I regarded as made by a deliberate process of manufacture into the fools I thought they were, and by the same process that I myself was being made one. I felt more and more that men were to be envied and women pitied. I lay

stress on this for it started in me a deliberate interest in women as women, I began to feel protective and kindly toward women.

As for Stekel's transvestite:

Until her sixth year, in spite of assertions of those around her, she thought she was a boy, dressed like a girl for reasons unknown to her . . . At 6, she told herself, "I'll be a lieutenant, and if God wills it, a marshal." She often dreamed of mounting a horse and riding out of town at the head of an army. Though very intelligent, she was miserable to be transferred from an ordinary school to a lycée . . . *she was afraid of becoming effeminate.*

This revolt by no means implies a sapphic predestination; most little girls feel the same indignation and despair when they learn that the accidental conformation of their bodies condemns their tastes and aspirations; Colette Audry angrily discovered at the age of twelve that she could never become a sailor;[3] the future woman naturally feels indignant about the limitations her sex imposes on her. The question is not why she rejects them: the real problem is rather to understand why she accepts them. Her conformism comes from her docility and timidity; but this resignation will easily turn to revolt if society's compensations are judged inadequate. This is what will happen in cases where the adolescent girl feels unattractive as a woman: anatomical configurations become particularly important when this happens; if she is, or believes she is, ugly or has a bad figure, woman rejects a feminine destiny for which she feels ill adapted; but it would be wrong to say that she acquires a mannish attitude to compensate for a lack of femininity: rather, the opportunities offered to the adolescent girl in exchange for the masculine advantages she is asked to sacrifice seem too meager to her. All little girls envy boys' practical clothes; it is their reflection in the mirror and the promises of things to come that make their furbelows little by little all the more precious; if the mirror harshly reflects an ordinary face, if it offers no promise, then lace and ribbons are an embarrassing, even ridiculous, livery, and the "tomboy" obstinately wishes to remain a boy.

Even if she has a good figure and is pretty, the woman who is involved in her own projects or who claims her freedom in general refuses to abdicate in favor of another human being; she recognizes herself in her acts,

---

3. *In the Eyes of Memory.*

not in her immanent presence: male desire reducing her to the limits of her body shocks her as much as it shocks a young boy; she feels the same disgust for her submissive female companions as the virile man feels for the passive homosexual. She adopts a masculine attitude in part to repudiate any involvement with them; she disguises her clothes, her looks, and her language, she forms a couple with a female friend where she assumes the male role: this playacting is in fact a "masculine protest"; but it is a secondary phenomenon; what is spontaneous is the conquering and sovereign subject's shame at the idea of changing into a carnal prey. Many women athletes are homosexual; they do not perceive this body that is muscle, movement, extension, and momentum as passive flesh; it does not magically beckon caresses, it is a hold on the world, not a thing of the world: the gap between the body for-itself and the body for-others seems in this case to be unbreachable. Analogous resistance is found in women of action, "brainy" types for whom even carnal submission is impossible. Were equality of the sexes concretely realized, this obstacle would be in large part eradicated; but man is still imbued with his own sense of superiority, which is a disturbing conviction for the woman who does not share it. It should be noted, however, that the most willful and domineering women seldom hesitate to confront the male: the woman considered "virile" is often clearly heterosexual. She does not want to renounce her claims as a human being; but she has no intention of mutilating her femininity either; she chooses to enter the masculine world, even to annex it for herself. Her robust sensuality has no fear of male roughness; she has fewer defenses to overcome than the timid virgin in finding joy in a man's body. A rude and animal nature will not feel the humiliation of coitus; an intellectual with an intrepid mind will challenge it; sure of herself and in a fighting mood, a woman will gladly engage in a duel she is sure to win. George Sand had a predilection for young and "feminine" men; but Mme de Staël looked for youth and beauty only in her later life: dominating men by her sharp mind and proudly accepting their admiration, she could hardly have felt a prey in their arms. A sovereign such as Catherine the Great could even allow herself masochistic ecstasies: she alone remained the master in these games. Isabelle Eberhardt, who dressed as a man and traversed the Sahara on horseback, felt no less diminished when she gave herself to some vigorous sharpshooter. The woman who refuses to be the man's vassal is far from always fleeing him; rather she tries to make him the instrument of her pleasure. In certain favorable circumstances—mainly dependent on her partner—the very notion of competition will disappear, and she will enjoy experiencing her woman's condition just as man experiences his.

But this arrangement between her active personality and her role as passive female is nevertheless more difficult for her than for man; rather than wear themselves out in this effort, many women will give up trying. There are numerous lesbians among women artists and writers. It is not because their sexual specificity is the source of creative energy or a manifestation of the existence of this superior energy; it is rather that being absorbed in serious work, they do not intend to waste their time playing the woman's role or struggling against men. Not admitting male superiority, they do not wish to pretend to accept it or tire themselves contesting it; they seek release, peace, and diversion in sexual pleasure: they could spend their time more profitably without a partner who acts like an adversary; and so they free themselves from the chains attached to femininity. Of course, the nature of her heterosexual experiences will often lead the "virile" woman to choose between assuming or repudiating her sex. Masculine disdain confirms the feeling of unattractiveness in an ugly woman; a lover's arrogance will wound a proud woman. All the motives for frigidity we have envisaged are found here: resentment, spite, fear of pregnancy, abortion trauma, and so on. They become all the weightier the more woman defies man.

However, homosexuality is not always an entirely satisfactory solution for a domineering woman; since she seeks to affirm herself, it vexes her not to fully realize her feminine possibilities; heterosexual relations seem to her at once an impoverishment and an enrichment; in repudiating the limitations implied by her sex, she may limit herself in another way. Just as the frigid woman desires pleasure even while rejecting it, the lesbian would often like to be a normal and complete woman while at the same time not wanting it. This hesitation is evident in the case of the transvestite studied by Stekel:

We have seen that she was only comfortable with boys and did not want to "become effeminate." At sixteen years of age, she formed her first relations with young girls; she had a profound contempt for them, which gave her eroticism a sadistic quality; she ardently, but platonically, courted a friend she respected: she felt disgust for those she possessed. She threw herself fiercely into difficult studies. Disappointed by her first serious Sapphic love affair, she frenetically indulged in purely sensual experiences and began to drink. At seventeen, she met the young man she married: but she thought of him as her wife; she dressed in a masculine way, and she continued to drink and study. At first she only had vaginismus and intercourse never produced an orgasm. She considered her position "humiliating"; she was always the one to take the aggressive and active role. She left her husband even while being "madly in love with him" and took up relations with women again. She met a male artist to whom she gave herself, but still without an orgasm. Her life was divided into clearly defined periods; for a while she wrote, worked creatively, and felt completely male; she episodically and sadistically slept with women during these periods. Then she would have a female period. She underwent analysis because she wanted to reach orgasm.

The lesbian would easily be able to consent to the loss of her femininity if in doing so she gained triumphant masculinity. But no. She obviously remains deprived of the virile organ; she can deflower her girlfriend with her hand or use an artificial penis to imitate possession; but she is still a eunuch. She may suffer acutely from this. Because she is incomplete as a woman, impotent as a man, her malaise sometimes manifests itself in psychoses. A patient told Roland Dalbiez, "It would be better if I had a thing to penetrate with."[4] Another wished that her breasts were rigid. The lesbian will often try to compensate for her virile inferiority by arrogance or exhibitionism, which in fact reveals inner imbalance. Sometimes, also, she will succeed in establishing with other women a type of relation completely analogous to those a "feminine" man or an adolescent still unsure of his virility might have with them. A striking case of such a destiny is that of Sandor reported by Krafft-Ebing. She used this means to attain a perfect balance destroyed only by the intervention of society:

Sarolta came of a titled Hungarian family known for its eccentricities. Her father had her reared as a boy, calling her Sandor; she rode horseback, hunted, and so on. She was under such influences until, at thirteen, she was placed in an institution. A little later she fell in love with an English girl, pretending to be a boy, and ran away with her. At home again, she resumed the name Sandor and wore boy's clothing, while being carefully educated. She went on long trips with her father, always in male attire; she was addicted to sports, drank, and visited brothels. She felt particularly drawn toward actresses and other such detached women, preferably not too young but "feminine

---

4. *La méthode psychanalytique et la doctrine freudienne* (*Psychoanalytical Method and the Doctrine of Freud*).

in nature." "It delighted me," she related "if the passion of a lady was disclosed under a poetic veil. All immodesty in a woman was disgusting to me. I had an indescribable aversion to female attire—indeed, for everything feminine. But only insofar as it concerned me; for, on the other hand, I was all enthusiasm for the beautiful Sex." She had numerous affairs with women and spent a good deal of money on them. At the same time, she was a valued contributor to two important journals.

She lived for three years in "marriage" with a woman ten years older than herself, from whom she broke away only with great difficulty. She was able to inspire violent passions. Falling in love with a young teacher, she was married to her in an elaborate cere-mony, the girl and her family believing her to be a man; her father-in-law on one occasion noticed what seemed to be an erection (probably a priapus); she shaved as a matter of form, but servants in the hotel room suspected the truth from seeing blood on her bedclothes and from spying through the keyhole.

Thus unmasked, Sandor was put in prison and later acquitted, after thorough investigation. She was greatly saddened by her enforced separation from her beloved Marie, to whom she wrote long and impassioned letters from her cell.

The examination showed that her conformation was not wholly feminine: her pelvis was small, and she had no waist. Her breasts were developed, her sexual parts quite feminine but not maturely formed. Her menstruation appeared late, at seventeen, and she felt a profound horror of the function. She was equally horrified at the thought of sexual relations with the male; her sense of modesty was developed only in regard to women and to the point that she would feel less shyness in going to bed with a man than with a woman. It was very embarrassing for her to be treated as a woman, and she was truly in anguish at having to wear feminine clothes. She felt that she was "drawn as by a magnetic force toward women of twenty-four to thirty." She found sexual satisfaction exclusively in caressing her loved one, never in being caressed. At times she made use of a stocking stuffed with oakum as a priapus. She detested men. She was very sensitive to the moral esteem of others, and she had much literary talent, wide culture, and a colossal memory.*

* Krafft-Ebing, *Psychopathia Sexualis.*—Trans.

Sandor was not psychoanalyzed but several salient points emerge just from the presentation of the facts. It seems that most spontaneously and "without a masculine protest," she always thought of herself as a man, thanks to the way she was brought up and her body's constitution; the way her father included her in his trips and his life obviously had a decisive influence on her; her virility was so confirmed that she did not show the slightest ambivalence toward women: she loved them like a man, without feeling compromised by them; she loved them in a purely dominating and active way, without accepting reciprocity. However, it is striking that she "detested men" and that she particularly cherished older women. This suggests that Sandor had a *masculine* Oedipus complex vis-à-vis her mother; she perpetuated the infantile attitude of the very young girl who, forming a couple with her mother, nourished the hope of one day protecting and dominating her. Very often the maternal tenderness a child has been deprived of haunts her whole adult life: raised by her father, Sandor must have dreamed of a loving and treasured mother, whom she sought afterward in other women; this explains her deep jealousy of other men, linked to her respect and "poetic" love for "isolated" and older women who were endowed in her eyes with a sacred quality. Her attitude was exactly that of Rousseau with Mme de Warens and the young Benjamin Constant concerning Mme de Charrière: sensitive, "feminine" adolescent boys also turn to maternal mistresses. This type of lesbian is found in more or less pronounced forms, one who has never identified with her mother—because she either admired her or detested her too much—but who, refusing to be a woman, desires the softness of feminine protection around her. From the bosom of this warm womb she can emerge into the world with boyish daring; she acts like a man, but as a man she has a fragility that makes her desire the love of an older mistress; the couple will reproduce the classic heterosexual couple: matron and adolescent boy.

Psychoanalysts have clearly noted the importance of the relationship a homosexual woman had earlier with her mother. There are two cases where the adolescent girl has difficulty escaping her influence: if she has been overly protected by an anxious mother; or if she was mistreated by a "bad mother" who inculcated a deep feeling of guilt in her. In the first case, their relations often bordered on homosexuality: they slept together, caressed, or kissed each other's breasts; the young girl will seek this same pleasure in new arms. In the second case, she will feel an ardent need of a "good mother" who protects her against her own mother, who removes the curse she feels weighing on her. One of the stories Havelock Ellis recounts concerns a subject who detested her mother throughout her childhood; she describes the love she felt at sixteen for an older woman:

I felt like an orphan child who had suddenly acquired a mother, and through her I began to feel less antagonistic to grown people and to feel . . . respect [for them] . . . My love for her was perfectly pure, and I thought of hers as simply maternal . . . I liked her to touch me and she sometimes held me in her arms or let me sit on her lap. At bedtime she used to come and say good-night and kiss me upon the mouth.*

If the older woman is willing, the younger one will joyfully abandon herself to more ardent embraces. She will usually assume the passive role because she desires to be dominated, protected, rocked, and caressed like a child. Whether these relations remain platonic or become carnal, they often have the characteristics of a truly passionate love. However, the very fact that they appear as a classic stage in the adolescent girl's development means that they cannot suffice to explain a determined choice of homosexuality. The young girl seeks in it both a liberation and a security she can also find in masculine arms. Once the period of amorous enthusiasm has passed, the younger one often experiences the ambivalent feeling for her older partner she felt toward her mother; she falls under her influence while at the same time wishing to extricate herself from it; if the other persists in holding her back, she will remain her "prisoner" for a time;[5] but either in violent scenes or amicably, she will manage to escape; having succeeded in expunging her adolescence, she feels ready to face a normal woman's life. For her lesbian vocation to affirm itself, either she has to reject her femininity—like Sandor—or her femininity has to flourish more happily in feminine arms. Thus, fixation on the mother is clearly not enough to explain homosexuality. And it can be chosen for completely different reasons. A woman may discover or sense through complete or tentative experiences that she will not derive pleasure from heterosexual relations, that only another woman is able to satisfy her: in particular, for the woman who worships her femininity, the sapphic embrace turns out to be the most satisfying.

It is very important to emphasize this: the refusal to make oneself an object is not always what leads a woman to homosexuality; most lesbians, on the contrary, seek to claim the treasures of their femininity. Consenting to metamorphose oneself into a passive thing does not mean renouncing all claims to subjectivity: the woman thereby hopes to realize herself as the in-

---

* *Studies in the Psychology of Sex*, Volume 2: *Sexual Inversion.*—TRANS.
5. As in Dorothy Baker's novel *Trio*, which is, moreover, very superficial.

itself; but she will then seek to grasp herself in her alterity. Alone, she does not succeed in separating herself in reality; she might caress her breasts, but she does not know how they would seem to a foreign hand, nor how they would come to life under the foreign hand; a man can reveal to her the existence *for itself* of her flesh, but not what it is *for an other*. It is only when her fingers caress a woman's body whose fingers in turn caress her body that the miracle of the mirror takes place. Between man and woman love is an act; each one torn from self becomes other: what delights the woman in love is that the passive listlessness of her flesh is reflected in the man's ardor; but the narcissistic woman is clearly baffled by the charms of the erect sex. Between women, love is contemplation; caresses are meant less to appropriate the other than to re-create oneself slowly through her; separation is eliminated, there is neither fight nor victory nor defeat; each one is both subject and object, sovereign and slave in exact reciprocity; this duality is complicity. "The close resemblance," says Colette, "validates even sensual pleasure. The woman friend basks in the certitude of caressing a body whose secrets she knows and whose own body tells her what she prefers."[6] And Renée Vivien:

> *Our heart is alike in our woman's breast,* *
> *Dearest! Our body is identically formed.*
> *The same heavy fate was laid on our soul*
> *I translate your smile and the shadow on your face.*
> *My softness is equal to your immense softness,*
> *At times it even seems we are of the same race*
> *I love in you my child, my friend, and my sister.*†

This uncoupling can occur in a maternal form; the mother who recognizes and alienates herself in her daughter often has a sexual attachment to her; the desire to protect and rock in her arms a soft object made of flesh is shared with the lesbian. Colette emphasizes this analogy, writing in *Les vrilles de la vigne* (*The Tender Shoot*): "You will give me pleasure, bent over me, your eyes full of maternal concern, you who seek, through your passionate woman friend, the child you never had."

---

6. *Ces plaisirs* (*The Pure and the Impure*).
* Discrepancy between Renée Vivien's poem quoted by Beauvoir and Vivien's published version, both translated by Gillian Spraggs.—TRANS.
† Cited incorrectly by Beauvoir as *Sortilèges*, which is nonexistent; poem from translation of *Sillages* (1908; Sea Wakes).—TRANS.

And Renée Vivien expresses the same feeling:

Come, I shall carry you off like a child who is sick,
Like a child who is plaintive and fearful and sick.
Within my firm arms I clasp your slight body,
You shall see that I know how to heal and protect,
And my arms are strong, the better to protect you.[7]

And again:

I love you to be weak and calm in my arms . . .
Like a warm cradle where you will take your rest. *

In all love—sexual or maternal—there is both greed and generosity, the desire to possess the other and to give the other everything; but when both women are narcissists, caressing an extension of themselves or their reflection in the child or the lover, the mother and the lesbian are notably similar.

However, narcissism does not always lead to homosexuality either, as Marie Bashkirtseff's example shows; there is not the slightest trace of affection for women in her writings; intellectual rather than sensual, extremely vain, she dreams from childhood of being validated by man: nothing interests her unless it contributes to her glory. A woman who idolizes only herself and who strives for abstract success is incapable of a warm complicity with other women; for her, they are only rivals and enemies.

In truth, there is never only one determining factor; it is always a question of a choice made from a complex whole, contingent on a free decision; no sexual destiny governs an individual's life: on the contrary, his eroticism expresses his general attitude to existence.

Circumstances, however, also have an important part in this choice. Today, the two sexes still live mostly separated: in boarding schools and in girls' schools the passage from intimacy to sexuality is quick; there are far fewer lesbians in circles where girl and boy camaraderie encourages heterosexual experiences. Many women who work among women in workshops and offices and who have little opportunity to be around men will

---

7. *At the Sweet Hour of Hand in Hand.*
* Discrepancy between Vivien's poem quoted by Beauvoir and Vivien's published version, both translated by Gillian Spraggs; from "Je t'aime d'être faible" ("I Love You to Be Weak"), in ibid.—TRANS.

form amorous friendships with women: it will be materially and morally practical to join their lives. The absence or failure of heterosexual relations will destine them to inversion. It is difficult to determine the boundary between resignation and predilection: a woman can devote herself to women because a man has disappointed her, but sometimes he disappoints her because she was looking for a woman in him. For all these reasons, it is wrong to establish a radical distinction between heterosexual and homosexual. Once the indecisive time of adolescence has passed, the normal male no longer allows himself homosexual peccadilloes; but the normal woman often returns to the loves—platonic or not—that enchanted her youth. Disappointed by men, she will seek in feminine arms the male lover who betrayed her; in *The Vagabond*, Colette wrote about this consoling role that forbidden sexual pleasures often play in the lives of women: some of them can spend their whole existence consoling each other. Even a woman fulfilled by male embraces might not refuse calmer sexual pleasures. Passive and sensual, a woman friend's caresses will not shock her since all she has to do is let herself go, let herself be fulfilled. Active and ardent, she will seem "androgynous," not because of a mysterious combination of hormones, but simply because aggressiveness and the taste for possession are looked on as virile attributes; Claudine in love with Renaud still covets Rézi's charms; as fully woman as she is, she still continues to desire to take and caress. Of course, these "perverse" desires are carefully repressed in "nice women"; they nonetheless manifest themselves as pure but passionate friendships or in the guise of maternal tenderness; sometimes they are suddenly revealed during a psychosis or a menopausal crisis.

So it is all the more useless to try to place lesbians in two definitive categories. Because social role-playing is sometimes superimposed on their real relations—taking pleasure in imitating a bisexual couple—they themselves suggest the division into virile and feminine. But the fact that one wears an austere suit and the other a flowing dress must not create an illusion. Looking more closely, one can ascertain—except in special cases—that their sexuality is ambiguous. A woman who becomes lesbian because she rejects male domination often experiences the joy of recognizing the same proud Amazon in another; not long ago many guilty loves flourished among the women students of Sèvres who lived together far from men; they were proud to belong to a feminine elite and wanted to remain autonomous subjects; this complexity that united them against the privileged caste enabled each one to admire in a friend this prestigious being she cherished in herself; embracing each other, each one was both man and woman and was enchanted with the other's androgynous virtues.

Inversely, a woman who wants to enjoy the pleasures of her femininity in feminine arms also knows the pride of obeying no master. Renée Vivien ardently loved feminine beauty, and she wanted to be beautiful; she took great care of her appearance, she was proud of her long hair; but she also liked to feel free and intact; in her poems she expresses scorn for those women who through marriage consent to become serfs of a male. Her taste for hard liquor and her sometimes obscene language manifested her desire for virility. The truth is that for most couples caresses are reciprocal. Thus it follows that the roles are distributed in very uncertain ways: the most infantile woman can play an adolescent boy toward a protective matron, or a mistress leaning on her lover's arm. They can love each other as equals. Because her partners are counterparts, all combinations, transpositions, exchanges, and scenarios are possible. Relations balance each other out depending on the psychological tendencies of each woman friend and on the situation as a whole. If there is one who helps or keeps the other, she assumes the male's functions: tyrannical protector, exploited dupe, respected lord, or even sometimes a pimp; a moral, social, and intellectual superiority will often confer authority on her; however, the one more loved will enjoy the privileges that the more loving one's passionate attachment invests her with. Like that of a man and a woman, the association of two women can take many different forms; it is based on feeling, interest, or habit; it is conjugal or romantic; it has room for sadism, masochism, generosity, faithfulness, devotion, caprice, egotism, and betrayal; there are prostitutes as well as great lovers among lesbians.

There are, however, certain circumstances that give these relations particular characteristics. They are not established by an institution or customs, nor regulated by conventions: they are lived more sincerely because of this. Men and women—even husband and wife—more or less play roles with each other, and woman, on whom the male always imposes some kind of directive, does so even more: exemplary virtue, charm, coquetry, childishness, or austerity; never in the presence of the husband and the lover does she feel fully herself; she does not show off to a woman friend, she has nothing to feign, they are too similar not to show themselves as they are. This similarity gives rise to the most complete intimacy. Eroticism often has only a very small part in these unions; sexual pleasure has a less striking character, less dizzying than between man and woman, it does not lead to such overwhelming metamorphoses; but when male and female lovers have separated into their individual flesh, they become strangers again; and even the male body is repulsive to the woman; and the man sometimes feels a kind of bland distaste for the woman's body; between women, carnal ten-

derness is more equal, continuous, they are not transported in frenetic
ecstasy, but they never fall into hostile indifference; seeing and touching
each other are calm pleasures discreetly prolonging those of the bed. Sarah
Posonby's union with her beloved lasted for almost fifty years without a
cloud: they seem to have been able to create a peaceful Eden on the fringes
of the world. But sincerity also has a price. Because they show themselves
freely, without caring either to hide or to control themselves, women incite
each other to incredible violence. Man and women intimidate each other
because they are different: he feels pity and apprehension toward her; he
strives to treat her courteously, indulgently, and circumspectly; she
respects him and somewhat fears him, she tries to control herself in front of
him; each one tries to spare the mysterious other whose feelings and reactions are hard to discern. Women among themselves are pitiless; they foil,
provoke, chase, attack, and lead each other on to the limits of abjection.
Masculine calm—be it indifference or self-control—is a barrier feminine
emotions come up against: but between two women friends, there is escala-
tion of tears and convulsions; their patience in endlessly going over criti-
cisms and explanations is insatiable. Demands, recriminations, jealousy,
tyranny—all these plagues of conjugal life pour out in heightened form. If
such love is often stormy, it is also usually more threatened than heterosexual love. It is criticized by the society into which it cannot always integrate.
A woman who assumes the masculine attitude—by her character, situation, and the force of her passion—will regret not giving her woman friend
a normal and respectable life, not being able to marry her, leading her
along unusual paths: these are the feelings Radclyffe Hall attributes to her
heroine in *The Well of Loneliness;* this remorse is conveyed by a morbid
anxiety and an even greater torturous jealousy. The more passive or less
infatuated woman will suffer from society's censure; she will think herself
degraded, perverted, frustrated, she will resent the one who has imposed
this lot on her. It might be that one of the two women desires a child; either
she sadly resigns herself to her childlessness or both adopt a child or the
one who desires motherhood asks a man for his services; the child is sometimes a link, sometimes also a new source of friction.

What gives women enclosed in homosexuality a masculine character
is not their erotic life, which, on the contrary, confines them to a feminine
universe: it is all the responsibilities they have to assume because they do
without men. Their situation is the opposite of that of the courtesan who
sometimes has a male mind by dint of living among males—like Ninon de
Lenclos—but who depends on them. The particular atmosphere around
lesbians stems from the contrast between the gynaeceum character of their

private life and the masculine independence of their public existence. They behave like men in a world without men. A woman alone always seems a little unusual; it is not true that men respect women: they respect each other through their women—wives, mistresses, "kept" women; when masculine protection no longer extends over her, woman is disarmed before a superior caste that is aggressive, sneering, or hostile. As an "erotic perversion," feminine homosexuality elicits smiles; but inasmuch as it implies a way of life, it provokes scorn or scandal. If there is an affectation in lesbians' attitudes, it is because they have no way of living their situation naturally: natural implies that one does not reflect on self, that one acts without representing one's acts to oneself; but people's behavior constantly makes the lesbian conscious of herself. She can only follow her path with calm indifference if she is older or secure in her social prestige.

It is difficult to determine, for example, if it is by taste or by defense mechanism that she so often dresses in a masculine way. It certainly comes in large part from a spontaneous choice. Nothing is less *natural* than dressing like a woman; no doubt masculine clothes are also artificial, but they are more comfortable and simple and made to favor action rather than impede it; George Sand and Isabelle Eberhardt wore men's suits; Thyde Monnier in her last book spoke of her predilection for wearing trousers;[8] all active women like flat shoes and sturdy clothes. The meaning of feminine attire is clear: it is a question of decoration, and decorating oneself is offering oneself; heterosexual feminists were formerly as intransigent as lesbians on this point: they refused to make themselves merchandise on display, they wore suits and felt hats; fancy low-cut dresses seemed to them the symbol of the social order they were fighting. Today they have succeeded in mastering reality, and the symbolic has less importance in their eyes. But it remains for the lesbian insofar as she must still assert her claim. It might also be—if physical particularities have motivated her vocation—that austere clothes suit her better. It must be added that one of the roles clothing plays is to gratify woman's tactile sensuality; but the lesbian disdains the consolations of velvet and silk: like Sandor she will appreciate them on her woman friend, or her friend's body may even replace them. This is why a lesbian often likes hard liquor, smokes strong tobacco, uses rough language, and imposes rigorous exercise on herself: erotically, she shares in feminine softness; by contrast, she likes an intense environment. This aspect can make her enjoy men's company. But a new factor enters here:

8. *Me.*

the often ambiguous relationship she has with them. A woman who is very sure of her masculinity will want only men as friends and associates: this assurance is rarely seen except in a woman who shares interests with men, who—in business, action, or art—works and succeeds like a man. When Gertrude Stein entertained, she only talked with the men and left to Alice Toklas the job of talking with their women companions.[9] It is toward women that the very masculine homosexual woman will have an ambivalent attitude: she scorns them, but she has an inferiority complex in relation to them both as a woman and as a man; she fears being perceived by them as a tomboy, an incomplete man, which leads her either to display a haughty superiority or to manifest—like Stekel's transvestite—a sadistic aggressiveness toward them. But this case is rather rare. We have seen that most lesbians partially reject men. For them as well as for the frigid woman, there is disgust, resentment, shyness, or pride; they do not really feel similar to men; to their feminine resentment is added a masculine inferiority complex; they are rivals, better armed to seduce, possess, and keep their prey; they detest their power over women, they detest the "soiling" to which they subject women. They also take exception to seeing men hold social privileges and to feeling that men are stronger than they: it is a crushing humiliation not to be able to fight with a rival, to know he can knock you down with one blow. This complex hostility is one of the reasons some homosexual women declare themselves as homosexuals; they see only other homosexual women; they group together to show they do not need men either socially or sexually. From there one easily slides into useless boastfulness and all the playacting of inauthenticity. The lesbian first plays at being a man; then being lesbian itself becomes a game; a transvestite goes from disguise to livery; and the woman under the pretext of freeing herself from man's oppression makes herself the slave of her personage; she did not want to confine herself in a woman's situation, but she imprisons herself in that of the lesbian. Nothing gives a worse impression of small-mindedness and mutilation than these clans of liberated women. It must be added that many women only declare themselves homosexual out of self-interest: they adopt equivocal appearances with exaggerated consciousness, hoping to catch men who like "perverts." These show-off zealots—who are obviously those one notices most—contribute to throwing discredit on what public opinion considers a vice and a pose.

---

9. A heterosexual woman who believes—or wants to persuade herself—that she transcends the difference of the sexes by her own worth will often have the same attitude; for example Mme de Staël.

In truth, homosexuality is no more a deliberate perversion than a fatal curse.[10] It is an attitude that is *chosen in situation;* it is both motivated and freely adopted. None of the factors the subject accepts in this choice— physiological facts, psychological history, or social circumstances—is determining, although all contribute to explaining it. It is one way among others for woman to solve the problems posed by her condition in general and by her erotic situation in particular. Like all human behavior, this will involve playacting, imbalance, failure, or lies, or, on the other hand, it will be the source of fruitful experiences, depending on whether it is lived in bad faith, laziness, and inauthenticity or in lucidity, generosity, and freedom.

---

10. *The Well of Loneliness* presents a heroine marked by a psychophysiological inevitability. But the documentary value of this novel is very insubstantial in spite of its reputation.

| PART TWO |

SITUATION

CHAPTER 5

The Married Woman

The destiny that society traditionally offers women is marriage. Even today, most women are, were, or plan to be married, or they suffer from not being so. Marriage is the reference by which the single woman is defined, whether she is frustrated by, disgusted at, or even indifferent to this institution. Thus we must continue this study by analyzing marriage.

The economic evolution of woman's condition is in the process of upsetting the institution of marriage: it is becoming a union freely entered into by two autonomous individuals; the commitments of the two parties are personal and reciprocal; adultery is a breach of contract for both parties; either of them can obtain a divorce on the same grounds. Woman is no longer limited to the reproductive function: it has lost, in large part, its character of natural servitude and has come to be regarded as a freely assumed responsibility;[1] and it is considered productive work since, in many cases, maternity leave necessitated by pregnancy must be paid to the mother by the state or the employer. For a few years in the U.S.S.R., marriage was a contract between individuals based on complete freedom of the spouses; today it seems to be a duty the state imposes on them both. Which of these tendencies prevails in tomorrow's world depends on the general structure of society: but in any case masculine guardianship is becoming extinct. Yet, from a feminist point of view, the period we are living through is still a period of transition. Only a part of the female population participates in production, and those same women belong to a society where ancient structures and values still survive. Modern marriage can be understood only in light of the past it perpetuates.

Marriage has always been presented in radically different ways for men and for women. The two sexes are necessary for each other, but this neces-

---

1. See Volume I.

sity has never fostered reciprocity; women have never constituted a caste establishing exchanges and contracts on an equal footing with men. Man is a socially autonomous and complete individual; he is regarded above all as a producer, and his existence is justified by the work he provides for the group; we have already seen the reasons why the reproductive and domestic role to which woman is confined has not guaranteed her an equal dignity.[2] Of course, the male needs her; with some primitive peoples, a bachelor, unable to support himself alone, may become a sort of pariah; in agricultural societies, a woman partner-worker is indispensable to the peasant; and for most men, it is advantageous to unload some of the chores onto a woman; the man himself wishes to have a stable sexual life, he desires posterity, and society requires him to contribute to its perpetuation. But man does not address his appeal to woman herself: it is men's society that allows each of its members to accomplish himself as husband and father; woman, integrated as slave or vassal into the family group dominated by fathers and brothers, has always been given in marriage to males by other males. In primitive times, the clan, the paternal gens, treats her almost like a thing: she is part of payments to which two groups mutually consent; her condition was not deeply modified when marriage evolved into a contractual form;[3] dowered or receiving her share of an inheritance, woman becomes a civil person: but a dowry or an inheritance still enslaves her to her family; for a long period, the contracts were signed between father-in-law and son-in-law, not between husband and wife; in those times, only the widow benefited from an economic independence.[4] A young girl's free choice was always highly restricted; and celibacy—except in rare cases where it bears a sacred connotation—ranked her as a parasite and pariah; marriage was her only means of survival and the only justification of her existence. It was doubly imposed on her: she must give children to the community; but rare are the cases where—as in Sparta and to some extent under the Nazi regime—the state takes her under its guardianship and asks only that she be a mother. Even civilizations that ignore the father's generative role demand that she be under the protection of a husband; and she also has the function of satisfying the male's sexual needs and caring for the home. The charge society imposes on her is considered a *service* rendered to the husband: and he owes his wife gifts or a marriage dowry and

---

2. See Volume I.

3. This evolution took place in a discontinuous manner. It was repeated in Egypt, in Rome, and in modern civilization: see Volume I.

4. Hence the special character of the young widow in erotic literature.

agrees to support her; using him as an intermediary, the community acquits itself of its responsibilities to the woman. The rights the wife acquires by fulfilling her duties have their counterpart in the obligations the male submits to. He cannot break the conjugal bond at whim; repudiation and divorce can only be granted by public authority, and then sometimes the husband owes a monetary compensation: the practice even becomes abusive in Bocchoris's Egypt, as it is today with alimony in the United States. Polygamy was always more or less tolerated: a man can have slaves, *pallakès*, concubines, mistresses, and prostitutes in his bed; but he is required to respect certain privileges of his legitimate wife. If she thinks she is maltreated or wronged, she has the option—more or less concretely guaranteed—to return to her family and to obtain a separation or divorce in her own right. Thus for both parties marriage is a charge and a benefit at the same time; but their situations are not symmetrical; for young girls, marriage is the only way to be integrated into the group, and if they are "rejects," they are social waste. This is why mothers have always at all costs tried to marry them off. Among the bourgeoisie of the last century, girls were barely consulted. They were offered to possible suitors through "interviews" set up in advance. Zola describes this custom in *Pot-Bouille:*

"A failure, it's a failure" said Mme Josserand, falling into her chair.

"Ah!" M. Josserand simply said.

"But you don't seem to understand," continued Mme Josserand in a shrill voice. "I'm telling you that here's another marriage gone down the river, and it's the fourth to fall through!

"Listen," went on Mme Josserand, advancing toward her daughter. "How did you spoil *this* marriage too?"

Berthe realized that her turn had come.

"I don't know, Mamma," she murmured.

"An assistant department head," continued her mother, "not yet thirty, a superb future. Every month it brings you money: solid, that's all that counts . . . You did something stupid, as you did with the others?"

"I swear I didn't, Mamma."

"When you were dancing, you slipped into the small parlor."

Berthe was unnerved: "Yes, Mamma . . . and as soon as we were alone, he wanted to do disgraceful things, he kissed me and grabbed me like this. So I got scared and pushed him against the furniture!"

Her mother interrupted her, "Pushed him against the furniture! Ah, you foolish girl, pushed him against the furniture!"

"But, Mamma, he was holding on to me."

"And what? He was holding on to you . . . how bad is that! Putting you idiots in boarding school! What do they teach you there, tell me! . . . For a kiss behind a door! Should you really even tell us about this, us, your parents? And you push people against furniture and you ruin your chances of getting married!"

Assuming a pontificating air, she continued:

"It's over, I give up, you are just stupid, my dear . . . Since you have no fortune, just understand that you have to catch men some other way. By being pleasant, gazing tenderly, forgetting your hand, allowing little indulgences without seeming to; in short, you have to fish a husband . . . And what bothers me is that she is not too bad when she wants," continued Mme Josserand. "Come now, dry your eyes, look at me as if I were a gentleman courting you. You see, you drop your fan so that when the gentleman picks it up he'll touch your fingers . . . And don't be stiff, let your waist bend. Men don't like boards. And above all, don't be a simpleton if they go too far. A man who goes too far is caught, my dear."

The clock in the parlor rang two o'clock; and in the excitement of the long evening, fired by her desire for an immediate marriage, the mother let herself think aloud, twisting and turning her daughter like a paper doll. The girl, docile and dispirited, gave in, but her heart was heavy and fear and shame wrung her breast.

This shows the young girl becoming absolutely passive; she is *married*, *given* in marriage by her parents. Boys *marry;* they *take* a wife. In marriage they seek an expansion, a confirmation of their existence but not the very right to exist; it is a charge they assume freely. So they can question its advantages and disadvantages just as the Greek and medieval satirists did; for them it is simply a way of life, not a destiny. They are just as free to prefer a celibate's solitude or to marry late or not at all.

In marrying, the woman receives a piece of the world as property; legal guaranties protect her from man's caprices; but she becomes his vassal. He is economically the head of the community, and he thus embodies it in society's eyes. She takes his name; she joins his religion, integrates into his class, his world; she belongs to his family, she becomes his other "half." She follows him where his work calls him: where he works essentially determines where they live; she breaks with her past more or less brutally, she is annexed to her husband's universe; she gives him her person: she owes him her virginity and strict fidelity. She loses part of the legal rights

of the unmarried woman. Roman law placed the woman in the hands of
her husband *loco filiae;* at the beginning of the nineteenth century, Bonald
declared that the woman is to her husband what the child is to the mother;
until the 1942 law, French law demanded a wife's obedience to her husband; law and customs still confer great authority on him: it is suggested by
her very situation within the conjugal society. Since he is the producer, it is
he who goes beyond family interest to the interest of society and who
opens a future to her by cooperating in the construction of the collective
future: it is he who embodies transcendence. Woman is destined to maintain the species and care for the home, which is to say, to immanence.[5] In
truth, all human existence is transcendence and immanence at the same
time; to go beyond itself, it must maintain itself; to thrust itself toward the
future, it must integrate the past into itself; and while relating to others, it
must confirm itself in itself. These two moments are implied in every living movement: for *man,* marriage provides the perfect synthesis of them;
in his work and political life, he finds change and progress, he experiences
his dispersion through time and the universe; and when he tires of this
wandering, he establishes a home, he settles down, he anchors himself in
the world; in the evening he restores himself in the house, where his wife
cares for the furniture and children and safeguards the past she keeps in
store. But the wife has no other task save the one of maintaining and caring
for life in its pure and identical generality; she perpetuates the immutable
species, she ensures the even rhythm of the days and the permanence of the
home she guards with locked doors; she is given no direct grasp on the
future, nor on the universe; she goes beyond herself toward the group only
through her husband as mouthpiece.

Marriage today still retains this traditional form. And, first of all, it is
imposed far more imperiously on the young girl than on the young man.
There are still many social strata where she is offered no other perspective;
for peasants, an unmarried woman is a pariah; she remains the servant of
her father, her brothers, and her brother-in-law; moving to the city is virtually impossible for her; marriage chains her to a man and makes her mistress of a home. In some bourgeois classes, a girl is still left incapable of
earning a living; she can only vegetate as a parasite in her father's home or
accept some lowly position in a stranger's home. Even when she is more
emancipated, the economic advantage held by males forces her to prefer

---

5. Cf. Volume I. This thesis is found in Saint Paul, the Church Fathers, Rousseau, Proudhon,
Auguste Comte, D. H. Lawrence, and others.

marriage over a career: she will look for a husband whose situation is superior to her own, a husband she hopes will "get ahead" faster and further than she could. It is still accepted that the love act is a *service* she renders to the man; he *takes* his pleasure, and he owes compensation in return. The woman's body is an object to be purchased; for her it represents capital she has the right to exploit. Sometimes she brings a dowry to her husband; she often agrees to provide some domestic work: she will keep the house, raise the children. In any case, she has the right to let herself be supported, and traditional morality even exhorts it. It is understandable that she is tempted by this easy solution, especially as women's professions are so unrewarding and badly paid; marriage is a more beneficial career than many others. Mores still make sexual enfranchisement for a single woman difficult; in France a wife's adultery was a crime until recent times, while no law forbade a woman free love; however, if she wanted to take a lover, she had to be married first. Many strictly controlled young bourgeois girls still marry "to be free." A good number of American women have won their sexual freedom; but their experiences are like those of the young primitive people described by Malinowski in "The Bachelors' House"—girls who engage in pleasures without consequences;* they are expected to marry, and only then will they be fully considered adults. A woman alone, in America even more than in France, is a socially incomplete being, even if she earns her living; she needs a ring on her finger to achieve the total dignity of a person and her full rights. Motherhood in particular is respected only in the married woman; the unwed mother remains an object of scandal, and a child is a severe handicap for her. For all these reasons, many Old and New World adolescent girls, when interviewed about their future projects, respond today just as they did in former times: "I want to get married." No young man, however, considers marriage as his fundamental project. Economic success is what will bring him to respectable adulthood: it may involve marriage—particularly for the peasant—but it may also exclude it. Modern life's conditions—less stable, more uncertain than in the past—make marriage's responsibilities particularly heavy for the young man; the benefits, on the other hand, have decreased since he can easily live on his own and sexual satisfaction is generally available. Without doubt, marriage brings material conveniences ("Eating home is better than eating out") and erotic ones ("This way we have a brothel at home"), and it frees the person from loneliness, it establishes him in space and time by providing him with

* In *The Sexual Life of Savages in North-Western Melanesia.*—TRANS.

a home and children; it is a definitive accomplishment of his existence. In spite of this, overall there is still less masculine demand than feminine supply. The father does not so much give his daughter as get rid of her; the young girl seeking a husband does not respond to a masculine call: she provokes it.

Arranged marriages have not disappeared; there is still a right-minded bourgeoisie perpetuating them. In France, near Napoleon's tomb, at the Opera, at balls, on the beach, or at a tea, the young hopeful with every hair in place, in a new dress, shyly exhibits her physical grace and modest conversation; her parents nag her: "You've already cost me enough in meeting people; make up your mind. The next time it's your sister's turn." The unhappy candidate knows her chances diminish the older she gets; there are not many suitors: she has no more freedom of choice than the young bedouin girl exchanged for a flock of sheep. As Colette says, "A young girl without a fortune or a trade, who is dependent on her brothers for everything, has only one choice: shut up, be grateful for her good luck, and thank God!"[6]

In a less crude way, high society permits young people to meet under mothers' watchful eyes. Somewhat more liberated, young girls go out more, attend university, take jobs that give them the chance to meet men. Between 1945 and 1947, Claire Leplae conducted a survey on the Belgian bourgeoisie, about the problem of matrimonial choice.[7] The author conducted interviews; I will cite some questions she asked and the responses given:

Q: *Are arranged marriages common?*
A: There are no more arranged marriages (51%).
   Arranged marriages are very rare, 1% at most (16%).
   1 to 3% marriages are arranged (28%).
   5 to 10% of marriages are arranged (5%).

The people interviewed point out that arranged marriages, frequent before 1945, have almost disappeared. Nonetheless, "specific interests, poor relations, self-interest, not much family, shyness, age, and the desire to make a good match are motives for some arranged marriages." These marriages are often conducted by priests; sometimes the young girl marries by correspondence. "They describe themselves in writing, and it is put on a special

---

6. *Claudine's House.*
7. Claire Leplae, *Les fiancailles* (The Engagement).

sheet with a number. This sheet is sent to all persons described. It includes, for example, two hundred female and an equal number of male candidates. They also write their own profiles. They can all freely choose a correspondent to whom they write through the agency."

Q: *How did young people meet their fiancées or fiancés over the past ten years?*
A: Social events (48%).
   School or clubs (22%).
   Personal acquaintances, travel (30%).

Everyone agrees that "marriages between childhood friends are very rare. Love is found in unexpected places."

Q: *Is money a primary factor in the choice of a spouse?*
A: 30% of marriages are based on money (48%).
   50% of marriages are based on money (35%).
   70% of marriages are based on money (17%).

Q: *Are parents anxious to marry their daughters?*
A: Parents are anxious to marry their daughters (58%).
   Parents are eager to marry their daughters (24%).
   Parents wish to keep their daughters at home (18%).

Q: *Are girls anxious to marry?*
A: Girls are anxious to marry (36%).
   Girls are eager to marry (38%).
   Girls prefer not to marry than to have a bad marriage (26%).

"Girls besiege boys. Girls marry the first boy to come along simply to get married. They all hope to marry and work at doing so. A girl is humiliated if she is not sought after: to escape this, she will often marry her first prospect. Girls marry to get married. Girls marry to be married. Girls settle down because marriage assures them more freedom." Almost all the interviews concur on this point.

Q: *Are girls more active than boys in seeking marriage?*
A: Girls declare their intentions to boys and ask them to marry them (43%).
   Girls are more active than boys in seeking marriage (43%).
   Girls are discreet (14%).

Here again the response is nearly unanimous: it is the girls who usually take the initiative in pursuing marriage. "Girls realize they are not equipped to get along on their own; not knowing how they can work to make a living, they seek a lifeline in marriage. Girls make declarations, throw themselves at boys. They are frightening! Girls use all their resources to get married . . . it's the woman who pursues the man," and so forth.

No such document exists in France; but as the situation of the bourgeoisie is similar in France and Belgium, the conclusions would probably be comparable; "arranged" marriages have always been more numerous in France than in any other country, and the famous Green Ribbon Club,* whose members have parties for the purpose of bringing people of both sexes together, is still flourishing; matrimonial announcements take up columns in many newspapers.

In France, as in America, mothers, older sisters, and women's magazines cynically teach girls the art of "catching" a husband like flypaper catching flies; this is "fishing" and "hunting," demanding great skill: do not aim too high or too low; be realistic, not romantic; mix coquetry with modesty; do not ask for too much or too little. Young men mistrust women who "want to get married." A young Belgian man declares, "There is nothing more unpleasant for a man than to feel himself pursued, to realize that a woman wants to get her hooks into him."[8] They try to avoid their traps. A girl's choice is often very limited: it would be truly free only if she felt free enough not to marry. Her decision is usually accompanied by calculation, distaste, and resignation rather than enthusiasm. "If the young man who proposes to her is more or less suitable (background, health, career), she accepts him without loving him. She will accept him without passion even if there are 'buts.' "

At the same time as she desires it, however, a girl is often apprehensive of marriage. It represents a more considerable benefit for her than for the man, which is why she desires it more fervently; but it demands weighty sacrifices as well; in particular, it implies a more brutal rupture with the past. We have seen that many adolescent girls are anguished by the idea of leaving the paternal home: when the event draws near, this anxiety is heightened. This is the moment when many neuroses develop; the same thing is true for young men who are frightened by the new responsibilities they are assuming, but such neuroses are much more widespread in girls

---

* Our translation of *"Club des lisières vertes,"* source unknown.—TRANS.
8. Ibid.

for the reasons we have already seen, and they become even more serious in this crisis. I will cite only one example, taken from Stekel. He treated a young girl from a good family who manifested several neurotic symptoms.

When Stekel meets her, she is suffering from vomiting, takes morphine every night, has fits of temper, refuses to wash, eats in bed, refuses to leave her room. She is engaged to be married and affirms that she loves her fiancé. She admits to Stekel that she gave herself to him. Later she says that she derived no pleasure from it: the memory of his kisses was even repugnant to her, and they are the cause of her vomiting. It is discovered that, in fact, she succumbed to him to punish her mother, who she felt never loved her enough; as a child, she spied on her parents at night because she was afraid they might give her a brother or sister; she adored her mother. "And now she had to get married, leave [her parents'] home, abandon her parents' bedroom? It was impossible." She lets herself grow fat, scratches and hurts her hands, deteriorates, falls ill, tries to offend her fiancé in all ways. The doctor heals her, but she pleads with her mother to give up this idea of marriage: "She wanted to stay home, to remain a child forever." Her mother insists that she marry. A week before the wedding day, she is found in her bed, dead; she shot herself with a revolver.

In other cases, the girl willfully falls into a protracted illness; she becomes desperate because her state keeps her from marrying the man "she adores"; in fact, she makes herself ill to avoid marrying him and finds her balance only by breaking her engagement. Sometimes the fear of marriage originates in former erotic experiences that have left their mark on her; in particular, she might dread that her loss of virginity will be discovered. But frequently the idea of submitting to a male stranger is unbearable because of her ardent feelings for her father and mother or a sister, or her attachment to her family home in general. And many of those who decide to marry because it is what they should do, because of the pressure on them, because they know it is the only reasonable solution, because they want a normal existence of wife and mother, nonetheless keep a secret and obstinate resistance in their deepest hearts, making the early days of their married lives difficult and even keeping themselves from ever finding a happy balance.

Marriages, then, are generally not based on love. "The husband is, so to speak, never more than a substitute for the loved man, and not that man himself," said Freud. This dissociation is not accidental. It is implicit in the very nature of the institution. The economic and sexual union of man and woman is a matter of transcending toward the collective interest and not of individual happiness. In patriarchal regimes, a fiancé chosen by parents had often never seen his future wife's face before the wedding day—and this still happens today with some Muslims. There would be no question of founding a lifelong enterprise, considered in its social aspect, on sentimental or erotic caprice. Montaigne says:

> In this sober contract the appetites are not so wanton; they are dull and more blunted. Love hates people to be attached to each other except by himself, and takes a laggard part in relations that are set up and maintained under another title, as marriage is. Connections and means have, with reason, as much weight in it as graces and beauty, or more. We do not marry for ourselves, whatever we say; we marry just as much or more for our posterity, for our family.*

Because it is the man who "takes" the woman—and especially when there is a good supply of women—he has rather more possibilities for choosing. But since the sexual act is considered a *service* imposed on the woman and upon which are founded the advantages conceded to her, it is logical to ignore her own preferences. Marriage is intended to defend her against man's freedom: but as there is neither love nor individuality without freedom, she must renounce the love of a particular individual to ensure the protection of a male for life. I heard a mother of a family teach her daughters that "love is a vulgar sentiment reserved for men and unknown to women of good standing." In a naive form, this was the very doctrine Hegel professed in *Phenomenology of Spirit:*

> The relationships of mother and wife, however, are those of particular individuals, partly in the form of something natural pertaining to desire, partly in the form of something negative which sees in those relationships only something evanescent and also, again, the particular individual is for that very reason a contingent element which can be replaced by another individual. In the ethical household, it is not a question of *this* particular husband, *this* particular child, but simply of husband and children generally; the relationships of the woman are based, not on feeling, but on the universal. The difference between the ethical life of the woman and that of the man consists just in this, that in her vocation as an individual and in her pleasure, her interest is centred on the universal and remains alien to the

---

* *Complete Essays of Montaigne,* translated by Donald M. Frame. All Montaigne quotations are from this book.—TRANS.

particularity of desire; whereas in the husband these two sides are separated; and since he possesses as a citizen the self-conscious power of universality, he thereby acquires the right of desire and, at the same time, preserves his freedom in regard to it. Since, then, in this relationship of the wife there is an admixture of particularity, her ethical life is not pure; but in so far as it *is* ethical, the particularity is a matter of indifference, and the wife is without the moment of knowing herself as *this* particular self in the other partner.

This points out that for a woman it is not at all a question of establishing individual relations with a chosen husband, but rather of justifying the exercise of her feminine functions in their generality; she should have sexual pleasure only in a generic form and not an individualized one; this results in two essential consequences that touch upon her erotic destiny. First, she has no right to sexual activity outside marriage; for both spouses, sexual congress becoming an institution, desire and pleasure are superseded by the interest of society; but man, as worker and citizen transcending toward the universal, can savor contingent pleasures prior to marriage and outside of married life: in any case, he finds satisfaction in other ways; but in a world where woman is essentially defined as female, she must be justified wholly as a female. Second, it has been seen that the connection between the general and the particular is biologically different for the male and the female: in accomplishing his specific task as husband and reproducer, the male unfailingly finds his sexual pleasure;[9] on the contrary, very often for the woman, there is a dissociation between the reproductive function and sexual pleasure. This is so to the extent that in claiming to give ethical dignity to her erotic life, marriage, in fact, means to suppress it.

Woman's sexual frustration has been deliberately accepted by men; it has been seen that men rely on an optimistic naturalism to tolerate her frustrations: it is her lot; the biblical curse confirms men's convenient opinion. Pregnancy's pains—the heavy ransom inflicted on the woman in exchange for a brief and uncertain pleasure—are often the object of various jokes. "Five minutes of pleasure: nine months of pain . . . It goes in more easily than it comes out." This contrast often makes them laugh. It is part of this sadistic philosophy: many men relish feminine misery and are repulsed by

---

9. Of course, the adage "A hole is always a hole" is vulgarly humorous; man does seek something other than brute pleasure; nonetheless, the success of certain "slaughterhouses" is enough to prove a man can find some satisfaction with the first available woman.

the idea of reducing it.[10] One can understand, then, that males have no scruples about denying their companion sexual happiness; and it even seems advantageous to them to deny woman the temptations of desire along with the autonomy of pleasure.[11]

This is what Montaigne expresses with a charming cynicism:

> And so it is a kind of incest to employ in this venerable and sacred alliance the efforts and extravagances of amorous license, as it seems to me I have said elsewhere. A man, says Aristotle, should touch his wife prudently and soberly, lest if he caresses her too lasciviously the pleasure should transport her outside the bounds of reason . . . I see no marriages that sooner are troubled and fail than those that progress by means of beauty and amorous desires. It needs more solid and stable foundations, and we need to go at it circumspectly; this ebullient ardor is no good for it . . . A good marriage, if such there be, rejects the company and conditions of love.

He also says:

> Even the pleasures they get in making love to their wives are condemned, unless moderation is observed; and . . . it is possible to err through licentiousness and debauchery, just as in an illicit affair.

---

10. There are some, for example, who support the idea that painful childbirth is necessary to awaken the maternal instinct: those who deliver under anesthesia have been known to abandon their fawns. Such alleged facts are at best vague; and a woman is in no way a doe. The truth is that some males are shocked that the burdens of womanhood might be lightened.

11. Still, in our times, woman's claim to pleasure incites male anger; a striking document on this subject is Dr. Grémillon's treatise *La vérité sur l'orgasme vénérien de la femme* (The Truth About the Genital Orgasm of the Woman). The preface informs us that the author, a World War I hero who saved the lives of fifty-five German prisoners, is a man of the highest moral standing. Taking serious issue with Stekel in *Frigidity in Woman*, he declares, "*The normal and fertile woman does not have a genital orgasm.* Many are the mothers (and the best of them) who have never experienced these wondrous spasms . . . the most latent erogenous zones are not natural but artificial. They are delighted to have them, but they are stigmas of decadence . . . Tell all that to a man seeking pleasure and he does not care. He wants his depraved partner to have a genital orgasm, and she will have it. If it does not exist, it will be made to exist. Modern woman wants a man to make her vibrate. To her we answer: Madam, we don't have the time, and hygiene forbids it! . . . The creator of erogenous zones works against himself: he creates insatiable women. The female ghoul can tirelessly exhaust innumerable husbands . . . the 'zoned' one becomes a new woman with a new spirit, sometimes a terrible woman capable of crime . . . there would be no neuroses, no psychoses if we understood that the 'two-backed beast' is an act as indifferent as eating, urinating, defecating, or sleeping."

Those shameless excesses that our first heat suggests to us in this sport are not only indecently but detrimentally practiced on our wives. Let them at least learn shamelessness from another hand. They are always aroused enough for our need . . . Marriage is a religious and holy bond. That is why the pleasure we derive from it should be a restrained pleasure, serious, and mixed with some austerity; it should be a somewhat discreet and conscientious voluptuousness.

In fact, if the husband awakens feminine sensuality, he awakens it in its general form, since he was not singularly chosen by her; he is preparing his wife to seek pleasure in other arms; "to love one's wife too well," says Montaigne, is to "shit in your hat and then put it on your head." He admits in good faith that masculine prudence puts the woman in a thankless situation:

Women are not wrong at all when they reject the rules of life that have been introduced into the world, inasmuch as it is the men who have made these without them. There is naturally strife and wrangling between them and us . . . we treat them inconsiderately in the following way. We have discovered . . . that they are incomparably more capable and ardent than we in the acts of love . . . we have gone and given women continence as their particular share, and upon utmost and extreme penalties . . . We, on the contrary, want them to be healthy, vigorous, plump, well-nourished, and chaste at the same time: that is to say, both hot and cold. For marriage, which we say has the function of keeping them from burning, brings them but little cooling off, according to our ways.

Proudhon is less scrupulous: according to him, separating love from marriage conforms to justice:

Love must be buried in justice . . . all love conversations, even between people who are engaged, even between husband and wife, are unsuitable, destructive of domestic respect, of the love of work, and of the practice of one's social duty . . . (once the function of love has been fulfilled) . . . we have to discard it like the shepherd who removes the rennet once the milk has coagulated.

Yet, during the nineteenth century, conceptions of the bourgeoisie changed somewhat; it ardently strove to defend and maintain marriage; and besides, the progress of individualism made it impossible to stifle feminine claims; Saint-Simon, Fourier, George Sand, and all the Romantics had too intensely proclaimed the right to love. The problem arose of integrating into marriage those individual feelings that had previously and carelessly been excluded. It was thus that the ambiguous notion of conjugal love was invented, miraculous fruit of the traditional marriage of convenience. Balzac expresses the ideas of the conservative bourgeoisie in all their inconsequence. He recognizes that the principle of marriage has nothing to do with love; but he finds it repugnant to assimilate a respectable institution with a simple business deal where the woman is treated like a thing; and he ends up with the disconcerting inconsistencies in *The Physiology of Marriage*, where we read:

> Marriage can be considered politically, civilly, or morally, as a law, a contract, or an institution . . .
>
> Thus marriage ought to be an object of general respect. Society has only considered it under these three heads—they dominate the marriage question.
>
> Most men who get married have only in view reproduction, propriety, or what is due to the child; yet neither reproduction, propriety, nor the child constitute happiness. "*Crescite et multiplicamini*"* does not imply love. To ask a girl whom one has seen fourteen times in a fortnight for her love on behalf of the law, the king and justice, is an absurdity only worthy of the fore-ordained!

This is as clear as Hegelian theory. But Balzac continues without any transition:

> Love is the union of desire and tenderness, and happiness in marriage comes from a perfect understanding between two souls. And from this it follows that to be happy a man is obliged to bind himself by certain rules of honour and delicacy. After having enjoyed the privilege of the social laws which consecrate desire, he should obey the secret laws of nature which bring to birth the affections. If his happiness depends on being loved, he himself must love sincerely; nothing can withstand true passion.
>
> But to be passionate is always to desire.
>
> Can one always desire one's wife?
>
> Yes.

---

* "Increase and multiply."—TRANS.

After that, Balzac exposes the science of marriage. But one quickly sees that for the husband it is not a question of being loved but of not being deceived: he will not hesitate to inflict a debilitating regime on his wife, to keep her uncultured, and to stultify her solely to safeguard his honor. Is this still about love? If one wants to find a meaning in these murky and incoherent ideas, it seems man has the right to choose a wife through whom he can satisfy his needs in their generality, a generality that is the guarantee of his faithfulness: then it is up to him to waken his wife's love by applying certain recipes. But is he really *in love* if he marries for his property or for his posterity? And if he is not, how can his passion be irresistible enough to bring about a reciprocal passion? And does Balzac really not know that an unshared love, on the contrary, annoys and disgusts? His bad faith is clearly visible in the *Letters of Two Brides*, an epistolary novel with a message. Louise de Chaulieu believes that marriage is based on love: she kills her first husband by her excessive passion; she dies from the jealous fixation she feels for her second. Renée de l'Estorade sacrifices her feelings to reason: but the joys of motherhood mostly compensate her, and she builds a stable happiness. One wonders first what curse—except the author's own decree—deprives the amorous Louise of the motherhood she desires: love has never prevented conception; and one also thinks that to accept her husband's embraces joyfully, Renée had to accept this "hypocrisy" Stendhal hated in "honest women." Balzac describes the wedding night in these words:

"The animal that we call a husband," to quote your words, disappeared, and one balmy evening I discovered in his stead a lover, whose words thrilled me and on whose arm I leant with pleasure beyond words . . . I felt a fluttering of curiosity in my heart . . . [Know that] nothing was lacking either of satisfaction for the most fastidious sentiment, or of that unexpectedness which brings, in a sense, its own sanction. Every witchery of imagination, of passion, of reluctance overcome, of the ideal passing into reality, played its part.

This beautiful miracle must not have occurred too often, since, several letters later, we find Renée in tears: "Formerly I was a person, now I am a chattel"; and she consoles herself after her nights "of conjugal love" by reading Bonald. But one would nevertheless like to know what recipe was used for the husband to change into an enchanter, during the most difficult moment of feminine initiation; those Balzac gives in *The Physiology of*

Marriage are succinct—"Never begin marriage by rape"—or vague: "The genius of the husband lies in deftly handling the various shades of pleasure, in developing them, and endowing them with a new style, an original expression." He quickly goes on to say, moreover, that "between two people who do not love one another, this genius is wanton"; then, precisely, Renée does not love Louis; and as he is depicted, where does this "genius" come from? In truth, Balzac has cynically skirted the problem. He underestimates the fact that there are no neutral feelings and that in the absence of love, constraints, together with boredom, engender tender friendship less easily than resentment, impatience, and hostility. He is more sincere in *The Lily in the Valley*, and the destiny of the unfortunate Mme de Mortsauf seems to be far less instructive.

Reconciling marriage and love is such a feat that at the very least divine intervention is necessary; this is the solution Kierkegaard adopts after complicated detours. He likes to denounce the paradox of marriage:

> Indeed, what a passing strange device is marriage! And what makes it all the stranger is that it could be a step taken without thought. And yet no step is more decisive . . . And such an important step as marriage ought to be taken without reflection![12]

> This is the difficulty: love and falling in love are spontaneous, marriage is a decision; yet falling in love should be awakened by marriage or by decision: wanting to marry; this means that what is the most spontaneous must at the same time be the freest decision, and what is, because of the spontaneity, so inexplicable that it must be attributed to a divinity, must at the same time take place because of reflection and such exhausting reflection that a decision results from it. Besides, these things must not follow each other, the decision must not come sneaking up behind; everything must occur simultaneously, the two things have to come together at the moment of dénouement.[13]

This underlines that loving is not marrying and it is quite difficult to understand how love can become duty. But paradoxes do not faze Kierkegaard: his whole essay on marriage is an attempt to elucidate this mystery. It is true, he agrees: "Reflection is the angel of death for spontane-

---

12. *In Vino Veritas.*
13. "Some Reflections on Marriage" [in *Stages on Life's Way.*—Trans.].

ity . . . If it were true that reflection must take precedence over falling in love, there would never be marriage." But "decision is a new spontaneity obtained through reflection, experienced in a purely ideal way, a spontaneity that precisely corresponds to that of falling in love. Decision is a religious view of life constructed upon ethical presuppositions, and must, so to speak, pave the way for falling in love and securing it against any danger, exterior or interior." This is why "a husband, a real husband, is himself a miracle! . . . Being able to keep the pleasure of love while existence focuses all the power of seriousness on him and his beloved!"

As for the wife, reason is not her lot, she is without "reflection"; so "she goes from the immediacy of love to the immediacy of the religious." Expressed in simple language, this doctrine means a man in love chooses marriage by an act of faith in God that guarantees him the accord of both feelings and duty; and the woman wishes to marry as soon as she is in love. I knew an old Catholic woman who, most naively, believed in a "sacramental falling in love"; she asserted that at the moment the couple pronounce the definitive "I do" at the altar, they feel their hearts burst into flame. Kierkegaard does admit there must previously be an "inclination," but that it be thought to last a whole lifetime is no less miraculous.

However, in France, late-nineteenth-century novelists and playwrights, less confident in the value of the holy vows, try to ensure conjugal happiness by more human means; more boldly than Balzac, they envisage the possibility of integrating eroticism with legitimate love. Porto-Riche affirms, in the play *Amoureuse* (*A Loving Wife*), the incompatibility of sexual love and home life: the husband, worn out by his wife's ardor, seeks peace with his more temperate mistress. But at Paul Hervieu's instigation, "love" between spouses is a legal duty. Marcel Prévost preaches to the young husband that he must treat his wife like a mistress, alluding to conjugal pleasures in a discreetly libidinous way. Bernstein is the playwright of legitimate love: the husband is put forward as a wise and generous being next to the amoral, lying, sensual, fickle, and mean wife; and he is also understood to be a virile and expert lover. Much romantic defense of marriage comes out in reaction to novels of adultery. Even Colette yields to this moralizing wave in *L'ingénue libertine* (*The Innocent Libertine*), when, after describing the cynical experiences of a clumsily deflowered young bride, she has her experience sexual pleasure in her husband's arms. Likewise, Martin Maurice, in a somewhat controversial book, brings the young woman, after a brief incursion into the bed of an experienced lover, to that of her husband, who benefits from her experience. For other reasons and in a different way, Americans today, who are both respectful of the institution of marriage and individualistic, endeavor to integrate sexuality into marriage. Many books on initiation into married life come out every year aimed at teaching couples to adapt to each other, and in particular teaching man how to create harmony with his wife. Psychoanalysts and doctors play the role of "marriage counselors"; it is accepted that the wife too has the right to pleasure and that the man must know the correct techniques to provide her with it. But we have seen that sexual success is not merely a technical question. The young man, even if he has memorized twenty textbooks such as *Ce que tout mari doit savoir* (What Every Husband Should Know), *Le secret du bonheur conjugal* (The Secret of Conjugal Happiness), and *L'amour sans peur* (Love Without Fear), is still not sure he will know how to make his new wife love him. She reacts to the psychological situation as a whole. And traditional marriage is far from creating the most propitious conditions for the awakening and blossoming of feminine eroticism.

In the past, in matriarchal communities, virginity was not demanded of the new wife, and for mystical reasons she was normally supposed to be deflowered before the wedding. In some French regions, these ancient prerogatives can still be observed; prenuptial chastity is not required of girls; and even girls who have "sinned" or unmarried mothers sometimes find a husband more easily than others. Moreover, in circles that accept woman's liberation, girls are granted the same sexual freedom as boys. However, paternalistic ethics imperiously demand that the bride be delivered to her husband as a virgin; he wants to be sure she does not carry within her a foreign germ; he wants the entire and exclusive property of this flesh he makes his own;[14] virginity has taken on a moral, religious, and mystical value, and this value is still widely recognized today. In France, there are regions where friends of the husband stay outside the door of the bridal suite, laughing and singing until the husband comes out triumphantly showing them the bloodstained sheet; or else the parents display it in the morning to the neighbors.[15] The custom of the "wedding night" is still widespread, albeit in a less brutal form. It is no coincidence that it has spawned a whole body of ribald literature: the separation of the social and the animal necessarily produces obscenity. A humanist morality demands that all living experience have a human meaning, that it be invested with freedom; in an

---

14. See "Myths" in Volume I.

15. "Today, in certain regions of the United States, first-generation immigrants still send the bloody sheet back to the family in Europe as proof of the consummation of the marriage," says the Kinsey Report.

authentically moral erotic life, there is the free assumption of desire and pleasure, or at least a deeply felt fight to regain freedom within sexuality: but this is only possible if a *singular* recognition of the other is accomplished in love or in desire. When sexuality is no longer redeemed by the individual, but God or society claims to justify it, the relationship of the two partners is no more than a bestial one. It is understandable that right-thinking matrons spurn adventures of the flesh: they have reduced them to the level of scatological functions. This is also why one hears so many sniggers at wedding parties. There is an obscene paradox in the super-imposing of a pompous ceremony on a brutally real animal function. The wedding presents its universal and abstract meaning: a man and a woman are united publicly according to symbolic rites; but in the secrecy of the bed it is concrete and singular individuals who confront each other face-to-face, and all gazes turn away from their embraces. Colette, attending a peasant wedding at the age of thirteen, was terribly consternated when a girlfriend took her to see the wedding chamber:

> The young couple's bedroom . . . Under its curtains of Adrianople red, the tall, narrow bed, the bed stuffed with down and crammed with goose-down pillows, the bed that is to be the final scene of this wedding day all steaming with sweat, incense, the breath of cattle, the aroma of different sauces . . . Shortly the young couple will be arriving here. I hadn't thought of that. They will dive into that deep mound of feathers . . . They will embark on that obscure struggle about which my mother's bold and direct language and the life of animals have taught me both too much and too little . . . And then? . . . I'm afraid of that bedroom, afraid of that bed which I hadn't thought of.[16]

In her childish distress, the girl felt the contrast between the pomp of the family feast and the animal mystery of the enclosed double bed. Marriage's comic and lewd side is scarcely found in civilizations that do not individualize woman: in the East, in Greece, in Rome; the animal function appears there in as generalized a form as do the social rites; but today in the West, men and women are grasped as individuals, and wedding guests snigger because it is this particular man and this particular woman who, in an altogether individual experience, are going to consummate the act that

---

16. *Claudine's House.*

we disguise in rites, speeches, and flowers. It is true that there is also a macabre contrast between the pomp of great funerals and the rot of the tomb. But the dead person does not awaken when he is put into the ground, while the bride is terribly surprised when she discovers the singularity and contingence of the *real* experience to which the mayor's tricolored sash and church organ pledged her. It is not only in vaudeville that one sees young women returning in tears to their mothers on their wedding night: psychiatric books are full of this type of account; several have been told to me directly: they concern young girls, too well brought up, without any sexual education, and whose sudden discovery of eroticism overwhelmed them. Last century, Mme Adam thought it was her duty to marry a man who had kissed her on the mouth because she believed that was the completed form of sexual union. More recently, Stekel writes about a young bride: "When during the honeymoon, her husband deflowered her, she thought he was of unsound mind and did not dare say a word for fear of dealing with an insane person."[17] It even happens that the young girl is so innocent she marries a woman invert and lives with her pseudo-husband for a long time without doubting that she is dealing with a man.

> If on your marriage day, returning home, you set your wife in a well to soak for the night, she will be dumbfounded. No comfort to her now that she has always had a vague uneasiness . . .
> "Well now!" she will say, "so that's what marriage is. That's why they keep it all so secret. I've let myself be taken in."
> But being annoyed, she will say nothing. That is why you will be able to dip her for long periods and often, without causing any scandal in the neighborhood.

This fragment of a poem by Michaux, called "Nuit de noces" (Bridal Night), accurately conveys the situation.[18] Today, many young girls are better informed; but their consent remains abstract; and their defloration has the characteristics of a rape. "There are certainly more rapes committed in marriage than outside of marriage," says Havelock Ellis. In his work *Monatsschrift für Geburtshülfe* (1889, vol. 9), Neugebauer found more than 150 cases of injuries inflicted on women by the penis during coitus; the causes were brutality, drunkenness, false position, and a disproportion of the organs. In England, Ellis reports, a woman asked six intelligent, mar-

---

17. *Conditions of Nervous Anxiety and Their Treatment.*
18. In *La nuit remue* (*Night Moves*).

ried, middle-class women about their reactions on their wedding night: for all of them intercourse was a shock; two of them had been ignorant of everything; the others thought they knew but were no less psychically wounded. Adler also emphasized the psychic importance of the act of defloration:

> The first moment man acquires his full rights often decides his whole life. The inexperienced and over-aroused husband can sow the germ of feminine insensitivity and through his continual clumsiness and brutality transform it into permanent desensitization.

Many examples of these unfortunate initiations were given in the previous chapter. Here is another case reported by Stekel:

> Mrs. H.N. . . . , raised very prudishly, trembled at the idea of her wedding night. Her husband undressed her almost violently without allowing her to get into bed. He undressed, asking her to look at him nude and to admire his penis. She hid her face in her hands. And so he exclaimed: "Why didn't you stay at home, you halfwit!" Then he threw her on the bed and brutally deflowered her. Naturally, she remained frigid forever.

We have, thus far, seen all the resistance the virgin has to overcome to accomplish her sexual destiny: her initiation demands "labor," both physiological and psychic. It is stupid and barbaric to want to put it all into one night; it is absurd to transform an operation as difficult as the first coitus into a duty. The woman is all the more terrorized by the fact that the strange operation she is subjected to is sacred; and that society, religion, family, and friends delivered her solemnly to the husband as to a master; and in addition, that the act seems to engage her whole future, because marriage still has a definitive character. This is when she feels truly revealed in the absolute: this man to whom she is pledged to the end of time embodies all of Man in her eyes; and he is revealed to her, too, as a figure she has not heretofore known, which is of immense importance since he will be her lifelong companion. However, the man himself is anguished by the duty weighing on him; he has his own difficulties and his own complexes that make him shy and clumsy or on the contrary brutal; many men are impotent on their wedding night because of the very solemnity of marriage. Janet writes in *Les obsessions et la psychasthénie* (Obsessions and Psychasthenia):

Who has not known these young grooms ashamed of their bad
fortune in not succeeding in accomplishing the conjugal act and
who are plagued by it with an obsession of shame and despair? We
witnessed a very curious tragicomic scene last year when a furious
father-in-law dragged his humble and resigned son-in-law to
Salpêtrière: the father-in-law demanded a medical attestation
enabling him to ask for a divorce. The poor boy explained that in
the past he had been potent, but since his wedding a feeling of
awkwardness and shame had made everything impossible.

Too much impetuousness frightens the virgin, too much respect
humiliates her; women forever hate the man who has taken his pleasure at
the expense of their suffering; but they feel an eternal resentment against
the one who seems to disdain them,[19] and often against the one who has not
attempted to deflower them the first night or who was unable to do it.
Helene Deutsch points out that some timid or clumsy husbands ask the
doctor to deflower their wife surgically on the pretext that she is not normally constituted; the reason is not usually valid.[20] Women, she says, har-
bor scorn and resentment for the husband unable to penetrate them
normally. One of Freud's observations shows that the husband's impotence can traumatize the woman:

> One patient would run from one room to another in which there was
> a table in the middle. She put on the tablecloth in a certain way, rang
> for the maid who was supposed to go toward the table, and then sent
> her away . . . When she tried to explain this obsession, she recalled
> that this cloth had a bad stain and that she arranged it each time so
> that the stain should jump out at the maid . . . The whole thing was
> a reproduction of the wedding night in which the husband had not
> shown himself as virile. He ran from his room to hers a thousand
> times to try again. Being ashamed in front of the maid who had to
> make the beds, he poured some red ink on the sheet to make her
> think there was blood.[21]

The "wedding night" transforms the erotic experience into an ordeal
that neither partner is able to surmount, too involved with personal prob-

19. See Stekel's observations quoted in the previous chapter.
20. *Psychology of Women.*
21. We summarize it following Stekel in *Frigidity in Woman.*

lems to think generously of each other; it is invested with a solemnity that makes it formidable; and it is not surprising that it often dooms the woman to frigidity forever. The difficult problem facing the husband is this: if he "titillates his wife too lasciviously," she might be scandalized or outraged; it seems this fear paralyzes American husbands, among others, especially in college-educated couples, says the Kinsey Report, because wives, more conscious of themselves, are more deeply inhibited. But if he "respects" her, he fails to waken her sensuality. This dilemma is created by the ambiguity of the feminine attitude: the young woman both wants and rejects pleasure; she demands a delicateness from which she suffers. Unless he is exceptionally lucky, the husband will necessarily appear as either clumsy or a libertine. It is thus not surprising that "conjugal duties" are often only a repugnant chore for the wife. According to Diderot,

> Submission to a master she dislikes is a torture to her. I have seen
> a virtuous wife shiver with horror at her husband's approach. I
> have seen her plunge into a bath and never think herself properly
> cleansed from the soilure of her duty. This sort of repugnance is
> almost unknown with us. Our organ is more indulgent. Many
> women die without having experienced the extreme of pleasure.
> This sensation which I am willing to consider a passing attack
> of epilepsy is rare with them, but never fails to come when we
> call for it. The sovereign happiness escapes them in the arms of
> the man they adore. We experience it with an easy woman we
> dislike. Less mistresses of their *sensations* than we are, their reward
> is less prompt and certain. A hundred times their expectation is
> deceived.[22]

Many women, indeed, become mothers and grandmothers without ever having experienced pleasure or even arousal; they try to get out of their soilure of duty by getting medical certificates or using other pretexts. The Kinsey Report says that in America, many wives "report that they consider their coital frequencies already too high and wish that their husbands did not desire intercourse so often. A very few wives wish for more frequent coitus." We have seen, though, that woman's erotic possibilities are almost indefinite. This contradiction points up the fact that marriage, claiming to regulate feminine eroticism, kills it.

---

22. "On Women."

In *Thérèse Desqueyroux,* Mauriac described the reactions of a young "reasonably married" woman to marriage in general and to conjugal duties in particular:

> Perhaps she was seeking less a dominion or a possession out of this marriage than a refuge. What finally pushed her into it, after all— wasn't it a kind of panic? A practical girl, a child housewife, she was in a hurry to take up her station in life, to find her definitive place; she wanted assurance against some peril that she could not name. She was never so rational and determined as she had been during the engagement period; she embedded herself in the family bloc, "she settled down," she entered into an order of life. She saved herself . . .
>
> The suffocating wedding day in the narrow Saint-Clair church, where the women's cackling drowned out the wheezing harmonium, and the body odor overpowered the incense—this was the day when Thérèse realized she was lost. She had entered the cage like a sleep-walker and, as the heavy door groaned shut, the miserable child in her reawakened. Nothing had changed, but she had the sensation that she would never again be able to be alone. In the thick of a family, she would smolder, like a hidden fire that leaps up onto a branch, lights up a pine tree, then another, then step by step creates a whole forest of torches . . .
>
> On the evening of that half-peasant, half-bourgeois wedding day, groups of the guests crowded around their car, forcing it to slow down; the girls' dresses fluttered in the crowd . . . Thérèse, thinking of the night that was coming, murmured, "It was horrible . . ." but then caught herself and said, "no—not so horrible." On their trip to the Italian lakes, had she suffered so much? No—she played the game; don't lie . . . Thérèse knew how to bend her body to these charades, and she took a bitter pleasure in the accomplishment. This unknown world of sensual pleasure into which the man forced her— her imagination helped her conceive that there was a real pleasure there for her too, a possible happiness—but what happiness? As when, before a country scene pouring with rain, we imagine to ourselves what it looks like in the sunshine—thus it was that Thérèse looked upon sensuality.
>
> Bernard, the boy with the vacant stare, . . . what an easy dupe! He was as sunk in his pleasure as those sweet little pigs you can watch through the fence, snorting with happiness in their trough

("and I was the trough," thought Thérèse) . . . Where had he
learned it, this ability to classify everything relating to the flesh,
to distinguish the honorable caress from that of the sadist? Never
a moment's hesitation . . .

"Poor Bernard! He's no worse than others. But desire transforms
the one who approaches us into a monster, a different being . . . I
played dead, as if the slightest movement on my part could make this
madman, this epileptic, strangle me."

Here is a blunter account. Stekel obtained this confession from which I
quote the passage about married life. It concerns a twenty-eight-year-old
woman, brought up in a refined and cultivated home:

I was a happy fiancée; I finally had the feeling I was safe, all at once I
was the focus of attention. I was spoiled, my fiancé admired me, all
this was new for me . . . our kisses (my fiancé had never attempted
any other caresses) had aroused me to such a point that I could not
wait for the wedding day . . . The morning of the wedding I was in
such a state of excitation that my camisole was soaking with sweat:
Just the idea that I was finally going to know the stranger I had
so desired. I had the infantile image that the man was supposed to
urinate in the woman's vagina . . . In our room, there was already a
little disappointment when my husband asked me if he should move
away. I asked him to do that because I was really ashamed in front of
him. The undressing scene had played such a role in my imagination. He came back, very embarrassed, when I was in bed. Later
on, he admitted that my appearance had intimidated him: I was the
incarnation of radiant and eager youth. Barely had he undressed
than he shut out the light. Barely kissing me, he immediately tried to
take me. I was frightened and asked him to let me alone. I wanted to
be very far from him. I was horrified at this attempt without prior
caresses. I found him brutal and often criticized him for it later. It
was not brutality but very great clumsiness and a lack of sensitivity.
All the attempts that night were in vain. I began to be very unhappy,
I was ashamed of my stupidity, I thought I was at fault and badly
formed . . . Finally, I settled for his kisses. Ten days later he succeeded in deflowering me, I had felt nothing. It was a major disappointment! Then I felt a little joy during coitus but success was
very disturbing, my husband laboring hard to reach his goal . . . In
Prague in my brother-in-law's bachelor apartment I imagined my

brother-in-law's feelings learning I had slept in his bed. That is when I had my first orgasm, making me very happy. My husband made love with me every day during the first weeks. I was still reaching orgasm but I was not satisfied because it was too short and I was excited to the point of crying . . . After two births . . . coitus became less and less satisfying. It rarely led to orgasm, my husband always reaching it before me; I followed each session anxiously (how long is it going to continue?). If he was satisfied leaving me at halfway, I hated him. Sometimes, I imagined my cousin during coitus or the doctor who had delivered me. My husband tried to excite me with his finger . . . I was very aroused but, at the same time, I found this means shameful and abnormal and experienced no pleasure . . . During the whole time of our marriage, he never caressed even one part of my body. One day he told me that he did not dare do anything with me . . . He never saw me naked because we always kept on our nightclothes, he performed coitus only at night.

This very sensual woman was later perfectly happy in the arms of a lover.

Engagements are specifically meant to create gradations in the young girl's initiation; but mores often impose extreme chastity on the engaged couple. When the virgin "knows" her future husband during this period, her situation is not very different from that of the young bride; she yields only because her engagement already seems to her as definitive as marriage and the first coitus has the characteristics of a test; once she has given herself—even if she is not pregnant, which would keep her in chains—it is very rare for her to assert herself again.

The difficulties of the first experiences are easily overcome if love or desire generates total consent from the two partners; physical love draws its strength and dignity from the joy lovers give each other and take in the reciprocal consciousness of their freedom; thus there are no degrading practices since, for both of them, their practices are not submitted to but generously desired. But the principle of marriage is obscene because it transforms an exchange that should be founded on a spontaneous impulse into rights and duties; it gives bodies an instrumental, thus degrading, side by dooming them to grasp themselves in their generality; the husband is often frozen by the idea that he is accomplishing a duty, and the wife is ashamed to feel delivered to someone who exercises a right over her. Of course, relations can become individualized at the beginning of married life; sexual apprenticeship is sometimes accomplished in slow gradations;

as of the first night, a happy physical attraction can be discovered between the spouses. Marriage facilitates the wife's abandon by suppressing the notion of sin still so often attached to the flesh; regular and frequent cohabitation engenders carnal intimacy that is favorable to sexual maturity: there are wives fully satisfied in their first years of marriage. It is to be noted that they remain grateful to their husbands, which makes it possible to pardon them later for the wrongs they might be responsible for. "Women who cannot get out of an unhappy home life have always been satisfied by their husbands," says Stekel. It remains that the young girl runs a terrible risk in promising to sleep exclusively and for her whole life with a man she does not know sexually, whereas her erotic destiny essentially depends on her partner's personality: this is the paradox Léon Blum rightfully denounced in his work *Marriage*.

To claim that a union founded on convention has much chance of engendering love is hypocritical; to ask two spouses bound by practical, social, and moral ties to satisfy each other sexually for their whole lives is pure absurdity. Yet advocates of marriages of reason have no trouble showing that marriages of love do not have much more chance of ensuring the spouses' happiness. In the first place, ideal love, which is often what the girl knows, does not always dispose her to sexual love; her platonic adorations, her daydreaming, and the passions into which she projects her infantile or juvenile obsessions are not meant to resist the tests of daily life nor to last for a long time. Even if there is a sincere and violent erotic attraction between her and her fiancé, that is not a solid basis on which to construct the enterprise of a life. Colette writes:

> But voluptuous pleasure is not the only thing. In the limitless desert
> of love it holds a very small place, so flaming that at first one sees
> nothing else . . . All about this flickering hearth there lies the
> unknown, there lies danger . . . After we have risen from a short
> embrace, or even from a long night, we shall have to begin to live
> at close quarters to each other, and in dependence on each other.[23]

Moreover, even in cases where carnal love exists before marriage or awakens at the beginning of the marriage, it is very rare for it to last many long years. Certainly fidelity is necessary for sexual love, since the two lovers' desire encompasses their singularity; they do not want it contested

---

23. *La vagabonde* (*The Vagabond*).

by outside experiences, they want to be irreplaceable for each other; but this fidelity has meaning only as long as it is spontaneous; and spontaneously, erotic magic dissolves rather quickly. The miracle is that it gives to each of the lovers, in the instant and in their carnal presence, a being whose existence is an unlimited transcendence: and *possession* of this being is undoubtedly impossible, but at least each of them is reached in a privileged and poignant way. But when individuals no longer want to reach each other because of hostility, disgust, or indifference between them, erotic attraction disappears; and it dies almost as surely in esteem and friendship: two human beings who come together in the very movement of their transcendence through the world and their common projects no longer need carnal union; and further, because this union has lost its meaning, they are repelled by it. The word "incest" that Montaigne pronounces is very significant. Eroticism is a movement toward the *Other,* and this is its essential character; but within the couple, spouses become, for each other, the *Same;* no exchange is possible between them anymore, no giving, no conquest. If they remain lovers, it is often in embarrassment: they feel the sexual act is no longer an intersubjective experience where each one goes beyond himself, but rather a kind of mutual masturbation. That they consider each other a necessary tool for the satisfaction of their needs is a fact conjugal politeness disguises but which bursts out when this politeness is rejected, for example in observations reported by Dr. Lagache in his work *The Nature and Forms of Jealousy:** the wife regards the male member as a certain source of pleasure that belongs to her, and she guards it in as miserly a way as the preserves she stores in the cupboard: if the man gives some away to a woman neighbor, there will be no more for her; she looks at his underwear to see if he has not wasted the precious semen. In *Chroniques maritales* (*Marcel and Élise: The Bold Chronicle of a Strange Marriage*), Jouhandeau notes this "daily censure practised by the legitimate wife who scrutinises your shirt and your sleep to discover the sign of ignominy." For his part, the man satisfies his desires on her without asking her opinion.

This brutal satisfaction of need is, in fact, not enough to satisfy human sexuality. That is why there is often an aftertaste of vice in these seemingly most legitimate embraces. The woman often helps herself along with erotic imaginings. Stekel cites a twenty-five-year-old woman who "could reach a slight orgasm with her husband by imagining that a strong, older man is taking her by force, so she cannot defend herself." She sees herself

---

* Beauvoir's title is mistaken. Lagache's work on jealousy is called *La jalousie amoureuse* (Jealousy in Love).—TRANS.

as being raped, beaten, and her husband is not himself but an Other. He indulges in the same dream: in his wife's body he possesses the legs of a dancer seen in a music hall, the breasts of this pinup whose photo he has dwelled on, a memory, an image; or else he imagines his wife desired, possessed, or raped, which is a way to give her back her lost alterity. "Marriage," says Stekel, "creates gross transpositions and inversions, refined actors, scenarios played out between the two partners who risk destroying the limits between appearance and reality." Pushed to the limit, real vices appear. The husband becomes a voyeur: he needs to see his wife, or know she is sleeping with a lover to feel a little of her magic again; or he sadistically strives to provoke her to refuse him, so her consciousness and freedom show through, assuring it is really a human being he is possessing. Inversely, masochistic behavior can develop in the wife who seeks to bring out in the man the master and tyrant he is not; I knew an extremely pious woman, brought up in a convent, who was authoritarian and dominating during the day and who, at night, begged her husband to whip her, which, though horrified, he consented to do. In marriage, vice itself takes on an organized and cold aspect, a somber aspect that makes it the saddest of possible choices.

The truth is that physical love can be treated neither as an absolute end in itself nor as a simple means; it cannot justify an existence: but it can receive no outside justification. It means it must play an episodic and autonomous role in all human life. This means it must above all be free.

———

Love, then, is not what bourgeois optimism promises the young bride: the ideal held up to her is happiness, that is, a peaceful equilibrium within immanence and repetition. At certain prosperous and secure times, this ideal was that of the whole bourgeoisie and specifically of landed property owners; their aim was not the conquest of the future and the world but the peaceful conservation of the past, the status quo. A gilded mediocrity with neither passion nor ambition, days leading nowhere, repeating themselves indefinitely, a life that slips toward death without looking for answers, this is what the author of "Sonnet to Happiness" prescribes; this pseudo-wisdom loosely inspired by Epicurus and Zeno has lost currency today: to conserve and repeat the world as it is seems neither desirable nor possible. The male's vocation is action; he needs to produce, fight, create, progress, go beyond himself toward the totality of the universe and the infinity of the future; but traditional marriage does not invite woman to transcend herself with him; it confines her in immanence. She has no choice but to build a stable life where the present, prolonging the past, escapes the threats of tomorrow, that is, precisely to create a happiness. In the place of love, she will feel for her husband a tender and respectful sentiment called conjugal love; within the walls of her home she will be in charge of managing, she will enclose the world; she will perpetuate the human species into the future. Yet no existent ever renounces his transcendence, especially when he stubbornly disavows it. The bourgeois of yesterday thought that by conserving the established order, displaying its virtue by his prosperity, he was serving God, his country, a regime, a civilization: to be happy was to fulfill his function as man. For woman as well, the harmonious home life has to be transcended toward other ends: it is man who will act as intermediary between woman's individuality and the universe; it is he who will imbue her contingent facticity with human worth. Finding in his wife the force to undertake, to act, to fight, he justifies her: she has only to put her existence in his hands, and he will give it its meaning. This presupposes humble renunciation on her end; but she is rewarded because guided and protected by male force, she will escape original abandonment; she will become necessary. Queen of her hive, tranquilly resting on herself within her domain, but carried by man's mediation through the universe and limitless time, wife, mother, and mistress of the house, woman finds in marriage both the force to live and life's meaning. We must see how this ideal is expressed in reality.

The home has always been the material realization of the ideal of happiness, be it a cottage or a château; it embodies permanence and separation. Inside its walls, the family constitutes an isolated cell and affirms its identity beyond the passage of generations; the past, preserved in the form of furniture and ancestral portraits, prefigures a risk-free future; in the garden, seasons mark their reassuring cycle with edible vegetables; every year the same spring adorned with the same flowers promises the summer's immutable return and autumn's fruits, identical to those of every autumn: neither time nor space escapes into infinity, but instead quietly goes round and round. In every civilization founded on landed property, an abundant literature sings of the poetry and virtues of the home; in Henry Bordeaux's novel precisely titled *La maison* (The Home), the home encapsulates all the bourgeois values: faithfulness to the past, patience, economy, caution, love of family, of native soil, and so forth; the home's champions are often women, since it is their task to ensure the happiness of the familial group; as in the days when the *domina* sat in the atrium, their role is to be "mistress of the house." Today the home has lost its patriarchal splendor; for most men, it is simply a place to live, no longer overrun by memories of deceased generations and no longer imprisoning the centuries to come. But woman still tries to give her "interior" the meaning and value a true home possessed. In *Cannery Row*, Steinbeck describes a woman hobo determined to decorate with rugs and curtains the old abandoned boiler she lives in with her husband: he objects in vain that not having windows makes curtains useless.

This concern is specifically feminine. A normal man considers objects around him as instruments; he arranges them according to the purpose for which they are intended; his "order"—where woman will often only see disorder—is to have his cigarettes, his papers, and his tools within reach. Artists—sculptors and painters, among others—whose work it is to re-create the world through material, are completely insensitive to the surroundings in which they live. Rilke writes about Rodin:

> When I first came to Rodin . . . I knew that his house was nothing to him, a paltry little necessity perhaps, a roof for time of rain and sleep; and that it was no care to him and no weight upon his solitude and composure. Deep in himself he bore the darkness, shelter, and peace of a house, and he himself had become sky above it, and wood around it, and distance and great stream always flowing by.*

But to find a home in oneself, one must first have realized oneself in works or acts. Man has only a middling interest in his domestic interior because he has access to the entire universe and because he can affirm himself in his projects. Woman, instead, is locked into the conjugal community: she has to change this prison into a kingdom. Her attitude to her home is dictated by this same dialectic that generally defines her condition: she takes by becoming prey, she liberates herself by abdicating; by renouncing the world, she means to conquer a world.

She regrets closing the doors of her home behind herself; as a young girl, the whole world was her kingdom; the forests belonged to her. Now she is confined to a restricted space; Nature is reduced to the size of a geranium pot; walls block out the horizon. One of Virginia Woolf's heroines murmurs:

> Whether it is summer, whether it is winter, I no longer know by the moor grass, and the heath flower; only by the steam on the window-pane, or the frost on the window-pane . . . I, who used to walk

---

* Rilke to Lou Andreas-Salomé, August 8, 1903.—TRANS.

through beech woods noting the jay's feather turning blue as it falls,
past the shepherd and the tramp, . . . go from room to room with a
duster.[24]

But she is going to make every attempt to refuse this limitation. She
encloses faraway countries and past times within her four walls in the form
of more or less expensive earthly flora and fauna; she encloses her husband, who personifies human society for her, and the child who gives her
the whole future in a portable form. The home becomes the center of the
world and even its own one truth; as Bachelard appropriately notes, it is "a
sort of counter- or exclusionary universe";* refuge, retreat, grotto, womb,
it protects against outside dangers: it is this confused exteriority that
becomes unreal. Especially at evening time, when the shutters are closed,
woman feels like a queen; the light shed at noon by the universal sun disturbs her; at night she is no longer dispossessed, because she does away
with that which she does not possess; from under the lamp shade she sees a
light that is her own and that illuminates her abode alone: nothing else
exists. Another text by Virginia Woolf shows us reality concentrated in the
house, while the outside space collapses:

> The night was now shut off by panes of glass, which, far from
> giving any accurate view of the outside world, rippled it so strangely
> that here, inside the room, seemed to be order and dry land; there,
> outside, a reflection in which things wavered and vanished, waterily.†

Thanks to the velvets, silks, and china with which she surrounds herself, woman can in part assuage this grasping sensuality that her erotic life
cannot usually satisfy; she will also find in this decor an expression of her
personality; it is she who has chosen, made, and "hunted down" furniture
and knickknacks, who has aesthetically arranged them in a way where
symmetry is important; they reflect her individuality while bearing social
witness to her standard of living. Her home is thus her earthly lot, the
expression of her social worth, and her intimate truth. Because she *does*
nothing, she avidly seeks herself in what she *has*.

It is through housework that the wife comes to make her "nest" her

---

24. *The Waves.*
* *La terre et les rêveries du repos* (Earth and Reveries of Repose), trans. Kenneth Haltman.
—TRANS.
† *To the Lighthouse.*—TRANS.

own; this is why, even if she has "help," she insists on doing things herself; at least by watching over, controlling, and criticizing, she endeavors to make her servants' results her own. By administrating her home, she achieves her social justification; her job is also to oversee the food, clothing, and care of the familial society in general. Thus she too realizes herself as an activity. But, as we will see, it is an activity that brings her no escape from her immanence and allows her no individual affirmation of herself.

The poetry of housework has been highly praised. It is true that housework makes the woman grapple with matter, and she finds an intimacy in objects that is the revelation of being and that consequently enriches her. In *A la recherche de Marie* (*Marie*), Madeleine Bourdouxhe describes her heroine's pleasure in spreading the cleaning paste on her stove. In her fingertips she feels the freedom and power that the brilliant image from scrubbed cast iron reflects back to her:

> When she comes up from the cellar, she enjoys the weight of the
> full coal-buckets, even though they seem heavier with every step.
> She has always felt affection for simple things that have their own
> particular smell, their own particular roughness, and she's always
> known how to handle them. Without fear or hesitation her hands
> plunge into dead fires or into soapy water, they rub the rust off a
> piece of metal and grease it, spread polish, and after a meal, sweep
> the scraps from a table in one great circular movement. It's a perfect
> harmony, a mutual understanding between the palms of her hands
> and the objects they touch.

Numerous women writers have lovingly spoken of freshly ironed linens, of the whitening agents of soapy water, of white sheets, of shining copper. When the housewife cleans and polishes furniture, "dreams of saturating penetration nourish the gentle patience of the hand striving to bring out the beauty of the wood with wax," says Bachelard. Once the job is finished, the housewife experiences the joy of contemplation. But for the precious qualities to show themselves—the polish of a table, the shine of a chandelier, the icy whiteness and starch of the laundry—a negative action must first be applied; all foul causes must be expelled. There, writes Bachelard, is the essential reverie to which the housewife surrenders: the dream of active cleanliness, that is, cleanliness conquering dirt. He describes it this way:

> It would seem that in imagination the struggle for tidiness requires
> provocation. The imagination needs to work itself up into a cunning

rage. With a nasty grin and dirty greasy rag one smears the copper faucet with a thick paste of scouring powder. Bitterness and hostility build up in the worker's heart. Why does the chore have to be so foul? But the moment for the dry cloth arrives and, along with it, a lighter-hearted malice, vigorous and talkative: faucet, you'll soon be like a mirror; kettle, you'll soon be like a sun! In the end, when the copper shines and laughs with the churlishness of an amiable fellow, peace is made. The housewife contemplates her gleaming victories.[25]

Ponge has evoked the struggle, in the heart of the laundry woman, between uncleanliness and purity:

Whoever has not lived for at least one winter in the company of a wash boiler knows nothing of a certain order of highly touching qualities and emotions.*

It is necessary—wincing—to have heaved it, brimful with soiled fabrics, off the ground and carried it over to the stove—where one must then drag it in a particular way so as to sit it right on top of the burner.

Beneath it one needs to have stirred up the fire, to set the boiler in motion gradually, touched its warm or burning sides often; next listened to the deep internal hum, from that point onward to have lifted the lid several times to check the tension of the spurts and the regularity of the wettings.

Finally, it is necessary to have embraced it once again, boiling hot, so as to set it back down on the ground . . .

The wash boiler is so conceived that, filled with a heap of disgusting rags, the inner emotion, the boiling indignation it feels, conducted toward the higher part of its being, rains back down on this heap of disgusting rags that turns its stomach—and this virtually endlessly—and that the outcome is a purification . . .

True, the linens, when the boiler received them, had already been soaked free of the worst of their filth.

Nonetheless, it has an idea or a feeling of the diffuse dirtiness of things inside it, which by dint of emotion, seethings, and exertions, it manages to get the best of—to remove the spots from the fabrics:

---

25. *Earth and Reveries of Repose.*
* In French "wash boiler," or *lessiveuse,* is feminine, and where English uses the pronoun "it," French uses *elle,* that is, "she." Playing on this ambiguity throughout his text, Ponge gives the wash boiler a feminine identity and presence.—TRANS.

so that these, rinsed in a catastrophe of cool water, will appear white
to an extreme . . .

And here in effect the miracle takes place:

Thousands of white flags are all at once deployed—which mark
not a capitulation but a victory—and are perhaps not merely the
sign of the bodily cleanness of this place's inhabitants.[26]

These dialectics can give housework the charm of a game: the little girl
readily enjoys shining the silver, polishing doorknobs. But for a woman to
find positive satisfaction, she must devote her efforts to an interior she can
be proud of; if not, she will never know the pleasure of contemplation, the
only pleasure that can repay her efforts. An American reporter, who lived
several months among American Southern "poor whites," has described
the pathetic destiny of one of these women, overwhelmed with burdens,
who labored in vain to make a hovel livable.[27] She lived with her husband
and seven children in a wooden shack, the walls covered with soot, crawl-
ing with cockroaches; she had tried to "make the house pretty," in the main
room, the fireplace covered with bluish plaster, a table, and a few pictures
hanging on the wall suggested a sort of altar. But the hovel remained a
hovel, and Mrs. G. said with tears in her eyes, "Oh, I do *hate* this house *so
bad*! Seems like they ain't nothing in the whole world I can do to make it
pretty!" Legions of women have in common only endlessly recurrent
fatigue in a battle that never leads to victory. Even in the most privileged
cases, this victory is never final. Few tasks are more similar to the torment
of Sisyphus than those of the housewife; day after day, one must wash
dishes, dust furniture, mend clothes that will be dirty, dusty, and torn
again. The housewife wears herself out running on the spot; she does
nothing; she only perpetuates the present; she never gains the sense that she
is conquering a positive Good, but struggles indefinitely against Evil. It is a
struggle that begins again every day. We know the story of the valet who
despondently refused to polish his master's boots. "What's the point?" he
asked. "You have to begin again the next day." Many still unresigned
young girls share this discouragement. I recall an essay of a sixteen-year-
old student that opened with words like these: "Today is housecleaning
day. I hear the noise of the vacuum Mama walks through the living room. I
would like to run away. I swear when I grow up, there will never be a

---

26. "The Wash Boiler," in *Liasse* (Sheaf). [This passage translated by Beverley Bie Brahic.
—TRANS.]

27. James Agee, *Let Us Now Praise Famous Men.*

housecleaning day in my house." The child thinks of the future as an indefinite ascent toward some unidentified summit. Suddenly in the kitchen, where her mother is washing dishes, the little girl realizes that over the years, every afternoon at the same time, these hands have plunged into greasy water and wiped the china with a rough dish towel. And until death they will be subjected to these rites. Eat, sleep, clean . . . the years no longer reach toward the sky, they spread out identical and gray as a horizontal tablecloth; every day looks like the previous one; the present is eternal, useless, and hopeless. In the short story "La poussière" (Dust), Colette Audry subtly describes the sad futility of an activity that stubbornly resists time:

> The next day while cleaning the sofa with a horsehair brush, she picked up something that she first took for an old morsel of cotton or a big feather. But it was only a dust ball like those that form on high wardrobes that you forget to dust or behind furniture between the wall and the wood. She remained pensive before this curious substance. So here they were living in these rooms for eight or ten weeks and already, in spite of Juliette's vigilance, a dust ball had had the time to take form, to grow, crouching in a shadow like those gray beasts that frightened her when she was small. A fine ash of dust proclaims negligence, the beginning of carelessness, it's the impalpable sediment from the air we breathe, clothes that flutter, from the wind coming through open windows; but this tuft already represented a second stage of dust, triumphant dust, a thickening that takes shape and from sediment becomes waste. It was almost pretty to look at, transparent and light like bramble puffs, but more drab . . .
>
> The dust had beaten out all the world's vacuum power. It had taken over the world and the vacuum cleaner was no more than a witness object destined to show everything the human race was capable of ruining in work, matter, and ingenuity in struggling against all-powerful dirt. It was waste made instrument . . .
>
> It was their life together that was the cause of everything, their little meals that left skin peelings, dust from both of them that mingled everywhere . . . Every couple secretes these little bits of litter that must be destroyed to make space for new ones . . . What a life one spends—and to be able to go out with a fresh little shirt, attractive to passersby, so your engineer husband looks good in his life. Mantras replayed in Marguerite's head: take care of the wooden

floors . . . for the care of brass, use . . . she was in charge of the care of two ordinary beings for the rest of their days.[28]

Washing, ironing, sweeping, routing out tufts of dust in the dark places behind the wardrobe, this is holding away death but also refusing life: for in one movement time is created and destroyed; the housewife only grasps the negative aspect of it. Hers is the attitude of a Manichaean. The essence of Manichaeism is not only to recognize two principles, one good and one evil: it is also to posit that good is attained by the abolition of evil and not by a positive movement; in this sense, Christianity is hardly Manichaean in spite of the existence of the devil, because it is in devoting oneself to God that one best fights the devil and not in trying to conquer him. All doctrines of transcendence and freedom subordinate the defeat of evil to progress toward good. But the wife is not called to build a better world; the house, the bedroom, the dirty laundry, the wooden floors, are fixed things: she can do no more than rout out indefinitely the foul causes that creep in; she attacks the dust, stains, mud, and filth; she fights sin, she fights with Satan. But it is a sad destiny to have to repel an enemy without respite instead of being turned toward positive aims; the housewife often submits to it in rage. Bachelard uses the word "malice" for it; psychoanalysts have written about it. For them, housekeeping mania is a form of sadomasochism; it is characteristic of mania and vice to make freedom want what it does not want; because the maniacal housewife detests having negativity, dirt, and evil as her lot, she furiously pursues dust, accepting a condition that revolts her. She attacks life itself through the rubbish left from any living growth. Whenever a living being enters her sphere, her eye shines with a wicked fire. "Wipe your feet; don't mess up everything; don't touch that." She would like to stop everyone from breathing: the least breath is a threat. Every movement threatens her with more thankless work: a child's somersault is a tear to sew up. Seeing life as a promise of decomposition demanding more endless work, she loses her joie de vivre; her eyes sharpen, her face looks preoccupied and serious, always on guard; she protects herself through prudence and avarice. She closes the windows because sun would bring in insects, germs, and dust; besides, the sun eats away at the silk wall coverings; the antique armchairs are hidden under loose covers and embalmed in mothballs: light would fade them. She does not even care to let her visitors see these treasures: admiration sullies. This defiance turns to bitterness and

---

28. *On joue perdant* (Playing a Losing Game).

causes hostility to everything that lives. In the provinces, some bourgeois women have been known to put on white gloves to make sure no invisible dust remains on the furniture: these were the kinds of women the Papin sisters murdered several years ago; their hatred of dirt was inseparable from their hatred of their servants, of the world, and of each other.

Few women choose such a gloomy vice when they are young. Those who generously love life are protected from it. Colette tells us about Sido:

> The fact is that, though she was active and always on the go, she was not a sedulous housewife. She was clean and tidy, fastidious even, but without a trace of that solitary, maniacal spirit that counts napkins, lumps of sugar, and full bottles. With a flannel in her hands, and one eye on the servant dawdling over her window-cleaning and smiling at the man next door, she would utter nervous exclamations like impatient cries for freedom.
> "When I take a lot of time and trouble wiping my Chinese cups," she would say, "I can actually feel myself getting older."
> But she always persevered loyally until the job was finished. Then off she would go, down the two steps that led into the garden, and at once her resentment and her nervous exasperation subsided.*

It is in this nervousness and resentment that frigid or frustrated women, old maids, desperate housewives, and those condemned by their husbands to a solitary and empty existence are satisfied. I knew, among others, an elderly woman who woke up every morning at five o'clock to inspect the wardrobes and begin rearranging them; it seems that at twenty she was gay and coquettish; closed up in her isolated estate, with a husband who neglected her and a single child, she took to arranging as others take to drink. For Élise in *The Bold Chronicle of a Strange Marriage*, the taste for housework stems from the exasperated desire to rule the universe, from a living exuberance, and from a will for domination, which, for lack of an outlet, leads nowhere; it is also a challenge to time, the universe, life, men, and everything that exists:

> Since dinner from nine o'clock onwards, she has been doing the washing. It is midnight. I have been dozing, but her fortitude annoys me because it insults my rest by making it look like laziness.
> *Élise:* "If you want things to be clean, you shouldn't be afraid of getting your hands dirty first."

---

* *Sido.*—TRANS.

And the house will soon be so spotless that we shall hardly dare live in it. There are divans, but you are expected to lie down beside them on the parquet floor. The cushions are too clean. You are afraid to soil or crumple them by putting your head or your feet on them, and every time I step on a carpet, I am followed with a carpet sweeper to remove the marks that I've made.

In the evening:
"It's done."
What is the point of her moving every object and every piece of furniture and going over all the floors, the walls, and the ceilings from the time she gets up till the time she goes to bed?
For the moment, it is the housewife who is uppermost in her. Once she has dusted the insides of her cupboards, she dusts the geraniums on the windowsills.

His mother: Élise always keeps so busy she does not notice she is alive.

Housework in fact allows the woman an indefinite escape far from herself. Chardonne rightly remarks:

Here is a meticulous and disordered task, with neither stops nor limits. In the home, a woman certain to please quickly reaches her breaking point, a state of distraction and mental void that effaces her.*

This escape, this sadomasochism in which woman persists against both objects and self, is often precisely sexual. "The kind of housecleaning that calls for bodily gymnastics amounts to a bordello for women," says Violette Leduc.[29] It is striking that the taste for cleanliness is of utmost importance in Holland where women are cold, and in puritanical civilizations that juxtapose the joys of the flesh with an ideal of order and purity. If the Mediterranean Midi lives in joyous filth, it is not only because water is scarce there: love of the flesh and its animality is conducive to tolerating human odor, squalor, and even vermin.
Preparing meals is more positive work and often more enjoyable than

---

* Jacques Chardonne, *L'épithalame* (*Epithalamium*).—TRANS.
29. *L'affamée* (The Starved Woman).

cleaning. First of all, it involves going to the market, which is for many housewives the best time of the day. The loneliness of the household weighs on the woman just as routine tasks leave her head empty. She is happy when, in Midi towns, she can sew, wash, and peel vegetables while chatting on her doorstep; fetching water from the river is a grand adventure for half-cloistered Muslim women: I saw a little village in Kabyle where the women tore down the fountain an official had built on the plaza; going down every morning to the wadi flowing at the foot of the hill was their only distraction. All the time they are doing their marketing, waiting in lines, in shops, on street corners, they talk about things that affirm their "homemaking worth" from which each one draws the sense of her own importance; they feel part of a community that—for an instant—is opposed to the society of men as the essential to the inessential. But above all, making a purchase is a profound pleasure: it is a discovery, almost an invention. Gide observes in his *Journals* that the Muslims, unfamiliar with games of chance, have replaced them with the discovery of hidden treasures; this is the poetry and adventure of mercantile civilizations. The housewife is oblivious to the gratuitousness of games: but a good firm cabbage and a ripe Camembert are treasures that must be subtly discovered in spite of the cunning shopkeeper; between seller and buyer, relations of dealing and ruse are established: for her, winning means getting the best goods for the lowest price; concern for a restricted budget is not enough to explain the extreme importance given to being economical: winning the game is what counts. When she suspiciously inspects the stalls, the housewife is queen; the world, with its riches and traps, is at her feet, for her taking. She tastes a fleeting triumph when she empties her shopping basket on the table. She puts her canned food and nonperishables in the larder, guarding her against the future, and she contemplates with satisfaction the raw vegetables and meats she is about to submit to her power.

Gas and electricity have killed the magic of fire; but in the countryside, many women still know the joys of kindling live flames from inert wood. With the fire lit, the woman changes into a sorceress. With a simple flip of the hand—beating the eggs or kneading the dough—or by the magic of fire, she effects transmutations of substances; matter becomes food. Colette, again, describes the enchantment of this alchemy:

> All is mystery, magic, spell, all that takes place between the time
> the casserole, kettle, stewpot, and their contents are put on the
> fire and the moment of sweet anxiety, of voluptuous expectation,
> when the dish is brought steaming to the table and its headdress
> removed.

Among other things, she lovingly depicts the metamorphoses that take place in the secret of hot ashes:

> Wood ash does a flavorsome job of cooking whatever it is given to cook. The apple, the pear nestling among the ashes, come out wrinkled and smoke-tanned but soft under the skin like a mole's belly, and however *bonne femme* the apple cooked in the stove might be, it is a far cry from this jam enclosed in its original robe, thick with flavor, and—if you go about it right—has oozed but a single tear of honey . . . a tall three-legged cauldron held sifted ash that never saw the fire. But stuffed with potatoes lying side by side without touching, its black claws planted in the embers, the cauldron laid tubers for us white as snow, burning hot, flaky.*

Women writers have particularly celebrated the poetry of making preserves: it is a grand undertaking, marrying pure solid sugar and the soft pulp of fruit in a copper preserving pan; foaming, viscous, boiling, the substance being made is dangerous: it is a bubbling lava the housewife proudly captures and pours into jars. When she covers them with parchment paper and inscribes the date of her victory, it is a triumph over time itself: she has captured the passage of time in the snare of sugar; she has put life in jars. Cooking is more than penetrating and revealing the intimacy of substances. It reshapes and re-creates them. In working the dough, she experiences her power. "The hand as well as the eye has its reveries and poetry," says Bachelard.[30] And he speaks of this "suppleness that fills one's hands, rebounding endlessly from matter to hand and from hand to matter." The hand of the cook who kneads is a "gratified hand," and cooking lends the dough a new value still. "Cooking is thus a great material transformation from whiteness to golden brown, from dough to crust."[31] Women can find a special satisfaction in a successful cake or a flaky pastry because not everyone can do it: it takes a gift. "Nothing is more complicated than the art of pastry," writes Michelet. "Nothing proceeds less according to rule, or is less dependent on education. One must be *born* with it. It is wholly a gift of the mother."

---

* Passage translated by Nina de Voogd Fuller.—TRANS.
30. Gaston Bachelard, *La terre et les rêveries de la volonté* (*Earth and Reveries of Will*).
31. Ibid.

Here again, it is clear that the little girl passionately enjoys imitating her female elders: with chalk and grass she plays at make-believe; she is happier still when she has a real little oven to play with, or when her mother lets her come into the kitchen and roll out the pastry with her palms or cut the hot burning caramel. But this is like housework: repetition soon dispels these pleasures. For Indians who get their nourishment essentially from tortillas, the women spend half their days kneading, cooking, reheating, and kneading again identical tortillas, under every roof, identical through-out the centuries: they are hardly sensitive to the magic of the oven. It is not possible to transform marketing into a treasure hunt every day, nor to delight in a shiny water tap. Women and men writers can lyrically exalt these triumphs because they never or rarely do housework. Done every day, this work becomes monotonous and mechanical; it is laden with wait-ing: waiting for the water to boil, for the roast to be cooked just right, for the laundry to dry; even if different tasks are well organized, there are long moments of passivity and emptiness; most of the time, they are accom-plished in boredom; between present life and the life of tomorrow, they are but an inessential intermediary. If the individual who executes them is him-self a producer or creator, they are integrated into his existence as naturally as body functions; this is why everyday chores seem less dismal when per-formed by men; they represent for them only a negative and contingent moment they hurry to escape. But what makes the lot of the wife-servant ungratifying is the division of labor that dooms her wholly to the general and inessential; home and food are useful for life but do not confer any meaning on it: the housekeeper's immediate goals are only means, not real ends, and they reflect no more than anonymous projects. It is understand-able that to give meaning to her work, she endeavors to give it her individ-uality and to attach an absolute value to the results obtained; she has her rituals, her superstitions, she has her ways of setting the table, arranging the living room, mending, cooking a dish; she persuades herself that in her place, no one could make such a good roast, or do the polishing as well; if her husband or daughter wants to help her or tries to do without her, she grabs the needle or the broom. "You don't know how to sew a button." Dorothy Parker described with a pitying irony the dismay of a young woman convinced she should bring a personal note to the arrangement of her house, but not knowing how:

> Mrs. Ernest Weldon wandered about the orderly living-room, giving it some of those little feminine touches. She was not espe-cially good as a touch-giver. The idea was pretty, and appealing to

482 | LIVED EXPERIENCE

her. Before she was married, she had dreamed of herself as moving softly about her new dwelling, deftly moving a vase here or straightening a flower there, and thus transforming it from a house to a home. Even now, after seven years of marriage, she liked to picture herself in the gracious act.

But, though she conscientiously made a try at it every night as soon as the rose-shaded lamps were lit, she was always a bit bewildered as to how one went about performing those tiny miracles that make all the difference in the world to a room . . . Touch-giving was a wife's job. And Mrs. Weldon was not one to shirk the business she had entered.

With an almost pitiable air of uncertainty, she strayed over to the mantel, lifted a small Japanese vase, and stood with it in her hand, gazing helplessly around the room . . .

Then she stepped back, and surveyed her innovations. It was amazing how little difference they made to the room.[32]

The wife wastes a great deal of time and effort searching for originality or her individual perfection; this gives her work the characteristic of a "meticulous and disordered task, with neither stops nor limits," as Chardonne points out, which makes it so difficult to measure the burden that household cares really mean. According to a recent report (published in 1947 by the newspaper *Combat*, written by C. Hébert), married women devote about three hours and forty-five minutes to housework (cleaning, food shopping, and so on) each working day, and eight hours on the day of rest, that is thirty hours a week, which corresponds to three-quarters of the working week of a woman worker or employee; this is enormous if it is added to a paid job; it is not much if the wife has nothing else to do (especially as woman workers and employees lose time traveling that has no equivalent here). Caring for children, if there are many, considerably adds to the wife's fatigue: a poor mother depletes her strength every one of her hectic days. By contrast, bourgeois women who have help are almost idle; and the ransom of this leisure is boredom. Because they are bored, many complicate and endlessly multiply their duties so that they become more stressful than a skilled job. A woman friend who had gone through nervous breakdowns told me that when she was in good health, she took care of her house almost without thinking of it, leaving her time for much more chal-

---

32. "Too Bad."

lenging occupations; when neurasthenia prevented her from giving herself to other jobs, she allowed herself to be swallowed up by household cares, devoting whole days to them without managing to finish.

The saddest thing is that this work does not even result in a lasting creation. Woman is tempted—all the more as she is so attentive to it—to consider her work as an end in itself. Contemplating the cake she takes out of the oven, she sighs: what a pity to eat it! What a pity husband and children drag their muddy feet on the waxed floor. As soon as things are used, they are dirtied or destroyed: she is tempted, as we have already seen, to withdraw them from being used; she keeps the jam until mold invades it; she locks the living room doors. But time cannot be stopped; supplies attract rats; worms start their work. Covers, curtains, and clothes are eaten by moths: the world is not a dream carved in stone, it is made of a suspicious-looking substance threatened by decomposition; edible stuff is as questionable as Dalí's meat monsters: it seemed inert and inorganic but hidden larvae have metamorphosed it into corpses. The housewife who alienates herself in things depends, like things, on the whole world: linens turn gray, the roast burns, china breaks; these are absolute disasters because when things disappear, they disappear irremediably. It is impossible to obtain permanence and security through them. Wars with their looting and bombs threaten wardrobes and the home.

Thus, the product of housework has to be consumed; constant renunciation is demanded of the wife whose work is finished only with its destruction. For her to consent to it without regret, these small holocausts must spark some joy or pleasure somewhere. But as housework is spent in maintaining the status quo, the husband—when he comes home—notices disorder and negligence but takes order and neatness for granted. He attaches more positive importance to a well-prepared meal. The triumphant moment of the cook is when she places a successful dish on the table: husband and children welcome it warmly, not only with words, but also by consuming it joyously. Culinary alchemy continues with the food becoming chyle and blood. Taking care of a body is of more concrete interest, is more vital than care of a parquet floor; the cook's effort transcends toward the future in an obvious way. However, while it is less futile to depend on an outside freedom than to alienate oneself in things, it is no less dangerous. It is only in the guests' mouths that the cook's work finds its truth; she needs their approval; she demands that they appreciate her dishes, that they take more; she is irritated if they are no longer hungry: to the point that one does not know if the fried potatoes are destined for the husband or the husband for the fried potatoes. This ambiguity is found in the housewife's whole attitude: she keeps the house for her husband; but she also insists on his devoting all the money he earns to buying furniture or a refrigerator. She wants to make him happy: but she approves of his activities only if they fit into the framework of the happiness she has constructed.

There have been periods when these claims were generally satisfied: periods when happiness was also the man's ideal, when he was primarily attached to his house and family, and when the children themselves chose to define themselves by family, their traditions, and their past. Then she who ruled the home, who presided over the table, was recognized as sovereign; she still plays this glorious role as wife in relation to some landowners, or some rich farmers who occasionally still perpetuate the patriarchal civilization. But on the whole, marriage today is the survival of obsolete customs with the wife's situation much more thankless than before since she still has the same duties while these no longer confer the same rights; she has the same chores without the rewards or honor from doing them. Today, man marries to anchor himself in immanence but not to confine himself in it; he wants a home but also to remain free to escape from it; he settles down, but he often remains a vagabond in his heart; he does not scorn happiness, but he does not make it an end in itself; repetition bores him; he seeks novelty, risk, resistance to overcome, camaraderie, friendships that wrest him from the solitude of the couple. Children even more than husbands want to go beyond the home's limits: their life is elsewhere, in front of them; the child always desires what is other. The wife tries to constitute a universe of permanence and continuity: husband and children want to go beyond the situation she creates and which for them is only a given. Thus, if she is loath to admit the precariousness of the activities to which her whole life is devoted, she is led to impose her services by force: from mother and housewife she becomes cruel mother and shrew.

So the wife's work within the home does not grant her autonomy; it is not directly useful to the group, it does not open onto the future, it does not produce anything. It becomes meaningful and dignified only if it is integrated into existences that go beyond themselves, toward the society in production or action: far from enfranchising the matron, it makes her dependent on her husband and children; she justifies her existence through them: she is no more than an inessential mediation in their lives. That the civil code erased "obedience" from her duties changes nothing in her situation; her situation is not based on what the couple wants but on the very structure of the conjugal community. The wife is not allowed to *do* any positive work and consequently to have herself known as a complete person. Regardless of how well she is respected, she is subjugated, secondary, parasitic. The heavy curse weighing on her is that the very meaning of her existence is not in her hands. This is the reason the successes and failures of her conjugal life have much more importance for her than for the man: he is a citizen, a producer, before being a husband; she is above all, and often exclusively, a wife; her work does not extract her from her condition; it is from her condition, on the contrary, that her work derives its price or not. Loving, generously devoted, she will carry out her tasks joyously; these chores will seem insipid to her if she accomplishes them with resentment. They will never play more than an inessential role in her destiny; in the misadventures of conjugal life they will be of no help. We thus have to see how this condition is concretely lived, one that is essentially defined by bed "service" and housework "service" in which the wife finds her dignity only in accepting her vassalage.

———

It is a crisis that pushes the young girl from childhood to adolescence; an even more acute crisis thrusts her into adult life. The anxieties inherent in all passages from one condition to another are superimposed on those that a somewhat brusque sexual initiation provokes in a woman. Nietzsche writes:

> And then to be hurled, as by a gruesome lightning bolt, into reality and knowledge, by marriage . . . To catch love and shame in a contradiction and to be forced to experience at the same time delight, surrender, duty, pity, terror, and who knows what else, in the face of the unexpected neighborliness of god and beast! . . . Thus a psychic knot has been tied that may have no equal.*

The excitement that surrounded the traditional "honeymoon" was meant in part to hide this confusion: thrown outside her everyday world for a few weeks, all connections with society being temporarily broken, the young woman was no longer situated in space, in time, in reality.[33] But sooner or later she has to take her place there again; and she finds herself in her new home, but never without apprehension. Her ties with her father's home are much stronger than her ties with the young man's. Tearing oneself away from one's family is a definitive weaning: this is when she experiences the anguish of abandon and the giddiness of freedom. The break is more or less painful, depending on the case; if she has already broken the

———

* *The Gay Science.*—TRANS.

33. Fin de siècle literature often has defloration take place in the sleeping car, which is a way of placing it "nowhere."

ties connecting her to her father, brothers and sisters, and above all her mother, she can leave painlessly; if, still dominated by them, she can practically remain in their protection, she will be less affected by her change in condition; but ordinarily, even if she wanted to escape from the paternal household, she feels disconcerted when she is separated from the little society in which she was integrated, cut off from her past, her child's universe with its familiar principles and unquestioned values. Only an ardent and full erotic life could make her bathe again in the peace of immanence; but usually she is at first more upset than fulfilled; that sexual initiation is more or less successful simply adds to her confusion. The day after her wedding finds many of the same reactions she had on her first menstruation: she often experiences disgust at this supreme revelation of her femininity, horror at the idea that this experience will be renewed. She also feels the bitter disappointment of the day after; once she began menstruating, the girl sadly realized she was not an adult; deflowered, now the young woman is an adult, and the last step is taken: Now what? This worrying disappointment is moreover linked as much to marriage itself as it is to defloration: a woman who had already "known" her fiancé, or who had "known" other men, but for whom marriage represents the full accession to adult life will often have the same reaction. Living the beginning of an enterprise is exalting; but nothing is more depressing than discovering a destiny over which one no longer has a hold. From this definitive, immutable background, freedom emerges with the most intolerable gratuitousness. Previously the girl, sheltered by her parents' authority, made use of her freedom in revolt and hope; she used it to refuse and go beyond a condition in which she nevertheless found security; her own transcendence toward marriage took place from within the warmth of the family; now she *is* married, there is no *other* future in front of her. The doors of home are closed around her: of all the earth, this will be her portion. She knows exactly what tasks lie ahead of her: the same as her mother's. Day after day, the same rites will be repeated. When she was a girl, her hands were empty: in hope, in dreams, she possessed everything. Now she has acquired a share of the world and she thinks in anguish: there is nothing more than this, forever. Forever this husband, this home. She has nothing more to expect, nothing more to want. However, she is afraid of her new responsibilities. Even if her husband is older and has authority, the fact that she has sexual relations with him removes some of his prestige: he cannot replace a father, and even less a mother, and he cannot give her her freedom. In the solitude of the new home, tied to a man who is more or less a stranger, no longer child but wife, and destined to become mother in turn, she feels numb; definitively removed from her mother's breast, lost in the middle of a world to which no aim calls her, abandoned in an icy present, she discovers the boredom and blandness of pure facticity. This is the distress so stunningly expressed in the young countess Tolstoy's diary;* she enthusiastically gave her hand to the great writer she admired; after the passionate embraces she submitted to on the wooden balcony at Yasnaya Polyana, she found herself disgusted by carnal love, far from her family, cut off from her past, at the side of a man to whom she had been engaged for one week, someone who was seventeen years her senior, with a totally foreign past and interests; everything seems empty, icy to her; her life is no more than an eternal sleep. Her diary account of the first years of her marriage must be quoted.

On September 23, 1862, Sophia gets married and leaves her family in the evening:

> A difficult and painful feeling gripped my throat and held me tight. I then felt that the time had come to leave forever my family and all those I loved deeply and with whom I had always lived . . . The farewells began and were ghastly . . . Now the last minutes. I had intentionally reserved the farewells to my mother till the end . . . When I pulled myself from her embrace and without turning around I went to take my place in the car, she uttered a heart-rending cry I have never forgotten all my life. Autumn rain did not cease to fall . . . Huddled in my corner, overwhelmed with fatigue and sorrow, I let my tears flow. Leon Nikolaivitch seemed very surprised, even discontent . . . When we left the city, I felt in the depths a sentiment of fear . . . The darkness oppressed me. We barely said anything to each other until the first stop, Birioulev, if I am not mistaken. I remember that Leon Nikolaivitch was very tender and attentive to my every need. At Birioulev, we were given the rooms said to be for the tsar, big rooms with furniture upholstered in red rep that was not very welcoming. We were brought the samovar. Cuddled up in a corner of the couch, I kept silent as a condemned person. "Well!" said Leon Nikolaivitch to me, "if you did the honors." I obeyed and served the tea. I was upset and could not free myself from a kind of fear. I did not dare address Leon Nikolaivitch in the familiar form and avoided calling him by his name. For a long time I continued to use the formal form.

---

* *Diaries of Sophia Tolstoy.*—TRANS.

Twenty-four hours later, they arrive at Yasnaya Polyana. She resumes her diary again on October 8. She feels anxious. She suffers from the fact that her husband has a past:

> I always dreamt of the man I would love as a completely whole, new *pure*, person . . . in these childish dreams, which I still find hard to give up . . . When he kisses me I am always thinking, "I am not the first woman he has loved."

The following day she notes:

> I feel downcast all the same. I had such a depressing dream last night, and it is weighing on me, although I do not remember it in detail. I thought of Maman today and grew dreadfully sad . . . I seem to be asleep all the time and unable to wake up . . . Something is weighing on me. I keep thinking that at any moment I might die. It is so strange to be thinking such things now that I have a husband. I can hear him in there sleeping. I am frightened of being on my own. He will not let me go into his room, which makes me very sad. All physical things disgust him.

> October 11: I am terribly, terribly sad, and withdrawing further and further into myself. My husband is ill and out of sorts and doesn't love me. I expected this, yet I could never have imagined it would be so terrible. Why do people always think I am so happy? What no one seems to realize is that I cannot create happiness, either for him or for myself. Before when I was feeling miserable I would ask myself, "What is the use of living when you make others unhappy and yourself wretched?" This thought keeps recurring to me now, and I am terrified. He grows colder and colder every day, while I, on the contrary, love him more and more . . . I keep thinking of my own family and how happy my life was with them; now, my God, it breaks my heart to think that nobody loves me. Darling Mother, Tanya—what wonderful people they were, why did I ever leave them? . . . it gnaws at my conscience . . . Lyovochka is a wonderful man . . . Now I have lost everything I once possessed, all my energy for work, life, and household tasks has been wasted. Now I want only to sit in silence all day, doing nothing but think bitter thoughts. I wanted to do some work, but could not; . . . I long to play the piano but it is so awkward in this place . . . He suggested today that I stay at home while he went off to Nikolskoe. I should have agreed and set him free from my presence, but I simply could not . . . Poor

man, he is always looking for something to divert him and take him away from me. What is the point of living?

November 13: It is true, I cannot find anything to occupy me. He is fortunate because he is talented and clever. I am neither . . . It is not difficult to find work, there is plenty to do, but first you have to enjoy such petty household tasks as breeding hens, tinkling on the piano, reading a lot of fourth-rate books and precious good ones, and pickling cucumbers. I am asleep now, since nothing brings me any excitement or joy—neither the trip to Moscow nor the thought of the baby. I wish I could take some remedy to refresh me and wake me up . . .

It is terrible to be alone. I am not used to it. There was so much life and love at home, and it's so lifeless here without him. He is almost always on his own . . . He . . . finds pleasure not in the company of those close to him, as I do, but in his work . . . he never had a family.

November 23: . . . Of course I am idle at present, but I am not so by nature; I simply have not discovered anything I could do . . . Sometimes I long to break free of his rather oppressive influence and stop worrying about him, but I cannot. I find his influence oppressive because I have begun thinking his thoughts and seeing with his eyes, trying to become like him, and losing myself. And I have changed too, which makes it even harder for me.

April 1: I have a very great misfortune: I have no inner resources to draw on . . . Lyova has his work and the estate to think about while I have nothing . . . What am I good for? I would like to *do* more, something *real*. At this wonderful time of year, I always used to long for things, aspire to things, dream about God knows what. But I no longer need anything, no longer have those foolish aspirations, for I know instinctively that I have all I need now and there is nothing left to strive for . . . Everything seems stupid now and I get irritable.

April 20:* . . . Lyova ignores me more and more. The physical side of love is very important for him. This is terrible, for me it is quite the opposite.

It is clear, during these first six months, that the young woman is suffering from her separation from her family, from solitude, and from the

---

* Discrepancy between the French and the English translations. In the English text of Tolstoy's diary the date is given as April 29.—TRANS.

definitive turn her destiny has taken; she detests her physical relations with her husband, and she is bored. This is the same ennui Colette's mother feels to the point of tears after the first marriage her brothers imposed on her:

> So she left the cosy Belgian house, the cellar-kitchen that smelled of gas, warm bread and coffee; she left her piano, her violin, the big Salvator Rosa she had inherited from her father, the tobacco jar and the fine long-stemmed clay pipes, the coke braziers, the books that lay open and the crumpled newspapers, and as a new bride entered the house with its flight of steps, isolated by the harsh winter of the forest lands all around . . . Here she found, to her surprise, a white and gold living room on the ground floor, but a first floor with barely even rough-cast walls, as abandoned as a loft . . . the bed-rooms were icy-cold and prompted no thoughts of either love or sweet sleep . . . Sido, who longed for friends and an innocent and cheerful social life, found on her estate only servants, cunning farmers . . . She filled the big house with flowers, had the dark kitchen whitewashed, oversaw in person the preparation of the Flemish dishes, kneaded cakes with raisins and looked forward to having her first child. The savage would smile at her between two outings and then set off once more . . . When she had exhausted her tasty recipes, her patience and her furniture polish, Sido—who had grown thin with loneliness—started to cry.[34]

In *Lettres à Françoise mariée* (Letters to Françoise, Married), Marcel Prévost describes the young woman's dismay upon her return from her honeymoon:

> She thinks of her mother's apartment with its Napoleon III and MacMahon furniture, its plush velvet, its wardrobes in black plum wood, everything she judged so old-fashioned, so ridiculous . . . In one instant all of that is evoked in her memory as a real haven, a true *nest*, the nest where she was watched over with disinterested tender-ness, sheltered from all storms and danger. This apartment with its new-carpet smell, its unadorned windows, the chairs in disarray, its whole air of improvisation and haste, no; it is not a nest. It is only

---

34. *Claudine's House.*

the place of the nest that has to be built . . . she suddenly felt horribly sad, as if she had been abandoned in a desert.

This distress is what often causes long depressions and various psychoses in the young woman. In particular, in the guise of different psychasthenic obsessions, she feels the giddiness of her empty freedom; she develops, for example, fantasies of prostitution we have already seen in young girls. Pierre Janet cites the case of a young bride who could not stand being alone in her apartment because she was tempted to go to the window and wink at passersby.[35] Others remain abulic faced with a universe that "no longer seems real," peopled only with ghosts and painted cardboard sets. There are those who try to refuse their adulthood, who will obstinately persist in refusing it their whole lives, like another patient whom Janet designates with the initials Qi:

> Qi, a thirty-six-year-old woman, is obsessed by the idea that she is a little ten- to twelve-year-old girl; especially when she is alone, she lets herself jump, laugh, dance; she lets her hair down, lets it loose on her shoulders, sometimes cuts it in places. She would like to lose herself completely in this dream of being a child: It is so unfortunate that she cannot play hide-and-seek, play tricks . . . in front of everyone . . . "I would like people to think I am nice, I am afraid of being the ugly duckling, I would like to be liked, talked to, petted, to be constantly told that I am loved as one loves little children . . . A child is loved for his mischievousness, for his good little heart, for his kindness, and what is asked of him in return? To love you, nothing more. That is what is good, but I cannot say that to my husband, he would not understand me. Look, I would so much like to be a little girl, have a father or a mother who would take me on their lap, caress my hair . . , but no, I am Madame, a mother; I have to keep the home, be serious, think on my own, oh, what a life!"[36]

Marriage is often a crisis for man as well: the proof is that many masculine psychoses develop during the engagement period or the early period of conjugal life. Less attached to his family than his sisters are, the young man

---

35. *Obsessions and Psychasthenia.*
36. Ibid.

belongs to some group: a special school, a university, a guild, a team, something that protects him from loneliness; he leaves it behind to begin his real existence as an adult; he is apprehensive of his future solitude, and it is often to exorcise it that he gets married. But he is fooled by the illusion maintained by the whole community that depicts the couple as a "conjugal *society*." Except in the brief fire of a passionate affair, two individuals cannot form a world that protects each of them against the world: this is what they both feel the day after the wedding. The wife, soon familiar, subjugated, does not obstruct her husband's freedom: she is a burden, not an alibi; she does not free him from the weight of his responsibilities, but on the contrary she exacerbates them. The difference of the sexes often means differences in age, education, and situation that do not bring about any real understanding: familiar, the spouses are still strangers. Previously, there was often a real chasm between them: the young girl, raised in a state of ignorance and innocence, had no "past," while her fiancé had "lived"; it was up to him to initiate her into the reality of life. Some males feel flattered by this delicate role; more lucid, they warily measure the distance that separates them from their future companion. In her novel *The Age of Innocence*, Edith Wharton describes the scruples of a young American of 1870 concerning the woman destined for him:

> With a new sense of awe he looked at the frank forehead, serious eyes and gay innocent mouth of the young creature whose soul's custodian he was to be. That terrifying product of the social system he belonged to and believed in, the young girl who knew nothing and expected everything, looked back at him like a stranger . . . What could he and she really know of each other, since it was his duty, as a "decent" fellow, to conceal his past from her, and hers, as a marriageable girl, to have no past to conceal? . . . The young girl who was the centre of this elaborate system of mystification remained the more inscrutable for her very frankness and assurance. She was frank, poor darling, because she had nothing to conceal, assured because she knew of nothing to be on her guard against; and with no better preparation than this, she was to be plunged overnight into what people evasively called "the facts of life" . . . But when he had gone the brief round of her he returned discouraged by the thought that all this frankness and innocence were only an artificial product . . . so cunningly manufactured by a conspiracy of mothers and aunts and grandmothers and long-dead ancestresses, because it was supposed to be what he wanted, what he had a right to, in order

that he might exercise his lordly pleasure in smashing it like an image made of snow.

Today, the gap is not as wide because the young girl is a less artificial being; she is better informed, better armed for life. But she is often much younger than her husband. The importance of this point has not been emphasized enough; the consequences of an unequal maturity are often taken as differences of sex; in many cases the wife is a child not because she is a woman but because she is in fact very young. The seriousness of her husband and his friends overwhelms her. Sophia Tolstoy wrote about one year after her wedding day:

> He is old and self-absorbed, whereas I feel young and long to do something wild. I'd like to turn somersaults instead of going to bed. But with whom?
> Old age hovers over me; everything here is old. I try to suppress all youthful feelings, for they would seem odd and out of place in this somber environment.*

As for the husband, he sees a "baby" in his wife; for him she is not the companion he expected, and he makes her feel it; she is humiliated by it. No doubt she likes finding a guide when she leaves her father's home, but she also wants to be seen as a "grown-up"; she wants to remain a child, she wants to become a woman; her older spouse can never treat her in a way that totally satisfies her.

Even if their age difference is slight, the fact remains that the young woman and young man have generally been brought up very differently; she is the product of a feminine universe where she was inculcated with feminine sagacity and respect for feminine values, whereas he is imbued with the male ethic. It is often very difficult for them to understand each other, and conflicts soon arise.

Because marriage usually subordinates the wife to the husband, the intensity of the problem of conjugal relations rests mainly on her. The paradox of marriage is that it brings into play an erotic function as well as a social one: this ambivalence is reflected in the figure the husband presents to the young wife. He is a demigod endowed with virile prestige and destined to replace her father: protector, overseer, tutor, guide; the wife has to thrive in his shadow; he is the holder of values, the guarantor of truth, the

---

* *Diaries of Sophia Tolstoy,* December 19, 1863.—TRANS.

ethical justification of the couple. But he is also a male with whom she must share an experience often shameful, bizarre, disgusting, or upsetting, and, in any case, contingent; he invites his wife to wallow with him in bestiality while directing her with a strong hand toward the ideal.

> One night in Paris—where they had come on their return journey—Bernard made a show of walking out of a nightclub, shocked at the revue: "To think that foreign visitors will see that! What shame! And that's how they'll judge us . . ." Thérèse could only marvel that this so chaste man was the same one who would be making her submit, in less than an hour, to his patient inventions in the dark.[37]

There are many hybrid forms between mentor and beast. Sometimes man is at once father and lover; the sexual act becomes a sacred orgy, and the loving wife finds ultimate salvation in the arms of her husband, redeemed by total abdication. This love-passion within married life is very rare. And at times the wife will love her husband platonically but will be unable to abandon herself in the arms of a man she respects too much. Such is this woman whose case Stekel reports. "Mrs. D.S., a great artist's widow, is now forty years old. Although she adored her husband, she was completely frigid with him." On the contrary, she may experience pleasure with him that she suffers as a common disgrace, killing all respect and esteem she has for him. Besides, an erotic failure relegates her husband to the ranks of a brute: hated in his flesh, he will be reviled in spirit; inversely, we have seen how scorn, antipathy, and rancor doomed the wife to frigidity. What often happens is that the husband remains a respected superior being after the sexual experience, excused of his animalistic weaknesses; it seems that this was the case, among others, of Adèle Hugo. Or else he is a pleasant partner, without prestige. Katherine Mansfield descried one of the forms this ambivalence can take in her short story "Prelude":

> For she really was fond of him; she loved and admired and respected him tremendously. Oh, better than anyone else in the world. She knew him through and through. He was the soul of truth and decency, and for all his practical experience he was awfully simple, easily pleased and easily hurt . . . If only he wouldn't jump at her so, and bark so loudly, and watch her with such eager, loving eyes. He

---

37. Mauriac, *Thérèse Desqueyroux*.

was too strong for her; she had always hated things that rushed at her, from a child. There were times when he was frightening—really frightening—when she just had not screamed at the top of her voice: "You are killing me." And at those times she had longed to say the most coarse, hateful things . . . Yes, yes, it was true . . . For all her love and respect and admiration she hated him . . . It had never been so plain to her as it was at this moment. There were all her feelings for him, sharp and defined, one as true as the other. And there was this other, this hatred, just as real as the rest. She could have done her feelings up in little packets and given them to Stanley. She longed to hand him that last one, for a surprise. She could see his eyes as he opened that.

The young wife rarely admits her feelings to herself with such sincerity. To love her husband and to be happy is a duty to herself and society; this is what her family expects of her; or if her parents were against the marriage, she wants to prove how wrong they were. She usually begins her conjugal life in bad faith; she easily persuades herself that she feels great love for her husband; and this passion takes on a more manic, possessive, and jealous form the less sexually satisfied she is; to console herself for this disappointment that she refuses at first to admit, she has an insatiable need for her husband's presence. Stekel cites numerous examples of these pathological attachments:

A woman remained frigid for the first years of her marriage, due to childhood fixations. She then developed a hypertrophic love as is frequently found in women who cannot bear to see that their husbands are indifferent to them. She lived only for her husband, and thought only of him. She lost all will. He had to plan her day every morning, tell her what to buy, etc. She carried out everything conscientiously. If he did not tell her what to do, she stayed in her room doing nothing and worried about him. She could not let him go anywhere without accompanying him. She could not stay alone, and she liked to hold his hand . . . She was unhappy and cried for hours, trembling for her husband and if there were no reasons to tremble, she created them.

My second case concerned a woman closed up in her room as if it were a prison for fear of going out alone. I found her holding her husband's hands, pleading with him to stay near her . . . Married for seven years, he was never able to have relations with his wife.

Sophia Tolstoy's case was similar; it comes out clearly in the passage I have cited and all throughout her diaries that as soon as she was married, she realized she did not love her husband. Sexual relations with him disgusted her; she reproached him for his past, found him old and boring, had nothing but hostility for his ideas; and it seems that greedy and brutal in bed, he neglected her and treated her harshly. To her hopeless cries, her confessions of ennui, sadness, and indifference, were nevertheless added Sophia's protestations of passionate love; she wanted her beloved husband near her always; as soon as he was away from her, she was tortured with jealousy. She writes:

January 11, 1863: My jealousy is a congenital illness, or it may be because in loving him I have nothing else to love; I have given myself so completely to him that my only happiness is with him and from him.

January 15, 1863:* I have been feeling [out of sorts and] angry that he should love everything and everyone, when I want him to love only me . . . The moment I think fondly of something or someone I tell myself no, I love only Lyovochka. But I absolutely *must* learn to love something else as he loves his *work* . . . but I hate being alone without him . . . My need to be near him grows stronger every day.

October 17, 1863: I feel I don't understand him properly, that's why I am always jealously following him.

July 31, 1868: It makes me laugh to read my diary. What a lot of contradictions—as though I were the unhappiest of women! . . . Could any marriage be more happy and harmonious than ours? I have been married six years now, but I love him more and more . . . I still love him with the same passionate, poetic, fevered, jealous love, and his composure occasionally irritates me.

September 16, 1876:† I avidly search his diaries for any reference to love, and am so tormented by jealously that I can no longer see anything clearly. I am afraid of my resentment of Lyovochka for leaving me . . . I choke back the tears, or hide away several times a

---

* *Diaries of Sophia Tolstoy.* Discrepancy between the French and the English translations. In the English text the date is given as January 17.—TRANS.
† Ibid. Discrepancy between the French and the English translations. In the English text the date is given as September 17.—TRANS.

day and weep with anxiety. I have a fever every day and a chill at
night . . . "What is he punishing me for?" I keep asking myself.
"Why, for loving him so much."

These pages convey the feeling of a vain effort to compensate for the
absence of a real love with moral and "poetic" exaltation; demands, anxieties, jealousy, are expressions of the emptiness in her heart. A great deal of
morbid jealousy develops in such conditions; in an indirect way, jealousy
conveys a dissatisfaction that woman objectifies by inventing a rival; never
feeling fulfillment with her husband, she rationalizes in some way her disappointment by imagining him deceiving her.

Very often, the wife persists in her pretense through morality,
hypocrisy, pride, or timidity. "Often, an aversion for the dear husband will
go unnoticed for a whole life: it is called melancholia or some other name,"
says Chardonne.[38] But the hostility is no less felt even though it is not
named. It is expressed with more or less violence in the young wife's effort
to refuse her husband's domination. After the honeymoon and the period
of confusion that often follows, she tries to win back her autonomy. This is
not an easy undertaking. The fact that her husband is often older than she
is, that he possesses in any case masculine prestige, and that he is the "head
of the family" according to the law means he bears moral and social superiority; very often he also possesses—or at least appears to—an intellectual superiority. He has the advantage of culture or at least professional
training over his wife; since adolescence, he has been interested in world
affairs: they are his affairs; he knows a little law, he follows politics, he
belongs to a party, a union, clubs; worker and citizen, his thinking is connected to action; he knows that one cannot cheat reality: that is, the average
man has the technique of reasoning, the taste for facts and experience, a
certain critical sense; here is what many girls lack; even if they have read,
listened to lectures, touched upon the fine arts, their knowledge amassed
here and there does not constitute culture; it is not because of an intellectual defect that they have not learned to reason: it is because they have not
had to practice it; for them thinking is more of a game than an instrument;
lacking intellectual training, even intelligent, sensitive, and sincere women
do not know how to present their opinions and draw conclusions from
them. That is why a husband—even if far more mediocre—will easily take
the lead over them; he knows how to prove himself right, even if he is

38. *Eva.*

wrong. Logic in masculine hands is often violence. Chardonne explained this kind of sly oppression well in *Epithalamium*. Older, more cultivated, and more educated than Berthe, Albert uses this pretext to deny any value to opinions of his wife that he does not share; he untiringly *proves* he is right; for her part she becomes adamant and refuses to accept that there is any substance in her husband's reasoning: he persists in his ideas, and that is the end of it. Thus a serious misunderstanding deepens between them. He does not try to understand feelings or deep-rooted reactions she cannot justify; she does not understand what lives behind her husband's pedantic and overwhelming logic. He even goes so far as to become irritated by the ignorance she never hid from him, and challenges her with questions about astronomy; he is flattered, nonetheless, to tell her what to read, to find in her a listener he can easily dominate. In a struggle where her intellectual shortcomings condemn her to losing every time, the young wife has no defense other than silence, or tears, or violence:

> Her head spinning, as if overcome by blows, Berthe could no longer think when she heard that erratic and strident voice, and Albert continued to envelop her in an imperious drone to confuse her, to injure her in the distress of her humiliated spirit . . . she was defeated, disarmed before the asperities of an inconceivable argumentation, and to release herself from this unjust power, she cried: Leave me alone! These words seemed too weak to her; she saw a crystal flask on her dressing table, and all at once threw the bottle at Albert.

Sometimes a wife will fight back. But often, with good or bad will, like Nora in *A Doll's House*,[39] she lets her husband think for her; it is he who will be the couple's consciousness. Through timidity, awkwardness, or laziness, she leaves it up to the man to formulate their common opinions on all general and abstract subjects. An intelligent woman, cultivated and independent but who, for fifteen years, had admired a husband she deemed

---

39. "When I was at home with papa, he told me his opinion about everything, and so I had the same opinions; and if I differed from him I concealed the fact, because he would not have liked it . . . I mean that I was simply transferred from papa's hands into yours. You arranged everything according to your own taste, and so I got the same tastes as yours—or else I pretended to, I am really not quite sure which—I think sometimes the one and sometimes the other . . . You and papa have committed a great sin against me. It is your fault that I have made nothing of my life."

superior, told me how, after his death she was obliged, to her dismay, to have her own convictions and behavior: she is still trying to guess what he would have thought and decided in each situation. The husband is generally comfortable in this role of mentor and chief.[40] In the evening after a difficult day dealing with his equals and obeying his superiors, he likes to feel absolutely superior and dispense incontestable truths.[41] Happy to find in his wife a double who shores up his self-confidence, he tells her about the day's events, tells her how he wins over his adversaries; he comments on the daily paper and the political news, he gladly reads aloud to his wife so that even her connection with culture should not be her own. To increase his authority, he likes to exaggerate feminine incapacity; she accepts this subordinate role with more or less docility. We have seen the surprised pleasure of women who, sincerely regretting their husbands' absence, discover in themselves at such times unsuspected possibilities; they run businesses, bring up children, decide and administer without help. They suffer when their husbands return and doom them again to incompetence.

Marriage incites man to a capricious imperialism: the temptation to dominate is the most universal and the most irresistible there is; to turn over a child to his mother or to turn over a wife to her husband is to cultivate tyranny in the world; it is often not enough for the husband to be supported and admired, to give counsel and guidance; he gives orders, he plays the sovereign; all the resentments accumulated in his childhood, throughout his life, accumulated daily among other men whose existence vexes and wounds him, he unloads at home by unleashing his authority over his wife;

---

40. Helmer says to Nora: "But do you suppose you are any the less dear to me, because you don't understand how to act on your own responsibility? No, no; only lean on me; I will advise you and direct you. I should not be a man if this womanly helplessness did not just give you a double attractiveness in my eyes . . . Be at rest, and feel secure; I have broad wings to shelter you under . . . There is something so indescribably sweet and satisfying, to a man, in the knowledge that he has forgiven his wife . . . she has in a way become both wife and child to him. So you shall be for me after this, my little scared, helpless darling. Have no anxiety about anything, Nora; only be frank and open with me, and I will serve as will and conscience both to you."

41. Cf. Lawrence, *Fantasia of the Unconscious:* "You'll have to fight to make a woman believe in you as a real man, a real pioneer. No man is a man unless to his woman he is a pioneer. You'll have to fight still harder to make her yield her goal to yours . . . ah, then, how wonderful it is! How wonderful it is to come back to her, at evening, as she sits half in fear and waits! How good it is to come home to her! . . . How rich you feel, tired, with all the burden of the day in your veins, turning home! . . . And you feel an unfathomable gratitude to the woman who loves you and believes in your purpose."

he acts out violence, power, intransigence; he issues orders in a severe tone, or he yells and hammers the table: this drama is a daily reality for the wife. He is so convinced of his rights that his wife's least show of autonomy seems a rebellion to him; he would keep her from breathing without his consent. She, nonetheless, rebels. Even if she started out recognizing masculine prestige, her dazzlement is soon dissipated; one day the child recognizes his father is but a contingent individual; the wife soon discovers she is not before the grand Suzerain, the Chief, the Master, but a man; she sees no reason to be subjugated to him; in her eyes, he merely represents unjust and unrewarding duty. Sometimes she submits with a masochistic pleasure: she takes on the role of victim, and her resignation is only a long and silent reproach; but she often fights openly against her master as well, and begins tyrannizing him back.

Man is being naive when he imagines he will easily make his wife bend to his wishes and "shape" her as he pleases. "A wife is what her husband makes her," says Balzac; but he says the opposite a few pages further on. In the area of abstraction and logic, the wife often resigns herself to accepting male authority; but when it is a question of ideas and habits she really clings to, she opposes him with covert tenacity. The influence of her childhood and youth is deeper for her than for the man, as she remains more closely confined in her own personal history. She usually does not lose what she acquires during these periods. The husband will impose a political opinion on his wife, but he will not change her religious convictions, nor will he shake her superstitions: this is what Jean Barois saw, he who imagined having a real influence on the devout little ninny who shared his life. Overcome, he says: "A little girl's brain, conserved in the shadows of a provincial town: all the assertions of ignorant stupidity: this can't be cleaned up." In spite of opinions she has learned and principles she reels off like a parrot, the wife retains her own vision of the world. This resistance can render her incapable of understanding a husband smarter than herself; or, on the contrary, she will rise above masculine seriousness like the heroines in Stendhal or Ibsen. Sometimes, out of hostility toward the man— either because he has sexually disappointed her or, on the contrary, because he dominates her and she wants revenge—she will clutch on to values that are not his; she relies on the authority of her mother, father, brother, or some masculine personality who seems "superior" to her, a confessor, or a sister to prove him wrong. Or rather than opposing him with anything positive, she continues to contradict him systematically, attack him, insult him; she strives to instill in him an inferiority complex. Of course, if she has the necessary capacity, she will delight in outshining her husband, imposing her advice, opinions, directives; she will seize all moral authority. In cases where it is impossible to contest her husband's intellectual superiority, she will try to take her revenge on a sexual level. Or she will refuse him, as Halévy tells us about Mme Michelet:

> She wanted to dominate everywhere: in bed because she had to do that and at the worktable. It was the table she aimed for, and Michelet defended it at first while she defended the bed. For several months, the couple was chaste. Finally Michelet got the bed and Athénaïs Mialaret soon after had the table: she was born a woman of letters and it was her true place.*

Either she stiffens in his arms and inflicts the insult of her frigidity on him; or she shows herself to be capricious and coquettish, imposing on him the attitude of suppliant; she flirts, she makes him jealous, she is unfaithful to him: in one way or another, she tries to humiliate him in his virility. While caution prevents her from pushing him too far, at least she preciously keeps in her heart the secret of her haughty coldness; she confides sometimes to her diary, more readily to her friends: many married women find it amusing to share "tricks" they use to feign pleasure they claim not to feel; and they laugh wildly at the vain naïveté of their dupes; these confidences are perhaps another form of playacting: between frigidity and willful frigidity, the boundaries are uncertain. In any case, they consider themselves to be unfeeling and satisfy their resentment this way. There are women—ones likened to the praying mantis—who want to triumph night and day: they are cold in embrace, contemptuous in conversations, and tyrannical in their behavior. This is how—according to Mabel Dodge's testimony—Frieda behaved with Lawrence. Unable to deny his intellectual superiority, she attempted to impose her own vision of the world on him where only sexual values counted:

> He must see through her and she had to see life from the sex center. She endorsed or repudiated experience from that angle.

One day she declared to Mabel Dodge:

> "He has to get it all from me. Unless I am there, he feels nothing. Nothing. And he gets his books from me," she continued,

---

* Daniel Halévy, *Jules Michelet*.—TRANS.

boastfully. "Nobody knows that. Why, I have done pages of his books for him."

Nonetheless, she bitterly and ceaselessly needs to prove this need he has for her; she demands he take care of her without respite: if he does not do it spontaneously, she corners him:

I discovered that Frieda would not let things slide. I mean between them. Their relationship was never allowed to become slack. When . . . they were going along smoothly . . . not noticing each other much, when the thing between them tended to slip into unconsciousness and *rest*, Frieda would burst a bombshell at him. She *never* let him forget her. What in the first days must have been the splendor of fresh and complete experience had become, when I knew them, the attack and the defense between enemies . . . Frieda would sting him in a tender place . . . At the end of an evening when he had not particularly noticed her, she would begin insulting him.*

Married life had become for them a series of scenes repeated over and over in which neither of them would give in, turning the least quarrel into a titanic duel between Man and Woman.

In a very different way, the same untamed will to dominate is found in Jouhandeau's Élise, driving her to undermine her husband as much as possible:

Élise: Right from the start, around me, I undermine everything. Afterwards, I don't have anything to worry about. I don't only have to deal with monkeys or monsters.
   When she wakes up she calls me:
   —My ugly one.
   It is a policy.
   She wants to humiliate me.
   She went about making me give up all my illusions about myself, one after the other, with such outright pleasure. She has never missed the chance to tell me that I am this or that miserable thing, in front of my astonished friends or our embarrassed servants. So I finally ended up believing her . . . To despise me, she never misses

---

* Luhan, *Lorenzo in Taos.*—TRANS.

an occasion to make me feel that my work interests her less than any of her own improvements.

It is she who dried up the source of my thoughts by patiently, slowly and purposefully discouraging me, methodically humiliating me, making me renounce my pride, in spite of myself, by chipping away with a precise, imperturbable, implacable logic.

—In the end, you earn less than a worker, she threw out at me one day in front of the polisher . . .

She wants to belittle me to seem superior or at least equal, and this disdain keeps her in her high place over me . . . She only has esteem for me insofar as what I do serves her as a stepping-stone or piece of merchandise.[42]

To posit themselves before the male as essential subjects, Frieda and Élise make use of a tactic men have often denounced: they try to deny them their transcendence. Men readily suppose that woman entertains dreams of castration against them; in fact, her attitude is ambiguous: she desires to humiliate the masculine sex rather than suppress it. Far more exact, she wishes to damage man in his projects, his future. She is triumphant when her husband or child is ill, tired, reduced to a bodily presence. They then appear to be no more than an object among others in the house over which she reigns; she treats them with a housewife's skill; she bandages them like she glues together a broken dish, she cleans them as one cleans a pot; nothing resists her angelic hands, friends of peelings and dishwater. In speaking about Frieda, Lawrence told Mabel Dodge, "You cannot imagine what it is to feel the hand of that woman on you if you are sick . . . The heavy, German hand of the flesh . . ." Consciously, the woman imposes her hand with all its weight to make the man feel he also is no more than a being of flesh. This attitude cannot be pushed further than it is with Jouhandeau's Élise:

I remember, for example, Tchang Tsen lice in the beginning of our marriage . . . I really only became intimate with a woman thanks to it, the day Élise took me naked on her lap to shave me like a sheep, lighting me up with a candle she moved around my body down to my secret parts. Oh, her close inspection of my armpits, my chest, my navel, the skin of my testicles taut like a drum between her fingers, her prolonged pauses along my thighs, between my feet and

---

42. *Bold Chronicle of a Strange Marriage* and *Nouvelles chroniques maritales* (New Marriage Chronicles).

the passage of the razor around my asshole: the final drop into the basket a tuft of blond hair where the lice were hiding, and that she burned, giving me over in one fell swoop, delivering me at the same time from the lice and their den, to a new nakedness and to the desert of isolation.

Woman loves man to be passive flesh and not a body that expresses subjectivity. She affirms life against existence, values of the flesh against values of the spirit; she readily adopts Pascal's humorous attitude to male enterprises; she thinks as well, "All man's miseries derive from not being able to sit quiet in a room alone"; she would gladly keep him shut up at home; all activity that does not directly benefit family life provokes her hostility; Bernard Palissy's wife is indignant when he burns the furniture to invent a new enamel without which the world had done very well until then; Mme Racine makes her husband take an interest in her red currants and refuses to read his tragedies. Jouhandeau is often peeved in *The Bold Chronicle of a Strange Marriage* because Élise stubbornly considers his literary work merely a source of material profit:

> I said to her: My latest story was published this morning. She replied (without in any way wishing to be cynical and merely because it is the only thing that matters to her): That means we shall have at least three hundred francs extra this month.

It happens that these conflicts worsen and then provoke a rupture. But generally the woman wants to "hold on to" her husband as well as to refuse his domination. She struggles against him to defend her autonomy, and she fights against the rest of the world to conserve the "situation" that dooms her to dependence. This double game is difficult to play, which explains in part the worried and nervous state in which multitudes of women spend their lives. Stekel gives a very significant example:

> Mrs. Z.T., who never had an orgasm, is married to a very cultivated man. But she cannot bear his superiority and she began to want to be his equal by studying his speciality. As it was too difficult, she gave up her studies as soon as they were engaged.
> The very famous man had many students chasing after him. She decides not to partake in this ridiculous cult. In her marriage she was insensitive from the start and she remained that way. She attained an orgasm only through masturbation when her husband had finished,

satisfied, and she would tell him about it. She refused his attempts
to excite her by his caresses . . . Soon she began to ridicule him and
undermine her husband's work. She could not "understand these
ninnies who pursued him, she who knew the behind-the-scenes of
the great man's private life." In their daily quarrels, expressions
arose such as: "You can't put anything over on me with your scrib-
bling!" Or: "You think you can do what you want with me because
you're a little writer." The husband spent more and more time with
his students, she surrounded herself with young men. She continued
this way for years until her husband fell in love with another woman.
She always stood for his little liaisons, she even made friends of his
abandoned "poor idiots" . . . But then she changed her attitude and
gave in, without orgasm, to the first adolescent who came along.
She admitted to her husband that she had cheated on him, which he
accepted without a problem. They could peacefully separate . . . She
refused the divorce. There followed a long explanation and reconcil-
iation. She broke down in tears and experienced her first intense
orgasm.

It is clear that in her struggle against her husband, she never intends to
leave him.

There is an art to "catching a husband": "keeping" him is a profession.
It takes a great deal of skill. A prudent sister said to a cranky young wife:
"Be careful, making scenes with Marcel will make you lose your *situation*."
The stakes are the highest: material and moral security, a home of one's
own, wifely dignity, a more or less successful substitute for love and happiness. The wife quickly learns that her erotic attraction is the weakest of her
weapons; it disappears with familiarity; and there are, alas, other desirable
women in the world; so she still works at being seductive and pleasing: she
is often torn between the pride that inclines her to frigidity and the notion
that her sensual ardor will flatter and keep her husband. She also counts on
the force of habit, on the charm he finds in a pleasant home, his taste for
good food, his affection for his children; she tries to "make him proud" by
her way of entertaining, dressing, and exercising authority over him with
her advice and her influence; as much as she can, she will make herself
indispensable, either by her social success or by her work. But, above all, a
whole tradition teaches wives the art of "how to catch a man"; one must
discover and flatter his weaknesses, cunningly use flattery and disdain,
docility and resistance, vigilance and indulgence. This last blend is especially subtle. One must not give a husband too much or too little freedom.

If she is too indulgent, the wife finds her husband escaping her; the money and passion he spends on other women are her loss; she runs the risk of having a mistress get enough power over him to seek a divorce or at least take first place in his life. Yet if she forbids him all adventure, if she overwhelms him by her close scrutiny, her scenes, her demands, she can seriously turn him against her. It is a question of knowing how to "make concessions" advisedly; if the husband puts "a few dents in the contract," she will close her eyes; but at other moments, she must open them wide; in particular the married woman mistrusts young girls who would be only too happy to take over her "position." To tear her husband from a worrying rival, she will take him on a trip, she will try to distract him; if necessary— following Mme de Pompadour's model—she will seek out another, less dangerous rival; if nothing succeeds, she will resort to crying, nervous fits, suicide attempts, and such; but too many scenes and recriminations will chase her husband from the house; the wife will make herself unbearable just when she most needs to seduce; if she wants to win her hand, she will skillfully combine touching tears and heroic smiles, blackmail and coquetry. Dissimulate, trick, hate, and fear in silence, bet on the vanity and weakness of a man, learn how to foil him, play him, manipulate him, it is all quite a sad science. The wife's great excuse is that she is forced to involve her whole self in marriage: she has no profession, no skills, no personal relations, even her name is not her own; she is nothing but her husband's "other half." If he abandons her, she will most often find no help, either within or outside of herself. It is easy to cast a stone at Sophia Tolstoy, as A. de Monzie and Montherlant do: But if she had refused the hypocrisy of conjugal life, where could she have gone? What destiny awaited her? True, she seems to have been a contemptible shrew: But could one ask her to love her tyrant and bless her enslavement? For there to be loyalty and friendship between spouses, the *sine qua non* is that both must be free vis-à-vis each other and concretely equal. As long as man alone possesses economic autonomy and holds—by law and custom—privileges conferred on him by his masculinity, it is natural that he should so often appear a tyrant, inciting woman to revolt and duplicity.

No one dreams of denying the tragedies and nastiness of married life: but advocates of marriage defend the idea that spouses' conflicts arise out of the bad faith of individuals and not out of the institution's. Tolstoy, among others, describes the ideal couple in the epilogue to *War and Peace:* Pierre and Natasha. She was a coquettish and romantic girl; when married, she astounds those who knew her by giving up her interest in her appearance, society, and pastimes and devoting herself exclusively to her husband and children; she becomes the very epitome of a matron:

In her face there was not, as formerly, that ceaselessly burning fire of animation that had constituted her charm. Now one often saw only her face and body, while her soul was not seen at all. One saw only a strong, beautiful, and fruitful female.

She demands from Pierre a love as exclusive as the one she swears to him; she is jealous of him; he gives up going out, all his old friends, and devotes himself entirely to his family as well.

Pierre's subjection consisted in his . . . not daring to go to clubs or dinners . . . not daring to leave for long periods of time except on business, in which his wife also included his intellectual pursuits, of which she understood nothing, but to which she ascribed great importance.

Pierre is "under the slipper of his wife," but in return:

At home Natasha put herself on the footing of her husband's slave . . . The entire household was governed only by the imaginary orders of the husband, that is, by Pierre's wishes, which Natasha tried to guess.

When Pierre goes far away from her, Natasha impatiently greets him upon his return because she suffers from his absence; but a wonderful harmony reigns over the couple; they understand each other with barely a few words. Between her children, her home, her loved and respected husband, she savors nearly untainted happiness.

This idyllic tableau merits closer scrutiny. Natasha and Pierre are united, says Tolstoy, like soul and body; but when the soul leaves the body, only one dies; what would happen if Pierre should cease to love Natasha? Lawrence, too, rejects the hypothesis of masculine inconstancy: Don Ramón will always love the little Indian girl Teresa, who gave him her soul. Yet one of the most ardent zealots of unique, absolute, eternal love, André Breton, is forced to admit that at least in present circumstances this love can mistake its object: error or inconstancy, it is the same abandonment for the woman. Pierre, robust and sensual, will be physically attracted to other women; Natasha is jealous; soon the relationship will sour; either he will leave her, which will ruin her life, or he will lie and resent her, which will spoil his life, or they will live with compromises and half measures, which will make them both unhappy. One might object that Natasha will at least have her children: but children are a source of joy only within a well-balanced structure, where the husband is one of its peaks; for the neglected, jealous wife they become a thankless burden. Tolstoy admires Natasha's blind devotion to Pierre's ideas; but another man, Lawrence, who also demands blind devotion from women, mocks Pierre and Natasha; so in the opinion of other men, a man can be a clay idol and not a real god; in worshipping him, one loses one's life instead of saving it; how is one to know? Masculine claims compete with each other, authority no longer plays a part: the wife must judge and criticize, she cannot be but a feeble echo. Moreover, it is degrading to her to impose principles and values on her that she does not believe in with her own free will; what she might share of her husband's thinking, she can only share through her own independent judgment; she should not have to accept or refuse what is foreign to her; she cannot borrow her own reasons for existing from another.

The most radical condemnation of the Pierre-Natasha myth comes from the Leon-Sophia couple. Sophia feels repulsion for her husband, she finds him "tedious"; he cheats on her with all the surrounding peasants, she is jealous and bored; she is frustrated by her multiple pregnancies, and her children do not fill the emptiness in her heart or her days; home for her is an arid desert; for him it is hell. And it ends up with an old hysterical woman lying half-naked in the humid night of the forest, with this old hounded man fleeing, renouncing finally the "union" of a whole life.

Of course, Tolstoy's case is exceptional; there are many marriages that "work well," that is, where the spouses reach a compromise; they live next to each other without antagonizing each other, without lying to each other too much. But there is a curse they rarely escape: boredom. Whether the husband succeeds in making his wife an echo of himself, or whether each one entrenches himself in his universe, they have nothing else to share with each other after a few months or years. The couple is a community whose members have lost their autonomy without escaping their solitude; they are statically assimilated to each other instead of sustaining a dynamic and lively relation together; this is why they can give nothing to each other, exchange nothing on a spiritual or erotic level. In one of her best short stories, "Too Bad," Dorothy Parker sums up the sad saga of many conjugal lives; it is night and Mr. Weldon comes home:

Mrs. Weldon opened the door at his ring.
"Well!" she said, cheerily.
They smiled brightly at each other.
"Hel-lo," he said. "Well! You home?"

They kissed, slightly. She watched with polite interest while he hung up his hat and coat, removed the evening papers from his pocket, and handed one to her.

"Bring the papers?" she said, taking it . . .

"Well, what have you been doing with yourself today?" he inquired.

She had been expecting the question. She had planned before he came in, how she would tell him all the little events of her day . . . But now . . . it seemed to her a long, dull story . . .

"Oh, nothing," she said, with a gay little laugh. "Did you have a nice day?"

"Why——" he began . . . But his interest waned, even as he started to speak. Besides, she was engrossed in breaking off a loose thread from the wool fringe of one of the pillows beside her.

"Oh, pretty fair," he said . . .

She could talk well enough to other people . . .

Ernest, too, seemed to be talkative enough when he was with others . . .

She tried to remember what they used to talk about before they were married, when they were engaged. It seemed to her that they never had had much to say to each other. But she hadn't worried about it then . . . Then, besides, there had been always kissing and things, to take up your mind . . . And you can't depend on kisses and all the rest of it to while away the evenings, after seven years.

You'd think that you would get used to it, in seven years, would realize that that was the way it was, and let it go at that. You don't, though. A thing like that gets on your nerves. It isn't one of those cozy, companionable silences that people occasionally fall into together. It makes you feel as if you must do something about it, as if you weren't performing your duty. You have the feeling a hostess has when her party is going badly . . .

Ernest would read industriously, and along toward the middle of the paper, he would start yawning aloud. Something happened inside Mrs. Weldon when he did this. She would murmur that she had to speak to Delia, and hurry to the kitchen. She would stay there rather a long time, looking vaguely into jars and inquiring half-heartedly about laundry lists, and, when she returned, he would have gone in to get ready for bed.

In a year, three hundred of their evenings were like this. Seven times three hundred is more than two thousand.

It is sometimes claimed this very silence is the sign of an intimacy deeper than any word; and obviously no one dreams of denying that conjugal life creates intimacy: this is true of all family relations, even those that include hatreds, jealousies, and resentments. Jouhandeau strongly emphasizes the difference between this intimacy and a real human fraternity, writing:

> Élise is my wife and it is probable that none of my friends, none of the members of my family, not a single one of my own limbs is more intimate with me than she; but however close to me is the place that she has made for herself and that I have made for her in my own most private universe; however deeply rooted she has become in the inextricable web of my body and soul (and there lies the whole mystery and the whole drama of our indissoluble union), the unknown person, whoever he may be, who happens to pass in the street at this particular moment and whom I can barely see from my window is less of a stranger to me than she is.

He says elsewhere:

> We discover that we are the victims of poisoning, but that we have grown used to it. How can we give it up without giving up ourselves?

Still more:

> When I think of her, I feel that married love has nothing to do with sympathy, with sensuality, with passion, with friendship, or with love. It alone is adequate to itself and cannot be reduced to one or other of these different feelings, it has its own nature, its particular essence, and its unique mode which depends on the couple that it brings together.

Advocates of conjugal love readily admit it is not love, which is precisely what makes it marvelous.[43] For in recent years the bourgeoisie has

---

43. There can be love within marriage; but then one does not speak of "conjugal love"; when these words are uttered, it means that love is missing; likewise, when one says of a man that he is "*very* communist," one means that he is not a communist; "a great gentleman" is a man who does not belong to the simple category of gentlemen, and so on.

invented an epic style: routine takes on the allure of adventure, faithfulness that of sublime madness, boredom becomes wisdom, and family hatreds are the deepest form of love. In truth, that two individuals hate each other without, however, being able to do without each other is not at all the truest, the most moving of all human relations; it is one of the most pitiful. The ideal would be, on the contrary, that each human being, perfectly self-sufficient, be attached to another by the free consent of their love alone. Tolstoy admires the fact that the link between Natasha and Pierre is something "indefinable, but firm, solid, as was the union of his own soul with his body." If one accepts the dualist hypothesis, the body represents only a pure facticity for the soul; so in the conjugal union, each one would have for the other the inevitable weight of contingent fact; one would have to assume and love the other as an absurd and unchosen presence as the necessary condition for and very matter of existence. There is a deliberate confusion between these two words—"assuming" and "loving"—and the mystification stems from this: one does not love what one assumes. One assumes one's body, past, and present situation: but love is a movement toward an other, toward an existence separated from one's own, toward a finality, a future; the way to assume or take on a load or a tyranny is not to love it but to revolt. A human relation has no value if it is lived in the immediacy; children's relations with their parents, for example, only have value when they are reflected in a consciousness; one cannot admire conjugal relations that degenerate into the immediate in which the spouses squander their freedom. One claims to respect this complex mixture of attachment, resentment, hatred, rules, resignation, laziness, and hypocrisy called conjugal love only because it serves as an alibi. But what is true of friendship is true of physical love: for friendship to be authentic, it must first be free. Freedom does not mean whim: a feeling is a commitment that goes beyond the instant; but it is up to the individual alone to compare his general will to his personal behavior so as either to uphold his decision or, on the contrary, to break it; feeling is free when it does not depend on any outside command, when it is lived in sincerity without fear. The message of "conjugal love" is an invitation, by contrast, to all kinds of repression and lies. And above all it keeps the husband and wife from genuinely knowing each other. Daily intimacy creates neither understanding nor sympathy. The husband respects his wife too much to be interested in the metamorphoses of her psychological life: that would mean recognizing in her a secret autonomy that could prove to be bothersome, dangerous; does she really get pleasure in bed? Does she really love her husband? Is she really happy to obey him? He prefers not to question himself; these questions even seem shocking to him. He married a "good woman"; by nature she is virtuous, devoted, faithful, pure, and happy, and she thinks what she should think. A sick man, after thanking his friends, his family, and his nurses, says to his young wife, who, for six months, had not left his bedside: "I do not have to thank you, you merely did your duty." He gives her no credit for any of her good qualities: they are guaranteed by society, they are implied by the very institution of marriage; he does not notice that his wife does not come out of a book by Bonald, that she is an individual of flesh and blood; he takes for granted her faithfulness to the orders she imposes on herself: he takes no account of the fact that she might have temptations to overcome, that she might succumb to them, that in any case, her patience, her chastity, and her decency might be difficult conquests; he ignores even more completely her dreams, her fantasies, her nostalgia, and the emotional climate in which she spends her days. Thus Chardonne shows us in *Eva* a husband who has for years kept a journal of his conjugal life: he speaks of his wife with delicate nuances; but only of his wife as he sees her, as she is for him without ever giving her dimensions as a free individual: he is stunned when he suddenly learns she does not love him, that she is leaving him. One often speaks of the naive and loyal man's disillusionment in the face of feminine perfidy: the husbands in Bernstein are scandalized to discover that the women in their lives are fickle, mean or adulterous; they take it with a virile courage, but the author does not fail to make them seem generous and strong: they seem more like boors to us, without sensitivity and goodwill; man criticizes women for their duplicity, but he must be very complacent to let himself be duped with so much constancy. Woman is doomed to immorality because morality for her consists in embodying an inhuman entity: the strong woman, the admirable mother, the virtuous woman, and so on. As soon as she thinks, dreams, sleeps, desires, and aspires without orders, she betrays the masculine ideal. This is why so many women do not let themselves "be themselves" except in their husbands' absence. Likewise, the woman does not know her husband: she thinks she perceives his true face because she grasps it in its daily contingency: but the man is first what he *does* in the world among other men. Refusing to understand the movement of his transcendence is denaturing it. "One marries a poet," says Élise, "and when one is his wife, the first thing she notices is he forgets to flush the toilet."[44] He nevertheless remains a poet, and the wife who is not interested in his works knows him

---

44. *Bold Chronicle of a Strange Marriage.*

less than a remote reader. It is often not the wife's fault that this complicity is forbidden to her: she cannot share her husband's affairs, she lacks the experience and the necessary culture to "follow" him: she fails to join him in the projects that are far more essential for him than the monotonous repetition of everyday life. In certain privileged cases the wife can succeed in becoming a real companion for her husband: she discusses his plans, gives him advice, participates in his work. But she is deluding herself if she thinks she can accomplish work of her own like that: he alone remains the active and responsible freedom. To find joy in serving him, she must love him; if not she will experience only vexation because she will feel frustrated by the fruit of her efforts. Men—faithful to the advice given by Balzac to treat the wife as a slave while persuading her she is queen—exaggerate to the utmost the importance of the influence women wield; deep down, they know well they are lying. Georgette Leblanc was duped by this mystification when she demanded of Maeterlinck that he write their two names on the book they had, or so she thought, written together; in the preface to the singer's *Souvenirs*, Grasset bluntly explains that any man is ready to hail the woman who shares his life as an associate and an inspiration but that he nevertheless still regards his work as belonging to him alone; rightfully. In any action, any work, what counts is the moment of choice and decision. The wife generally plays the role of the crystal ball clairvoyants use: another would do just as well. And the proof is that often the man welcomes another adviser, another collaborator, with the same confidence. Sophia Tolstoy copied her husband's manuscripts and put them in order: he later gave the job to one of his daughters; she understood that even her zeal had not made her indispensable. Only autonomous work can assure the wife an authentic autonomy.[45]

Conjugal life takes different forms depending on the case. But for many wives, the day begins approximately in the same way. The husband leaves his wife hurriedly in the morning: she is happy to hear the door close after him; she likes to find herself free, without duties, sovereign in her home. The children in turn leave for school: she will stay alone all day; the baby squirming in his crib or playing in his playpen is not company. She spends more or less time getting dressed, doing the housework; if she has a

---

45. There is sometimes a *real* collaboration between a man and a woman, in which the two are equally autonomous: in the Joliot-Curie couple, for example. But then the wife who is as skilled as the husband goes out of her wifely role; their relation is no longer of a conjugal order. There are also wives who use the man to achieve personal aims; they escape the condition of the married woman.

maid, she gives her instructions, lingers a little in the kitchen while chatting; or else she will stroll in the market, exchanging comments on the cost of living with her neighbors or shopkeepers. If her husband and children come home for lunch, she cannot take advantage of their presence very much; she has too much to do to get the meal ready, serve, and clean up; most often, they do not come back for lunch. In any case, she has a long, empty afternoon in front of her. She takes her youngest children to the public park and knits or sews while keeping an eye on them; or, sitting at the window at home, she does her mending; her hands work, but her mind is not occupied; she ruminates over her worries; she makes plans; she daydreams, she is bored; none of her occupations suffices in itself; her thoughts are directed toward her husband and her children, who will wear these shirts, who will eat the meal she is preparing; she lives for them alone; and are they at all grateful to her? Little by little her boredom changes into impatience; she begins to wait for their return anxiously. The children come back from school, she kisses them, questions them; but they have homework to do, they want to have fun together, they escape, they are not a distraction. And then they have bad grades, they have lost a scarf, they are noisy, messy, they fight with each other: she almost always has to scold them. Their presence annoys the mother more than it soothes her. She waits for her husband more and more urgently. What is he doing? Why is he not home already? He has worked, seen the world, chatted with people, he has not thought of her; she starts ruminating nervously that she is stupid to sacrifice her youth to him; he is not grateful to her. The husband making his way toward the house where his wife is closed up feels vaguely guilty; early in the marriage, he would bring a bunch of flowers, a little gift, as an offering; but this ritual soon loses any meaning; now he arrives empty-handed, and he is even less in a hurry when he anticipates the usual greeting. Indeed, the wife often takes revenge with a scene of boredom, of the daily wait; this is how she wards off the disappointment of a presence that does not satisfy the expectation of her waiting. Even if she does not express her grievances, her husband too is disappointed. He has not had a good time at his office, he is tired; he has a contradictory desire for stimulation and for rest. His wife's too familiar face does not free him from himself; he feels she would like to share his worries with him, that she also expects distraction and relaxation from him: her presence weighs on him without satisfying him, he does not find real abandon with her. Nor do the children bring entertainment or peace; during the meal and the evening there is a vague bad mood; reading, listening to the radio, chatting idly, each one under the cover of intimacy, will remain alone. Yet the wife wonders with an anxious hope—or a no less anxious apprehension—if tonight—finally! again!—something will happen. She goes to sleep disappointed, irritated, or relieved; she will be happy to hear the door slam shut tomorrow. The lot of wives is even harsher if they are poor and overburdened with chores; it lightens when they have both leisure and distractions. But this pattern—boredom, waiting, and disappointment—is found in many cases.

There are some escapes available to the wife;[46] but in practice they are not available to all. The chains of marriage are heavy, particularly in the provinces; a wife has to find a way of coming to grips with a situation she cannot escape. Some, as we have seen, are puffed up with importance and become tyrannical matrons and shrews. Others take refuge in the role of the victim, they make themselves their husbands' and children's pathetic slaves and find a masochistic joy in it. Others perpetuate the narcissistic behavior we have described in relation to the young girl: they also suffer from not realizing themselves in any undertaking, and, being able to do nothing, they are nothing; undefined, they feel undetermined and consider themselves misunderstood; they worship melancholy; they take refuge in dreams, playacting, illnesses, fads, scenes; they create problems around them or close themselves up in an imaginary world; the "smiling Mme Beudet" that Amiel depicted is one of these. Shut up in provincial monotony with a boorish husband, with no chance to act or to love, she is devoured by the feeling of her life's emptiness and uselessness; she tries to find compensation in romantic musings, in the flowers she surrounds herself with, in her clothes, her person: her husband interferes even with these games. She ends up trying to kill him. The symbolic behavior into which the wife escapes can bring about perversions, and these obsessions can lead to crime. There are conjugal crimes dictated less by interest than by pure hatred. Thus, Mauriac shows us Thérèse Desqueyroux trying to poison her husband as Mme Lafarge did previously. A forty-year-old woman who had endured an odious husband for twenty years was recently acquitted for having coldly strangled her husband with the help of her elder son. There had been no other way for her to free herself from an intolerable situation.

For a wife who wants to live her situation in lucidity, in authenticity, her only resort is often to stoic pride. Because she is totally dependent, she can only have a deeply interior and therefore abstract freedom; she refuses ready-made principles and values, she judges, she questions, and thus escapes conjugal slavery; but her haughty reserve and her acceptance of the

---

46. See Chapter 7 of this volume.

saying "Suffer and be still" constitute no more than a negative attitude. Confined in denial, in cynicism, she lacks a positive use of her strength; as long as she is passionate and living, she finds ways to use it: she helps others, she consoles, protects, gives, she has many interests; but she suffers from not finding any truly demanding job, from not devoting her activity to an end. Often eaten away by loneliness and sterility, she ends up by giving up, destroying herself. Mme de Charrière provides us with a notable example of such a destiny. In the sympathetic book he devotes to her, Geoffrey Scott depicts her with "a frond of flame; a frond of frost."[47] But it is not her reason that put out this flame of life that Hermenches said could "warm the heart of a Laplander," it is marriage that slowly assassinates the brilliant Belle de Zuylen; she resigned herself and called it reason: either heroism or genius would have been necessary to invent a different outcome. That her lofty and rare qualities were not sufficient to save her is one of the most stunning condemnations of the conjugal institution found in history.

Brilliant, cultivated, intelligent, and ardent, Mlle de Zuylen astonished Europe; she frightened away suitors; she rejected more than twelve of them, but others, perhaps more acceptable, backed off. Hermenches was the only man who interested her, but it was out of the question to make him her husband: she carried on a twelve-year correspondence with him; but this friendship and her studies no longer satisfied her. "Virgin and martyr" was a pleonasm, she said; and the constraints of Zuylen's life were unbearable; she wanted to become a woman, a free being. At thirty, she married M. de Charrière; she liked the "honesty of heart" she found in him, his "sense of justice," and she first decided to make him "the most tenderly loved husband in the world." Later, Benjamin Constant recounts that "she had tormented him greatly to impress upon him reactions equal to hers"; she did not manage to overcome his methodical impassivity; shut up in Colombier with this honest and dull husband, a senile father-in-law, two dull sisters-in-law, Mme de Charrière began to be bored; the narrow-mindedness of Neufchâtel provincial society displeased her; she killed her days in washing the household linen and playing "Comet" in the evening. A young man briefly crossed her life and left her lonelier than before. "Taking ennui as muse," she wrote four novels on the customs of Neufchâtel, and the circle of her friends grew narrower. In one of her works, she described the long sadness of a marriage between a lively and sensitive woman and a good but ponderous and cold man: conjugal life seemed to

---

47. Geoffrey Scott, *The Portrait of Zélide*.

her like a chain of misunderstandings, disappointments, petty resentments. It was clear she herself was unhappy; she fell ill, recovered, returned to the long accompanied solitude that was her life. "It is clear that the routine of the life at Colombier and the negative, unresisting smoothness of her husband's temperament were like a perpetual pause which no activity of Mme de Charrière's could fill," writes her biographer. And then appears Benjamin Constant, who passionately occupied her for eight years. When, too proud to wrest him from Mme de Staël, she gave him up, her pride hardened. She wrote to him one day: "The stay at Colombier was abhorrent to me, and I never went back there without despair. I decided not to leave it anymore and made it bearable for myself." She closed herself up there and did not leave her garden for fifteen years; this is how she applied the stoic precept: seek to conquer one's heart rather than fortune. As a prisoner, she could only find freedom by choosing her prison. "She accepted M. de Charrière at her side as she accepted the Alps," says Scott. But she was too lucid not to understand that this resignation was, after all, only deception; she became so withdrawn, so hard, she was thought to be so despairing that she was frightening. She had opened her house to the immigrants who were pouring into Neufchâtel; she protected them, helped them, guided them; she wrote elegant and disillusioned works that Huber, a poor German philosopher, translated; she lavished advice on a circle of young women and taught Locke to her favorite one, Henriette; she loved to play the role of divine protection for the peasants of the area; avoiding Neufchâtel society more and more carefully, she preciously limited her life; she "sought only to create routine, and to endure it. Even her infinite acts of kindness had something frightening about them, in the chill of her self-control . . . She seemed to those around her like one moving in an empty room."[48] On rare occasions—a visit, for example—the flame of life awakened. But "the years passed aridly. Ageing side by side lived M. and Mme de Charrière, a whole universe apart; and often a visitor would turn from the house with relief, and hearing the gate clang behind him, would feel that he was leaving a shut tomb . . . The clock ticked; M. de Charrière sat below, alone, poring over his mathematics. Rhythmically, from the barn outside, came the sound of the threshers. It throbbed, and it ceased. Life went on, though it was threshed out . . . A life of small things, desperately compelled to fill every crevice of the day: to this Zélide, who hated littleness, had come."

---

48. Ibid.

One might say M. de Charrière's life was no livelier than his wife's: at least he had chosen it; and it seems it suited his mediocrity. If one imagines a man endowed with the exceptional qualities of the Belle de Zuylen, he surely would not be consumed in Colombier's arid solitude. He would have carved out a place for himself in the world where he would undertake things, fight, act, and live. How many wives swallowed up in marriage have been, in Stendhal's words, "lost to humanity"! It is said marriage diminishes man: it is often true; but it almost always destroys woman. Marcel Prévost, advocate of marriage, admits it himself:

> How many times have I met after a few months or years of marriage a young woman I had known as a girl and been struck by the ordinariness of her character, the meaninglessness of her life.

Sophia Tolstoy uses almost the same words six months after her marriage:

> December 23, 1863:* My life is so mundane, and my death. But he has such a rich internal life, talent and immortality.

A few months earlier, she had uttered another complaint:

> May 9, 1863: You simply cannot be happy just sitting there sewing or playing the piano alone, completely *alone*, and gradually realizing, or rather becoming convinced that even though your husband may not love you, you are stuck there forever and there you must sit.

Twelve years later, she writes these words that many women today subscribe to:

> October 22, 1875:† Day after day, month after month, year after year—nothing ever changes. I wake up in the morning and just lie there wondering who will get me up, who is waiting for me. The cook is bound to come in, then the nurse, . . . so then I get up, . . . and sit silently darning holes, and then it's time for the

---

* *Diaries of Sophia Tolstoy*. Discrepancy between the French and the English translations. In the English text the date is given as November 13, 1863.—TRANS.

† Ibid. Discrepancy between the French and the English translations. In the English text the date is given as October 12, 1863.—TRANS.

children's grammar and piano lessons. Then in the evening more darning, with Auntie and Lyovochka playing endless . . . games of patience.

Mme Proudhon's complaint resonates with the same sound. "You have your ideas," she said to her husband. "And I, when you are at work, when the children are in school, I have nothing."

In the first years the wife often lulls herself with illusions, she tries to admire her husband unconditionally, to love him unreservedly, to feel she is indispensable to him and her children; and then her true feelings emerge; she sees her husband can get along without her, that her children are made to break away from her: they are always more or less thankless. The home no longer protects her from her empty freedom; she finds herself alone, abandoned, a subject, and she finds nothing to do with herself. Affections and habits can still be of great help, but not salvation. All sincere women writers have noted this melancholy that inhabits the heart of "thirty-year-old women"; this is a characteristic common to the heroines of Katherine Mansfield, Dorothy Parker, and Virginia Woolf. Cécile Sauvage, who sang so gaily of marriage and children at the beginning of her life, later expresses a subtle distress. It is noteworthy that the number of single women who commit suicide, compared with married women, shows that the latter are solidly protected from revulsion against life between twenty and thirty years of age (especially between twenty-five and thirty) but not in the following years. "As for marriage," writes Halbwachs, "it protects provincial as well as Parisian women until thirty years of age but not after."[49]

The drama of marriage is not that it does not guarantee the wife the promised happiness—there is no guarantee of happiness—it is that it mutilates her; it dooms her to repetition and routine. The first twenty years of a woman's life are extraordinarily rich; she experiences menstruation, sexuality, marriage, and motherhood; she discovers the world and her destiny. She is mistress of a home at twenty, linked from then on to one man, a child in her arms, now her life is finished forever. Real activity, real work, are the privilege of man: her only occupations are sometimes exhausting but never fulfill her. Renunciation and devotion have been extolled; but it often seems highly futile to devote herself to "the upkeep of any two beings until the end of their lives." It is all very grand to forget oneself, but

---

49. *Les causes du suicide* (*The Causes of Suicide*). The comment applies to France and Switzerland but not to Hungary or Oldenburg.

one must know for whom and for what. Worst of all is that her devotion itself is exasperating; in her husband's eyes, it changes into a tyranny from which he tries to escape; and yet it is he who imposes his presence on woman as her supreme, one justification; by marrying her, he obliges her to give herself to him completely; he does not accept the reciprocal obligation, which is to accept this gift. Sophia Tolstoy's words "I live through him and for him, I demand the same thing for me" are certainly revolting; but Tolstoy demanded she only live for him and through him, an attitude reciprocity alone can justify. It is the husband's duplicity that dooms the wife to a misfortune of which he later complains to be the victim. Just as he wants her both hot and cold in bed, he claims her totally given and yet weightless; he asks her to fix him to earth and to let him be free, to ensure the daily monotonous repetition and not to bother him, always to be present and never nag him; he wants her entirely for himself and not to belong to him, to live in a couple and to remain alone. Thus, as soon as he marries her, he mystifies her. She spends her life measuring the extent of this betrayal. What D. H. Lawrence says about sexual love is generally valid: the union of two human beings is doomed to failure if it requires an effort for each of them to complete each other, which supposes a primal mutilation; marriage must combine two autonomous existences, not be a withdrawal, an annexation, an escape, a remedy. This is what Nora understands when she decides that before being able to be a wife and mother, she has to be a person.[50] The couple should not consider itself a community, a closed cell: instead, the individual as individual has to be integrated into a society in which he can thrive without assistance; he will then be able to create links in pure generosity with another individual equally adapted to the group, links founded on the recognition of two freedoms.

This balanced couple is not a utopia; such couples exist sometimes even within marriage, more often outside of it; some are united by a great sexual love that leaves them free in their friendships and occupations; others are linked by a friendship that does not hamper their sexual freedom; more rarely there are still others who are both lovers and friends but without seeking in each other their exclusive reason for living. Many nuances are possible in the relations of a man and a woman: in companionship, pleasure, confidence, tenderness, complicity, and love, they can be for each other the most fruitful source of joy, richness, and strength offered to a human being. It is not the individuals who are responsible for the failure of

---

50. Ibsen, *A Doll's House.*

marriage: it is—unlike what Bonald, Comte, and Tolstoy claim—the institution that is perverted at its base. Declaring that a man and a woman who do not even choose each other *must* meet each other's needs in all respects, at once, for their whole life, is a monstrosity that necessarily gives rise to hypocrisy, hostility, and unhappiness.

The traditional form of marriage is changing: but it still constitutes an oppression that both spouses feel in different ways. Considering the abstract rights they enjoy, they are almost equals; they choose each other more freely than before, they can separate much more easily, especially in America, where divorce is commonplace; there is less difference in age and culture between the spouses than previously; the husband more easily acknowledges the autonomy his wife claims; they might even share housework equally; they have the same leisure interests: camping, bicycling, swimming, and so on. She does not spend her days waiting for her spouse's return: she practices sports, she belongs to associations and clubs, she has outside occupations, sometimes she even has a little job that brings her some money. Many young couples give the impression of perfect equality. But as long as the man has economic responsibility for the couple, it is just an illusion. He is the one who determines the conjugal domicile according to the demands of his job: she *follows* him from the provinces to Paris, from Paris to the provinces, the colonies, abroad; the standard of living is fixed according to his income; the rhythm of the days, the weeks, and the year is organized on the basis of his occupations; relations and friendships most often depend on his profession. Being more positively integrated than his wife into society, he leads the couple in intellectual, political, and moral areas. Divorce is only an abstract possibility for the wife, if she does not have the means to earn her own living: while alimony in America is a heavy burden for the husband, in France the lot of the wife and mother abandoned with a derisory pension is scandalous. But the deep inequality stems from the fact that the husband finds concrete accomplishment in work or action while for the wife in her role as wife, freedom has only a negative form: the situation of American girls, among others, recalls that of the emancipated girls of the Roman decadence. We saw that they had the choice between two types of behavior: some perpetuated the style of life and the virtues of their grandmothers; others spent their time in futile activity; likewise, many American women remain "housewives" in conformity with the traditional model; the others mostly whittle away their energy and time. In France, even if the husband has all the goodwill in the world, the burdens of the home do not weigh on him anymore once the young wife is a mother.

It is a commonplace to say that in modern households, and especially in the United States, the wife has reduced the husband to slavery. The fact is not new. Since the Greeks, males have complained of Xanthippe's tyranny; what is true is that the wife intervenes in areas that previously were forbidden to her; I know, for example, of students' wives who contribute to the success of their man with frenetic determination; they organize their schedules, their diet, they watch over their work; they cut out all distractions, and almost keep them under lock and key. It is also true that man is more defenseless than previously against this despotism; he recognizes his wife's abstract rights, and he understands that she can concretize them only through him: it is at his own expense that he will compensate for the powerlessness and the sterility the wife is condemned to; to realize an apparent equality in their association, he has to give her more because he possesses more. But precisely because she receives, takes, and demands, she is the poorer. The dialectic of the master and slave has its most concrete application here: in oppressing, one becomes oppressed. Males are in chains by their very sovereignty; it is because they alone earn money that the wife demands checks, because men alone practice a profession that the wife demands that they succeed, because they alone embody transcendence that the wife wants to steal it from them by taking over their projects and successes. And inversely, the tyranny wielded by the woman only manifests her dependence: she knows the success of the couple, its future, its happiness, and its justification, resides in the hands of the other; if she bitterly seeks to subjugate him to her will, it is because she is alienated in him. She makes a weapon of her weakness; but the fact is she is weak. Conjugal slavery is ordinary and irritating for the husband; but it is deeper for the wife; the wife who keeps her husband near her for hours out of boredom irritates him and weighs on him; but in the end, he can do without her more easily than she him; if he leaves her, it is she whose life will be ruined. The big difference is that for the wife, dependence is interiorized; she *is* a slave even when she conducts herself with apparent freedom, while the husband is essentially autonomous and enchained from the outside. If he has the impression he is the victim, it is because the burdens he bears are more obvious: the wife feeds on him like a parasite; but a parasite is not a triumphant master. In reality, just as biologically males and females are never victims of each other but all together of the species, the spouses together submit to the oppression of an institution they have not created. If it is said *men* oppress *women*, the husband reacts indignantly; he feels oppressed: he is; but in fact, it is the masculine code, the society developed by males and in their interest, that has defined the feminine condition in a form that is now for both sexes a source of distress.

The situation has to be changed in their common interest by prohibiting marriage as a "career" for the woman. Men who declare themselves antifeminist with the excuse that "women are already annoying enough as it is" are not very logical: it is precisely because marriage makes them "praying mantises," "bloodsuckers," and "poison" that marriage has to be changed and, as a consequence, the feminine condition in general. Woman weighs so heavily on man because she is forbidden to rely on herself; he will free himself by freeing her, that is, by giving her something *to do* in this world.

There are young women who are already trying to win this positive freedom; but seldom do they persevere in their studies or their jobs for long: they know the interests of their work will most often be sacrificed to their husband's career; their salary will only "help out" at home; they hesitate to commit themselves to undertakings that do not pull them away from conjugal enslavement. Those who do have a serious profession will not draw the same social advantages as men: lawyers' wives, for example, are entitled to a pension on their husbands' death; women lawyers are prohibited from paying a corresponding pension to their husbands in case of death. This shows that the woman who works cannot keep the couple at the same level as the man. There are women who find real independence in their profession; but many discover that work "outside" only represents another source of fatigue within the framework of marriage. Moreover and most often, the birth of a child forces them to confine themselves to their role of matron; it is still very difficult to reconcile work and motherhood.

According to tradition, it is the child who should ensure the wife a concrete autonomy that dispenses her from devoting herself to any other aim. If she is not a complete individual as a wife, she becomes it as a mother: the child is her joy and justification. She reaches sexual and social self-realization through him; it is thus through him that the institution of marriage has meaning and reaches its aim. Let us examine this ultimate step in woman's development.

CHAPTER 6

The Mother

It is through motherhood that woman fully achieves her physiological destiny; that is her "natural" vocation, since her whole organism is directed toward the perpetuation of the species. But we have already shown that human society is never left to nature. And in particular, for about a century, the reproductive function has no longer been controlled by biological chance alone but by design.[1] Some countries have officially adopted specific methods of birth control; in Catholic countries, it takes place clandestinely: either man practices coitus interruptus, or woman rids her body of the sperm after the sexual act. This is often a source of conflict or resentment between lovers or married partners; the man gets irritated at having to check his pleasure; the woman detests the chore of douching; he begrudges her too-fertile womb; she dreads these living germs he risks leaving in her. And for both of them there is consternation when, in spite of precautions, she finds herself "caught." This happens frequently in countries where contraceptive methods are rudimentary. Then anti-physis takes a particularly acute form: abortion. As it is even banned in countries that authorize birth control, there are many fewer occasions to have recourse to it. But in France, many women are forced to have this operation, which haunts the love lives of most of them.

There are few subjects on which bourgeois society exhibits more hypocrisy: abortion is a repugnant crime to which it is indecent to make an allusion. For an author to describe the joys and suffering of a woman giving birth is perfectly fine; if he talks about a woman who has had an abortion, he is accused of wallowing in filth and describing humanity in an abject light: meanwhile, in France every year there are as many abortions as births. It is such a widespread phenomenon that it has to be considered

---

1. See Volume I, Part Two, "History," Chapter 5, where a historical account of the question of birth control and abortion can be found.

one of the risks normally involved in the feminine condition. The law persists, however, in making it a misdemeanor: it demands that this delicate operation be executed clandestinely. Nothing is more absurd than the arguments used against legislating abortion. It is claimed to be a dangerous operation. But honest doctors recognize, along with Dr. Magnus Hirschfeld, that "abortion performed by a competent specialist, in a clinic and with proper preventative measures, does not involve the serious dangers penal law asserts." It is, on the contrary, its present form that makes it a serious risk for women. The incompetence of "back-alley" abortionists and their operating conditions cause many accidents, some of them fatal. Forced motherhood results in bringing miserable children into the world, children whose parents cannot feed them, who become victims of public assistance or "martyr children." It must be pointed out that the same society so determined to defend the rights of the fetus shows no interest in children after they are born; instead of trying to reform this scandalous institution called public assistance, society prosecutes abortionists; those responsible for delivering orphans to torturers are left free; society closes its eyes to the horrible tyranny practiced in "reform schools" or in the private homes of child abusers; and while it refuses to accept that the fetus belongs to the mother carrying it, it nevertheless agrees that the child is his parents' thing; this very week, a surgeon committed suicide because he was convicted of performing abortions, and a father who had beaten his son nearly to death has been condemned to three months of prison *with a suspended sentence*. Recently a father let his son die of whooping cough by not providing medical care; a mother refused to call a doctor for her daughter in the name of unconditional submission to God's will: in the cemetery, other children threw stones at her; but when some journalists showed their indignation, a group of right-thinking people protested that children belong to their parents, that outside control would be unacceptable. Today there are "a million children in danger," says the newspaper *Ce Soir;* and *France-Soir* writes: "Five hundred thousand children are *reported* to be in physical or moral danger." In North Africa, the Arab woman has no recourse to abortion: out of ten children she gives birth to, seven or eight die, and no one is disturbed because painful and absurd childbirth has killed maternal sentiments. If this is morality, then what kind of morality is it? It must be added that the men who most respect embryonic life are the same ones who do not hesitate to send adults to death in war.

The practical reasons invoked against legal abortion are completely unfounded; as with moral reasons, they are reduced to the old Catholic argument: the fetus has a soul, and the gates to paradise are closed to it without baptism. It is worth noting that the Church authorizes the killing of adult men in war, or when it is a question of the death penalty; but it stands on intransigent humanitarianism for the fetus. It is not redeemed by baptism: but in the times of the holy wars against the infidel, the infidels were not baptized either, and massacre was still strongly encouraged. Victims of the Inquisition were undoubtedly not all in a state of grace, nor are criminals who are guillotined and soldiers killed on the battlefield. In all these cases, the Church leaves it to the grace of God; it accepts that man is only an instrument in his hands and that the soul's salvation depends on the Church and God. Why, then, keep God from welcoming the embryonic soul into his heaven? If a council authorized it, he would not protest against the pious massacre of the Indians any more than in the good old days. The truth is that this is a conflict with a stubborn old tradition that has nothing to do with morality. The masculine sadism I have already discussed also has to be taken into account. The book Dr. Roy dedicated to Pétain in 1943 is a striking example; it is a monument of bad faith. In a paternalistic way it underlines the dangers of abortion; but nothing seems more hygienic to him than a Cesarean. He wants abortion to be considered a crime and not a misdemeanor; and he wishes to have it banned even in its therapeutic form, that is, when the mother's life or health is in danger: it is immoral to choose between one life and another, he declares, and bolstered by this argument, he advises sacrificing the mother. He declares that the fetus does not belong to the mother, that it is an autonomous being. But when these same "right-thinking" doctors exalt motherhood, they affirm that the fetus is part of the mother's body, that it is not a parasite nourished at the mother's expense. This fervor on the part of some men to reject everything that might liberate women shows how alive antifeminism still is.

Besides, the law that dooms young women to death, sterility, and illness is totally powerless to ensure an increase of births. A point of agreement for both partisans and enemies of legal abortion is the total failure of repression. According to Professors Doléris, Balthazard, and Lacassagne, there were 500,000 abortions a year around 1933; a statistic (cited by Dr. Roy) established in 1938 estimated the number at 1 million. In 1941, Dr. Aubertin from Bordeaux hesitated between 800,000 and 1 million. This last figure seems closest to the truth. In a March 1948 article in *Combat*, Dr. Desplas wrote:

Abortion has entered into our customs . . . Repression has practically failed . . . In the Seine district, in 1943, 1,300 investigations found 750 charged and of them, 360 women were arrested, 513 condemned to a minimum of one to five years in prison, which is low compared with the 15,000 presumed abortions in the district. There are 10,000 reported cases in the territory.

He adds:

So-called criminal abortion is as familiar to all social classes as the contraceptive policies accepted by our hypocritical society. Two-thirds of abortions are performed on married women . . . it can be roughly estimated that there are as many abortions as births in France.

Due to the fact that the operation is often carried out in disastrous conditions, many abortions end in these women's deaths:

Two bodies of women who had abortions arrive per week at the medical-legal institute in Paris; many abortions result in permanent illnesses.

It is sometimes said that abortion is a "class crime," and this is very often true. Contraceptive practices are more prevalent in the bourgeoisie; the existence of bathrooms makes their use easier than for workers or farmers deprived of running water; young girls in the bourgeoisie are more careful than others; a child is less of a burden in these households: poverty, insufficient housing, and the necessity for the wife to work outside the home are among the most common reasons for abortions. It seems that most often couples decide to limit births after two children; an ugly woman can have an abortion just as can this magnificent mother rocking her two blond angels in her arms: she is the same woman. In a document published in *Les Temps Modernes* in October 1945, under the title "Common Ward," Mme Geneviève Serreau describes a hospital room where she had to go once, and where many of the patients had just undergone curettages: fifteen out of eighteen had had miscarriages, half of which were induced. Number 9 was the wife of a market porter; she had had ten children in two marriages, of which only three were still living, and she had seven miscarriages, five of which were induced; she regularly used the "coat hanger" technique that she complaisantly displayed, as well as pills whose names she shared with her companions. Number 16, sixteen years old and married, had had affairs and contracted salpingitis as the result of an abortion.

Number 7, thirty-five, explained: "I've been married twenty years. I never loved him: for twenty years I behaved properly. Three months ago I took a lover. One time, in a hotel room. I got pregnant . . . So what else could I do? I had it taken out. No one knows anything, not my husband, not . . . him. Now it's over; I'll never go through it again. I've suffered too much . . . I'm not speaking about the curettage . . . No, no, it's something else: it's . . . it's self-respect, you see." Number 14 had had five children in five years; at forty she looked like an old woman. All of them had an air of resignation that comes from despair. "Women are made to suffer," they said sadly.

The seriousness of this ordeal varies a great deal depending on the circumstances. The conventionally married woman or one comfortably provided for, supported by a man, having money and relations, is better off: first, she finds ways to have a "therapeutic" abortion much more easily; if necessary, she has the means to pay for a trip to Switzerland, where abortion is liberally tolerated; gynecology today is such that it is a benign operation when performed by a specialist with all hygienic guarantees and, if necessary, anesthetic resources; failing official approval, she can find unofficial help that is just as safe: she has the right addresses, she has enough money to pay for conscientious care, without waiting until her pregnancy is advanced; she will be treated respectfully; some of these privileged people even maintain that this little accident can be beneficial to one's health and improve the complexion. On the other hand, there is little distress more pathetic than that of an isolated and penniless girl who sees herself ensnared in a "crime" to erase a "fault" that people around her consider unpardonable: in France this is the case of approximately 300,000 women employees, secretaries, students, workers, and peasants; illegitimate motherhood is still so terrible a stain that many prefer suicide or infanticide to being an unmarried mother: proof that no punishment will ever stop them from "getting rid of the infant." A typical case heard thousands of times is one related by Dr. Liepmann. It concerns a young Berlin woman, the natural child of a shoemaker and a maid:

I became friendly with a neighbor's son ten years older than
myself . . . His caresses were so new to me that, well, I let myself go.
However, in no way was it a question of love. But he continued to
teach me a lot of things, giving me books to read on women; and
finally I gave him the gift of my virginity. When, two months later, I
accepted a situation as a teacher in a nursery school in Speuze, I was
pregnant. I didn't see my period for two more months. My seducer

wrote to me that I absolutely had to make my period come back by drinking gasoline and eating black soap. I can no longer now describe the torments I went through . . . I had to see this misery through to the end on my own. The fear of having a child made me do the awful thing. This is how I learned to hate men.

The school pastor, having learned the story from a letter gone astray, gave her a long sermon, and she left the young man; she was called a black sheep:

That was how I ended up doing eighteen months in a reformatory.

Afterward, she became a children's maid in a professor's home and stayed for four years:

At that period, I came to know a judge. I was happy to have a real man to love. I gave him all my love. Our relations were such that at twenty-four years old, I gave birth to a healthy boy. Today that child is ten. I have not seen the father for nine and a half years . . . as I found the sum of twenty-five hundred marks insufficient, and as he refused to give the child his name and denied paternity, everything was over between us. No other man has aroused my desire since.[2]

It is often the seducer himself who convinces the woman that she should rid herself of the child. Either he has already abandoned her when she learns she is pregnant, or she altruistically wants to hide her disgrace from him, or else she finds no support from him. Sometimes it is not without regret that she refuses to have the child; either because she does not decide to abort early enough, or because she does not know where to go to do it, or because she does not have the money at hand and she has wasted her time trying ineffective drugs, she is in the third, fourth, fifth month of her pregnancy when she tries to eliminate it; the miscarriage will be infinitely more dangerous, more painful, more compromising than in the course of the first weeks. The woman knows this; in anguish and fear, she tries to find a way out. In the countryside, using a catheter is hardly known; the peasant woman who has "sinned" accidentally lets herself fall off an attic ladder, throws herself from the top of a staircase, often hurts herself

2. *Youth and Sexuality.*

with no result; it also happens that a small strangled corpse is found in the bushes, in a ditch, or in an outhouse. In towns, women help each other out. But it is not always easy to get hold of a backstreet abortionist, and still less easy to get the money demanded; the pregnant woman requests help from a friend, or she may perform the operation herself; these cut-price women surgeons are often incompetent; it does not take long to perforate oneself with a coat hanger or knitting needle; a doctor told me that an ignorant woman, trying to inject vinegar into her uterus, injected it into her bladder instead, provoking unspeakable pain. Brutally begun and poorly treated, the miscarriage, often more painful than an ordinary delivery, is accompanied by nervous disorders that can verge on epileptic fits, sometimes provoke serious internal illnesses, and bring on fatal hemorrhaging. In *Gribiche*, Colette recounts the harsh agony of a little music-hall dancer abandoned to the ignorant hands of her mother; a standard remedy, she says, is to drink a concentrated soap solution and then to run for a quarter of an hour: with such treatments, it is often by killing the mother that one gets rid of the child. I was told about a secretary who stayed in her room for four days, lying in her blood, without eating or drinking, because she did not dare call anyone. It is difficult to imagine abandonment more frightful than the kind where the threat of death converges with that of crime and shame. The ordeal is less harsh in the case of poor but married women who act in accord with their husbands and without being tormented by useless scruples: a social worker told me that in "poor neighborhoods" women share advice, borrow and lend instruments, and help each other out as simply as if they were removing corns. But they undergo severe physical suffering; hospitals are obliged to accept a woman whose miscarriage has already commenced; but she is sadistically *punished* by being refused sedatives during labor and during the final curettage procedure. As seen in reports by Serreau, for example, these persecutions do not even shock women all too used to suffering: but they are sensitive to the humiliations heaped on them. The fact that the operation they undergo is a clandestine and criminal one multiplies the dangers and makes it abject and anguishing. Pain, sickness, and death seem like chastisement: we know what distance separates suffering from torture, accident from punishment; with the risks she assumes, the woman feels guilty, and it is this interpretation of pain and blame that is particularly distressful.

This moral aspect of the drama is more or less intensely felt depending on the circumstances. For very "liberated" women, thanks to their financial resources, their social situation, the free milieu they belong to, or for those who have learned through poverty and misery to disdain bourgeois morality, the question hardly arises: there is a difficult moment to go through, but it must be gone through, and that is all. But many women are intimidated by a morality that maintains its prestige in their eyes, even though their behavior cannot conform to it; inwardly, they respect the law they are breaking, and they suffer from committing a crime; they suffer even more for having to find accomplices. In the first place, they undergo the humiliation of begging: they beg for an address, a doctor's care, a midwife; they risk being haughtily snubbed; or they expose themselves to a degrading connivance. To deliberately invite another to commit a crime is a situation that most men never know and that the woman experiences with a mixture of fear and shame. This intervention she demands is one she often rejects in her own heart. She is divided inside herself. It might be that her spontaneous desire is to keep this child whose birth she is preventing; even if she does not positively want this motherhood, she feels ill at ease with the ambiguity of the act she is about to perform. For even if abortion is not murder, it cannot be assimilated to a simple contraceptive practice; an event has taken place that is an absolute commencement and whose development is being halted. Some women are haunted by the memory of this child who did not come to be. Helene Deutsch cites the case of a psychologically normal married woman who, having twice lost third-month fetuses due to her physical condition, made them little tombs that she treated with great piety even after the birth of many other children.[3] If the miscarriage was induced, this is all the more reason to feel she has committed a sin. The childhood remorse that follows the jealous desire for the death of a newborn little brother is revived, and the woman blames herself for really killing a child. This feeling of guilt can be expressed in pathological melancholies. In addition to women who think they tried to kill a living thing, there are many who feel they have mutilated a part of themselves; from here stems a resentment against the man who accepted or solicited this mutilation. Deutsch, once again, cites the case of a young girl who, deeply infatuated with her lover, herself insisted on eliminating a child who would have been an obstacle to their happiness; leaving the hospital, she refused to see the man she loved from then on. Even if such a definitive rupture is rare, it is, on the contrary, common for a woman to become frigid, either with all men or with the one who made her pregnant.

Men tend to take abortion lightly; they consider it one of those numerous accidents to which the malignity of nature has destined women: they

---

3. *Psychology of Women.*

do not grasp the values involved in it. The woman repudiates feminine values, her values, at the moment the male ethic is contested in the most radical way. Her whole moral future is shaken by it. Indeed, from childhood woman is repeatedly told she is made to bear children, and the praises of motherhood are sung; the disadvantages of her condition—periods, illness, and such—the boredom of household tasks, all this is justified by this marvelous privilege she holds, that of bringing children into the world. And in an instant, the man, to keep his freedom and not to handicap his future, in the interest of his job, asks the woman to renounce her female triumph. The child is no longer a priceless treasure: giving birth is no longer a sacred function: this proliferation becomes contingent and inopportune, and it is again one of femininity's defects. The monthly labor of menstruation becomes a blessing by comparison: now the return of the red flow that once plunged the girl into horror is anxiously awaited; it was in promising her the joys of childbearing that she had been consoled. Even consenting to and wanting an abortion, woman feels her femininity sacrificed: she will from now on definitively see in her sex a malediction, a kind of infirmity, a danger. Taking this denial to its extreme, some women become homosexual after the trauma of abortion. Yet when man asks woman to sacrifice her bodily possibilities for the success of his male destiny, he is denouncing the hypocrisy of the male moral code at the same time. Men universally forbid abortion; but they accept it individually as a convenient solution; they can contradict themselves with dizzying cynicism; but woman feels the contradictions in her wounded flesh; she is generally too shy to deliberately revolt against masculine bad faith; while seeing herself as a victim of an injustice that decrees her to be a criminal in spite of herself, she still feels dirtied and humiliated; it is she who embodies man's fault in a concrete and immediate form, in herself; he commits the fault, but unloads it onto her; he just says words in a pleading, threatening, reasonable, or furious tone: he forgets them quickly; it is she who translates these phrases into pain and blood. Sometimes he says nothing, he just walks away; but his silence and avoidance are a far more obvious indictment of the whole moral code instituted by men. What is called immorality in women, a favorite theme with misogynists, should surprise no one; how could women not feel inwardly defiant against the arrogant principles men publicly advocate and secretly denounce? Women learn to believe men no longer when they exalt women or when they exalt men; the one sure thing is the manipulated and bleeding womb, those shreds of red life, that absence of a child. With her first abortion, the woman begins to "understand." For many women, the world will never be the same. And yet, for lack of access to contraceptives, abortion is the only way out today in

France for women who do not want to bring into the world children condemned to death and misery. Stekel said it correctly: "Prohibition of abortion is an immoral law, since it must be forcibly broken every day, every hour."[4]

Birth control and legal abortion would allow women to control their pregnancies freely. In fact, what decides woman's fecundity is in part a considered desire and in part chance. As long as artificial insemination is not widely practiced, a woman might desire to become pregnant but be unable to—because either she does not have relations with men, or her husband is sterile, or she is unable to conceive. And, on the other hand, she is often forced to give birth against her will. Pregnancy and motherhood are experienced in very different ways depending on whether they take place in revolt, resignation, satisfaction, or enthusiasm. One must keep in mind that the decisions and feelings the young mother expresses do not always correspond to her deep desires. An unwed mother can be overwhelmed in material terms by the burden suddenly imposed on her, be openly distressed by it, and yet find in the child the satisfaction of secretly harbored dreams; inversely, a young married woman who joyfully and proudly welcomes her pregnancy can fear it in silence, hate it with obsessions, fantasies, and infantile memories that she herself refuses to recognize. This is one of the reasons why women are so secretive on this subject. Their silence comes in part from liking to surround an experience that is theirs alone in mystery; but they are also disconcerted by the contradictions and conflicts of which they themselves are the center. "The preoccupations of pregnancy are a dream that is forgotten as entirely as the dream of birth pains," one woman said.[5] These are complex truths that come to the fore in women and that they endeavor to bury in oblivion.

We have seen that in childhood and adolescence woman goes through several phases in connection with motherhood. When she is a little girl, it is a miracle and a game: she sees in the doll and she feels in the future child an object to possess and dominate. As an adolescent girl, on the contrary, she sees in it a threat to the integrity of her precious person. Either she rejects it violently, like Colette Audry's heroine who confides to us:

Each little child playing in the sand, I loathed him for coming out of a woman . . . I loathed the adults too for lording it over the children, purging them, spanking them, dressing them, shaming them in all

---

4. *Frigidity in Woman.*
5. N. Hale.

ways: women with their soft bodies always ready to bud out with new little ones, men who looked at all this pulp of their women and children belonging to them with a satisfied and independent air. My body was mine alone, I only liked it brown, encrusted with sea salt, scratched by the rushes. It had to stay hard and sealed.[6]

Or else she fears it at the same time as she wishes it, which leads to pregnancy fantasies and all kinds of anxieties. Some girls enjoy exercising maternal authority but are not at all disposed to assume the responsibilities fully. Such is the case of Lydia cited by Helene Deutsch who, at sixteen, placed as a maid with foreigners, took the most extraordinarily devoted care of the children entrusted to her: it was a prolongation of her childish dreams in which she formed a couple with her mother to raise a child; suddenly she began to neglect her service, to be indifferent to the children, to go out, flirt; the time of games was finished, and she was beginning to pay attention to her real life, where desire for motherhood did not hold a great place. Some women have the desire to dominate children their whole lives, but they are horrified by the biological labor of parturition: they become midwives, nurses, grammar school teachers; they are devoted aunts, but they refuse to have children. Others too, without being disgusted by maternity, are too absorbed by their love lives or careers to make a place for it in their existence. Or they are afraid of the burden a child would mean for them or their husbands.

Often a woman deliberately ensures her sterility either by refusing all sexual relations or by birth-control practices; but there are also cases where she does not admit her fear of the infant and where conception is prevented by a psychic defense mechanism; functional problems of nervous origin occur that can be detected in a medical examination. Dr. Arthus cites a striking example, among others:

Mme H. . . . had been poorly prepared for her life as a woman by her mother; who had always warned her of the worst catastrophes if she became pregnant . . . When Mme H. . . . was married she thought she was pregnant the following month; she realized her error; then once more after three months; new mistake. A year later she went to a gynecologist, who did not see any cause of infertility in her or her husband. Three years later, she saw another one who told her: "You

---

6. "L'enfant" (The Child), in *Playing a Losing Game*.

will get pregnant when you talk less." After five years of marriage, Mme H. . . . and her husband had accepted that they would not have a child. A baby was born after six years of marriage.[7]

The acceptance or refusal of conception is influenced by the same factors as pregnancy in general. The subject's infantile dreams and her adolescent anxieties are revived during pregnancy; it is experienced in different ways depending on the woman's relations with her mother, her husband, and herself.

Becoming a mother in turn, woman somehow takes the place of the one who gave birth to her: this means total emancipation for her. If she sincerely desires her pregnancy, it will be of utmost importance for her to carry it out without assistance; still dominated and consenting to it, she will put herself, on the contrary, in her mother's hands: the newborn will seem like a brother or sister to her rather than her own offspring; if at the same time she wants and does not dare to liberate herself, she fears that the child, instead of saving her, will make her fall back under the yoke: this anguish can cause miscarriages; Deutsch cites the case of a young woman who, having to accompany her husband on a trip and leaving the child with her mother, gave birth to a stillborn child; she wondered why she had not mourned it more because she had ardently desired it; but she would have hated giving it over to her mother, who would have dominated her through this child. Guilt feelings toward one's mother are common, as was seen, in the adolescent girl; if they are still strong, the wife imagines that a curse weighs on her offspring or on herself: the child, she thinks, will kill her upon coming into the world, or he will die in birth. This anguish that they will not carry their pregnancy to term—so frequent in young women—is often provoked by remorse. This example reported in H. Deutsch shows how the relationship to the mother can have a negative importance:

Mrs. Smith was the youngest in a family with many other children, one boy and several girls. After this boy had disappointed the ambitious hopes of the parents, they wanted to have another son, but instead my patient was born. Her mother never concealed her disappointment over this fact . . . the patient was saved from traumatic reactions to this attitude by two compensations—her father's deep and tender love for her, and the maternal affection of one of her sisters . . . As a little girl she had reacted to her mother's rejections with conscious hatred . . . Up to her pregnancy she had been able to disregard her mother problem; but this method no longer worked when she herself was about to become a mother . . . she gave birth one month before term to a stillborn child. Soon she was again pregnant; and her joy was now even more mixed with fear of loss than during her first pregnancy. By this time she had come into close relation with a former friend of hers who was also pregnant . . . The friend had a mother who was the opposite of her own . . . full to the brim with maternal warmth. She spread her motherly wings both over her own loving daughter and Mrs. Smith. [But] her friend had conceived a whole month before her; thus during the last month she would be left to her own fate . . . to the surprise of everyone concerned, her friend did not have her child at the expected time . . . and gave birth to a boy overdue by a whole month on the very day that Mrs. Smith expected her own delivery.[8] The two friends now consciously adjusted themselves to each other in regard to their next pregnancies and conceived in the same month. This second time, Mrs. Smith had no fears or doubts. But during the third month of her pregnancy her friend told her that her husband had been offered a position in another town and that the family would probably move there. That very day Mrs. Smith started on a miscarriage. This woman could not manage to have a second child . . . After her friend had failed her she could no longer chase away the shadow of the mother she had rejected.

The woman's relationship with her child's father is no less important. An already mature and independent woman can desire a child belonging wholly to herself: I knew one whose eyes lit up at the sight of a handsome male, not out of sensual desire, but because she judged his stud-like capacities; there are maternal Amazons who enthusiastically welcome the miracle of artificial insemination. Even if the child's father shares their life, they deny him any right over their offspring; they try—like Paul's mother in *Sons and Lovers*—to form a closed couple with their child. But in most cases, a woman needs masculine support to accept her new responsibilities; she will only devote herself joyously to a newborn if a man devotes himself to her.

---

8. H. Deutsch affirms that she verified the fact that the child was really born ten months after conception.

The more infantile and shy she is, the more she needs this. Deutsch thus recounts the story of a young woman who at fifteen years of age married a sixteen-year-old boy who had got her pregnant. As a little girl, she had always loved babies and helped her mother take care of her brothers and sisters. But once she herself became a mother of two children, she panicked. She demanded that her husband constantly stay with her; he had to take a job that allowed him to remain home for long periods. She lived in a state of constant anxiety, exaggerating her children's fights, giving excessive importance to the slightest incidents of their days. Many young mothers demand so much help from their husbands that they drive them away by overburdening them with their problems. Deutsch cites other curious cases, like this one:

> A young married woman thought she was pregnant and was extremely happy about it; separated from her husband by a trip, she had a very brief adventure that she accepted specifically because, delighted by her pregnancy, nothing else seemed to be of consequence; back with her husband, she learned later on that in truth, she had been mistaken about the conception date: it dated from his trip. When the child was born, she suddenly wondered if he was her husband's son or her fleeting lover's; she became incapable of feeling anything for the desired child; anguished and unhappy, she resorted to a psychiatrist and was not interested in the baby until she decided to consider her husband as the newborn's father.*

The woman who feels affection for her husband will often tailor her feelings to his: she will welcome pregnancy and motherhood with joy or misery depending on whether he is proud or put upon. Sometimes a child is desired to strengthen a relationship or a marriage, and the mother's attachment depends on the success or failure of her plans. If she feels hostility toward the husband, the situation is quite different: she can fiercely devote herself to the child, denying the father possession, or, on the other hand, hate the offspring of the detested man. Mrs. H.N., whose wedding night we recounted as reported by Stekel, immediately became pregnant, and she detested the little girl conceived in the horror of this brutal initiation her whole life. In Sophia Tolstoy's *Diaries* too, the ambivalence of her feelings for her husband is reflected in her first pregnancy. She writes:

---

* *Psychology of Women.*—TRANS.

I am in an unbearable state, physically and mentally. Physically I am always ill with something, mentally there is this awful emptiness and boredom, like a dreadful depression. As far as Lyova is concerned I do not exist . . . I can do nothing to make him happy, because I am pregnant.

The only pleasure she feels in this state is masochistic: it is probably the failure of her sexual relations that gives her an infantile need for self-punishment.

I have been ill since yesterday. I am afraid I may miscarry, yet I even take pleasure from the pain in my stomach. It is like when I did something naughty as a child, and Maman would always forgive me but I could never forgive myself, and would pinch and prick my hand. The pain would become unbearable but I would take intense pleasure in enduring it . . . I shall enjoy my new baby and also enjoy physical pleasures again—how disgusting . . . Everything here seems so depressing. Even the clock sounds melancholy when it strikes the hour; . . . everything is dead. But if Lyova . . . !

But pregnancy is above all a drama playing itself out in the woman between her and herself. She experiences it both as an enrichment and a mutilation; the fetus is part of her body, and it is a parasite exploiting her; she possesses it, and she is possessed by it; it encapsulates the whole future, and in carrying it, she feels as vast as the world; but this very richness annihilates her, she has the impression of not being anything else. A new existence is going to manifest itself and justify her own existence, she is proud of it; but she also feels like the plaything of obscure forces, she is tossed about, assaulted. What is unique about the pregnant woman is that at the very moment her body transcends itself, it is grasped as immanent: it withdraws into itself in nausea and discomfort; it no longer exists for itself alone and then becomes bigger than it has ever been. The transcendence of an artisan or a man of action is driven by a subjectivity, but for the future mother the opposition between subject and object disappears; she and this child who swells in her form an ambivalent couple that life submerges; snared by nature, she is plant and animal, a collection of colloids, an incubator, an egg; she frightens children who are concerned with their own bodies and provokes sniggers from young men because she is a human being, consciousness and freedom, who has become a passive instrument of life. Life is usually just a condition of existence; in gestation it is creation; but it is a strange creation that takes place in contingence and facticity. For some women the joys of pregnancy and nursing are so strong they want to repeat them indefinitely; as soon as the baby is weaned, they feel frustrated. These "breeders" rather than mothers eagerly seek the possibility of alienating their liberty to the benefit of their flesh: their existence appears to them to be tranquilly justified by the passive fertility of their body. If flesh is pure inertia, it cannot embody transcendence, even in a degraded form; it is idleness and ennui, but as soon as it burgeons, it becomes progenitor, source, flower, it goes beyond itself, it is movement toward the future while being a thickened presence at the same time. The separation woman suffered from in the past during her weaning is compensated for; it is submerged again in the current of life, reintegrated into the whole, a link in the endless chain of generations, flesh that exists for and through another flesh. When she feels the child in her heavy belly or when she presses it against her swollen breasts, the mother accomplishes the fusion she sought in the arms of the male, and that is refused as soon as it is granted. She is no longer an object subjugated by a subject; nor is she any longer a subject anguished by her freedom, she is this ambivalent reality: life. Her body is finally her own since it is the child's that belongs to her. Society recognizes this possession in her and endows it with a sacred character. She can display her breast that was previously an erotic object, it is a source of life: to such an extent that pious paintings show the Virgin Mary uncovering her breast and begging her Son to save humanity. Alienated in her body and her social dignity, the mother has the pacifying illusion of feeling she is a being *in itself*, a ready-made *value*.

But this is only an illusion. Because she does not really make the child: it is made in her; her flesh only engenders flesh: she is incapable of founding an existence that will have to found itself; creations that spring from freedom posit the object as a value and endow it with a necessity: in the maternal breast, the child is unjustified, it is still only a gratuitous proliferation, a raw fact whose contingence is symmetrical with that of death. The mother can have *her* reasons for wanting *a* child, but she cannot give to *this* other—who tomorrow is going to be—his own raisons d'être; she engenders him in the generality of his body, not in the specificity of his existence. This is what Colette Audry's heroine understands when she says:

> I never thought he could give meaning to my life . . . His being
> had grown in me and I had to go through with it to term, whatever
> happened, without being able to hasten things, even if I had to die

from it. Then he was there, born from me; so he was like the work I might have done in my life . . . but after all he was not.[9]

In one sense the mystery of incarnation is repeated in each woman; every child who is born is a god who becomes man: he could not realize himself as consciousness and freedom if he did not come into the world; the mother lends herself to this mystery, but she does not control it; the supreme truth of this being taking shape in her womb escapes her. This is the ambivalence she expresses in two contradictory fantasies: all mothers have the idea that their child will be a hero; they thus express their wonderment at the idea of giving birth to a consciousness and a liberty; but they also fear giving birth to a cripple, a monster, because they know the awful contingency of flesh, and this embryo who inhabits them is merely flesh. There are cases where one of these myths wins out: but often the woman wavers between them. She is also susceptible to another ambivalence. Trapped in the great cycle of the species, she affirms life against time and death: she is thus promised to immortality; but she also experiences in her flesh the reality of Hegel's words: "The birth of children is the death of parents." The child, he also says, is for the parents "the being for itself of their love that falls outside of them"; and inversely, he will obtain his being for himself "in separating from the source, a separation in which this source dries up." Going beyond self for woman is also the prefiguration of her death. She manifests this truth in the fear she feels when imagining the birth: she fears losing her own life in it.

As the meaning of pregnancy is thus ambiguous, it is natural for the woman's attitude to be ambivalent as well: it changes moreover with the various stages of the fetus's evolution. It has to be noted first that at the beginning of the process the child is not present; he has only an imaginary existence; the mother can dream of this little individual who will be born in a few months, be busy preparing his cradle and layette: she grasps concretely only the organic and worrisome phenomena of which she is the seat. Some priests of Life and Fecundity mystically claim that woman knows the man has just made her a mother by the quality of the pleasure she experiences: this is one of the myths to be put into the trash heap. She never has a decisive intuition of the event: she deduces it from uncertain signs. Her periods stop, she thickens, her breasts become heavy and hurt, she has dizzy spells and is nauseous; sometimes she thinks she is simply ill, and it is the doctor who informs her. Then she knows her body has been

9. "The Child," in *Playing a Losing Game.*

given a destination that transcends it; day after day a polyp born of her flesh and foreign to it is going to fatten in her; she is the prey of the species that will impose its mysterious laws on her, and generally this alienation frightens her: her fright manifests itself in vomiting. It is partially provoked by modifications in the gastric secretions then produced; but if this reaction, unknown in other female mammals, becomes more serious, it is for psychic reasons; it expresses the acute character of the conflict between species and individual in the human female.[10] Even if the woman deeply desires the child, her body revolts at first when it has to deliver. In *Conditions of Nervous Anxiety and Their Treatment,* Stekel asserts that the pregnant woman's vomiting always expresses a certain rejection of the child; and if the child is greeted with hostility—often for unavowed reasons—gastric troubles are exacerbated.

"Psychoanalysis has taught us that psychogenic intensification of the oral pregnancy symptom of vomiting takes place only when the oral expulsion tendencies are accompanied by unconscious and sometimes even manifest emotions of hostility to pregnancy or to the fetus," says Deutsch. She adds, "The psychologic content in pregnancy vomiting was exactly the same as that in the hysterical vomiting of young girls that is induced by an unconscious pregnancy fantasy and not by a real condition."[11] In both cases, the old idea that children have of fertilization through the mouth comes back to life. For infantile women in particular, pregnancy is, as in the past, assimilated to an illness of the digestive apparatus. Deutsch cites a woman patient who anxiously studied her vomit to see if there were not fragments of the fetus; but she *knew,* she said, that this obsession was absurd. Bulimia, lack of appetite, and feeling sick signal the same hesitation between the desire to conserve and the desire to destroy the embryo. I knew a young woman who suffered both from excessive vomiting and fierce constipation; she told me that one day she had the impression both of trying to reject the fetus and of striving to keep it, corresponding exactly to her avowed desires. Dr. Arthus cites the following example, which I have summarized:

Mme T. . . . presents serious pregnancy problems with irrepressible vomiting . . . The situation is so worrisome that an abortion is being

---

10. See Volume I, Chapter 1. [In Part One, "Destiny."—TRANS.]

11. I was specifically told about the case of a man who for the first months of his wife's pregnancy—a wife he did not even love very much—presented the exact symptoms of nausea, dizziness, and vomiting seen in pregnant women. They obviously express unconscious conflicts in a hysterical form.

considered . . . The young woman is disconsolate . . . The brief analysis that can be practiced shows [that] Mme T. subconsciously identifies with one of her former boarding school friends who had played a great role in her emotional life and who died during her first pregnancy. As soon as this cause could be uncovered, the symptoms improved; vomiting continued somewhat for two weeks but does not present any more danger.[12]

Constipation, diarrhea, and expulsion tendencies always express the same mixture of desire and anguish; the result is sometimes a miscarriage: almost all spontaneous miscarriages have a psychic origin. The more importance woman gives these malaises and the more she coddles herself, the more intense they are. In particular, pregnant women's famous "cravings" are indulgently nurtured infantile obsessions: they are always focused on food, and have to do with the old idea of fertilization by food; feeling distressed in her body, woman expresses, as often happens in psychasthenies, this feeling of strangeness through a desire that fascinates her. There is moreover a "culture," a tradition, of these cravings as there once was a culture of hysteria; woman expects to have these cravings, she waits for them, she invents them for herself. I was told of a teenage mother who had such a frenetic craving for spinach that she ran to the market to buy it and jumped up and down in impatience watching it cook: she was thus expressing the anxiety of her solitude; knowing she could only count on herself, she was in a feverish rush to satisfy her desires. The duchesse d'Abrantès described very amusingly in her *Memoirs* a case where the craving is imperiously suggested by the woman's circle of friends. She complains of having been surrounded by too much solicitude during her pregnancy:

These cares and kind attentions increased the discomfort, nausea, nervousness, and thousands of sufferings that almost always accompany first pregnancies. I found it so . . . It was my mother who started it one day when I was having dinner at her house . . . "Good heavens," she cried suddenly, putting down her fork and looking at me with dismay. "Good heavens! I forgot to ask what you especially *craved*."

"But there is nothing in particular," I replied.

"You have no special craving," exclaimed my mother, "nothing!

---

12. *Marriage.*

But that is unheard of. You must be wrong. You haven't noticed. I'll speak to your mother-in-law about it."

And so there were my two mothers in consultation. And there was Junot, afraid I would bear him a child with a wild boar's head . . . asking me every morning: "Laura, what do you crave?" My sister-in-law came back from Versailles and added her voice to the choir of questions, saying that she had seen innumerable people disfigured because of unsatisfied longings . . . I finally got frightened myself . . . I tried to think of what would please me most and couldn't think of a thing. Then, one day, it occurred to me when I was eating pineapple lozenges that a pineapple had to be a very excellent thing . . . Once I persuaded myself that I had a *longing* for a pineapple, I felt at first a very lively desire, increased when Corcelet declared that . . . they were not in season. Ah, then I felt that mad desire which makes you feel that you will die if it is not satisfied.

(Junot, after many attempts, finally received a pineapple from Mme Bonaparte. The duchess of Abrantès welcomed it joyously and spent the night feeling and touching it as the doctor had ordered her not to eat it until morning, when Junot finally served it to her.)

I pushed the plate away. "But—I don't know what is the matter with me. I can't eat pineapple." He put my nose into the cursed plate, which made it clear that I could not eat pineapple. They not only had to take it away but also had to open the windows and perfume my room in order to remove the least traces of an odor that had become hateful to me in an instant. The strangest part of it is that since then I have never been able to eat pineapple without practically forcing myself.

Women who are too coddled or who coddle themselves too much are the ones who present the most morbid phenomena. Those that go through the ordeal of pregnancy the most easily are, on one hand, matrons totally devoted to their function as breeders and, on the other hand, mannish women who are not fascinated by the adventures of their bodies and who do everything they can to triumph over them with ease: Mme de Staël went through pregnancy as easily as a conversation.

As the pregnancy proceeds, the relation between mother and fetus changes. It is solidly settled in the maternal womb, the two organisms adapt to each other, and there are biological exchanges between them allowing the woman to regain her balance. She no longer feels possessed by the species: she herself possesses the fruit of her womb. The first months she was an ordinary woman, and diminished by the secret labor taking place in her; later she is obviously a mother, and her malfunctions are the reverse of her glory. The increasing weakness she suffers from becomes an excuse. Many women then find a marvelous peace in their pregnancy: they feel justified; they always liked to observe themselves, to spy on their bodies; because of their sense of social duty, they did not dare to focus on their body with too much self-indulgence: now they have the right to; everything they do for their own well-being they also do for the child. They are not required to work or make an effort; they no longer have to pay attention to the rest of the world; the dreams of the future they cherish have meaning for the present moment; they only have to enjoy the moment: they are on vacation. The reason for their existence is there, in their womb, and gives them a perfect impression of plenitude. "It is like a stove in winter that is always lit, that is there for you alone, entirely subject to your will. It is also like a constantly gushing cold shower in the summer, refreshing you. It is there," says a woman quoted by Helene Deutsch. Fulfilled, woman also experiences the satisfaction of feeling "interesting," which has been, since her adolescence, her deepest desire; as a wife, she suffered from her dependence on man; at present she is no longer sex object or servant, but she embodies the species, she is the promise of life, of eternity; her friends and family respect her; even her caprices become sacred: this is what encourages her, as we have seen, to invent "cravings." "Pregnancy permits woman to rationalize performances which otherwise would appear absurd," says Helene Deutsch. Justified by the presence within her of another, she finally fully enjoys being herself.

Colette wrote about this phase of her pregnancy in *L'étoile vesper* (*The Evening Star*):

> Insidiously, unhurriedly, I was invaded by the beatitude of the woman great with child. I was no longer the prey of any malaise, any unhappiness. Euphoria, purring—what scientific or familiar name can one give to this saving grace? It must certainly have filled me to overflowing, for I haven't forgotten it . . . One grows weary of suppressing what one has never said—such as the state of pride, of banal magnificence which I savoured in ripening my fruit . . . Every evening I said a small farewell to one of the good periods of my life. I was well aware that I should regret it. But the cheerfulness, the purring, the euphoria submerged everything, and I was governed by the calm animality, the unconcern, with which I was charged by my increasing weight and the muffled call of the being I was forming.

Sixth, seventh month . . . the first strawberries, the first roses . . . Can I call pregnancy anything but a long holiday? One forgets the anguish of the term, one doesn't forget a unique long holiday; I've forgotten none of it. I particularly recall that sleep used to overwhelm me at capricious hours, and that I would be seized, as in my childhood, by the desire to sleep on the ground, on the grass, on warm straw. Unique "craving," healthy craving . . .

Towards the end I had the air of a rat that drags a stolen egg. Uncomfortable in myself, I would be too tired to go to bed . . . Even then, the weight and the tiredness did not interrupt my long holiday. I was borne on a shield of privilege and solicitude.

This happy pregnancy was called by one of Colette's friends "a man's pregnancy." And she seemed to be the epitome of these women who valiantly support their state because they are not absorbed in it. She continued her work as a writer at the same time. "The child showed signs of coming first and I screwed on the top of my pen."

Other women are more weighed down; they mull indefinitely over their new importance. With just a little encouragement they adopt masculine myths: they juxtapose the lucidity of the mind to the fertile night of Life, clear consciousness to the mysteries of interiority, sterile freedom to the weight of this womb there in its enormous facticity; the future mother smells of humus and earth, spring and root; when she dozes, her sleep is that of chaos where worlds ferment. There are those more forgetful of self who are especially enchanted with the treasure of life growing in them. This is the joy Cécile Sauvage expresses in her poems in *L'âme en bourgeon* (The Soul in Bud):

> *You belong to me as dawn to the plain*
> *Around you my life is a warm fleece*
> *Where your chilly limbs grow in secret.*

And further on:

> *Oh you whom I fearfully cuddle in fleecy cotton*
> *Little soul in bud attached to my flower*
> *With a piece of my heart I fashion your heart*
> *Oh my cottony fruit, little moist mouth.* *

---

* Translated by Beverley Bie Brahic.—TRANS.

And in a letter to her husband:

> It's funny, it seems to me I am watching the formation of a tiny
> planet and that I am kneading its frail globe. I have never been so
> close to life. I have never so felt I am sister of the earth with all
> vegetation and sap. My feet walk on the earth as on a living beast. I
> dream of the day full of flutes, of awakened bees, of dew because
> here he is bucking and stirring in me. If you knew what springtime
> freshness and what youth this soul in bud puts in my heart. And to
> think this is Pierrot's infant soul and that in the night of my being it
> is elaborating two big eyes of infinity like his.

In contrast are women who are very flirtatious, who grasp themselves
essentially as erotic objects, who love themselves in the beauty of their
bodies, and who suffer from seeing themselves deformed, ungainly, incapable of arousing desire. Pregnancy does not at all appear to them as a celebration or an enrichment, but as a diminishing of their self.

In *My Life* by Isadora Duncan one can read, among other observations:

> The child asserted itself now, more and more. It was strange to see
> my beautiful marble body softened and broken and stretched and
> deformed . . . As I walked beside the sea, I sometimes felt an excess
> of strength and prowess, and I thought this creature would be mine,
> mine alone, but on other days . . . I felt myself some poor animal in
> a mighty trap . . . With alternate hope and despair, I often thought
> of the pilgrimage of my childhood, my youth, my wanderings . . .
> my discoveries in Art, and they were as a misty, far-away prologue,
> leading up to this—the before-birth of a child. What any peasant
> woman could have! . . . I began to be assailed with all sorts of fears.
> In vain I told myself that every woman had children . . . It was all in
> the course of life, etc. I was, nevertheless, conscious of fear. Of
> what? Certainly not of death, nor even of pain—some unknown
> fear, of what I did not know . . . More and more my lovely body
> bulged under my astonished gaze . . . Where was my lovely, youth-
> ful naiad form? Where my ambition? My fame? Often, in spite
> of myself, I felt very miserable and defeated. This game with the
> giant Life was too much. But then I thought of the child to come,
> and all such painful thoughts ceased . . . Helpless, cruel hours of
> waiting in the night . . . With what a price we pay for the glory of
> motherhood.

In the last stage of pregnancy begins the separation between mother and child. Women experience his first movement differently, his kick knocking at the doors of the world, knocking against the wall of the womb that encloses him away from the world. Some women welcome and marvel at this signal announcing the presence of an autonomous life; others think of themselves with repugnance as the receptacle of a foreign individual. Once again, the union of fetus and maternal body is disturbed: the uterus descends, the woman has a feeling of pressure, tension, respiratory trouble. She is possessed this time not by the indistinct species but by this child who is going to be born; until then, he was just an image, a hope; he becomes heavily present. His reality creates new problems. Every passage is anguishing: the birth appears particularly frightening. When the woman comes close to term, all the infantile terrors come back to life; if, from a feeling of guilt, she thinks she is cursed by her mother, she persuades herself she is going to die or that the child will die. In *War and Peace,* Tolstoy painted in the character of Lise one of these infantile women who see a death sentence in birth: and she does die.

Depending on the case, the birth takes many different forms: the mother wants both to keep in her womb the treasure of her flesh that is a precious piece of her self and to get rid of an intruder; she wants finally to hold her dream in her hands, but she is afraid of new responsibilities this materialization will create: either desire can win, but she is often divided. Often, also, she does not come to the anguishing ordeal with a determined heart: she intends to prove to herself and to her family—her mother, her husband—that she is capable of surmounting it without help; but at the same time she resents the world, life, and her family for the suffering inflicted on her, and in protest she adopts a passive attitude. Independent women—matrons or masculine women—attach great importance to playing an active role in the period preceding and even during the birth; very infantile women let themselves passively go to the midwife, to their mother; some take pride in not crying out; others refuse to follow any recommendations. On the whole, it can be said that in this crisis they express their deepest attitude to the world in general, and to their motherhood in particular: they are stoic, resigned, demanding, imperious, revolted, inert, tense . . . These psychological dispositions have an enormous influence on the length and difficulty of the birth (which also, of course, depends on purely organic factors). What is significant is that normally woman—like some domesticated female animals—needs help to accomplish the function to which nature destines her; there are peasants in rough conditions and shamed young unmarried mothers who give birth alone: but their solitude often brings about the death of the child or for the mother incurable ill-nesses. At the very moment woman completes the realization of her femi-nine destiny, she is still dependent: which also proves that in the human species nature can never be separated from artifice. With respect to nature, the conflict between the interest of the feminine person and that of the species is so acute it often brings about the death of either the mother or the child: human interventions by doctors and surgeons have considerably reduced—and even almost eliminated—the accidents that were previously so frequent. Anesthetic methods are in the process of giving the lie to the biblical affirmation "In sorrow thou shalt bring forth children"; they are commonly used in America and are beginning to spread to France; in March 1949, a decree has just made them compulsory in England.[13]

It is difficult to know exactly what suffering these methods save women from. The fact that delivery sometimes lasts more than twenty-four hours and sometimes is completed in two or three hours prevents any generaliza-tion. For some women, childbirth is martyrdom. Such is the case of Isadora Duncan: she lived through her pregnancy in anxiety, and psychic resistance undoubtedly aggravated the pains of childbirth even more. She writes:

> Talk about the Spanish Inquisition! No woman who has borne a child would have to fear it. It must have been a mild sport in compar-ison. Relentless, cruel, knowing no release, no pity, this terrible, unseen genie had me in his grip, and was, in continued spasms, tearing my bones and my sinews apart. They say such suffering is soon forgotten. All I have to reply is that I have only to shut my eyes and I hear again my shrieks and groans as they were then.

On the other hand, some women think it is a relatively easy ordeal to bear. A small number experience sensual pleasure in it. One woman writes:

---

13. I have already said that some antifeminists, in the name of nature and the Bible, were indig-nant at the attempt to eliminate the suffering of childbirth; it is supposed to be one of the sources of the maternal "instinct." Helene Deutsch seems tempted by this opinion; she writes that when the mother has not felt the labor of childbirth, she does not profoundly recognize the child as her own at the moment she is presented with him; however, she agrees that the same feeling of emptiness and strangeness is encountered in women who have given birth and suf-fered; and she maintains all through her book that maternal love is a feeling, a conscious atti-tude, and not an instinct; that it is not necessarily linked to pregnancy; according to her, a woman can maternally love an adopted child or one her husband has had from a first marriage, and so on. This contradiction obviously comes from the fact that she has destined woman to masochism and her thesis demands she grant a high value to feminine suffering.

I am so strongly sexed that even childbirth means to me a sexual act . . . I had a very pretty "madame" for a nurse. She bathed me and gave me my vaginal douches. This was enough for me—it kept me in such a high state of sexual agitation that I trembled.[14]

Some women say they felt creative power during childbirth; they truly accomplished a voluntary and productive piece of work; many others feel passive, a suffering and tortured instrument.

The mother's first relations with the newborn vary as well. Some women suffer from this emptiness they now feel in their bodies: it seems to them that someone has stolen their treasure. Cécile Sauvage writes:

> *I am the hive without speech*
> *Whose swarm has flown into the air*
> *No longer do I bring back the beakful*
> *Of my blood to your frail body*
> *My being is a closed-up house*
> *From which they have removed a body.*

And more:

> *No longer are you mine alone. Your head*
> *Already reflects other skies.*

And also:

> *He is born, I have lost my young beloved*
> *Now that he is born, I am alone, I feel*
> *Terrifying within me the void of my blood.* *

Yet, at the same time, there is a wondrous curiosity in every young mother. It is a strange miracle to see, to hold a living being formed in and coming out of one's self. But what part has the mother really had in the extraordinary event that brings a new existence into the world? She does not know. The being would not exist without her, and yet he escapes her. There is a surprising sadness in seeing him outside, cut off from herself. And there is almost always a disappointment. The woman would like to

---

14. Stekel recorded this subject's confession, which I have partially summarized.
* Translated by Beverley Bie Brahic.—TRANS.

feel him *hers* as surely as her own hand: but everything he feels is closed up inside him, he is opaque, impenetrable, apart; she does not even recognize him, since she does not know him; she lived her pregnancy without him: she has no common past with this little stranger; she expected to be familiar right away; but no, he is a newcomer, and she is stupefied by the indifference with which she receives him. In her pregnancy reveries he was an image, he was infinite, and the mother mentally played out her future motherhood; now he is a tiny, finite individual, he is really there, contingent, fragile, demanding. The joy that he is finally here, quite real, is mingled with the regret that this is all he is.

After the initial separation, many young mothers regain an intimate animal relationship with their children through nursing; this is a more stressful fatigue than that of pregnancy, but it allows the nursing mother to prolong the "vacation" state of peace and plenitude she relished in pregnancy. Colette Audry says of one of her heroines:

> When the baby was suckling, there was really nothing else to do, and it could last for hours; she did not even think of what would come after. She could only wait for him to release her breast like a big bee.[15]

But there are women who cannot nurse, and in whom the surprising indifference of the first hours continues until they regain concrete bonds with the child. This was the case, among others, with Colette, who was not able to nurse her daughter and who describes her first maternal feelings with her customary sincerity:

> The outcome is the contemplation of a new person who has entered the house without coming in from outside . . . Did I devote enough love to my contemplation? I should not like to say so. True, I had the capacity—I still have—for wonder. I exercised it on that assembly of marvels which is the newborn. Her nails, resembling in their transparency the convex scale of the pink shrimp—the soles of her feet, which have reached us without touching the ground . . . The light plumage of her lashes, lowered over her cheek, interposed between the scenes of earth and the bluish dream of her eye . . . The small sex, a barely incised almond, a bivalve precisely closed, lip to lip . . . But the meticulous admiration I devoted to my daughter—

---

15. *Playing a Losing Game.*

I did not call it, I did not feel it as love. I waited . . . I did not derive from these scenes, so long awaited in my life, the vigilance and emulation of besotted mothers. When, then, would be vouchsafed to me the sign that was to mark my second, more difficult, violation? I had to accept that an accumulation of warnings, of furtive, jealous outbursts, of false premonitions—and even of real ones—the pride in managing an existence of which I was the humble creditor, the somewhat perfidious awareness of giving the other love a lesson in modesty, would eventually change me into an ordinary mother. Yet I only regained my equanimity when intelligible speech blossomed on those ravishing lips, when recognition, malice, and even tenderness turned a run-of-the-mill baby into a little girl, and a little girl into my daughter![16]

There are also many mothers who are terrified of their new responsibilities. During pregnancy, they had only to abandon themselves to their flesh; no initiative was demanded of them. Now in front of them is a person who has rights to them. Some women happily caress their babies while they are still in the hospital, still gay and carefree, but upon returning home, they start to regard them as burdens. Even nursing brings them no joy, and, on the contrary, they worry about ruining their breasts; they resent feeling their cracked breasts, their painful glands; the baby's mouth hurts them: he seems to be sucking their strength, life, and happiness from them. He inflicts a harsh servitude on them, and he is no longer part of his mother: he is like a tyrant; she feels hostility for this little individual who threatens her flesh, her freedom, her whole self.

Many other factors are involved. The woman's relations with her mother are still of great importance. Helene Deutsch cites the case of a young nursing mother whose milk dried up whenever her mother came to see her; she often solicits help, but is jealous of the care someone else gives to the baby and feels depressed about this. Her relations with the infant's father and the feelings he himself fosters also have a strong influence. A whole set of economic and sentimental considerations define the infant as a burden, a shackle, or a liberation, a jewel, a form of security. There are cases where hostility becomes outright hatred resulting in extreme neglect or bad treatment. Most often the mother, conscious of her duties, combats this hostility; she feels remorse that gives rise to anxieties prolonging the

16. *Evening Star.*

apprehensions of pregnancy. All psychoanalysts agree that mothers who are obsessed about harming their children, or who imagine horrible accidents, feel an enmity toward them they force themselves to repress. What is nonetheless remarkable and distinguishes this relationship from all other human relationships is that in the beginning the child himself does not play a part: his smiles, his babbling, have no meaning other than the one his mother gives them; it depends on her, not him, whether he seems charming, unique, bothersome, ordinary, or obnoxious. This is why cold, unsatisfied, melancholic women who expect a child to be a companion, or to provide warmth and excitement that draw them out of themselves, are always deeply disappointed. Like the "passage" into puberty, sexual initiation, and marriage, motherhood generates morose disappointment for subjects who are waiting for an external event to renew and justify their lives. This is the sentiment found in Sophia Tolstoy. She writes:

> "These past nine months have been practically the worst in my life," to say nothing of the tenth.*

She tries in vain to express a conventional joy; we are struck by her sadness and fear of responsibilities:

> It is all over, the baby has been born and my ordeal is at last at an end. I have risen from my bed and am gradually entering into life again, but with a constant feeling of fear and dread about my baby and especially my husband. Something within me seems to have collapsed, and I sense that whatever it is it will always be there to torment me; it is probably the fear of not doing my duty towards *my family* . . . I have become insincere, for I am frightened by the womb's vulgar love for its offspring, and frightened by my somewhat unnatural love for my husband . . . I sometimes comfort myself with the thought that most people see this love of one's husband and children as a virtue . . . But how strong these maternal feelings are! . . . He is Lyovochka's child, that's why I love him.

But we know very well that she only exhibits so much love for her husband because she does not love him; this antipathy marks the child conceived in embraces that disgusted her.

---

* *Diaries of Sophia Tolstoy.* Beauvoir attributes this quotation to Sophia, but it is in fact Leo's.—TRANS.

Katherine Mansfield describes the hesitation of a young mother who loves her husband but is repulsed by his caresses. For her children she feels tenderness and at the same time has an impression of emptiness she sadly interprets as complete indifference. Linda, resting in the garden next to her newborn, thinks about her husband, Stanley:

Well, she was married to him. And what was more she loved him. Not the Stanley whom everyone saw, not the everyday one; but a timid, sensitive, innocent Stanley who knelt down every night to say his prayers . . . But the trouble was . . . she saw her Stanley so seldom. There were glimpses, moments, breathing spaces of calm, but all the rest of the time it was like living in a house that couldn't be cured of the habit of catching on fire, on a ship that got wrecked every day. And it was always Stanley who was in the thick of the danger. Her whole time was spent in rescuing him, and restoring him, and calming him down, and listening to his story. And what was left of her time was spent in the dread of having children . . . It was all very well to say it was the common lot of women to bear children. It wasn't true. She, for one, could prove that wrong. She was broken, made weak, her courage was gone, through child-bearing. And what made it doubly hard to bear was, she did not love her children. It was useless pretending . . . No, it was as though a cold breath had chilled her through and through on each of those awful journeys; she had no warmth left to give them. As to the boy—well, thank Heaven, mother had taken him; he was mother's, or Beryl's, or anybody's who wanted him. She had hardly held him in her arms. She was so indifferent about him that as he lay there . . . Linda glanced down . . . There was something so quaint, so unexpected about that smile that Linda smiled herself. But she checked herself and said to the boy coldly, "I don't like babies." "Don't like babies?" The boy couldn't believe her. "Don't like me?" He waved his arms foolishly at his mother. Linda dropped off her chair on to the grass. "Why do you keep on smiling?" she said severely. "If you knew what I was thinking about, you wouldn't" . . . Linda was so astonished at the confidence of this little creature . . . Ah no, be sincere. That was not what she felt; it was something far different, it was something so new, so . . . The tears danced in her eyes; she breathed in a small whisper to the boy, "Hallo, my funny!"[17]

---

17. "At the Bay."

These examples all prove that there is no such thing as maternal "instinct": the word does not in any case apply to the human species. The mother's attitude is defined by her total situation and by the way she accepts it. It is, as we have seen, extremely variable.

But the fact is that if circumstances are not positively unfavorable, the mother will find herself enriched by a child. "It was like a response to the reality of her own existence . . . through him she had a grasp on all things and on herself to begin with," wrote Colette Audry about a young mother. And she has another character say these words:

> He was heavy in my arms, and on my breast, like the heaviest thing
> in the world, to the limit of my strength. He buried me in silence
> and darkness. All at once he had put the weight of the world on my
> shoulders. That was indeed why I wanted him. I was too light
> myself. Alone, I was too light.

While some women are "breeders" rather than mothers and lose interest in their child as soon as it is weaned, or as soon as it is born, and only desire another pregnancy, many others by contrast feel that it is the separation itself that gives them the child; it is no longer an indistinct part of themselves but a piece of the world; it no longer secretly haunts the body but can be seen, touched; after the melancholy of delivery, Cécile Sauvage expresses the joy of possessive motherhood:

> *Here you are my little lover*
> *On your mother's big bed*
> *I can kiss you, hold you,*
> *Feel the weight of your fine future;*
> *Good day my little statue*
> *Of blood, of joy and naked flesh,*
> *My little* double, *my excitement . . .*

It has been said again and again that woman happily finds an equivalent of the penis in the infant: this is completely wrong. In fact, the adult man no longer sees his penis as a wonderful toy: his organ is valued in relation to the desirable objects it allows him to possess; by the same token, the adult woman envies the male for the prey he acquires, not the instrument of this acquisition; the infant satisfies this aggressive eroticism that the male embrace does not fulfill: the infant is homologous to this mistress that she is for the male and that he is not for her; of course there is no exact correspondence; every relation is unique; but the mother finds in the child—like the lover in the beloved—a carnal plenitude, not in surrender but in domination; she grasps in the child what man seeks in woman: an other, both nature and consciousness, who is her prey, her *double*. He embodies all of nature. Audry's heroine tells us she found in her child:

> The skin that was for my fingers to touch, that fulfilled the promise of all little kittens, all flowers . . .

His skin has that sweetness, that warm elasticity that, as a little girl, the woman coveted in her mother's flesh and, later, everywhere in the world. He is plant and animal, he holds rains and rivers in his eyes, the azure of the sky and the sea, his fingernails are coral, his hair a silky growth, he is a living doll, a bird, a kitten; my flower, my pearl, my chick, my lamb . . . His mother murmurs words almost of a lover and uses, like a lover, the possessive adjective; she uses the same words of appropriation: caresses, kisses; she hugs the infant to her body, she envelops him in the warmth of her arms, of her bed. At times these relations have a clearly sexual cast. Thus in the confession collected by Stekel I have already cited, we read:

> I nursed my baby but I took no particular joy in doing so because he did not thrive well. We were both losing ground. The act of nursing seemed something sexual to me. I was always ashamed of it . . . it was for me a majestic experience to feel the warm little body snuggling up to me . . . The touch of his little hands thrilled me . . . My whole love went out to him . . . The child would cling to me and did not leave my side. It was troublesome to try to keep him away from me . . . When he saw me in bed he crawled up at once—he was two years of age at the time—and tried to lie on top of me. At the same time his little hands wandered over my breasts and tried to reach down. I found this very pleasurable; it was not easy for me to send the child away. Frequently I fought against the temptation of playing with his genitals.

Motherhood takes on a new aspect when the child grows older; at first he is only a "standard baby," existing in his generality: little by little he becomes individualized. Very dominating or very carnal women grow cold toward him; it is then that some others—like Colette—begin to take an interest in him. The mother's relation to the child becomes more and more complex: he is a double, and at times she is tempted to alienate herself completely in him, but he is an autonomous subject, and therefore rebellious; today he is warmly real, but in the far-off future he is an adolescent, an imaginary adult; he is her wealth, a treasure: but he is also a responsibility, a tyrant. The joy the mother can find in him is a joy of generosity; she must take pleasure in serving, giving, creating happiness, such as the mother depicted by Colette Audry:

> Thus, he had a happy storybook infancy, but his infancy was to storybook infancy as real roses were to postcard roses. And this happiness of his came out of me like the milk with which I nourished him.

Like the woman in love, the mother is delighted to feel needed; she is justified by the demands she responds to; but what makes maternal love difficult and great is that it implies no reciprocity; the woman is not before a man, a hero, a demigod, but a little stammering consciousness, lost in a fragile and contingent body; the infant possesses no value, and he can bestow none; the woman remains alone before him; she expects no compensation in exchange for her gifts, she justifies them with her own freedom. This generosity deserves the praise that men forever bestow on her; but mystification begins when the religion of Motherhood proclaims that all mothers are exemplary. For maternal devotion can be experienced in perfect authenticity; but in fact, this is rarely the case. Ordinarily, maternity is a strange compromise of narcissism, altruism, dream, sincerity, bad faith, devotion, and cynicism.

The great risk our mores present for the infant is that the mother to whom he is tied and bound is almost always an unfulfilled woman: sexually she is frigid or unsatisfied; socially she feels inferior to man; she has no hold on the world or the future; she will try to compensate for her frustrations through the child; when one recognizes how the present situation of woman makes her full development difficult, how many desires, revolts, pretensions, and claims she secretly harbors, one is frightened that helpless little children are given over to her. Just as when she both pampered and tortured her dolls, her behavior is symbolic: but these symbols become bitter reality for the child. A mother who beats her child does not only beat the child, and in a way she does not beat him at all: she is taking her vengeance on man, on the world, or on herself; but it is the child who receives the blows. Mouloudji expresses this painful misunderstanding in *Enrico*: Enrico well understands it is not he whom his mother beats so wildly; and waking from her delirium, she sobs with remorse and tenderness; he does not hold it against her, but he is no less disfigured by her blows. And the mother described in Violette Leduc's *In the Prison of Her*

Skin, in lashing out against her daughter, is in fact taking revenge on the seducer who abandoned her, on life that humiliated and defeated her. This cruel aspect of motherhood has always been known; but with hypocritical prudishness, the idea of the "bad mother" has been defused by inventing the cruel stepmother; the father's second wife torments the child of the deceased "good mother." Indeed, Mme Fichini is a mother figure, the exact counterpart of the edifying Mme de Fleurville described by Mme de Ségur. Since Jules Renard's *Poil de carotte* (*Carrot Top*), there have been more and more accusations: *Enrico, In the Prison of Her Skin*, Simone de Tervagne's *Maternal Hatred*, Hervé Bazin's *Viper in the Fist*. While the types sketched in these novels are somewhat exaggerated, the majority of women suppress their spontaneous impulses out of morality and decency; but these impulses flare up in scenes, slaps, anger fits, insults, punishments, and so on. In addition to frankly sadistic women, there are many who are especially capricious; what delights them is to dominate; when the baby is tiny, he is a toy: if it is a boy, they shamelessly play with his penis; if it is a girl, they treat her like a doll; later they only want a little slave who will blindly obey them: vain, they show the child off like a trained pet; jealous and exclusive, they set him apart from the rest of the world. Also, the woman often continues to expect gratitude for the care she gives the child: she shapes an imaginary being through him who will recognize her with gratitude for being an admirable mother and one in whom she recognizes herself. When Cornelia, proudly showing her children, said, "These are my jewels," she gave an ill-fated example to posterity; too many mothers live in the hope of one day repeating this arrogant gesture; and they do not hesitate to sacrifice the little flesh-and-blood individual whose contingent and indecisive existence does not fulfill them. They force him to resemble their husbands, or, on the contrary, not to resemble them, or to reincarnate a father, a mother, or a venerated ancestor; they model him on someone prestigious: a German socialist deeply admired Lily Braun, recounts Helene Deutsch; the famous activist had a brilliant son who died young; her imitator was determined to treat her own son like a future genius, and as a result he became a bandit. Harmful to the child, this ill-adapted tyranny is always a source of disappointment for the mother. Deutsch cites another striking example, of an Italian woman whose case history she followed for several years.

> Mrs. Mazzetti . . . had a number of small children . . . who caused
> her difficulties, all of them, one after the other. Personal contact with
> Mrs. Mazzetti soon revealed that although she sought help it was

difficult to influence her . . . Her entire bearing . . . was consistently
used only in face of the outside world, but . . . in relations with her
family, she gave way to uncontrolled emotional outbursts . . . we
learned that coming from a poor, uncultured milieu, she had always
had the urge to become something "better." She always attended
night schools and would perhaps have achieved something in
harmony with her aspirations if she had not met her husband.
He . . . exerted an irresistible sexual attraction upon her. At the age
of sixteen she had sexual relations with him, soon became pregnant,
and found herself compelled to marry him . . . She continually tried
to raise herself again . . . she went to night school, etc. The man was
a first class workman . . . Mrs. Mazzetti evidently had emphasized
her superiority to him in a very aggressive way, which drove this
simple man to . . . alcoholism. He tried to devaluate his wife's
superiority by . . . making her repeatedly pregnant . . . After
her separation from her husband she turned all her emotions
to the children, and began to treat them as she had treated her
husband . . . As long as the children were small she appeared to be
attaining her goal. They were very ambitious, successful in school,
etc. When Louise, the oldest child, approached the age of sixteen,
her mother seems to have fallen into a state of anxiety that was
based upon her own past experiences. This anxiety was expressed in
heightened watchfulness and strictness, to which Louise reacted with
protests, and had an illegitimate child . . . The children emotionally
clung to their father and were against their mother who tried to
impose her moral standards on them . . . She could never be kind to
more than one of her older children at a time, and always indulged
her negative, aggressive emotions at the expense of the others. Since
the children thus alternated as objects of her love, the child who had
just been loved was driven to rage, jealousy, and revenge . . . one
daughter after another became promiscuous, they brought syphilis
and illegitimate children into the home, the little boys began to steal,
and Mrs. Mazzetti could not understand that ideal demands instead
of tender harmony pushed them in that direction.

This authoritarian upbringing and capricious sadism I spoke of are often
mixed together; to justify her anger, the mother uses the pretext of wanting
to "shape" the child; and inversely, failure in her endeavor exasperates her
hostility.

Masochistic devotion is another quite common attitude, and no less harmful for the child; some mothers make themselves slaves of their off-spring to compensate for the emptiness in their hearts and to punish them-selves for the hostility they do not want to admit; they endlessly cultivate a morbid anxiety, they cannot bear to let their child do anything on his own; they give up all pleasure, all personal life, enabling them to assume the role of victim; and from these sacrifices they derive the right to deny the child all independence; this renunciation is easily reconciled with a tyrannical will to domination; the *mater dolorosa* turns her suffering into a weapon she uses sadistically; her displays of resignation spur guilt feelings in the child, which he will often carry through his whole life: they are more harmful than aggressive displays. Tossed about, baffled, the child finds no defense mechanism: sometimes blows, sometimes tears, show him to be a criminal. The mother's main excuse is that the child is far from bringing her that sat-isfying self-accomplishment she was promised since childhood: she takes out on him the mystification of which she was a victim and that the child innocently exposes. She did what she wanted with her dolls; when she helped care for her sister's or a friend's baby, it was without responsibility. But now society, her husband, her mother, and her own pride hold her responsible for this little foreign life as if it were her own composition: the husband in particular is irritated by the child's faults just as he is by a spoiled dinner or his wife's improper behavior; his abstract demands often weigh heavily on the mother's relation to the child; an independent woman—thanks to her solitude, her carefree state, or her authority in the household—will be much more serene than those carrying the weight of dominating demands in making her child obey. For the great difficulty is to contain within a fixed framework a mysterious existence like that of ani-mals, turbulent and disorderly, like the forces of nature, but human nonetheless; one cannot train a child in silence like training a dog, nor per-suade him with adult words: he plays on this ambiguity, pitting words against the animality of sobs and tantrums, and constraints against the insolence of language. Of course, the problem thus posed is challenging, and when she has time for it, the mother enjoys being an educator: peace-fully settled in a park, the baby is still as good an excuse as he was when he nestled in her stomach; often still more or less infantile herself, she delights in being silly with him, reviving games, words, interests, and joys of days gone by. But when she is washing, cooking, nursing another infant, shop-ping, entertaining callers, and mainly when she is taking care of her hus-band, the child is no more than a bothersome, harassing presence; she does not have the leisure time to "train" him; she must first keep him from mak-ing trouble; he demolishes, tears, dirties, he is a constant danger to objects and to himself; he fidgets, he screams, he talks, he makes noise: he lives for himself; and this life disturbs his parents' life. Their interest and his do not converge: therein lies the drama. Forever burdened by him, parents inflict sacrifices on him for reasons he does not understand: they sacrifice him for their tranquillity and his own future. It is natural for him to rebel. He does not understand the explanations his mother tries to give him: she cannot penetrate his consciousness; his dreams, his phobias, his obsessions, and his desires shape an opaque world: the mother can only gropingly control a being who sees these abstract laws as absurd violence from the outside. As the child grows older, this lack of comprehension remains: he enters a world of interests and values from which his mother is excluded; he often scorns her for it. The boy in particular, proud of his masculine prerogatives, laughs off a woman's orders: she insists on him doing his homework, but she cannot solve his problems, translate his Latin text; she cannot "keep up" with him. The mother is sometimes driven to tears over this task whose difficulty the husband rarely appreciates: raising an individual with whom one does not communicate but who is nonetheless a human being; interfering in a foreign freedom that defines and affirms itself only by rebelling against you.

The situation differs, depending on whether the child is a boy or a girl; and while boys are more "difficult," the mother generally gets along better with them. Because of the prestige woman attributes to men, and also the privileges they hold concretely, many women wish for a son. "It's marvelous to bring a man into the world," they say; as has been seen, they dream of giving birth to a "hero," and the hero is obviously of the male sex. The son will be a chief, a leader of men, a soldier, a creator; he will impose his will on the face of the earth, and his mother will share in his immortality; the houses she did not build, the countries she did not explore, the books she did not read, he will give to her. Through him she will possess the world: but on condition that she possesses her son. This is the source of her paradoxical attitude. Freud believes that the mother-son relationship contains the least ambivalence; but in fact in motherhood, as in marriage and love, woman has an ambiguous attitude to masculine transcendence; if her conjugal or love life has made her hostile to men, she will find satisfaction in dominating the male reduced to his infantile figure; she will treat the arrogantly pretentious sex organ with an ironic familiarity: at times she will frighten the child by announcing she will cut it off if he does not behave. Even if she is humble and more peaceful and respects the future hero in her son, she does what she can to reduce him to his immanent reality in order to ensure that he is really hers: just as she treats her husband like a child, she treats her child like a baby. It is too rational, too simple, to think she wishes to castrate her son; her dream is more contradictory: she wants him to be infinite and yet fit in the palm of her hand, dominating the whole world and kneeling before her. She encourages him to be soft, greedy, selfish, shy, sedentary, she forbids sports and friends, and she makes him unsure of himself because she wants to have him for herself; but she is disappointed if he does not at the same time become an adventurer, a champion, a genius she can be proud of. There is no doubt that her influence is often harmful—as Montherlant maintains and as Mauriac demonstrates in *Génitrix*. Luckily, boys can fairly easily escape this hold; customs and society encourage them to. And the mother herself is resigned to it: she knows very well that the struggle against man is unfair. She consoles herself by acting the *mater dolorosa* or by pondering the pride of having given birth to one of her conquerors.

The little girl is more wholly under the control of her mother; her claims on her daughter are greater. Their relations assume a much more dramatic character. The mother does not greet a daughter as a member of the chosen caste: she seeks a double in her. She projects onto her all the ambiguity of her relationship with her self; and when the alterity of this alter ego affirms itself, she feels betrayed. The conflicts we have discussed become all the more intensified between mother and daughter.

There are women who are satisfied enough with their lives to want to reincarnate themselves in a daughter, or at least welcome her without disappointment; they would like to give their child the same chances they had, as well as those they did not have: they will give her a happy youth. Colette traced the portrait of one of those well-balanced and generous mothers; Sido cherishes her daughter in her freedom; she fulfills her without ever making demands in return because her joy comes from her own heart. It can happen that in devoting herself to this double in whom she recognizes and transcends herself, the mother ends up totally alienating herself in her; she renounces herself, her only care is for her child's happiness; she will even be egotistical and hard toward the rest of the world; she runs the danger of becoming annoying to the one she adores, as did Mme de Sévigné for Mme de Grignan; the disgruntled daughter will try to rid herself from such tyrannical devotion; often she is unsuccessful, and she lives her whole life as a child, frightened of responsibilities because she has been too "sheltered." But it is especially a certain masochistic form of motherhood that risks weighing heavily on the young daughter. Some women feel their femininity as an absolute curse: they wish for or accept a daughter with the bitter pleasure of finding another victim; and at the same time they feel guilt at having brought her into the world; their remorse and the pity they feel for themselves through their daughter are manifested in endless anxieties; they will never take a step away from the child; they will sleep in the same bed for fifteen or twenty years; the little girl will be destroyed by the fire of this disquieting passion.

Most women both claim and detest their feminine condition; they experience it in resentment. The disgust they feel for their sex could incite them to give their daughters a virile education: they are rarely generous enough to do so. Irritated at having given birth to a female, the mother accepts her with this ambiguous curse: "You will be a woman." She hopes to redeem her inferiority by turning this person she considers a double into a superior being; and she also has a tendency to inflict on her the defect she has had to bear. At times she tries to impose exactly her own destiny on her child: "What was good enough for me is good enough for you; this is the way I was brought up, so you will share my lot." And at times, by contrast, she fiercely forbids her to resemble her: she wants her own experience to be useful, it is a way to get even. The courtesan will send her daughter to a convent, the ignorant woman will give her an education. In *In the Prison of Her Skin*, the mother who sees the hated consequence of a youthful error in her daughter tells her with fury:

> Try to understand. If such a thing happened to you, I would disown you. I did not know a thing. Sin! A vague idea, sin! If a man calls you, don't go. Go on your way. Don't turn back. Do you hear me? You've been warned, this must not happen to you, and if it happened, I would have no pity, I would leave you in the gutter.

We have seen that Mrs. Mazzetti, because she wanted to spare her daughter from her own error, precipitated it. Stekel recounts a complex case of "maternal hatred" of a daughter:

> I know a mother who disliked at birth her fourth daughter, a quiet charming girl . . . She claimed that this child had inherited, in concentrated measure, all her father's unpleasant traits . . . The child was born to her during the year when this exalted, dreamy woman had fallen passionately in love with another man, a poet, who was courting her . . . during her husband's embraces she permitted her mind to dwell on the poet, hoping that the child would thus become endowed with her beloved's traits—as in Goethe's *Elective Affinities*. However, the child looked so much like its father, from the

moment of its birth, that its paternity was obvious . . . She saw in the child a reflection of herself—a reflection of the dreamy, tender, yielding, sensual side of herself. She despised these qualities, scorned them in herself. She would have preferred to have been strong, unyielding, vigorous, prudish, and energetic. Thus she hated herself even more than she hated her husband through her hatred of the child.*

It is when the girl grows up that real conflicts arise; we have seen that she wishes to affirm her autonomy from her mother: this is, in her mother's eyes, a mark of detestable ingratitude; she obstinately tries to "tame" this determination that is lurking; she cannot accept that her double becomes *an other*. The pleasure man savors in women—feeling absolutely superior—is something a woman experiences only toward her children, and her daughters in particular; she feels frustration if she renounces these privileges and her authority. Whether she is a passionate or a hostile mother, her child's independence ruins her hopes. She is doubly jealous: of the world that takes her daughter, and of her daughter who, in conquering part of the world, robs her of it. This jealousy first involves the father-daughter relationship; sometimes the mother uses the child to keep her husband home: if this fails, she is vexed, but if her maneuver succeeds, she is sure to revive her infantile complex in an inverted form: she becomes irritated by her daughter as she was once by her own mother; she sulks, she feels abandoned and misunderstood. A French woman, married to a foreigner who loved his daughters very much, angrily said one day: "I've had enough of living with these 'wogs'!" Often the eldest daughter, the father's favorite, is the target of the mother's persecution. The mother heaps the worst chores on her, demands a seriousness beyond her age: since she is a rival, she will be treated as an adult; she too will learn that "life is not a storybook romance, everything is not rosy, you can't do whatever you please, you're not on earth to have fun." Very often, the mother strikes the child for no reason, simply "to teach her a lesson"; she wants to show her she is still in charge: for what vexes her the most is that she does not have any real superiority to set against a girl of eleven or twelve; the latter can already perform household tasks perfectly well, she is "a little woman"; she even has a liveliness, curiosity, and lucidity that, in many regards, make her superior to adult women. The mother likes to rule over her feminine universe with-

---

* *Conditions of Nervous Anxiety and Their Treatment.*—Trans.

out competition; she wants to be unique, irreplaceable; and yet here her young assistant reduces her to the pure generality of her function. She scolds her daughter sternly if, after being away for two days, she finds her household in disorder; but she goes into fits of anger if it so happens that family life continued along well without her. She cannot accept that her daughter will really become her double, a substitute of herself. Yet it is still more intolerable that she should boldly assert herself as an other. She systematically detests the girlfriends in whom her daughter seeks succor against family oppression, friends who "spur her on"; she criticizes them, prevents her daughter from seeing them too often, or even uses the pretext of their "bad influence" to radically forbid her to be with them. All influence that is not her own is bad; she has a particular animosity toward women of her own age—teachers, girlfriends' mothers—toward whom her daughter turns her affection: she declares these sentiments absurd or unhealthy. At times, gaiety, silliness, or children's games and laughter are enough to exasperate her; she more readily accepts this of boys; they are exercising their male privilege, as is natural, and she has long given up this impossible competition. But why should this other woman enjoy advantages that she has been refused? Imprisoned in the snares of seriousness, she envies all occupations and amusements that wrench her daughter from the boredom of the household; this escape makes a sham of all the values to which she has sacrificed herself. The older the child gets, the more this bitterness eats at the mother's heart; every year brings the mother closer to her decline; from year to year the youthful body develops and flourishes; this future opening up to her daughter seems to be stolen from the mother; this is why some mothers become irritated when their daughters first get their period: they begrudge their consecration from now on as newly become women. This new woman is offered still-indefinite possibilities in contrast to the repetition and routine that are the lot of the older woman: these chances are what the mother envies and detests; not able to take them herself, she tries to diminish or suppress them: she keeps her daughter home, watches over her, tyrannizes her, dresses her like a frump on purpose, refuses her all pastimes, goes into rages if the adolescent puts on makeup, if she "goes out"; she turns all her own rage toward life against this young life who is embarking on a new future; she tries to humiliate the young girl, she ridicules her ventures, she bullies her. Open war is often declared between them, and it is usually the younger woman who wins as time is on her side; but victory has a guilty taste: her mother's attitude gives rise to both revolt and remorse; her mother's presence alone makes her the guilty one: we have seen how this sentiment can seriously affect her future. Willy-nilly, the mother accepts her defeat in the end; when her daughter becomes an adult, they reestablish a more or less distressed friendship. But one of them will forever be disappointed and frustrated; the other will often be haunted by a curse.

We will return later to the older woman's relations with her adult children: but it is clear that for their first twenty years they occupy a most important place in the mother's life. A dangerous misconception about two currently accepted preconceived ideas strongly emerges from the descriptions we have made. The first is that motherhood is enough in all cases to fulfill a woman: this is not at all true. Many are the mothers who are unhappy, bitter, and unsatisfied. The example of Sophia Tolstoy, who gave birth more than twelve times, is significant; she never stops repeating, all through her diary, that everything seems useless and empty in the world and in herself. Children bring a kind of masochistic peace for her. "With the children, I do not feel young anymore. I am calm and happy." Renouncing her youth, her beauty, and her personal life brings her some calm; she feels old, justified. "The feeling of being indispensable to them is my greatest happiness." They are weapons enabling her to reject her husband's superiority. "My only resources, my only weapons to establish equality between us, are the children, energy, joy, health . . ." But they are absolutely not enough to give meaning to an existence worn down by boredom. On January 25, 1875, after a moment of exaltation, she writes:

> *I too want and can do everything.*[18] But as soon as this feeling goes away, I realize that I don't want and can't do anything, except care for my babies, eat, drink, sleep, love my husband and my children, which should really be happiness but which makes me sad and like yesterday makes me want to cry.

And eleven years later:

> I devote myself energetically to my children's upbringing and education and have an ardent desire to do it well. But my God! How impatient and irascible I am, how I yell! . . . This eternal fighting with the children is so sad.

The mother's relation with her children is defined within the overall context of her life; it depends on her relations with her husband, her past, her occupations, herself; it is a fatal and absurd error to claim to see a child

---

18. S. Tolstoy's emphasis.

as a panacea. This is also Helene Deutsch's conclusion in the work I have often cited, where she studies phenomena of motherhood on the basis of her experience in psychiatry. She ranks this function highly; she believes woman accomplishes herself totally through it: but under the condition that it is freely assumed and sincerely desired; the young woman must be in a psychological, moral, and material situation that allows her to bear the responsibility; if not, the consequences will be disastrous. In particular, it is criminal to advise having a child as a remedy for melancholia or neuroses; it causes unhappiness for mother and child. Only a balanced, healthy woman, conscious of her responsibilities, is capable of becoming a "good mother."

I have said that the curse weighing on marriage is that individuals too often join together in their weakness and not in their strength, that each one asks of the other rather than finding pleasure in giving. It is an even more deceptive lure to dream of attaining through a child a plenitude, warmth, and value one is incapable of creating oneself; it can bring joy only to the woman capable of disinterestedly wanting the happiness of another, to the woman who seeks to transcend her own existence without any reward for her. To be sure, a child is an undertaking one can validly aspire to; but like any other undertaking, it does not represent a justification in itself; and it must be desired for itself, not for hypothetical benefits. Stekel quite rightly says:

> Children are not substitutes for one's disappointed love; they are
> not substitutes for one's thwarted ideal in life, children are not mere
> material to fill out an empty existence. Children are a responsibility
> and an opportunity. Children are the loftiest blossoms upon the tree
> of untrammeled love . . . They are neither playthings, nor tools for
> the fulfillment of parental needs or ungratified ambitions. Children
> are obligations; they should be brought up so as to become happy
> human beings.

Such an obligation is not at all *natural:* nature could never dictate a moral choice; this implies an engagement. To have a child is to take on a commitment; if the mother shrinks from it, she commits an offense against human existence, against a freedom; but no one can impose it on her. The relation of parents to children, like that of spouses, must be freely chosen. And it is not even true that the child is a privileged accomplishment for a woman; it is often said that a woman is coquettish, or amorous, or lesbian, or ambitious as a result of "being childless"; her sexual life, her goals, and the values she pursues are deemed to be substitutes for the child. In fact, from the beginning there is indetermination: one can just as well say that lacking love, an occupation, or the power to satisfy her homosexual tendencies, a woman wants to have a child. A social and artificial morality hides behind this pseudo-naturalism. That the child is the ultimate end for woman is an affirmation worthy of an advertising slogan.

The second preconceived idea immediately following the first is that the child is sure to find happiness in his mother's arms. There is no such thing as an "unnatural mother," since maternal love has nothing natural about it: but precisely because of that, there are bad mothers. And one of the great truths that psychoanalysis has proclaimed is the danger "normal" parents constitute for a child. The complexes, obsessions, and neuroses adults suffer from have their roots in their family past; parents who have their own conflicts, quarrels, and dramas are the least desirable company for children. Deeply marked by the paternal household, they approach their own children through complexes and frustrations: and this chain of misery perpetuates itself indefinitely. In particular, maternal sado-masochism creates guilt feelings for the daughter that will express themselves in sadomasochistic behavior toward her own children, without end. There is extravagant bad faith in the conflation of contempt for women and respect shown for mothers. It is a criminal paradox to deny women all public activity, to close masculine careers to them, to proclaim them incapable in all domains, and to nonetheless entrust to them the most delicate and most serious of all undertakings: the formation of a human being. There are many women who, out of custom and tradition, are still refused education, culture, responsibilities, and activities that are the privileges of men, and in whose arms, nevertheless, babies are placed without scruple, as in earlier life they were consoled for their inferiority to boys with dolls; they are deprived of living their lives; as compensation, they are allowed to play with flesh-and-blood toys. A woman would have to be perfectly happy or a saint to resist the temptation of abusing her rights. Montesquieu was perhaps right when he said it would be better to entrust women with the government of state than with a family; for as soon as she is given the opportunity, woman is as reasonable and efficient as man: it is in abstract thought, in concerted action that she most easily rises above her sex; it is far more difficult in this day and age to free herself from her feminine past, to find an emotional balance that nothing in her situation favors. Man is also much more balanced and rational in his work than at home; he calculates with mathematical precision: he "lets himself go" with his wife, becoming illogical, a liar, capricious; likewise, she "lets herself go" with her child.

And this self-indulgence is more dangerous because she can better defend herself against her husband than the child can defend himself against her. It would obviously be better for the child if his mother were a complete person and not a mutilated one, a woman who finds in her work and her relations with the group a self-accomplishment she could not attain through his tyranny; and it would be preferable also for the child to be left infinitely less to his parents than he is now, that his studies and amusements take place with other children under the control of adults whose links with him are only impersonal and dispassionate.

Even in cases where the child is a treasure within a happy or at least balanced life, he cannot be the full extent of his mother's horizons. He does not wrest her from her immanence; she shapes his flesh, she supports him, she cares for him: she can do no more than create a situation that solely the child's freedom can transcend; when she invests in his future, it is again by proxy that she transcends herself through the universe and time; that is, once again she dooms herself to dependency. Not only his ingratitude but the failure of her son will refute all of her hopes: as in marriage or love, she puts the care of justifying her life in the hands of another, whereas the only authentic behavior is to assume it freely herself. Woman's inferiority, as we have seen, originally came from the fact that she was restricted to repeating life, while man invented reasons for living, in his eyes more essential than the pure facticity of existence; confining woman to motherhood is the perpetuation of this situation. But today she demands participation in the movement by which humanity ceaselessly tries to find justification by surpassing itself; she can only consent to give life if life has meaning; she cannot try to be a mother without playing a role in economic, political, or social life. It is not the same thing to produce cannon fodder, slaves, victims, as to give birth to free men. In a properly organized society where the child would in great part be taken charge of by the group, where the mother would be cared for and helped, motherhood would absolutely not be incompatible with women's work. On the contrary, a woman who works—farmer, chemist, or writer—has the easiest pregnancy because she is not centered on her own person; it is the woman who has the richest personal life who will give the most to her child and who will ask for the least, she who acquires real human values through effort and struggle will be the most fit to bring up children. If too often today a woman has a hard time reconciling the interests of her children with a profession that demands long hours away from home and all her strength, it is because, on the one hand, woman's work is still too often a kind of slavery; on the other hand, no effort has been made to ensure children's health, care, and education outside the home. This is social neglect: but it is a sophism to justify it by pretending that a law was written in heaven or in the bowels of the earth that requires that the mother and child belong to each other exclusively; this mutual belonging in reality only constitutes a double and harmful oppression.

It is a mystification to maintain that woman becomes man's equal through motherhood. Psychoanalysts have tried hard to prove that the child provides the equivalent of the penis for her: but enviable as this attribute may be, no one believes that possessing one can justify an existence or that such possession can be a supreme end in itself. There has been an enormous amount of talk about the sacred rights of women, but being a mother is not how women gained the right to vote; the unwed mother is still scorned; it is only in marriage that the mother is glorified—in other words, as long as she is subordinate to the husband. As long as he is the economic head of the family, even though it is she who cares for the children, they depend far more on him than on her. This is why, as has been seen, the mother's relationship with her children is deeply influenced by the one she maintains with her husband.

So conjugal relations, homemaking, and motherhood form a whole in which all the parts are determinant; tenderly united to her husband, the wife can cheerfully carry out the duties of the home; happy with her children, she will be understanding of her husband. But this harmony is not easy to attain, for the different functions assigned to the wife conflict with each other. Women's magazines amply advise the housewife on the art of maintaining her sexual attraction while doing the dishes, of remaining elegant throughout pregnancy, of reconciling flirtation, motherhood, and economy; but if she conscientiously follows their advice, she will soon be overwhelmed and disfigured by care; it is very difficult to remain desirable with chapped hands and a body deformed by pregnancies; this is why a woman in love often feels resentment of the children who ruin her seduction and deprive her of her husband's caresses; if she is, by contrast, deeply maternal, she is jealous of the man who also claims the children as his. But then, the perfect homemaker, as has been seen, contradicts the movement of life: the child is the enemy of waxed floors. Maternal love is often lost in the reprimands and outbursts that underlie the concern for a well-kept home. It is not surprising that the woman torn between these contradictions often spends her day in a state of nervousness and bitterness; she always loses on some level, and her gains are precarious, they do not count as any sure success. She can never save herself by her work alone; it keeps her occupied, but does not constitute her justification: her justification rests on outside freedoms. The wife shut up in her home cannot establish her existence on her own; she does not have the means to affirm herself in her singularity: and this singularity is consequently not acknowledged. For Arabs or Indians, and in many rural populations, a wife is only a female servant appreciated according to the work she provides, and who is replaced without regret if she disappears. In modern civilization, she is more or less individualized in her husband's eyes; but unless she completely renounces her self, swallowed up like Natasha in a passionate and tyrannical devotion to her family, she suffers from being reduced to pure generality. She is *the* mistress of the house, the wife, the unique and indistinct mother; Natasha delights in this supreme self-effacement, and in rejecting all confrontation, she negates others. But the modern Western woman, by contrast, wants to be noticed by others as *this* mistress of the house, *this* wife, *this* mother, *this* woman. Herein lies the satisfaction she will seek in her social life.

CHAPTER 7

Social Life

The family is not a closed community: notwithstanding its separateness, it establishes relations with other social units; the home is not only an "interior" in which the couple is confined; it is also the expression of its living standard, its wealth, its tastes: it must be exhibited for others to see. It is essentially the woman who will organize this social life. The man is connected to the community as producer and citizen, by ties of an organic solidarity based on the division of labor; the couple is a social person, defined by the family, class, milieu, and race to which it belongs, attached by ties of mechanical solidarity to groups socially similar to themselves; the woman is the one most likely to embody this most purely: the husband's professional relations often do not reflect his social level, while the wife, who does not have the obligations brought about by work, can limit herself to the company of her peers; besides, she has the leisure, through her "visits" and "receptions," to promote these relations, useless in practice, and that, of course, matter only in categories of people wanting to hold their rank in the social hierarchy, that is, who consider themselves superior to certain others. She delights in showing off her home and even herself, which her husband and children do not see because they have a vested interest in them. Her social duty, which is to "represent," will become part of the pleasure she has in showing herself to others.

First, she has to represent herself; at home, going about her occupations, she merely dresses: to go out, to entertain, she "dresses up." Dressing has a twofold significance: it is meant to show the woman's social standing (her standard of living, her wealth, the social class she belongs to), but at the same time it concretizes feminine narcissism; it is her uniform and her attire; the woman who suffers from not *doing* anything thinks she is expressing her *being* through her dress. Beauty treatments and dressing are kinds of work that allow her to appropriate her person as she appropriates her home through housework; she thus believes that she is choosing and re-creating her own self. And social customs encourage her to alienate herself in her image. Like his body, a man's clothes must convey his transcendence and not attract attention;[1] for him neither elegance nor beauty constitutes him as object; thus he does not usually consider his appearance a reflection of his being. By contrast, society even requires woman to make herself an erotic object. The goal of the fashion to which she is in thrall is not to reveal her as an autonomous individual but, on the contrary, to cut her from her transcendence so as to offer her as a prey to male desires: fashion does not serve to fulfill her projects but on the contrary to thwart them. A skirt is less convenient than trousers, and high-heeled shoes impede walking; the least practical dresses and high heels, the most fragile hats and stockings, are the most elegant; whether the outfit disguises, deforms, or molds the body, in any case, it delivers it to view. This explains why dressing is an enchanting game for the little girl who wants to look at herself; later her child's autonomy rises up against the constraints of light-colored muslin and patent-leather shoes; at the awkward age she is torn between the desire and the refusal to show herself off; once she has accepted her vocation as sex object, she enjoys adorning herself.

As we have said, by adorning herself, woman is akin to nature, while attesting to nature's need for artifice; she becomes flower and jewel for man and for herself as well.[2] Before giving him rippling water or the soft warmth of furs, she takes them for herself. More intimately than her knick-knacks, rugs, cushions, and bouquets, she prizes feathers, pearls, brocade, and silks that she mingles with her flesh; their shimmer and their gentle contact compensate for the harshness of the erotic universe that is her lot: the more her sensuality is unsatiated, the more importance she gives to it. If many lesbians dress in a masculine way, it is not only out of imitation of males and defiance of society: they do not need the caresses of velvet and satin, because they grasp such passive qualities on a feminine body.[3] The woman given to the harsh masculine embrace—even if she savors it and even more if she gets no pleasure from it—can embrace no carnal prey other than her own body: she perfumes it to change it into a flower, and the shine of the diamonds she puts around her neck is no different from that of

---

1. See Volume I. Homosexuals are an exception as they specifically grasp themselves as sexual objects; dandies also, who must be studied separately. Today, in particular, the "zoot-suitism" of the American blacks who dress in light-colored, noticeable suits is explained with very complex reasons.

2. See Volume I, Part Three, "Myths," Chapter 1.

3. Sandor, whose case Krafft-Ebing detailed, adored well-dressed women but did not "dress up."

her skin; in order to possess them, she identifies with all the riches of the world. She covets not only sensual treasures but sometimes also sentimental values and ideals. This jewel is a souvenir; that one is a symbol. Some women make themselves bouquets, aviaries; others are museums and still others hieroglyphs. Georgette Leblanc tells us in her memoirs, evoking her youth:

> I was always dressed like a painting. I walked around in van Eyck, in an allegory of Rubens, or in the Virgin of Memling. I still see myself crossing a street in Brussels one winter day in a dress of amethyst velvet embellished with old silver binding taken from some tunic. Dragging insouciantly my long train behind me, I was conscientiously sweeping the pavement. My folly of yellow fur framed my blond hair, but the most unusual thing was the diamond placed on the frontlet on my forehead. Why all this? Simply because it pleased me, and so I thought I was living outside of all convention. The more I was laughed at as I went by, the more extravagant my burlesque inventions. I would have been ashamed to change anything in my appearance just because I was being mocked. That would have seemed to me to be a degrading capitulation . . . At home it was something else again. The angels of Gozzoli, Fra Angelico, Burne-Jones, and Watts were my models. I was always attired in azure and aurora; my flowing dresses spread out in manifold trains around me.

The best examples of this magical appropriation of the universe are found in mental institutions. A woman who does not control her love for precious objects and symbols forgets her own appearance and risks dressing outlandishly. The very little girl thus sees in dressing a disguise that changes her into a fairy, a queen, a flower; she thinks she is beautiful as soon as she is laden with garlands and ribbons because she identifies with these flashy clothes; charmed by the color of a piece of material, the naive young girl does not notice the wan complexion it gives her; one also finds this excessive bad taste in women artists or intellectuals more fascinated by the outside world than conscious of their own appearance: infatuated by these old materials and antique jewels, they delight in conjuring up China or the Middle Ages and give the mirror no more than a cursory or passing glance. It is sometimes surprising to see the strange getups elderly women like: tiaras, lace, bright dresses, and extravagant necklaces unfortunately draw attention to their ravaged features. Now that they have given up seduction, clothes often become once again a gratuitous game for them as in their childhood. An elegant woman by contrast can seek sensual or aesthetic pleasures in her clothes if need be, but she must reconcile them in harmony with her image: the color of her dress will flatter her complexion, the cut will emphasize or improve her figure; arrayed, she complaisantly cherishes her adorned self and not the objects that adorn her.

Dressing is not only adornment: it expresses, as we have said, woman's social situation. Only the prostitute whose function is exclusively that of a sex object displays herself exclusively in this light; in the past it was her saffron hair and the flowers that dotted her dress; today it is her high heels, skimpy satin, harsh makeup, and heavy perfume that are the signature of her profession. Any other woman is criticized for dressing "like a strumpet." Her erotic qualities are integrated into social life and can only appear in this toned-down form. But it must be emphasized that decency does not mean dressing with strict modesty. A woman who teases male desire too blatantly is considered vulgar; but a woman who is seen to repudiate this is disreputable as well: she is seen as wanting to look like a man: she's a lesbian; or to single herself out: she's an eccentric; refusing her role as object, she defies society: she's an anarchist. If she simply does not want to be noticed, she must still conserve her femininity. Custom dictates the compromise between exhibitionism and modesty; sometimes it is the neckline and sometimes the ankle that the "virtuous woman" must hide; sometimes the young girl has the right to highlight her charms so as to attract suitors, while the married woman gives up all adornment: such is the usage in many peasant civilizations; sometimes young girls have to dress in flowing clothes of baby colors and modest cut, while their elders are allowed tight-fitting dresses, heavy material, rich hues, and daring cuts; on a sixteen-year-old, black stands out because the rule at that age is not to wear it.[4] One must, of course, conform to these laws; but in any case, and even in the most austere circles, woman's sexual attributes will be emphasized: the pastor's wife curls her hair, wears some makeup, is discreetly fashion-conscious, indicating through the attention to her physical charm that she accepts her female role. This integration of eroticism into social life is particularly obvious in the "evening gown." To mark a social gathering, that is, luxury and waste, these dresses must be costly and delicate, they must be as uncomfortable as possible; skirts are long and so wide or so complicated

---

4. In a film set last century—and a rather stupid one—Bette Davis created a scandal by wearing a red dress to the ball whereas white was de rigueur until marriage. Her act was considered a rebellion against the established order.

that they impede walking; under the jewels, ruffles, sequins, flowers, feathers, and false hair, woman is changed into a flesh-doll; even this flesh is
exposed; just as flowers bloom gratuitously, the woman displays her shoulders, back, bosom; except in orgies, the man must not indicate that he covets her: he only has the right to looks and the embraces of the dance; but he
can take delight in being the king of a world of such tender treasures. From
one man to another, the festivity takes on the appearance of a potlatch;
each of them gives the vision of this body that is his property to all the others as a gift. In her evening dress, the woman is disguised as woman for all
the males' pleasure and the pride of her owner.

This social significance of the toilette allows woman to express her
attitude to society by the way she dresses; subject to the established order,
she confers on herself a discreet and tasteful personality; many nuances are
possible: she will make herself fragile, childlike, mysterious, candid, austere, gay, poised, a little daring, self-effacing, as she chooses. Or, on the
contrary, she will affirm her rejection of conventions by her originality. It
is striking that in many novels the "liberated" woman distinguishes herself
by an audacity in dressing that emphasizes her character as sex object, and
thus of dependence: so in Edith Wharton's *The Age of Innocence*, the young
divorced woman with an adventuresome past and a bold heart is first presented with a plunging décolletage; the whiff of scandal she provokes
becomes the tangible reflection of her scorn for conformity. Thus the
young girl will enjoy dressing as a woman, the older woman as a little girl,
the courtesan as a sophisticated woman of the world, and the woman of the
world as a vamp. Even if every woman dresses according to her status,
there is still play in it. Artifice like art is situated in the imagination. Not
only do girdle, bra, hair dyes, and makeup disguise body and face; but as
soon as she is "dressed up," the least sophisticated woman is not concerned
with perception: she is like a painting, a statue, like an actor on stage, an
analogon through which is suggested an absent subject who is her character
but is not she. It is this confusion with an unreal object—necessary, perfect
like a hero in a novel, like a portrait or a bust—that flatters her; she strives
to alienate herself in it and so to appear frozen, justified to herself.

Page by page we see Marie Bashkirtseff in *Ecrits intimes* (Intimate
Writings) endlessly remaking her image. She does not spare us any of her
dresses: for each new outfit, she believes she is an other and she adores herself anew:

I took one of Mama's great shawls, I made a slit for my head, and I
sewed up the two sides. This shawl that falls in classic folds gives me
an Oriental, biblical, strange look.

I go to the Laferrières', and in just three hours Caroline makes me a dress in which I look as if I'm enveloped in a cloud. This is a piece of English crepe that she drapes over me, making me thin, elegant, and long.

Enveloped in a warm wool dress hanging in harmonious folds, a character out of Lefebvre who knows so well how to draw these lithe and young bodies in modest fabrics.

This refrain is repeated day after day: "I was charming in black . . . In gray, I was charming . . . I was in white, charming."

Mme de Noailles, who also accorded much importance to her dress, speaks sadly in her *Memoirs* of the crisis of a failed dress:

I loved the vividness of the colours, their daring contrast, a dress seemed like a landscape, the beginning of adventure. Just as I was putting on the dress made by unsure hands, I suffered from all the defects I saw.

If the toilette has so much importance for many women, it is because they are under the illusion that it provides them both with the world and with their own self. A German novel, *The Artificial Silk Girl*,[5] tells the story of a poor girl's passion for a vair coat; sensually she loved the caressing warmth of it, the furry tenderness; in precious skins it is her transfigured self she cherishes; she finally possesses the beauty of the world she had never embraced and the radiant destiny that had never been hers:

And then I saw a coat hanging from a hook, a fur so soft, so smooth, so tender, so gray, so shy: I felt like kissing it I loved it so much. It looked like consolation and All Saints' Day and total safety, like the sky. It was genuine vair. Silently, I took off my raincoat and put on the vair. This fur was like a diamond on my skin that loved it and what one loves, one doesn't give it back once one has it. Inside, a Moroccan crepe lining, pure silk, with hand embroidery. The coat enveloped me and spoke more than I to Hubert's heart . . . I am so elegant in this fur. It is like the rare man who would make me precious through his love for me. This coat wants me and I want it: we have each other.

---

5. By Irmgard Keun.

As woman is an object, it is obvious that how she is adorned and dressed affects her intrinsic value. It is not pure frivolousness for her to attach so much importance to silk stockings, gloves, and a hat: keeping her rank is an imperious obligation. In America, a great part of the working woman's budget is devoted to beauty care and clothes; in France, this expense is lighter; nevertheless, a woman is all the more respected if she "presents well"; the more she needs to find work, the more useful it is to look well-off: elegance is a weapon, a sign, a banner of respect, a letter of recommendation.

It is a servitude; the values it confers have a price; they sometimes have such a high price that a detective catches a socialite or an actress shoplifting perfumes, silk stockings, or underwear. Many women prostitute themselves or "get help" in order to keep themselves well dressed; it is their clothes that determine their need for money. Being well dressed also requires time and care; it is a chore that is sometimes a source of positive joy: in this area there is also the "discovery of hidden treasures," trades, ruses, arrangements, and invention; a clever woman can even be creative. Showroom days—especially the sales—are frenetic adventures. A new dress is a celebration in itself. Makeup and hair are substitutes for a work of art. Today, more than before, woman knows the joys of shaping her body by sports, gymnastics, swimming, massage, and diets;[6] she decides on her weight, her figure, and her complexion; modern beauty treatments allow her to combine beauty and activity: she has the right to toned muscles, she refuses to put on weight; in physical culture, she affirms herself as subject; this gives her a kind of liberation from her contingent flesh; but this liberation easily lapses back into dependence. The Hollywood star triumphs over nature: but she finds herself a passive object in the producer's hands.

Next to these victories in which woman rightly takes delight, taking care of one's appearance implies—like household tasks—a fight against time, because her body too is an object eroded by time. Colette Audry describes this fight, comparable to the one the housewife engages against dust:

Already it was no longer the compact flesh of youth; along her arms and thighs the pattern of her muscles showed through a layer of fat and slightly flabby skin. Upset, she once again changed her schedule:

---

6. According to recent studies, however, it seems that women's gymnasiums in France are almost empty; it was especially between 1920 and 1940 that French women indulged in physical culture. Household problems weigh too heavy on them at this time.

her day would begin with half an hour of gymnastics and in the evening, before getting into bed, a quarter of an hour of massage. She took to reading medical books and fashion magazines, to watching her waistline. She prepared fruit juices, took a laxative from time to time, and did the dishes with rubber gloves. Her two concerns—rejuvenating her body and refurbishing her home— finally became one so that one day she would reach a kind of steadiness, a kind of dead center . . . the world would be as if stopped, suspended outside of aging and decay . . . At the swimming pool, she now took serious lessons to improve her style, and the beauty magazines kept her breathless with infinitely renewed recipes. Ginger Rogers confides to us: "I brush my hair one hundred strokes every morning, it takes exactly two and a half minutes and I have silky hair . . ." How to get thinner ankles: stand on your toes every day, thirty times in a row, without putting your heels down, this exercise only takes a minute; what is a minute in a day? Another time it is an oil bath for nails, lemon paste for hands, crushed strawberries on cheeks.[7]

Routine, here again, turns beauty care and wardrobe maintenance into chores. The horror of degradation that all living change involves in some cold or frustrated women arouses a horror of life itself: they seek to preserve themselves as others preserve furniture or jam; this negative stubbornness makes them enemies of their own existence and hostile to others: good meals damage their figures, wine spoils their complexions, smiling too much gives you wrinkles, the sun hurts the skin, rest makes you lethargic, work wears you out, love gives you circles under your eyes, kisses make your cheeks red, caresses deform your breasts, embraces shrivel the flesh, pregnancies disfigure your face and body; you know how young mothers angrily push away the child marveling at their ball gown. "Don't touch me, your hands are all sticky, you're going to get me dirty"; the appearance-conscious rejects her husband's or lover's ardor with the same rebuffs. Just as one covers furniture with loose covers, she would like to withdraw from men, the world, time. But none of these precautions prevents the appearance of gray hair and crow's-feet. Starting from youth, woman knows this destiny is inevitable. And, regardless of her vigilance, she is a victim of accidents: a drop of wine falls on her dress, a cigarette

7. *Playing a Losing Game.*

burns it; and so the creature of luxury and parties who smilingly struts about the living room disappears: she turns into the serious and hard housewife; suddenly one discovers that her toilette was not a bouquet of flowers, fireworks, a gratuitous and perishable splendor destined to generously light up an instant: it is an asset, capital, an investment, it demands sacrifices; its loss is an irreparable disaster. Stains, holes, dresses that are failures, and ruined perms are far more serious catastrophes than a burned roast or a broken vase: because the coquettish woman is not only alienated in things, she wants to be a thing, and without an intermediary she feels insecure in the world. The relations she maintains with her dressmaker and milliner, her impatience, her demands, are manifestations of her seriousness and insecurity. A successful dress creates in her the character of her dreams; but in a soiled, ruined outfit, she feels demeaned.

Marie Bashkirtseff writes: "My mood, my manners, the expression on my face, everything depended on my dress." And then: "Either you have to go around naked, or you have to dress according to your body, taste, and character. When they are not right, I feel gauche, common, and therefore humiliated. What happens to the mood and mind? They think about clothes and so one becomes stupid, boring, and one does not know what to do with oneself."

Many women prefer to miss a party than go badly dressed, even if they are not going to be noticed.

However, although some women affirm "I dress for myself only," we have seen that even in narcissism the gaze of the other is involved. Only in asylums do the fashion-conscious stubbornly keep their faith in absent gazes; normally, they demand witnesses. After ten years of marriage, Sophia Tolstoy writes:

> I want people to admire me and say how pretty I am, and I want
> Lyova to see and hear them too . . . I hate people who tell me I am
> beautiful. I never believed them . . . what would be the point of it?
> My darling little Petya loves his old nanny just as much as he would
> love a great beauty . . . I am having my hair curled today, and have
> been happily imagining how nice it will look, even though nobody
> will see me and it is quite unnecessary. I adore ribbons, and I would
> like a new leather belt—and now I have written this I feel like
> crying.

Husbands do not perform this role well. Here again the husband's demands are duplicitous. If his wife is too attractive, he becomes jealous;

but every husband is more or less King Candaules; he wants his wife to make him proud; for her to be elegant, pretty, or at least "presentable"; if not, he will humorously tell her these words of Pére Ubu: "You are quite ugly today! Is it because we are expecting company?" In marriage, as we have seen, erotic and social values are not very compatible; such antagonism is reflected in this situation. The wife who accentuates her sexual attraction is considered vulgar in her husband's eyes; he criticizes this boldness that would seduce him in an unknown woman, and this criticism kills all desire for her; if his wife dresses decently, he approves but coldly: he does not find her attractive and vaguely reproaches her for it. Because of that, he rarely looks at her on his own account: he inspects her through the eyes of others. "What will they say about her?" He does not see clearly because he projects his spousal point of view onto others. Nothing is more irritating for a woman than to see him appreciate in another the dresses or way of dressing he criticizes in her. Naturally, of course, he is too close to her to see her; her face is immutable for him; nor does he notice her outfits or hairstyle. Even a husband in love or an infatuated lover is often indifferent to a woman's clothes. If they love her ardently in her nudity, the most attractive adornments merely disguise her; and they will cherish her whether badly dressed, tired, or dazzling. If they no longer love her, the most flattering dresses will be of no avail. Clothes can be an instrument of conquest but not a weapon of defense; their art is to create mirages, they offer the viewer an imaginary object: in the erotic embrace and in daily relations mirages fade; conjugal feelings like physical love exist in the realm of reality. Women do not dress for the loved man. Dorothy Parker, in one of her short stories, describes a young woman who, waiting impatiently for her husband, who is on leave, decides to make herself beautiful to welcome him:

> She bought a new dress; black—he liked black dresses—simple—he liked plain dresses—and so expensive that she would not think of its price . . .
>   "Do you . . . like my dress?"
>   "Oh, yes," he said. "I always liked that dress on you."
>   It was as if she turned to wood. "This dress," she said, enunciating with insulting distinctness, "is brand new. I have never had it on before in my life. In case you are interested, I bought it especially for this occasion."
>   "I'm sorry, honey," he said. "Oh, sure, now I see it's not the other one at all. I think it's great. I like you in black."

"At moments like this," she said, "I almost wish I were in it for another reason."[8]

It is often said that women dress to arouse jealousy in other women: this jealousy is really a clear sign of success; but this is not its only aim. Through envious or admiring approbation, woman seeks an absolute affirmation of her beauty, her elegance, her taste: of herself. She dresses to display herself; she displays herself to make herself be. She thus submits herself to a painful dependence; the housewife's devotion is useful even if it is not recognized; the effort of the fashion-conscious woman is in vain unless consciousness is involved. She is looking for a definitive valorization of herself; it is this attempt at the absolute that makes her quest so exhausting; criticized by only one voice—this hat *is* not beautiful—she is flattered by a compliment, but a contradiction demolishes her; and as the absolute only manifests itself in an indefinite series of appearances, she will never have entirely won; this is why the fashion-conscious woman is sensitive; it is also why some pretty and much-admired women can be sadly convinced they are neither beautiful nor elegant, that this supreme approbation of an unknown judge is exactly what is missing: they are aiming for an in-itself that is unrealizable. Rare are the gorgeous stylish women who embody in themselves the laws of elegance, whom no one can fault because they are the ones who define success or failure; as long as their reign endures, they can think of themselves as an exemplary success. What is unfortunate is that this success serves nothing and no one.

Clothes immediately imply going out and receptions, and besides, that is their original intent. The woman parades her new outfit from place to place and invites other women to see her reign over her "interior." In certain particularly important situations, the husband accompanies her on her "calls"; but most often she fulfills her "social obligations" while he is at work. The implacable ennui weighing on these gatherings has been described hundreds of times. It comes from the fact that these women gathered there by "social obligations" have nothing to say to each other. There is no common interest linking the lawyer's wife to the doctor's—and none between Dr. Dupont's and Dr. Durand's. It is bad taste in a general conversation to talk of one's children's pranks or problems with the help. What is left is discussion of the weather, the latest novel, and a few general ideas borrowed from their husbands. This custom of "calling" is tending to

---

8. "The Lovely Eva." [The real title of this short story is "The Lovely Leave."—TRANS.]

disappear; but the chore of the "call" in various forms survives in France. American women often replace conversation with bridge, which is an advantage only for women who enjoy this game.

However, social life has more attractive forms than carrying out this idle duty of etiquette. Entertaining is not just welcoming others into one's own home; it is changing one's home into an enchanted domain; the social event is both festivity and potlatch. The mistress of the house displays her treasures: silver, table linen, crystal; she dresses the house with flowers: ephemeral and useless, flowers exemplify the gratuitousness of occasions that mean expenses and luxury; blooming in vases, doomed to a rapid death, flowers are ceremonial bonfires, incense and myrrh, libation, sacrifice. The table is laden with fine food, precious wines; it means satisfying the guests' needs, it is a question of inventing gracious gifts that anticipate their desires; the meal becomes a mysterious ceremony. Virginia Woolf emphasizes this aspect in this passage from *Mrs. Dalloway:*

> And so there began a soundless and exquisite passing to and fro
> through swing doors of aproned white-capped maids, handmaidens
> not of necessity, but adepts in a mystery or grand deception prac-
> ticed by hostesses in Mayfair from one-thirty to two, when, with
> a wave of the hand, the traffic ceases, and there rises instead this
> profound illusion in the first place about the food—how it is not paid
> for; and then that the table spreads itself voluntarily with glass and
> silver, little mats, saucers of red fruit; films of brown cream mask
> turbot; in casseroles severed chickens swim; coloured, undomestic,
> the fire burns; and with the wine and the coffee (not paid for) rise
> jocund visions before musing eyes; gently speculative eyes; eyes to
> whom life appears musical, mysterious.

The woman who presides over these mysteries is proud to feel she is the creator of a perfect moment, the dispenser of happiness and gaiety. She is the one bringing the guests together, she is the one making the event take place, she is the gratuitous source of joy and harmony.

This is exactly what Mrs. Dalloway feels:

> But suppose Peter said to her, "Yes, yes, but your parties—what's
> the sense of your parties?" all she could say was (and nobody could
> be expected to understand): They're an offering; . . . Here was So-
> and-so in South Kensington; someone up in Bayswater; and some-
> body else, say, in Mayfair. And she felt quite continuously a sense of

their existence; and she felt what a waste; and she felt what a pity;
and she felt if only they could be brought together; so she did it.
And it was an offering; to combine, to create; but to whom? . . . An
offering for the sake of offering, perhaps. Anyhow, it was her gift.
Nothing else had she of the slightest importance . . . anybody could
do it; yet this anybody she did a little admire, couldn't help feeling
that she had, anyhow, made this happen.

If there is pure generosity in this homage to others, the party is really a
party. But social routine quickly changes the potlatch into an institution,
the gift into an obligation, and the party hardens into a rite. All the while
savoring the "dinner out," the invited woman ponders having to return the
invitation: she sometimes complains of having been entertained too well.
"The Xs . . . wanted to impress us," she says bitterly to her husband. I
have been told that during the last war in a little Portuguese city, tea parties
had become the most costly of potlatches: at each gathering the mistress of
the house had to serve more varied cakes and in greater number than the
previous one; this burden became so heavy that one day all the women
decided together not to serve anything anymore with the tea. The party
loses its generous and magnificent character in such circumstances; it is one
more chore; the accessories that make up a party are only a source of
worry: you have to check the crystal and the tablecloth, measure the cham-
pagne and petits fours; a broken cup, the silk upholstering of a burned armchair, are a disaster; tomorrow you have to clean, put away, put in order:
the woman dreads this extra work. She feels this multiple dependence that
defines the housewife's destiny: she is dependent on the soufflé, the roast,
the butcher, the cook, the extra help; she is dependent on the husband, who
frowns every time something goes wrong; she is dependent on the guests,
who judge the furniture and wine and who decide if the evening has been a
success or not. Only generous or self-confident women will go through this
ordeal with a light heart. A triumph can give them a heady satisfaction. But
in this respect many resemble Mrs. Dalloway, about whom Woolf tells us:
Although she loved these triumphs . . . and their brilliance and the excitement they brought, she also felt the hollowness, the sham. The woman can
only take pleasure in it if she does not attach too much importance to it; if
she does, she will be tormented by a perpetually unsatisfied vanity. Besides,
few women are wealthy enough to find their life's occupation in "socializ-
ing." Those who devote themselves to it entirely usually try not only to
make a cult of it but also to go beyond this social life toward other aims:
genuine salons have a literary or political side. These women try to influ-

ence men and to play a personal role. They escape from the condition of the married woman. She is not usually fulfilled by the pleasures and ephemeral triumphs rarely bestowed on her and that often mean as much fatigue as distraction. Social life demands that woman "represent," that she show off, but does not create between her and others real communication. It does not wrest her from her solitude.

"It is painful to think," writes Michelet, "that woman, the relative being who can only live in a couple, is more often alone than man. He finds social life everywhere, makes new contacts. As for her, she is nothing with-. out her family. And the family weighs her down; all weight is on her." And, in fact, the woman kept confined, isolated, does not have the joys of a comradeship that involves pursuing aims together; her work does not occupy her mind, her education did not give her either the taste or the habit of independence, and yet she spends her days in solitude; we have seen that this is one of the miseries Sophia Tolstoy complained of. Her marriage often took her away from her father's home and the friends of her youth. In *Mes apprentissages* (*My Apprenticeships*), Colette described the uprooting of a bride transported from her province to Paris; only the long correspondence she exchanged with her mother provided any relief; but letters are no substitute for presence, and she cannot admit her disappointments to Sido. Often, there is no longer any real closeness between the young woman and her family: neither her mother nor her sisters are her friends. Nowadays, due to a housing crisis, many young couples live with their families or in-laws; but this enforced presence is far from ever providing real companionship for the young woman.

The feminine friendships she is able to keep or make are precious for a woman; they are very different from relations men have; men relate to each other as individuals through their ideas, their own personal projects; women, confined within the generality of their destiny as women, are united by a kind of immanent complicity. And what they seek first of all from each other is the affirmation of their common universe. They do not discuss opinions: they exchange confidences and recipes; they join together to create a kind of counter-universe whose values outweigh male values; when they meet, they find the strength to shake off their chains; they negate male sexual domination by confiding their frigidity to each other and cynically deriding the appetites or the clumsiness of their males; they also contest with irony the moral and intellectual superiority of their husbands and men in general. They compare their experiences: pregnancies, deliveries, children's illnesses, their own illnesses, and housework become the essential events of human history. Their work is not technical: in transmitting recipes for cooking or housework, they give them the dignity of a secret science founded in oral traditions. Sometimes they examine moral problems together. Letters to the editor in women's magazines are a good example of these exchanges; we can hardly imagine a Lonely Hearts column reserved for men; they meet in *the* world, which is *their* world, whereas women must define, measure, and explore their own space; mostly they share beauty tips or cooking or knitting recipes, and they ask each other for advice; real anxieties can sometimes be perceived in women's tendency to talk and show off. The woman knows the male code is not hers, that man even expects she will not observe it since he pushes her to abortion, adultery, misdeeds, betrayal, and lies he officially condemns; she then asks other women to help her to define a sort of "parallel law," a specifically feminine moral code. It is not only out of malevolence that women comment on and criticize the conduct of their girlfriends so much: to judge them and to lead their own lives, they need much more moral invention than men.

What makes these relationships valuable is their truthfulness. When confronting man, woman is always onstage; she lies when pretending to accept herself as the inessential other, she lies when she presents to him an imaginary personage through impersonations, clothes, and catchphrases; this act demands constant tension; every woman thinks more or less "I am not myself" around her husband or her lover; the male world is hard, there are sharp angles, voices are too loud, lights are too bright, contacts brusque. When with other women, the wife is backstage; she sharpens her weapons, she does not enter combat; she plans her clothes, devises makeup, prepares her ruses: she lies around in slippers and robe in the wings before going onstage; she likes this lukewarm, soft, relaxed atmosphere. Colette describes the moments she spends with her girlfriend Marco like this: "Brief confidences, the amusements of two women shut away from the world, hours that were now like those in a sewing room, now like the idle ones of convalescence."[9]

She enjoys playing the adviser to the older woman:

As we sat under the balcony awning on those hot afternoons, Marco mended her underclothes. She sewed badly, but conscientiously, and I flattered my vanity by giving her pieces of advice, such as: "You're using too coarse a thread for fine needles . . . You shouldn't put blue

---

9. *Le képi* (*The Kepi*).

baby ribbon in chemises, pink is much prettier in lingerie and up against the skin." It was not long before I gave her others, concerning her face powder, the color of her lipstick, a hard line she penciled around the edge of her beautifully shaped eyelids. "D'you think so? D'you think so?" she would say. My youthful authority was adamant. I took the comb, I made a charming little gap in her tight, sponge-like fringe, I proved expert at softly shadowing her eyes and putting a faint pink glow high up on her cheekbones, near her temples.

A bit further on, she shows us Marco anxiously preparing to face a young man she wants to win over:

She was about to wipe her wet eyes but I stopped her.

"Let me do it, Marco."

With my two thumbs, I raised her upper eyelids so that the two tears about to fall should be reabsorbed and not smudge the mascara on her lashes by wetting them.

"There! Wait, I haven't finished."

I retouched all her features. Her mouth was trembling a little. She submitted patiently, sighing as if I were dressing a wound. To complete everything, I filled the puff in her handbag with a rosier shade of powder. Neither of us uttered a word meanwhile.

"Whatever happens," I told her, "don't cry. At all costs, don't let yourself give way to tears" . . .

She pressed her hand to her forehead, under her fringe.

"I *ought* to have bought that black dress last Saturday—the one I saw in the secondhand shop . . . Tell me, could you possibly lend me some very fine stockings? I've left it too late now to . . ."

"Yes, yes, of course."

"Thank you. Don't you think a flower to brighten up my dress? No, *not* a flower on the bodice. Is it true that iris is a scent that's gone out of fashion? I'm sure I had heaps of other things to ask you . . . heaps of things."

And in still another of her books, *Le toutounier,* Colette evoked this other side of women's life. Three sisters, unhappy or troubled in their loves, gather every night around the old sofa from their childhood; there they relax, pondering the worries of the day, preparing tomorrow's battles, tasting the ephemeral pleasures of a reparative rest, a good sleep, a warm bath, a crying session, they barely speak, but each one creates a nesting space for the others; and everything taking place with them is real.

For some women, this frivolous and warm intimacy is more precious than the serious pomp of their relations with men. It is in another woman that the narcissist, as in the days of her adolescence, sees a favorite double; it is through her attentive and competent eyes that she can admire her well-cut dress, her elegant interior. Over and above marriage, the best friend remains her favorite witness: she can still continue to be a desirable and desired object. In almost every young girl, as we have seen, there are homosexual tendencies; the often awkward embraces of her husband do not efface these tendencies; this is the source of the sensual softness woman feels for her counterparts and that has no equal in ordinary men. Sensual attachment between two women friends can be sublimated into exalted sentimentality or expressed in diffuse or real caresses. Their embraces can also be no more than a distracting pastime—such is the case for harem women whose principal concern is to kill time—or they can become of primary importance.

It is nonetheless rare for feminine complicity to reach true friendship; women feel more spontaneous solidarity with each other than men do, but from within this solidarity they do not transcend toward each other: together they are turned toward the masculine world, whose values each hopes to monopolize for herself. Their relations are not built on their singularity, but are lived immediately in their generality: and from there, the element of hostility comes into play. Natasha, who cherished the women in her family because they could witness the births of her babies, nevertheless felt jealous of them: every one of them could embody *the* woman in Pierre's eyes.[10] Women's mutual understanding lies in the fact that they identify with each other: but then each one competes with her companion. A housewife has a more intimate relationship with her maid than a man—unless he is homosexual—has with his valet or chauffeur; they tell each other secrets, and sometimes they are accomplices; but there are also hostile rivalries between them, because while freeing herself from the actual work, the mistress of the house wants to assume the responsibility and credit for the work she assigns; she wants to think of herself as irreplaceable, indispensable. "Everything goes wrong as soon as I'm not there." She harasses her maid in order to find fault with her; if she does her job too well, the mistress cannot be proud of feeling unique. Likewise, she system-

10. Tolstoy, *War and Peace*.

atically becomes irritated with teachers, governesses, nurses, and children's maids who care for her offspring, with parents and friends who help her out; she gives the excuse that they do not respect "her will," that they do not carry out "her ideas"; the truth is that she has neither particular will nor ideas; what irritates her, on the contrary, is that others carry out her functions exactly as she would. This is one of the main sources of family and domestic discussions that poison the life of the home: the less able she is to show her own merits, the fiercer she is in wanting to be sovereign. But where women especially see each other as enemies is in the area of seduction and love; I have pointed out this rivalry in girls: it often continues throughout life. We have seen how they seek absolute validation in the ideal of the fashionable woman or the socialite; she suffers from not being surrounded by glory; she cannot bear to perceive the slightest halo around someone else's head; she steals all the credit others receive; and what is an absolute if not unique? A woman who truly loves is satisfied to be glorified in one heart, she will not envy her friends' superficial success; but she feels threatened in her very love. The fact is that the theme of the woman betrayed by her best friend is not only a literary cliché; the closer two women are as friends, the more their duality becomes dangerous. The confidante is invited to see through the eyes of the woman in love, to feel with her heart, with her flesh: she is attracted by the lover, fascinated by the man who seduces her friend; she feels protected enough by her loyalty to let her feelings go; she does not like playing an inessential role: soon she is ready to surrender, to offer herself. Many women prudently avoid their "intimate girlfriends" as soon as they fall in love. This ambivalence keeps women from relying on their mutual feelings. The shadow of the male always weighs heavily on them. Even when not mentioning him, the verse of Saint-John Perse applies: "And the sun is not named, but its presence is among us."

Together women take revenge on him, set traps for him, malign him, insult him: but they wait for him. As long as they stagnate in the gynaeceum, they bask in contingency, in blandness, in boredom; this limbo has retained some of the warmth of the mother's breast: but it is still limbo. Woman is content to linger there on condition that she will soon be able to emerge from it. She is thus content enough in the dampness of her bathroom imagining she will later make her entrance into the luminous salon. Women are comrades for each other in captivity, they help each other endure their prison, even prepare their escape: but their liberator will come from the masculine world.

For most women, this world keeps its glow after marriage; only the husband loses his prestige; the wife discovers that his pure manly essence tarnishes: but man still remains the truth of the universe, the supreme authority, the wonderful, adventure, master, gaze, prey, pleasure, salvation; he still embodies transcendence, he is the answer to all questions. And the most loyal wife never consents to give him up completely and close herself in a dismal tête-à-tête with a contingent individual. Her childhood left her in absolute need of a guide; when the husband fails to fulfill this role, she turns to another man. Sometimes her father, a brother, an uncle, a relative, or an old friend has kept his former prestige: so she will lean on him. There are two categories of men whose professions destine them to become confidants and mentors: priests and doctors. The first have that great advantage of not having to be paid for these consultations; the confessional renders them defenseless in the face of the babbling of the pious; they avoid "sacristy pests" and "holy Marys" as best they can; but their duty is to lead their flock on the moral path, a most urgent duty as women gain social and political importance and the Church endeavors to make instruments of them. The "spiritual guide" dictates his political opinions to his penitent and influences her vote; and many husbands are irritated by his interference in their conjugal life: it is he who defines what they do in the privacy of the bedroom as licit or illicit; he is concerned in the education of the children; he advises the woman on her conduct with her husband; she who always hailed man as a god kneels with pleasure before the male who is the earthly substitute for God. The doctor is better protected as he requires payment; and he can close his door to clients who are too indiscreet; but he is the target of more specific, more stubborn aims; three-quarters of the men harassed by nymphomaniacs are doctors; to undress in front of a man is a great exhibitionistic pleasure for many women.

Stekel says: I know some women who find satisfaction only in an examination by a doctor they like. In particular, there are among spinsters many rich women who see their doctor for "a very careful" examination because of minor discharges or a banal problem. Others suffer from a cancer phobia or infections from toilets, and these phobias provide them with the pretext to have an examination.

He cites two cases, among others:

A spinster, B.V. . . . , 43 years old and rich, goes to see a doctor once a month, after her period, demanding a very careful examination because she believed that something was wrong. She changes doctors every month and plays the same game each time. The doctor asks her to undress and lie down on the table or couch. She refuses, saying that she is too modest, that she cannot do such a thing, that it is against nature! The doctor forces her or gently persuades her, and she finally undresses, explaining she is a virgin and he should not hurt her. He promises to give her a rectal exam. Her orgasm often comes as soon as the doctor examines her; it is repeated, intensified, during the rectal exam. She always uses a false name and pays right away . . . She admits to having entertained the hope of being raped by a doctor.

Mrs. L.M. . . . , 38 years old, married, tells me she is completely unfeeling when with her husband. She comes to be analyzed. After two sessions only, she admits to having a lover. But he cannot make her reach orgasm. She could only have one by being examined by a gynecologist (her father was a gynecologist!). Every two or three sessions or so, she had the urge to go to the doctor and have an examination. From time to time, she requested a treatment and those were the happiest times. The last time, a gynecologist massaged her at length because of a supposed fallen womb. Each massage brought about several orgasms. She explains her passion for these examinations by the first touch that had caused the first orgasm of her life.

The woman easily imagines that the man to whom she has exhibited herself is impressed by her physical charm or her soul's beauty, and she thus is persuaded, in pathological cases, that she is loved by a priest or doctor. Even if she is normal, she has the impression that a subtle bond exists between them; she basks in respectful obedience to him; in addition, she sometimes finds in him a source of security that helps her accept her life.

There are women, nonetheless, who are not content to prop up their existence with moral authority; they also need romantic exaltation in their lives. If they do not want to cheat on or leave their husbands, they will seek recourse in the same tactic as a girl who fears flesh-and-blood males: they give themselves over to imaginary passions. Stekel gives several examples of this:

A decent married woman of the better social class suffers from "nervous anxiety" and is predisposed to depressions. One evening during the performance at the opera she falls in love with the tenor. His singing suffuses her with a strange warmth. She becomes the singer's fanatic admirer. Thenceforth she does not miss a single performance in which he appears. She obtains his photograph, she dreams of him, and once she sent him an imposing bouquet of roses with the inscription: "From a grateful unknown admirer!" She even goes so far as to write him a letter . . . This letter she also signs, "From an unknown admirer!" but she keeps at a distance. An occasion unexpectedly arises, making it possible for her to meet this singer at a social gathering. She decides very promptly that she will not go. She does not care to become personally acquainted with him. She does not require closer contact. She is happy to be able to love so warmly and still remain a faithful wife!

I became acquainted with a woman obsessed with the most remarkable Kainz, a famous actor from Vienna. She had a special Kainz room, embellished with numerous portraits of the famous artist. There was a Kainz library in one corner. Here there was to be found everything in the shape of his books, pamphlets, and clippings which she could gather bearing on her hero. She had also gathered in this library a collection of theatre programs, including, of course, Kainz festivals and premières. A particularly precious possession was the portrait of the great artist bearing his autograph. This woman wore mourning for a whole year after the artist's death. She took long journeys to attend lectures on Kainz . . . This Kainz cult served to preserve the woman's physical chastity, it protected her against all temptation, leaving no room for any other erotic thoughts.[11]

We recall what tears Rudolph Valentino's death brought forth. Married women and young girls alike worship cinema heroes. Women often evoke their images when engaged in solitary pleasures, or they call up such fantasies in conjugal lovemaking; these images also often revive some childhood memory in the figure of a grandfather, a brother, a teacher, and so on.

Nevertheless, there are also men of flesh and blood in women's circles; whether she is sexually fulfilled, frigid, or frustrated—except in the rare case of a complete, absolute, and exclusive love—the woman places great value on their approbation. Her husband's too mundane gaze no longer nurtures her image; she needs eyes still full of mystery to discover her as mystery; she needs a sovereign consciousness before her to receive her confidences, to revive the faded photographs, to bring to life that dimple in the corner of her mouth, the fluttering eyelashes that are hers alone; she is only desirable, lovable, if she is desired, loved. While she more or less

---

11. *Frigidity in Woman.*

makes the best of her marriage, she looks to other men mainly to satisfy her vanity: she invites them to share in her cult; she seduces, she pleases, happy to dream about forbidden loves, to think: If I wanted to . . . ; she prefers to charm many admirers than to attach herself deeply to any one; more ardent, less shy than a young girl, her coquetry needs males to confirm her in the consciousness of her worth and power; she is often all the bolder as, anchored in her home and having succeeded in conquering one man, she leads him on without great expectations and without great risks.

It happens that after a longer or shorter period of fidelity, the woman no longer confines herself to these flirtations or coquetries. Often, she decides to deceive her husband out of resentment. Adler maintains that woman's infidelity always stems from revenge; this is going too far; but the fact is that she often yields less to a lover's seduction than to a desire to defy her husband: "He is not the only man in the world—I can attract others— I am not his slave, he thinks he is clever but he can be duped." It may happen that the derided husband retains his primordial importance for the wife; just as the girl will sometimes take a lover to rebel against her mother or protest against her parents, disobey them, affirm herself, so a woman whose very resentment attaches her to her husband seeks a confidant in her lover, an observer who considers her a victim, an accomplice who helps her humiliate her husband; she talks to him endlessly about her husband under the pretext of subjecting him to his scorn; and if the lover does not play his role well, she moodily turns from him either to go back to her husband or to find another consoler. But very often, it is less resentment than disappointment that drives her into the arms of a lover; she does not find love in marriage; she resigns herself with difficulty to never knowing the sensual pleasures and joys whose expectations charmed her youth. Marriage, by frustrating women's erotic satisfaction, denies them the freedom and individuality of their feelings, drives them to adultery by way of a necessary and ironic dialectic.

Montaigne says:

> We train them from childhood to the ways of love. Their grace, their dressing up, their knowledge, their language, all their instruction, has only this end in view. Their governesses imprint in them nothing else but the idea of love, if only by continually depicting it to them in order to disgust them with it.

Thus it is folly to try to bridle women's desire, which is so burning and natural.

And Engels declares:

With monogamous marriage, two constant social types, unknown hitherto, make their appearance on the scene—the wife's attendant lover and the cuckold husband . . . Together with monogamous marriage and hetaerism, adultery became an unavoidable social institution—denounced, severely penalised, but impossible to suppress.*

If conjugal sex has excited the wife's curiosity without satisfying her senses, like in Colette's *The Innocent Libertine*, she tries to complete her education in the beds of strangers. If she has no singular attachment to her husband, but he has succeeded in awakening her sexuality, she will want to taste the pleasures she has discovered through him with others.

Some moralists have been outraged by the preference shown to the lover, and I have pointed out the efforts of bourgeois literature to rehabilitate the figure of the husband; but it is absurd to defend him by showing that often in the eyes of society—that is to say, other men—he is better than his rival: what is important here is what he represents for the wife. So there are two traits that make him detestable. First of all, it is he who assumes the thankless role of initiator; the contradictory demands of the virgin who dreams of being both violated and respected almost surely condemn him to failure; she remains forever frigid in his arms; with her lover she experiences neither the torment of defloration nor the initial humiliation of modesty overcome; she is spared the trauma of surprise: she knows more or less what to expect; more honest, less vulnerable, less naive than on her wedding night, she does not confuse ideal love and physical hunger, sentiment and sexual excitement: when she takes a lover, it is a lover she wants. This lucidity is an aspect of the freedom of her choice. For here lies the other defect weighing on her husband: he was usually imposed and not chosen. Either she accepted him in resignation, or she was given over to him by her family; in any case, even if she married him for love, she makes him her master by marrying him; their relations have become a duty, and he often takes on the figure of tyrant. Her choice of lover is doubtless limited by circumstances, but there is an element of freedom in this relationship; to marry is an obligation, to take a lover is a luxury; it is because he has solicited her that the woman yields to him: she is sure, if not of his love, at least of his desire; it is not for the purpose of obeying laws that he acts upon his desire. He also has this advantage: that his seduction and prestige are not tarnished by the frictions of everyday life; he remains removed, an

---

* *Origin of the Family.*—Trans.

other. Thus the woman has the impression of getting out of herself in their meetings, of finding new riches: she feels other. This is above all what some women seek in a liaison: to be involved, surprised, rescued from themselves by the other. A rupture leaves them with a desperate empty feeling. Janet cites several cases of this melancholia that show us bluntly what the woman looks for and finds in her lover:

> A thirty-nine-year-old woman, heartbroken at having been aban-doned by a writer with whom she worked for five years, writes to Janet: "He had such a rich life and was so tyrannical that all I could do was take care of him, and I could not think of anything else."

> Another woman, thirty-one, fell ill after breaking with a lover she adored. "I wanted to be an inkwell on his desk to see him, hear him," she writes. And she explains: "Alone, I am bored, my husband brings me no intellectual stimulation, he knows nothing, he teaches me nothing, he does not *surprise* me . . . , he has nothing but common sense, it crushes me." But by contrast, she writes about her lover: "He is an *astonishing* man, I never saw in him a moment of confu-sion, emotion, gaiety, carelessness, always in control, mocking, cold enough to make you die of shame. In addition, an impudence, sangfroid, a sharp mind, a lively intelligence that made my head spin . . ."[12]

There are women who savor this feeling of plenitude and joyful excite-ment only in the first moments of a liaison; if a lover does not give them instant pleasure—and this frequently happens the first time as the partners are intimidated and ill adapted to each other—they feel resentment and disgust toward him; these "Messalinas" have multiple affairs and leave one lover after another. But it also happens that a woman, enlightened by the failure of her marriage, is attracted this time by a man who suits her well, and a lasting relation is created between them. Often he will appeal to her because he is of a radically different type from her husband. This is with-out a doubt the contrast that Sainte-Beuve, who seduced Adèle, provides with Victor Hugo. Stekel cites the following case:

> Mrs. P.H. has been married for the past eight years to a man who is a member of an athletic club. She visits the gynecologic clinic on account of a slight inflammation of the ovaries. There she complains

---

that her husband gives her no peace . . . She perceives only pain and does not know the meaning of gratification. The man is rough and violent . . . Finally he takes a sweetheart . . . [This does not trouble her in the least.] She is happy . . . she wants a divorce and calls on an attorney. In his office she meets a clerk who is the exact opposite of her husband. The clerk is humble, delicate, weak, but he is also loving and tender. They become closely acquainted and he begins to court her. He writes her tender letters. His petty attentions flatter and please her . . . They find that they have similar intellectual interests . . . With his first kiss her anaesthesia vanishes . . . This man's relatively weak *potentia* has roused the keenest orgasm in the woman. After the divorce they married; now they live very happily together . . . He is also able to rouse this woman's orgasm with kisses and other caresses. This was the same woman whose frigidity in the embrace of a highly potent man drove her to take a lover!

Not all affairs have fairy-tale endings. It happens that just as the young girl dreams of a liberator who will wrest her from under her father's roof, the wife awaits the lover who will save her from the conjugal yoke: an often-told story is that of the ardent lover who cools off and flees when his mistress starts talking about marriage; she is often hurt by his reluctance, and from then on, their relations become distorted by resentment and hostility. If a relationship becomes a stable one, it often takes on a familiar conjugal character in the end; all the vices of marriage—boredom, jealousy, prudence, deception—can be found in it. And the woman dreams of another man who will rescue her from this routine.

Adultery, furthermore, has very different characteristics according to customs and circumstances. In our civilization of enduring patriarchal traditions, marital infidelity is still more serious for the woman than for the man. Montaigne says:

Iniquitous appraisal of vices! . . . But we create and weigh vices not according to nature but according to our interest, whereby they assume so many unequal shapes. The severity of our decrees makes women's addiction to this vice more exacerbated and vicious than its nature calls for, and involves it in consequences that are worse than their cause.

We have seen the primary reasons for this severity: women's adultery risks introducing the child of a stranger into a family, dispossessing legitimate heirs; the husband is master, the wife his property. Social changes and the practice of birth control have taken much of the force out of these motives. But the will to keep woman in a state of dependency perpetuates the proscriptions that still surround her. She often interiorizes them; she closes her eyes to the conjugal escapades that her religion, her morality, and her "virtue" do not permit her to envisage with reciprocity. The control imposed by her social environment—in particular in "small towns" in the Old as well as the New World—is far more severe for her than for her husband: he goes out more, he travels, and his dalliances are more indulgently tolerated; she risks losing her reputation and her situation as a married woman. The ruses women use to thwart this scrutiny have often been described; I know a small Portuguese town of ancient severity where young women only go out in the company of a mother-in-law or sister-in-law; but the hairdresser rents out rooms above his shop; between hair being set and combed out, lovers steal a furtive embrace. In large cities, women have far fewer wardens: but the old custom of "afternoon dalliances" was hardly more conducive to the happy fulfillment of illicit feelings. Furtive and clandestine, adultery does not create human and free relationships; the lies it entails rob conjugal relations of what is left of their dignity.

In many circles today, women have partially gained sexual freedom. But it is still a difficult problem for them to reconcile their conjugal life with sexual satisfaction. As marriage generally does not mean physical love, it would seem reasonable to clearly differentiate one from the other. A man can admittedly make an excellent husband and still be inconstant: his sexual caprices do not in fact keep him from carrying out the enterprise of a friendly communal life with his wife; this amity will be all the purer, less ambivalent if it does not represent a shackle. One might allow that it could be the same for the wife; she often wishes to share in her husband's existence, create a home with him for their children, and still experience other embraces. It is the compromises of prudence and hypocrisy that make adultery degrading; a pact of freedom and sincerity would abolish one of the defects of marriages. It must be recognized, however, that *today* the irritating formula that inspired *Francillon* by Dumas fils—"It is not the same thing for women"—retains a certain truth. There is nothing *natural* about the difference. It is claimed that woman needs sexual activity less than man: nothing is less sure. Repressed women make shrewish wives, sadistic mothers, fanatical housekeepers, unhappy and dangerous creatures; in any case, even if her desires were more infrequent, there is no reason to consider it superfluous for her to satisfy them. The difference stems from the overall erotic situation of man and woman as defined by tradition and today's society. For woman, the love act is still considered a *service* woman renders to man, thus giving him the status of master; we have seen that he can always *take* an inferior woman, but she degrades herself if she *gives herself* to a male who is not her equal; her consent, in any case, is of the same nature as a surrender, a fall. A woman often graciously accepts her husband having other women: she is even flattered; Adèle Hugo apparently saw her fiery husband take his ardors to other beds without regret; some women even copy Mme de Pompadour and act as procurers.[13] By contrast, in lovemaking, the woman is changed into object, into prey; it seems to the husband that she is possessed by a foreign mana, that she ceases to belong to him, she is stolen from him. And the fact is that in bed the woman often feels, wants to be, and, consequently, is dominated; the fact also is that because of virile prestige, she tends to approve, to imitate the male who, having possessed her, embodies in her eyes all men. The husband is irritated, not without reason, to hear in his wife's familiar mouth the echo of a stranger's thinking: it seems to him in a way that it is he who is possessed, violated. If Mme de Charrière broke with the young Benjamin Constant—who played the feminine role between two virile women—it was because she could not bear to feel him marked by the hated influence of Mme de Staël. As long as the woman acts like a slave and the reflection of the man to whom she "gives herself," she must recognize the fact that her infidelities wrest her from her husband more radically than do his reciprocal infidelities.

If she does preserve her integrity, she may nonetheless fear that her husband will be compromised in her lover's consciousness. Even a woman is quick to imagine that in sleeping with a man—if only once, in haste, on a sofa—she has gained a certain superiority over the legitimate spouse; a man who believes he possesses a mistress thinks, with even more reason, that he has trumped her husband. This is why the woman is careful to choose her lover from a lower social class in Bataille's *Tenderness* or Kessel's *Belle de nuit*,* she seeks sexual satisfaction from him, but she does not want to give him an advantage over her respected husband. In *Man's Fate*, Malraux shows us a couple where man and woman make a pact for reciprocal freedom: yet when May tells Kyo she has slept with a friend, he grieves over the fact that this man thinks he "had" her; he chooses to respect her independence because he knows very well that one never *has*

---

13. I am speaking here of marriage. We will see that the attitude of the couple is reversed in a love affair.

* The correct title is *Belle de jour.*—Trans.

anyone; but the complaisant ideas held by another man hurt and humiliate him through May. Society confuses the free woman and the loose woman; the lover himself may not recognize the freedom from which he profits; he would rather believe his mistress has yielded, let herself go, that he has conquered her, seduced her. A proud woman might personally come to terms with her partner's vanity; but it would be detestable for her that her esteemed husband should stand such arrogance. For as long as this equality is not universally recognized and concretely realized, it is very difficult for a woman to act as an equal to a man.

In any case, adultery, friendships, and social life are but diversions within married life; they can help its constraints to be endured, but they do not break them. They are only artificial escapes that in no way authentically allow the woman to take her destiny into her own hands.

CHAPTER 8

Prostitutes and Hetaeras

Marriage, as we have seen, has an immediate corollary in prostitution.[1] "Hetaerism," says Morgan, "follows mankind in civilization as a dark shadow upon the family." Man, out of prudence, destines his wife to chastity, but he does not derive satisfaction from the regime he imposes on her. Montaigne says:

> The kings of Persia used to invite their wives to join them at their feasts; but when the wine began to heat them in good earnest and they had to give completely free rein to sensuality, they sent them back to their private rooms, so as not to make them participants in their immoderate appetites, and sent for other women in their place, to whom they did not have this obligation of respect.*

Sewers are necessary to guarantee the sanitation of palaces, said the Church Fathers. And Mandeville, in a very popular book, said: "It is obvious that some women must be sacrificed to save others and to prevent an even more abject filth." One of the arguments of American slaveholders and defenders of slavery is that, released from slavish drudgery, Southern whites could establish the most democratic and refined relations with each other; likewise, the existence of a caste of "lost women" makes it possible to treat "the virtuous woman" with the most chivalric respect. The prostitute is a scapegoat; man unloads his turpitude onto her, and he repudiates her. Whether a legal status puts her under police surveillance or she works clandestinely, she is in any case treated as a pariah.

From the economic point of view, her situation is symmetrical to the married woman's. "Between those who sell themselves through prostitu-

---

1. Volume I, Part Two.
* *Complete Essays of Montaigne.*—TRANS.

tion and those who sell themselves through marriage, the only difference resides in the price and length of the contract," says Marro.[2] For both, the sexual act is a service; the latter is engaged for life by one man; the former has several clients who pay her per item. One male against all the others protects the former; the latter is defended by all against the exclusive tyranny of each one. In any case, the advantages they derive from giving their bodies are limited by competition; the husband knows he could have had another wife: the accomplishment of his "conjugal duties" is not a favor; it is the execution of a contract. In prostitution, masculine desire can be satisfied on any body as it is specific and not individual. Wives or courtesans do not succeed in exploiting man unless they wield a singular power over him. The main difference between them is that the legitimate woman, oppressed as a married woman, is respected as a human person; this respect begins seriously to bring a halt to oppression. However, the prostitute does not have the rights of a person; she is the sum of all types of feminine slavery at once.

It is naive to wonder what motives drive a woman to prostitution; Lombroso's theory that assimilated prostitutes with criminals and that saw them both as degenerates is no longer accepted; it is possible, as the statistics show, that in general prostitutes have a slightly below-average mental level and that some are clearly retarded: women with fewer mental faculties readily choose jobs that do not demand of them any specialization; but most are normal and some very intelligent. No hereditary fate, no physiological defect, weighs on them. In reality, as soon as a profession opens in a world where misery and unemployment are rife, there are people to enter it; as long as there are police and prostitution, there will be policemen and prostitutes. Especially because these professions are, on average, more lucrative than many others. It is very hypocritical to be surprised by the supply masculine demand creates; this is a rudimentary and universal economic process. "Of all the causes of prostitution," wrote Parent-Duchâtelet in his study in 1857, "none is more active than the lack of work and the misery that is the inevitable consequence of inadequate salaries."[*] Right-thinking moralists respond sneeringly that the pitiful accounts of prostitutes are just stories for the naive client. It is true that in many cases a

---

2. *Puberty.* [A. Marro, "The Psychology of Puberty," *British Journal of Psychiatry* (1910). —TRANS.]

* A. J. B. Parent-Duchâtelet, *De la prostitution dans la ville de Paris* (Prostitution in the City of Paris). Brussels: Société Encyclographique des Sciences Médicales, 1836. Beauvoir's dates are erroneous. The study was republished in 1857.—TRANS.

prostitute could earn her living in a different way: that the living she has chosen does not seem the worst to her does not prove she has this vice in her blood; rather, it condemns a society where this profession is still one that seems the least repellent to many women. One asks, why did she choose it? The question should be: Why should she not choose it? It has been noted that, among other things, many "girls" were once servants; this is what Parent-Duchâtelet established for all countries, what Lily Braun noted in Germany and Ryckère in Belgium. About 50 percent of prostitutes were first servants. One look at "maids' rooms" is enough to explain this fact. Exploited, enslaved, treated as an object rather than as a person, the maid or chambermaid cannot look forward to any improvement of her lot; sometimes she has to submit to the whims of the master of the house: from domestic slavery and sexual subordination to the master, she slides into a slavery that could not be more degrading and that she dreams will be better. In addition, women in domestic service are very often uprooted; it is estimated that 80 percent of Parisian prostitutes come from the provinces or the countryside. Proximity to one's family and concern for one's reputation are thought to prevent a woman from turning to a generally discredited profession; but if she is lost in a big city, no longer integrated into society, the abstract idea of "morality" does not provide any obstacle. While the bourgeoisie invests the sexual act—and above all virginity—with daunting taboos, the working class and peasantry treat it with indifference. Numerous studies agree on this point: many girls let themselves be deflowered by the first comer and then find it natural to give themselves to anyone who comes along. In a study of one hundred prostitutes, Dr. Bizard recorded the following facts: one had been deflowered at eleven, two at twelve, two at thirteen, six at fourteen, seven at fifteen, twenty-one at sixteen, nineteen at seventeen, seventeen at eighteen, six at nineteen; the others, after twenty-one. There were thus 5 percent who had been raped before puberty. More than half said they gave themselves out of love; the others consented out of ignorance. The first seducer is often young. Usually it is someone from the workshop, an office colleague, a childhood friend; then come soldiers, foremen, valets, and students; Dr. Bizard's list also included two lawyers, an architect, a doctor, and a pharmacist. It is rather rare, as legend has it, for the employer himself to play this initiating role: but often it is his son or nephew or one of his friends. Commenge, in his study, also reports on forty-five girls from twelve to seventeen who were deflowered by strangers whom they never saw again; they had consented with indifference, and without experiencing pleasure. Dr. Bizard recorded the following, more detailed cases, among others:

Mlle G. de Bordeaux, leaving the convent at eighteen, is persuaded, out of curiosity and without thinking of any danger, to follow a stranger from the fair into his caravan, where she is deflowered.

Without thinking, a thirteen-year-old child gives herself to a man she has met in the street, whom she does not know and whom she will never see again.

M. . . . tells us explicitly that she was deflowered at seventeen by a young man she did not know . . . she let it happen out of total ignorance.

R. . . . , deflowered at seventeen and a half by a young man she had never seen whom she had met by chance at the doctor's, where she had gone to get the doctor for her sick sister; he brought her back by car so that she could get home more quickly, but in fact he left her in the middle of the street after getting what he wanted from her.

B. . . . deflowered at fifteen and a half "without thinking about what she was doing," in our client's words, by a young man she never saw again; nine months later, she gave birth to a healthy boy.

S. . . . , deflowered at fourteen by a young man who drew her to his house under the pretext that he wanted her to meet his sister. The young man in reality did not have a sister, but he had syphilis and contaminated the girl.

R. . . . deflowered at eighteen in an old trench from the front by a married cousin with whom she was visiting the battlefields; he got her pregnant and made her leave her family.

C. . . . at seventeen, deflowered on the beach one summer evening by a young man whom she had just met at the hotel and at a hundred meters from their two mothers, who were talking about trifles. Contaminated with gonorrhea.

L. . . . deflowered at thirteen by her uncle while listening to the radio at the same time as her aunt, who liked to go to bed early, was sleeping quietly in the next room.*

We can be sure that these girls who gave in passively nevertheless suffered the trauma of defloration; one would like to know what psychological influence this brutal experience had on their future; but "girls" are not psychoanalyzed, they are inarticulate in describing themselves and take

---

* Léon Bizard, *Souvenirs d'un médecin . . . des prisons de Paris* (1925; Memoirs of a Doctor of Paris Prisons)—TRANS.

refuge behind clichés. For some, the facility of giving themselves to the first comer can be explained by the existence of prostitution fantasies about which we have spoken: out of family resentment, horror of their budding sexuality, the desire to act grown-up, some young girls imitate prostitutes; they use harsh makeup, see boys, act flirtatiously and provocatively; they who are still infantile, asexual, and cold think they can play with fire with impunity; one day a man takes them at their word, and they slip from dreams to acts.

"When a door has been broken open, it is then hard to keep it closed," said one fourteen-year-old prostitute.[3] However, the girl rarely decides to be a streetwalker immediately following her defloration. In some cases, she remains attached to her first lover and continues to live with him; she takes an "honest" job; when the lover abandons her, another consoles her; since she no longer belongs to one man, she decides she can give herself to all; sometimes it is the lover—the first, the second—who suggests this means of earning money. There are also many girls who are prostituted by their parents: in some families, like the famous American family the Jukes, all the women are doomed to this job. Among young female vagabonds, there are also many girls abandoned by their families who begin by begging and slip from there to the streets. In 1857, out of 5,000 prostitutes, Parent-Duchâtelet found that 1,441 were influenced by poverty, 1,425 seduced and abandoned, 1,255 abandoned and left penniless by their parents.* Contemporary studies suggest approximately the same conclusions. Illness often leads to prostitution as the woman has become unable to hold down a real job or has lost her place; it destroys her precarious budget, it forces the woman to come up with new resources quickly. So it is with the birth of a child. More than half the women of Saint-Lazare had at least one child; many raised from three to six children; Dr. Bizard points out one who brought fourteen into the world, of whom eight were still living when he knew her. Few of them, he says, abandon their children; and sometimes the unwed mother becomes a prostitute in order to feed the child. He cites this case, among others:

> Deflowered in the provinces, at nineteen, by a sixty-year-old direc-
> tor while she was still living at home, she had to leave her family,
> as she was pregnant, and she gave birth to a healthy girl that she

---

3. Cited by Marro, "Puberty."

* Parent-Duchâtelet's study was written in 1836 and republished in 1857.

brought up well. After nursing, she went to Paris, found a job as a nanny, and began to carouse at the age of twenty-nine. She has been a prostitute for thirty-three years. Weak and exhausted, she is now asking to be hospitalized in Saint-Lazare.

It is well-known that there is an increase of prostitution in wars and the crises of their aftermath.

The author of *The Life of a Prostitute*, published in part in *Les Temps Modernes*,[4] tells of her beginnings:

I got married at sixteen to a man thirteen years older than I. I did it to get out of my parents' house. My husband only thought of making me have kids. "Like that, you'll stay at home, you won't go out," he said. He wouldn't let me wear makeup, didn't want to take me to the movies. I had to stand my mother-in-law, who came to the house every day and always took the side of her bastardly son. My first child was a boy, Jacques; fourteen months later, I gave birth to another, Pierre . . . As I was very bored, I took courses in nursing, which I liked a lot . . . I got work at a hospital on the outskirts of Paris, working with women. A nurse who was just a girl taught me things I hadn't known about before. Sleeping with my husband was mostly a chore. As for men, I didn't have a fling with anyone for six months. Then one day, a real tough guy, a cad but good-looking, came into my own room. He convinced me I could change my life, that I could go with him to Paris, that I wouldn't work anymore . . . He knew how to fool me . . . I decided to go off with him . . . I was really happy for a month . . . One day he brought along a well-dressed, chic woman, saying: "So here, this one does all right for herself." At the beginning, I didn't go along with it. I even found a job as a nurse in a local hospital to show him that I didn't want to walk the streets, but I couldn't carry on for long. He would say: "You don't love me. When you love a man, you work for him." I cried. At the hospital, I was sad. Finally, I was persuaded to go to the hairdresser's . . . I began to turn tricks! Julot followed me to see if I was doing well and to be able to warn me if the cops were onto me.*

---

4. She had this story published in secret under the pseudonym Marie-Thérèse; I will refer to her by this name.
* Julot is a pet name for a prostitute's pimp.—TRANS.

In some ways, this story is the classic one of the girl doomed to the street by a pimp. This role might also be played by the husband. And sometimes, by a woman as well. L. Faivre made a study in 1931 of 510 young prostitutes; he found that 284 of them lived alone, 132 with a male friend, and 94 with a female friend with whom they usually had homosexual ties.[5] He cites (with their spelling)* extracts of the following letters:

Suzanne, seventeen. I gave myself to prostitution, especially with women prostitutes. One of them who kept me for a long time was very jealous, and so I left that street.

Andrée, fifteen and a half. I left my parents to live with a friend I met at a dance, I understood right away that she wanted to love me like a man, I stayed with her four months, then . . .

Jeanne, fourteen. My poor sweet papa's name was X. . . . he died in the hospital from war wounds in 1922. My mother got married again. I was going to school to get my primary school diploma, then having got it, I went to study sewing . . . then as I earned very little, the fights with my stepfather began . . . I had to be placed as a maid at Mme X.'s, on X. street . . . I was alone with a girl who was probably twenty-five for about ten days; I noticed a very big change in her. Then one day, just like a boy, she admitted her great love. I hesitated, then afraid of being let go, I finally gave in; I understood then certain things . . . I worked, then finding myself without a job, I had to go to the Bois, where I continued with women. I met a very generous lady, and so forth.

Quite often, the woman only envisages prostitution as a temporary way of increasing her resources. But the way in which she then finds herself enslaved to it has been described many times. While cases of the "white slave trade," where she is dragged into the spiral by violence, false promises, mystifications, and so on, are relatively rare, what happens more often is that she is kept in this career against her will. The capital necessary to get her started is provided by a pimp or a madam who acquires rights over her,

---

5. "Les jeunes prostituées vagabondes en prison" (Young Vagabond Prostitutes in Prison) (1931).

* In the French text of these passages there are grammar and spelling errors that we have not reproduced in English.—TRANS.

who gets most of her profits, and from whom she is not able to free herself. Marie-Thérèse carried on a real fight for several years before succeeding:

> I finally understood that Julot didn't want anything but my dough, and I thought that far from him, I could save a bit of money . . . At home in the beginning, I was shy, I didn't dare go up to clients and tell them "come on up." The wife of one of Julot's buddies watched me closely and even counted my tricks . . . So Julot writes to me that I should give my money every evening to the madam: "Like that, nobody will steal it from you." When I wanted to buy a dress, the hotel manager told me that Julot had forbidden her to give my dough . . . I decided to get out of this trick house as fast as I could. When the boss lady found out I wanted to leave, she didn't give me the tampon before the visit like the other times, and I was stopped and put into the hospital[6] . . . I had to return to the brothel to earn some money for my trip . . . but I only stayed in the house for four weeks . . . I worked a few days in Barbès like before but I was too furious at Julot to stay in Paris: we fought, he beat me, once he almost threw me out of the window . . . I made an arrangement with a go-between to go to the provinces. When I realized he knew Julot, I didn't show up at the rendezvous. The agent's two broads met me on rue Belhomme and gave me a thrashing . . . The next day, I packed my bags and left alone for the isle of T. . . . Three weeks later I was fed up with the brothel, I wrote to the doctor to mark me as going out when he came for the visit . . . Julot saw me on Boulevard de Magenta and beat me . . . My face was scarred after the thrashing on Boulevard de Magenta. I was fed up with Julot. So I signed a contract to go to Germany.

Literature has popularized the character of the fancy man. He plays a protective role in the girl's life. He advances her money to buy outfits, then he defends her against the competition of other women and the police— sometimes he himself is a policeman—and against the clients. They would like to be able to consume without paying; there are those who would readily satisfy their sadism on a woman. In Madrid a few years ago Fascist and gilded youth amused themselves by throwing prostitutes into the river on cold nights; in France students having fun sometimes brought women into

---

6. "A tampon to anesthetize the gono was given to prostitutes before the doctor's visit so that he only found a woman to be sick if the madam wanted to get rid of her."

the countryside and abandoned them, entirely naked, at night; in order to get her money and avoid bad treatment, the prostitute needs a man. He also provides her with moral support: "You work less well alone, you don't have your heart in it, you let yourself go," some say. She often feels love for him; she takes on this job or justifies it out of love; in this milieu, man's superiority over woman is enormous: this distance favors love-religion, which explains some prostitutes' passionate abnegation. They see in their male's violence the sign of his virility and submit to him even more docilely. They experience jealousy and torment with him, but also the joys of the woman in love.

But sometimes they feel only hostility and resentment for him: it is out of fear, because he has a hold over them, that they remain under his thumb, as we just saw in the case of Marie-Thérèse. So sometimes they console themselves with a "fling" with one of their clients. Marie-Thérèse writes:

> All the women have flings, me too, in addition to their Julot. He was a very handsome sailor. Even though he was a good lover, he didn't turn me on, but we felt a lot of friendship for each other. Often he came up with me without making love, just to talk; he told me I should get out of this, that my place wasn't here.

They also find consolation with women. Many prostitutes are homosexual. We saw that there was often a homosexual adventure at the beginning of their careers and that many continued to live with a woman. According to Anna Rueling, about 20 percent of prostitutes in Germany are homosexual. Faivre points out that in prison young women prisoners correspond with each other with pornographic and passionate letters that they sign "United for life." These letters are similar to those schoolgirls write to each other, feeding the "flames" in their hearts; these girls are less aware, shyer; prisoners carry their feelings to the limit, both in their words and their actions. We can see in the life of Marie-Thérèse—who was launched into lovemaking by a woman—what special role the female "pal" plays in comparison to the despised male client or the authoritarian pimp:

> Julot brought around a girl, a poor drudge who didn't even have a pair of shoes to wear. At the flea market they buy what she needed, and then she comes to work with me. She was sweet, and in addition she liked women, so we got along well. She reminded me of everything I learned with the nurse. We had a lot of fun, and instead of working, we went to the movies. I was happy to have her with us.

One can see that the girlfriend plays approximately the same role that the best friend plays for the virtuous woman surrounded by women: she is the companion in pleasure, she is the one with whom she has free, gratuitous relations, that can thus be chosen; tired of men, disgusted by them, or wishing for a diversion, the prostitute will often seek relief and pleasure in the arms of another woman. In any case, the complicity I spoke of and that immediately unites women exists more strongly in this case than in any other. Because their relations with half of humanity are commercial, because the whole of society treats them as pariahs, there is great solidarity among prostitutes; they might be rivals, jealous of each other, insult each other, fight with each other; but they have a great need of each other to form a "counter-universe" in which they regain their human dignity; the friend is the confidante and the privileged witness; she is the one who approves of the dress and hairdo meant to seduce the man, but which are ends in themselves in other women's envious or admiring gazes.

As for the prostitute's relations with her clients, opinions vary and cases undoubtedly vary. It is often emphasized that she reserves kissing on the lips, the expression of real tenderness, for her true love, and she makes no connection between amorous embraces and professional ones. Men's views are dubious because their vanity incites them to let themselves be duped by simulated orgasm. It must be said that the circumstances are very different when it is a question of a "mass turnover," often physically exhausting, a quick trick, or regular relations with a familiar client. Marie-Thérèse generally did her job indifferently, but she mentions some nights of delights; she had "crushes" and says that all her friends did too; a woman might refuse to be paid by a client she liked, and sometimes, if he is in a difficult situation, she offers to help him. In general, however, the woman works "cold." Some only feel indifference tinged with scorn for their clientele. "Oh! What saps men are! Women can put anything they want into men's heads!" writes Marie-Thérèse. But many feel a disgusted resentment of men; they are sickened, for one thing, by their perversions, either because they go to the brothel to satisfy the perversions they do not dare to admit to their wives or mistresses or because being at a brothel incites them to invent perversions; many men demand "fantasies" from the woman. Marie-Thérèse complained in particular that the French have an insatiable imagination. The sick women treated by Dr. Bizard confided in him that "all men are more or less perverted." One of my female friends spoke at great length at the Beaujon hospital with a young, very intelligent prostitute who started off as a servant and who lived with a pimp she adored. "*All* men are perverted," she said, "except mine. That's why I love him. If I ever discover he's a pervert, I'll leave him. The first time the client doesn't always dare, he seems normal; but when he comes back, he begins to want things . . . You say your husband isn't a pervert: you'll see. They all are." Because of these perversions she detested them. Another of my female friends, in 1943 in Fresnes, became intimate with a prostitute. She emphasized that 90 percent of her clients were perverts and about 50 percent were self-hating pederasts. Those who showed too much imagination terrified her. A German officer asked her to walk about the room naked with flowers in her arms while he imitated the flight of a bird; in spite of her courtesy and generosity, she ran away every time she caught sight of him. Marie-Thérèse hated "fantasy" even though it had a much higher rate than simple coitus, and was often less demanding for the woman. These three women were particularly intelligent and sensitive. They certainly understood that as soon as they were no longer protected by the routine of the job, as soon as man stopped being a client in general and became individualized, they were prey to consciousness, to a capricious freedom: it was no longer just a simple business transaction. Some prostitutes, though, specialize in "fantasy" because it brings in more money. In their hostility to the client there is often class resentment. Helene Deutsch speaks at great length about the story of Anna, a pretty blond prostitute, childlike, generally very gentle, but who had fierce fits of anger against some men. She was from a working-class family; her father drank, her mother was sickly: this unhappy household gave her such a horrible idea of family life that she rejected all proposals to marry, even though throughout her career she had many opportunities. The young men of the neighborhood debauched her; she liked her job well enough; but when, ill with tuberculosis, she was sent to the hospital, she developed a fierce hatred of doctors; "respectable" men were abhorrent to her; she could not stand gentility, her doctor's solicitude. "Don't we know better than anyone that these men easily drop their masks of gentility, self-control, and behave like brutes?" she said. Other than that, she was mentally perfectly well-balanced. She pretended to have a child that she left with a wet nurse, but otherwise she did not lie. She died of tuberculosis. Another young prostitute, Julia, who gave herself to every boy she met from the age of fifteen, only liked poor and weak men; she was gentle and nice with them; she considered the others "wicked beasts who deserved harsh treatment." (She had an obvious complex that manifested an unsatisfied maternal vocation: she had fits as soon as "mother," "child," or similar-sounding words were uttered.)

Most prostitutes are morally adapted to their condition; that does not mean they are hereditarily or congenitally immoral, but they rightly feel integrated into a society that demands their services. They know well that the edifying lecture of the policeman who puts them through an inspection is pure verbiage, and the lofty principles their clients pronounce outside the brothel do little to intimidate them. Marie-Thérèse explains to the baker woman with whom she lives in Berlin:

> Myself, I like everyone. When it's a question of dough,
> madame . . . Yes, because sleeping with a man for free, for nothing,
> says the same thing about you, that one's a whore; if you get paid,
> they call you a whore, yes, but a smart one; because when you ask a
> man for money, you can be sure that he'll tell you right off: "Oh! I
> didn't know you did that kind of work," or "Do you have a man?"
> There you are. Paid or not, for me it's the same thing. "Ah yes!" she
> answers. "You're right." Because, I tell her, you're going to stand in
> line for a half hour to have a ticket for shoes. Myself, for a half hour,
> I'll turn a trick. I get the shoes without paying, and on the contrary,
> if I do my thing right, I'm paid as well. So you see, I'm right.

It is not their moral and psychological situation that makes prostitutes' existence miserable. It is their material condition that is deplorable for the most part. Exploited by their pimps and hotel keepers, they have no security, and three-quarters of them are penniless. After five years in the trade, around 75 percent of them have syphilis, says Dr. Bizard, who has treated thousands; among others, inexperienced minors are frighteningly susceptible to contamination; close to 25 percent must be operated on for complications resulting from gonorrhea. One in twenty has tuberculosis; 60 percent become alcoholics or drug addicts; 40 percent die before forty. It must be added that in spite of precautions, they do become pregnant from time to time, and they are generally operated on in bad conditions. Common prostitution is a hard job where the sexually and economically oppressed woman—subjected to the arbitrariness of the police, humiliating medical checkups, the whims of her clients, and the prospect of germs, sickness, and misery—is really reduced to the level of a thing.[7]

There are many degrees between the common prostitute and the grand hetaera. The main difference is that the former trades in her pure general-

---

7. Obviously, it is not through negative and hypocritical measures that this situation can be changed. For prostitution to disappear, two conditions are necessary: a decent job must be guaranteed to all women; customs must not place any obstacles to free love. Prostitution will be suppressed only by suppressing the needs to which it responds.

ity, so that competition keeps her at a miserable level of living, while the latter tries to be recognized in her singularity: if she succeeds, she can aspire to a lofty future. Beauty, charm, and sex appeal are necessary for this, but they are not sufficient: the woman must be considered *distinguished*. Her value will often be revealed through a man's desire: but she will be "launched" only when the man declares her price to the eyes of the world. In the last century, it was the town house, carriage and pair, and pearls that proved the influence of the cocotte on her protector and that raised her to the rank of demimondaine; her worth was confirmed as long as men continued to ruin themselves for her. Social and economic changes abolished the Blanche d'Antigny types. There is no longer a demimonde in which a reputation can be established. An ambitious woman has to try to attain fame in other ways. The most recent incarnation of the hetaera is the movie star. Flanked by her husband or serious male friend—rigorously required by Hollywood—she is no less related to Phryne, Imperia, or Casque d'Or. She delivers Woman to the dreams of men who give her fortune and glory in exchange.

There has always been a vague connection between prostitution and art, because beauty and sexuality are ambiguously associated with each other. In fact, it is not Beauty that arouses desire: but the Platonic theory of love suggests hypocritical justifications for lust. Phryne baring her breast offers Areopagus the contemplation of a pure idea. Exhibiting an unveiled body becomes an art show; American burlesque has turned undressing into a stage show. "Nudity is chaste," proclaim those old gentlemen who collect obscene photographs in the name of "artistic nudes." In the brothel, the moment of choice begins as a display; if choosing is more complicated, *tableaux vivants* and "artistic poses" are offered to the client. The prostitute who wishes to acquire a singular distinction does not limit herself to showing her flesh passively; she tries to have her own talents. Greek flute-playing women charmed men with their music and dances. The Ouled Nails performing belly dances and Spanish women dancing and singing in the Barrio Chino are simply offering themselves in a refined manner to enthusiasts. Nana goes onstage to find herself a "protector." Some music halls, like some concert cafés before them, are simply brothels. All occupations where a woman displays herself can be used for amatory purposes. Of course there are showgirls, taxi dancers, nude dancers, escorts, pinups, models, singers, and actresses who do not let their sexual lives interfere with their occupations; the more skill and invention involved in their work, the more it can be taken as a goal in itself; but a woman who "goes onstage" to earn a living is often tempted to use her charms for more intimate commercial ends. Inversely, the courtesan wishes to have an occupation that will serve as her alibi. Rare are those like Colette's Léa who, addressed by a friend as "Dear artist," would respond: "Artist? My lovers are truly most indiscreet." We have said that her reputation confers a market value on her: the stage or screen where she makes a "name" for herself will become her capital.

Cinderella does not always dream of Prince Charming: husband or lover, she fears he may change into a tyrant; she prefers to dream of her own smiling face on a movie theater marquee. But it is more often thanks to her masculine "protection" that she will attain her goal; and it is men—husbands, lovers, suitors—who confirm her triumph by letting her share their fortune or their fame. It is this need to *please* another or a crowd that connects the movie star to the hetaera. They play a similar role in society: I will use the word "hetaera" to designate women who use not only their bodies but also their entire person as exploitable capital. Their attitude is very different from that of a creator who, transcending himself in a work, goes beyond the given and appeals to a freedom in others to whom he opens up the future; the hetaera does not uncover the world, she opens no road to human transcendence:[8] on the contrary, she seeks to take possession of it for her profit; offering herself for the approval of her admirers, she does not disavow this passive femininity that dooms her to man: she endows it with a magic power that allows her to take males into the trap of her presence, and to feed herself on them; she engulfs them with herself in immanence.

In this way, woman succeeds in acquiring a certain independence. Giving herself to many men, she belongs to none definitively; the money she accumulates, the name she "launches" as one launches a product, ensure her economic autonomy. The freest women in ancient Greece were neither matrons nor common prostitutes but hetaeras. Renaissance courtesans and Japanese geishas enjoy an infinitely greater freedom than their contemporaries. In France, the woman who seems to be the most virile and independent is perhaps Ninon de Lenclos. Paradoxically, those women who exploit their femininity to the extreme create a situation for themselves nearly equal to that of a man; moving from this sex that delivers them to men as objects, they become subjects. They not only earn their living like men but also live in nearly exclusively masculine company; free in their mores and

---

8. It may happen that she is *also* an artist, and seeking to please, she invents and creates. She can either combine these two functions or go beyond the amatory level and class herself in the category of actress, opera singer, dancer, and so on, which will be discussed later.

speech, they can rise to the rarest intellectual freedom—like Ninon de Lenclos. The most distinguished among them are often surrounded with artists and writers who find "virtuous women" boring. Masculine myths find their most seductive incarnation in the hetaera; more than any other woman, she is flesh and consciousness, idol, inspiration, muse; painters and sculptors want her as their model; she will nourish poets' dreams; it is in her that the intellectual will explore the treasures of feminine "intuition"; she is more readily intelligent than the matron, because she is less set in hypocrisy. Women who are extremely talented will not readily settle for the role of Egeria; they will feel the need to show autonomously the value that the admiration of others confers on them; they will try to transform their passive virtues into activities. Emerging in the world as sovereign subjects, they write poems, prose; they paint and compose music. Thus Imperia became famous among Italian courtesans. A woman might also use man as an instrument, so as to practice through him masculine functions: the "favorite royal mistresses" participated in the government of the world through their powerful lovers.[9]

This liberation can be conveyed on the erotic level as well. Woman might find compensation for the feminine inferiority complex in the money and services she extorts from man; money has a purifying role; it abolishes the war of the sexes. If many nonprofessional women insist on extracting checks and gifts from their lovers—making the man pay—and paying him, as we will see further on, it is not out of cupidity alone: it is to change him into an instrument. In that way, the woman defends herself from becoming one herself; perhaps he believes he "has" her, but this sexual possession is illusory; it is she who *has* him on the far more solid economic ground. Her self-esteem is satisfied. She can abandon herself to her lover's embraces; she is not yielding to a foreign will; pleasure will not be "inflicted" on her, it will become rather a supplementary benefit; she will not be "taken," because she is paid.

Nevertheless, the courtesan has the reputation of being frigid. It is useful for her to know how to govern her heart and her sexual appetite: sentimental or sensual, she risks being under the influence of a man who will exploit or dominate her or make her suffer. Among the sexual acts she accepts, there are many—especially early in her career—that humiliate her; her revolt against male arrogance is expressed by her frigidity. He-

9. Just as some women use marriage to serve their own ends, others use their lovers as means for attaining a political or economic aim. They go beyond the hetaera's situation as others go beyond the matron's.

taeras, like matrons, freely confide "tricks" to each other that enable them to "fake" their work. This contempt, this disgust for men clearly shows they are not at all sure they have won the game of exploiter-exploited. And in fact, in the great majority of cases, dependence is still their lot.

No man is their definitive master. But they have the most urgent need of man. The courtesan loses all her means of existence if he ceases to desire her: the novice knows that her whole future is in his hands; deprived of masculine support, even the movie star sees her prestige fade: abandoned by Orson Welles, Rita Hayworth wandered over Europe like a sickly orphan until she found Aly Khan. The most beautiful woman is never sure of tomorrow, because her weapons are magic, and magic is capricious; she is bound to her protector—husband or lover—nearly as tightly as a "virtuous" wife is bound to her husband. She not only owes him bed service but also is subjected to his presence, conversation, friends, and especially his vanity's demands. By paying for his steady's high heels and satin skirts, the pimp makes an investment that will bring a return; by offering his girlfriend pearls and furs, the industrialist or the producer displays his wealth and power through her: whether the woman is a means for earning money or a pretext for spending it, it is the same servitude. The gifts showered on her are chains. And are these clothes and jewels she wears really hers? The man sometimes reclaims them after they break up, as Sacha Guitry once did with elegance. To "keep" her protector without renouncing her pleasures, the woman uses ruses, maneuvers, lies, and hypocrisy that dishonor conjugal life; even if she only feigns servility, this game is itself servile. Beautiful and famous, she can choose another if the master of the moment becomes odious. But beauty is a worry, a fragile treasure; the hetaera is totally dependent on her body, which time pitilessly degrades; the fight against aging is most dramatic for her. If she is endowed with great prestige, she will be able to survive the ruin of her face and figure. But caring for this renown, her surest asset, subjects her to the hardest of tyrannies: that of public opinion. We know that Hollywood stars fall into slavery. Their bodies are no longer their own; the producer decides on their hair color, weight, figure, and type; teeth are pulled out to change the shape of a cheek. Diets, exercise, fittings, and makeup are daily chores. Going out and flirting are part of "personal appearances"; private life is just a moment in their public life. In France there is no written contract, but a careful and clever woman knows what "promotion" demands of her. The star who refuses to give in to these demands will face a brutal or slow but ineluctable decline. The prostitute who only gives her body is perhaps less of a slave than the woman whose occupation it is to entertain. A woman who has "arrived" through a real profession and whose talent is recognized—actress, opera singer, dancer—escapes the hetaera's condition; she can experience true independence; but most spend their entire lives in danger; they must seduce the public and men over and over without respite.

Very often the kept woman interiorizes her dependence; subjected to public opinion, she accepts its values; she admires the "fashionable world" and adopts its customs; she wants to be regarded according to bourgeois standards. She is a parasite of the rich bourgeoisie, and she adheres to its ideas; she is "right thinking"; in former times she would readily send her daughters to a convent school, and as she got older, she even went to Mass and openly converted. She is on the conservatives' side. She is too proud to have made her place in this world to want to change. The struggle she wages to "arrive" does not dispose her to feelings of brotherhood and human solidarity; she paid for her success with too much slavish compliance to sincerely wish for universal freedom. Zola highlights this trait in Nana:

> As for books and plays, Nana had very definite opinions: she wanted tender and noble works, things to make her dream and elevate her soul . . . she was riled up against the republicans. What on earth did those dirty people who never washed want? Weren't people happy, didn't the emperor do everything he could for the people? A pretty bit of filth, the people! She knew them, she could talk about them: No, you see, their republic would be a great misfortune for everyone. Oh, may God preserve the emperor as long as possible!

In times of war, no one displays a more aggressive patriotism than high-level prostitutes; they hope to rise to the level of duchess through the noble sentiments they affect. Commonplaces, clichés, prejudices, and conventional feelings form the basis of their public conversations, and they have often lost all sincerity deep in their hearts. Between lies and hyperbole, language is destroyed. The hetaera's whole life is a show: her words, her gestures, are intended not to express her thoughts but to produce an effect. She plays a comedy of love for her protector: at times she plays it for herself. She plays comedies of respectability and prestige for the public: she ends up believing herself to be a paragon of virtue and a sacred idol. Stubborn bad faith governs her inner life and permits her studied lies to seem true. There are moments of spontaneity in her life: she does experience love; she has "flings" and "infatuations"; sometimes she is even "mad about" someone. But the one who spends too much time on caprices, feelings, or pleasure will soon lose her "position." Generally, she composes her fantasies with the prudence of an adulterous wife; she hides from her producer and the public; thus, she cannot give too much of herself to her "true loves"; they can only be a distraction, a respite. Besides, she is usually too obsessed with her own success to be able to lose herself in a real love affair. As for other women, it often happens that the hetaera loves them sensually; as an enemy of men who impose their domination on her, she will find sensual relaxation as well as revenge in the arms of a woman friend: so it was with Nana and her dear Satin. Just as she wishes to play an active role in the world to put her freedom to positive use, she likes to possess other beings: very young men whom she enjoys "helping," or young women she will willingly support and, in any case, for whom she will be a virile personage. Whether she is homosexual or not, she will have the complex relations I have discussed with women in general: she needs them as judges and witnesses, as confidantes and accomplices, to create this "counter-universe" that every woman oppressed by man must have. But feminine rivalry reaches its paroxysm here. The prostitute who trades on her generality has competition; but if there is enough work for everyone, they feel solidarity, even with their disputes. The hetaera who seeks to "distinguish" herself is a priori hostile to the one who, like her, lusts for a privileged place. This is where the well-known theme of feminine "cattiness" proves true.

The greatest misfortune for the hetaera is that not only is her independence the deceptive reverse side of a thousand dependencies, but this very freedom is negative. An actress like Rachel, a dancer like Isadora Duncan, even if they are aided by men, have occupations that are demanding and justify them; they attain concrete freedom from the work they choose and love. But for the great majority of them, their art, their occupations are only a means; they are not involved in real projects. Cinema in particular, which subjects the star to the director, allows her no invention, no progress, in creative activity. *Others* exploit what she *is;* she does not create a new object. Still it is quite rare to become a star. In "amorous adventures," properly speaking, no road opens onto transcendence. Here again, ennui accompanies the confinement of woman in immanence. Zola shows this with Nana:

> However, in the midst of all this luxury, and surrounded by her
> courtiers, Nana was bored to tears. She had men for every minute
> of the night, and money all over the house, even among the brushes
> and combs in the drawers of her dressing-table. But all this had

ceased to satisfy her; and she was conscious of a void in her existence, a gap which made her yawn. Her life dragged on without occupation, each day bringing back the same monotonous hours. The next day did not exist: she lived like a bird, sure of having enough to eat, and ready to perch on the first branch she came to. This certainty of being fed caused her to stretch out in languid ease all day, lulled to sleep in conventional idleness and submission as if she were the prisoner of her own profession. Never going out except in her carriage, she began to lose the use of her legs. She reverted to her childish habits, kissing Bijou from morning to night and killing time with stupid pleasures, as she waited for some man or other.

American literature abounds with this opaque ennui that stifles Hollywood and chokes the traveler as soon as he arrives there: actors and extras are as bored as the women whose condition they share. Even in France, official events are often burdensome. The protector who rules the starlet's life is an older man whose friends are his age: their preoccupations are foreign to the young woman, their conversations weary her; there is a chasm far deeper than in bourgeois marriages between the twenty-year-old novice and the forty-five-year-old banker who spend their days and nights side by side.

The Moloch to whom the hetaera sacrifices pleasure, love, and freedom is her career. The matron's ideal is static happiness that envelops her relations with her husband and children. Her "career" stretches across time, but it is nonetheless an immanent object that is summed up in a name. The name gets bigger on billboards and on people's lips as the steps mounted up the social ladder get higher. According to her temperament, the woman administers her enterprise prudently or boldly. One woman will find satisfaction in housekeeping, folding laundry in her closet, the other in the headiness of adventure. Sometimes the woman limits herself to perpetually balancing a perpetually threatened situation that sometimes breaks down; or sometimes she endlessly builds—like a Tower of Babel aiming in vain for the sky—her renown. Some of them, mixing amorous commerce with other activities, are true adventurers: they are spies, like Mata Hari, or secret agents; they generally are not the ones who initiate the projects, they are rather instruments in men's hands. But overall, the hetaera's attitude is similar to that of the adventurer; like him, she is often halfway between the *serious* and the *adventure* as such; she seeks ready-made values—money and glory—but she attaches as much value to winning them as to possessing them; and finally, the supreme value in her eyes is subjective success. She, too, justifies this individualism by a more or less systematic nihilism, but experienced with all the more conviction as she is hostile to men and sees enemies in other women. If she is intelligent enough to feel the need for moral justification, she will invoke a more or less well assimilated Nietzscheism; she will affirm the right of the elite being over the vulgar. Her person belongs to her like a treasure whose mere existence is a gift: so much so that in being dedicated to herself, she will claim to serve the group. The destiny of the woman devoted to man is haunted by love: she who exploits the male fulfills herself in the cult of self-adoration. If she attaches such a price to her glory, it is not only for economic interest: she seeks there the apotheosis of her narcissism.

CHAPTER 9

From Maturity to Old Age

The history of woman—because she is still trapped in her female functions—depends much more than man's on her physiological destiny; and the arc of this destiny is more erratic, more discontinuous, than the masculine one. Every period of woman's life is fixed and monotonous: but the passages from one stage to another are dangerously abrupt; they reveal themselves in far more decisive crises than those of the male: puberty, sexual initiation, menopause. While the male grows older continuously, the woman is brusquely stripped of her femininity; still young, she loses sexual attraction and fertility, from which, in society's and her own eyes, she derives the justification of her existence and her chances of happiness: bereft of all future, she has approximately half of her adult life still to live.

The "dangerous age" is characterized by certain organic troubles,[1] but the symbolic value they embody gives them their importance. The crisis is felt much less acutely by women who have not essentially staked everything on their femininity; those who work hard—in their home or outside—are relieved when their menstrual servitude ends; peasants and workers' wives who are constantly threatened with new pregnancies are happy when, finally, that risk no longer exists. In this situation as in many others, women's disorders come less from the body itself than from their anxious consciousness of it. The moral drama usually begins before the onset of the physiological phenomena, and it does not end until long after they have been eliminated.

Well before the definitive mutilation, woman is haunted by the horror of aging. The mature man is engaged in more important enterprises than those of love; his sexual ardor is less pressing than in his youth; and as he is not expected to have the passive qualities of an object, the alteration of his

---

1. Cf. Volume I, Chapter i. [In Part One, "Destiny."—TRANS.]

face and body does not spoil his possibilities of seduction. By contrast, woman reaches her full sexual blossoming at about thirty-five, having finally overcome all her inhibitions: this is when her desires are the most intense and when she wants to satisfy them the most ardently; she has counted on her sexual attributes far more than man has; to keep her husband, to be assured of protection, and to succeed in most jobs she holds, she has to please; she has not been allowed a hold on the world except through man's mediation: What will become of her when she no longer has a hold on him? This is what she anxiously wonders while she witnesses, powerless, the degradation of this object of flesh with which she is one; she fights; but dyes, peeling, and plastic surgery can never do more than prolong her dying youth. At least she can play tricks with the mirror. But when the inevitable, irreversible process starts, which is going to destroy in her the whole edifice constructed during puberty, she feels touched by the very inevitability of death.

One might think that the woman who experiences the greatest distress is the one who has been the most passionately enraptured by her beauty and youth; but no; the narcissist is too attentive to her person not to have envisaged the ineluctable moment and not to have worked out an alternative position; she will certainly suffer from her mutilation: but at least she will not be caught short and will adapt rather quickly. The woman who has forgotten, devoted, and sacrificed herself will be disrupted much more by the sudden revelation. "I had only one life to live; this was my lot, so here I am!" To the surprise of her family and friends, a radical change takes place in her: expelled from her shelter, torn away from her projects, she brusquely finds herself, without resources, face-to-face with herself. Beyond this barrier she has unexpectedly struck, she has the feeling that she will do no more than survive; her body will be without promise; the dreams and desires she has not realized will forever remain unaccomplished; she will look back on the past from this new perspective; the time has come to draw the line, to take stock. And she is horrified by the narrow strictures inflicted on her life. Faced with this, her brief and disappointing story, she behaves like an adolescent girl on the threshold of a still inaccessible future: she denies her finitude; to the poverty of her existence she contrasts the nebulous treasures of her personality. Because as a woman she endured her destiny more or less passively, she feels that her chances were taken from her, that she was duped, that she slid from youth to maturity without being aware of it. She discovers that her husband, her milieu, and her occupations were not worthy of her; she feels misunderstood. She withdraws from the surroundings to which she esteems herself superior; she shuts herself up with the secret she carries in her heart and which is the mysterious key to her unfortunate lot; she tries to see the possibilities she has not exhausted. She begins to keep a diary; if she has understanding confidantes, she pours out her heart in endless conversations; and she ruminates on her regrets, her grievances, all day and all night. Just as the young girl dreams of what her future *will be*, she recalls what her past *could have been;* she remembers the missed occasions and constructs beautiful retrospective romances. Helene Deutsch cites the case of a woman who had broken off an unhappy marriage very early and who had then spent long serene years with a second husband: at forty-five, she painfully began to miss her first husband and to sink into melancholy. The cares of childhood and puberty come back to life, the woman constantly mulls over the story of her youth, and forgotten feelings for her parents, brothers and sisters, and childhood friends come alive once again. Sometimes she indulges in dreamy and passive moroseness. But more often she is jolted into saving her wasted existence. She displays, exhibits, and praises the merits of this personality she has just discovered in contrast with the pettiness of her destiny. Matured by experience, she believes she is finally able to prove her worth; she would like to have another chance. And first in a pathetic effort, she tries to stop time. A maternal woman is sure she can still have a child: she passionately seeks to create life once more. A sensual woman strives to conquer a new lover. The coquette is more than ever determined to please. They all declare they have never felt so young. They want to persuade others that the passage of time has not really touched them; they begin to "dress young," they act childishly. The aging woman well knows that if she has ceased being a sexual object, it is not only because her flesh no longer provides man with fresh treasures: it is also that her past and her experience make a person of her whether she likes it or not; she has fought, loved, wanted, suffered, and taken pleasure for herself: this autonomy is intimidating; she tries to disavow it; she exaggerates her femininity, she adorns herself, wears perfume, she becomes totally charming, gracious, pure immanence; she admires her male interlocutor with a naive eye and childish intonations; she ostentatiously brings up her memories of girlhood; instead of speaking, she chirps, claps her hands, bursts out laughing. She plays this game with a kind of sincerity. This newfound interest in herself and her desire to wrench herself from old routines and start over again give her the impression of a new beginning.

In fact, it is not really a question of a new start; she discovers no goals in the world toward which she could project herself in a free and effective movement. Her agitation is more eccentric, incoherent, and useless because it only serves as symbolic compensation for past errors and failures. Among other things and before it is too late, the woman will try to realize all her childhood and adolescent desires: this one goes back to the piano, that one begins to sculpt, to write, to travel; she takes up skiing, foreign languages. She welcomes everything she had refused until then—again before it is too late. She admits her repugnance for a husband she had previously tolerated, and she becomes frigid in his arms; or by contrast, she abandons herself to the passions she repressed; she overwhelms the husband with her demands; she goes back to practicing masturbation, which she had given up since childhood. Her homosexual tendencies—which are latent in almost all women—come out. The subject often carries them over to her daughter; but sometimes unusual feelings arise for a woman friend. In his work *Sex, Life, and Faith*, Rom Landau tells the following story, confided to him by the person herself:

> Mrs. X., a woman in the late forties, married for over twenty-five years, mother of three grown-up children, occupied a prominent position in . . . the social and charitable activities of the town in which she lived. Mrs. X. met a woman in London some ten years her junior who, like herself, was a leading social worker. The two . . . became friends. Miss Y. invited Mrs. X. to stay as her guest during her next visit to London, and Mrs. X. . . . accepted. During the second evening of her visit—Mrs. X. assured me repeatedly that she had not the least idea how it happened—she suddenly found herself passionately embracing her hostess, and subsequently she spent the whole night with her . . . she was terrified . . . and left London the same day . . . Never in her life had she read or heard anything about homosexuality and had had no idea that "such things" existed . . . she could do nothing to stifle her ever-growing feelings for Miss Y. . . . For the first time in her life she found [her husband's] caresses unwelcome, even his routine kiss . . . Finally, she decided to revisit Miss Y. and "clear up" the situation . . . she only found herself more deeply involved in it; . . . to be with her filled her with a delight that she had never experienced before . . . she was troubled by a profound sin-consciousness, and was anxious to discover whether there was a "scientific explanation" of her state and any moral justification for it.

In this case, the subject gave in to a spontaneous drive and was herself deeply disconcerted by it. But often the woman deliberately seeks to live the romances she has not experienced and that soon she will no longer be able to experience. She leaves her home, both because it seems unworthy of her and because she desires solitude as well as the chance to seek adventure. If she finds it, she throws herself into it greedily. Thus, in this story by Stekel:

> Mrs. B.Z. was forty years old, had three children and twenty years of married life behind her when she began to think she was misunderstood, that she had wasted her life; she took up various new activities among which was going skiing in the mountains; there she met a thirty-year-old man and became his mistress; but soon after, he fell in love with Mrs. B.Z.'s daughter . . . she agreed to their marriage so as to keep her lover near her; there was an unacknowledged but very strong homosexual love between mother and daughter, which partially explains this decision. Nevertheless, the situation soon became intolerable, the lover sometimes leaving the mother's bed during the night to be with the daughter. Mrs. B.Z. . . . attempted suicide. It was then—she was forty-six—that she was treated by Stekel. She decided to break it off and while her daughter gave up her marriage plans Mrs. B.Z. . . . then became an exemplary wife and fell into piousness.

A woman influenced by a tradition of decency and honesty does not always follow through with action. But her dreams are peopled with erotic fantasies that she calls up during waking hours as well; she manifests an exalted and sensual tenderness to her children; she cultivates incestuous obsessions with her son; she secretly falls in love with one young man after another; like an adolescent girl, she is haunted by ideas of rape; she also feels the attraction of prostitution; the ambivalence of her desires and fears produces an anxiety that sometimes leads to neuroses: she scandalizes her family and friends by bizarre behavior that in fact merely expresses her imaginary life.

The boundary between the imaginary and the real is even less distinct in this troubled period than during puberty. One of the most salient characteristics in the aging woman is the feeling of depersonalization that makes her lose all objective landmarks. People in good health who have come close to death also say they have felt a curious impression of doubling; when one feels oneself to be consciousness, activity, and freedom, the passive object affected by fate seems necessarily like another: *I* am not the one run over by a car; *I* am not the old woman the mirror shows me. The woman who "never felt so young" and who never saw herself so old is not able to reconcile these two aspects of herself; time passes and diminishes her in dreams. So reality fades and becomes less important: likewise, she can no longer tell herself apart from the illusion. The woman relies on interior proof rather than on this strange world where time proceeds in reverse, where her double no longer resembles her, where events have betrayed her. She is thus inclined to ecstasies, visions, and deliriums. And since love is even more than ever her essential preoccupation, it is understandable that she lets herself go to the illusion that she is loved. Nine out of ten erotomaniacs are women; and they are almost all between forty and fifty years old.

However, not everyone is able to cross over the wall of reality so boldly. Deprived of all human love, even in their dreams, many women seek relief in God; the flirt, the lover, and the dissolute become pious around menopause. The vague ideas of destiny, secrecy, and misunderstood personality of woman in her autumn years find a rational unity in religion. The devotee considers her wasted life as a test sent by the Lord; in her unhappiness, her soul has drawn exceptional advantages from misfortune, making her worthy of being visited by the grace of God; she will readily believe that heaven sends her illuminations or even—like Mme Krüdener—that it imperiously entrusts her with a mission. As she has more or less lost the sense of reality during this crisis, the woman is open to any suggestion: any spiritual guide is in a strong position to wield power over her soul. She will also enthusiastically accept more questionable authorities; she is an obvious prey for religious sects, spirits, prophets, faith healers, and any charlatan. Not only has she lost all critical sense by losing contact with the given world, but she is also desperate for a definitive truth: she has to have the remedy, the formula, the key, that will suddenly save her by saving the universe. She scorns more than ever a logic that obviously could not possibly apply to her own case; the only arguments that seem convincing to her are those that are particularly destined for her: revelations, inspirations, messages, signs, or even miracles begin to appear around her. Her discoveries sometimes draw her into paths of action: she throws herself into schemes, undertakings, and adventures whose idea is whispered to her by some adviser or inner voices. Sometimes, she simply deems herself the holder of the truth and absolute wisdom. Whether she is active or contemplative, her attitude is accompanied by feverish exaltation. The crisis of menopause brutally cuts feminine life into two: it is this discontinuity that gives woman the illusion of a "new life"; it is an *other* time opening before her: she approaches it with the fervor of a convert; she is converted to love, life, God, art, and humanity: she loses and magnifies herself in these entities. She is dead and resuscitated, she views the earth with a gaze that has pierced the secrets of the beyond, and she thinks she is flying toward uncharted heights.

Yet the earth does not change; the summits remain out of reach; the messages received—even in blinding clarity—are hard to decipher; the inner lights go out; what remains before the mirror is a woman one day older than yesterday. Doleful hours of depression follow moments of fervor. The body determines this rhythm since a reduction in hormonal secretions is offset by a hyperactive hypophysis; but it is above all the psychological state that orders this alternation. For the agitation, illusions, and fervor are merely a defense against the inevitability of what has been. Once again, anxiety grabs the throat of the one whose life is already finished, even though death is not imminent. Instead of fighting against despair, she often chooses to intoxicate herself with it. She rehashes grievances, regrets, and recriminations; she imagines that her neighbors and family are engaging in dark machinations; if she has a sister or woman friend of her age who is associated with her life, they may construct persecution fantasies together. But above all she becomes morbidly jealous of her husband: she is jealous of his friends, his sisters, his job; and rightly or wrongly, she accuses some rival of being responsible for all her problems. Cases of pathological jealousy mostly occur between fifty and fifty-five years of age.

The problems of menopause will last—sometimes until death—if the woman does not decide to let herself grow old; if she does not have any resources other than the use of her charms, she will fight tooth and nail to maintain them; she will also fight with rage if her sex drives remain alive. This is not unusual. Princess Metternich was asked at what age a woman stops being tormented by the flesh. "I don't know," she said, "I'm only sixty-five." Marriage, which Montaigne thought provided "little relief" for woman, becomes a more and more inadequate solution as a woman gets older; she often pays for the resistance and coldness of her youth in maturity; when she finally begins to experience the fevers of desire, her husband has been resigned to her indifference for a long time: he has found a solution for himself. Stripped of her attraction by habit and time, the wife seldom has the opportunity to awaken the conjugal flame. Vexed, determined to "live her life," she will have fewer scruples than before—if she ever had any—in taking lovers; but there again they have to let themselves be taken: it is a manhunt. She deploys a thousand ruses: feigning to offer herself, she imposes herself; she uses charm, friendship, and gratitude as traps. It is not only out of a desire for fresh flesh that she goes after young men: they are the only ones from whom she can hope for this disinterested tenderness the adolescent male can sometimes feel for a maternal mistress; she has become aggressive and domineering: Léa is fulfilled by Chéri's docility as well as by his beauty. Once she reached her forties, Mme de Staël chose pages whom she overwhelmed with her prestige; and a shy man, a novice, is also easier to capture. When seduction and intrigue really prove useless, there is still one resource: paying. The tale of the little knife, popular in the Middle Ages, illustrates these insatiable ogresses' fate: a young woman, as thanks for her favors, asked each of her lovers for a little knife, which she kept in a cupboard; the day came when the cupboard was full: but it was then that the lovers began to demand from her a little knife after each night of love; the cupboard was soon emptied; all the little knives had been returned: others had to be bought. Some women take a cynical view of the situation: they have had their moment; now it is their turn to "return the little knives." Money in their eyes can even play the opposite—but equally purifying—role of the one it plays for the courtesan: it changes the male into an instrument and provides woman with the erotic freedom that her young pride used to deny her. But more romantic than lucid, the mistress-benefactress often attempts to buy a mirage of tenderness, admiration, and respect; she even persuades herself that she gives for the pleasure of giving, without being asked: here too a young man is the perfect choice because a woman can pride herself on maternal generosity toward him; and then there is a little of this "mystery" the man also asks of the woman he "helps" so that this crude deal is thus camouflaged as enigma. But it is rare for this bad faith to be moderate for long; the battle of the sexes changes into a duel between exploiter and exploited where woman, disappointed and ridiculed, risks suffering cruel defeats. If she is prudent, she will resign herself to "disarming," without waiting too long, even if all her passions are not yet spent.

From the day woman agrees to grow old, her situation changes. Until then, she was still young, determined to fight against an evil that mysteriously made her ugly and deformed her; now she becomes a different being, asexual but complete: an elderly woman. It may be thought that the change-of-life crisis is then finished. But one must not conclude that it will be easy to live from then on. When she has given up the fight against the inevitability of time, another combat opens: she has to keep a place on earth.

Woman frees herself from her chains in her autumn and winter years; she uses the pretext of her age to escape burdensome chores; she knows her husband too well to let herself still be intimidated by him, she avoids his embraces, she carves out—in friendship, indifference, or hostility—a real life of her own alongside him; if he declines more quickly than she, she takes the lead in the couple. She can also allow herself to disdain fashion and public opinion; she refuses social obligations, diets, and beauty treatment: like Léa, whom Chéri finds liberated from dressmakers, corset makers, and hairdressers, and happily settled down indulging herself in food. As for her children, they are old enough not to need her, they get married, they leave home. Relieved of her duties, she finally discovers her freedom. Unfortunately, every woman's history repeats the fact we have observed throughout the history of woman: she discovers this freedom when she can find nothing more to do with it. This repetition has nothing coincidental about it: patriarchal society has made all feminine functions servile; woman escapes slavery only when she loses all productivity. At fifty, she is in full possession of her strength, she feels rich in experience; this is the age when man rises to the highest positions, the most important jobs: and as for her, she is forced into retirement. She has only been taught to devote herself, and there is no one who requires her devotion anymore. Useless, unjustified, she contemplates these long years without promise she still has to live and murmurs: "No one needs me!"

She does not resign herself right away. Sometimes, out of despair, she clings to her husband; she overwhelms him more imperiously than ever with her ministrations; but the routine of conjugal life has been too well established; either she has known for a long time that her husband does not need her, or he does not seem precious enough to her to justify her any longer. Assuring the maintenance of their shared life is as contingent a task as watching over herself alone. She turns to her children with hope: for them the die is not yet cast; the world, the future, are open to them; she would like to dive into it after them. The woman who has had the chance of giving birth at an advanced age finds herself privileged: she is still a young mother when the others are becoming grandparents. But in general, between forty and fifty, the mother sees her little ones become adults. It is at the very instant they are escaping her that she passionately attempts to live through them.

Her attitude is different depending on whether she is counting on being saved by a son or a daughter; she usually puts her strongest hope in her son. Here he finally comes to her from the far past, the man whose marvelous appearance she waited to see coming over the horizon; from the first scream of the newborn she has waited for this day when he will hand out all the treasures the father was never able to satisfy her with. During that time, she has doled out slaps and purges, but she has forgotten them; he whom she carried in her womb was already one of these demigods who govern the world and women's destiny: now he will recognize her in the glory of her motherhood. He will defend her against her spouse's supremacy, avenge her for the lovers she has had and those she has not had; he will be her liberator, her savior. She will behave like the seductive and ostentatious girl waiting for Prince Charming; when she is walking beside him, elegant and still charming, she thinks she looks like his "older sister"; she is delighted if—taking after the heroes of American films—he teases and jostles her, laughing and respectful: with proud humility she recognizes the virile superiority of the one she carried in her womb. To what extent can these feelings be considered incestuous? It is sure that when she thinks of herself complaisantly on her son's arm, the expression "older sister" prudishly expresses ambivalent fantasies; when she sleeps, when she does not control herself, her musings sometimes carry her very far; but I have already said that dreams and fantasies are far from always expressing the hidden desire of a real act: they are often sufficient; they are the completion of a desire that only requires an imaginary satisfaction. When the mother plays in a more or less veiled way at seeing her son as a lover, it is just a game. Real eroticism usually has little place in this couple. But it is a couple; it is from the depths of her femininity that the mother hails in her son the sovereign man; she puts herself in his hands with as much fervor as a lover, and in exchange for this gift, she counts on being raised to the right hand of the god. To gain this assumption, the woman in love appeals to the lover's freedom: she generously assumes a risk; her anxious demands are the ransom. The mother reckons she has acquired holy rights by the simple fact of giving birth; she does not expect her son to see himself in her in order for her to consider him her creation, her property; she is less demanding than the woman lover because she is of a more tranquil bad faith; having made a being of flesh, she makes an existence her own: she appropriates its acts, accomplishments, and merits. In exalting her fruit, she is carrying her own person to the heights.

Living by proxy is always a precarious expedient. Things may not turn out as one wished. It often happens that a son is no more than a good-for-nothing, a hooligan, a failure, a lost cause, an empty promise, ungrateful. The mother has her own ideas about the hero her son is supposed to embody. Nothing is rarer than a mother who authentically respects the human person her child is, who recognizes his freedom even in his failures, who assumes with him the risks implied by any engagement. One more often encounters mothers who emulate that over-glorified Spartan woman who cavalierly condemns her son to glory or death; on earth, the son has to

justify his mother's existence by taking hold of values she herself respects
for their mutual advantage. The mother demands that the child-god's projects conform to her own ideal and that their success be assured. Every
woman wants to give birth to a hero, a genius; but all mothers of heroes
and geniuses began by proclaiming they were breaking their mothers'
hearts. It is in reaction to his mother that man most often wins the trophies
she dreamed of displaying for herself and that she does not recognize even
when he lays them at her feet. Though she may approve in principle of her
son's undertakings, she is torn by a contradiction similar to one that tortures the woman in love. To justify his life—and his mother's—the son
must surpass her toward his ends; and to attain them, he is led to risk his
health and put himself in danger: but he contests the value of the gift she
gave him when he places certain goals above the pure fact of living. She is
shocked by this; she reigns sovereign over man only if this flesh she has
engendered is for him the supreme good: he does not have the right to
destroy this work she has produced through suffering. "You'll tire yourself
out, you'll make yourself ill, you'll be sorry," she drones in his ears. Yet she
knows very well that to live is not enough, or else procreation itself would
be superfluous; she is the first to be irritated if her offspring is a loafer, a
coward. She is never at rest. When he goes to war, she wants him home
alive but decorated. In his career, she wishes him to "make it" but trembles
when he overworks. Whatever he does, she always worries that she will
stand by powerless in the unfolding of a story that is hers but over which
she has no control: she fears he will make the wrong decision, that he will
not succeed, that if he succeeds, he will ruin his health. Even if she has confidence in him, differences of age and sex keep a real complicity from being
established between her son and her; she is not informed about his work;
no collaboration is demanded of her.

This is why the mother remains unsatisfied, even if she admires her son
with inordinate pride. Believing that she has not only engendered a being
of flesh but also founded an absolutely necessary existence, she feels retro-
spectively justified; but having rights is not an occupation: to fill her days,
she needs to perpetuate her beneficent activity; she wants to feel indispensable to her god; the mystification of devotion in this case is denounced in
the most brutal manner: his wife will strip her of her functions. The hostility she feels to this stranger who "steals" her child has often been described.
The mother has raised the contingent facticity of parturition to the height
of divine mystery: she refuses to accept that a human decision can have
more weight. In her eyes, values are preestablished, they proceed from
nature, from the past: she does not understand the value of a freely made
engagement. Her son owes her his life; what does he owe this woman he

did not know until yesterday? It is through some evil spell that she convinced him of the existence of a bond that until now did not *exist;* she is devious, calculating, and dangerous. The mother impatiently waits for the imposture to be revealed; encouraged by the old myth of the good mother with healing hands who binds the wounds inflicted on him by the bad wife, she watches her son's face for signs of unhappiness: she finds them, even if he denies it; she feels sorry for him even when he complains of nothing; she spies on her daughter-in-law, she criticizes her, she counters all her innovations with the past and the customs that condemn the intruder's very presence. Each woman understands the beloved's happiness in her own way: the wife wants to see in him a man through whom she will control the world; the mother tries to keep him by taking him back to his childhood; to the projects of the young wife who expects her husband to *become* rich or important, the mother counters with the laws of his unchanging essence: he *is* fragile, he must not tire himself. The conflict between the past and the future is exacerbated when it is the newcomer's turn to get pregnant. "The birth of children is the death of parents"; here this truth is at its cruelest: the mother who had hoped to live on through her son understands he has condemned her to death. She gave life: life will continue without her; she is no longer *the* Mother: simply a link; she falls from the heaven of timeless idols; she is no more than a finished, outdated individual. It is then that in pathological cases her hatred intensifies to the point where she has a neurosis or is driven to commit a crime; it was when her daughter-in-law's pregnancy was announced that Mme Lefebvre, who had long hated her, decided to kill her.[2]

Normally, the grandmother overcomes her hostility; sometimes she obstinately sees the newborn as her son's alone, and she loves it tyrannically; but generally the young mother and her own mother claim it for their own; the jealous grandmother cultivates an ambiguous affection for the baby, where hostility hides in the guise of concern.

---

2. In August 1925, a sixty-year-old bourgeois woman from the North, Mme Lefebvre, who lived with her husband and her children, killed her daughter-in-law, six months pregnant, during a car trip while her son was driving. Condemned to death and then pardoned, she spent the rest of her life in a reformatory where she showed no remorse; she believed God approved of her when she killed her daughter-in-law "as one kills a weed, a bad seed, as one kills a savage beast." The only savagery she gave as proof was that the young woman one day said to her: "You have me now, so you now have to take me into account." It was when she suspected her daughter-in-law's pregnancy that she bought a revolver, supposedly to defend herself against robbers. After her menopause, she was desperately attached to her maternity: for twelve years she had suffered from malaises that manifested themselves symbolically in an imaginary pregnancy.

The mother's attitude to her grown daughter is very ambivalent: she seeks a god in her son; in her daughter, she finds a double. The "double" is an ambiguous personage; it assassinates the one from which it emanates, as can be seen in the tales of Poe, in *The Picture of Dorian Gray*, and in the story told by Marcel Schwob. Thus the girl condemns her mother to death by becoming a woman; and yet she permits her to survive. The mother's behavior depends on whether she grasps her child's healthy development as a promise of ruin or of resurrection.

Many mothers become rigid in hostility; they do not accept being supplanted by the ingrate who owes them her life; we have often pointed out the coquette's jealousy of the fresh adolescent who denounces her artifices: a woman who has detested a rival in any woman will hate the rival even in her child; she sends her away, hides her, or finds ways to deprive her of opportunities. A woman who took pride in being the Wife and the Mother in an exemplary and unique way will refuse no less fiercely to give up her throne; she continues to affirm that her daughter is merely a child, and she considers her undertakings to be childish games; she is too young to marry, too delicate to give birth; if she insists on wanting a husband, a home, and children, they will never be more than look-alikes; the mother tirelessly criticizes, derides, or prophesies misfortune. If she can, she condemns her daughter to eternal childhood; if not, she tries to ruin this adult life the daughter is trying to lead on her own. We have seen that she often succeeds: many young women remain sterile, have miscarriages, prove incapable of nursing and raising their children or running their homes because of this evil influence. Their conjugal life becomes impossible. Unhappy and isolated, they will find refuge in the sovereign arms of their mothers. If they resist her, a perpetual conflict will pit them against each other; the frustrated mother largely transfers onto her son-in-law the irritation her insolent daughter's independence provokes in her.

The mother who passionately identifies with her daughter is no less tyrannical; what she wants, having acquired mature experience, is to relive her youth: thus will she save her past while saving herself from it; she herself will choose a son-in-law who conforms to the perfect husband she never had; flirtatious and tender, she will easily imagine somewhere in her heart that it is she he is marrying; through her daughter, she will satisfy her old desires for wealth, success, and glory; such women, who ardently "push" their children along the paths of seduction, cinema, or theater, have often been described; under the pretext of watching over them, they take over their lives: I have been told about some who go so far as to take the girl's suitor to bed with them. But it is rare for the girl to put up with this guardianship indefinitely; the day she finds a husband or a serious protector, she will rebel. The mother-in-law who had begun by cherishing her son-in-law then becomes hostile to him; she moans about human ingratitude, takes the role of victim herself; she becomes in her turn an enemy mother. Foreseeing these disappointments, many women feign indifference when they see their children grow up: but they take little joy from it. A mother must have a rare mixture of generosity and detachment to find enrichment in her children's lives without becoming a tyrant or turning them into her tormentors.

The grandmother's feelings toward her grandchildren are an extension of those she has for her daughter: she often transfers her hostility onto them. It is not only out of fear of public opinion that so many women force their seduced daughter to have an abortion, to abandon the child, to do away with it: they are only too happy to keep her from motherhood; they obstinately wish to keep the privilege for themselves. They readily advise even a legitimate mother to provoke a miscarriage, not to breast-feed the child, or to rid herself of it. They themselves will deny the existence of this impudent little being by their indifference; or else they will spend their time endlessly scolding the child, punishing him, even mistreating him. By contrast, the mother who identifies with her daughter often welcomes the children more avidly than the young woman does; the daughter is disconcerted by the arrival of the little stranger; the grandmother recognizes him: she goes back twenty years in time, she becomes the young woman giving birth again; all the joys of ·possession and domination her children long ago ceased to give her are returned to her, all the desires of motherhood she had renounced with menopause are miraculously fulfilled; she is the real mother, she takes charge of the baby with authority, and if the baby is given over to her, she will passionately devote herself to him. Unfortunately for her, the young woman is keen to hold on to her rights: the grandmother is authorized only to play the role of assistant that her elders formerly played with her; she feels dethroned; and besides she has to share this with her son-in-law's mother, of whom she is naturally jealous. Resentment often distorts the spontaneous love she felt at first for the child. The anxiety often observed in grandmothers expresses the ambivalence of their feelings: they cherish the baby insofar as it belongs to them, they are hostile to the little stranger that he is to them, they are ashamed of this enmity. Yet if the grandmother maintains her warm affection for her grandchildren while giving up the idea of entirely possessing them, she can play the privileged role of guardian angel in their lives: recognizing neither rights nor responsibilities, she loves them out of pure generosity; she does not entertain narcissistic dreams through them, she asks nothing of them, she does not sacrifice their future in which she will not be present: what she loves are the little flesh-and-blood beings who are there today in their contingency and their gratuitousness; she is not an educator; she does not represent abstract justice or law. This is where the conflicts that at times set her in opposition to the parents will sometimes arise.

It may be that the woman has no descendants or is not interested in posterity; lacking natural bonds with children or grandchildren, she sometimes tries to create them artificially with counterparts. She offers maternal tenderness to young people; whether or not her affection remains platonic, it is not necessarily hypocrisy that makes her declare that she loves her young protégé "like a son": the mother's feelings, inversely, are love feelings. It is true that Mme de Warens's competitors take pleasure in generously satisfying, helping, and shaping a man: they want to be the source, the necessary condition, and the foundation of an existence that has passed them by; they become mothers and find their identity in their lovers far more in this role than in the role of mistress. Very often also the maternal woman adopts girls: here again their relations take more or less sexual forms; but whether platonic or carnal, what she seeks in her protégées is her own double, miraculously rejuvenated. The actress, the dancer, the singer, become teachers—they form pupils—and the intellectual woman—such as Mme de Charrière, alone in Colombier—indoctrinates disciples; the devotee gathers spiritual daughters around her; the seductress becomes a madam. It is never pure self-interest that brings such ardent zeal to their proselytizing: they are passionately seeking to reincarnate themselves. Their tyrannical generosity gives rise to more or less the same conflicts as between mothers and daughters united by blood. It is also possible to adopt grandchildren: great-aunts and godmothers gladly play a role similar to that of grandmothers. But in any case, it is rare for a woman to find in posterity—natural or selected—a justification of her declining life: she fails to make the enterprise of these young existences her own. Either she persists in the effort to appropriate it, consumed in the struggles and dramas that leave her disappointed and broken; or she resigns herself to a modest participation. This is the most common case. The aged mother and grandmother repress their dominating desires, they conceal their resentments; they are satisfied with whatever their children choose to give them. But then they get little help from them. They remain available facing the desert of the future, prey to solitude, regret, and ennui.

Here we touch upon the older woman's tragedy: she realizes she is useless; all through her life, the bourgeois woman often has to resolve the derisory problem: How to kill time? For once the children are raised and the husband has become successful, or at least settled, days drag on.

"Women's handiwork" was invented to mask this horrible idleness; hands embroider, knit, they are busy hands, and they move; it is not a question here of real work, because the object produced is not the goal; it has little importance, and it is often a problem to know what to do with it: one gets rid of it by giving it to a friend or a charitable organization or by cluttering mantelpieces or coffee tables; neither is it a game that reveals the pure joy of existence in its gratuitousness; and it is hardly a diversion because the mind is vacant: it is an absurd distraction, as Pascal described it; with needle or hook, woman sadly weaves the very nothingness of her days. Watercolors, music, or reading have the very same role; the unoccupied woman does not try to extend her grasp on the world in giving herself over to such activities, but only to relieve boredom; an activity that does not open up the future slides into the vanity of immanence; the idle woman begins a book, then puts it down, opens the piano, closes it, returns to her embroidery, yawns, and ends up on the telephone. In fact, she is more likely to seek relief in social life; she goes out, makes visits, and—like Mrs. Dalloway—attaches enormous importance to her parties; she goes to every wedding, every funeral; no longer having any existence of her own, she feeds on the company of others; she goes from being a coquette to a gossip: she watches, she comments; she compensates for her inaction by dispensing criticism and advice to those around her. She gives her experienced advice even to those around her who do not seek it. If she has the means, she holds a salon; in this way she hopes to appropriate undertakings and successes that are not hers; Mme du Deffand's and Mme Verdurin's despotism over their subjects is well-known. To be a center of attraction, a crossroads, an inspiration, or to create an "atmosphere" is in itself an ersatz activity. There are other, more direct ways to intervene in the course of the world; in France, there are "charities" and a few "clubs," but it is particularly true in America that women group together in clubs where they play bridge, hand out literary prizes, or reflect on social improvement. What characterizes most of these organizations on the two continents is that they are in themselves their own reason for existence: the aims they claim to pursue serve only as a pretext. Things happen exactly as in Kafka's fable: no one is concerned about building the Tower of Babel; a vast city is built around its ideal place, consuming all its resources for administration, growth, and resolving internal dissensions.[3] So charity women spend most of their time organizing their organization; they elect a board, discuss its statutes, dis-

---

3. "The City Coat of Arms."

pute among themselves, and struggle to keep their prestige over rival associations: no one must steal *their* poor, *their* sick, *their* wounded, *their* orphans; they would rather leave them to die than yield them to their neighbors. And they are far from wanting a regime that, in doing away with injustice and abuse, would make their dedication useless; they bless the wars and famines that transform them into benefactresses of humanity. It is clear that in their eyes the knit hats and parcels are not intended for soldiers and the hungry: instead, the soldiers and the hungry are made expressly to receive knit goods and parcels.

In spite of everything, some of these groups attain positive results. In the United States, the influence of venerated "Moms" is strong; this is explained by the leisure time their parasitic existence leaves them: and this is why it is harmful. "Knowing nothing about medicine, art, science, religion, law, sanitation," says Philip Wylie, speaking of the American Mom, "she seldom has any especial interest in *what,* exactly, she is doing as a member of any of these endless organizations, so long as it is *something*."[4] Their effort is not integrated into a coherent and constructive plan, it does not aim at objective ends: imperiously, it tends only to show their tastes and prejudices or to serve their interests. They play a considerable role in the domain of culture, for example: it is they who buy the most books; but they read as one plays the game of solitaire; literature takes its meaning and dignity when it is addressed to individuals committed to projects, when it helps them surpass themselves toward greater horizons; it must be integrated into the movement of human transcendence; instead, woman devalues books and works of art by swallowing them into her immanence; a painting becomes a knickknack, music an old song, a novel a reverie as useless as crocheted antimacassars. It is American women who are responsible for the degradation of best sellers: these books are only intended to please, and worse to please idle women who need escape. As for their activities in general, Philip Wylie defines them like this:

> They frighten politicians to sniveling servility and they terrify pastors; they bother bank presidents and they pulverize school boards. Mom has many such organizations, the real purpose of which is to compel an abject compliance of her environs to her personal desires . . . she drives out of the town and the state, if possible, all young harlots . . . she causes bus lines to run where they

---

4. *Generation of Vipers.*

are convenient for her rather than for workers . . . throws prodigious fairs and parties for charity and gives the proceeds . . . to
the janitor to buy the committee some beer for its headache on
the morning after . . . clubs afford mom an infinite opportunity
for nosing into other people's business.

There is much truth in this aggressive satire. Not being specialized in
politics or economics or any technical discipline, old women have no concrete hold on society; they are unaware of the problems action poses; they
are incapable of elaborating a constructive program. Their morality is
abstract and formal, like Kant's imperatives; they issue prohibitions instead
of trying to discover the paths of progress; they do not positively try to
create new situations; they attack what already exists in order to do away
with the evil in it; this explains why they are always forming coalitions
against something—against alcohol, prostitution, or pornography—they
do not understand that a purely negative effort is doomed to be unsuccessful, as evidenced by the failure of prohibition in America or the law in
France voted by Marthe Richard. As long as woman remains a parasite, she
cannot effectively participate in the building of a better world.

It does happen that in spite of everything, some women entirely committed to a cause truly have an impact; these women are not merely seeking
to keep themselves busy, they have ends in view; autonomous producers,
they escape from the parasitic category we are considering here: but this
conversion is rare. In their private or public activities, most women do not
aim for a goal that can be reached but for a way to keep busy: and no occupation is meaningful if it is only a pastime. Many of them suffer from this;
with a life already behind them, they feel the same distress as adolescent
boys whose lives have not yet opened up; nothing is calling them, around
them both is a desert; faced with any action, they murmur: What's the use?
But the adolescent boy is drawn, willingly or not, into a man's existence
that reveals responsibilities, goals, and values; he is thrown into the world,
he takes a stand, he becomes committed. If it is suggested to the older
woman that she begin to move toward the future, she responds sadly: it's
too late. It is not that her time is limited from here on: a woman is made to
retire very early; but she lacks the drive, confidence, hope, and anger that
would allow her to discover new goals in her own life. She takes refuge in
the routine that has always been her lot; she makes repetition her system,
she throws herself into household obsessions; she becomes more deeply
religious; she becomes rigidly stoic, like Mme de Charrière. She becomes
brittle, indifferent, egotistical.

The old woman often finds serenity toward the end of her life when she has given up the fight, when death's approach frees her from anxiety about the future. Her husband was often older than she, she witnesses his decline with silent complacency: it is her revenge; if he dies first, she cheerfully bears the mourning; it has often been observed that men are far more overwhelmed by being widowed late in life: they profit more from marriage than women do, and particularly in their old age, because then the universe is concentrated within the limits of the home; the present does not spill over into the future: it is their wife who assures their monotonous rhythm and reigns over them; when he loses his public functions, man becomes totally useless; woman continues at least to run the home; she is necessary to her husband, whereas he is only a nuisance. Women are proud of their independence, they finally begin to view the world through their own eyes; they realize they have been duped and mystified their whole lives; now lucid and wary, they often attain a delicious cynicism. In particular, the woman who "has lived" has a knowledge of men that no man shares: for she has seen not their public image but the contingent individual that every one of them lets show in the absence of their counterparts; she also knows women, who only show themselves in their spontaneity to other women: she knows what happens behind the scenes. But even if her experience allows her to denounce mystifications and lies, it is not enough to reveal the truth to her. Whether she is amused or bitter, the old woman's wisdom still remains completely negative: it is contestation, accusation, refusal; it is sterile. In her thoughts as in her acts, the highest form of freedom a woman-parasite can have is stoic defiance or skeptical irony. At no time in her life does she succeed in being both effective and independent.

CHAPTER 10

Woman's Situation and Character

We can now understand why, from ancient Greece to today, there are so many common features in the indictments against woman; her condition has remained the same throughout superficial changes, and this condition defines what is called the woman's "character": she "wallows in immanence," she is argumentative, she is cautious and petty, she does not have the sense either of truth or of accuracy, she lacks morality, she is vulgarly self-serving, selfish, she is a liar and an actress. There is some truth in all these affirmations. But the types of behaviors denounced are not dictated to woman by her hormones or predestined in her brain's compartments: they are suggested in negative form by her situation. We will attempt to take a synthetic point of view of her situation, necessarily leading to some repetition, but making it possible to grasp the Eternal Feminine in her economic, social, and historical conditioning as a whole.

The "feminine world" is sometimes contrasted with the masculine universe, but it must be reiterated that women have never formed an autonomous and closed society; they are integrated into the group governed by males, where they occupy a subordinate position; they are united by a mechanical solidarity only insofar as they are similar: they do not share that organic solidarity upon which any unified community is founded; they have always endeavored—in the period of the Eleusinian mysteries just like today in clubs, salons, and recreation rooms—to band together to assert a "counter-universe," but it is still within the masculine universe that they frame it. And this is where the paradox of their situation comes in: they belong both to the male world and to a sphere in which this world is challenged; enclosed in this sphere, involved in the male world, they cannot peacefully establish themselves anywhere. Their docility is always accompanied by refusal, their refusal by acceptance; this is similar to the girl's attitude; but it is more difficult to maintain because it is no longer simply a question of the adult woman dreaming her life through symbols, but of living it.

The woman herself recognizes that the universe as a whole is masculine; it is men who have shaped it and ruled it and who still today dominate it; as for her, she does not consider herself responsible for it; it is understood that she is inferior and dependent; she has not learned the lessons of violence, she has never emerged as a subject in front of other members of the group; enclosed in her flesh, in her home, she grasps herself as passive opposite to these human-faced gods who set goals and standards. In this sense there is truth in the saying that condemns her to remaining "an eternal child"; it has also been said of workers, black slaves, and colonized natives that they were "big children" as long as they were not threatening; that meant they had to accept without argument the truths and laws that other men gave them. Woman's lot is obedience and respect. She has no grasp, even in thought, on this reality that involves her. It is an opaque presence in her eyes. That means she has not learned the technology that would enable her to dominate matter; as for her, she is not fighting with matter but with life, and life cannot be mastered by tools: one can only submit to its secret laws. The world does not appear to the woman as a "set of tools" halfway between her will and her goals, as Heidegger defines it: on the contrary, it is a stubborn, indomitable resistance; it is dominated by fate and run through with mysterious caprices. No mathematics can make an equation out of this mystery of a spot of blood that changes into a human being in the mother's womb, no machine can rush it or slow it down; she experiences the resistance of a duration that the most ingenious machines fail to divide or multiply; she experiences it in her flesh that is subjected to the rhythm of the moon, and that the years first ripen and then corrode. Daily cooking teaches her patience and passivity; it is alchemy; one must obey fire, water, "wait for the sugar to melt," the dough to rise, and also the clothes to dry, the fruit to ripen. Housework comes close to a technical activity; but it is too rudimentary, too monotonous, to convince the woman of the laws of mechanical causality. Besides, even in this area, things are capricious; there is material that "revives" and material that does not "revive" in the wash, spots that come out and others that persist, objects that break on their own, dust that grows like plants. Woman's mentality perpetuates that of agricultural civilizations that worship the earth's magical qualities: she believes in magic. Her passive eroticism reveals her desire not as will and aggression but as an attraction similar to that which makes the dowser's pendulum quiver; the mere presence of her flesh makes the male sex swell and rise; why should hidden water not make the dowser's wand jump? She feels surrounded by waves, radiation, fluid; she believes in telepathy, astrology, divination, Mesmer's *baquet*, theosophy, table turning, mind readers, and healers; she introduces primitive superstitions into religion—candles, ex-votos, and such—she embodies ancient spirits of nature in the saints—this one protects travelers, that one women who have just given birth, another one finds lost objects—and of course no marvel surprises her. Her attitude will be that of conjuration and prayer; to obtain a certain result, she will follow certain time-tested rites. It is easy to understand why she is ruled by routine; time has no dimension of novelty for her, it is not a creative spring; because she is doomed to repetition, she does not see in the future anything but a duplication of the past; if one knows the word and the recipe, duration is allied with the powers of fecundity: but this too obeys the rhythm of months and seasons; the cycle of each pregnancy, of each flowering, reproduces the preceding one identically; in this circular movement, time's sole becoming is slow degradation: it eats at furniture and clothes just as it disfigures the face; fertile powers are destroyed little by little by the flight of years. So the woman does not trust this force driven to destroy.

Not only is she unaware of what real action is, that is able to change the face of the world, but she is lost in the middle of this world as in the heart of an immense and confused mass. She does not know how to use masculine logic well. Stendhal noted that she handles it as skillfully as man if she has to. But it is an instrument she does not often have the occasion to use. A syllogism is not useful in making mayonnaise or calming a child's tears; masculine reasoning is not relevant to the reality she experiences. And in the man's world, since she does not *do* anything, her thinking, as it does not flow into any project, is no different from a dream; she does not have the sense of truth, because she lacks efficacy; she struggles only by means of images and words: that is why she accepts the most contradictory assertions without a problem; she does not care about clarifying the mysteries of a sphere, which in any case is beyond her scope; she settles for horribly vague knowledge when it concerns her: she confuses parties, opinions, places, people, and events; there is a strange jumble in her head. But after all, seeing clearly is not her business: she was taught to accept masculine authority; she thus forgoes criticizing, examining, and judging for herself. She leaves it to the superior caste. This is why the masculine world seems to be a transcendent reality, an absolute to her. "Men make gods," says Frazer, "and women worship them." Men cannot kneel with total conviction in front of idols they themselves have created, but when women come across these imposing statues on their path, they cannot imagine any hand making them, and they meekly bow down before them.[1] They specifically like Law and Order to be embodied in a chief. In all Olympus, there is one sovereign god; the prestigious virile essence must be gathered in one archetype of which father, husband, and lovers are merely vague reflections. It is somewhat humorous to say that their worship of this great totem is sexual; what is true is that women fully realize their infantile dream of abdication and prostration. In France, the generals Boulanger, Pétain, and de Gaulle have always had the support of women;[2] one remembers the purple prose of L'Humanité's women journalists when writing about Tito and his beautiful uniform. The general or the dictator—eagle eye, prominent chin—is the celestial father the serious universe demands, the absolute guarantor of all values. The respect women grant to heroes and to the masculine world's laws stems from their powerlessness and ignorance; they acknowledge these laws not through judgment but through an act of faith: faith draws its fanatical power from the fact that it is not knowledge: it is blind, passionate, stubborn, and stupid; what it puts forward is done unconditionally, against reason, against history, against all refutation. This stubborn reverence can take two forms depending on circumstances: sometimes it is the content of the law and sometimes the empty form alone that the woman passionately abides by. If she belongs to the privileged elite that profits from the given social order, she wants it unshakable, and she is seen as intransigent. The man knows he can reconstruct other institutions, another ethics, another code; grasping himself as transcendence, he also envisages history as a becoming; even the most conservative knows that some change is inevitable and that he has to adapt his action and thinking to it; as the woman does not participate in history, she does not understand its necessities; she mistrusts the future and wants to stop time. If the idols her father, brothers, and husband propose are knocked down, she cannot imagine any way of repopulating the heavens; she is determined to defend them. Among the Southerners during the Civil War, no one was as passionately in favor of slavery as the women; in

---

1. Cf. J.-P. Sartre, Les mains sales (Dirty Hands): "HŒDERER: They need props, you understand, they are given ready-made ideas, then they believe in them as they do in God. We're the ones who make these ideas and we know how they are cooked up; we are never quite sure of being right."

2. "On the general's passage, the public was made up mostly of women and children" (Les Journaux, about the September 1948 tour in Savoy).

"The men applauded the general's speech, but the women stood out by their enthusiasm. Some were literally in ecstasy, singling out almost every word and clapping and shouting with a fervor that made their faces turn poppy red" (Aux Ecoutes, April 11, 1947).

England during the Boer War, and in France against the Commune, it was the women who were the most enraged; they seek to compensate for their inaction by the force of the feelings they display; in victory they are as wild as hyenas against the beaten enemy; in defeat, they bitterly refuse any arrangement; as their ideas are only attitudes, they do not mind defending the most outdated causes: they can be legitimists in 1914, tsarists in 1949. Sometimes the man smilingly encourages them: it pleases him to see his measured opinions reflected in a fanatical form; but sometimes he is also bothered by the stupid and stubborn way his own ideas are transformed.

It is only in strongly integrated civilizations and classes that the woman looks so intransigent. Generally, as her faith is blind, she respects the laws simply because they are laws; the laws may change, but they keep their prestige; in the eyes of women, power creates law since the laws they recognize in men come from their power; that is why they are the first to throw themselves at the victors' feet when a group collapses. In general, they accept what is. One of their typical features is resignation. When the ashes of Pompeii's statues were dug out, it was observed that the men were caught in movements of revolt, defying the sky or trying to flee, while the women were bent, withdrawn into themselves, turning their faces toward the earth. They know they are powerless against things: volcanoes, police-men, employers, or men. "Women are made to suffer," they say. "That's life; nothing can be done about it." This resignation engenders the patience often admired in women. They withstand physical suffering much better than men; they are capable of stoic courage when circumstances demand it: without the aggressive daring of the male, many women are distinguished by the calm tenacity of their passive resistance; they deal with crises, mis-ery, and misfortune more energetically than their husbands; respectful of duration that no haste can conquer, they do not measure their time; when they apply their calm stubbornness to any undertaking, they are sometimes brilliantly successful. "Whatever woman wants," says the proverb.* In a generous woman, resignation looks like indulgence: she accepts every-thing; she condemns no one because she thinks that neither people nor things can be different from what they are. A proud woman can make a lofty virtue of it, like Mme de Charrière, rigid in her stoicism. But she also engenders a sterile prudence; women always try to keep, to fix, to arrange rather than to destroy and reconstruct anew; they prefer compromises and exchanges to revolutions. In the nineteenth century, they constituted one of

---

* French proverb: "What woman wants, God wants."—TRANS.

the biggest obstacles to the effort of women workers' emancipation: for every Flora Tristan or Louise Michel, how many utterly timid housewives begged their husbands not to take any risk! They were afraid not only of strikes, unemployment, and misery; they also feared that the revolt was a mistake. Submission for submission, it is understandable that they prefer routine to adventure: they eke out for themselves a more meager happiness at home than on the streets. Their lot is one with that of perishable things: they would lose everything in losing them. Only a free subject, asserting himself beyond time, can foil destruction; this supreme recourse is forbidden to the woman. It is mainly because she has never experienced the powers of liberty that she does not believe in liberation: the world to her seems governed by an obscure destiny against which it is presumptuous to react. These dangerous paths that she is compelled to follow are ones she herself has not traced: it is understandable that she does not take them enthusiastically.[3] When the future is open to her, she no longer hangs on to the past. When women are concretely called to action, when they identify with the designated aims, they are as strong and brave as men.[4]

Many of the faults for which they are reproached—mediocrity, meanness, shyness, pettiness, laziness, frivolity, and servility—simply express the fact that the horizon is blocked for them. Woman, it is said, is sensual, she wallows in immanence; but first she was enclosed in it. The slave imprisoned in the harem does not feel any morbid passion for rose jelly and perfumed baths: she has to kill time somehow; inasmuch as the woman is stifling in a dismal gynaeceum—brothel or bourgeois home—she will also take refuge in comfort and well-being; moreover, if she avidly pursues sexual pleasure, it is often because she is frustrated; sexually unsatisfied, destined to male brutality, "condemned to masculine ugliness," she consoles herself with creamy sauces, heady wines, velvets, the caresses of water, sun, a woman friend, or a young lover. If she appears to man as such a "physical" being, it is because her condition incites her to attach a great

---

3. Cf. Gide, *Journals:* "Creusa or Lot's wife: one tarries and the other looks back, which is a worse way of tarrying . . . There is no greater cry of passion than this:

And Phaedra having braved the Labyrinth with you
Would have been found with you or lost with you.

But passion blinds her; after a few steps, to tell the truth, she would have sat down, or else would have wanted to go back—or even would have made him carry her."

4. This is how the attitude of the proletarian women has changed over the century; during the recent strikes in the mines of the North, for example, they showed as much passion and energy as men, demonstrating and fighting side by side.

deal of importance to her animality. Carnality does not cry out any more strongly in her than in the male: but she watches out for its slightest signs and amplifies it; sexual pleasure, like the wrenching of suffering, is the devastating triumph of immediacy; the violence of the instant negates the future and the universe: outside of the carnal blaze, what is there is nothing; during this brief apotheosis, she is no longer mutilated or frustrated. But once again, she attaches such importance to these triumphs of immanence because it is her only lot. Her frivolity has the same cause as her "sordid materialism"; she gives importance to little things because she lacks access to big ones: moreover the futilities that fill her days are often of great seriousness; she owes her charm and her opportunities to her toilette and beauty. She often seems lazy, indolent; but the occupations that are offered her are as useless as the pure flowing of time; if she is talkative or a scribbler, it is to while away her time: she substitutes words for impossible acts. The fact is that when a woman is engaged in an undertaking worthy of a human being, she knows how to be as active, effective, and silent, as ascetic, as a man. She is accused of being servile; she is always willing, it is said, to lie at her master's feet and to kiss the hand that has beaten her. It is true that she generally lacks real self-regard; advice to the "lovelorn," to betrayed wives, and to abandoned lovers is inspired by a spirit of abject submission; the woman exhausts herself in arrogant scenes and in the end gathers up the crumbs the male is willing to throw her. But what can a woman—for whom the man is both the only means and the only reason for living—do without masculine help? She has no choice but to endure all humiliations; a slave cannot understand the meaning of "human dignity"; for him it is enough if he manages to survive. Finally, if she is "down-to-earth," a homebody, simply useful, it is because she has no choice but to devote her existence to preparing food and cleaning diapers: she cannot draw the meaning of grandeur from this. She must ensure the monotonous repetition of life in its contingence and facticity: it is natural for her to repeat herself, to begin again, without ever inventing, to feel that time seems to be going around in circles without going anywhere; she is busy without ever *doing* anything: so she is alienated in what she *has;* this dependence on things, a consequence of the dependence in which she is held by men, explains her cautious management, her avarice. Her life is not directed toward goals: she is absorbed in producing or maintaining things that are never more than means—food, clothes, lodging—these are inessential intermediaries between animal life and free existence; the only value that is attached to inessential means is usefulness; the housewife lives at the level of utility, and she takes credit for herself only when she is useful to her family. But no existent is able to satisfy itself with an inessential role: he quickly makes ends out of means—as can be observed in politicians, among others—and in his eyes the value of the means becomes an absolute value. Thus utility reigns higher than truth, beauty, and freedom in the housewife's heaven; and this is the point of view from which she envisages the whole universe; and this is why she adopts the Aristotelian morality of the golden mean, of mediocrity. How could one find daring, ardor, detachment, and grandeur in her? These qualities appear only where a freedom throws itself across an open future, emerging beyond any given. A woman is shut up in a kitchen or a boudoir, and one is surprised her horizon is limited; her wings are cut, and then she is blamed for not knowing how to fly. Let a future be open to her and she will no longer be obliged to settle in the present.

The same foolishness is seen when, closed up in the limits of her self or her home, she is criticized for her narcissism and egotism with their corollaries: vanity, touchiness, meanness, and so forth. All possibility of concrete communication with others is removed from her; in her experience she does not recognize either the appeal or the advantages of solidarity, since, separated, she is entirely devoted to her own family; she cannot be expected therefore to go beyond herself toward the general interest. She obstinately confines herself in the only familiar area where she has the power to grasp things and where she finds a precarious sovereignty.

Although she might close the doors and cover the windows, the woman does not find absolute security in her home; this masculine universe that she respects from afar without daring to venture into it involves her; and because she is unable to grasp it through technology, sound logic, or coherent knowledge, she feels like a child and a primitive surrounded with dangerous mysteries. She projects her magic conception of reality: the flow of things seems inevitable to her, and yet anything can happen; she has difficulty differentiating the possible and the impossible, she is ready to believe anyone; she welcomes and spreads rumors, she sets off panics; even in calm periods she lives in worry; at night, half-asleep, the inert body is frightened by the nightmare images reality acquires: so for the woman condemned to passivity, the opaque future is haunted by phantoms of war, revolution, famine, and misery; not being able to act, she worries. When her husband and son embark on a job, when they are passionately involved in an event, they take their own risks: their projects and the orders they follow show them a sure way even in darkness; but the woman struggles in the blurry night; she "worries" because she does not do anything; in imagination all possibilities are equally real: the train may derail, the operation may be unsuccessful, the affair may fail; what she vainly tries to ward off in her long, despondent ruminations is the specter of her own powerlessness.

Worry expresses her mistrust of the given world; if it seems threatening, ready to sink into obscure catastrophes, it is because she does not feel happy in it. Most often, she is not resigned to being resigned; she knows what she is going through, she goes through it in spite of herself: she is woman without being asked; she does not dare revolt; she submits against her will; her attitude is a constant recrimination. Everyone who receives women's confidences—doctors, priests, social workers—knows that complaint is the commonest mode of expression; together, women friends groan individually about their own ills and all together about the injustice of their lot, the world, and men in general. A free individual takes the blame for his failures on himself, he takes responsibility for them: but what happens to the woman comes from others, it is others who are responsible for her misfortune. Her furious despair rejects all remedies; suggesting solutions to a woman determined to complain does not help: no solution seems acceptable. She wants to live her situation exactly as she lives it: in impotent anger. If a change is suggested to her, she throws her arms up: "That's all I need!" She knows that her malaise is deeper than the pretexts she gives for it, and that one expedient is not enough to get rid of it; she takes it out on the whole world because it was put together without her, and against her; since adolescence, since childhood, she has protested against her condition; she was promised compensations, she was assured that if she abdicated her opportunities into the hands of the man, they would be returned to her a hundredfold, and she considers herself duped; she accuses the whole masculine universe; resentment is the other side of dependence: when one gives everything, one never receives enough in return. But she also needs to respect the male universe; if she contested it entirely, she would feel in danger, and without a roof over her head: she adopts the Manichaean attitude also suggested to her by her experience as a housewife. The individual who acts accepts responsibility for good and evil just like the others, he knows that it is up to him to define ends, to see that they triumph; in action he experiences the ambiguity of all solutions; justice and injustice, gains and losses, are inextricably intermingled. But whoever is passive puts himself on the sidelines and refuses to pose, even in thought, ethical problems: good *must* be realized, and if it is not, there is wrongdoing for which the guilty must be punished. Like the child, the woman imagines good and evil in simple storybook images; Manichaeism reassures the mind by eliminating the anguish of choice; deciding between one scourge and a lesser one, between a benefit today and a greater benefit tomorrow, having to define by oneself what is defeat and what is victory: this means taking terrible risks; for the Manichaean, the wheat is clearly distinguishable from the chaff, and the chaff has to be eliminated; dust condemns itself, and cleanliness is the absolute absence of filth; cleaning means getting rid of waste and mud. Thus the woman thinks that "everything is the Jews' fault" or the Masons' or the Bolsheviks' or the government's; she is always *against* someone or something; women were even more violently anti-Dreyfusard than men; they do not always know what the evil principle is; but what they expect from a "good government" is that it get rid of it as one gets rid of dust from the house. For fervent Gaullists, de Gaulle is the king sweeper; they imagine him, dust mops and rags in hand, scrubbing and polishing to make a "clean" France.

But these hopes are always placed in an uncertain future; meanwhile, evil continues to eat away at good; and as woman does not have Jews, Masons, and Bolsheviks to hand, she seeks someone against whom she can rise up concretely: the husband is the perfect victim. He embodies the masculine universe, it is through him that the male society took the woman in hand and duped her; he bears the weight of the world, and if things go wrong, it is his fault. When he comes home in the evening, she complains to him about the children, the suppliers, the housework, the cost of living, her rheumatism, and the weather: and she wants him to feel guilty. She often harbors specific complaints about him; but he is particularly guilty of being a man; he might well have illnesses and problems too—"It just isn't the same thing"—he is privy to a privilege she constantly resents as an injustice. It is noteworthy that the hostility she feels for the husband or the lover binds her to him instead of moving her away from him; a man who begins to detest wife or mistress tries to get away from her: but she wants to have the man she hates nearby to make him pay. Choosing to recriminate is choosing not to get rid of one's misfortunes but to wallow in them; her supreme consolation is to set herself up as martyr. Life and men have conquered her: she will make a victory of this very defeat. Thus, as she did in childhood, she quickly gives way to the frenzy of tears and scenes.

It is surely because her life takes place against a background of powerless revolt that the woman cries so easily; she undoubtedly has less physiological control of her nervous and sympathetic systems than the man; her education taught her to let herself go: orders and instruction play a great role here since, although Diderot and Benjamin Constant shed rivers of tears, men stopped crying when custom forbade it for them. But the woman is still inclined to be defeatist vis-à-vis the world because she has never frankly assumed it. The man accepts the world; even misfortune will not change his attitude, he will cope with it, he will "not let it get him down," while a little setback is enough for the woman to rediscover the universe's hostility and the injustice of her lot; so she throws herself into her safest refuge: herself; this moist trace on her cheeks, this burning in her eyes, are the tangible presence of her suffering soul; gentle on one's skin, barely salty on one's tongue, tears are also a tender and bitter caress; the face burns under a stream of mild water; tears are both complaint and consolation, fever and soothing coolness. They are also a supreme alibi; sudden as a storm, coming out in fits, a cyclone, shower, deluge, they metamorphose the woman into a complaining fountain, a stormy sky; her eyes can no longer see, mist blurs them: they are no longer even a gaze, they melt in rain; blinded, the woman returns to the passivity of natural things. She must be vanquished: she is lost in her defeat; she sinks, she drowns, she escapes man who contemplates her, powerless as if before a cataract. He judges this way of behaving as unfair: but she thinks that the battle has been unfair from the beginning because no effective weapon has been put into her hands. She resorts once again to magical conjuration. And the fact that these sobs exasperate the male provides her with one more reason to indulge herself in them.

If tears are not sufficient to express her revolt, she will carry on in such incoherent violence that it will disconcert the man even more. In some circles, the man might strike his wife with actual blows; in others, because he is the stronger and his fist an effective instrument, he will forgo all violence. But the woman, like the child, indulges in symbolic outbursts: she might throw herself on the man, scratch him; these are only gestures. But above all, through nervous fits in her body she attempts to express the refusals she cannot carry out concretely. It is not only for physiological reasons that she is subject to convulsive manifestations: a convulsion is an interiorization of an energy that, thrown into the world, fails to grasp any object; it is a useless expenditure of all the powers of negation caused by the situation. The mother rarely has crying fits in front of her young children because she can beat or punish them: it is in front of her older son, her husband, or her lover, on whom she has no hold, that the woman gives vent to furious hopelessness. Sophia Tolstoy's hysterical scenes are significant; it is true that she made the big mistake of never trying to understand her husband and in her diary she does not seem generous, sensitive, or sincere, she is far from coming across as an endearing person; but whether she was right or wrong does not change the horror of her situation at all: she never did anything in her whole life but submit to the conjugal embraces, pregnancies, solitude, and mode of life that her husband imposed on her while receiving constant recriminations; when new decisions of Tolstoy's worsened the conflict, she found herself weaponless against the enemy's will, which she rejected with all her powerless will; she threw herself into rejection scenes—fake suicides, false escapes, false illnesses—unpleasant to her family and friends, exhausting for herself: it is hard to see any other solution available to her since she had no positive reason to silence her feelings of revolt and no effective way of expressing them.

There is only one solution available to the woman when rejection runs its course: suicide. But it would seem that she resorts to it less than the man. The statistics are very ambiguous: if one considers successful suicides, there are many more men than women who put an end to their lives; but suicide attempts are more frequent in women.[5] This may be because they settle more often for playacting: they *play* at suicide more often than man, but they *want* it more rarely. It is also in part because such brutal means are repugnant to them: they almost never use knives or firearms. They drown themselves more readily, like Ophelia, showing woman's affinity for water, passive and full of darkness, where it seems that life might be able to dissolve passively. On the whole, this is the ambiguity I already mentioned: the woman does not sincerely seek to take leave of what she detests. She plays at rupture but in the end remains with the man who makes her suffer; she pretends to leave the life that mistreats her, but it is relatively rare for her to kill herself. She does not favor definitive solutions: she protests against man, against life, against her condition, but she does not escape from it.

There is much feminine behavior that has to be interpreted as protest. We have seen that the woman often cheats on her husband by defiance and not for pleasure; she will be absentminded and a spendthrift on purpose because he is methodical and careful. Misogynists who accuse woman of "always being late" think she lacks "the sense of exactitude." In truth, we have seen how docilely she adapts to the demands of time. Being late is deliberate. Some flirtatious women think that this is the way to excite the desire of the man, who will thus attach more importance to their presence; but above all, in keeping a man waiting for a few minutes, the woman protests against this long wait that is her own life. In one sense, her whole existence is a waiting since she is enclosed in the limbo of immanence and contingency and her justification is always in someone else's hands: she is waiting for a tribute, men's approval, she is waiting for love, she is waiting

---

5. See Halbwachs, *The Causes of Suicide*.

for gratitude and her husband's or lover's praise; she expects to gain from them her reasons to exist, her worth, and her very being. She awaits her subsistence from them; whether she has her own checkbook or receives the money her husband allocates to her every week or month, he has to have been paid, obtained the raise for her to pay the grocer or buy a new dress. She awaits men's presence: her economic dependence puts her at their disposal; she is only one element of masculine life, whereas the man is her whole life; the husband has occupations outside the home, the woman endures his absence every day; it is the lover—even if passionate—who decides on the separation and meetings according to his obligations. In bed, she awaits the male's desire; she awaits—sometimes anxiously—her own pleasure. The only thing she can do is to be late for the date the lover set up; or not to be ready at the time the husband fixed; this is the way she asserts the importance of her own occupations, she claims her independence, she becomes the essential subject for a moment while the other passively submits to her will. But this is meager revenge; no matter how determined she might be to make men stew, she will never compensate for the infinite hours she has spent being subjected to and watching out and hoping for the male's goodwill.

In general, while more or less acknowledging men's supremacy and accepting their authority, worshipping their idols, she will contest their reign tooth and nail; hence the famous "contrariness" for which she is so often criticized; as she does not possess an autonomous domain, she cannot put forward truths or positive values different from those that males assert; she can only negate them. Her negation is more or less systematic depending on her particular balance of respect and resentment. But the fact is, she knows all the fault lines of the masculine system and she hastens to denounce them.

Women do not have a hold on the world of men, because their experience does not teach them to deal with logic and technology: conversely, the power of male instruments disappears at the borders of the feminine domain. There is a whole region of human experience that the male deliberately chooses to ignore because he fails to *think* it: this experience, the woman *lives* it. The engineer, so precise when making his plans, behaves like a demigod at home: one word and his meal is served, his shirts starched, his children silenced: procreating is an act that is as quick as Moses's magic rod; he sees nothing surprising in these miracles. The notion of miracle differs from the idea of magic: from within a rationally determined world a miracle posits the radical discontinuity of an event without cause against which any thinking shatters, whereas magic phenomena are united by secret forces of which a docile consciousness can embrace the continuous becoming—without understanding it. The new-born is miraculous for the demigod father, magic for the mother who has undergone the ripening in her womb. Man's experience is intelligible but full of holes; that of the wife is, in its own limits, obscure but complete. This opacity weighs her down; the male is light in his relations with her: he has the lightness of dictators, generals, judges, bureaucrats, codes, and abstract principles. This is undoubtedly what this housewife meant when, shrugging her shoulders, she murmured: "Men, they don't think!" Women also say: "Men, they don't know; they don't know life." As a contrast to the myth of the praying mantis, they juxtapose the symbol of the frivolous and importunate bumblebee.

It is understandable why, from this perspective, woman objects to mas-culine logic. Not only does it have no bearing on her experience, but she also knows that in men's hands reason becomes an insidious form of vio-lence; their peremptory affirmations are intended to mystify her. They want to confine her in a dilemma: either you agree or you don't; she has to agree in the name of the whole system of accepted principles: in refusing to agree, she rejects the whole system; she cannot allow herself such a dra-matic move; she does not have the means to create another society: yet she does not agree with this one. Halfway between revolt and slavery, she unwillingly resigns herself to masculine authority. He continuously uses force to make her shoulder the consequences of her reluctant submission. He pursues the chimera of a freely enslaved companion: he wants her to yield to him as yielding to the proof of a theorem; but she knows he him-self has chosen the postulates on which his vigorous deductions are hung; as long as she avoids questioning them, he will easily silence her; neverthe-less, he will not convince her, because she senses their arbitrariness. Thus will he accuse her, with stubborn irritation, of being illogical: she refuses to play the game because she knows the dice are loaded.

The woman does not positively think that the truth is *other* than what men claim: rather, she holds that there *is* no truth. It is not only life's becoming that makes her suspicious of the principle of identity, nor the magic phenomena surrounding her that ruin the notion of causality: it is at the heart of the masculine world itself, it is in her as belonging to this world, that she grasps the ambiguity of all principles, of all values, of all that exists. She knows that when it comes to her, masculine morality is a vast mystification. The man pompously drums his code of virtue and honor into her; but secretly he invites her to disobey it: he even counts on this disobedience; the whole lovely facade he hides behind would collapse without it.

The man readily uses the pretext of the Hegelian idea that the male citizen acquires his ethical dignity by transcending himself toward the universal: as a singular individual, he has the right to desire and pleasure. His relations with woman thus lie in a contingent region where morality no longer applies, where conduct is inconsequential. His relations with other men are based on certain values; he is a freedom confronting other freedoms according to laws universally recognized by all; but with woman—she was invented for this reason—he ceases to assume his existence, he abandons himself to the mirage of the in-itself, he situates himself on an inauthentic plane; he is tyrannical, sadistic, violent or puerile, masochistic or querulous; he tries to satisfy his obsessions, his manias; he "relaxes," he "lets go" in the name of rights he has acquired in his public life. His wife is often surprised—like Thérèse Desqueyroux—by the contrast between the lofty tone of his remarks, of his public conduct, and "his patient inventions in the dark."* He preaches population growth: but he is clever at not having more children than are convenient for him. He praises chaste and faithful wives: but he invites his neighbor's wife to commit adultery. We have seen the hypocrisy of men decreeing abortion to be criminal when every year in France a million women are put by men into the situation where they have to abort; very often the husband or lover imposes this solution on them; and often these men tacitly assume that it will be used if necessary. They openly count on the woman to consent to making herself guilty of a crime: her "immorality" is necessary for the harmony of moral society, respected by men. The most flagrant example of this duplicity is man's attitude to prostitution: it is his demand that creates the offer; I have spoken of the disgusted skepticism with which prostitutes view respectable gentlemen who condemn vice in general but show great indulgence for their personal foibles; they consider girls who make a living with their bodies perverse and debauched, and not the men who use them. An anecdote illustrates this state of mind: at the end of the last century, the police discovered two little girls of twelve or thirteen in a bordello; a trial was held where they testified; they spoke of their clients, who were important gentlemen; one of them opened her mouth to give a name. The judge abruptly stopped her: *Do not sully the name of an honest man!* A gentleman decorated with the Legion of Honor remains an honest man while deflowering a little girl; he has his weaknesses, but who does not? However, the little girl who has no access to the ethical region of the universal—who is neither judge nor general nor a great French man, nothing but a little girl—gambles her moral

---

* Mauriac, *Thérèse Desqueyroux*.—TRANS.

value in the contingent region of sexuality: she is perverted, corrupted, depraved, and good only for the reformatory. In many cases, the man can commit acts with woman's complicity that degrade her without tarnishing his lofty image. She does not understand these subtleties very well; what she does understand is that the man's actions do not conform to the principles he professes and that he asks her to disobey them; he does not want what he says he wants: she therefore does not give him what she pretends to give him. She will be a chaste and faithful wife: and in secret she will give in to her desires; she will be an admirable mother: but she will carefully practice birth control, and she will have an abortion if she must. Officially the man renounces her, those are the rules of the game; but he is clandestinely grateful to one for her "easy virtue," to another for her sterility. The woman has the role of those secret agents who are left to the firing squad if they are caught, and who are covered with rewards if they succeed; it is for her to shoulder all of males' immorality: it is not only the prostitute; it is all the women who serve as the gutter to the luminous and clean palaces where respectable people live. When one speaks to these women of dignity, honor, loyalty, and all the lofty virile virtues, one should not be surprised if they refuse to "go along." They particularly snigger when virtuous males reproach them for being calculating, actresses, liars:[6] they know well that no other way is open to them. The man also is "calculating" about money and success: but he has the means to acquire them through his work: the woman has been assigned the role of parasite: all parasites are necessarily exploiters; she needs the male to acquire human dignity, to eat, to feel pleasure, to procreate; she uses the service of sex to ensure her benefits; and since she is trapped in this function, she is entirely an instrument of exploitation. As for falsehoods, except in the case of prostitution, there is no fair arrangement between her and her protector. Man even requires her to playact: he wants her to be the *Other;* but every existent, as desperately as he may disavow himself, remains a subject; he wants her to be object: she *makes* herself object; at the moment she makes herself being, she is exercising a free activity; this is her original treason; the most docile, the most passive woman is still consciousness; and it is sometimes enough to make him feel duped by her for the male to glimpse that in giving herself to him she is watching and judging him; she should be no more than an offered thing, a prey. Nonetheless, he also demands that she surrender this thing to him

6. "All these women with this little delicate and touch-me-not air accumulated by a whole past of slavery, with no other means of salvation and livelihood than this unintentional seductive air biding its time" (Jules Laforgue).

freely: in bed, he asks her to feel pleasure; at home, she must sincerely recognize his superiority and his strengths; at the very moment she obeys, she must also feign independence, even though she actively plays the role of passivity at other moments. She lies to keep her man and ensure her daily bread—scenes and tears, uncontrollable transports of love, hysterics—and she lies as well to escape the tyranny she accepts out of self-interest. He encourages playacting as it feeds his imperialism and vanity: she uses her powers of dissimulation against him; revenge is thus doubly delicious: for in deceiving him, she satisfies her own particular desires and she savors the pleasure of mocking him. The wife and the courtesan lie in feigning transports they do not feel; afterward, with their lovers or girlfriends, they make fun of the naive vanity of their dupe: "Not only do they 'botch it,' but they want us to wear ourselves out moaning with pleasure," they say resentfully. These conversations resemble those of servants who criticize their "bosses" in the servants' kitchen. The woman has the same faults because she is a victim of the same paternalistic oppression; she has the same cynicism because she sees the man from head to toe as a valet sees his master. But it is clear that none of these traits manifests a perverted essence or perverted original will; they reflect a situation. "There is duplicity wherever there is a coercive regime," says Fourier. "Prohibition and contraband are inseparable in love as in business." And men know so well that the woman's faults show her condition that, careful to maintain the hierarchy of the sexes, they encourage these very traits in their companion that allow them to scorn her. Doubtless the husband or lover is irritated by the faults of the particular woman he lives with; yet, extolling the charms of femininity in general, he considers it to be inseparable from its flaws. If the woman is not perfidious, futile, cowardly, or indolent, she loses her seduction. In *A Doll's House*, Helmer explains how just, strong, understanding, and indulgent man feels when he pardons his weak wife for her puerile faults. Thus Bernstein's husbands are moved—with the author's complicity—by the thieving, cruel, adulterous wife; bowing indulgently to her, they prove their virile wisdom. American racists and French colonialists wish the black man to be thieving, indolent, and lying: he proves his indignity, putting the oppressors in the right; if he insists on being honest and loyal, he is regarded as quarrelsome. Woman's faults are amplified all the more to the extent that she will not try to combat them but, on the contrary, make an ornament of them.

Rejecting logical principles and moral imperatives, skeptical about the laws of nature, woman lacks a sense of the universal; the world seems to her a confused collection of individual cases; this is why she more readily accepts a neighbor's gossip than a scientific explanation; she doubt-less respects the printed book, but this respect skims along the written pages without grasping the content; by contrast, the anecdote told by an unknown person waiting in a line or in a drawing room instantly takes on overwhelming authority; in her domain, everything is magic; outside, everything is mystery; she is ignorant of the criterion for credibility; only immediate experience convinces her: her own experience or another's, as long as it is forcefully affirmed. As for herself, she feels she is a special case because she is isolated in her home and has no active contact with other women; she always expects destiny and men to make an exception in her favor; she believes in whatever insights come her way far more than in rea-soning that is valid for everyone; she readily admits that they have been sent by God or by some obscure world spirit; in relation to misfortunes or accidents, she calmly thinks, "That can't happen to me," or else she imag-ines, "I'll be the exception": she enjoys special favors; the shopkeeper will give her a discount, the policeman will let her go to the head of the line; she has been taught to overestimate the value of her smile, but no one told her that all women smiled. It is not that she thinks herself more special than her neighbor: it is that she does not make comparisons; for the same reason experience rarely proves her wrong: she suffers one failure, then another, but she does not add them up.

This is why women do not succeed in building a solid "counter-universe" where they can defy males; they sporadically rant against men in general, they tell stories about the bedroom or childbirth, they exchange horoscopes and beauty secrets. But to truly build this "world of griev-ances" that their resentment calls for, they lack conviction; their attitude to man is too ambivalent. Indeed, he is a child, a contingent and vulnerable body, an innocent, an unwanted drone, a mean tyrant, an egotist, a vain man: and he is also the liberating hero, the divinity who sets the standards. His desire is a gross appetite, his embraces a degrading chore: yet his ardor and virile force are also a demiurgic energy. When a woman ecstatically utters, "This is a man!" she is evoking both the sexual vigor and the social effectiveness of the male she admires: in both are expressed the same cre-ative sovereignty; she does not think he can be a great artist, a grand busi-nessman, a general, or a chief without being a great lover: his social success is always a sexual attraction; inversely, she is ready to recognize genius in the man who satisfies her. She is, in fact, turning to a masculine myth here. The phallus for Lawrence and many others is both living energy and human transcendence. Thus in the pleasures of the bed, woman can see a communion with the spirit of the world. Worshipping man as in a mystical

cult, she loses and finds herself in his glory. The contradiction is easily perceived here due to the different types of individuals who are virile.
Some—whose contingence she encounters in everyday life—are the incarnation of human misery; in others, man's grandeur is exalted. But the
woman even accepts that these two figures be fused into one. "If I become
famous," wrote a girl in love with a man she considered superior,
"R. . . . will surely marry me because it will flatter his vanity; his chest will
swell with me on his arm." Yet she admired him madly. The same individual, in the eyes of the woman, may very well be stingy, mean, vain, foolish,
and a god; after all, gods have their weaknesses. One feels a demanding
severity—the opposite of authentic esteem—for an individual who is
loved in his freedom and humanity, whereas a woman kneeling before her
male can very well pride herself on "knowing how to deal with him," or
"handle him," and she complaisantly flatters his "weaknesses" without his
losing prestige; this is the proof that she does not feel friendship for his
individual person as expressed in his real acts; blindly she bows to the general essence her idol is part of: virility is a sacred aura, a given fixed value,
which is affirmed despite the weaknesses of the individual who bears it;
this individual does not count; by contrast, the woman, jealous of his privilege, is delighted to exercise sly superiority over him.

The same ambiguity of woman's feelings for man is found in her general attitude concerning her self and the world; the domain in which she is
enclosed is invested by the masculine universe; but it is haunted by obscure
forces of which men themselves are the playthings; if she allies herself
with these magical virtues, she will, in her turn, acquire power. Society
subjugates Nature; but Nature dominates it; the Spirit affirms itself over
Life; but it dies if life no longer supports it. Woman uses this ambivalence
to assign more truth to a garden than a city, to an illness than an idea, to a
birth than a revolution; she tries to reestablish this reign of the earth, of the
Mother, imagined by Bachofen, to be able to find herself as the essential
facing the inessential. But as she herself is an existent that a transcendence
inhabits, she will only be able to valorize this region where she is confined
by transfiguring it: she lends it a transcendent dimension. Man lives in a
coherent universe that is a thought reality. Woman struggles with a magic
reality that does not allow thinking: she escapes through thoughts lacking
real content. Instead of assuming her existence, she contemplates in the
heavens the pure Idea of her destiny; instead of acting, she erects her statue
in her imagination; instead of reasoning, she dreams. From here comes the
fact that while being so "physical," she is also so artificial, while being so
terrestrial, she can be so ethereal. Her life is spent scrubbing pots and pans,

and it is a marvelous romance; vassal to man, she believes she is his idol; debased in her flesh, she exalts Love. Because she is condemned to know only life's contingent facticity, she becomes priestess of the Ideal.

This ambivalence is marked by the way woman deals with her body. It is a burden: weakened by the species, bleeding every month, passively propagating, for her it is not the pure instrument of her grasp on the world but rather an opaque presence; it is not certain that it will give her pleasure, and it creates pains that tear her apart; it contains threats: she feels danger in her "insides." Her body is "hysterical" because of the close connection between endocrine secretions and nervous and sympathetic systems commanding muscles and viscera; it expresses reactions the woman refuses to accept: in sobs, convulsions, and vomiting, her body escapes her, it betrays her; it is her most intimate reality, but it is a shameful reality that she keeps hidden. And yet it is her marvelous double; she contemplates it in the mirror with amazement; it is the promise of happiness, a work of art, a living statue; she shapes it, adorns it, displays it. When she smiles into the mirror, she forgets her carnal contingence; in love's embrace, in motherhood, her image disappears. But often, dreaming about herself, she is surprised to be both that heroine and that flesh.

Nature symmetrically provides her with a double face: it supplies the stew and incites mystical effusions. In becoming a housewife and mother, woman gave up her free getaways into fields and woods, she preferred the calm cultivation of the kitchen garden, she tamed flowers and put them in vases: yet she is still exalted by moonlights and sunsets. In the terrestrial fauna and flora, she sees food and ornamentation before all; yet a sap flows that is generosity and magic. Life is not only immanence and repetition: it is also a dazzling face of light; in flowering meadows, it is revealed as Beauty. In tune with nature by the fertility of her womb, woman also feels swept by the breath that animates her and is spirit. And insofar as she is unsatisfied and feels like the uncompleted and unlimited girl, her soul will then rush forward on endlessly unwinding roads toward limitless horizons. Slave to her husband, children, and home, she finds it intoxicating to be alone, sovereign on the hillside; she is no longer spouse, mother, housewife, but a human being; she contemplates the passive world: and she recalls that she is a whole consciousness, an irreducible freedom. In front of the mystery of water and the mountain summit's thrust, male supremacy is abolished; walking through the heather, dipping her hand in the river, she lives not for others but for herself. The woman who maintained her independence through all her servitudes will ardently love her own freedom in Nature. The others will find in it only the pretext for refined raptures, and they will hesitate at twilight between the fear of catching a cold and a swooning soul.

This double belonging to the carnal world and to a "poetic" world defines the metaphysics and wisdom to which the woman more or less explicitly adheres. She tries to combine life and transcendence; this is to say she rejects Cartesianism and all doctrines connected to it; she is comfortable in a naturalism similar to that of the Stoics or Neoplatonists of the sixteenth century: it is not surprising that women, Margaret of Navarre being the first of them, should be attached to such a philosophy, at once so material and so spiritual. Socially Manichaean, the woman has a deep need to be ontologically optimistic: the moralities of action do not suit her, since it is forbidden for her to act; she submits to the given: so the given must be Good; but a Good recognized by reason like that of Spinoza or by calculation like that of Leibniz cannot touch her. She requires a good that is a living Harmony and within which she situates herself by the mere fact of living. The notion of harmony is one of the keys of the feminine universe: it implies perfection in immobility, the immediate justification of each element as part of the whole, and her passive participation in the totality. In a harmonious world, woman thus attains what man will seek in action: she has purchase on the world, she is necessary to it, she cooperates in the triumph of Good. Moments women consider revelations are those where they discover they are in harmony with a reality based on peace with one's self. These are the moments of luminous happiness that Virginia Woolf—in *Mrs. Dalloway*, in *To the Lighthouse*—that Katherine Mansfield, all through her work, grant to their heroines as a supreme recompense. The joy that is a surge of freedom is reserved for the man; what the woman knows is an impression of smiling plenitude.[7] One understands that simple ataraxia, in her eyes, can be of utmost importance, as she normally lives in the tension of denial, recrimination, and demands; one could never reproach her for savoring a beautiful afternoon or the sweetness of an evening. But it is a delusion to try to find here the true definition of the hidden soul of the world. Good *is* not; the world is not harmony, and no individual has a necessary place in it.

---

7. Out of reams of texts, I will cite Mabel Dodge's lines where the passage to a global vision of the world is not explicit but is clearly suggested: "It was a still, autumn day, all yellow and crimson. Frieda and I, in a lapse of antagonism, sat on the ground together, with the red apples piled all around us. We were warmed and scented by the sun and the rich earth—and the apples were living tokens of plenitude and peace and rich living; the rich, natural flow of the earth, like the sappy blood in our veins, made us feel gay, indomitable, and fruitful like orchards. We were united for a moment, Frieda and I, in a mutual assurance of self-sufficiency, made certain, as women are sometimes, of our completeness by the sheer force of our bountiful health."

There is a justification, a supreme compensation, that society has always been bent on dispensing to woman: religion. There must be religion for women as for the people, for exactly the same reasons: when a sex or a class is condemned to immanence, the mirage of transcendence must be offered to it. It is to man's total advantage to have God endorse the codes he creates: and specifically because he exercises sovereign authority over the woman, it is only right that this authority be conferred on him by the sovereign being. Among others, for Jews, Muslims, and Christians, man is the master by divine right: fear of God will stifle the slightest inclination of revolt in the oppressed. Their credulity can be counted on. Woman adopts an attitude of respect and faith before the masculine universe: God in his heaven seems barely farther from her than a government minister, and the mystery of Genesis matches that of an electrical power station. But more important, if she throws herself so willingly into religion, it is because religion fills a profound need. In modern civilization, where freedom plays an important role—even for the woman—religion becomes less of an instrument of constraint than of mystification. The woman is less often asked to accept her inferiority in the name of God than to believe, thanks to him, that she is equal to the male lord; even the temptation to revolt is avoided by pretending to overcome injustice. The woman is no longer robbed of her transcendence, since she will dedicate her immanence to God; souls' merits are judged only in heaven and not according to their terrestrial accomplishments; here below, as Dostoevsky would have said, they are never more than occupations: shining shoes or building a bridge is the same vanity; over and above social discriminations, equality of the sexes is reestablished. This is why the little girl and the adolescent girl throw themselves into devotion with an infinitely greater fervor than their brothers; God's gaze that transcends his transcendence humiliates the boy: he will forever remain a child under this powerful guardianship, it is a more radical castration than that with which he feels his father's existence threatens him. But the "eternal girl child" finds her salvation in this gaze that metamorphoses her into a sister of the angels; it cancels out the privilege of the penis. A sincere faith helps the girl avoid all inferiority complexes: she is neither male nor female, but God's creature. This is why we find a virile steadfastness in the great female saints: Saint Bridget and Saint Catherine of Siena arrogantly tried to rule the world; they recognized no male authority: Catherine even directed her directors very severely; Joan of Arc and Saint Teresa followed their own paths with an intrepidness surpassed by no man. The Church sees to it that God never authorizes women to escape from male guardianship; it has put these powerful weapons in masculine hands only: refusal of absolution and excommunication; for her obstinate visions, Joan of Arc was burned at the stake. Nevertheless, even subjected by God's will to men's laws, the woman finds a solid recourse against them through him. Masculine logic is refuted by mysteries; males' pride becomes a sin, their agitation is not only absurd but culpable: Why remodel this world created by God himself? The passivity to which woman is doomed is sanctified. Reciting her rosary by the fire, she knows she is closer to heaven than her husband, who is out at political meetings. There is no need to *do* anything to save her soul, it is enough to *live* without disobeying. The synthesis of life and spirit is completed: the mother not only engenders body but also gives God a soul; this is higher work than penetrating the secrets of the atom. With the complicity of the heavenly Father, woman can make a claim to the glory of her femininity against man.

Not only does God thus reestablish the dignity of the feminine sex in general, but every woman will find special support in the celestial absence; as a human person, she carries little weight; but as soon as she acts in the name of divine inspiration, her desires become sacred. Mme Guyon says that, concerning a nun's illness, she learned "what it meant to command by the Word and obey by the same Word"; thus the devotee camouflages her authority in humble obedience; raising her children, governing a convent, or organizing a charity, she is but a docile tool in supernatural hands; one cannot disobey her without offending God himself. To be sure, men do not disdain this support either; but it loses its force when they encounter other men who make equal claim to it: the conflict finishes by being solved on a human level. Woman invokes divine will to justify her authority absolutely in the eyes of those who are naturally subordinated to her, and to justify it in her own eyes. If this cooperation is useful for her, it is because she is above all concerned with her relations with herself—even when those relations interest others; it is only in these totally interior debates that the Supreme Silence can have the force of law. In truth, woman uses the pretext of religion to satisfy her desires. Frigid, masochistic, or sadistic, she sanctifies herself by renouncing the flesh, playing the victim, stifling every living impulse around her; mutilating and annihilating herself, she rises in the ranks of the chosen; when she martyrs husband and children by depriving them of all terrestrial happiness, she is preparing them for a choice place in paradise; "to punish herself for having sinned," Margaret of Cortona's pious biographers recount, she maltreated the child of her sin; she fed him only after feeding all the beggars she passed; we have seen that hatred of the unwanted child is common: it is a godsend to be able to express it in a virtuous rage. On her side, a woman whose morals are loose conveniently makes an arrangement with God; the certainty of being puri-

fied from sin by absolution tomorrow often helps the pious woman conquer her scruples now. Whether she has chosen asceticism or sensuality,
pride or humility, the concern she has for her salvation encourages her to
give in to this pleasure that she prefers over all others: taking care of self;
she listens to her heart beat, she watches every quiver of her flesh, justified
by the presence of grace within herself, like the pregnant woman with her
fruit. Not only does she examine herself with tender vigilance, but she
reports to her confessor; in days gone by, she could savor the headiness of
public confessions. We are told that Margaret of Cortona, to punish herself
for an act of vanity, climbed onto her terrace and began to cry out like a
woman in labor: "Wake up, people of Cortona, wake up and bring candles
and lanterns and come out to hear the sinner!" She enumerated all her sins,
proclaiming her misery to the stars. By this noisy humility, she satisfied this
need for exhibitionism, found in so many examples of narcissistic women.
For the woman, religion authorizes self-indulgence; it gives her the guide,
father, lover, titular divinity she nostalgically needs; it feeds her reveries; it
fills her empty hours. But especially, it confirms the world order; it justifies
resignation by bringing hope for a better future in an asexual heaven. This
is why today women are still a powerful asset in the hands of the Church; it
is why the Church is so hostile to any measure that might facilitate their
emancipation. Women must have religion; there must be women, "real
women," to perpetuate religion.

It is clear that woman's whole "character"—her convictions, values,
wisdom, morality, tastes, and behavior—is explained by her situation. The
fact that she is denied transcendence usually prohibits her from having
access to the loftiest human attitudes—heroism, revolt, detachment, invention, and creation—but they are not so common even in men. There are
many men who are, like woman, confined within the domain of the intermediary, of inessential means; the worker escapes from it through political
action, expressing a revolutionary will; but men from what we precisely
call the "middle" class settle in this sphere deliberately; destined like the
woman to the repetition of daily tasks, alienated in ready-made values,
respecting public opinion, and only seeking vague comforts on earth, the
employee, the shopkeeper, and the bureaucrat hold no superiority over
their women companions; cooking, washing, running her home, raising
her children, the woman shows more initiative and independence than the
man enslaved to orders; he must obey his superiors every day, wear a
removable collar, and affirm his social rank; she can lie about in a housecoat
in her apartment, sing, laugh with her women neighbors; she acts as she
pleases, takes small risks, and efficiently tries to attain a few results. She

lives much less according to convention and appearances than does her husband. The bureaucratic world described by Kafka—among others—this universe of ceremonies, absurd gestures, meaningless behavior, is essentially masculine; she has greater purchase on reality; when he lines up his figures, or converts sardine boxes into money, he grasps nothing but abstracts; the child content in his cradle, clean laundry, the roast, are more tangible things; yet, just because she feels their contingence—and consequently her own contingence—in the concrete pursuit of these objectives, it often happens that she does not alienate herself in them: she remains available. Man's undertakings are both projects and escapes: he lets himself be overwhelmed by his career, his personage; he is readily self-important, serious; contesting masculine logic and morality, woman does not fall into these traps: that is what Stendhal appreciated so strongly in her; she does not resort to pride to elude the ambiguity of her condition; she does not hide behind the mask of human dignity; she reveals her undisciplined thoughts, her emotions, her spontaneous reactions with more sincerity. This is why her conversation is far less boring than her husband's whenever she speaks in her own name and not as her seigneur's loyal half; he recites so-called general ideas, meaning words and formulas found in the columns of his newspaper or in specialist works; she brings experience, limited but concrete. The famous "feminine sensitivity" is part myth, part theater; but the fact remains that woman is more attentive than man to herself and the world. Sexually, she lives in a crude masculine climate: she compensates by appreciating "pretty things," which can lead to sentimentality, but also to refinement; because her sphere is limited, the objects she touches are precious to her: by not binding them in concepts or projects, she displays their splendor; her desire for escape is expressed in her taste for festiveness: she enjoys the gratuitousness of a bouquet of flowers, a cake, a well-laid table, she is pleased to transform the emptiness of her idle hours into a generous offering; loving laughter, songs, adornment, and knickknacks, she is also ready to welcome everything that palpitates around her: the spectacle of the street, of the sky; an invitation or an excursion offers her new horizons; the man often refuses to participate in these pleasures; when he comes home, joyous voices become silent, and the women in the family assume the bored and proper air expected of them. From the depths of solitude, of separation, the woman finds the sense of the singularity of her life: she has a more intimate experience than the man of the past, death, of time passing; she is concerned with the adventures of her heart, her flesh, her mind, because she knows that on earth she has but one lot; and also, because she is passive, she bears the reality that submerges her in a more passionate manner, with more pathos than the individual absorbed by an ambition or job; she has the leisure and the tendency to abandon herself to her emotions, study her feelings, and draw conclusions from them. When her imagination is not lost in vain dreams, she becomes full of sympathy: she tries to understand the other in his uniqueness and re-create him in herself; regarding her husband, her lover, she is capable of true identification: she makes his projects and his cares her own in a way he could not imitate. She watches anxiously over the whole world; it seems to be an enigma to her: each being, every object, can be a reply; she questions avidly. When she grows older, her disenchanted expectation is converted into irony and an often piquant cynicism; she refuses masculine mystifications, she sees the contingent, absurd, gratuitous reverse side of the imposing structure built by males. Her dependence prohibits detachment for her; but she draws real generosity from her imposed devotion; she forgets herself in favor of her husband, her lover, her child, she ceases to think of herself, she is pure offering, gift. Being poorly adapted to men's society, she is often forced to invent her own conduct; she is less able to settle for ready-made patterns and clichés; if she is of goodwill, her apprehensions are closer to authenticity than is her husband's self-confidence.

But she will only have these advantages over her husband if she rejects the mystifications he offers her. In the upper classes, women are willing accomplices to their masters because they stand to profit from the benefits they are guaranteed. We have seen that women of the high bourgeoisie and aristocracy have always defended their class interests more stubbornly than their husbands: they do not hesitate to radically sacrifice their autonomy as human beings; they stifle all thinking, all critical judgment, all spontaneity; they parrot conventional wisdom, they identify with the ideal imposed on them by the male code; in their hearts, and even on their faces, all sincerity is dead. The housewife regains independence in her work, in caring for the children: she draws a limited but concrete experience from it: a woman who is "waited on" no longer has any grasp on the world; she lives in dreams and abstraction, in a void. She is unaware of the reach of the ideas she professes; the words she rattles off have lost all meaning in her mouth; the banker, the businessman, and even at times the general take risks, accepting exhaustion and problems; they purchase their privileges in an unfair market, but at least they pay for them themselves; for all they receive, their wives give nothing, do nothing in return; and they even more righteously believe in their imprescriptible rights with a blind faith. Their vain arrogance, their radical incapability, their stubborn ignorance, turn them into the most useless beings, the most idiotic that the human species has ever produced.

It is thus as absurd to speak of "the woman" in general as of "the eternal man." And we can see why all comparisons where we try to decide if the woman is superior, inferior, or equal to the man are pointless: their situations are profoundly different. If these same situations are compared, it is obvious that the man's is infinitely preferable, that is to say, he has far more concrete opportunities to project his freedom in the world; the inevitable result is that masculine realizations outweigh by far those of women: for women, it is practically forbidden to *do* anything. But to compare the use that, within their limits, men and women make of their freedom is a priori meaningless, precisely because they use it freely. In various forms, the traps of bad faith and the mystifications of seriousness are lying in wait for both of them; freedom is entire in each. However, because of the fact that in woman this freedom remains abstract and empty, it cannot authentically assume itself except in revolt: this is the only way open to those who have no chance to build anything; they must refuse the limits of their situation and seek to open paths to the future; resignation is only a surrender and an evasion; for woman there is no other way out than to work for her liberation.

This liberation can only be collective, and it demands above all that the economic evolution of the feminine condition be accomplished. There have been and there still are many women who do seek to attain individual salvation on their own. They try to justify their existence within their own immanence, that is, to achieve transcendence through immanence. It is this ultimate effort—sometimes ridiculous, often pathetic—of the imprisoned woman to convert her prison into a heaven of glory, her servitude into sovereign freedom, that we find in the narcissist, the woman in love, and the mystic.

PART THREE

JUSTIFICATIONS

CHAPTER 11

The Narcissist

It has sometimes been asserted that narcissism is the fundamental attitude of all women;[1] but overextending this notion destroys it as La Rochefoucauld destroyed the notion of egotism. In fact, narcissism is a well-defined process of alienation: the self is posited as an absolute end, and the subject escapes itself in it. There are many other—authentic or inauthentic—attitudes found in woman: we have already studied some of them. What is true is that circumstances invite woman more than man to turn toward self and to dedicate her love to herself.

All love demands the duality of a subject and an object. Woman is led to narcissism by two convergent paths. As subject, she is frustrated; as a little girl, she was deprived of this alter ego that the penis is for the boy; later, her aggressive sexuality remained unsatisfied. Of far greater importance is that she is forbidden virile activities. She is busy, but she does not *do* anything; in her functions as wife, mother, and housewife, she is not recognized in her singularity. Man's truth is in the houses he builds, the forests he clears, the patients he cures: not being able to accomplish herself in projects and aims, woman attempts to grasp herself in the immanence of her person. Parodying Sieyès's words, Marie Bashkirtseff wrote: "Who am I? Nothing. What would I like to be? All." It is because they are nothing that many women fiercely limit their interests to their self alone, that their self becomes hypertrophied so as to be confounded with All. "I am my own heroine," continues Marie Bashkirtseff. A man who acts necessarily confronts himself. Inefficient and separated, woman can neither situate nor assess herself; she gives herself sovereign importance because no important object is accessible to her.

If she can put *herself* forward in her own desires, it is because since

---

1. Cf. Helene Deutsch, *Psychology of Women.*

childhood she has seen herself as an object. Her education has encouraged her to alienate herself wholly in her body, puberty having revealed this body as passive and desirable; it is a thing she can touch, that satin or velvet arouses, and that she can contemplate with a lover's gaze. In solitary pleasure, it may happen that the woman splits into a male subject and a female object; Dalbiez studied the case of Irène, who said to herself, "I'm going to love myself," or more passionately, "I'm going to possess myself," or in a paroxysm, "I'm going to fecundate myself."[2] Marie Bashkirtseff is also both subject and object when she writes, "It's really a pity that no one sees my arms and torso, all this freshness and youth."

In truth, it is not possible to be *for self* positively Other and grasp oneself as object in the light of consciousness. Doubling is only dreamed. For the child, it is the doll that materializes this dream; she recognizes herself in it more concretely than in her own body because there is separation between the two. Mme de Noailles expresses this need to be two so as to establish a tender dialogue between self and self in, among other works, *Le livre de ma vie* (The Book of My Life):

> I loved dolls, I endowed their immobility with the life of my own existence; I could not have slept under the warmth of a cover if they were not also wrapped in wool and feathers . . . I dreamed of truly savoring pure solitude as two . . . This need to persist intact, to be twice myself, I felt it avidly as a little child . . . Oh! How I wanted in the tragic instants where my dreamy sweetness was the plaything of hurtful tears to have another little Anna next to me who would throw her arms around my neck, who would console me, understand me . . . during my life I met her in my heart and I held her tight: she helped me not in the form of hoped-for consolation but in the form of courage.

The adolescent girl leaves her dolls dormant. But throughout her life, woman will be vigorously encouraged to leave and come back to herself by the magic of the mirror. Otto Rank brought to light the mirror-double relation in myths and dreams. It is above all in woman that the reflection allows itself to be assimilated to the self. Male beauty is a sign of transcen-

---

2. Dalbiez, *La méthode psychanalytique et la doctrine freudienne* (*Psychoanalytical Method and the Doctrine of Freud*). In her childhood, Irène liked to urinate like boys; she often sees herself in her dreams in undine form, which confirms Havelock Ellis's ideas on the relation between narcissism and what he calls "undinism"; that is, a certain urinary eroticism.

dence, that of woman has the passivity of immanence: the latter alone is made to arrest man's gaze and can thus be caught in the immobile trap of the mirror's silvering; man who feels and wants himself to be activity and subjectivity does not recognize himself in his immobile image; it does not appeal to him, since the man's body does not appear to him as an object of desire; while the woman, knowing she is and making herself object, really believes she is seeing *herself* in the mirror: passive and given, the reflection is a thing like herself; and as she covets feminine flesh, her flesh, she enlivens the inert qualities she sees with her admiration and desire. Mme de Noailles, who knew about this, confides to us:

> I was less vain about the gifts of the mind, so vigorous in me that I did not doubt them, than about the image reflected by a frequently consulted mirror . . . Only physical pleasure satisfies the soul fully.

The words "physical pleasure" are vague and inadequate here. What satisfies the soul is that, while the mind will have to prove its worth, the contemplated face is here, today, given and indubitable. The whole future is concentrated in this rectangle of light, and its frame makes a universe; outside these narrow limits, things are no more than disorganized chaos; the world is reduced to this piece of glass where one image shines: the One and Only. Every woman drowned in her reflection reigns over space and time, alone, sovereign; she has total rights over men, fortune, glory, and sensual pleasure. Marie Bashkirtseff was so intoxicated by her beauty that she wanted to fix it in indestructible marble; it is herself she would have thus destined to immortality:

> Coming home I get undressed, I am naked and am struck by the beauty of my body as if I had never seen it. A statue has to be made of me, but how? Without getting married, it is almost impossible. And I have to, I would only get ugly, spoiled . . . I have to take a husband, if only to have my statue made.

Cécile Sorel, preparing for an amorous rendezvous, depicts herself like this:

> I am in front of my mirror. I would like to be more beautiful. I fight with my lion's mane. Sparks fly from my comb. My head is a sun in the middle of my tresses set like golden rays.

I also recall a young woman I saw one morning in the restroom of a café; she was holding a rose, and she looked a little drunk; she brought her lips to the mirror as if to drink her image, and she was murmuring while smiling: "Adorable, I find myself adorable." Both priestess and idol, the narcissist crowned with glory hovers in the heart of eternity, and on the other side of the clouds kneeling creatures worship her: she is God contemplating himself. "I love myself, I am my God!" said Mme Mejerowsky. To become God is to realize the impossible synthesis of the in-itself and for-itself: the moments an individual thinks he has succeeded are special times of joy, exaltation, and plenitude. One day in an attic, Roussel, at nineteen, felt the aura of glory around his head: he never got over it. The girl who saw beauty, desire, love, and happiness deep in her mirror, endowed with her own features—animated, so she thinks, by her own consciousness—will try her whole life to use the promises of this blinding revelation. "It is you I love," confides Marie Bashkirtseff to her reflection one day. Another day she writes: "I love myself so much, I make myself so happy that I was as if crazy at dinner." Even if the woman is not of irreproachable beauty, she will see her soul's unique riches appear on her face, and that will be enough to make her drunk. In the novel where she portrayed herself as Valérie, Mme Krüdener describes herself like this:

> She has something special that I have never yet seen in any woman.
> One can be as graceful, much more beautiful, and be far from her.
> She is perhaps not admired, but she has something ideal and charming that makes one pay attention. Seeing her so delicate, so svelte that she is a thought . . .

It should not be surprising that those less advantaged might sometimes experience the ecstasy of the mirror: they are moved by the mere fact of being a thing of flesh, which is there; like man, all they need is the pure generosity of young feminine flesh; and since they grasp themselves as a singular subject, with a little bad faith they will also endow their generic qualities with an individual charm; they will discover some gracious, rare, or amusing feature in their face or body; they will think they are beautiful just because they feel they are women.

Moreover, the mirror is not the only instrument of doubling, although it is the favored one. Each person can try to create a twin brother in his inner dialogue. Alone most of the day, fed up with household tasks, woman has the leisure to shape her own figure in dreams. As a young girl, she dreamed of the future; trapped in an uncertain present, she tells her story

to herself; she retouches it so as to introduce an aesthetic order, transforming her contingent life into a destiny well before her death.

We know, for example, how attached women are to their childhood
memories; women's literature makes it clear; in general, childhood takes a
secondary place in men's autobiographies; women, on the other hand,
often go no further than recounting their early years; these are the favorite
subjects of their novels and stories. A woman who confides in a woman
friend or a lover almost always begins her stories with these words: "When
I was a little girl . . ." They are nostalgic for this period when they felt their
father's beneficent and imposing hand on their head while tasting the joys
of independence; protected and justified by adults, they were autonomous
individuals with a free future opening before them: now, however, they are
poorly protected by marriage and love and have become servants or
objects, imprisoned in the present. They reigned over the world, conquering it day after day: and now they are separated from the universe, doomed
to immanence and repetition. They feel dispossessed. But what they suffer
from the most is being swallowed up in generality: a wife, mother, housewife, or one woman among millions of others; as a child, by contrast, the
woman lived her condition in an individual way; she was unaware of the
analogies between her apprenticeship to the world and that of her friends;
through her parents, teachers, and friends, she was recognized in her individuality, she thought herself incomparable to any other woman, unique,
promised to unique possibilities. She returns emotionally to this younger
sister whose freedom, demands, and sovereignty she abdicated and whom
she more or less betrayed. The woman she has become misses this human
being she was; she tries to find this dead child in her deepest self. The
words "little girl" move her; but "What a funny little girl" do even more,
words that revive her lost originality.

She is not satisfied with marveling from afar at this precious childhood:
she tries to revive it in her. She tries to convince herself that her tastes,
ideas, and feelings have kept their exceptional freshness. Perplexed, quizzi-
cal, and playing with her necklace or twisting her ring, she murmurs:
"That's funny . . . That's just how I am . . . You know? Water fascinates
me . . . Oh! I adore the countryside." Each preference seems like an eccen-
tricity, each opinion a challenge to the world. Dorothy Parker captured this
widespread true-to-life characteristic:

> She liked to think of herself as one for whom flowers would thrive,
> who must always have blossoms about her, if she would be truly
> happy . . . She told people, in little bursts of confidence, that she

loved flowers. There was something almost apologetic in her way of uttering her tender avowal, as if she would beg her listeners not to consider her too bizarre in her taste. It seemed rather as though she expected the hearer to fall back, startled, at her words, crying, "Not really! Well, what *are* we coming to?" She had other little confessions of affection . . . always with a little hesitation, as if understandably delicate about baring her heart, she told her love for color, the country, a good time, a really interesting play, nice materials, well-made clothes, and sunshine. But it was her fondness for flowers that she acknowledged oftenest. She seemed to feel that this, even more than her other predilections, set her apart from the general.*

The woman eagerly tries to confirm these analyses in her behavior; she chooses a color: "Green is really my color"; she has a favorite flower, perfume, musician, superstitions, and fetishes that she treats with respect; she does not have to be beautiful to express her personality in her outfits and home. The character she portrays is more or less coherent and original according to her intelligence, obstinacy, and depth of alienation. Some women just randomly put together a few sparse and mismatched traits; others systematically create a figure whose role they consistently play: it has already been said that women have trouble differentiating this game from the truth. Around this heroine, life goes on like a sad or marvelous novel, always somewhat strange. Sometimes it is a novel already written. I do not know how many girls have told me they see themselves in Judy of "Dust."† I remember an old, very ugly lady who used to say: "Read *The Lily in the Valley*:‡ it's my story"; as a child I used to contemplate this wilted lily for hours. Others, more vaguely, murmur: "My life is a novel." A good or bad star hovers over them. "Things like this only happen to me," they say. Rotten luck dogs them, or good luck smiles on them: in any case, they have a destiny. Cécile Sorel writes with the naïveté that characterizes her *Mémoires*: "This is how I made my debut in the world. My first friends were genius and beauty." And in *The Book of My Life*, a fabulous narcissistic monument, Mme de Noailles writes:

The governesses disappeared one day: chance took their place. It mistreated the creature both powerful and weak as much as it had

---

satisfied it, it kept it from shipwrecks, where it was like a combative Ophelia, saving her flowers and whose voice ever rises. It asked the creature to hope that this final promise be kept: The Greeks use death.

This other example of narcissistic literature must be cited:

From the sturdy little girl I was with delicate but rounded arms and legs and healthy cheeks, I acquired a more frail physique, more evanescent that made me a pathetic adolescent, in spite of the source of life that can spring forth from my desert, my famine, and my brief and mysterious deaths as strangely as Moses's rock. I will not boast of my courage as I have the right to. It is part of my strengths, my luck. I could describe it as one says: I have green eyes, black hair, a small and powerful hand.

And these lines too:

Today I can recognize that, bolstered by my soul and its harmonious powers, I have lived to the sound of my voice.

Without beauty, brilliance, or happiness, woman will choose the character of a victim; she will obstinately embody the *mater dolorosa*, the misunderstood wife, she will be "the unhappiest woman in the world." This is the case of this melancholic woman Stekel describes:

Each time around Christmas, Mrs. H.W. appears at my office, palefaced, clad in somber black and complains of her fate. She relates a sad story while tears stream down her face. A thwarted existence, an unfortunate marriage! . . . The first time I was moved to tears and would have almost wept with her . . . Two years have since flown* . . . but she is still at the threshold of her hopes, still bewailing her misspent life . . . her face begins to show the early signs of the disintegration brought on by age. She thus has an additional reason for bemoaning her fate . . . "What has become of me! I was once so beautiful and so much admired" . . . Her complaints are cumulative; she stresses her despair. Her friends . . . are well familiar with her sad

---

* Stekel says "Ten years."—TRANS.

plight . . . She makes herself a nuisance to everybody with her perpetual complaints . . . this in turn again furnishes her the opportunity to feel herself lonely, abandoned, not understood . . . This woman found her satisfaction in the *tragic role*. The thought that she was the unhappiest woman on earth intoxicated her . . . All attempts to awaken her interest in the active current life ended in failure.[3]

A trait shared by young Mrs. Weldon, stunning Anna de Noailles, Stekel's unfortunate patient, and the multitude of women marked by an exceptional destiny is that they feel misunderstood; their family and friends do not recognize—or inadequately recognize—their singularity; they transform this ignorance, this indifference of others, into the positive idea that they hold a secret inside them. The fact is that many have silently buried childhood and youthful memories that had a great importance for them; they know their official biography is not to be confused with their real history. But above all, because she has not realized herself in her life, the heroine cherished by the narcissist is merely an imaginary character; her unity does not come from the concrete world: it is a hidden principle, a kind of "strength," "virtue" as obscure as phlogistonism; the woman believes in its presence, but if she wanted to show it to others, she would be as bothered as the psychasthenic determined to confess to intangible crimes. In both cases, the "secret" is reduced to the empty conviction of possessing in one's deepest self a key to decipher and justify feelings and behavior. It is their abulia and inertia that give this illusion to psychasthenics; and it is because of her inability to express herself in daily action that woman believes an inexpressible mystery inhabits her: the famous myth of the eternal feminine encourages her in this and is thus, in turn, confirmed.

Enriched by these misunderstood treasures, whether she be under a lucky or an unlucky star, woman, in her own eyes, adopts the tragic hero's need to be governed by destiny. Her whole life is transfigured into a sacred drama. In her solemnly chosen dress emerges both a priestess clothed in holy garb and an idol attired by faithful hands, offered for the adoration of devotees. Her home becomes her temple of worship. Marie Bashkirtseff gives as much care to the decoration she places around her as to her dresses:

Near the desk, an old-style armchair, so that upon entering, I need make only a small movement in the chair to find myself facing the

---

3. *Frigidity in Woman.*

people . . . near the pedantic-looking desk with books in the background, in between, paintings and plants, legs and feet visible
instead of being cut in two as before by this black wood. Hanging
above the divan are two mandolins and the guitar. Put a blond and
white girl with fine small blue-veined hands in the middle of this.

When she parades in salons, when she abandons herself on the arm of
a lover, the woman accomplishes her mission: she is Venus dispensing the
treasures of her beauty to the world. It is not she herself, it is Beauty that
Cécile Sorel defended when she broke the glass covering Bib's caricature of
her; one can see in her *Mémoires* that she invited mortals to the cult of Art
at each moment of her life. Likewise, Isadora Duncan, as she depicts herself in *My Life:*

After a performance, in my tunic, with my hair crowned with roses,
I was so lovely. Why should not this loveliness be enjoyed? . . . A
man who labours all day with his brain . . . why should he not be
taken in those beautiful arms and find comfort for his pain and a few
hours of beauty and forgetfulness?

The narcissist's generosity is profitable to her: better than in mirrors, it
is in others' admiring eyes she sees her double haloed in glory. Without a
complaisant audience, she opens her heart to a confessor, doctor, or psycho-
analyst; she will consult chiromancers, mediums. "It's not that I believe in
it," said an aspiring starlet, "but I love it so much when I'm spoken about!"
She talks about herself to her women friends; more avidly than in anything
else, she seeks a witness in the lover. The woman in love quickly forgets
herself; but many women are incapable of real love, precisely because they
never forget themselves. They prefer the wider stage to the privacy of the
bedroom. Thus the importance of society life for them: they need gazes to
contemplate them, ears to listen to them; they need the widest possible audience for their personage. Describing her room once more, Marie Bashkirtseff reveals: "Like this, *I am on stage* when someone enters and finds me
writing." And further on: "I decided to buy myself a *considerable mise en
scène.* I am going to build a more beautiful townhouse and grander workshops than Sarah's."
And Mme de Noailles writes:

I loved and love the agora . . . And so I have often reassured my
friends who apologized for the many guests they feared I would be

importuned by with this sincere admission: I don't like *to play to empty seats.*

Dressing up and conversation largely satisfy this feminine taste for display. But an ambitious narcissist wants to exhibit herself in a more recherché and varied way. In particular, making her life a play offered to public applause, she will take delight in really staging herself. In *Corinne*, Mme de Staël recounts at length how she charmed Italian crowds by reciting poems that she accompanied on a harp. At Coppet, one of her favorite pastimes was to declaim tragic roles; playing Phaedra, she would readily make ardent declarations to young lovers whom she dressed up as Hippolytus. Mme Krüdener specialized in the dance of the shawl that she describes in *Valérie*:

> Valérie required a dark blue muslin shawl, she took her hair away
> from her forehead; she put the shawl on her head; it went down
> along her temples and shoulders; her forehead appeared in an
> antique manner, her hair disappeared, her eyelids lowered, her usual
> smile faded little by little: her head bent, her shawl fell softly on her
> crossed arms, on her bust, and this blue piece of clothing and this
> pure and gentle figure seem to have been drawn by Correggio to
> express tranquil resignation; and when her eyes looked up, and her
> lips dared a smile, one could say that one was seeing, as Shakespeare
> described it, Patience smiling at Pain in front of a monument . . .
>   One has to see Valérie. She is simultaneously timid, noble, and
> profoundly sensitive, and she troubles, leads, moves, draws tears,
> and makes the heart beat as it beats when dominated by a great
> ascendant; it is she who possesses this charming grace that cannot
> be taught but that nature secretly reveals to some superior beings.

If circumstances allow it, nothing will give the narcissist deeper satisfaction than devoting herself publicly to the theater. "The theatre," says Georgette Leblanc, "provided me what I had sought in it: a reason for exaltation. Today, it is for me the *caricature of action*, something indispensable for excessive temperaments." The expression she uses is striking: if she cannot take action, the woman invents substitutes for action; the theater represents a privileged substitute for some women. The actress can have very different aims. For some, acting is a means of earning one's living, a simple profession; for others, it is access to fame that will be exploited for amorous aims; for still others, the triumph of their narcissism; the greatest—Rachel, Eleonora Duse—are authentic artists who transcend themselves in the roles they create; the ham, by contrast, cares not for what she accomplishes but for the glory that will cascade over her; she seeks above all to put herself in the limelight. The stubborn narcissist will be as limited in art as in love because she does not know how to give herself.

This failing will be seriously felt in all her activities. She will be tempted by all roads leading to glory; but she will never unreservedly take any. Painting, sculpture, and literature are disciplines requiring strict training and demanding solitary work; many women try such work but quickly abandon it if they are not driven by a positive desire to create; and many of those who persevere never do more than "play" at working. Marie Bashkirtseff, so avid for glory, spent hours in front of her easel; but she loved herself too much to seriously love to paint. She admits it herself after years of bitterness. "Yes, I don't take the trouble to paint, I watched myself today, I *cheat*." When a woman succeeds, like Mme de Staël or Mme de Noailles, in building a body of work, it is because she is not exclusively absorbed by self-worship: but one of the burdens that weighs on many women writers is a self-indulgence that hurts their sincerity, limits and diminishes them.

Many women imbued with a feeling of superiority, however, are not able to show it to the world; their ambition will thus be to use a man whom they convince of their worth as their means of intervention; they do not aim for specific values through free projects; they want to attach ready-made values to their egos; they will thus turn—by becoming muses, inspiration, and stimulation—to those who hold influence and glory in the hope of being identified with them. A striking example is Mabel Dodge in her relations with Lawrence:

> I wanted to seduce his spirit so that I could make him carry out certain things . . . It was his soul I needed for my purpose, his soul, his will, his creative imagination, and his lighted vision. The only way to obtain the ascendancy over these essential tools was by way of the blood . . . I was always trying to get things done: I didn't often even try to do anything myself. I seemed to want to use all my power upon delegates to carry out the work. This way—*perhaps a compensation for that desolate and barren feeling of having nothing to do!*—I achieved a sense of fruitfulness and activity vicariously.*

---

* Luhan, *Lorenzo in Taos*, Simone de Beauvoir's italics.—TRANS.

And further on:

> I wanted Lawrence to understand things for me. To take *my* experience, *my* material, *my* Taos, and to formulate it all into a magnificent creation.

In a similar way, Georgette Leblanc wanted to be "food and flame" for Maeterlinck; but she also wanted to see her name inscribed in the poet's book. This is not, here, a question of ambitious women having chosen personal aims and using men to reach them—as did Mme de Staël and the princesse des Ursins—but rather of women animated by a wholly subjective desire for *importance,* with no objective aim, trying to appropriate for themselves the transcendence of another. They do not always succeed—far from it—but they are skillful in hiding their failure and in persuading themselves that they are endowed with irresistible seduction. Knowing they are lovable, desirable, and admirable, they feel certain of being loved, desired, and admired. Bélise is wholly narcissistic. Even the innocent Brett, devoted to Lawrence, invents for herself a little personage she endows with weighty seduction:

> I raise my eyes and see that you are looking at me with your mischievous faun-like air, a provocative gleam in your eyes, Pan. I stare back at you with a solemn and dignified air until the gleam goes out of your face.

These illusions can give rise to real derangement; Clérambault had good reason to consider erotomania "a kind of professional derangement"; to feel like a woman is to feel like a desirable object, to believe oneself desired and loved. It is significant that nine out of ten patients with "illusions of being loved" are women. They are clearly seeking in their imaginary lover the apotheosis of their narcissism. They want him to be endowed with unconditional distinction: priest, doctor, lawyer, superior man; and the unquestionable truth his behavior reveals is that his ideal mistress is superior to all other women, that she possesses irresistible and sovereign virtues.

Erotomania can be part of various psychoses; but its content is always the same. The subject is illuminated and glorified by the love of an admirable man who was suddenly fascinated by her charms—though she expected nothing from him—and displays his feelings in a circuitous but imperious way; this relation at times remains ideal and at other times

assumes a sexual form; but what characterizes it essentially is that the powerful and glorious demigod loves more than he is loved and he displays his
passion in bizarre and ambiguous behavior. Among the great number of
cases reported by psychiatrists, here is a typical one adapted from Ferdière.[4] It concerns a forty-eight-year-old woman, Marie-Yvonne, who
makes the following confession:

> This is about Mr. Achille, Esq., former deputy and undersecretary of
> state, member of the bar and the Conseil de l'Ordre. I have known
> him since May 12, 1920; the evening before, I tried to meet him at the
> courts; from afar I had noticed his strong stature, but I did not know
> who he was; it sent chills up my spine . . . Yes, there is an affair of
> feeling between us, a reciprocal feeling: our eyes, our gazes, met.
> From the moment I saw him, I had a liking for him; it is the same for
> him . . . In any case, he declared his feeling first: it was early in 1922;
> he received me in his home, always alone; one day he even sent his
> son out . . . One day . . . he got up and came toward me, carrying on
> with his conversation. I understood right away that it was a senti-
> mental surge . . . His words made me understand. By various
> kindnesses he made me understand we had reciprocal feelings.
> Another time, once again in his office, he approached me saying:
> "It is you, it is you alone and no one else, Madam, you understand
> clearly." I was so taken aback that I did not know what to answer; I
> simply said, "Thank you, sir!" Then another time he accompanied
> me from his office to the street; he even got rid of a man who was
> with him, he gave him twenty sous in the staircase and told him:
> "Leave me, my boy, you see I am with Madam!" All of that was to
> accompany me and be alone with me. He always shook my hands
> tightly. During his first court pleading, he made a comment to let
> me know he was a bachelor.
>
> He sent a singer to my courtyard to demonstrate his love
> to me . . . He watched my windows; I could sing you his
> romance . . . He had a town band march by my door. I was foolish.
> I should have responded to his advances. I gave M. Achille the cold
> shoulder . . . he thus thought I was rejecting him and he took action;
> he should have spoken out openly; he took revenge on me.
> M. Achille thought that I had feelings for B. . . . and he was

---

4. *L'érotomanie* (Erotomania).

jealous . . . He made me suffer by putting a magic spell on my photograph; at least that is what I discovered this year through studies in books and dictionaries. He worked enough on this photo: it all comes from that.

This delusion easily changes, in fact, into a persecution complex. And this process is found even in normal cases. The narcissist cannot accept that others are not passionately interested in her; if she has the clear proof she is not adored, she immediately supposes she is hated. She attributes all criticism to jealousy or spite. Her failures are the result of dark machinations: and thus they confirm her in the idea of her importance. She easily slips into megalomania or the opposite, persecution delirium: as center of her universe and aware of no other universe except her own, she becomes the absolute center of the world.

But narcissist drama plays itself out at the expense of real life; an imaginary personage solicits the admiration of an imaginary public; a woman tormented by her ego loses all hold on the concrete world, she does not care about establishing any real relationship with others; Mme de Staël would not declaim *Phaedra* so wholeheartedly if she had foreseen the mockeries her "admirers" noted that night in their notebooks; but the narcissist refuses to accept she can be seen other than as she shows herself: this is what explains why, so busy contemplating herself, she totally fails to judge herself, and she falls so easily into ridiculousness. She no longer listens, she talks, and when she talks, she recites her lines. Marie Bashkirtseff writes: "It amuses me. I don't speak with him, I *act* and, feeling I am in front of a receptive audience, I am excellent at childlike and fanciful intonations and attitudes."

She looks at herself too much to see anything; she understands in others only what she recognizes about them; whatever she cannot assimilate to her own case, to her own story, remains foreign to her. She likes to expand her experiences: she wants to experience the headiness and torments of being in love, the pure joys of motherhood, friendship, solitude, tears, and laughter; but because she can never give herself, her sentiments and emotions are fabricated. Isadora Duncan undoubtedly cried real tears on the death of her children. But when she cast their ashes into the sea with a great theatrical gesture, she was merely being an actress; and one cannot read this passage where she evokes her sorrow in *My Life* without embarrassment:

I feel the warmth of my own body. I look down on my bare legs—stretching them out. The softness of my breasts, my arms that are never still, but continually waving about in soft undulations, and I realize that for twelve years I have been weary, this breast has harboured a never-ending ache, these hands before me have been marked with sorrow, and when I am alone these eyes are seldom dry.

In the worship of self, the adolescent girl can muster the courage to face the disturbing future; but it is a stage she must go beyond quickly: if not, the future closes up. The woman in love who encloses her lover in the couple's immanence dooms him to death with herself: the narcissist, alienating herself in her imaginary double, destroys herself. Her memories become fixed, her behavior stereotyped, she dwells on the same words, repeats gestures that have lost all meaning: this is what gives the impression of poverty found in "secret diaries" or "feminine autobiographies"; so occupied in flattering herself, the woman who does nothing becomes nothing and flatters a nothing.

Her misfortune is that, in spite of all her bad faith, she is aware of this nothingness. There cannot be a real relationship between an individual and his double, because this double does not exist. The woman narcissist suffers a radical failure. She cannot grasp herself as a totality, as plenitude; she cannot maintain the illusion of being in itself—for itself. Her solitude, like that of every human being, is felt as contingence and abandonment. And this is why—unless there is a conversion—she is condemned to hide relentlessly from herself in crowds, noise, and others. It would be a grave error to believe that in choosing herself as the supreme end, she escapes dependence: on the contrary, she dooms herself to the most severe slavery; she does not make the most of her freedom, she makes herself an endangered object in the world and in foreign consciousnesses. Not only are her body and face vulnerable flesh worn by time, but from a practical point of view it is a costly enterprise to adorn the idol, to put her on a pedestal, to erect a temple to her: we have seen that to preserve her form in immortal marble, Marie Bashkirtseff had to consent to marry for money. Masculine fortunes paid for the gold, incense, and myrrh that Isadora Duncan and Cécile Sorel laid at the foot of their thrones. As it is man who incarnates destiny for woman, women usually gauge their success by the number and quality of men subjected to their power. But reciprocity comes into play again here; the "praying mantis," attempting to make the male her instrument, does not free herself from him like this, because to catch him, she must please him. The American woman, trying to be an idol, makes herself the slave of her admirers, does not dress, live, or breathe other than through the man and for him. In fact, the narcissist is as dependent as the hetaera. If she escapes an individual man's domination, it is by accepting the tyranny of public opinion. This link that rivets her to others does not imply reciprocity; if she sought recognition by others' freedom while also recognizing that freedom as an end through activity, she would cease to be narcissistic. The paradox of her attitude is that she demands to be valued by a world to which she denies all value, since she alone counts in her own eyes. Outside approbation is an inhuman, mysterious, and capricious force that must be tapped magically. In spite of her superficial arrogance, the narcissistic woman knows she is threatened; it is why she is uneasy, susceptible, irritable, and constantly suspicious; her vanity is never satisfied; the older she grows, the more anxiously she seeks praise and success, the more she suspects plots around her; lost and obsessed, she sinks into the darkness of bad faith and often ends up by building a paranoid delirium around herself. The words "Whosoever shall save his life will lose it" apply specifically to her.

CHAPTER 12

The Woman in Love

The word "love" has not at all the same meaning for both sexes, and this is a source of the grave misunderstandings that separate them. Byron rightly said that love is merely an occupation in the life of the man, while it is life itself for the woman. The same idea is expressed by Nietzsche in *The Gay Science*. The same word "love," he says, means, in fact, two different things for the man and for the woman:

> What woman means by love is clear enough: total devotion (not mere surrender) with soul and body, without any consideration or reserve . . . In this absence of conditions her love is a faith; woman has no other *faith*.[1] Man, when he loves a woman, *wants*[2] precisely this love from her and is thus himself as far as can be from the presupposition of feminine love. Supposing, however, that there should also be men to whom the desire for total devotion is not alien; well, then they simply are not men.

Men might be passionate lovers at certain moments of their existence, but there is not one who could be defined as "a man in love"; in their most violent passions, they never abandon themselves completely; even if they fall on their knees before their mistresses, they still wish to possess them, annex them; at the heart of their lives, they remain sovereign subjects; the woman they love is merely one value among others; they want to integrate her into their existence, not submerge their entire existence in her. By contrast, love for the woman is a total abdication for the benefit of a master.

Cécile Sauvage writes: "When the woman loves, she must forget her own personality. This is a law of nature. A woman does not exist without a master. Without a master, she is a scattered bouquet."

---

1. Nietzsche's emphasis.
2. Also Nietzsche's emphasis.

In reality, this has nothing to do with a law of nature. It is the difference in their situations that is reflected in the conceptions man and woman have of love. The individual who is a subject, who is himself, endeavors to extend his grasp on the world if he has the generous inclination for transcendence: he is ambitious, he acts. But an inessential being cannot discover the absolute in the heart of his subjectivity; a being doomed to immanence could not realize himself in his acts. Closed off in the sphere of the relative, destined for the male from her earliest childhood, used to seeing him as a sovereign, with whom equality is not permitted, the woman who has not suppressed her claim to be human will dream of surpassing her being toward one of those superior beings, of becoming one, of fusing with the sovereign subject; there is no other way out for her than losing herself body and soul in the one designated to her as the absolute, as the essential. Since she is, in any case, condemned to dependence, she would rather serve a god than obey tyrants—parents, husband, protector; she chooses to want her enslavement so ardently that it will seem to her to be the expression of her freedom; she will try to overcome her situation as inessential object by radically assuming it; through her flesh, her feelings, and her behavior, she will exalt as sovereign the one she loves, she will posit him as value and supreme reality: she will efface herself before him. Love becomes a religion for her.

We have seen that the adolescent girl at first wishes to identify with males; once she renounces this, she then seeks to participate in their virility by being loved by one of them; it is not the individuality of one man or another that seduces her; she is in love with man in general. "And you, the men I will love, how I await you," writes Irène Reweliotty. "How I rejoice in soon knowing you. You, especially, the first one." Of course, the man must belong to the same class and the same race as her own: the privilege of sex works only within this framework; for him to be a demigod, he must obviously be a human being first; for the daughter of a colonial officer, the native is not a man; if the young girl gives herself to an "inferior," she is trying to degrade herself because she does not think she is worthy of love. Normally, she looks for the man who represents male superiority; she is rapidly led to discover that many individuals of the chosen sex are sadly contingent and mundane; but first she is favorably disposed toward them; they have less to prove their value than to keep from grossly disavowing it: this explains many often lamentable errors; the naive young girl is taken in by virility. According to the circumstances, male worth will appear to her as physical force, elegance, wealth, culture, intelligence, authority, social situation, or a military uniform: but what she always hopes for is that her lover will be the summation of the essence of man. Familiarity often is enough to destroy his prestige; it breaks down with the first kiss, or in everyday contact, or on the wedding night. Love at a distance is nonetheless merely a fantasy, not a real experience. When it is carnally consummated, desire for love becomes passionate love. Inversely, love can arise from making love, the sexually dominated woman exalting the man who first seemed insignificant to her. But it often happens that the woman is unable to transform any of the men she knows into a god. Love holds less place in feminine life than is often believed. Husband, children, home, pleasures, social life, vanity, sexuality, and career are far more important. Almost all women have dreamed of the "great love": they have had imitations, they have come close to it; it has come to them in incomplete, bruised, trifling, imperfect, and false forms; but very few have really dedicated their existence to it. The great women lovers are often those who did not waste their emotions on juvenile crushes; they first accepted the traditional feminine destiny: husband, home, children; or they lived in difficult solitude; or they counted on some venture that more or less failed; when they glimpse the chance to save their disappointing life by dedicating it to an elite being, they desperately give themselves up to this hope. Mlle Aïssé, Juliette Drouet, and Mme d'Agoult were nearly thirty when they began their love lives, Julie de Lespinasse was close to forty; no goal was available to them, they were unprepared to undertake any venture that seemed worthwhile to them, love was their only way out.

Even if they are allowed independence, this road is still the one that seems the most attractive to most women; it is agonizing to take responsibility for one's life endeavor; the adolescent boy too readily turns to older women, seeking a guide, a tutor, a mother in them; but his education, customs, and the inner constraints he faces prevent him from definitively accepting the easy solution of abdication; he views such loves merely as a phase. It is man's luck—in adulthood as in childhood—to be made to take the most arduous roads but the surest ones; woman's misfortune is that she is surrounded by nearly irresistible temptations; everything incites her to take the easy way out: instead of being encouraged to fight on her own account, she is told that she can let herself get by and she will reach enchanted paradises; when she realizes she was fooled by a mirage, it is too late; she has been worn out in this adventure.

Psychoanalysts like to claim that the woman seeks her father's image in her lover; but it is because he is man, not father, that he dazzles the child, and every man shares this magic; the woman wishes not to reincarnate one individual in another but to bring back to life a situation: one she knew as a little girl, sheltered by adults; she was an integral part of her family home life, she felt the peace of quasi-passivity; love will bring her mother as well as her father back to her, and her childhood as well; what she wishes is to find a roof over her head, walls that hide her from her abandonment within the world, laws that protect her from her freedom. This childish dream haunts many feminine loves; the woman is happy when her lover calls her "my little girl, my dear child"; men know the words well: "You look like a little girl" are among the words that most surely touch the hearts of women: we have seen how many of them have suffered becoming adults; many persist in "acting like a child," and indefinitely prolonging their childhood in their attitude and dress. To become a child again in the arms of a man brings them great satisfaction. It is the theme of this popular tune:

> *I feel so small in your arms*
> *So small, o my love . . .*

a theme tirelessly repeated in lovers' conversations and correspondence. "Baby, my baby," murmurs the lover, and the woman calls herself "little one, your little one." Irène Reweliotty writes: "When, then, will he come, the one who will be able to dominate me?" And thinking she had met him: "I love feeling you a man and better than me."

A psychasthenic woman studied by Janet illustrates this attitude in the most striking way:

> As far back as I can recall, all the foolish acts or all the good deeds I
> have done stem from the same cause, an aspiration to the perfect and
> ideal love where I can give myself entirely, confide all my being to
> another being, God, man, or woman, so superior to me that I would
> no longer think of leading my life or watching over myself. To find
> someone who would love me enough to take the trouble to make me
> live, someone whom I would blindly and confidently obey, sure that
> he would keep me from all failure and would put me on the right
> track, very gently and with much love, toward perfection. How I
> envy the ideal love of Mary Magdalene and Jesus: to be the ardent
> disciple of an adored and worthy master; to live and die for one's
> idol, believe in him without any possible shadow of doubt, to hold
> at last the final victory of the Angel over the beast, to be held in his
> enveloping arms, so small, so pressed in his protection, and so much
> his that I no longer exist.[3]

---

3. Pierre Janet, *Obsessions and Psychasthenia.*

Many examples have already proven to us that this dream of annihilation is in fact an avid will to be. In all religions, the adoration of God is part of the devotee's desire for his own salvation; by giving herself up entirely to the idol, the woman hopes he will give her possession both of herself and of the universe contained in him. In most cases, it is first the justification, the exaltation of her ego, she asks of her lover. Many women do not abandon themselves to love unless they are loved in return: and the love they are shown is sometimes enough to make them fall in love. The young girl has dreamed of herself as seen through the man's eyes: it is in man's eyes that the woman believes she has at last found herself.

Cécile Sauvage writes:

Walking beside you, moving my tiny little feet that you loved, feeling them so slender in their high felt-topped shoes, made me love all the love you surrounded them with. The slightest movements of my hands in my muff, of my arms, of my face, the inflections of my voice, filled me with happiness.*

The woman feels endowed with a sure and high value; at last she has the right to cherish herself through the love she inspires. She is exhilarated at finding a witness in her lover. This is what Colette's Vagabond admits:

I must confess that, in allowing this man to return tomorrow, I was giving way to my desire to keep, not an admirer, not a friend, but an eager spectator of my life and my person. "One has to get terribly old," said Margot to me one day, "before one can give up the vanity of living in the presence of someone else."†

In one of her letters to Middleton Murry, Katherine Mansfield recounts that she has just bought a ravishing mauve corset; she quickly adds: "What a pity there is no one to *see* it!" Nothing is more discouraging than to feel that one is the flower, the perfume, the treasure that no desire seeks: What good is an asset that does not enrich me and that no one wants as a gift? Love is the revealer that shows up in positive and clear traits the dull negative image as empty as a blank print; the woman's face, the curves of her body, her childhood memories, her dried tears, her dresses, her habits, her

---

* Translated by Beverley Bie Brahic.—TRANS.
† Colette, *The Vagabond*.—TRANS.

universe, everything she is, everything that belongs to her, escapes contingence and becomes necessary: she is a marvelous gift at the foot of her god's altar:

> Before his hands were laid gently on her shoulders, before his eyes took their fill of hers, she had been a plain dull woman in a plain dull world. He kissed her, and she stood in the rose-light of immortality.[4]

Thus, men endowed with social prestige and good at flattering feminine vanity will arouse passion even if they have no physical charm. Because of their lofty situation, they incarnate Law and Truth: their consciousness discloses an uncontested reality. The woman they praise feels transformed into a priceless treasure. According to Isadora Duncan, D'Annunzio's success came from this:

> When D'Annunzio loves a woman, he lifts her spirit from this earth to the divine regions where Beatrice moves and shines. In turn he transforms each woman to a part of the divine essence, he carries her aloft until she believes herself really with Beatrice . . . he flung over each favourite in turn a shining veil. She rose above the heads of ordinary mortals and walked surrounded by a strange radiance. But when the caprice of the poet ended, this veil vanished, the radiance was eclipsed, and the woman turned again to common clay . . . To hear oneself praised with that magic peculiar to D'Annunzio is, I imagine, something like the experience of Eve when she heard the voice of the serpent in Paradise. D'Annunzio can make any woman feel that she is the centre of the universe.[5]

Only in love can woman harmoniously reconcile her eroticism and her narcissism; we have already seen an opposition between these two systems that makes the woman's adaptation to her sexual destiny very difficult. Making herself carnal object and prey contradicts her self-adoration: it seems to her that lovemaking disfigures and defiles her body or degrades her soul. Some women, therefore, choose frigidity, thinking they can thus preserve the integrity of their ego. Others dissociate animal sensuality and lofty sentiments. A very characteristic case is Mrs. D.S.'s, reported by Stekel and which I have already cited concerning marriage:

---

4. Mary Webb, *The House in Dormer Forest*.
5. Isadora Duncan, *My Life*.

Frigid, and married to a respected man, after his death, there came into her life a young man . . . he, too, was an artist and a wonderful musician . . . She became his mistress. Her love was and is to this day so great that she feels happy only in his presence. Her whole life is wrapped in her Lothar. In spite of her great love for him she has remained cool in his arms. Another man, too, crossed her path. He was a forester, a powerful, rough individual who, on finding himself alone with her one day, took possession of her without saying a word. She was so consternated that she didn't object. In his embrace she experienced the keenest orgasm. "In his arms," she states, "I have regained my health for the past months. It is like a wild intoxication, but followed by an indescribable disgust when I think of my Lothar. Paul I hate; Lothar I love. Nevertheless, Paul is the one who gratifies me. Everything about Lothar holds me to him; but it seems I must act like a harlot in order to feel. As a lady I can never respond." [She refuses to marry Paul but continues to sleep with him; in those moments] she becomes like a person transformed and the raw words which escape her lips she would never be guilty of using on any other occasion.

Stekel adds that "for many women, the descent into animality is the condition for orgasm." They see an abasement in physical love impossible to reconcile with feelings of esteem and affection. For others, by contrast, it is by the man's esteem, tenderness, and admiration that this abasement can be abolished. They only consent to give themselves to a man if they believe they are deeply loved by him; a woman has to be very cynical, indifferent, or proud to consider physical relations as an exchange of pleasures in which each partner equally gets something out of it. The man revolts as much as—and perhaps more than—the woman against anyone who wants to exploit him sexually;[6] but she is the one who generally has the impression that her partner is using her as an instrument. Only exalted admiration can make up for the humiliation of an act she considers a defeat. We have seen that the love act requires a woman's profound alienation; she is awash in the indolence of passivity; eyes closed, anonymous, lost, she feels transported by waves, caught up in torment, buried in the night: night of flesh, of the womb, of the tomb; reduced to nothing, she reaches the

---

6. See, among others, *Lady Chatterley's Lover*. Through Mellors, Lawrence expresses his horror of women who make him a tool of pleasure.

Whole, her self effaced. But when the man separates himself from her, she finds herself thrown back to earth, on a bed, in the light; she has a name and a face again: she is a conquered person, a prey, an object. This is when love becomes necessary to her. Just as after being weaned the child seeks the reassuring gaze of his parents, it is in the eyes of the lover who contemplates her that the woman whose flesh has been painfully detached has to feel reunited with the Whole. She is rarely completely satisfied; even if she experienced the relief of pleasure, she is not entirely freed from the carnal spell, her arousal becomes feeling; in providing her with sensuality, the man attaches her to him and does not liberate her. He, though, no longer feels desire for her: she only forgives him for this momentary indifference if he has vowed timeless and absolute feeling to her. Then the immanence of the instant is transcended; the burning memories are no longer a regret but a treasure; as it dies down, the sensuality becomes hope and promise; sexual pleasure is justified; the woman can gloriously assume her sexuality because she transcends it; arousal, pleasure, and desire are no longer a state but a gift; her body is no longer an object: it is a song, a flame. Thus she can abandon herself passionately to the magic of eroticism; night becomes light; the woman in love can open her eyes, look at the man who loves her and whose gaze glorifies her; through him nothingness becomes plenitude of being, and being is transfigured into value; she no longer sinks into a sea of darkness, she is transported on wings, exalted to the sky. Abandon becomes holy ecstasy. When she *receives* the loved man, the woman is inhabited, visited like the Virgin by the Holy Spirit, like the believer by the wafer; this explains the obscene analogy between holy hymns and ribald songs: it is not that mystical love always has a sexual side; but the sexuality of the woman in love takes on a mystical tone. "My God, my beloved, my master": the same words spill from the lips of the kneeling saint and the woman in love lying on the bed; the saint offers her flesh to Christ's arrows, she holds out her hands to receive the stigmata, she implores the burning of divine Love; the woman in love also offers and waits: darts, stinger, and arrows are embodied in the male sex. In both of them there is the same dream, the infantile, mystical, love dream: to exist sovereignly by effacing oneself within the other.

It has sometimes been claimed that this desire for effacement leads to masochism.[7] But as I have noted concerning eroticism, one can only speak of masochism if I try "to cause myself to be fascinated by my objectivity-for-others,"[8] that is, if the consciousness of the subject turns back to the

---

7. It is, among others, H. Deutsch's theory in *Psychology of Women*.
8. Cf. Sartre, *Being and Nothingness*.

ego to grasp it in its humiliated situation. But the woman in love is not only a narcissist alienated in her self: she also experiences a passionate desire to go beyond her own limits and become infinite, thanks to the intervention of another who has access to infinite reality. She abandons herself first to love to save *herself;* but the paradox of idolatrous love is that in order to save herself, she ends up totally disavowing *herself.* Her feeling takes on a mystical dimension; she no longer asks God to admire her or approve her; she wants to melt into him, forget herself in his arms. "I would have liked to be a love saint," writes Mme d'Agoult. "I envied the martyr in such moments of exaltation and ascetic furor." What comes through in these words is the desire for a radical destruction of the self, abolishing the frontiers that separate her from her beloved: it is not masochism but a dream of ecstatic union. The same dream inspires these words of Georgette Leblanc: "At that time, had I been asked what I most wanted in the world, without any hesitation I would have said: to be food and flame for his spirit."

To achieve this union, the woman first wants to serve; she will feel necessary in responding to her lover's demands; she will be integrated into his existence, she will be a part of his value, she will be justified; even mystics like to believe, according to Angelus Silesius, that God needs man, otherwise the gift they make of themselves would be in vain. The more demands the man makes, the more fulfilled the woman feels. Although the seclusion Hugo imposed on Juliette Drouet weighed on the young woman, one feels she is happy to obey him: staying seated close to the fire is doing something for the master's happiness. She passionately tries to be positively useful to him. She prepares special dishes for him, creates a home for him: your little "nest for two," she said sweetly; she takes care of his clothes.

She writes to him: "I want you to stain and tear all your clothes as much as possible and that I alone should mend and clean them and nobody else."

For him she reads newspapers, cuts out articles, organizes letters and notes, copies manuscripts. She is upset when the poet entrusts part of this work to his daughter Léopoldine. Similar characteristics are found in all women in love. If need be she tyrannizes herself in the lover's name; everything she is, everything she has, every second of her life, must be devoted to him and thus find their raison d'être; she does not want to possess anything except in him; what would make her unhappy is that he demand nothing of her, and so an attentive lover invents demands. She first sought in love a confirmation of what she was, her past, her personage; but she also commits her future: to justify it, she destines it to the one who possesses all values; she thus gives up her transcendence: she subordinates it to that of the essential other whose vassal and slave she makes herself. It is to find herself, to save herself, that she began by losing herself in him: the fact is that little by little she loses herself; all reality is in the other. Love that was originally defined as a narcissistic apotheosis is accomplished in the bitter joys of a devotion that often leads to self-mutilation. At the outset of a consuming passion, the woman becomes prettier, more elegant than before. "When Adèle does my hair, I look at my forehead because you love it," writes Mme d'Agoult. This face, this body, this room, this me, she has found a raison d'être for them; she cherishes them through the mediation of this beloved man who loves her. But later, she gives up all coquetry; if the lover so desires, she changes this face that had once been more precious than love itself; she loses interest in it; she makes what she is and what she has the fief of her lord; what he disdains, she disavows; she would like to devote to him each beat of her heart, each drop of blood, the marrow of her bones; this is what a dream of martyrdom expresses: to exaggerate the gift of self to the point of torture, of death, to be the ground the beloved treads on, to be nothing but that which responds to his call. She vigorously eliminates everything the beloved finds useless. If this gift she makes of self is totally accepted, there is no masochism: few traces of it are seen in Juliette Drouet. In her excessive adoration she sometimes knelt before the poet's portrait and asked him to excuse the mistakes she might have committed; she did not angrily turn against herself. But the slide from generous enthusiasm to masochistic rage is easy. The woman in love who finds herself before her lover in the same situation as the child before his parents also recovers the feeling of guilt she experienced around them; she does not choose to revolt against him as long as she loves him: she revolts against her self. If he loves her less than she desires, if she fails to interest him, to make him happy, to be sufficient to him, all her narcissism turns into disgust, humiliation, and self-hatred that push her to self-punishment. During a longer or shorter crisis, sometimes for a whole life, she will be a willing victim; she will go out of her way to harm this self that has not been able to satisfy the lover. Then her attitude is specifically masochistic. But cases where the woman in love seeks her own suffering so as to get revenge on herself and those where she seeks confirmation of the man's freedom and power must not be confused. It is a commonplace—and seems to be a reality—that the prostitute is proud to be beaten by her man: but it is not the idea of her battered and enslaved person that exalts her, it is the strength, authority, and sovereignty of the male on whom she depends; she also likes to see him mistreat another male, she often pushes him into dangerous competitions: she wants her master to hold the values recognized in the milieu to which she belongs. The woman who gladly submits to masculine caprices also admires the proof of a sovereign freedom in the tyranny that is wielded over her. One must be careful to note that if for some reason the lover's prestige is ruined, his blows and demands become odious to her: they are only worth something if they manifest the beloved's divinity. In that case, it is intoxicatingly joyous to feel oneself the prey of a foreign freedom: for any existent the most surprising adventure is to find oneself sustained by the diverse and imperious will of another; one is tired of inhabiting the same skin all the time; blind obedience is the only chance of radical change that a human being might experience. So here is the woman slave, queen, flower, doe, stained-glass window, doormat, servant, courtesan, muse, companion, mother, sister, or child depending on the lover's fleeting dreams, the lover's imperious orders: she complies with delight with these metamorphoses as long as she does not recognize that she still has the same taste of submission on her lips. In love as well as in eroticism, it appears that masochism is one of the paths the unsatisfied woman takes, disappointed by the other and by herself; but this is not the natural slope of a happy resignation. Masochism perpetuates the presence of the self as a hurt, fallen figure; love aims at the forgetting of self in favor of the essential subject.

The supreme aim of human love, like mystical love, is identification with the loved one. The measure of values and the truth of the world are in his own consciousness; that is why serving him is still not enough. The woman tries to see with his eyes; she reads the books he reads, prefers the paintings and music he prefers, she is only interested in the landscapes she sees with him, in the ideas that come from him; she adopts his friends, his enemies, and his opinions; when she questions herself, she endeavors to hear the answer he gives; she wants the air he has already breathed in her lungs; the fruits and flowers she has not received from his hands have neither fragrance nor taste; even her hodological space is upset: the center of the world is no longer where she is but where the beloved is; all roads leave from and lead to his house. She uses his words, she repeats his gestures, adopts his manias and tics. "I *am* Heathcliff," says Catherine in *Wuthering Heights;* this is the cry of all women in love; she is another incarnation of the beloved, his reflection, his double: she is *he*. She lets her own world founder in contingence: she lives in his universe.

The supreme happiness of the woman in love is to be recognized by the beloved as part of him; when he says "we," she is associated and identified with him, she shares his prestige and reigns with him over the rest of the world; she does not tire of saying—even if it is excessive—this delicious "we." Necessary to a being who is absolute necessity, who projects himself in the world toward necessary goals, and who reconstitutes the world as necessity, the woman in love experiences in her resignation the magnificent possession of the absolute. It is this certitude that gives her such great joys; she feels exalted at the right hand of the god; what does it matter that she is always in second place as long as it is *her* place, forever, in a marvelously ordered world? As long as she loves, as she is loved and necessary for the beloved, she feels completely justified: she savors peace and happiness. Such was perhaps Mlle Aïssé's lot at Knight d'Aydie's side before religious scruples troubled her soul, of Juliette Drouet's in Hugo's shadow.

But this glorious felicity is seldom stable. No man is God. The relations the mystic has with the divine absence depend on his fervor alone: but the deified man—who is not God—is present. That is where the torments of the woman in love stem from. Her most ordinary destiny can be summarized in Julie de Lespinasse's famous words: "At every instant of my life, my friend, I love you, I suffer, and I await you." Of course for men too suffering is linked to love; but their heartbreaks either do not last long or are not all consuming; Benjamin Constant wanted to die for Juliette Récamier: in one year, he was cured. Stendhal missed Métilde for years, but it was a regret that enriched his life more than destroying it. In accepting herself as the inessential and as total dependence, the woman creates a hell for herself; all women in love see themselves in Andersen's Little Mermaid, who, having exchanged her fish tail for a woman's legs out of love, walked on needles and burning coals. It is not true that the beloved man is unconditionally necessary and that she is not necessary to him; it is not up to him to justify the woman who worships him, and he does not let himself be possessed by her.

An authentic love should take on the other's contingence, that is, his lacks, limitations, and originary gratuitousness; it would claim to be not a salvation but an inter-human relation. Idolatrous love confers an absolute value on the loved one: this is the first lie strikingly apparent to all outsiders: "*He* doesn't deserve so much love," people whisper around the woman in love; posterity smiles pityingly when evoking the pale figure of Count Guibert. It is a heartrending disappointment for the woman to discover her idol's weaknesses and mediocrity. Colette—in *The Vagabond* and *Mes apprentissages* (*My Apprenticeships*)—often alludes to this bitter agony; this disillusion is even crueler than the child's at seeing paternal prestige crumble, because the woman herself chose the one to whom she made a gift of her whole being. Even if the chosen one is worthy of the deepest attachment, his truth is earthbound: it is not he whom the woman kneeling before a supreme being loves; she is duped by that spirit of seriousness which refuses to put values "in parentheses," not recognizing that they stem from human existence; her bad faith erects barriers between her and the one she worships. She flatters him, she bows down before him, but she is not a friend for him, since she does not realize he is in danger in the world, that his projects and finalities are as fragile as he himself is; considering him the Law and Truth, she misunderstands his freedom, which is hesitation and anguish. This refusal to apply a human measure to the lover explains many feminine paradoxes. The woman demands a favor from the lover, he grants it: he is generous, rich, magnificent, he is royal, he is divine; if he refuses, he is suddenly stingy, mean, and cruel, he is a devilish being or bestial. One might be tempted to counter: If a yes is understood as a superb extravagance, why should one be surprised by a no? If the no manifests such an abject egotism, why admire the yes so much? Between the superhuman and the inhuman is there not room for the human?

A fallen god, then, is not a man: it is an imposture; the lover has no alternative other than to prove he is really the king one adulates or to denounce himself as a usurper. When he is no longer worshipped, he has to be trampled on. In the name of this halo with which the woman in love adorns her beloved, she forbids him all weakness; she is disappointed and irritated if he does not conform to this image she put in his place; if he is tired, confused, if he is hungry or thirsty when he should not be, if he makes a mistake, if he contradicts himself, she decrees he is "not himself," and she reproaches him for this. Likewise, she will go so far as to reproach him for all the initiatives she does not appreciate; she judges her judge, and in order for him to deserve to remain her master, she refuses him his freedom. Her adoration is sometimes better served by his absence than his presence; there are women, as we have seen, who devote themselves to dead or inaccessible heroes so that they never have to compare them with flesh-and-blood beings; the latter inevitably fail to live up to their dreams. Hence the disillusioned sayings: "You shouldn't believe in Prince Charming. Men are just poor things." They would not seem like dwarfs if they were not required to be giants.

This is one of the curses weighing on the passionate woman: her generosity is immediately converted into demands. Being alienated in another, she also wants to salvage herself: she has to annex this other who holds her being. She gives herself to him entirely: but he has to be totally available to receive this gift honorably. She dedicates all her moments to him: he has to be present at every moment; she only wants to live through him: but she wants to live; he has to devote himself to making her live.

Mme d'Agoult writes to Liszt: "I love you sometimes stupidly, and at such times I do not understand that I could not, would not be able to, and

should not be for you the same absorbing thought as you are for me." She
tries to curtail her spontaneous wish: to be everything for him. There is the
same appeal in Mlle de Lespinasse's complaint:

> My God! If you only knew what the days are like, what life is like
> without the interest and pleasure of seeing you! My friend, dissipa-
> tion, occupation, and movement satisfy you; and I, my happiness is
> you, it is only you; I would not want to live if I could not see you
> and love you every minute of my life.

At first, the woman in love is delighted to satisfy her lover's desire;
then—like the legendary fireman who out of love for his job lights fires
everywhere—she works at awakening this desire so as to have to satisfy it;
if she does not succeed, she feels humiliated, useless to such an extent that
the lover will feign passion he does not feel. In making herself a slave, she
has found the surest means of subjugating him. This is another lie of love
that many men—Lawrence, Montherlant—have resentfully denounced:
he takes himself for a gift when he is a tyranny. In *Adolphe*, Benjamin Constant fiercely painted the chains the overly generous passion of a woman
entwines around the man. "She did not count her sacrifices because she was
busy making me accept them," he says cruelly about Ellénore. Acceptance
is thus a commitment that ties the lover up, without his even having the
benefit of appearing to be the one who gives; the woman demands that he
graciously welcome the loads she burdens him with. And her tyranny is
insatiable. The man in love is authoritarian: but when he has obtained what
he wanted, he is satisfied; but there are no limits to the demanding devotion
of the woman. A lover who has confidence in his mistress shows no displeasure at her absences or if she is occupied when away from him: sure
that she belongs to him, he prefers to possess a freedom more than a thing.
By contrast, the absence of the lover is always torture for the woman: he is
a gaze, a judge, as soon as he looks at something other than her, he frus-
trates her; everything he sees, he steals from her; far from him, she is dispossessed both of herself and of the world; even seated at her side,
reading, writing, he abandons her, he betrays her. She hates his sleep.
Baudelaire is touched by the sleeping woman: "Your beautiful eyes are
weary, poor lover." Proust delights in watching Albertine sleep;[9] male jealousy is thus simply the desire for exclusive possession; the woman beloved,
when sleep gives her back the disarming candor of childhood, belongs to

---

9. That Albertine is an Albert does not change anything; Proust's attitude here is in any case
the masculine attitude.

no one: for the man, this certitude suffices. But the god, the master, must not abandon himself to the repose of immanence; it is with a hostile look that the woman contemplates this destroyed transcendence; she detests his animal inertia, this body that no longer exists *for her* but *in itself*, abandoned to a contingence whose ransom is her own contingence. Violette Leduc forcefully expressed this feeling:

> I hate sleepers. I lean over them with bad intent. Their submission exasperates me. I hate their unconscious serenity, their false anesthesia, their studiously blind face, their reasonable drunkenness, their incompetent earnestness . . . I hovered, I waited for a long time for the pink bubble that would come out of my sleeper's mouth. I only wanted a bubble of presence from him. I didn't get it . . . I saw that his night eyelids were eyelids of death . . . I took refuge in his eyelids' gaiety when this man was impossible. Sleep is hard when it wants to be. He walked off with everything. I hate my sleeper who can create peace for himself with an unconsciousness that is alien to me. I hate his sweet forehead . . . He is deep down inside himself busy with his rest. He is recapitulating who knows what . . . We had left posthaste. We wanted to leave the earth by using our personality. We had taken off, climbed up, watched out, waited, hummed, arrived, whined, won, and lost together. It was a serious school for playing hooky. We had uncovered a new kind of nothingness. Now you're sleeping. Your effacement is not honest . . . If my sleeper moves, my hand touches, in spite of itself, the seed. It is the barn with fifty sacks of grain that is stifling, despotic. The scrotum of a sleeping man fell on my hand . . . I have the little bags of seed. I have in my hand the fields that will be plowed, the orchards that will be pruned, the force of the waters that will be transformed, the four boards that will be nailed, the tarpaulins that will be lifted. I have in my hand the fruits, flowers, and chosen animals. I have in my hand the lancet, the clippers, the probe, the revolver, the forceps, and all that does not fill my hand. The seed of the sleeping world is only the dangling extra of the soul's prolongation . . .
>
> You, when you sleep, I hate you.[10]

The god must not sleep, or he becomes clay and flesh; he must not cease to be present, or his creature founders in nothingness. For woman,

---

10. *Je hais les dormeurs* (I Hate Sleepers).

man's sleep is avarice and betrayal. At times the lover wakes his mistress: it is to make love to her; she wakes him simply to keep him from sleeping, to keep him nearby, thinking only of her, there, closed up in the room, in the bed, in her arms—like God in the tabernacle—this is what the woman desires: she is a jailer.

And yet, she does not really consent to have the man be nothing else but her prisoner. Here is one of the painful paradoxes of love: captive, the god sheds his divinity. The woman preserves her transcendence by handing it over to him: but he must bring it to the whole world. If two lovers disappear into the absolute of passion together, all freedom deteriorates into immanence; only death can provide a solution: this is one of the meanings of the Tristan and Isolde myth. Two lovers who are exclusively destined for each other are already dead: they die of boredom. Marcel Arland in *Terres étrangères* (Foreign Lands) described this slow agony of a love that devours itself. The woman understands this danger. Except for cases of jealous frenzy, she herself demands that man be project and action: he has to accomplish exploits to remain a hero. The chevalier who embarks on new feats of prowess offends his lady; but she scorns him if he stays seated at her feet. This is the torture of impossible love; woman wants to *have* man all to herself, but she demands that he go beyond all the givens he could possibly possess; one does not *have* a freedom; she wants to lock up *here* an existent who is, in Heidegger's words, a "being from afar," she knows full well that this effort is futile. "My friend, I love you as one should love, with excess, madness, rapture, and despair," writes Julie de Lespinasse. Idolatrous love, if lucid, can only be hopeless. For the woman in love who asks her lover to be a hero, giant, demigod, demands not to be everything for him, whereas she can find happiness only if she contains him entirely within herself.

Nietzsche says:

A woman's passion in its unconditional renunciation of rights of her own presupposes precisely that . . . there is no equal pathos, no equal will to renunciation; for if both partners felt impelled by love to renounce themselves, we should then get—I do not know what; perhaps an empty space? Woman wants to be taken . . . she wants someone who *takes*, who does not give himself or give himself away; on the contrary, he is supposed to become richer in "himself" . . . Woman gives herself away, man acquires more.[11]

---

11. *The Gay Science.*

In any case, the woman will be able to find her joy in this enrichment she brings to her loved one; she is not All for him: but she will try to believe herself indispensable; there are no degrees in necessity. If he cannot "get along without her," she considers herself the foundation of his precious existence, and she derives her own worth from that. Her joy is to serve him: but he must gratefully recognize this service; giving becomes demand according to the customary dialectic of devotion.[12] And a woman of scrupulous mind asks herself: Is it really *me* he needs? The man cherishes her, desires her with singular tenderness and desire: But would he not have just as singular feelings for another? Many women in love let themselves be deluded; they want to ignore the fact that the general is enveloped in the particular, and the man facilitates this illusion because he shares it at first; there is often in his desire a passion that seems to defy time; at the moment he desires this woman, he desires her with passion, he wants only her: and certainly the moment is an absolute, but a momentary absolute. Duped, the woman passes into the eternal. Deified by the embrace of the master, she believes she has always been divine and destined for the god: she alone. But male desire is as fleeting as it is imperious; once satisfied, it dies rather quickly, while it is most often after love that the woman becomes his prisoner. This is the theme of a whole type of shallow literature and songs. "A young man was passing by, a girl was singing . . . A young man was singing, a girl was crying." And even if the man is seriously attached to the woman, it still does not mean that she is necessary to him. Yet this is what she demands: her abdication only saves her if it reinstates her empire; one cannot escape the play of reciprocity. So she must suffer or lie to herself. Most often she clutches first at the lie. She imagines the man's love as the exact counterpart of the love she bears him; with bad faith, she takes desire for love, an erection for desire, love for religion. She forces the man to lie to her. Do you love me? As much as yesterday? Will you always love me? She cleverly asks the questions just when there is not enough time to give nuanced and sincere answers or when circumstances prevent them; imperiously she asks her questions during lovemaking, at the moment of convalescence, when sobbing, or on a railway station platform; she makes trophies of the answers she extorts; and in the absence of responses, she interprets the silences; every genuine woman in love is more or less paranoid. I remember a woman friend who, when faced with the long silence from a far-off lover, declared, "When one wants to break up, one writes to

---

12. I have tried to show this in *Pyrrhus et Cinéas*.

announce it"; then upon receiving an unambiguous letter: "When one really wants to break up, one doesn't write." It is often very difficult to decide where pathological delirium begins when hearing such confidences. Described by the panicking woman in love, the man's behavior always seems extravagant: he's neurotic, sadistic, repressed, a masochist, a devil, unstable, cowardly, or all of these together; he defies the most subtle psychological explanations. "X. . . . adores me, he's wildly jealous, he wants me to wear a mask when I go out; but he's such a strange being and so suspicious of love that he keeps me in the hallway and doesn't invite me in when I ring his bell." Or: "Z. . . . adored me. But he was too proud to ask me to go to Lyon, where he lives: I went there, I moved in with him. After eight days, without an argument, he threw me out. I saw him twice afterward. The third time I called him and he hung up in the middle of the conversation. He's a neurotic." These mysterious stories become clearer when the man explains: "I absolutely did not love her," or "I liked her well enough, but I could not have lived one month with her." Bad faith in excess leads to the mental asylum: one of the constants of erotomania is that the lover's behavior seems enigmatic and paradoxical; from this slant, the patient's delirium always succeeds in breaking down the resistance of reality. A normal woman sometimes finally realizes the truth, recognizing that she is no longer loved. But as long as her back is not to the wall, she always cheats a little. Even in reciprocal love, there is a fundamental difference between the lovers' feelings that she tries to hide. The man must of course be capable of justifying himself without her since she hopes to be justified through him. If he is necessary to her, it is because she is fleeing her freedom: but if he assumes the freedom without which he would be neither a hero nor simply man, nothing and no one will be necessary for him. The dependence woman accepts comes from her weakness: How could she find a reciprocal dependence in the man she loves in his strength?

A passionately demanding soul cannot find tranquillity in love, because she sets her sights on a contradictory aim. Torn and tormented, she risks being a burden to the one for whom she dreamed of being a slave; she becomes importunate and obnoxious for want of feeling indispensable. Here is a common tragedy. Wiser and less intransigent, the woman in love resigns herself. She is not all, she is not necessary: it is enough for her to be useful; another can easily take her place: she is satisfied to be the one who is there. She recognizes her servitude without asking for reciprocity. She can thus enjoy modest happiness; but even in these limits, it will not be cloudless. Far more painfully than the wife, the woman in love waits. If the wife herself is exclusively a woman in love, the responsibilities of the home, motherhood, her occupations, and her pleasures will have little value in her eyes: it is the presence of her husband that lifts her out of the limbo of ennui. "When you are not there, it seems not even worthwhile to greet the day; everything that happens to me seems lifeless, I am no more than a little empty dress thrown on a chair," writes Cécile Sauvage early in her marriage.[13] And we have seen that, very often, it is outside marriage that passionate love arises and blooms. One of the most remarkable examples of a life entirely devoted to love is Juliette Drouet's: it is an endless wait. "I must always come back to the same starting point, meaning eternally waiting for you," she writes to Victor Hugo. "I wait for you like a squirrel in a cage." "My God! How sad it is for someone with my nature to wait from one end of life to another." "What a day! I thought it would never end waiting for you, and now I feel it went too quickly since I did not see you." "I find the day eternal." "I wait for you because after all I would rather wait than believe you are not coming at all." It is true that Hugo, after having made her break off from her rich protector, Prince Demidoff, confined Juliette to a small apartment and forbade her to go out alone for twelve years, to prevent her from seeing her former friends. But even when her lot—she called herself "your poor cloistered victim"—had improved, she still continued to have no other reason to live than her lover and not to see him very much. "I love you, my dearest Victor," she wrote in 1841, "but my heart is sad and full of bitterness; I see you so little, so little, and the little I see you, you belong to me so little that all these littles make a whole of sadness that fills my heart and mind." She dreams of reconciling independence and love. "I would like to be both independent and slave, independent through a state that nourishes me and slave only to my love." But having totally failed in her career as an actress, she had to resign herself to being no more than a lover "from one end of life to the other." Despite her efforts to be of service to her idol, the hours were too empty: the seventeen thousand letters she wrote to Hugo at the rate of three to four hundred every year are proof of this. Between visits from the master, she could only kill time. The worst horror of woman's condition in a harem is that her days are deserts of boredom: when the male is not using this object that she is for him, she is absolutely nothing. The situation of the woman in love is analogous: she only wants to be this loved woman, and nothing else has value in her eyes. For her to exist, then, her lover must be by her side, taken care of by her; she awaits his return, his desire, his waking; and as soon as

---

13. The case is different if the wife has found her autonomy in the marriage; in such a case, love between the two spouses can be a free exchange of two self-sufficient beings.

he leaves her, she starts again to wait for him. Such is the curse that weighs on the heroines of *Back Street*[14] and *The Weather in the Streets*,[15] priestesses and victims of pure love. It is the harsh punishment inflicted on those who have not taken their destiny in their own hands.

Waiting can be a joy; for the woman who watches for her loved one, knowing he is hurrying to her, that he loves her, the wait is a dazzling promise. But over and above the confident intoxication of love that changes absence itself into presence, the torment of worry gets confused with the emptiness of absence: the man might never return. I knew a woman who greeted her lover with surprise each time they met: "I thought you would never return," she would say. And if he asked her why: "Because you *could* never return; when I wait, I always have the impression that I will never see you again." Above all, he may cease to love her: he may love another woman. The vehemence with which she tries to fool herself by saying "He loves me madly, he can love no one but me" does not exclude the torture of jealousy. It is characteristic of bad faith that it allows passionate and contradictory affirmations. Thus the madman who stubbornly takes himself for Napoleon does not mind admitting he is also a barber. The woman rarely consents to ask herself, does he really love me? but asks herself a hundred times: Does he love another? She does not accept that her lover's fervor could have dimmed little by little, nor that he gives less value to love than she does: she immediately invents rivals. She considers love both a free feeling and a magic spell; and she assumes that "her" male continues to love her in his freedom while being "snared" or "tricked" by some clever schemer. The man grasps the woman as being assimilated to him, in her immanence; here is why he easily plays the Boubouroche; he cannot imagine that she too could be someone who slips away from him; jealousy for him is ordinarily just a passing crisis, like love itself: the crisis may be violent and even murderous, but rarely does it last long in him. Jealousy for him mainly appears derivative: when things go badly for him or when he feels threatened by life, he feels derided by his wife.[16] By contrast, a woman loving a man in his alterity and transcendence feels in danger at every moment. There is no great distance between betrayal by absence and infidelity. As soon as she feels unloved, she becomes jealous: given her demands, it is always more or less true; her

---

14. Fanny Hurst, *Back Street*.
15. Rosamond Lehmann, *The Weather in the Streets*.
16. This comes to the fore, for example, in Lagache's work *The Nature and Forms of Jealousy*. [The correct title of Lagache's book is *La jalousie amoureuse*—*Jealousy in Love.*—TRANS.]

reproaches and her grievances, whatever their pretexts, are converted into jealous scenes: this is how she will express her impatience, the ennui of waiting, the bitter feeling of her dependence, the regret of having only a mutilated existence. Her whole destiny is at stake in every glance her lover casts at another woman since she has alienated her entire being in him. And she becomes irritated if for one instant her lover turns his eyes to another woman; if he reminds her that she has just been dwelling on a stranger for a long time, she firmly answers: "It's not the same thing." She is right. A man looked at by a woman receives nothing: giving begins only at the moment when the feminine flesh becomes prey. But the coveted woman is immediately metamorphosed into a desirable and desired object; and the neglected woman in love "returns to ordinary clay." Thus she is always on the lookout. What is he doing? At whom is he looking? To whom is he talking? What one smile gave her, another smile can take back from her; an instant is enough to hurl her from "the pearly light of immortality" to everyday dusk. She has received everything from love; she can lose everything by losing it. Vague or definite, unfounded or justified, jealousy is frightening torture for the woman because it is a radical contestation of love: if the betrayal is certain, it is necessary to either renounce making a religion of love or renounce that love; it is such a radical upheaval that one can understand how the woman in love, both doubting and deceived, can be obsessed by the desire and fear of discovering the mortal truth.

Being both arrogant and anxious, the woman is often constantly jealous but wrongly so: Juliette Drouet had pangs of suspicion toward all the women who came near Hugo, only forgetting to fear Léonie Biard, who was his mistress for eight years. When unsure, every woman is a rival and a danger. Love kills friendship insofar as the woman in love encloses herself in the universe of the loved man; jealousy exasperates her solitude, thus constricting her dependence even more. But she finds there recourse against boredom; keeping a husband is work; keeping a lover is a kind of vocation. The woman who, lost in happy adoration, neglected her personal appearance begins to worry about it again the moment she senses a threat. Dressing, caring for her home, or social appearances become moments of combat. Fighting is stimulating activity; as long as she is fairly certain to win, the woman warrior finds a poignant pleasure in it. But the tormented fear of defeat transforms the generously consented gift into a humiliating servitude. The man attacks in defense. Even a proud woman is forced to be gentle and passive; maneuvers, prudence, trickery, smiles, charm, and docility are her best weapons. I still see this young woman whose bell I unexpectedly rang; I had just left her two hours before, badly made up, sloppily dressed, her eyes dull; but now she was waiting for *him;* when she saw me, she put on her ordinary face again, but for an instant I had the time to see her, prepared for him, her face contracted in fear and hypocrisy, ready for any suffering behind her breezy smile; her hair was carefully coiffed, special makeup brightened her cheeks and lips, and she was dressed up in a sparkling white lace blouse. Party clothes, fighting clothes. The masseuse, beauty consultant, and "aesthetician" know how tragically serious their women clients are about treatments that seem useless; new seductions have to be invented for the lover, she has to become that woman he wishes to meet and possess. But all effort is in vain: she will not resurrect in herself that image of the Other that first attracted him, that might attract him to another. There is the same duplicitous and impossible imperative in the lover as in the husband; he wants his mistress absolutely his and yet another; he wants her to be the answer to his dreams and still be different from anything his imagination could invent, a response to his expectations and an unexpected surprise. This contradiction tears the woman apart and dooms her to failure. She tries to model herself on her lover's desire; many women who bloomed at the beginning of a love affair that reinforced their narcissism become frightening in their maniacal servility when they feel less loved; obsessed and diminished, they irritate their lover; giving herself blindly to him, the woman loses that dimension of freedom that made her fascinating at first. He was looking for his own reflection in her: but if he finds it too faithful, he becomes bored. One of the misfortunes of the woman in love is that her love itself disfigures her, demolishes her; she is no more than this slave, this servant, this too-docile mirror, this too-faithful echo. When she realizes it, her distress reduces her worth even more; she ends up losing all attraction with her tears, demands, and scenes. An existent is what he does; to be, she has to put her trust in a foreign consciousness and give up doing anything. "I only know how to love," writes Julie de Lespinasse. *I who am only love:* this title of a novel is the motto of the woman in love;[17] she is only love, and when love is deprived of its object, she is nothing.

Often she understands her mistake; and so she tries to reaffirm her freedom, to find her alterity; she becomes flirtatious. Desired by other men, she interests her blasé lover again: such is the hackneyed theme of many awful novels, absence is sometimes enough to bring back her prestige; Albertine seems insipid when she is present and docile; from afar she

17. Dominique Rolin, *Moi qui ne suis qu'amour.*

becomes mysterious again, and the jealous Proust appreciates her again. But these maneuvers are delicate; if the man sees through them, they only serve to reveal to him how ridiculous his slave's servitude is. And even their success can be dangerous: because she is his the lover disdains his mistress, but he is attached to her because she is his; is it disdain or is it attachment that an infidelity will kill? It may be that, vexed, the man turns away from the indifferent one: he wants her free, yes; but he wants her given. She knows this risk: it paralyzes her flirtatiousness. It is almost impossible for a woman in love to play this game skillfully; she is too afraid to be caught in her own trap. And insofar as she still reveres her lover, she is loath to dupe him: How can he remain a god in her eyes? If she wins the match, she destroys her idol; if she loses it, she loses herself. There is no salvation.

A cautious woman in love—but these words clash—tries to convert the lover's passion into tenderness, friendship, habit; or she tries to attach him with solid ties: a child or marriage; this desire of marriage haunts many liaisons: it is one of security; the clever mistress takes advantage of the generosity of young love to take out insurance on the future: but when she gives herself over to these speculations, she no longer deserves the name of woman in love. For she madly dreams of securing the lover's freedom forever, but not of destroying it. And this is why, except in the rare case where free commitment lasts a whole life, love-religion leads to catastrophe. With Mora, Mlle de Lespinasse was lucky enough to tire of him first: she tired of him because she had met Guibert, who in return promptly tired of her. The love between Mme d'Agoult and Liszt died of this implacable dialectic: the passion, vitality, and ambition that made Liszt so easy to love destined him to other loves. The Portuguese nun could only be abandoned. The fire that made D'Annunzio so captivating[18] had a price: his infidelity. A rupture can deeply mark a man: but in the end, he has his life as man to live. The abandoned woman is nothing, has nothing. If she is asked "How did you live before?" she cannot even remember. She let fall into ashes the world that was hers to adopt a new land from which she is brutally expelled; she gave up all the values she believed in, broke off her friendships; she finds herself without a roof over her head and the desert all around her. How could she begin a new life when outside her lover there is nothing? She takes refuge in delirious imaginings as in former times in the convent; or if she is too reasonable, there is nothing left but to die: very quickly, like Mlle de Lespinasse, or little by little; the agony can last a long time. When a woman has been devoted to a man body and soul for ten or twenty years, when he

---

18. According to Isadora Duncan.

has remained firmly on the pedestal where she put him, being abandoned is a crushing catastrophe. "What can I do," asks this forty-year-old woman, "what can I do if Jacques no longer loves me?" She dressed, fixed her hair, and made herself up meticulously; but her hardened face, already undone, could barely arouse a new love; and she herself, after twenty years spent in the shadow of a man, could she ever love another? There are many years still to live at forty. I still see that other woman who kept her beautiful eyes and noble features in spite of a face swollen with suffering and who let her tears flow down her cheeks in public, blind and deaf, without even realizing it. Now the god is telling another the words invented for her; dethroned queen, she no longer knows if she ever reigned over a true kingdom. If the woman is still young, she has the chance of healing; a new love will heal her; sometimes she will give herself to it with somewhat more reserve, realizing that what is not unique cannot be absolute; but often she will be crushed even more violently than the first time because she will have to redeem herself for her past defeat. The failure of absolute love is a productive ordeal only if the woman is capable of taking herself in hand again; separated from Abélard, Héloïse was not a wreck, because, directing an abbey, she constructed an autonomous existence. Colette's heroines have too much pride and too many resources to let themselves be broken by an amorous disillusion; Renée Néré is saved by her work. And Sido tells her daughter that she was not too worried about her emotional destiny because she knew that Colette was much more than a woman in love. But there are few crimes that bring worse punishment than this generous mistake: to put one's self entirely in another's hands.

Authentic love must be founded on reciprocal recognition of two freedoms; each lover would then experience himself as himself and as the other; neither would abdicate his transcendence, they would not mutilate themselves; together they would both reveal values and ends in the world. For each of them, love would be the revelation of self through the gift of self and the enrichment of the universe. In his work *La connaissance de soi* (The Discovery of Self),* Georges Gusdorf summarizes precisely what *man* demands of love:

Love reveals us to ourselves by making us come out of ourselves. We affirm ourselves by contact with that which is foreign and complementary to us. Love as a form of understanding discovers

---

* The correct title of the work is *La découverte de soi.*—TRANS.

new heavens and new earths even in the very landscape where we have always lived. Here is the great secret: the world is other, *I myself am other*. And I am no longer alone in knowing it. Even better: someone taught me this. Woman therefore plays an indispensable and capital role in the consciousness man has of himself.

This accounts for the importance the young man gives to love's apprenticeship;[19] we have seen how Stendhal and Malraux marvel at the miracle that "I myself am another." But Gusdorf is wrong to write "and *in the same way* man represents for the woman an indispensable intermediary of herself to herself," because today her situation is not *the same;* man is revealed in the guise of another, but he remains himself, and his new face is integrated into the whole of his personality. It would only be the same for woman if she also existed essentially for-herself; this would imply that she possessed an economic independence, that she projected herself toward her own ends and surpassed herself without intermediary toward the group. Thus equal loves are possible, such as the one Malraux describes between Kyo and May. It can even happen that the woman plays the virile and dominating role like Mme de Warens with Rousseau, Léa with Chéri. But in most cases, the woman knows herself only as other: her for-others merges with her very being; love is not for her an intermediary between self and self, because she does not find herself in her subjective existence; she remains engulfed in this loving woman that man has not only revealed but also created; her salvation depends on this despotic freedom that formed her and can destroy her in an instant. She spends her life trembling in fear of the one who holds her destiny in his hands without completely realizing it and without completely wanting it; she is in danger in an other, an anguished and powerless witness of her own destiny. Tyrant and executioner in spite of himself, this other wears the face of the enemy in spite of her and himself: instead of the sought-after union, the woman in love experiences the bitterest of solitudes; instead of complicity, struggle and often hate. Love, for the woman, is a supreme attempt to overcome the dependence to which she is condemned by assuming it; but even consented to, dependence can only be lived in fear and servility.

Men have rivaled each other proclaiming that love is a woman's supreme accomplishment. "A woman who loves like a woman becomes *a more perfect woman*," says Nietzsche; and Balzac: "In the higher order,

---

19. See Volume I.

man's life is glory, woman's is love. Woman is equal to man only in making her life a perpetual offering, as his is perpetual action." But there again is a cruel mystification since what she offers, he cares not at all to accept. Man does not need the unconditional devotion he demands, nor the idolatrous love that flatters his vanity; he only accepts them on the condition that he does not satisfy the demands these attitudes reciprocally imply. He preaches to the woman about giving: and her gifts exasperate him; she finds herself disconcerted by her useless gifts, disconcerted by her vain existence. The day when it will be possible for the woman to love in her strength and not in her weakness, not to escape from herself but to find herself, not out of resignation but to affirm herself, love will become for her as for man the source of life and not a mortal danger. For the time being, love epitomizes in its most moving form the curse that weighs on woman trapped in the feminine universe, the mutilated woman, incapable of being self-sufficient. Innumerable martyrs to love attest to the injustice of a destiny that offers them as ultimate salvation a sterile hell.

CHAPTER 13

The Mystic

Love has been assigned to woman as her supreme vocation, and when she addresses it to a man, she is seeking God in him: if circumstances deny her human love, if she is disappointed or demanding, she will choose to worship the divinity in God himself. It is true that there are also men who have burned with this flame; but they are rare, and their fervor has been of a highly refined intellectual form. Women, though, who abandon themselves to the delights of celestial marriages are legion: and they experience them in a strangely affective way. Women are accustomed to living on their knees; normally, they expect their salvation to descend from heaven, where males reign; men too are enveloped in clouds: their majesty is revealed from beyond the veils of their bodily presence. The Beloved is always more or less absent; he communicates with her, his worshipper, in ambiguous signs; she only knows his heart by an act of faith; and the more superior to her he seems, the more impenetrable his behavior seems to her. We have seen that in erotomania this faith resisted all refutations. A woman does not need to see or touch to feel the Presence at her side. Whether it be a doctor, a priest, or God, she will find the same incontestable proof; she will welcome as a slave the waves of a love that falls from on high into her heart. Human love and divine love melt into one not because the latter is a sublimation of the former but because the former is also a movement toward a transcendent, toward the absolute. In any case, the woman in love has to save her contingent existence by uniting with the Whole incarnated in a sovereign Person.

This ambiguity is flagrant in many cases—pathological or normal—where the lover is deified, where God has human traits. I will only cite this one reported by Ferdière in his work on erotomania. It is the patient who is speaking:

In 1923, I corresponded with a journalist from *La Presse;* every day I read his articles about morality. I read between the lines; it seemed to me that he was answering me, giving me advice; I wrote him love letters; I wrote to him a lot . . . In 1924, it suddenly came to me: it seemed to me that God was looking for a woman, that he was going to come and speak to me; I had the impression he had given me a mission, chosen me to found a temple; I believed myself to be the center of a big complex where doctors would take care of women . . . It was then that . . . I was transferred to the Clermont mental institution . . . There were young doctors who wanted to change the world: in my cabin, I felt their kisses on my fingers, I felt their sex organs in my hands; once, they told me: "You are not sensitive, but sensual; turn over"; I turned over and I felt them in me: it was very pleasant . . . The head doctor, Dr. D. . . . , was like a god; I really felt there was something when he came near my bed; he looked at me as if to say: I am all yours. He really loved me: one day, he looked at me insistently in a truly extraordinary way . . . his green eyes became blue as the sky; they widened intensely in an incredible way . . . he saw the effect that produced all the while speaking to another woman patient and he smiled . . . and I thus remained fixated, fixated on Dr. D. . . . one nail does not replace another and in spite of all my lovers (I have had fifteen or sixteen), I could not separate myself from him; that's why he's guilty . . . For more than twelve years, I have been having mental conversations with him . . . when I wanted to forget him, he reappeared . . . he was sometimes a bit mocking . . . "You see, I frighten you," he said again, "you can love others, but you will always come back to me . . ." I often wrote him letters, even making appointments I would keep. Last year, I went to see him; he was remote; there was no warmth; I felt so silly and I left . . . People tell me he married another woman, but he will always love me . . . he is my husband, and yet the act has never taken place, the act that would make the fusion . . . "Abandon everything," he sometimes says, "with me you will always rise upward, you will not be like a being of the earth." You see: each time I look for God, I find a man; now I don't know what religion I should turn to.*

This is a pathological case. But there is this inextricable confusion in many devotees between man and God. In particular, the confessor occupies an ambiguous place between heaven and earth. He listens with carnal

---

* *Erotomania.*—TRANS.

ears to the penitent who bares her soul, but it is a supernatural light that shines in the gaze with which he enfolds her; he is a divine man, he is God in the appearance of a man. Mme Guyon describes her meeting with Father La Combe in these terms: "It seemed to me that an effect of grace came from him to me by the most intimate soul and returned from me to him so that he felt the same thing." The priest's intercession pulled her out of the drought she had been suffering from for years and inflamed her soul once again with ardor. She lived by his side during her entire great mystical period. And she admits: "There was nothing but one whole unity, so that *I could no longer tell him apart from God*." It would be too simple to say she was really in love with a man and she feigned to love God: she also loved this man because he was something other than himself in her eyes. Like Ferdière's patient, she was groping for the supreme source of values. That is what every mystic is aiming for. The male intermediary is sometimes useful for her to launch herself toward heaven's desert; but he is not indispensable. Having difficulty separating reality from play, the act from magical behavior, the object from imagination, woman is singularly likely to presentify through her body an absence. What is much less humorous is confusing mysticism with erotomania, as has sometimes been done: the erotomaniac feels glorified by the love of a sovereign being; he is the one who takes the initiative in the love relationship, he loves more passionately than he is loved; he makes his feelings known by clear but secret signs; he is jealous and irritated by the chosen woman's lack of fervor: he does not hesitate then to punish her; he almost never manifests himself in a carnal and concrete form. All these characteristics are found in mystics; in particular, God cherishes for all eternity the soul he inflames with his love, he shed his blood for her, he prepares splendid apotheoses for her; the only thing she can do is abandon herself to his flames without resistance.

It is accepted today that erotomania takes a sometimes platonic and sometimes sexual form. Likewise, the body has a greater or lesser role in the feelings the mystic devotes to God. Her effusions are modeled on those that earthly lovers experience. While Angela of Foligno contemplates an image of Christ holding Saint Francis in his arms, he tells her: "This is how I will hold you tight and much more than can be seen by the body's eyes . . . I will never leave you if you love me." Mme Guyon writes: "Love gave me no respite. I said to him: Oh my love, enough, leave me." "I want the love that thrills my soul with ineffable tremors, the love that makes me swoon." "Oh my God! If you made the most sensual of women feel what I feel, they would soon quit their false pleasures to partake of such true riches." Saint Teresa's vision is well-known:

In [an angel's] hands I saw a great golden spear . . . This he plunged into my heart several times so that it penetrated my entrails. When he pulled it out I felt that he took them with it, and left me utterly consumed by the great love of God. The pain was so severe that it made me utter several moans. What I am certain of is that the pain penetrates the depths of my entrails and it seems to me that they are torn when my spiritual spouse withdraws the arrow he uses to enter them.

It is sometimes piously claimed that the poverty of language makes it necessary for the mystic to borrow this erotic vocabulary; but she also has only one body, and she borrows from earthly love not only words but also physical attitudes; she has the same behavior when offering herself to God as offering herself to a man. This, however, does not at all diminish the validity of her feelings. When Angela of Foligno becomes "pale and dry" or then "full and flushed," according to the rhythm of her heart, when she breaks down in deluges of tears,[1] when she comes back to earth, it is hardly possible to consider these phenomena as purely "spiritual"; but to explain them by her excessive "emotivity" alone is to invoke the poppy's "sleep-inducing virtue"; the body is never the *cause* of subjective experiences, since it is the subject himself in his objective form: the subject experiences his attitudes in the unity of his existence. Both adversaries and admirers of mystics think that giving a sexual content to Saint Teresa's ecstasies is to reduce her to the rank of a hysteric. But what diminishes the hysterical subject is not the fact that his body actively expresses his obsessions: it is that he is obsessed, that his freedom is subjugated and annulled; the mastery a fakir acquires over his body does not make him its slave; bodily gestures can be part of the expression of a freedom. Saint Teresa's texts are not at all ambiguous, and they justify Bernini's statue showing us the swooning saint in thrall to a stunning sensuality; it would be no less false to interpret her emotions as simple "sexual sublimation"; there is not first an unavowed sexual desire that takes the form of divine love; the woman in love herself is not first the prey of a desire without object that then fixes itself on an individual; it is the presence of the lover that arouses an excitement in her immediately intended to him; thus, in one movement, Saint Teresa seeks to unite with God and experiences this union in her body; she is not slave to her nerves and hormones: rather, she should be admired for the intensity of

---

1. "Tears burned her cheeks to such an extent that she had to apply cold water," says one of her biographers.

a faith that penetrates to the most intimate regions of her flesh. In truth, as Saint Teresa herself understood, the value of a mystical experience is measured not by how it has been subjectively experienced but by its objective scope. The phenomena of ecstasy are approximately the same for Saint Teresa and Marie Alacoque: the interest of their message is very different. Saint Teresa situates the dramatic problem of the relationship between the individual and the transcendent Being in a highly intellectual way; she lived an experience as a woman whose meaning extends beyond any sexual specification; it has to be classified along with that of Saint John of the Cross. But it is a striking exception. What her minor sisters provide is an essentially feminine vision of the world and of salvation; it is not transcendence they are aiming for: it is the redemption of their femininity.[2]

The woman first seeks in divine love what the woman asks for in man's love: the apotheosis of her narcissism; this sovereign gaze fixed on her attentively and lovingly is a miraculous chance for her. Throughout her life as a girl and young woman, Mme Guyon had always been tormented by the desire to be loved and admired. A modern Protestant mystic, Mlle Vé, writes: "Nothing makes me unhappier than having no one interested in me in a special and sympathetic way, in what is taking place in me." Mme Krüdener imagined that God was constantly occupied with her, to such an extent that, says Sainte-Beuve, "in the most decisive moments with her lover she moaned: 'My God, how happy I am! I ask you to forgive my extreme happiness!' " One can understand the intoxication that permeates the heart of the narcissist when all of heaven becomes her mirror; her deified image is infinite like God himself, it will never disappear; and at the same time she feels in her burning, palpitating, and love-drowned breast her soul created, redeemed, and cherished by the adoring Father; it is her double, it is she herself she is embracing, infinitely magnified by God's mediation. These texts of Saint Angela of Foligno are particularly significant. This is how Jesus speaks to her:

> My daughter, sweeter to me than I am to you, my temple, my
> delight. My daughter, my beloved, *love me because you are very much
> loved by me;* much more than you could love me. Your whole life,
> your eating, drinking, your sleeping, and all that you do are pleasing
> to me. I will do great things in you in the sight of the nations.

2. For Catherine of Siena, theological preoccupations nevertheless remain very important. She also is of a rather virile type.

Through you, I shall be known and my name will be praised by many nations. My daughter and my sweet spouse, I love you so much more than any other women.

And again:

My daughter, sweeter to me than I am to you, . . . my delight, the heart of God almighty is now upon your heart . . . God almighty has deposited much love in you, more than in any woman of this city. He takes delight in you.

And once more:

Such is the love I have for you that I am totally unable to remember your faults and my eyes no longer see them. In you I have deposited a great treasure.

The chosen woman cannot fail to respond passionately to such ardent declarations falling from such a lofty place. She tries to connect with the lover using the usual technique of the woman in love: annihilation. "I have only one concern, which is to love, to forget myself, and to annihilate myself," writes Marie Alacoque. Ecstasy bodily mimics this abolition of self; the subject no longer sees or feels, he forgets his body, disavows it. The blinding and sovereign Presence is indirectly indicated by the intensity of this abandon, by the hopeless acceptance of passivity. Mme Guyon's quietism erected this passivity into a system: as for her, she spent a great deal of her time in a kind of catalepsy; she slept wide awake.

Most women mystics are not satisfied with abandoning themselves passively to God: they actively apply themselves to self-annihilation by the destruction of their flesh. Of course, asceticism was also practiced by monks and brothers. But woman's relentlessness in violating her flesh has specific characteristics. We have seen how ambiguous the woman's attitude to her body is: it is through humiliation and suffering that she metamorphoses it into glory. Given over to a lover as a thing of pleasure, she becomes a temple, an idol; torn by the pain of childbirth, she creates heroes. The mystic will torture her flesh to have the right to claim it; reducing it to abjection, she exalts it as the instrument of her salvation. This accounts for the strange excesses of some women saints. Saint Angela of Foligno recounts her delectation in drinking the water in which she had just washed the lepers' hands and feet:

This concoction filled us with such sweetness that joy followed us and brought it home with us. Never had I drunk with such delight. A piece of scaly skin from one of the lepers' wounds had stuck in my throat. Rather than spitting it out, I tried very had to swallow it and I succeeded. It seemed to me that I had just received communion. Never will I be able to express the delights that flooded over me.

It is known that Marie Alacoque cleaned a sick person's vomit with her tongue; she describes in her autobiography her happiness when she had filled her mouth with the excrement of a man with diarrhea; Jesus rewarded her by keeping her lips glued to his Sacred Heart for three hours. Devotion has a carnal coloration in countries of ardent sensuality like Italy and Spain: in a village in Abruzzo, even today women tear their tongues by licking the rocks on the ground along the stations of the cross. In all these practices they are only imitating the Redeemer, who saved flesh by the abasement of his own flesh: women show their sensitivity to this great mystery in a much more concrete way than males.

God appears to woman more readily in the figure of the husband; sometimes he reveals himself in his glory, dazzlingly white and beautiful, and dominating; he clothes her in a wedding dress, he crowns her, takes her by the hand, and promises her a celestial apotheosis. But most often he is a being of flesh: the wedding ring Jesus had given to Saint Catherine and that she wore, invisible, on her finger, was this "ring of flesh" that circumcision had cut off. Above all, he is a mistreated and bloody body: it is in the contemplation of the Crucified that she drowns herself the most fervently; she identifies with the Virgin Mary holding the corpse of her Son in her arms, or with Magdalene standing at the foot of the cross and being sprinkled with the Beloved's blood. Thus does she satisfy her sadomasochistic fantasies. In the humiliation of God, she admires Man's fall: inert, passive, covered with sores, the crucified is the inverted image of the white and red martyr offered to wild beasts, to the knife, to males, and with whom the little girl has so often identified: she is thrown into confusion seeing that Man, Man-God, has assumed his role. It is she who is placed on the wood, promised the splendor of the Resurrection. It is she: she proves it; her forehead bleeds under the crown of thorns; her hands, her feet, her side, are transpierced by an invisible iron. Out of the 321 people with stigmata recognized by the Catholic Church, only 47 are men; the others—including Helen of Hungary, Joan of the Cross, G. van Oosten, Osanna of Mantua, and Clare of Montefalco—are women, who are, on average, past the age of menopause. Catherine Emmerich, the most famous, was marked prematurely. At the age of twenty-four, having desired the sufferings of the crown of thorns, she saw coming toward her a dazzling young man who pushed this crown onto her head. The next day, her temples and forehead swelled and blood began to flow. Four years later, in ecstasy, she saw Christ with rays pointed like fine blades coming from his wounds, and drops of blood then sprang from the saint's hands, feet, and side. She sweated blood, she spat blood. Still today, every Good Friday, Therese Neumann turns a face dripping with Christ's blood toward her visitors. The mysterious alchemy that changes flesh into glory ends in the stigmata since, in the form of a bloody pain, they are the presence of divine love itself. It is quite understandable why women particularly are attached to the metamorphosis of the red flow into pure golden flame. They have a horror of this blood that runs out of the side of the King of men. Saint Catherine of Siena speaks of it in almost all her letters. Angela of Foligno lost herself in the contemplation of the heart of Jesus and the gaping wound in his side. Catherine Emmerich put on a red shirt so as to resemble Jesus when he was like "a cloth soaked in blood"; she saw all things "through Jesus's blood." We have seen in which circumstances Marie Alacoque quenched her thirst for three hours from the Sacred Heart of Jesus. It was she who offered the enormous red clot surrounded by flamboyant darts of love to the adoration of the faithful. That is the emblem symbolizing the great feminine dream: from blood to glory through love.

Ecstasies, visions, and dialogues with God, this interior experience is sufficient for some women. Others feel the need to communicate it to the world through acts. The connection between action and contemplation takes two very different forms. There are women of action like Saint Catherine, Saint Teresa, and Joan of Arc who are well aware of the goals they set themselves and who lucidly invent the means to reach them: their revelations merely give an objective form to their certainties; they encourage them to take the paths they have carefully planned. There are women narcissists like Mme Guyon and Mme Krüdener who, at the limit of silent fervor, feel suddenly "in an apostolic state."[3] They are not very precise concerning their tasks; and—like patronesses seeking excitement—they do not care too much what they do as long as it is *something*. Thus after displaying herself as ambassador and novelist, Mme Krüdener interiorized the conception she had of her own worth: it was not to see definite ideas triumph but to see herself confirmed in her role as God's inspired one that

3. Mme Guyon.

she took the destiny of Alexander I in hand. If a little beauty and intelligence are often enough for a woman to feel endowed with a holy character, it is even more so when she knows she is God's chosen; she feels filled with a mission: she preaches dubious doctrines, she eagerly founds sects, and this allows her to effectuate, through the members of the group she inspires, a thrilling multiplication of her personality.

Mystical fervor, like love and even narcissism, can be integrated into active and independent lives. But in themselves these attempts at individual salvation can only result in failures; either the woman establishes a relation with an unreal: her double or God; or she creates an unreal relation with a real being; in any case, she has no grasp on the world; she does not escape her subjectivity; her freedom remains mystified; there is only one way of accomplishing it authentically: it is to project it by a positive action into human society.

PART FOUR

TOWARD LIBERATION

CHAPTER 14

The Independent Woman

French law no longer includes obedience among a wife's duties, and every woman citizen has become a voter; these civic liberties remain abstract if there is no corresponding economic autonomy; the kept woman—wife or mistress—is not freed from the male just because she has a ballot paper in her hands; while today's customs impose fewer constraints on her than in the past, such negative licenses have not fundamentally changed her situation; she remains a vassal, imprisoned in her condition. It is through work that woman has been able, to a large extent, to close the gap separating her from the male; work alone can guarantee her concrete freedom. The system based on her dependence collapses as soon as she ceases to be a parasite; there is no longer need for a masculine mediator between her and the universe. The curse on the woman vassal is that she is not allowed to do anything; so she stubbornly pursues the impossible quest for being through narcissism, love, or religion; when she is productive and active, she regains her transcendence; she affirms herself concretely as subject in her projects; she senses her responsibility relative to the goals she pursues and to the money and rights she appropriates. Many women are conscious of these advantages, even those with the lowest-level jobs. I heard a cleaning woman as she was washing a hotel lobby floor say, "I never asked anyone for anything. I made it on my own." She was as proud of being self-sufficient as a Rockefeller. However, one must not think that the simple juxtaposition of the right to vote and a job amounts to total liberation; work today is not freedom. Only in a socialist world would the woman who has one be sure of the other. Today, the majority of workers are exploited. Moreover, social structures have not been deeply modified by the changes in women's condition. This world has always belonged to men and still retains the form they have imprinted on it. It is important not to lose sight of these facts that make the question of women's work complex. An important and self-righteous woman recently carried out a study on women workers at a Renault factory: she asserts that they would rather stay at home than work in a factory. Without a doubt, they are economically independent only within an economically oppressed class; and besides, tasks carried out in a factory do not free them from household chores.[1] If they had been able to choose between forty hours of weekly work in a factory *or* at home, they would undoubtedly have responded quite differently; and they might even accept both jobs eagerly if, as women workers, they would become part of a world that would be their world, that they would proudly and happily participate in building. In today's work, without even mentioning women who work on the land,[2] most working women do not escape the traditional feminine world; neither society nor their husbands give them the help needed to become, in concrete terms, the equals of men. Only those women with political convictions, active in trade unions, who are confident in the future, can give an ethical meaning to the thankless daily labor; but as women deprived of leisure time and inheriting a tradition of submissiveness, it is understandable that they are just beginning to develop their political and social awareness. It is understandable that since they do not receive the moral and social benefits they could legitimately expect in exchange for their work, they simply resign themselves to its constraints. It is also understandable that a shopgirl, an office worker, or a secretary should not want to give up the advantages of having a male to lean on. I have already said that it is an almost irresistible temptation for a young woman to be part of a privileged caste when she can do so simply by surrendering her body; she is doomed to have love affairs because her wages are minimal for the very high standard of living society demands of her; if she settles for what she earns, she will be no more than a pariah: without decent living accommodations or clothes, all amusement and even love will be refused her. Virtuous people preach asceticism to her; in fact, her diet is often as austere as a Carmelite's; but not everyone can have God as a lover: she needs to please men to succeed in her life as a woman. So she will accept help: her employer cynically counts on this when he pays her a pittance. Sometimes this help will enable her to improve her situation and achieve real independence; but sometimes she will give up her job to become a kept woman. She often does both: she frees herself from her lover through work, and she escapes work thanks to her lover; but then she experiences the double servitude of a job and mas-

---

1. I said in Volume I, Part Two, "History," pp. 71–156, how burdensome these are for the woman who works outside the home.

2. Whose condition we examined, ibid., p. 153.

culine protection. For the married woman, her salary usually only means extra income; for the "woman who is helped," it is the man's protection that seems inessential; but neither woman buys total independence through her own efforts.

However, there are quite a lot of privileged women today who have gained economic and social autonomy in their professions. They are the ones who are at issue when the question of women's possibilities and their future is raised. While they are still only a minority, it is particularly interesting to study their situation closely; they are the subject of continuing debate between feminists and antifeminists. The latter maintain that today's emancipated women do not accomplish anything important, and that besides they have trouble finding their inner balance. The former exaggerate the emancipated women's achievements and are blind to their frustrations. In fact, there is no reason to assume that they are on the wrong track; and yet it is obvious that they are not comfortably settled in their new condition: they have come only halfway as yet. Even the woman who has emancipated herself economically from man is still not in a moral, social, or psychological situation identical to his. Her commitment to and focus on her profession depend on the context of her life as a whole. And, when she starts her adult life, she does not have the same past as a boy; society does not see her with the same eyes; she has a different perspective on the universe. Being a woman poses unique problems to an autonomous human being today.

The advantage man enjoys and which manifests itself from childhood onward is that his vocation as a human being in no way contradicts his destiny as a male. The fact that the phallus is assimilated with transcendence means that man's social and spiritual successes endow him with virile prestige. He is not divided. However, for a woman to accomplish her femininity, she is required to be object and prey; that is, she must renounce her claims as a sovereign subject. This is the conflict that singularly characterizes the situation of the emancipated woman. She refuses to confine herself to her role as female because she does not want to mutilate herself; but it would also be a mutilation to repudiate her sex. Man is a sexed human being; woman is a complete individual, and equal to the male, only if she too is a sexed human being. Renouncing her femininity means renouncing part of her humanity. Misogynists have often reproached intellectual women for "letting themselves go"; but they also preach to them: if you want to be our equals, stop wearing makeup and polishing your nails. This advice is absurd. Precisely because the idea of femininity is artificially defined by customs and fashion, it is imposed on every woman from the outside; it may evolve so that its fashion standards come closer to those of men: on the beach, women now wear trousers. That does not change the core of the problem: the individual is not free to shape the idea of femininity at will. By not conforming, a woman devalues herself sexually and consequently socially because society has incorporated sexual values. Rejecting feminine attributes does not mean acquiring virile ones; even a transvestite cannot turn herself into a man: she is a transvestite. We have seen that homosexuality also constitutes a specification: neutrality is impossible. There is no negative attitude that does not imply a positive counterpart. The adolescent girl often thinks she can simply scorn convention; but by doing so, she is making a statement; she is creating a new situation involving consequences she will have to assume. Whenever one ignores an established convention, one becomes a rebel. A flamboyantly dressed woman is lying when she ingenuously claims she is simply dressing to suit herself, and that is all: she knows perfectly well that suiting herself is an absurdity. Inversely, if she does not want to look eccentric, she follows the rules. Choosing defiance is a risky tactic unless it is a positively effective action; more time and energy are spent than saved. A woman who has no desire to shock, no intention to devalue herself socially, has to live her woman's condition as a woman: very often her professional success even requires it. But while conformity is quite natural for a man—custom being based on his needs as an autonomous and active individual—the woman who is herself also subject and activity has to fit into a world that has doomed her to passivity. This servitude is even greater since women confined to the feminine sphere have magnified its importance: they have made dressing and housekeeping difficult arts. The man barely has to care about his clothes; they are comfortable, adapted to his active life, and need not be original; they are hardly part of his personality; what's more, no one expects him to take care of them himself: some woman, volunteer or paid, delivers him from this chore. The woman, on the other hand, knows that when people look at her, they do not distinguish her from her appearance: she is judged, respected, or desired in relation to how she looks. Her clothes were originally meant to doom her to impotence, and they still remain fragile: stockings run; heels wear down; light-colored blouses and dresses get dirty; pleats unpleat; but she must still repair most of these accidents herself; her peers will never volunteer to help her out, and she will have second thoughts about straining her budget for work she *can* do herself: perm, hairdos, makeup, and new dresses are already expensive enough. Whether she is a secretary or a student, when she goes home at night, there is always a stocking to mend, a blouse to wash, a skirt to iron.

The woman who earns a good living will spare herself these chores; but she will be held to a higher standard of elegance, she will waste time on shopping and dress fittings, and such. Tradition also demands that the woman, even unmarried, pay attention to her home; a government official sent to a new city thinks nothing of living in a hotel; his woman colleague will try to "set up house"; she has to keep it spotless because her negligence will not be excused, whereas a man's will be overlooked. However, public opinion is not the only concern that makes her devote so much time and care to her looks and home. She wants to feel like a real woman for her own personal satisfaction. She only succeeds in accepting herself from the perspective of both the present and the past by combining the life she has made for herself with the destiny prepared for her by her mother, her childhood games, and her adolescent fantasies. She has cultivated narcissistic dreams; she continues to pit the cult of her image against the phallic pride of the male; she wants to show off, to charm. Her mother and other older women have fostered her nesting instinct: a home of her own was the earliest form of her dream of independence; she would not think of discarding it, even when she finds freedom in other ways. And not yet feeling secure in the male universe, she still needs a retreat, a symbol of that interior refuge she has been used to finding in herself. Following docilely in the feminine tradition, she will wax her floors or do her own cooking instead of going to a restaurant like her male colleague. She wants to live both like a man and like a woman; her workload and her fatigue are multiplied as a result.

If she intends to remain fully woman, it also means she intends to approach the opposite sex with the maximum of odds on her side. It is in the area of sex that the most difficult problems will arise. To be a complete individual, equal to man, woman has to have access to the male world as man does to the female one, access to the *other;* but the demands of the *other* are not symmetrical in the two cases. Once acquired, the seemingly immanent virtues of fame and fortune can enhance the woman's sexual attraction; but being an autonomous activity contradicts her femininity: she knows this. The independent woman—and especially the intellectual who thinks through her situation—will suffer from an inferiority complex as a female; she does not have as much free time for beauty care as a flirt, whose only preoccupation is to seduce; while she might follow all the experts' advice, she will never be more than an amateur in the elegance department; feminine charm demands that transcendence deteriorating into immanence no longer be anything more than a subtle carnal throb; she must be a spontaneously offered prey: the intellectual woman knows she is offering herself, she knows she is a consciousness, a subject; one cannot willfully kill one's gaze and change one's eyes into empty pools; a body that reaches out to the world cannot be thwarted and metamorphosed into a statue animated by hidden vibrations. The more the intellectual woman fears failure, the more zealously she will try; but this conscious zeal remains an activity and falls short of its goal. She makes mistakes like those blamed on menopause: she tries to deny her intelligence as an aging woman tries to deny her age; she dresses like a girl, she overdoes the flowers, the frills, and the loud materials; she carries childish and wide-eyed mimicry too far. She romps, skips, prattles, acts overly casual, scatterbrained, and impulsive. But she looks like those actors who, failing to feel the emotion that would relax certain muscles, purposely contract antagonistic ones instead, lowering their eyelids or the corners of their mouths instead of letting them drop; thus the intelligent woman, wishing to appear uninhibited, stiffens instead. She senses this, and it irritates her; suddenly an unintended piercing spark of intelligence passes over her totally naive face; her lips full of promise become pursed. If she has trouble pleasing men, it is because she is not like her little slave sisters, a pure will to please; her desire to seduce may be strong, but it has not penetrated into the marrow of her bones; as soon as she feels awkward, she gets fed up with her servility; she tries to take her revenge by playing the game with masculine weapons: she talks instead of listening, she flaunts clever ideas, unusual feelings; she contradicts her interlocutor instead of going along with him, she tries to outdo him. Mme de Staël cleverly mixed both methods with stunning triumphs: she was almost always irresistible. But defiance, so frequent, for example, among American women, irritates men more than it wins them over; it is men, however, who provoke it by their own defiance; if men were content to love a peer instead of a slave—as indeed some men do who are without either arrogance or an inferiority complex—then women would be far less obsessed with their femininity; they would become more natural and simple and would easily rediscover themselves as women, which, after all, they are.

The fact is that men are beginning to come to terms with the new condition of women; no longer feeling condemned a priori, women feel more at ease; today the working woman does not neglect her femininity, nor does she lose her sexual attraction. This success—already a step toward equality—remains, nonetheless, incomplete; it is still much harder for a woman than for a man to have the type of relationship she would like with the other sex. Many obstacles stand in the way of her sex and love life. And the vassal woman is no better off: sexually and emotionally, most wives and mistresses are radically frustrated. These difficulties are more obvious for the independent woman because she has chosen not resignation but combat. All living problems find a silent solution in death; so a woman who works at living is more torn than one who buries her will and desires; but she will not accept being offered this as an example. She will consider herself at a disadvantage only when she compares herself with man.

A woman who works hard, who has responsibilities, and who knows how harsh the struggle is against the world's obstacles needs—like the male—not only to satisfy her physical desires but also to experience the relaxation and diversion provided by enjoyable sexual adventures. Now, there are still some environments where it is not concretely recognized that she should have this freedom; if she avails herself of it, she risks compromising her reputation and career; at the least, a burdensome hypocrisy is demanded of her. The more she has succeeded in making her mark socially, the more willingly will people close their eyes; but she is severely scrutinized, especially in the provinces. Even in the most favorable circumstances—when fear of public opinion is not an issue—her situation is not the same in this area as the man's. Differences stem from both tradition and the problems posed by the particular nature of feminine sexuality.

The man can easily engage in casual sex that at least calms his physical needs and is good for his morale. There have been women—a small number—who have demanded the opening of bordellos for women; in a novel titled *Le numéro 17* (Number 17), a woman proposed creating houses where women could go and find "sexual relief" with a sort of "taxi-boy."[3] It seems that such an establishment once existed in San Francisco; it was frequented only by the girls from the bordellos, amused by the idea of paying instead of being paid: their pimps had them closed. Besides the fact that this solution is utopian and undesirable, it would also probably have little success: we have seen that woman does not attain "relief" as mechanically as man; most women would hardly consider this solution favorable to sexual abandon. In any case, the fact is that this recourse is not open to them today. The solution of women picking up a partner for a night or an hour—assuming that the woman, endowed with a strong temperament and having overcome all her inhibitions, can consider it without disgust—is far more dangerous for her than for the male. The risk of venereal disease is more serious for her in that it is up to him to take precautions to avoid con-

---

3. The author—whose name I have forgotten, but it is unimportant—explains at length how they could be trained to satisfy any client, what kind of life should be imposed on them, and so forth.

tamination; and, however prudent she may be, she is never completely covered against the threat of becoming pregnant. But the difference in physical strength is also very significant, especially in relations between strangers—relations that take place on a physical level. A man has little to fear from the woman he takes home; a little vigilance is enough. It is not the same for the woman who lets a man into her house. I have been told of two young women, newly arrived in Paris and avid to "see life," who, after doing the town, invited two seductive Montmartre pimps to a late supper: in the morning they found themselves robbed, brutalized, and threatened with blackmail. A worse case is that of a divorced woman of about forty who worked hard all day to feed her three grown children and elderly parents. Still beautiful and attractive, she had absolutely no leisure time to have a social life, to flirt, or to make any of the usual efforts necessary for seduction, which in any case would have bored her. Yet she had strong physical desires; and she felt that, like a man, she had the right to satisfy them. Some evenings she went out to roam the streets and managed to pick up a man. But one night, after an hour or two spent in a thicket in the Bois de Boulogne, her lover refused to let her leave: he wanted her name, her address, to see her again, to live with her; when she refused, he beat her violently and only left her when she was wounded and terrorized. As for taking on a lover by supporting him or helping him out, as men often take on a mistress, it is possible only for wealthy women. There are some for whom this deal works: by paying the male, they make an instrument of him, permitting them to use him with disdainful abandon. But women must usually be older to dissociate eroticism from sentiment so crudely, because in feminine adolescence this connection is, as we have seen, so deep. There are also many men who never accept this division between flesh and consciousness. For even more reasons, the majority of women will refuse to consider it. Besides, there is an element of deception they are more aware of than men: the paying client is an instrument as well, used by the partner as a livelihood. Virile arrogance hides the ambiguities of the erotic drama from the male: he spontaneously lies to himself; the woman is more easily humiliated, more susceptible, and also more lucid; she will succeed in blinding herself only at the price of a more cunning bad faith. Even supposing she has the means, she will not find it generally satisfying to buy a man.

For most women—and also for some men—it is a question not only of satisfying their desires but of maintaining their dignity as human beings while satisfying them. When the male gets sexual satisfaction from the woman, or when he satisfies her, he posits himself as the unique subject:

imperious victor, generous donor, or both. She wants to affirm reciprocally that she submits her partner to her pleasure and covers him with her gifts. Thus when she convinces the man of her worth, either by the benefits she promises him or by relying on his courtesy or by skillfully arousing his desire in its pure generality, she easily persuades herself that she is satisfying him. Thanks to this beneficial conviction, she can solicit him without feeling humiliated since she claims she is acting out of generosity. Thus in *Green Wheat*, the "woman in white" who lusts for Phil's caresses archly tells him: "I only like beggars and the hungry." In fact, she is cleverly angling for him to act imploringly. So, says Colette, "she rushed toward the narrow and dark kingdom where her pride could believe that a moan is a confession of distress, and where the aggressive beggars of her sort drink the illusion of generosity." Mme de Warens exemplifies these women who choose their lovers young, unhappy, or of a lower social class to make their appetite look like generosity. But there are also fearless women who take on the challenge of the most robust males and who are delighted to have satisfied them even though they may have succumbed only out of politeness or fear.

On the other hand, while the woman who traps the man likes to imagine herself giving, the woman who gives herself wants it understood that she takes. "As for me, I am a woman who takes," a young woman journalist told me one day. The truth in these cases is that, except for rape, no one really takes the other; but the woman is lying doubly to herself. For the fact is that man does often seduce by his passion and aggressiveness, thereby actively gaining his partner's consent. Except in special cases—like Mme de Staël, to whom I have already referred—it is otherwise for the woman: she can do little else than offer herself; for most males are fiercely jealous of their role; they want to awaken a personal sexual response in the woman, not to be selected to satisfy her need in its generality: chosen, they feel exploited.[4] "A woman who is not afraid of men frightens them," a young man told me. And I have often heard adults declare: "I am horrified by a woman who takes the initiative." If the woman proposes herself too boldly, the man flees: he insists on conquering. The woman can thus take only when she is prey: she must become a passive thing, a promise of submission. If she succeeds, she will think she has willingly performed this magic conjuration; she will see herself become subject again. But she runs the risk of being turned into a fixed and useless object by the male's dis-

4. This feeling corresponds to the one we have pointed out in the girl. Only she resigns herself to her destiny in the end.

dain. This is why she is so deeply humiliated if he rejects her advances. The man also sometimes gets angry when he feels he has been taken in; nonetheless, he has only failed in an enterprise, nothing more. The woman, on the other hand, has consented to make herself flesh through her sexual arousal, anticipation, and promise; she could only win by losing: she remains lost. One must be particularly blind or exceptionally lucid to choose such a defeat. And even when seduction succeeds, victory remains ambiguous; thus, according to public opinion, it is the man who conquers, who *has* the woman. It does not accept that she can, like the man, assume her desires: she is their prey. It is understood that the male has integrated the forces of the species into his individuality, whereas the woman is the slave of the species.[5] She is represented alternately as pure passivity: she is a "slut; open for business"; ready and willing, she is a utensil; she limply gives in to the spell of arousal, she is fascinated by the male who picks her like a fruit. Or else she is seen as an alienated activity: there is a devil raging in her womb, a serpent lurks in her vagina, craving to devour male sperm. In any case, it is out of the question to think of her as simply free. In France especially, the free woman and the easy woman are stubbornly confused, as the idea of easy implies an absence of resistance and control, a lack, the very negation of freedom. Women authors try to combat this prejudice: for example, in *Grisélidis* (Portrait of Grisela), Clara Malraux emphasizes that her heroine does not let herself be drawn in, but accomplishes an act for which she accepts full responsibility. In America, a freedom is recognized in woman's sexual activity, which is very favorable to her. But in France, men's disdain for women who "sleep around," the very men who profit from their favors, paralyzes many women. They fear the remonstrances they would incite, the remarks they would provoke.

Even if the woman scorns anonymous rumors, she has concrete difficulties in her relations with her partner, for public opinion is embodied in him. Very often, he considers the bed the terrain for asserting his aggressive superiority. He wants to take and not receive, not exchange but ravish. He seeks to possess the woman beyond that which she gives him; he demands that her consent be a defeat, and that the words she murmurs be avowals that he extracts from her; if she admits her pleasure, she is acknowledging her submission. When Claudine defies Renaud by her promptness in submitting to him, he anticipates her: he rushes to rape her

---

5. We have seen in Volume I, Chapter 1 that there is a certain truth in this opinion. But it is precisely not at the moment of desire that this asymmetry appears: it is in procreation. In desire man and woman assume their natural function identically.

when she was going to offer herself; he forces her to keep her eyes open to contemplate his triumph in their torment. Thus, in *Man's Fate*, the over-bearing Ferral insists on switching on the lamp Valérie wants to put out.* Proud and demanding, the woman faces the male as an adversary; she is far less well armed in this battle than he; first of all, he has physical force, and it is easier for him to impose his desires; we have also noted that tension and activity correspond to his eroticism, whereas the woman who refuses pas-sivity breaks the spell that brings her sexual satisfaction; if she mimics domination in her attitudes and movements, she fails to reach a climax: most women who surrender to their pride become frigid. Rare are those lovers who allow their mistresses to satisfy their dominating or sadistic ten-dencies; and even rarer still are those women who derive full erotic satis-faction from this male docility.

There is a road that seems much less thorny for the woman, that of masochism. When one works, struggles, and takes responsibilities and risks during the day, it is relaxing to abandon oneself at night to vigorous caprices. In love or naive, the woman in fact is often happy to annihilate herself for the benefit of a tyrannical will. But she still has to feel truly dominated. It is not easy for a woman who lives daily among men to believe in the unconditional supremacy of males. I have been told about the case of a not really masochistic but very "feminine" woman, that is, one who deeply appreciated the pleasure of abdication in masculine arms; from the age of seventeen, she had had several husbands and numerous lovers, all of whom gave her great satisfaction; having successfully carried out a difficult project where she managed men, she complained of having become frigid: her once-blissful submission became impossible for her because she had become used to dominating males and because their pres-tige had vanished. When the woman begins to doubt men's superiority, their claims can only diminish her esteem for them. In bed, at moments where the man feels he is most fiercely male, the very fact of his miming virility makes him look infantile to knowing eyes: he is merely warding off the old castration complex, the shadow of his father, or some other fantasy. It is not always out of pride that the mistress refuses to give in to her lover's caprices: she wants to interact with an adult who is living a real moment of his life, not a little boy fooling himself. The masochistic woman is particu-larly disappointed: a maternal, exasperated, or indulgent complaisance is not the abdication she dreams of. Either she herself will also have to make

---

* André Malraux, *Man's Fate*—TRANS.

do with meaningless games, pretending to be dominated and subjugated, or she will run after men considered "superior" in the hope of coming across a master, or else she will become frigid.

We have seen that it is possible to escape the temptations of sadism and masochism when both partners recognize each other as equals; as soon as there is a little modesty and some generosity between men and women, ideas of victory and defeat are abolished: the act of love becomes a free exchange. But, paradoxically, it is harder for woman than for man to recognize an individual of the opposite sex as her equal. Precisely because the male caste enjoys superiority, man can hold many individual women in affectionate esteem: a woman is easy to love; she has, first of all, the privilege of introducing her lover to a world different from his own and one that he is pleased to explore at her side; she fascinates, she amuses, at least for a little while; and then, because her situation is limited and subordinate, all her qualities seem like conquests while her errors are excusable. Stendhal admires Mme de Rênal and Mme de Chasteller in spite of their detestable prejudices; the man does not hold a woman responsible for not being very intelligent, clear-sighted, or courageous: she is a victim, he thinks—often rightly—of her situation; he dreams of what she could have been, of what she will perhaps be: she can be given credit, one can grant her a great deal because she *is* nothing definite in particular; this lack is what will cause the lover to grow tired of her quickly: but it is the source of her mystery, the charm that seduces him and inclines him to feel superficial tenderness for her. It is far less easy to show friendship for a man: for he is what he made himself be, without help; he must be loved in his presence and his reality, not in his promises and uncertain possibilities; he is responsible for his behavior, his ideas; he has no excuse. There is fraternity with him only if his acts, goals, and opinions are approved; Julien can love a legitimist; a Lamiel could not cherish a man whose ideas she detests. Even ready to compromise, the woman has trouble adopting a tolerant attitude. For the man does not offer her a green paradise of childhood, she meets him in this world that is common to both of them: he brings only himself. Closed in on himself, defined, decided, he does not inspire dreams; when he speaks, one must listen; he takes himself seriously: if he does not prove interesting, he becomes bothersome, his presence weighs heavily. Only very young men allow themselves to appear adorned by the marvelous; one can seek mystery and promise in them, find excuses for them, take them lightly: this is one of the reasons mature women find them so seductive. But they themselves prefer young women in most cases. The thirty-year-old woman has no choice but to turn to adult males. And she will undoubtedly meet some who deserve both her esteem and her friendship; but she will be lucky if they do not then display arrogance. The problem she has when looking for an affair or an adventure involving her heart as well as her body is meeting a man she can consider her equal, without his seeing himself as superior.

One might say that in general women do not make such a fuss; they seize the occasion without much questioning, and then they make do with their pride and sensuality. That is true. But it is also true that they bury in the secret of their hearts many disappointments, humiliations, regrets, and grievances whose equivalents are unknown—on the whole—to men. The man will almost surely get the benefit of pleasure from a more or less unsuccessful affair; the woman might well not profit from it at all; even if indifferent, she politely lends herself to lovemaking when the decisive moment arrives. The lover might prove to be impotent, and she will suffer from having compromised herself in a ludicrous escapade; if she does not reach arousal, then she feels "had," deceived; if she is satisfied, she will want to hold on to her lover for a longer time. She is rarely completely sincere when she claims to envisage nothing more than a short-term adventure just for pleasure, because pleasure, far from freeing her, binds her; separation, even a so-called friendly one, wounds her. It is far more rare to hear a woman talk good-naturedly about a former lover than a man about his mistresses.

The nature of her eroticism and the difficulties of a free sexual life push the woman toward monogamy. Nonetheless, a liaison or marriage is far less easily reconciled with a career for her than for the man. The lover or husband may ask her to give up her career: she hesitates, like Colette's Vagabond who ardently wishes to have a man's warmth at her side but who dreads the conjugal shackles; if she gives in, she is once again a vassal; if she refuses, she condemns herself to a withering solitude. Today, the man generally accepts the idea that his partner should continue working; novels by Colette Yver that show young women cornered into sacrificing their professions to maintain peace at home are somewhat outdated; living together is an enrichment for two free beings, who find a guarantee of their own independence in the partner's occupations; the self-sufficient wife frees her husband from the conjugal slavery that was the price of her own. If the man is scrupulously well-intentioned, lovers and spouses can attain perfect equality in undemanding generosity.[6] Sometimes the man himself plays the role of devoted servant; thus did Lewes create for George Eliot

---

6. Clara and Robert Schumann's life seems to have had this kind of success for a certain time.

the favorable atmosphere the wife usually creates around the lord-husband. But most of the time, it is still the woman who pays the price for harmony at home. It seems natural to the man that she run the house and oversee the care and raising of the children alone. The woman herself believes that her personal life does not dispense her from the duties she assumed in marrying; she does not want her husband to be deprived of the advantages he would have had in marrying a "real woman": she wants to be elegant, a good housekeeper, and a devoted mother as wives traditionally are. It is a task that easily becomes overwhelming. She assumes it out of both consideration for her partner and fidelity to herself: for she insists, as we have seen, on fulfilling every aspect of her destiny as woman. She will be a double for her husband at the same time as being herself; she will take charge of his worries, she will participate in his successes just as much as taking care of her own lot, and sometimes even more so. Taught to respect male superiority, she may still believe that man takes first place; and sometimes she fears that claiming it would ruin her family; split between the desire to affirm herself and self-effacement, she is divided and torn.

There is nonetheless one advantage woman can gain from her very inferiority: since from the start she has fewer chances than man, she does not feel a priori guilty toward him; it is not up to her to compensate for social injustice, and she is not called upon to do so. A man of goodwill feels it his duty to "help" women because he is more favored than they are; he will let himself be caught up in scruples or pity, and he risks being the prey of "clinging" or "devouring" women because they are at a disadvantage. The woman who achieves a virile independence has the great privilege of dealing sexually with autonomous and active individuals who—generally—will not play a parasite's role in her life, who will not bind her by their weaknesses and the demands of their needs. But women who know how to create a free relation with their partners are in truth rare; they themselves forge the chains with which men do not wish to burden them: they adopt toward their partner the attitude of the woman in love. For twenty years of waiting, dreaming, and hoping, the young girl has embraced the myth of the liberating hero and savior: independence won through work is not enough to abolish her desire for a glorious abdication. She would have had to be brought up exactly like a boy[7] to be able to comfortably overcome adolescent narcissism: but in her adult life she perpetuates this cult of self toward which her whole youth has predis-

---

7. That is, not only with the same methods, but in the same climate, which today is impossible in spite of all the efforts of educators.

posed her; she uses the merits of her professional success to enrich her image; she needs a gaze from above to reveal and consecrate her worth. Even if she is severe on men whom she judges daily, she reveres Man nonetheless, and if she encounters him, she is ready to fall on her knees. To be justified by a god is easier than to be justified by her own effort; the world encourages her to believe in the possibility of a *given* salvation: she chooses to believe in it. At times she entirely renounces her autonomy, she is no more than a woman in love; more often she tries conciliation; but adoring love, the love of abdication, is devastating: it takes up all thoughts, all instants, it is obsessive, tyrannical. If she encounters a professional disappointment, the woman passionately seeks refuge in love: her failures find expression in scenes and demands at the lover's expense. But her heartbreaks in no way have the effect of increasing her professional zeal: generally she becomes irritated, on the contrary, by the kind of life that keeps her from the royal road of the great love. A woman who worked ten years ago for a political magazine run by women told me that in the office people talked rarely about politics but incessantly about love: one would complain that she was loved only for her body, ignoring her fine intelligence; another would whine that she was only appreciated for her mind and no one ever appreciated her physical charms. Here again, for the woman to be in love like a man—that is to say, without putting her very *being* into question, freely—she would have to think herself his equal, and be his equal concretely: she would have to commit herself with the same decisiveness to her enterprises, which, as we will see, is still not common.

There is one female function that is still almost impossible to undertake in complete freedom, and that is motherhood; in England and in America, the woman can at least refuse it at will, thanks to the practice of birth control; we have seen that in France she is often compelled to have painful and costly abortions; she often finds herself burdened with a child she did not want, ruining her professional life. If this burden is a heavy one, it is because, inversely, social norms do not allow the woman to procreate as she pleases: the unwed mother causes scandal, and for the child an illegitimate birth is a stain; it is rare for a woman to become a mother without accepting the chains of marriage or lowering herself. If the idea of artificial insemination interests women so much, it is not because they wish to avoid male lovemaking: it is because they hope that voluntary motherhood will finally be accepted by society. It must be added that given the lack of well-organized day nurseries and kindergartens, even one child is enough to entirely paralyze a woman's activity; she can continue to work only by abandoning the child to her parents, friends, or servants. She has to choose between sterility, often experienced as a painful frustration, and burdens hardly compatible with a career.

Thus the independent woman today is divided between her professional interests and the concerns of her sexual vocation; she has trouble finding her balance; if she does, it is at the price of concessions, sacrifices, and juggling that keep her in constant tension. More than in physiological facts, it is here that one must seek the reason for the nervousness and frailty often observed in her. It is difficult to decide how much woman's physical makeup in itself represents a handicap. The obstacle created by menstruation, for example, has often been examined. Women known for their work or activities seem to attach little importance to it: Is this because they owe their success to the fact that their monthly problems are so mild? One may ask if it is not on the contrary the choice of an active and ambitious life that confers this privilege on them: the attention women pay to their ailments exacerbates them; athletic women and women of action suffer less than the others because they pass over their sufferings. It is clear that menstrual pain does have organic causes, and I have seen the most energetic women spend twenty-four hours in bed every month in the throes of pitiless tortures; but their enterprises were never hindered by them. I am convinced that most ailments and illnesses that weigh women down have psychic causes: this is in fact what gynecologists have told me. Women are constantly overwhelmed by the psychological tension I have spoken about, because of all the tasks they take on and the contradictions they struggle against; this does not mean that their ills are imaginary: they are as real and devouring as the situation they convey. But a situation does not depend on the body; it is rather the body that depends on it. So woman's health will not detract from her work when the working woman has the place she deserves in society; on the contrary, work will strongly reinforce her physical balance by keeping her from being endlessly preoccupied with it.

When we judge the professional accomplishments of women and try to speculate on their future on that basis, we must not lose sight of all these facts. The woman embarks on a career in the context of a highly problematic situation, subjugated still by the burdens traditionally implied by her femininity. Objective circumstances are no more favorable to her either. It is always hard to be a newcomer trying to make one's way in a hostile society, or at least a mistrustful one. Richard Wright showed in *Black Boy* how blocked from the start the ambitions of a young American black man are and what struggle he has to endure merely to raise himself to the level where whites begin to have problems; the blacks who came to France from

Africa also have—within themselves as well as from outside—difficulties similar to those encountered by women.

The woman first finds herself in a state of inferiority during her period of apprenticeship: I have already pointed this out in relation to the period of girlhood, but it must be dealt with in more detail. During her studies and in the early, decisive years of her career, it is rare for the woman to be able to make full use of her possibilities: many will later be handicapped by a bad start. In fact, the conflicts I have discussed will reach their greatest intensity between the ages of eighteen and thirty: and this is when their professional future is determined. Whether the woman lives with her family or is married, her friends and family will rarely respect her efforts as they respect a man's; they will impose duties and chores on her, and curtail her freedom; she herself is still profoundly marked by her upbringing, respectful of the values the older women around her represent, haunted by childhood and adolescent dreams; she has difficulty reconciling the inheritance of her past with the interest of her future. Sometimes she rejects her femininity, she hesitates between chastity, homosexuality, or a provocative virago attitude, she dresses badly or like a man: she wastes a lot of time and energy in defiance, scenes, and anger. More often she wants, on the contrary, to assert her femininity: she dresses up, goes out, and flirts, she is in love, wavering between masochism and aggressiveness. In all cases, she questions herself, is agitated and scattered. By the very fact that she is in thrall to outside preoccupations, she does not commit herself entirely to her enterprise; thus she profits from it less, and is more tempted to give it up. What is extremely demoralizing for the woman trying to be self-sufficient is the existence of other women of her class, having from the start the same situation and chances, and who live as parasites; the man might resent privileged people: but he feels solidarity with his class; on the whole, those who begin on an equal footing with equal chances arrive at approximately the same standard of living, while women in similar situations have greatly differing fortunes because of man's mediation; the woman friend who is married or comfortably kept is a temptation for the woman who has to ensure her success alone; she feels she is arbitrarily condemning herself to the most difficult paths: at each obstacle she wonders if it would not be better to choose a different way. "When I think I have to get everything from my brain!" a young, poor student told me indignantly. The man obeys an imperious necessity: the woman must constantly renew her decision; she goes forward, not with her eye fixed on a goal directly in front of her, but letting her attention wander all around her; thus her progress is timid and uncertain. And moreover—as I have already said—it seems to her that the further she advances, the more she renounces her other chances; in becoming a bluestocking, a cerebral woman, she will either displease men in general or humiliate her husband or lover by being too dazzling a success. Not only will she apply herself all the more to appearing elegant and frivolous, but she will also hold herself back. The hope of one day being free from looking after herself and the fear of having to give up this hope by coping with this anxiety come together to prevent her from devoting herself single-mindedly to her studies and career.

Inasmuch as the woman wants to be woman, her independent status produces an inferiority complex; inversely, her femininity leads her to doubt her professional opportunities. This is a most important point. A study showed that fourteen-year-old girls believed: "Boys are better; they find it easier to work." The girl is convinced that she has limited capacities. Because parents and teachers accept that the girl's level is lower than the boy's, students readily accept it too; and in truth, in spite of the fact that the curricula are identical, girls' intellectual growth in secondary schools is given less importance. With few exceptions, the students in a female philosophy class overall have a markedly lower achievement level than a class of boys: many female students do not intend to continue their studies, they work superficially, and others suffer from a lack of competitiveness. As long as the exams are fairly easy, their inadequacy will not be noticed too much; but when serious competitive exams are in question, the female student will become aware of her weaknesses; she will attribute them to the unjust curse of femaleness and not to the mediocrity of her education; resigning herself to this inequality, she exacerbates it; she persuades herself that her chances of success are related to her patience and assiduity; she decides to use her strength sparingly: this is a bad calculation. Above all, in studies and professions requiring a degree of inventiveness, originality, and some small discoveries, a utilitarian attitude is disastrous; conversations, reading outside the syllabus, or a walk that allows the mind to wander freely can be far more profitable even for the translation of a Greek text than the dreary compilation of complex syntaxes. Crushed by respect for those in authority and the weight of erudition, her vision blocked by blinkers, the overly conscientious female student kills her critical sense and even her intelligence. Her methodical determination gives rise to tension and ennui: in classes where female secondary school students prepare for the Sèvres examination, there is a stifling atmosphere that discourages even slightly spirited individuality. Having created her own jail, the female examination candidate wants nothing more than to escape from it; as soon as she closes her books, she thinks about any other subject. She does not experience those rich moments where study and amusement merge, where adventures of the mind acquire living warmth. Overwhelmed by the thanklessness of her chores, she feels less and less able to carry them out. I remember a female student doing the *agrégation* who said, at the time when there was a coed competitive exam in philosophy: "Boys can succeed in one or two years; we need at least four." Another—who was recommended a book on Kant, a writer on the curriculum—commented: "This book is too difficult: it's for Normalians!"* She seemed to think that women could take easier exams; beaten before even trying, she was in effect giving all chances of success to the men.

Because of this defeatist attitude, the woman easily settles for a mediocre success; she does not dare to aim higher. Starting out in her job with a superficial education, she very quickly curtails her ambitions. She often considers the very fact of earning her own living a great enough feat; like so many others, she could have entrusted her future to a man; to continue to want her independence she needs to take pride in her effort, but it exhausts her. It seems to her she has done enough just in choosing to do something. "That's not so bad for a woman," she thinks. A woman in an unusual profession said: "If I were a man, I would feel obliged to be in the top rank; but I am the only woman in France holding such a position: that's enough for me." There is prudence in her modesty. In trying to go further, the woman is afraid of failing miserably. She is bothered, and rightly so, by the idea that no one has confidence in her. In general, the superior caste is hostile to the parvenus of the inferior caste: whites will not go to see a black doctor, nor men a woman doctor; but individuals from the lower caste, imbued with the feeling of their generic inferiority and often full of resentment of someone who has prevailed over destiny, will also prefer to turn to the masters; in particular, most women, steeped in the adoration of the male, avidly seek him in the doctor, lawyer, office manager. Neither men nor women like working under a woman's orders. Even if her superiors appreciate her, they will always be somewhat condescending; to be a woman is, if not a defect, at least a peculiarity. The woman must ceaselessly earn a confidence not initially granted to her: at the outset she is suspect; she has to prove herself. If she is any good, she will, people say. But worth is not a given essence: it is the result of a favorable development. Feeling a negative judgment weighing on one rarely helps one to overcome it. The initial inferiority complex most usually leads to the defensive reaction of

---

* Students or graduates from the Ecole Normale Supérieure, prestigious school of higher education in France.—TRANS.

an exaggerated affectation of authority. Most women doctors, for example, have too much or too little. If they are natural, they are not intimidating, because their life as a whole disposes them more to seduce than to command; the patient who likes to be dominated will be disappointed by advice simply given; conscious of this, the woman doctor uses a low voice, a decisive tone, but then she does not have the cheerful simplicity that is so seductive in the confident doctor. The man is used to being imposing; his clients believe in his competence; he can let himself go: he is sure to impress. The woman does not inspire the same feeling of security; she stiffens, exaggerates, overdoes it. In business, in the office, she is scrupulous, a stickler, and easily aggressive. Just as she is in her studies, she lacks confidence, inspiration, and daring. In an effort to succeed, she becomes tense. Her behavior is a series of provocations and abstract self-affirmations. The greatest failure a lack of self-assurance brings about is that the subject cannot forget himself. He does not generously aim for a goal: he tries to prove he is worth what is demanded of him. Throwing oneself boldly toward goals risks setbacks: but one also attains unexpected results; prudence necessarily leads to mediocrity. It is rare to see in the woman a taste for adventure, gratuitous experience, or disinterested curiosity; she seeks "to build a career" the way others construct a happy life; she remains dominated, invested by the male universe, she lacks the audacity to break through the ceiling, she does not passionately lose herself in her projects; she still considers her life an immanent enterprise: she aims not for an object, but through an object for her subjective success. This is a very striking attitude in, among others, American women; it pleases them to have a job and to prove to themselves they are able to carry it out properly: but they do not become passionate about the *content* of their tasks. Likewise, the woman has a tendency to attach too much importance to minor failures and modest successes; she either gets discouraged or swells with vanity; when success is expected, it is welcomed with simplicity; but it becomes an intoxicating triumph if one doubted obtaining it; that is the excuse of women who get carried away with their own importance and who ostentatiously display their least accomplishments. They constantly look back to see how far they have come: this curbs their drive. They can have honorable careers with such methods, but will not accomplish great things. It should be said that many men too are only able to build mediocre careers. It is only in relation to the best of them that the woman—with very rare exceptions—seems to us still to be bringing up the rear. The reasons I have given sufficiently explain this and do not in any way compromise the future. To do great things, today's woman needs above all forgetfulness of self: but to forget oneself one must first be solidly sure that one has already found oneself. Newly arrived in the world of men, barely supported by them, the woman is still much too busy looking for herself.

There is one category of women to whom these remarks do not apply because their careers, far from harming the affirmation of their femininity, reinforce it; through artistic expression they seek to go beyond the very given they constitute: actresses, dancers, and singers. For three centuries they have almost been the only ones to possess concrete independence in society, and today they still hold a privileged place in it. In the past, actresses were cursed by the Church: this excessive severity allowed them great freedom of behavior; they are often involved in seduction, and like courtesans they spend much of their days in the company of men: but as they earn their living themselves, finding the meaning of their existence in their work, they escape men's yoke. Their great advantage is that their professional successes contribute—as for males—to their sexual worth; by realizing themselves as human beings, they accomplish themselves as women: they are not torn between contradictory aspirations; on the contrary, they find in their jobs a justification for their narcissism: clothes, beauty care, and charm are part of their professional duties; a woman infatuated with her image finds great satisfaction in *doing* something simply by exhibiting what she *is;* and this exhibition requires sufficient amounts of both artifice and study if it is to be, in Georgette Leblanc's words, a substitute for action. A great actress will aim even higher: she will go beyond the given in the way she expresses it, she will really be an artist, a creator who gives meaning to her life by lending meaning to the world.

But these rare advantages also conceal traps: instead of integrating her narcissistic indulgence and the sexual freedom she enjoys into her artistic life, the actress often falls into self-worship or seduction; I have already spoken of these pseudo-artists who seek only "to make a name for themselves" in the cinema or theater by representing capital to exploit in a man's arms; the comfort of masculine support is very tempting compared with the risks of a career and the harshness any real work involves. The desire for a feminine destiny—a husband, a home, children—and the spell of love are not always easily reconcilable with the desire to succeed. But above all, the admiration she feels for herself limits the actress's talent in many cases; she deludes herself as to the value of her mere presence to the extent that serious work seems useless to her; more than anything else, she prefers to place herself in the limelight and sacrifices the character she is interpreting to ham acting; she, like others, does not have the generosity to forget herself, which keeps her from going beyond herself: rare are the

Rachels or the Duses who overcome this risk and who make of their person the instrument of their art instead of seeing in art a servant of their self. In her private life, though, the ham will exaggerate all her narcissistic defects: she will appear vain, touchy, and a phony; she will treat the whole world as a stage.

––––––––

Today the expressive arts are not the only ones open to women: many try their hand at creative activities. Woman's situation encourages her to seek salvation in literature and in art. Living on the margin of the masculine world, she does not grasp it in its universal guise but through a particular vision; for her it is not a group of implements and concepts but a source of feelings and emotions; she is interested in the qualities of things inasmuch as they are gratuitous and secret; taking on a negative attitude, one of refusal, she does not lose herself in the real: she protests against it, with words; she looks for the image of her soul in nature, she abandons herself to her reveries, she wants to reach her *being:* she is doomed to failure; she can only recover it in the realm of imagination. So as not to allow an inner life that does not *serve* any purpose to sink into nothingness, so as to assert herself against the given that she endures in revolt, so as to create a world other than the one in which she cannot succeed in reaching herself, she needs *to express herself.* Thus it is well-known that she is talkative and a scribbler; she pours out her feelings in conversations, letters, and diaries. If she is at all ambitious, she will be writing her memoirs, transposing her biography into a novel, breathing her feelings into poems. She enjoys vast leisure time that favors these activities.

But the very circumstances that orient the woman toward creation also constitute obstacles she will often be unable to overcome. When she decides to paint or write just to fill the emptiness of her days, paintings and essays will be treated as "ladies' work"; she will devote little time or care to them, and they will be worth about as much. To compensate for the flaws in her existence, often the woman at menopause feverishly takes up the brush or pen: it is late; without serious training, she will never be more than an amateur. But even if she begins quite young, she rarely envisages art as serious work; used to idleness, never having experienced in her life the austere necessity of a discipline, she will not be capable of a steady and persevering effort, she will not compel herself to acquire a solid technique; she balks at the thankless and solitary trials and errors of work that is never exhibited, that has to be destroyed and done over again a hundred times; and as from childhood she was taught to cheat in order to please, she hopes to get by with a few ruses. This is what Marie Bashkirtseff admits. "Yes, I don't take the trouble to paint, I watched myself today, I *cheat*." The woman easily *plays* at working, but she does not work; believing in the magic virtues of passivity, she confuses conjurations and acts, symbolic gestures and effective behavior; she disguises herself as a Beaux-Arts student, she arms herself with her arsenal of brushes; planted in front of her easel, she allows her gaze to wander from the blank canvas to her mirror; but the bouquet of flowers, the bowl of apples, do not appear on their own on the canvas. Seated at her desk, musing over vague stories, the woman acquires a peaceful alibi in imagining she is a writer: but she must at some point make signs on the blank page; they have to have a meaning in the eyes of others. So the trickery is exposed. To please one need only to create mirages: but a work of art is not a mirage, it is a solid object; to construct it, one must know one's craft. It is not only thanks to her gifts or personality that Colette became a great writer; her pen was often her livelihood, and she demanded of it the careful work that a good artisan demands of his tool; from *Claudine* to *La naissance du jour* (*Break of Day*), the amateur became professional: the progress brilliantly shows the advantages of a strict apprenticeship. Most women, though, do not understand the problems that their desire for communication poses: and this is what largely explains their laziness. They have always considered themselves as givens; they believe their worth comes from an inner grace, and they do not imagine that value can be acquired; to seduce, they know only how to display themselves: their charm works or does not work, they have no grasp on its success or failure; they suppose that in a similar way, to express oneself, one need only show what one is; instead of constituting their work by a thoughtful effort, they put their confidence in spontaneity; writing or smiling is all one to them: they try their luck, success will come or will not. Sure of themselves, they reckon that the book or painting will be successful without effort; timid, they are discouraged by the least criticism; they do not know that error can open the road to progress, they take it for an irreparable catastrophe, like a malformation. This is why they often overreact, which is harmful to themselves: they become irritated and discouraged when recognizing their errors rather than drawing valuable lessons from them. Unfortunately, spontaneity is not as simple as it appears: the paradox of the commonplace—as Paulhan explains in *Les fleurs de Tarbes* (*The Flowers of Tarbes*)—is that it is nothing more than the immediate translation of the subjective impression. Thus, when the woman produces the image she creates without taking others into account, she thinks she is most unusual, but she is merely reinventing a banal cliché; if she is told, she is surprised and vexed and throws down her pen; she is not aware that the public reads with its own eyes and its own mind and that a brand-new epithet can awaken in it many old memories; of course, it is a precious gift to be able to dig down into oneself and bring up vibrant impressions to the surface of language; one admires Colette for a spontaneity not found in any male writer; but—although these two terms seem to contradict each other—hers is a thoughtful spontaneity: she refuses some of its contributions and accepts others as she sees fit; the amateur, rather than seizing words as an interindividual relation, an appeal to the other, sees in them the direct revelation of her feelings; editing or crossing out for her means repudiating a part of self; she does not want to sacrifice anything both because she delights in what she *is* and because she hopes not to become other. Her sterile vanity comes from the fact that she cherishes herself without daring to construct herself.

Thus, very few of the legions of women who attempt to dabble in literature and art persevere; those who overcome this first obstacle very often remain divided between their narcissism and an inferiority complex. Not being able to forget oneself is a failure that will weigh on them more heavily than in any other career; if their essential goal is an abstract self-affirmation, the formal satisfaction of success, they will not abandon themselves to the contemplation of the world: they will be incapable of creating it anew. Marie Bashkirtseff decided to paint because she wanted to become famous; the obsession with glory comes between her and reality; she does not really like to paint: art is merely a means; it is not her ambitious and empty dreams that will reveal to her the meaning of a color or face. Instead of giving herself generously to the work she undertakes, the woman all too often considers it a simple ornament of her life; books and paintings are only an inessential intermediary allowing her to exhibit this essential reality publicly: her own person. Thus it is her person that is the main—sometimes only—subject that interests her: Mme Vigée-Lebrun does not tire of putting her smiling maternity on her canvases. Even if she speaks of general themes, the woman writer will still speak of herself: one cannot read such and such theater reviews without being informed of the size and corpulence of their author, the color of her hair, and the peculiarities of her personality. Of course, the self is not always detestable. Few books are as fascinating as certain confessions: but they have to be sincere, and the author has to have something to confess. Instead of enriching the woman, her narcissism impoverishes her; involved in nothing but self-contemplation, she eliminates herself; even the love she bestows on herself becomes stereotyped: she does not discover in her writings her authentic experience but an imaginary idol constructed from clichés. She cannot be criticized for projecting herself in her novels as Benjamin Constant and Stendhal did: but unfortunately, she sees her story too often as a silly fairy tale; the young girl hides the brutal and frightening reality from herself with good doses of fantasizing: it is a pity that once she is an adult, she still buries the world, its characters, and herself in the fogginess of poetry. When the truth emerges from this travesty, there are sometimes charming successes, but next to *Dusty Answer** or *The Constant Nymph*, how many bland and dull escapist novels there are!

It is natural for women to try to escape this world where they often feel unrecognized and misunderstood; what is regrettable is that they do not dare the bold flights of a Gérard de Nerval or a Poe. Many reasons excuse woman's timidity. Her great concern is to please; and as a woman she is often already afraid of displeasing just because she writes: the term "bluestocking," albeit a bit overused, still has a disagreeable connotation; she lacks the courage to displease even more as a writer. The writer who is original, as long as he is not dead, is always scandalous; what is new disturbs and antagonizes; women are still astonished and flattered to be accepted into the world of thinking and art, a masculine world: the woman watches her manners; she does not dare to irritate, explore, explode; she thinks she has to excuse her literary pretensions by her modesty and good taste; she relies on the proven values of conformism; she introduces just the personal note that is expected of her into her literature: she points out that she is a woman with some well-chosen affectations, simpering, and preciosities; so she will excel at producing "best sellers," but she cannot be counted on to blaze new trails. Women do not lack originality in their behavior and feelings: there are some so singular that they have to be locked up; on the whole, many of them are more baroque and eccentric than the men whose strictures they reject. But they put their bizarre genius into their lives, conversation, and correspondence; if they try to write, they feel crushed by the universe of culture because it is a universe of men: they just babble. Inversely, the woman who chooses to reason, to express herself using masculine techniques, will do her best to stifle an originality she distrusts; like a female student, she will be assiduous and pedantic; she will imitate rigor and virile vigor. She may become an excellent theoretician and acquire a solid talent; but she will make herself repudiate everything in her that is "different." There are women who are mad, and there are women of talent: none of them have this madness in talent called genius.

---

* *Poussières* in the French: Beauvoir does not specify the author, but this is probably a reference to Rosamond Lehmann's *Dusty Answer*.—TRANS.

This reasonable modesty is what has above all defined the limits of feminine talent until now. Many women have eluded—and they increasingly elude—the traps of narcissism and faux wonderment; but no woman has ever thrown prudence to the wind to try to *emerge* beyond the given world. In the first place, there are, of course, many who accept society just as it is; they are par excellence the champions of the bourgeoisie since they represent the most conservative element of this threatened class; with well-chosen adjectives, they evoke the refinements of a civilization "of quality"; they extol the bourgeois ideal of happiness and disguise their class interests under the banner of poetry; they orchestrate the mystification intended to persuade women to "remain women"; old houses, parks and kitchen gardens, picturesque grandparents, mischievous children, laundry, jams and jellies, family gatherings, clothes, salons, balls, suffering but exemplary wives, the beauty of devotion and sacrifice, small disappointments and great joys of conjugal love, dreams of youth, mature resignation—women novelists from England, France, America, Canada, and Scandinavia have exploited these themes to the utmost; they have attained glory and wealth but have not enriched our vision of the world. Far more interesting are the women insurgents who have indicted this unjust society; protest literature can give rise to strong and sincere works; George Eliot drew from her revolt a detailed and dramatic vision of Victorian England; however, as Virginia Woolf shows, Jane Austen, the Brontë sisters, and George Eliot had to spend so much negative energy freeing themselves from external constraints that they arrived out of breath at the point where the major masculine writers were starting out; they have little strength left to benefit from their victory and break all the ties that bind them: for example, they lack the irony, the nonchalance, of a Stendhal or his calm sincerity. Nor have they had the wealth of experience of a Dostoevsky, a Tolstoy: it is why the great book *Middlemarch* does not equal *War and Peace; Wuthering Heights*, in spite of its stature, does not have the scope of *Brothers Karamazov*. Today, women already have less trouble asserting themselves; but they have not totally overcome the age-old specification that confines them in their femininity. Lucidity, for example, is a conquest they are justly proud of but with which they are a little too quickly satisfied. The fact is that the traditional woman is a mystified consciousness and an instrument of mystification; she tries to conceal her dependence from herself, which is a way of consenting to it; to denounce this dependence is already a liberation; cynicism is a defense against humiliation and shame: it is the first stage of assuming responsibility. In trying to be lucid, women writers render the greatest service to the cause of women; but—without generally realizing it—they remain too attached to serving this cause to adopt, in front of the whole world, the disinterested attitude that opens up wider horizons. When they pull away the veils of illusion and lies, they think they have done enough: nonetheless, this negative daring still leaves us with an enigma; for truth itself is ambiguity, depth, mystery: after its presence is acknowledged, it must be thought, re-created. It is all well and good not to be duped: but this is where it all begins; the woman exhausts her courage in dissipating mirages, and she stops in fear at the threshold of reality. This is why, for example, there are sincere and endearing women's autobiographies: but none can compare with *Confessions* or *Memoirs of an Egotist*. We women are still too preoccupied with seeing clearly to try to penetrate other shadows beyond that clarity.

"Women never go beyond the pretext," a writer told me. This is true enough. Still amazed at having had permission to explore the world, they take its inventory without trying to discover its meaning. Where they sometimes excel is in the observation of facts: they make remarkable reporters; no male journalist has outdone Andrée Viollis's eyewitness reports on Indochina and India. They know how to describe atmosphere and people, to show the subtle relations between them, and let us share in the secret workings of their souls: Willa Cather, Edith Wharton, Dorothy Parker, and Katherine Mansfield have sharply and sensitively brought to life individuals, climates, and civilizations. They have rarely succeeded in creating as convincing a masculine hero as Heathcliff: they grasp little more than the male in man; but they often describe their own interior lives, experiences, and universe very well; attached to the secret side of objects, fascinated by the uniqueness of their own sensations, they convey their fresh experience through the use of savory adjectives and sensual images; their vocabulary is usually more noticeable than their syntax because they are interested in things more than in their relations; they do not aim for abstract elegance; instead, their words speak to the senses. One area they have most lovingly explored is Nature; for the girl or the woman who has not completely abdicated, nature represents what woman represents for man: herself and her negation, a kingdom and a place of exile; she is all in the guise of the other. The woman writer will most intimately reveal her experience and dreams in speaking of moors or kitchen gardens. There are many who enclose the miracles of sap and seasons in pots, vases, and flower beds; others, without imprisoning plants and animals, nonetheless try to appropriate them by the attentive love they dispense to them: so it is with Colette and Katherine Mansfield; very rare are those who approach nature in its inhuman freedom, who try to decipher its foreign meanings and lose themselves in order to unite with this other presence: hardly any women venture down these roads Rousseau invented, except for Emily Brontë, Virginia Woolf, and sometimes Mary Webb. And to an even greater extent we can count on the fingers of one hand the women who have traversed the given in search of its secret dimension: Emily Brontë explored death, Virginia Woolf life, and Katherine Mansfield sometimes—not very often—daily contingence and suffering. No woman ever wrote *The Trial, Moby-Dick, Ulysses,* or *Seven Pillars of Wisdom.* Women do not challenge the human condition because they have barely begun to be able to assume it entirely. This explains why their works generally lack metaphysical resonance and black humor as well; they do not set the world apart, they do not question it, they do not denounce its contradictions: they take it seriously. The fact is that most men have the same limitations as well; it is when she is compared with the few rare artists who deserve to be called "great" that woman comes out as mediocre. Destiny is not what limits her: it is easy to understand why it has not been possible for her to reach the highest summits, and why it will perhaps not be possible for some time.

Art, literature, and philosophy are attempts to found the world anew on a human freedom: that of the creator; to foster such an aim, one must first unequivocally posit oneself as a freedom. The restrictions that education and custom impose on woman limit her grasp of the universe; when the struggle to claim a place in this world gets too rough, there can be no question of tearing oneself away from it; one must first emerge within it in sovereign solitude if one wants to try to grasp it anew: what woman primarily lacks is learning from the practice of abandonment and transcendence, in anguish and pride. Marie Bashkirtseff writes:

> What I want is the freedom to walk around alone, come and go, sit on park benches in the Tuileries Gardens. Without this freedom you cannot become a true artist. You think you can profit from what you see when you are being accompanied or when you must wait for your car, your nursemaid, your family to go to the Louvre! . . . This is the freedom that is missing and without which one cannot seriously become something. *Thinking is imprisoned by this stupid and incessant constraint . . . That is all it takes to clip one's wings.* This is one of the reasons there are no women artists.

Indeed, for one to become a creator, it is not enough to be cultivated, that is, to make going to shows and meeting people part of one's life; culture must be apprehended through the free movement of a transcendence;

the spirit with all its riches must project itself in an empty sky that is its to fill; but if a thousand fine bonds tie it to the earth, its surge is broken. The girl today can certainly go out alone, stroll in the Tuileries; but I have already said how hostile the street is: eyes everywhere, hands waiting; if she wanders absentmindedly, her thoughts elsewhere, if she lights a cigarette in a café, if she goes to the cinema alone, an unpleasant incident can quickly occur; she must inspire respect by the way she dresses and behaves: this concern rivets her to the ground and to self. "Her wings are clipped." At eighteen, T. E. Lawrence went on a grand tour through France by bicycle; a young girl would never be permitted to take on such an adventure: still less would it be possible for her to take off on foot for a half-desert and dangerous country as Lawrence did. Yet such experiences have an inestimable impact: this is how an individual in the headiness of freedom and discovery learns to look at the entire world as his fief. The woman is already naturally deprived of the lessons of violence: I have said how physical weakness disposes her to passivity; when a boy settles a fight with punches, he feels he can rely on himself in his own interest; at least the girl should be allowed to compensate by sports, adventure, and the pride of obstacles overcome. But no. She may feel alone *within* the world: she never stands up *in front* of it, unique and sovereign. Everything encourages her to be invested and dominated by foreign existences: and particularly in love, she disavows rather than asserts herself. Misfortune and distress are often learning experiences in this sense: it was isolation that enabled Emily Brontë to write a powerful and unbridled book; in the face of nature, death, and destiny, she relied on no one's help but her own. Rosa Luxemburg was ugly; she was never tempted to wallow in the cult of her image, to make herself object, prey, and trap: from her youth she was wholly mind and freedom. Even then, it is rare for a woman to fully assume the agonizing tête-à-tête with the given world. The constraints that surround her and the whole tradition that weighs on her keep her from feeling responsible for the universe: this is the profound reason for her mediocrity.

Men we call great are those who—in one way or another—take the weight of the world on their shoulders; they have done more or less well, they have succeeded in re-creating it or they have failed; but they took on this enormous burden in the first place. This is what no woman has ever done, what no woman has ever been *able* to do. It takes belonging to the privileged caste to view the universe as one's own, to consider oneself as guilty of its faults and take pride in its progress; those alone who are at the controls have the opportunity to justify it by changing, thinking, and revealing it; only they can identify with it and try to leave their imprint on it. Until now it has only been possible for Man to be incarnated in the man, not the woman. Moreover, individuals who appear exceptional to us, the ones we honor with the name of genius, are those who tried to work out the fate of all humanity in their particular lives. No woman has thought herself authorized to do that. How could van Gogh have been born woman? A woman would not have been sent on mission to Borinage, she would not have felt men's misery as her own crime, she would not have sought redemption; so she would never have painted van Gogh's sunflowers. And this is without taking into account that the painter's kind of life—the solitude in Arles, going to cafés, whorehouses, everything that fed into van Gogh's art by feeding his sensibility—would have been prohibited to her. A woman could never have become Kafka: in her doubts and anxieties, she would never have recognized the anguish of Man driven from paradise. Saint Teresa is one of the only women to have lived the human condition for herself, in total abandonment: we have seen why. Placing herself beyond earthly hierarchies, she, like Saint John of the Cross, felt no reassuring sky over her head. For both of them it was the same night, the same flashes of light, in each the same nothingness, in God the same plenitude. When finally it is possible for every human being to place his pride above sexual differences in the difficult glory of his free existence, only then will woman be able to make her history, her problems, her doubts, and her hopes those of humanity; only then will she be able to attempt to discover in her life and her works all of reality and not only her own person. As long as she still has to fight to become a human being, she cannot be a creator.

Once again, to explain her limits, we must refer to her situation and not to a mysterious essence: the future remains wide open. The idea that woman has no "creative genius" has been defended ad nauseam; Mme Marthe Borély, a noted antifeminist of former times, defends this thesis, among others: but it looks as if she tried to make her books the living proof of incoherence and feminine silliness, and so they contradict themselves. Besides, the idea of a given creative "instinct" must be rejected like that of the "eternal feminine" and put away in the attic of entities. Some misogynists affirm a bit more concretely that because women are neurotic, they will never create anything of value: but these same people often declare that genius is a neurosis. In any case, the example of Proust shows clearly enough that psychophysiological imbalance does not mean powerlessness or mediocrity. As for the argument drawn from history, we have just seen what we should think of it; the historical past cannot be considered as defining an eternal truth; it merely translates a situation that is showing itself to be historical precisely in that it is in the process of changing. How could women ever have had genius when all possibility of accomplishing a work of genius—or just a work—was refused them? Old Europe formerly heaped its contempt on barbarian Americans for possessing neither artists nor writers. "Let us live before asking us to justify our existence," Jefferson wrote, in essence. Blacks give the same answers to racists who reproach them for not having produced a Whitman or Melville. Neither can the French proletariat invoke a name like Racine or Mallarmé. The free woman is just being born; when she conquers herself, she will perhaps justify Rimbaud's prophecy: "Poets will be. When woman's infinite servitude is broken, when she lives for herself and by herself, man—abominable until now—giving her her freedom, she too will be a poet! Woman will find the unknown! Will her worlds of ideas differ from ours? She will find strange, unfathomable, repugnant, delicious things, we will take them, we will understand them."[8] Her "worlds of ideas" are not necessarily different from men's, because she will free herself by assimilating them; to know how singular she will remain and how important these singularities will continue to be, one would have to make some foolhardy predictions. What is beyond doubt is that until now women's possibilities have been stifled and lost to humanity, and in her and everyone's interest it is high time she be left to take her own chances.

---

8. Rimbaud to Paul Demeny, May 15, 1871.

Conclusion

"No, woman is not our brother; through negligence and corruption, we have made her a being apart, unknown, having no weapon but her sex, which is not only perpetual war but in addition an unfair weapon—adoring or hating, but not a frank companion or a being with *esprit de corps* and freemasonry—of the eternal little slave's defiances."

Many men would still subscribe to these words of Jules Laforgue; many think that there will always be Sturm und Drang between the two sexes and that fraternity will never be possible for them. The fact is that neither men nor women are satisfied with each other today. But the question is whether it is an original curse that condemns them to tear each other apart or whether the conflicts that pit them against each other express a transitory moment in human history.

We have seen that in spite of legends, no physiological destiny imposes eternal hostility on the Male and Female as such; even the notorious praying mantis devours her male only for lack of other food and for the good of the species: in the animal kingdom, from the top of the ladder to the bottom, all individuals are subordinated to the species. Moreover, humanity is something other than a species: it is a historical becoming; it is defined by the way it assumes natural facticity. Indeed, even with the greatest bad faith in the world, it is impossible to detect a rivalry between the male and the female human that is specifically physiological. And so their hostility is located on that ground that is intermediate between biology and psychology, namely, psychoanalysis. Woman, it is said, envies man's penis and desires to castrate him, but the infantile desire for the penis only has importance in the adult woman's life if she experiences her femininity as a mutilation; and it is only to the extent that the penis embodies all the privileges of virility that she wishes to appropriate the male organ for herself. It is generally agreed that her dream of castration has a symbolic significance: she wishes, so it is thought, to deprive the male of his transcendence. Her wish, as we have seen, is much more ambiguous: she wishes, in a contradictory way, *to have* this transcendence, which presupposes that she both respects and denies it, and that she intends both to throw herself into it and to keep it within herself. This is to say that the drama does not unfold on a sexual level; sexuality, moreover, has never seemed to us to define a destiny or to provide in itself the key to human behavior, but to express the totality of a situation it helps define. The battle of the sexes is not immediately implied by the anatomy of man and woman. In fact, when it is mentioned, it is taken for granted that in the timeless heaven of Ideas a battle rages between these uncertain essences: the Eternal Feminine and the Eternal Masculine; and it is not noticed that this titanic combat assumes two totally different forms on earth, corresponding to different historical moments.

The woman confined to immanence tries to keep man in this prison as well; thus the prison will merge with the world, and she will no longer suffer from being shut up in it: the mother, the wife, the lover, are the jailers; society codified by men decrees that woman is inferior: she can only abolish this inferiority by destroying male superiority. She does her utmost to mutilate, to dominate man, she contradicts him, she denies his truth and values. But in doing that, she is only defending herself; neither immutable essence nor flawed choice has doomed her to immanence and inferiority. They were imposed on her. All oppression creates a state of war. This particular case is no exception. The existent considered as inessential cannot fail to attempt to reestablish his sovereignty.

Today, the combat is taking another form; instead of wanting to put man in prison, woman is trying to escape from it; she no longer seeks to drag him into the realms of immanence but to emerge into the light of transcendence. And the male attitude here creates a new conflict: the man petulantly "dumps" the woman. He is pleased to remain the sovereign subject, the absolute superior, the essential being; he refuses to consider his companion concretely as an equal; she responds to his defiance by an aggressive attitude. It is no longer a war between individuals imprisoned in their respective spheres: a caste claiming its rights lays siege but is held in check by the privileged caste. Two transcendences confront each other; instead of mutually recognizing each other, each freedom wants to dominate the other.

This difference in attitude is manifest on the sexual as well as the spiritual level; the "feminine" woman, by becoming a passive prey, tries to reduce the male to carnal passivity as well; she works at entrapping him, at imprisoning him, by the desire she arouses, docilely making herself a thing; the "emancipated" woman, on the contrary, wants to be active and prehensile and refuses the passivity the man attempts to impose on her.

Likewise, Élise and her followers do not accord any value to virile activities;* they place flesh above spirit, contingence above freedom, conventional wisdom above creative daring. But the "modern" woman accepts masculine values: she prides herself on thinking, acting, working, and creating on the same basis as males; instead of trying to belittle them, she declares herself their equal.

This claim is legitimate insofar as it is expressed in concrete ways; and it is men's insolence that is then reprehensible. But in their defense it must be said that women themselves tend to confuse the issue. A Mabel Dodge attempted to enslave Lawrence by her feminine wiles in order to then dominate him spiritually; to show by their successes that they equal a man, many women strive to secure masculine support through sex; they play both sides, demanding both old-fashioned respect and modern esteem, relying on their old magic and their fledgling rights; it is understandable that the irritated man should go on the defensive, but he too is duplicitous when he demands that the woman play the game loyally whereas he, in his hostility and distrust, refuses to grant her indispensable trump cards. In reality, the struggle between them cannot be clear-cut, since woman's very being is opacity; she does not stand in front of man as a subject but as an object paradoxically endowed with subjectivity; she assumes herself as both *self* and *other*, which is a contradiction with disconcerting consequences. When she makes a weapon of both her weakness and her strength, it is not a deliberate calculation: she is spontaneously seeking her salvation in the path imposed on her, that of passivity, at the same time as she is actively demanding her sovereignty; and this process is undoubtedly not "fair play," but it is dictated by the ambiguous situation assigned to her. Man, though, when he treats her like a freedom, is indignant that she is still a trap for him; while he flatters and satisfies her in her role as his prey, he gets annoyed at her claims to autonomy; whatever he does, he feels duped and she feels wronged.

The conflict will last as long as men and women do not recognize each other as peers, that is, as long as femininity is perpetuated as such; which of them is the most determined to maintain it? The woman who frees herself from it nevertheless wants to conserve its prerogatives; and the man then demands that she assume its limitations. "It is easier to accuse one sex than to excuse the other," says Montaigne. Meting out blame and approbation is useless. In fact, the vicious circle is so difficult to break here because each sex is victim both of the other and of itself; between two adversaries confronting each other in their pure freedom, an agreement could easily be

---

* *Bold Chronicle of a Strange Marriage.*—Trans.

found, especially as this war does not benefit anyone; but the complexity of this whole business comes from the fact that each camp is its enemy's accomplice; the woman pursues a dream of resignation, the man a dream of alienation; inauthenticity does not pay: each one blames the other for the unhappiness brought on himself by taking the easy way out; what the man and the woman hate in each other is the striking failure of their own bad faith or their own cowardice.

We have seen why men originally enslaved women; the devaluation of femininity was a necessary step in human development; but this step could have brought about a collaboration between the two sexes; oppression is explained by the tendency of the existent to flee from himself by alienating himself in the other that he oppresses for that purpose; this tendency can be found in each individual man today: and the vast majority give in to it; a husband looks for himself in his wife, a lover in his mistress, in the guise of a stone statue; he seeks in her the myth of his virility, his sovereignty, his unmediated reality. "My husband never goes to the movies," says the woman, and the dubious masculine pronouncement is engraved in the marble of eternity. But he himself is a slave to his double: what effort to build up an image in which he is always in danger! After all, it is founded on the capricious freedom of women: it must constantly be made favorable; man is consumed by the concern to appear male, important, superior; he play-acts so that others will playact with him; he is also aggressive and nervous; he feels hostility for women because he is afraid of them, and he is afraid of them because he is afraid of the character with whom he is assimilated. What time and energy he wastes in getting rid of, idealizing, and transposing complexes, in speaking about women, seducing, and fearing them! He would be liberated with their liberation. But that is exactly what he fears. And he persists in the mystifications meant to maintain woman in her chains.

That she is mystified is something of which many men are conscious. "What a curse to be a woman! And yet the very worst curse when one is a woman is, in fact, not to understand that it is one," says Kierkegaard.[1] Attempts have been made to disguise this misfortune for a long time. Guardianship, for example, was eliminated: the woman was given "protec-

---

1. *In Vino Veritas*. He also says: "Gallantry is essentially woman's due; and the fact that she unconsciously accepts it may be explained by the solicitude of nature for the weak and the disadvantaged, those who feel more than recompensed by an illusion. But this illusion is precisely fatal . . . Is it not an even worse mockery to feel freed from misery—thanks to one's imagination, to be the dupe of imagination? Woman certainly is far from being *verwahrlost* [abandoned]; but inasmuch as she never can free herself from the illusion with which nature consoles her, she is."

tors," and if they were endowed with the rights of the old guardians, it was in her best interest. Forbidding her to work and keeping her at home is intended to defend her against herself and ensure her happiness. We have seen the poetic veils used to hide the monotonous burdens she bears: housework and maternity; in exchange for her freedom she was given fallacious treasures of "femininity" as a gift. Balzac described this maneuver very well in advising a man to treat her as a slave while persuading her she is a queen. Less cynical, many men endeavor to convince themselves she is truly privileged. There are American sociologists seriously teaching today the theory of "low-class gain," that is, the "advantages of the lower castes." In France as well it has often been proclaimed—albeit less scientifically—that workers are indeed lucky not to be obliged to "present well," and even more so tramps who could dress in rags and sleep on the streets, pleasures that were forbidden to the comte de Beaumont and those poor Wendel gentlemen. Like the filthy carefree souls cheerfully scratching their vermin, like the joyful Negroes laughing while being lashed, and like these gay Arabs of Sousse with a smile on their lips, burying their children who starved to death, the woman enjoys this incomparable privilege: irresponsibility. Without difficulties, without responsibility, without cares, she obviously has "the best part." What is troubling is that by a stubborn perversity— undoubtedly linked to original sin—across centuries and countries, the people who have the best part always shout to their benefactors: It's too much! I'll settle for yours! But the magnanimous capitalists, the generous colonialists, the superb males persist: Keep the best part, keep it!

The fact is that men encounter more complicity in their woman companions than the oppressor usually finds in the oppressed; and in bad faith they use it as a pretext to declare that woman *wanted* the destiny they imposed on her. We have seen that in reality her whole education conspires to bar her from paths of revolt and adventure; all of society—beginning with her respected parents—lies to her in extolling the high value of love, devotion, and the gift of self and in concealing the fact that neither lover, husband, nor children will be disposed to bear the burdensome responsibility of it. She cheerfully accepts these lies because they invite her to take the easy slope: and that is the worst of the crimes committed against her; from her childhood and throughout her life, she is spoiled, she is corrupted by the fact that this resignation, tempting to any existent anxious about her freedom, is meant to be her vocation; if one encourages a child to be lazy by entertaining him all day, without giving him the occasion to study, without showing him its value, no one will say when he reaches the age of man that he chose to be incapable and ignorant; this is how the woman is raised, without ever being taught the necessity of assuming her own existence; she readily lets herself count on the protection, love, help, and guidance of others; she lets herself be fascinated by the hope of being able to realize her being without *doing* anything. She is wrong to yield to this temptation; but the man is ill advised to reproach her for it since it is he himself who tempted her. When a conflict breaks out between them, each one will blame the other for the situation; she will blame him for creating it: no one taught me to reason, to earn my living . . . He will blame her for accepting it: you know nothing, you are incompetent . . . Each sex thinks it can justify itself by taking the offensive: but the wrongs of one do not absolve the other.

The innumerable conflicts that set men and women against each other stem from the fact that neither sex assumes all the consequences of this situation that one proposes and the other undergoes: this problematic notion of "equality in inequality" that one uses to hide his despotism and the other her cowardice does not withstand the test of experience: in their exchanges, woman counts on the abstract equality she was guaranteed, and man the concrete inequality he observes. From there ensues the endless debate on the ambiguity of the words "give" and "take" in all relationships: she complains of giving everything; he protests that she takes everything from him. The woman has to understand that an exchange—a basic law of political economy—is negotiated according to the value the proposed merchandise has for the buyer and not for the seller: she was duped by being persuaded she was priceless; in reality she is merely a distraction, a pleasure, company, an inessential article for the man; for her he is the meaning, the justification of her existence; the two objects exchanged are thus not of the same quality; this inequality will be particularly noticeable because the time they spend together—and that fallaciously seems to be the same time—does not have the same value for both partners; during the evening the lover spends with his mistress, he might be doing something useful for his career, seeing friends, cultivating relations, entertaining himself; for a man normally integrated into his society, time is a positive asset: money, reputation, pleasure. By contrast, for the idle and bored woman time is a burden she aspires to get rid of; she considers it a benefit to succeed in killing time: the man's presence is pure profit; in many cases, what interests man the most in a relationship is the sexual gain he draws from it: he can, at worst, settle for spending just enough time with his mistress to perform the sex act, but what she herself wants—with rare exceptions—is to "dispose of" all this excess time she has on her hands: and—like the shopkeeper who will not sell his potatoes if one does not "take" his turnips—she only gives her body if the lover "takes" hours of conversation and outings into the bargain. Balance can be established if the cost of the whole matter does not seem too high to the man: that depends, of course, on how intense is his desire and how important to him the occupations he sacrifices; but if the woman demands—offers—too much time, she becomes completely importunate, like the river that overflows its banks, and the man will choose to have nothing rather than to have too much. So she moderates her demands; but very often a balance is found at the price of a twofold tension: she believes that the man *has* her at a bargain price; he thinks he is paying too much. Of course this explanation is somewhat humorous; but—except in cases of jealous and exclusive passion where the man wants the woman in her entirety—this conflict, in tenderness, desire, even love, is always present; the man always has "something else to do" with his time, whereas she is trying to get rid of hers; and he does not consider the hours she devotes to him as a gift but as a burden. Generally, he consents to tolerate it because he knows he is on the privileged side, he has a "guilty conscience"; and if he has any goodwill, he tries to compensate for the unequal conditions with generosity; however, he gives himself credit for being compassionate, and at the first clash he treats the woman as ungrateful, he gets irritated: I am too generous. She feels she is acting like a beggar while she is convinced of the high value of her gifts, and this humiliates her. This explains the cruelty of which the woman often shows herself capable; she feels "self-righteous" because she has the bad role; she does not feel any obligation to accommodate the privileged caste, she thinks only of defending herself; she will even be very happy if she has the opportunity to display her resentment to the lover who has not been able to satisfy her: since he does not give enough, she will take everything back with fierce pleasure. Then the wounded man discovers the total price of the relationship whose every minute he disdained: he agrees to all the promises, even if it means he will again consider himself exploited when he has to honor them; he accuses his mistress of blackmailing him: she blames him for his stinginess; both consider themselves frustrated. Here too it is useless to allocate excuses and criticism: justice can never be created within injustice. It is impossible for a colonial administrator to conduct himself well with the indigenous population, or a general with his soldiers; the only solution is to be neither colonialist nor military leader; but a man cannot prevent himself from being a man. So here he is, thus guilty in spite of himself and oppressed by this fault that he has not committed himself; likewise, she is a victim and a shrew in spite of herself; sometimes he revolts, he chooses cruelty, but then he makes himself an accomplice of injustice, and the fault really becomes his; sometimes he allows himself to be destroyed, devoured, by his protesting victim: but then he feels duped; often he settles for a compromise that both diminishes him and puts him ill at ease. A man of goodwill will be more torn by the situation than the woman herself: in one sense, one is always better off being on the side of the defeated; but if she is also of goodwill, unable to be self-sufficient, unwilling to crush the man with the weight of her destiny, she struggles with herself in an inextricable confusion. One meets so many of these cases in daily life for which there are no satisfactory solutions because they are defined by unsatisfactory conditions: a man who sees himself as obligated to maintain a woman he no longer loves materially and morally feels he is a victim; but if he abandoned without resources the one who has committed her whole life to him, she would be a victim in an equally unjust manner. The wrong does not come from individual perversity—and bad faith arises when each person attacks the other—it comes from a situation in the face of which all individual behavior is powerless. Women are "clingy," they are a burden, and they suffer from it; their lot is that of a parasite that sucks the life from a foreign organism; were they endowed with an autonomous organism, were they able to fight against the world and wrest their subsistence from it, their dependence would be abolished: the man's also. Both would undoubtedly be much better off for it.

A world where men and women would be equal is easy to imagine because it is exactly the one the Soviet revolution *promised:* women raised and educated exactly like men would work under the same conditions and for the same salaries;[2] erotic freedom would be accepted by custom, but the sexual act would no longer be considered a remunerable "service"; women would be *obliged* to provide another livelihood for themselves; marriage would be based on a free engagement that the spouses could break when they wanted to; motherhood would be freely chosen—that is, birth control and abortion would be allowed—and in return all mothers and their children would be given the same rights; maternity leave would be paid for by the society that would have responsibility for the children, which does not mean that they would be *taken* from their parents but that they would not be *abandoned* to them.

But is it enough to change laws, institutions, customs, public opinion, and the whole social context for men and women to really become peers? "Women will always be women," say the skeptics; other seers prophesy that in shedding their femininity, they will not succeed in changing into men and will become monsters. This would mean that today's woman is nature's

---

2. That some arduous professions are prohibited to them does not contradict this idea: even men are seeking professional training more and more; their physical and intellectual capacities limit their choices; in any case, what is demanded is that no boundaries of sex or caste be drawn.

creation; it must be repeated again that within the human collectivity nothing is natural, and woman, among others, is a product developed by civilization; the intervention of others in her destiny is originary: if this process were driven in another way, it would produce a very different result. Woman is defined neither by her hormones nor by mysterious instincts but by the way she grasps, through foreign consciousnesses, her body and her relation to the world; the abyss that separates adolescent girls from adolescent boys was purposely dug out from early infancy; later, it would be impossible to keep woman from being what she *was made*, and she will always trail this past behind her; if the weight of this past is accurately measured, it is obvious that her destiny is not fixed in eternity. One must certainly not think that modifying her economic situation is enough to transform woman: this factor has been and remains the primordial factor of her development, but until it brings about the moral, social, and cultural consequences it heralds and requires, the new woman cannot appear; as of now, these consequences have been realized nowhere: in the U.S.S.R. no more than in France or the United States; and this is why today's woman is torn between the past and the present; most often, she appears as a "real woman" disguised as a man, and she feels as awkward in her woman's body as in her masculine garb. She has to shed her old skin and cut her own clothes. She will only be able to do this if there is a collective change. No one teacher can today shape a "female human being" that would be an exact homologue to the "male human being": if raised like a boy, the young girl feels she is an exception, and that subjects her to a new kind of specification. Stendhal understood this, saying: "The forest must be planted all at once." But if we suppose, by contrast, a society where sexual equality is concretely realized, this equality would newly assert itself in each individual.

If, from the earliest age, the little girl were raised with the same demands and honors, the same severity and freedom, as her brothers, taking part in the same studies and games, promised the same future, surrounded by women and men who are unambiguously equal to her, the meanings of the "castration complex" and the "Oedipus complex" would be profoundly modified. The mother would enjoy the same lasting prestige as the father if she assumed equal material and moral responsibility for the couple; the child would feel an androgynous world around her and not a masculine world; were she more affectively attracted to her father—which is not even certain—her love for him would be nuanced by a will to emulate him and not a feeling of weakness: she would not turn to passivity; if she were allowed to prove her worth in work and sports, actively rivaling boys, the absence of a penis—compensated for by the promise of a child—

would not suffice to cause an "inferiority complex"; correlatively, the boy would not have a natural "superiority complex" if it were not instilled in him and if he held women in the same esteem as men.[3] The little girl would not seek sterile compensations in narcissism and dreams, she would not take herself as given, she would be interested in what she does, she would throw herself into her pursuits. I have said how much easier puberty would be if she surpassed it, like the boy, toward a free adult future; menstruation horrifies her only because it signifies a brutal descent into femininity; she would also assume her youthful eroticism more peacefully if she did not feel a frightening disgust for the rest of her destiny; a coherent sexual education would greatly help her to surmount this crisis. And thanks to coeducation, the august mystery of Man would have no occasion to arise: it would be killed by everyday familiarity and open competition. Objections to this system always imply respect for sexual taboos; but it is useless to try to inhibit curiosity and pleasure in children; this only results in creating repression, obsessions, and neuroses; exalted sentimentality, homosexual fervor, and the platonic passions of adolescent girls along with the whole procession of nonsense and dissipation are far more harmful than a few childish games and actual experiences. What would really be profitable for the young girl is that, not seeking in the male a demigod—but only a pal, a friend, a partner—she not be diverted from assuming her own existence; eroticism and love would be a free surpassing and not a resignation; she could experience them in a relationship of equal to equal. Of course, there is no question of writing off all the difficulties a child must overcome to become an adult; the most intelligent, tolerant education could not free her from having her own experiences at her own expense; what one would want is that obstacles should not accumulate gratuitously on her path. It is already an improvement that "depraved" little girls are no longer cauterized with red-hot irons; psychoanalysis has enlightened parents somewhat; yet the conditions in which woman's sexual education and initiation take place today are so deplorable that none of the objections to the idea of a radical change are valid. It is not a question of abolishing the contingencies and miseries of the human condition in her but of giving her the means to go beyond them.

Woman is the victim of no mysterious fate; the singularities that make her different derive their importance from the meaning applied to them;

---

3. I know a little boy of eight who lives with a mother, aunt, and grandmother, all three independent and active, and a grandfather who is half-senile. He has a crushing inferiority complex in relation to the female sex, though his mother tries to combat it. In his lycée he scorns his friends and professors because they are poor males.

they can be overcome as soon as they are grasped from new perspectives; we have seen that in her erotic experience, the woman feels—and often detests—male domination: it must not be concluded that her ovaries condemn her to living on her knees eternally. Virile aggressiveness is a lordly privilege only within a system where everything conspires to affirm masculine sovereignty; and woman *feels* so deeply passive in the love act only because she already *thinks* herself that way. Many modern women who claim their dignity as human beings still grasp their sexual lives by referring back to a tradition of slavery: so it seems humiliating to them to lie under the man and be penetrated by him, and they tense up into frigidity; but if reality were different, the meaning sexual gestures and postures symbolically express would be different as well: a woman who pays, who dominates her lover, can, for example, feel proud of her superb inertia and think that she is enslaving the male who is actively exerting himself; and today there are already many sexually balanced couples for whom notions of victory and defeat yield to an idea of exchange. In fact, man is, like woman, a flesh, thus a passivity, the plaything of his hormones and the species, uneasy prey to his desire; and she, like him, in the heart of carnal fever, is consent, voluntary gift, and activity; each of them lives the strange ambiguity of existence made body in his or her own way. In these combats where they believe they are tackling each other, they are fighting their own self, projecting onto their partner the part of themselves they repudiate; instead of living the ambiguity of their condition, each one tries to make the other accept the abjection of this condition and reserves the honor of it for one's self. If, however, both assumed it with lucid modesty, as the correlate of authentic pride, they would recognize each other as peers and live the erotic drama in harmony. The fact of being a human being is infinitely more important than all the singularities that distinguish human beings; it is never the given that confers superiority: "virtue," as the ancients called it, is defined at the level of "what depends on us." The same drama of flesh and spirit, and of finitude and transcendence, plays itself out in both sexes; both are eaten away by time, stalked by death, they have the same essential need of the other; and they can take the same glory from their freedom; if they knew how to savor it, they would no longer be tempted to contend for false privileges; and fraternity could then be born between them.

People will say that all these considerations are merely utopian because to "remake woman," society would have had to have already made her *really* man's equal; conservatives have never missed the chance to denounce this vicious circle in all analogous circumstances: yet history does not go round in circles. Without a doubt, if a caste is maintained in an inferior position, it remains inferior: but freedom can break the circle; let blacks vote and they become worthy of the vote; give woman responsibilities and she knows how to assume them; the fact is, one would not think of expecting gratuitous generosity from oppressors; but the revolt of the oppressed at times and changes in the privileged caste at other times create new situations; and this is how men, in their own interest, have been led to partially emancipate women: women need only pursue their rise, and the success they obtain encourages them; it seems most certain that they will sooner or later attain perfect economic and social equality, which will bring about an inner metamorphosis.

In any case, some will object that if such a world is possible, it is not desirable. When woman is "the same" as her male, life will lose "its spice." This argument is not new either: those who have an interest in perpetuating the present always shed tears for the marvelous past about to disappear without casting a smile on the young future. It is true that by doing away with slave markets, we destroyed those great plantations lined with azaleas and camellias, we dismantled the whole delicate Southern civilization; old lace was put away in the attics of time along with the pure timbres of the Sistine castrati, and there is a certain "feminine charm" that risks turning to dust as well. I grant that only a barbarian would not appreciate rare flowers, lace, the crystal clear voice of a eunuch, or feminine charm. When shown in her splendor, the "charming woman" is a far more exalting object than "the idiotic paintings, over-doors, decors, circus backdrops, sideboards, or popular illuminations" that maddened Rimbaud; adorned with the most modern of artifices, worked on with the newest techniques, she comes from the remotest ages, from Thebes, Minos, Chichén Itzá; and she is also the totem planted in the heart of the African jungle; she is a helicopter and she is a bird; and here is the greatest wonder: beneath her painted hair, the rustling of leaves becomes a thought and words escape from her breasts. Men reach out their eager hands to the marvel; but as soon as they grasp it, it vanishes; the wife and the mistress speak like everyone else, with their mouths: their words are worth exactly what they are worth; their breasts as well. Does such a fleeting miracle—and one so rare—justify perpetuating a situation that is so damaging for both sexes? The beauty of flowers and women's charms can be appreciated for what they are worth; if these treasures are paid for with blood or misery, one must be willing to sacrifice them.

The fact is that this sacrifice appears particularly heavy to men; few of them really wish in their hearts to see women accomplish themselves; those who scorn woman do not see what they would have to gain, and those who cherish her see too well what they have to lose; and it is true that present-day developments not only threaten feminine charm: in deciding to live for herself, woman will abdicate the functions as double and mediator that provide her with her privileged place within the masculine universe; for the man caught between the silence of nature and the demanding presence of other freedoms, a being who is both his peer and a passive thing appears as a great treasure; he may well perceive his companion in a mythical form, but the experiences of which she is the source or pretext are no less real: and there are hardly more precious, intimate, or urgent ones; it cannot be denied that feminine dependence, inferiority, and misfortune give women their unique character; assuredly, women's autonomy, even if it spares men a good number of problems, will also deny them many conveniences; assuredly, there are certain ways of living the sexual adventure that will be lost in the world of tomorrow: but this does not mean that love, happiness, poetry, and dreams will be banished from it. Let us beware lest our lack of imagination impoverish the future; the future is only an abstraction for us; each of us secretly laments the absence in it of what was; but tomorrow's humankind will live the future in its flesh and in its freedom; that future will be its present, and humankind will in turn prefer it; new carnal and affective relations of which we cannot conceive will be born between the sexes: friendships, rivalries, complicities, chaste or sexual companionships that past centuries would not have dreamed of are already appearing. For example, nothing seems more questionable to me than a catchphrase that dooms the new world to uniformity and then to boredom. I do not see an absence of boredom in this world of ours nor that freedom has ever created uniformity. First of all, certain differences between man and woman will always exist; her eroticism, and thus her sexual world, possessing a singular form, cannot fail to engender in her a sensuality, a singular sensitivity: her relation to her body, to the male body, and to the child will never be the same as those man has with his body, with the female body, and with the child; those who talk so much about "equality in difference" would be hard put not to grant me that there are differences in equality. Besides, it is institutions that create monotony: young and pretty, slaves of the harem are all the same in the sultan's arms; Christianity gave eroticism its flavor of sin and legend by endowing the human female with a soul; restoring woman's singular sovereignty will not remove the emotional value from amorous embraces. It is absurd to contend that orgies, vice, ecstasy, and passion would become impossible if man and woman were concretely peers; the contradictions opposing flesh to spirit, instant to time, the vertigo of immanence to the appeal of transcendence, the absolute of pleasure to the nothingness of oblivion will never disappear; tension, suffering, joy, and the

766 | LIVED EXPERIENCE

failure and triumph of existence will always be materialized in sexuality. To emancipate woman is to refuse to enclose her in the relations she sustains with man, but not to deny them; while she posits herself for herself, she will nonetheless continue to exist for him *as well:* recognizing each other as subject, each will remain an *other* for the other; reciprocity in their relations will not do away with the miracles that the division of human beings into two separate categories engenders: desire, possession, love, dreams, adventure; and the words that move us: "to give," "to conquer," and "to unite" will keep their meaning; on the contrary, it is when the slavery of half of humanity is abolished and with it the whole hypocritical system it implies that the "division" of humanity will reveal its authentic meaning and the human couple will discover its true form.

"The direct, natural, and necessary relation of person to person is the *relation of man to woman,*" said Marx.[4] From the character of this relationship follows how much man as *a species-being,* as man, has come to be himself and to comprehend himself; the relation of man to woman is the most natural relation of human being to human being. It therefore reveals the extent to which man's *natural* behavior has become *human,* or the extent to which the *human* essence in him has become a *natural* essence—the extent to which his *human nature* has come to be *natural* to him.

This could not be better said. Within the given world, it is up to man to make the reign of freedom triumph; to carry off this supreme victory, men and women must, among other things and beyond their natural differentiations, unequivocally affirm their brotherhood.

---

4. *Philosophical Works,* Volume 6. Marx's italics. [Marx and Engels, *Collected Works,* Volume 6. —Trans.]

Selected Sources

The works listed below are the published English translations that the translators consulted for Simone de Beauvoir's French quotes, as well as the English-language books and publications to which she makes reference. In some instances, the translators translated Beauvoir's citations themselves, for example, when she paraphrases an author. But the works are also included here as "selected sources."

Abrantès, Laure Junot. *Memoirs of the Duchess d'Abrantès (Madame Junot)*. J. & J. Harper, 1832.

Aeschylus. *Eumenides*. Translated by Richard Lattimore. University of Chicago Press, 1969.

Angela of Foligno. *Complete Works*. Paulist Press, 1993.

Bachelard, Gaston. *Earth and Reveries of Repose*. Translated by Kenneth Haltman. Unpublished.

———. *Earth and Reveries of Will*. Translated by Kenneth Haltman. Dallas Institute of Humanities and Culture, 2002.

Bálint, Alice. *The Psychoanalysis of the Nursery*. Routledge and Kegan Paul, 1953.

Balzac, Honoré de. *Letters of Two Brides*. Translated by R. S. Scott. Hard Press, 2006.

———. *The Lily in the Valley*. Translated by Lucienne Hill. Carroll & Graf, 1997.

———. *The Physiology of Marriage*. With an introduction by Sharon Marcus. Johns Hopkins University Press, 1997.

Bashkirtseff, Marie. *I Am the Most Interesting Book of All: The Diary of Marie Bashkirtseff*. Translated by Phyllis Howard Kernberger and Katherine Kernberger. Chronicle Books, 1997.

Bazin, Hervé. *Viper in the Fist*. Translated by W. J. Strachan. Prentice-Hall, 1951.

Bloch, Jean-Richard. *A Night in Kurdistan*. Translated by Stephen Haden Guest. Victor Gollancz, 1930.

Bourdouxhe, Madeleine. *Marie*. Translated by Faith Evans. Bloomsbury, 1997.

Breton, André. *Arcanum 17*. Translated by Zack Rogow. Green Integer, 2004.

———. *Communicating Vessels*. Translated by Mary Ann Caws and Geoffrey Harris. Nebraska University Press, 1990.

———. *Mad Love*. Translated by Mary Ann Caws. Bison Books, 1988.

———. *Nadja*. Translated by Richard Howard. Grove Press, 1994.

———. *Poems of André Breton: A Bilingual Anthology*. Translated by Mary Ann Caws. University of Texas Press, 1982.

Colette. *Break of Day*. Translated by Enid McLeod. Limited Editions Club, 1983.

———. *Claudine at School*. Translated by Antonia White. Farrar, Straus and Giroux, 2001.

———. *Claudine's House*. Translated by Andrew Brown. Hesperus Press Limited, 2006.

———. *The Evening Star: Recollections*. Translated by David Le Vay. Bobbs-Merrill, 1973.

————. *Green Wheat*. Translated by Zack Rogow. Sarabande Books, 2004.

————. *The Innocent Libertine*. Translated by Antonia White. New York: Farrar, Straus and Giroux, 1978.

————. *The Kepi*. Translated by Antonia White. Secker and Warburg, 1984.

————. *My Apprenticeships & Music-Hall Sidelights*. Translated by Helen Beauclerk. Penguin Books, 1967.

————. *The Pure and the Impure*. Translated by Herma Briffault. New York Review of Books, 2000.

————. *Sido*. Translated by Una Vicenzo Troubridge and Enid McLeod. Farrar, Straus and Giroux, 2002.

————. *The Tender Shoot*. Translated by Antonia White. Farrar, Straus and Giroux, 1975.

————. *The Vagabond*. Translated by Enid McLeod. Farrar, Straus and Giroux, 1955.

Dalbiez, Roland. *Psychoanalytical Method and the Doctrine of Freud*. Longmans, Green, 1941.

Deutsch, Helene. *The Psychology of Women*. Bantam Books, 1973.

Diderot, Denis. "On Women." *In Dialogues*. Translated by Francis Birrell. Routledge, 1927.

Duncan, Isadora. *My Life*. Boni & Liveright, 1955.

Ellis, Havelock. *Studies in the Psychology of Sex: Sexual Inversion*. University Press of the Paçific, 2001.

Engels, Friedrich. *The Origin of the Family, Private Property, and the State*. Translated by Alick West and Dona Torr. Marxist-Leninist Library, 1942.

Flaubert, Gustave. *Sentimental Education*. Translated by Robert Baldich. Penguin Books, 1964.

Freud, Sigmund. *Moses and Monotheism*. Translated by Katherine Jones. Knopf, 1939.

Gide, André. *The Coiners*. Translated by Dorothy Bussy. Cassell, 1950.

————. *The Journals of André Gide*. Translated by Justin O'Brien. Penguin Modern Classics, 1967.

Halbwachs, Maurice. *The Causes of Suicide*. Translated by Harold Goldblatt. Free Press, 1978.

Halévy, Daniel. *Jules Michelet*. Hachette, 1928 and 1947.

Hall, Radclyffe. *The Well of Loneliness*. Wordsworth Editions, 2005.

Hegel, G. W. F. *Phenomenology of Spirit*. Translated by A. V. Miller. Oxford University Press, 1977.

————. *The Philosophy of Nature*. Translated by J. N. Findlay and A. V. Miller. Oxford University Press, 1979.

Huart, Clément. *Ancient Persia and Iranian Civilization*. Knopf, 1927.

Hughes, Richard. *A High Wind in Jamaica*. Harper & Brothers, 1929.

Hurst, Fannie. *Back Street*. Grosset, 1931.

Ibsen, Henrik. *A Doll's House*. In *Eleven Plays of Henrik Ibsen*. Modern Library, 1935.

Jouhandeau, Marcel. *Marcel and Élise: The Bold Chronicle of a Strange Marriage*. Translated by Martin Turnell. Pantheon Books, 1953.

Jung, Carl. *The Development of Personality*. Translated by R. F. C. Hull. Princeton University Press, 1970.

————. *Symbols of Transformation*. (Originally published as *Metamorphoses and Symbols of the Libido*.) Translated by R. F. C. Hull. Pantheon Books, 1956.

Kennedy, Margaret. *The Constant Nymph*. Doubleday, Page,1925.

Kierkegaard, Søren. *Stages on Life's Way*. Translated by H. V. and E. H. Hong. Princeton University Press, 2009.

Krafft-Ebing, Richard von. *Psychopathia Sexualis*. Rebman Kessinger, 1906.

Landau, Rom. *Sex, Life, and Faith*. Faber and Faber, 1946.

Lawrence, D. H. *Fantasia of the Unconscious*. Dover Publications, 2006.

————. *Lady Chatterley's Lover*. Modern Library, 2003.

————. *Sons and Lovers*. Modern Library, 1999.

————. *The Plumed Serpent*. Vintage, 1992.

Lehmann, Rosamond. *Dusty Answer.* Virago, 2008.

———. *Invitation to the Waltz.* Virago, 2006.

———. *The Weather in the Street.* Virago, 1981.

Levinas, Emmanuel. *Time and the Other.* Translated by Richard Cohen. Duquesne University Press, 1987.

Lévi-Strauss, Claude. *The Elementary Structures of Kinship.* Translated by James Harle Bell, Rodney Needham, and John Richard von Sturmer. Beacon Press, 1969.

Luhan, Mabel Dodge. *Lorenzo in Taos.* Knopf, 1932.

Malinowski, Bronislaw. "The Bachelors' House." In *The Sexual Life of Savages in North-Western Melanesia.* Horace Liveright, 1929.

Malraux, André. *Man's Fate.* Translated by Haakon M. Chevalier. Modern Library, 1934.

Mansfield, Katherine. "Prelude." In *The Short Stories of Katherine Mansfield.* Knopf, 1937.

Marx, Karl, and Friederich Engels. *Collected Works.* Vol. 6. www.marxists.org/archive/marx/works/1844/manuscripts/comm.htm.

Mauriac, François. *A Kiss for the Leper* and *Genetrix.* Translated by Gerard Hopkins. Eyre and Spottiswood, 1950.

———. *Thérèse Desqueyroux.* Translated by Raymond MacKenzie. Rowman & Littlefield, 2005.

McCullers, Carson. *The Member of the Wedding.* Penguin Classics, 1962.

Merleau-Ponty, Maurice. *Phenomenology of Perception.* Translated by Colin Smith. Routledge, 2005.

Michaux, Henri. "Bridal Night." In *Selected Writings.* New Directions, 1968.

Michelet, Jules. *The Mountain.* Translated by W. H. Davenport Adams. T. Nelson & Sons, 1872.

Mill, John Stuart. "The Subjection of Women," as reprinted in *Philosophy of Women*, edited by Mary Briody Mahowald. Hackett, 1994.

Montaigne, Michel de. *The Complete Essays of Montaigne.* Translated by Donald M. Frame. Stanford University Press, 1965.

Montherlant, Henry de. *The Bachelors.* Translated by Terence Kilmartin. Greenwood Press, 1977.

———. *The Dream.* Translated by Terence Kilmartin. Macmillan, 1963.

———. *The Girls.* Translated by Terence Kilmartin. Harper & Row, 1968.

———. *The Master of Santiago.* Translated by Jonathan Griffin. Knopf, 1951.

———. *La Petite Infánte de Castille.* French & European Publications, 1973.

Nietzsche, Friedrich. *The Gay Science.* Translated by Walter Kaufmann. Vintage, 1974.

———. *Thus Spoke Zarathustra.* Translated by R. J. Hollingdale. Penguin Classics, 1961.

Parker, Dorothy. "Too Bad" and "The Lovely Leave." In *The Portable Dorothy Parker.* Penguin Books, 1944.

Rabelais, François. *The Complete Works.* Translated by Donald M. Frame. University of California Press, 1991.

Rimbaud, Arthur. *Illuminations.* Translated by Helen Rootham. New Directions, 1943.

———. *A Season in Hell.* Translated by Delmore Schwartz. New Directions, 1939.

Rougemont, Denis de. *The Devil's Share.* Translated by Haakon M. Chevalier. Pantheon Books, 1944.

Sachs, Maurice. *Witches' Sabbath.* Translated by Richard Howard. Jonathan Cape, 1965.

Sade, Marquis de. *Philosophy in the Boudoir.* Translated by Joachim Neugroschel. Penguin Classics, 2006.

Sartre, Jean-Paul. *Anti-Semite and Jew.* Translated by George J. Becker. Schocken, 1948.

———. *Being and Nothingness.* Translated by Hazel Barnes. Citadel Press, 2001.

———. *Dirty Hands.* In *Three Plays.* Translated by Lionel Abel. Knopf, 1949.

Scott, Geoffrey. *The Portrait of Zélide.* Turtle Point Press, 1997.

Senghor, Leopold Sédar. *The Collected Poetry*. Translated by Melvin Dixon. University of Virginia Press, 1998.

Stekel, Wilhelm. *Conditions of Nervous Anxiety and Their Treatment*. Liveright, 1950.

———. *Frigidity in Woman*. Translated by James S. Van Teslaar. Liveright, 1943.

Stendhal. *Memoirs of an Egotist*. Translated by David Ellis. Horizon Press, 1975.

———. *The Red and the Black*. Translated by Roger Gard. Penguin Classics, 2002.

———. *Three Italian Chronicles*. Translated by C. K. Scott-Moncrieff. New Directions, 1991.

Tolstoy, Leo. *War and Peace*. Translated by Richard Pevear and Larissa Volokhonsky. Knopf, 2008.

Tolstoy, Sophia. *The Diaries of Sophia Tolstoy*. Translated by Cathy Porter. Random House, 1985.

Webb, Mary. *The House in Dormer Forest*. Jonathan Cape, 1928.

———. *Precious Bane*. E. P. Dutton, 1926.

Wharton, Edith. *The Age of Innocence*. Random House, 1999.

Woolf, Virginia. *Mrs. Dalloway*. Penguin Books, 1967.

———. *To the Lighthouse*. In *The Selected Works of Virginia Woolf*. Wordsworth Editions, 2005.

———. *The Waves*. Harcourt, Brace, 1931.

Zola, Emile. *Nana*. Unpublished translation by Constance Borde and Sheila Malovany-Chevallier.

———. *Pot-Bouille*. Everyman, 1999.

Index

abjection, 185, 223, 433, 763
abortion, 106, 137–9, 147, 148, 153, 407, 524–33, 541–2, 610, 632, 652, 653, 735, 760
Abraham, Karl, 287n, 289, 292n
Abrantès, Laure Junot, duchesse d', 542–3
actresses, 616, 676–7, 741–2
Adam, 5, 15, 88, 104, 116, 122, 123, 160–1, 171, 182, 186, 303
Adler, Alfred, 53, 55, 60, 216n, 287n, 292, 301, 397, 419, 460, 592
Adlerians, 58, 61, 263
adolescence, 165, 212, 278, 295n, 300, 326, 329, 341, 344, 346, 350, 587, 684, 685, 724, 761
Adolescent Girl, The (Evard), 356
Adolphe (Constant), 696
adultery, 63, 91, 92, 94, 96, 101, 103, 109, 112, 128, 129, 148, 149–50, 205, 439, 444, 512, 592–8, 652
    of men vs. women, 207–8
adults
    children's solidarity with, 300
    child's perception of, 285
    girls' amorous dreams about, 307–8
    sexual practices of, 366
Aeschylus, 87, 112, 163, 164
Africa, 178, 737
Agee, James, 474n
Age of Innocence, The (Wharton), 492–3, 575
aggressiveness, 37, 737
    in girls, 347
Agoult, Marie d', 685, 691, 692, 695–6, 705
agricultural society, 76–9, 84, 126, 440, 639
agriculture, 63, 100, 179, 722
Agrippa, Cornelius, 122–3
Aiguillon, duchesse d', 119
Aïssé, Charlotte, 685, 694
Alacoque, Marie, 713, 714–16
Alain-Fournier (Henri Alban-Fournier), 209
A la recherche de Marie (*Marie*) (Bourdouxhe), 472

Alcott, Louisa May, 303, 347–8, 362
Alembert, Jean Le Rond d', 124
Alexander I, tsar of Russia, 717
alienation, 57, 59, 77
alimony, 441, 521
alterity, 80n, 83, 88, 159, 187, 260, 266, 271, 311, 329, 411, 415, 429, 468, 702, 704
altruism, 264–5, 267–8
Amazons, 71–2, 201, 208
    maternal, 536
Ambrose, Saint, 104, 186
âme en bourgeon, L' (*The Soul in Bud*) (Sauvage), 545–6
amenorrhea, 40
Amiel, Denys, 515
Amoureuse (*A Loving Wife*) (Porto-Riche), 205, 456
amour fou, L' (*Mad Love*) (Breton), 247, 248
anal phase, Freudian, 50
Andersen, Hans Christian, 216, 303, 694
androgyny, 431, 761
Andromache, 80
Andromeda, 200
Angela of Foligno, Saint, 711–16
animals, animality
    male sexual aggression in, 385
    orgasm and, 689
    sexual organs of, 318
    transcendence of, 73–5
    women compared to, 222, 223, 644
Anna (psychoanalytic subject), 297–9
Anne of Austria, 119
annonce faite à Marie, L' (*The Tidings Brought to Mary*) (Claudel), 238n, 239n
annulments, 107
Anouilh, Jean, 371
Anthony, Susan B., 144
antifeminists, antifeminism, 4, 12, 80n, 104, 122–3, 129, 131–2, 142, 152, 153, 254, 523, 526, 548n, 638, 723, 750

Antigny, Blanche d', 611
Antigone (Anouilh), 371
ants, 30, 32, 33
anxiety, 59, 562, 623
Apollo, 87
A Propos of "Lady Chatterley's Lover" (Lawrence), 230
Arabs, 91, 172, 525, 570, 757
  poetry of, 218
Aragon, Louis, 161–2
Arcanum 17 (Breton), 175, 248–9, 251
Archilochus, 98
Aristophanes, 9, 98
Aristotle, 5, 11, 23, 25, 40, 87, 163, 217, 451, 645
Arland, Marcel, 364, 698
Arnould, Sophie, 120
Arria, 103, 188
art, 346, 470, 677, 742–4
  prostitution and, 611–12
Arthus, André, 534–5, 541–2
artifice, fashion and, 177–8
artificial insemination, 139, 533, 536, 735
Artificial Silk Girl, The (Keun), 576
asceticism, 661, 714, 722
asexual reproduction, 21–2, 24, 26
Asia, 79, 97
Asia Minor, 79, 85
Aspasia, 98, 118, 150, 162, 199, 267
Asquith, Lord, 143
Astarte, 79, 85, 168, 171, 189
Astrée, L', 123, 200
Atala, 306
Athena, 162, 165
Aton, 88
"At the Bay" (Mansfield), 553
Attis, 85
Auclert, Hubertine, 141
Audry, Colette, 307–9, 324–5, 336, 422, 475–6, 533–4, 539–40, 550, 556, 577–8, 672
Augustine, Saint, 11, 111, 112, 137, 139*n*, 185*n*, 186
Augustus, emperor of Rome, 91
Aurélia (Breton), 247
Austen, Jane, 142, 746
autoerotic stage, 50–1
autonomy, 293, 311, 706
  vs. Otherness, 294–5
  women and, 723
Aux fontaines du désir (*At the Fountains of Desire*) (Montherlant), 222, 224*n*, 225*n*
aventures de Sophie, Les (*The Adventures of Sophie*) (Claudel), 237*n*, 238*n*, 245–6
Aydie, Chevalier d', 694

Babylon, 79, 85, 93, 97, 195
bacchantes, 171

Bachelard, Gaston, 55, 65*n*, 176*n*, 289, 471, 472–3, 476, 480
Bachofen, Johann Jakob, 80, 656
Back Street (Hurst), 702
Baer, Karl Ernst von, 25
Bakri, Abu 'Ubayd al-, 172
Bálint, Alice, 57*n*, 287*n*, 288*n*
Balthazard, Victor, 526
Balzac, Honoré de, 129, 200, 268*n*, 397, 453–6, 500, 513, 672*n*, 707–8, 757
barbarians, 104, 105, 137
Barois, Jean, 500
Barrès, Maurice, 195
Barry, Mme du, 120
Bashkirtseff, Marie, 152, 293–4, 350, 351–2, 361, 378, 413, 430, 575–6, 579, 667–70, 674–5, 677, 680–1, 742–4, 748
Bataille, Georges, 171, 211
Bataille, Henry, 209, 597
Baudelaire, Charles, 696
Baudoche, Colette, 195
Baudouin, Charles, 310
Bayard, Pierre Terrail, seigneur de, 303
Bazard, Claire, 130
Bazin, Hervé, 308*n*, 557
Beatrice, 196, 203, 245, 246, 247, 252, 267
Beaumanoir, Philippe de, 108, 109, 110
beauty, 350, 644, 675
  female, 249, 252, 669
  male, 176, 668–9
  of self, 669–70
  sexuality and, 611
Bebel, August, 8, 64, 133, 135, 146, 194
Beccaria, Cesare, 138
bedouins, 80, 170
bees, 22, 30, 32, 33
Behn, Aphra, 121
Being and Nothingness (Sartre), 55, 413*n*, 690*n*
Belgium, 445–7, 601
Bel-Marduk, 85, 88
Benda, Julien, 5–6
Benedict XV, Pope, 142
Bernini, Gian Lorenzo, 712
Bernstein, Henri, 205, 456, 512
Bible, 89, 195, 303, 311, 315, 548
biology, 9, 21–48, 62, 66, 68, 74, 77, 345
  infantilism in, 129
  male aggressive role in, 387
  values and, 47–8
  vs. social inculcation, 294–6
birds, 23, 27, 35, 36
birth control, 72, 136–7, 139, 149, 152–3, 399, 524, 527, 531, 532–3, 534, 596, 653, 735, 760
Bizard, Léon, 601–2, 603, 608, 610
Black Boy (Wright), 736

blacks, 4, 572n, 639, 751, 757, 763–74
  in France, 736–7
  in U.S., 6, 7–8, 12, 13, 135, 144, 148, 223,
    311–12, 343–4, 386, 654, 736
Blake, William, 164
Blanche of Castile, 115
Blanche of Navarre, 109
Blandine, Saint, 305–6
Blanqui, Louis-Auguste, 133
blé en herbe, Le (Green Wheat) (Colette), 364–5,
  404, 729
Bloch, Jean-Richard, 183–4
blood, 42, 169, 313
  menstrual, 169–70, 268, 326, 366
  virginal, 172–3
Bloomerists, 131
Bluebeard, 306, 361
bluestockings, 121–2, 347, 738, 745
Blum, Léon, 466
blushing, 323
Bocchoris, pharaoh of Egypt, 94, 441
body, 396, 643–4, 657, 668, 761
  aging of, 178–9, 614
  artificial shaping of, 577
  as capital, 155, 612, 614
  carnal presence of, 350
  female, expectations of, 274
  feminine, 185–6, 358
  of girls, 312
  hysterical, 345, 405, 657
  loss of confidence in, 344
  organic difficulties of, 349
  powerlessness of, 177
  shame of, 326
body hair, 320, 322
Boileau-Despréaux, Nicolas, 123
Bonald, Louis de, 128, 233, 443, 454, 512, 521
Bonellia viridis, 29–30
Bordeaux, Henry, 469
boredom, 347, 701, 703
  in marriage, 508, 511
  of wives, 514–15, 516, 522, 532
Borély, Marthe, 750
Boscq, Father du, 123
Bossuet, Jacques-Bénigne, 5, 123
bottle-feeding, 284
Boulanger, Georges Ernest, 641
Bourdouxhe, Madeleine, 411, 472
bourgeoisie, 1, 6, 8, 12, 13, 68, 115, 119, 126,
  129, 140, 194, 246, 254, 255, 441, 443, 444,
  452, 524, 527, 615, 617, 663
  boredom and idleness among, 482–3
  ideals of marriage among, 468–9, 593
  marriage inequality in, 110, 233
  morality of wives among, 120
  sexual morality of, 601
  women of, 127, 129–30, 141, 386, 477

Bourget, Paul, 209
boys, 309–10, 343, 348, 352, 723
  adolescent, 329, 341, 344, 350, 685, 761
  competition and power in, 343, 344
  desire to be girls by, 286
  erotic drives in, 344, 397
  future and freedom for, 312, 341, 346, 348,
    762
  girls' envy of, 300–1
  girls raised like, 295, 734
  happiness of, 310
  mystery of motherhood admired by, 299
  prestige and privilege given to, 292–3
  puberty in, 320, 329
  religion and, 659
  self-love and eroticism not identical in,
    350
  sexual freedom for, 457
  superiority of, 567, 738, 762
  violence and aggressiveness in, 343, 367
  virility of, 285–7, 329, 334
  women as a dream of, 341
Brahmans, 80, 89, 173, 188
brain weight, 44–5
Braun, Lily, 557, 601
breast-feeding, 42, 73, 284, 386, 632
breasts, 177, 320, 321, 322, 323, 342, 349, 358,
  392, 395, 402, 429, 539, 540
Breton, André, 175, 214, 246, 252, 262–5, 507
Brontë, Emily, 142, 376, 377, 693, 746, 747, 748,
  749
Brontë sisters, 746
brothels, 606, 610, 611, 643, 652
Brothers Karamazov, The (Dostoevsky), 746
Brunschvicg, Cécile, 141–2
Buisson, Ferdinand, 141
business, women in, 128, 135, 144, 154
butterflies, 30, 33
buttocks, 177, 392
Byron, George Gordon, Lord, 683

Cabet, Étienne, 130–1
Calderón de la Barca, Pedro, 207
Candaules, King, 193, 580
canon law, 89, 105, 112, 138
cantate à trois voix, La (Cantata for Three
  Voices) (Claudel), 237n, 240n
capital, women's bodies as, 155
capitalism, 64, 140, 757
Carnot, Hippolyte, 130–1
Carolingians, 106
Carrouges, Michel, 14n, 160n, 164n
Cartesianism, 658
Casque d'Or, 611
castration, 33, 40, 187, 503, 560
  fear of, 293, 418

castration complex, 51–2, 53, 55, 287, 292, 731, 753, 761
Castro, Inès de, 228
catabolic glands, 43
Cathar heresies, 108
Cather, Willa, 747
Catherine of Siena, Saint, 115, 118, 150, 377, 659, 715, 716
Catherine the Great, 81, 120, 150, 423
Cat, The (Colette), 175–6
Cato, 101, 102
celibacy, 117, 377, 440, 442
　clerical, 105, 149
célibataires, Les (*The Bachelors*) (Montherlant), 214–15
Celts, 79
central nervous system, 41
Cesarean sections, 526
Chardonne, Jacques, 478, 482, 497, 498, 512
charities, 634–5
Charlemagne, 106, 107, 113
Charles IX, king of France, 113
charm, 348, 350, 364, 625, 628, 644, 764–5
Charrière, Charles-Emmanuel de, 516–18
Charrière, Isabelle de, *see* Zuylen, Belle de
chastity, 89, 91, 97, 106, 173, 179, 206, 386, 398, 451, 457, 465, 591, 599, 652, 653, 737
Châtelet, Emilie du, 120, 124n
Chaucer, Geoffrey, 166
Chevreuse, duchesse de, 119, 327
Cheyney, Peter, 201n, 272
childbirth, 42, 72, 134, 165, 178, 269, 312–13, 316, 317, 323, 330, 386, 524, 527, 534, 547–9
　anesthesia and, 548
　decreased dangers of, 139
　fear of, 318, 331, 547
　pain of, 412, 714
child care, 153–4, 296–7, 444, 482, 523, 534, 661, 734–6, 760
　older sisters in, 300, 348
child-care centers, 147
childhood, 165, 283–340
children, 106, 187, 194, 379–80, 433, 440, 445, 484, 505, 507–8, 515, 519, 523, 531, 532, 533, 588, 596, 603, 652, 663, 680, 685, 741, 757
　adult, 565
　approbation sought by, 285
　artificialism of, 292
　awareness of male superiority in, 301–4
　daily routine of, 513–14
　death rate of, 525
　illegitimate, 398, 735
　independence of, 563
　inheritance and, 95, 96
　limiting number of, *see* birth control
　male, 96
　mothers and, 556–69
　newborn, 549–51
　older vs. younger, 302n
　of older women, 627–33
　as Other, 555
　overburdened, 300
　parental control over, 101–2, 105, 525
　paternal control over, 90
　response to abandonment by, 284–5
　as substitute for penis, 60, 554, 569, 761
　value attached to, 73, 76
　welfare of, 525
child-woman, 252
China, 89n, 178
chivalry, 200
Christianity, 49, 89, 104–5, 110, 118, 148, 150, 160, 185, 196, 197–8, 208, 237, 305, 476, 659, 765
　abortion and, 137–8
　feminism in, 142
　flesh as enemy in, 185–6
　gender quality in, 188–9
　on prostitution, 112–13
　Protestant, 304n
　women depicted by, 194
Christian Science Church, 144
Christine, Queen, 119
Christine de Pizan, 115–17, 148, 152
Chroniques italiennes (*Italian Chronicles*) (Stendhal), 256
Chroniques maritales (*The Bold Chronicle of a Strange Marriage*) (Jouhandeau), 467, 477–8, 503–4, 512, 755
Church Fathers, 105, 123, 186, 237, 443n, 599
Cinderella myth, 155, 201, 208, 305, 612
Circe, 183, 203, 207
Citizen Kane, 201, 208
Citoyenne, La, 141
civil rights, women's, 141
Civil War, U.S., 144, 150, 641
clans, 77, 79, 82, 440
Clare of Montefalco, 715
class, 141, 737, 757
　gender and, 63, 66, 663
　lovers and, 597
　sexuality and, 601
Claudel, Paul, 188, 195n, 214, 237–46, 262–5
Claudia Rufina, 103
Claudine (Colette), 743
Claudine à l'école (*Claudine at School*) (Colette), 355, 364
Clérambault, Gaetan Gatian de, 678
clitoral orgasm, 384, 406

clitoris, 30, 49, 50, 51, 52, 54, 68, 283, 332, 384, 385, 418
cloaca, 31, 34
clothing and appearance, 154, 177–8, 274, 296, 310, 323, 346, 348, 349, 364, 381, 569, 585–6, 627, 644, 723–6, 737, 741
    affirmation sought in, 581
    balance between exhibitionism and modesty in, 574
    of children, 290, 306
    fear of aging and decay in, 577–9
    female narcissism and, 571, 579
    of lesbians, 572
    male, 422, 434, 572
    social situation reflected by, 571–81
    woman as erotic object and, 572, 577, 579–80
clubs, women's, 634, 638
Clytemnestra, 88
Cocteau, Jean, 183
coitus, 35, 37, 47, 187, 383, 390, 405, 406, 409, 411, 423, 464, 465
    first, 385, 460
    injuries during, 459
    man's response to, 411
    as sacred act, 179
coitus interruptus, 137, 139*n*, 524
Colette, 175–6, 313, 355, 364–5, 374–5, 377, 396, 404, 414, 420, 429, 431, 445, 456, 458–9, 477, 479–80, 490, 530, 544–5, 550–1, 555, 561, 585–7, 593, 612, 626, 627, 687, 694–5, 706, 707, 729, 730–1, 733, 743–4, 747
collective unconscious, 56
colonialism, 6, 639, 757
Colonna, Vittoria, 118
Combat, 482, 526, 526–7
communal regimes, 76–7, 130
Commune, 150, 642
communism, 161–2
Communist International, 147
Communist Youth Organization, 148*n*
communitarian regimes, 64
Compagnons de la Femme, 130
Comte, Auguste, 128–9, 191, 233, 265, 268, 443*n*, 521
concentration camps, 223
conception, psychic defense mechanism against, 534–5
concubines, 95, 128, 441
Condé, princesse de, 119
condition humaine, La (Man's Fate) (Malraux), 597–8, 731
Conditions of Nervous Anxiety and Their Treatment (Stekel), 541
Condorcet, Marie Jean Antoine Nicolas de Caritat, marquis de, 124–5, 127, 152

confessors, 675, 710–11
conjugal love, 453, 456, 510–11, 625, 746
conjugal relations, 569, 600, 648
consciousness, 74
    imperialism of human, 66
    women's submissive, 161
Constant, Benjamin, 427, 516–17, 597, 647, 694, 696, 745
Constant Nymph, The (Kennedy), 319*n*, 373–4, 745
Constitutional Assembly of 1848, 128
contingency, 652, 657
contracts
    adultery as breach of, 439
    marriage and, 94, 440, 600
    women and, 105, 440
convents, 111, 114, 115, 120, 706
Conversations in Sicily (Vittorini), 185
cooking, 478–81, 483, 505, 639, 661
copulation, 23, 31
coquetry, 59, 115, 283, 364, 379, 421, 447, 501, 506, 567, 592, 621, 631
    childhood, 348–9
    infantile, 293–4
Corday, Charlotte, 127, 150
Coriolanus, 100
Cornelia, 101, 122, 188, 557
couple
    as a social person, 571
    woman dependent on being part of, 584
courage, 377
courtesans, 97, 103*n*, 114, 118–19, 131, 205, 267, 417, 562, 600, 612, 626, 654
courtly love, 108–9, 115, 117, 151, 197, 204, 205
courtship, 391, 392
cowardice, 347, 758
creation, male principle and, 163
Crete, 79, 85
crying, 647–8
Curie, Marie, 151
Cybele, 79, 85, 163–4, 189, 195

Dahomey, 71
Dalbiez, Roland, 50, 425, 668
Dalí, Salvador, 483
Damietta, 113
Dane, Clemence, 357
D'Annunzio, Gabriele, 688, 705
Dante Alighieri, 196, 245, 246, 252
Danton, Georges, 151
Darwin, Charles, 36
daughters
    adulthood for, 565
    marrying off of, 441–2
    mothers and, 561–4

daughters *(continued)*
    older women and, 631–2
    rebellion by, 632
daughters-in-law, 630
David, 303
death
    fertility and, 166, 181
    life and, 165–6
    love and, 183
death penalty, 526
Debesse, Maurice, 352*n*, 379*n*
Decameron, 200, 206
*Declaration on the Nobility and Preeminence of
    the Female Sex* (Agrippa), 122
"Declaration of the Rights of Woman and the
    Female Citizen," 127
découverte de soi, La (*The Discovery of Self*)
    (Gusdorf), 706–7
defloration, 384, 393–6, 404–5, 412, 425, 456,
    459, 461, 464, 485*n*, 486, 601–2, 603
Defoe, Daniel, 121
Delilah, 162
dementia, precocious, 399–400
Demeter, 85, 163, 166*n*, 179, 363
Demetrius Poliorcetes, king of Macedonia, 97
Demidoff, Prince, 701
democracy, 101, 124, 161, 599
Demosthenes, 95
depersonalization, in aging women, 623–4
depression, 401, 491, 625
Deraismes, Maria, 140–1, 151*n*
Deroin, Jeanne, 131
Deschamps, Eustache, 123
Desdemona, 206
Desmoulins, Lucile, 127
Desplas, Dr., 526–7
detective novels, 201
Deutsch, Helene, 287*n*, 288, 292, 324, 330–1,
    334*n*, 336*n*, 360, 417–18, 461, 531, 534,
    535–7, 541, 544, 548, 551, 557–8, 566, 609,
    621, 667*n*, 690*n*
devotion, 519–20, 699
dialectic, 212, 363, 592, 705
    of devotion, 699
    of housework, 474
    master-slave, 74, 159, 160, 271, 522
diaries, 351–2, 487, 501, 565, 621, 648
Dickinson, Emily, 355–6
Diderot, Denis, 11, 124, 377, 462, 647
Dionysus, 171
Directoire, 149
disgust, attraction and, 182, 366
divine right, 151
divorce, 94, 96, 101, 102, 103, 105, 128, 129, 141,
    147, 148, 439, 441, 461, 506, 521, 595, 760
    abolition of, 128
    in U.S., 140

docility, 412, 421, 422, 653
doctors, 675
    women, 740
    women's relationships with, 589–90
Dodge, Mabel, *see* Luhan, Mabel Dodge
dolls, 293–7, 298, 352, 533, 559, 567, 668
Doll's House, A (Ibsen), 498, 520*n*, 654
domesticity, 105, 129–30, 131, 194, 267, 301,
    309, 443, 445, 469, 484, 505, 570, 643
domestic labor, 73, 78–9, 92, 100, 127, 132, 136,
    153, 154, 299–300, 310, 348, 379, 440, 444,
    471–84, 513–14, 532, 569, 571, 639, 656,
    661, 734, 757
    daughters and, 299–300, 563–4
    status quo maintained in, 483–4
    working women and, 147, 157, 346, 482, 722,
        723–5, 737
Donaldson, Sir James, 60
Donkey Skin, 200, 305
Dostoevsky, Fyodor, 659, 746
doubles, 668–70
    grown daughters as, 631
dowry, 93, 95, 96, 102, 105, 112, 440, 444
dreaming, daydreaming, 307–8, 310–11, 352–5,
    360–1, 371, 381, 392, 395, 514, 590–1, 623,
    663, 686, 690, 725, 734, 746, 762
    marital sex and, 467–8
    by men, 162
    mirror-double in, 668
Drouet, Juliette, 685, 691–2, 694, 701, 703
dualist hypothesis, 511
duality, 6, 10
Duguesclin, Bertrand, 303
Du Guillet, Pernette, 118–19
Dumas, Alexandre, fils, 140–1, 596
Dumézil, Georges, 187–8
Duncan, Isadora, 387, 396, 546, 548, 616, 675,
    680–1, 688
Duse, Eleonora, 677, 742
Dusty Answer (Lehmann), 355, 373, 745

earth, 65, 87, 163–4, 166, 171
Eberhardt, Isabelle, 423, 434
Ecclesiastes, 92, 123, 216
échange, L' (*The Trade*) (Claudel), 238*n*,
    242*n*
economic feminism, 124
economics, 9–10, 11, 13, 48, 61, 62–6, 68, 78,
    100, 102, 103, 129, 147, 149, 206, 279, 415,
    761
    men's privilege in, 156, 341, 442
    oppression and equality in, 114, 126
    oppression of workers and, 721–72
    prostitute and, 599–600
    U.S. women and, 144
    of woman's condition, 439, 664

women as parasites in, 127, 130, 149, 382, 443–4, 446, 448, 484, 521, 522, 599–600, 615, 618, 636, 637, 650, 653, 721, 734, 737, 755
women's emancipation in, 723
economy, political, 758
Ecrits intimes (*Intimate Writings*) (Bashkirtseff), 575–6
Eddy, Mary Baker, 144
education, 117, 125, 147, 685
coeducational, 300–1, 310n, 762
of girls, 295, 734
by mothers, 93, 129, 215, 559, 562, 569
of women, 114, 118, 120, 122, 123, 124, 130–1, 142, 145, 155, 254, 279, 296, 346, 381, 398, 430, 492, 523, 647, 667, 737–8, 757, 760
Egeria, 199, 613
eggs, 25–34, 36, 38, 39–42, 49, 72, 316
ego, 68, 691
egotism, 645, 667
Egypt, 79, 85, 94–5, 95, 97, 164, 167, 188, 272, 440n, 441
eighteenth century, 119–21, 124–5, 128, 129, 136, 149, 150, 151, 273
ejaculation, 180, 181, 293, 409
Eleanor of Aquitaine, 109
Elective Affinities (Goethe), 562–3
Electra complex, 51, 52, 302
Eleusinian mysteries, 171, 638
Eliot, George, 142, 347, 372–3, 377, 733–4, 746
Elizabeth I, queen of England, 118, 150
Ellis, Havelock, 289–91, 310, 324, 385n, 421–2, 427–8, 459–60, 668n
emancipation, 12, 13, 103
of women, 131, 261, 723
embryos, 137–8
evolution of, 38–9
Emerson, Ralph Waldo, 144
Emmerich, Catherine, 715–16
endocrine system, 42, 43, 657
endogamy, 83n
Enfantin, Barthélemy-Prosper (Père), 130
engagement, 391, 448, 465
Engels, Friedrich, 63–6, 68, 80, 86, 109, 132, 135, 139, 592–3
England, 135, 136, 139, 140, 155n, 459–60, 548, 642, 735, 746
suffragism in, 141, 142–3, 148
Enlightenment, 4
Enrico (Mouloudji), 556, 557
entoniscid, 32
epiklerate, 96
Epinay, Mme d', 120
Epistle to the God of Love, The (Christine de Pisan), 115n, 117
équinoxe de septembre, L' (*September Equinox*) (Montherlant), 224n

Erasmus, Desiderius, 122
erections, 180, 293, 318, 334, 392, 699
erogenous zones, 390, 409–11, 451n
sensitivity of, in adolescents, 332
undeveloped, 418
erotic fantasies, 623
eroticism, 171, 176, 187, 246, 353, 690, 693, 728, 733, 762, 765
active, 389–91
childhood, 388
female, 52, 348
feminine, 418, 419, 462
immanent, 360
as lacking in marriage, 204–5
lesbian, 432
male, 269, 430
Other and, 415, 467–8
passive, 389–91, 639
sophistication and, 178
sudden discovery of, 459
working women and, 274
erotomania, 624, 678–80, 700, 709–11
érotomanie, L' (*Erotomania*) (Ferdière), 679n, 710n
Esther, 303
estrus cycle, 34, 37
eternal feminine, 3, 4–5, 12, 197, 214, 217, 253, 266, 267, 638, 750, 754
étoile vesper, L' (*The Evening Star*), 544–5
Eumenides (Aeschylus), 87, 88, 112
eunuchs, 389, 421, 425, 764
Eurydice, 200
Evard, Marguerite, 353n, 356, 357n
Eve, 5, 7, 11, 15, 89, 104, 108, 116, 122, 123, 160–1, 162, 171, 182, 186, 189, 203, 237, 303
Evil, 88, 89, 186, 206, 207, 209, 211, 476
Other and, 163
excretory function, 288, 294, 313
exercise, 296, 300–1, 310, 342, 343
exhibitionism, 317–18
existentialism, 61, 376
alienation and identification, 77
being vs. existence in, 160
ethnographic data and, 71
morality and, 16–17
sexuality and, 50, 55–7
transcendence and, 74
existents, 213, 756
interiority of, 203
women as, 74–5, 312, 419, 656, 754, 757, 762
exogamy, 83, 99, 170

fabliaux, 115, 117, 192
factories, 132–4

family, 37, 571
  bourgeois, 113
  as isolated cell, 469
  men in, 14
  patriarchal, 63
family-state conflict, 148, 185
Fantasia of the Unconscious (Lawrence), 232n,
  233n, 234n, 499n
farces, 115, 117
Farewell to Arms, A (Hemingway), 273
fascism, 606
  in Italy, 146, 176
fathers, 112, 486, 761
  activities of, 300
  adolescent girls and, 335, 369
  authority of, 296, 359
  children and, 101, 112
  daughters and, 563, 671
  as demigods, 651
  girls raised by, 295
  identification with, 54
  initiation by, 287
  little girls and, 286, 341, 348
  lovers and, 685–6
  power of, 53, 58
  role in procreation of, 77
  seduction of, 51
Faulkner, William, 186
Faust (Goethe), 164, 197
Fawcett, Millicent Garrett, 140, 143
feminine principle, 47, 170, 172, 189
feminine sensitivity, 662
feminine world, masculine universe vs., 638
femininity, 4, 16–17, 54, 58, 60, 152, 185, 195,
  196, 209, 210, 266, 279, 296, 344, 348–9,
  415, 450, 574, 619, 660, 726, 731, 738, 746,
  754, 755, 757
  adulthood and, 340, 762
  aging women and, 621
  as artificially defined, 723–4
  boys' choice of, 286
  in courtly poetry, 117
  cult of, 355
  as curse, 561–2
  defects of, 295
  defined as binary with masculinity, 420
  devaluation of, 756
  duties of, 346
  as ideal, 176
  inculcated in daughters, 283, 294–6, 300,
    302, 340, 561–2
  individuality vs., 421–2
  and lesbian desire, 417, 419–20, 423, 425,
    428–30, 432
  limits of, 329–30
  loss of, 425

and misery, 450–1
  Montherlant on, 217
  as mutilation, 753
  mystics and, 713
  as myth, 266–7, 272
  nature of, 3–4
  passivity in, 294, 572, 612
  as prolonged childhood, 129
  rejection of, 428, 723–4, 737
  servility and, 627
  social construct of, 283, 420–1, 760–1
  woman as object and prey in, 723
  of working women, 726, 736
feminism, 10, 11, 127, 131, 141, 149, 434, 439,
  457, 723
  Christian, 142
  critiquing arguments by, 15
  economic, 124
  and female education, 296
  founding of, 141
  nationalist, 146
  quarrels over, 3
  revolutionary, 141
  sentimental, 146
  socialism and, 131, 141
Feminist Congress of 1892, 141
Femme Nouvelle, La, 130
Fénelon, Bernard de, 124
Ferdière, Gaston, 679–80, 709–11
fertility, 96, 106, 164, 169n, 170, 171, 172, 173,
  179, 183, 657
  aging and, 619
  death and, 166
  regulation of, 136
  unregulated, 139
fertility goddesses, 163–4
fertilization, 22, 27, 29–36, 41, 42, 47, 385
fetus, 313, 538
  rights of, 525–6
feudalism, 106–11, 185
  military service in, 107
fidelity, 91, 95, 104, 108, 442, 466–7, 511, 592,
  653
Fifteen Joys of Marriage, The, 117
Finland, 135, 145
Fioramenti, Hippolyta, 117
fish, 34, 36, 37, 38, 73
fishing, 72, 83, 179
flesh, 376
  hatred of, 222
  shame of, 392–3
Fleury, Abbot, 124
flirtation, 347, 392, 501, 534, 546, 569, 592, 649,
  704, 725, 737
Florrie (psychoanalytic subject), 289–91
Fontenelle, Barnard de, 124

food manias, 366
Fouillée, Alfred, 29
Fourier, Charles, 130, 453, 654
France, 89n, 109, 136, 138, 139, 140, 141–3, 152, 153, 155n, 168, 173, 192, 195, 300, 302, 304n, 444, 445, 447, 456, 457, 521, 533, 548, 577, 606, 614, 616, 634, 641, 642, 730, 735, 746, 757, 761
  abortion in, 524, 527
  colonialism in, 654
  healthy sexual initiation in, 404
  Occupation of, 222, 224, 226, 228, 344
  sexual freedom lacking in, 730
  social calls in, 582
  virginity in, 399
  women's wages in, 134–5
France-Soir, 525
Francis of Assisi, Saint, 164, 711
Frazer, Sir James George, 640
freedom, 159, 188, 205, 207–8, 262–3, 274, 284, 295, 312, 329, 346, 348, 376, 415, 416, 449, 476, 485, 486, 491, 505–6, 515, 520, 532, 561, 566, 646, 664, 682, 684, 693, 702, 721, 754, 765
  "easy" as negation of, 730
  of elderly women, 626–7
  erotic, 626
  giving up of, 362–3
  of the hysteric, 712
  infidelity as, 205–6
  motherhood and, 735
  without object, 216
  protection from, 686
  in relationships, 733–4
  woman's, 657
free love, 131, 147, 149, 444, 596, 610n
free woman, 130, 160, 730, 751
French Revolution, 126–7, 150
French Union for Women's Suffrage, 141
Freud, Sigmund, 50–3, 55–6, 58, 67–8, 287n, 288, 291, 297, 302, 448
  on female erotic maturation, 418
  masculine model of, 52
  on mother-son relationships, 560
Freudians, Freudianism, 52, 54, 57, 58, 61, 411, 413
friendships, 159, 501, 598, 608, 625, 643, 646, 732, 733
  freedom and, 511
  of girls, 309, 338, 347, 353, 381, 564
  immanent complicity in, 584, 587
  intimacy in, 587
  love and, 588, 703
  male, 347, 584
  with men, 588–92
  romantic schoolgirl, 355–9

  sexual, 337, 338
  women's, 584–8
frigidity, 52, 393–4, 404–8, 414, 415, 424, 435, 460, 462, 494, 495, 501, 505, 556, 595, 613–14, 622, 660, 688–9, 731–2, 763

Gaea, 79, 85, 163n
Galais, Yvonne de, 209
Gambara, Veronica, 118
gametes, 27, 28–9, 31, 36, 47
  heterogenic, 22–3, 30
Gandhi, Mohandas K., 143
Gantillon, Simon, 210
"Garden of Paradise, The" (Andersen), 303
Gauclère, Yassu, 285n, 304n, 318n, 332
Gaulle, Charles de, 641, 647
Gay Science, The (Nietzsche), 683, 698
gaze, 350, 579, 726
  male, 364, 391, 392, 393, 735
  paternal, 357
gender dimorphism, 38
gender division, as myth, 266
Generation of Vipers (Wylie), 155n, 191, 201, 635n
Genesis, 5, 160, 659
Geneviève de Brabant, 206, 305
genital phase, Freudian, 50
genital system, 409–10
Génitrix (Mauriac), 561
geniuses, lost women, 152, 254
genos, 91, 96
genotypes, 30
gens, 100, 105, 107, 440
Germanic tribes, 105–6, 107
Germany, 109, 139, 151, 195, 601, 607
  feminism in, 146
  women's wages in, 135
germination, 166
gestation, 42, 47, 165
Gide, André, 195, 270, 479, 643n
giggling, 365–6
Girard de Vienne, 107
Giraudoux, Jean, 370
girls, 287, 341–82
  adolescent, 344, 346, 348, 587, 684, 724, 761
  adolescent, lesbianism in, 355–9, 382, 420, 428, 587, 762
  adoption of, 633
  adults of interest to, 307–8, 309
  alienation of self in, 293
  anxiety in, 292–3, 368, 371
  attitudes of, towards boys, 309–10
  autonomy of, 295–6, 348–9, 362, 368, 381, 671

girls *(continued)*
    boys' freedom envied by, 300–1, 310, 361, 684, 738
    career and marriage both desired by, 381
    clothing and appearance of, 290, 306
    control lacking in, 371–2
    dependence in, 372
    desire for domination in, 411
    dolls given to, 293–5, 297
    domestic chores assigned to, 299–300
    dreaming by, *see* dreaming, daydreaming
    early development of, 283
    early privileging of, 285–6
    education of, 346
    emotions in, 310–11, 321–2, 342–3, 370–2
    encouragement lacking for, 346
    erotic experiences of, 383–416
    fathers and, 563, 671
    feminine vocation accepted by, 301
    femininity inculcated in, 283, 294–6, 300, 302, 340, 561–2
    friendships of, 309, 338, 347, 353, 381, 564
    genitals of, 287
    humanity vs. femininity in, 348
    hysterical body of, 345
    imitation of elders by, 481
    inaccessibility as appealing to, 360–3
    independence and, 734
    inferiority of, 311, 340, 342, 346, 567, 738
    laughter and giggling in, 365–6
    limitations on freedom of, 346–7
    and limits of femininity, 329–30
    male admiration as prize for, 341–2, 350
    marriage and motherhood as inevitable career for, 312–13
    marriage feared by, 447–8
    marriage pursued by, 446–7
    on motherhood, 533
    as object, 349
    passivity of, 304n, 308, 312, 334–5, 341–4, 347–50, 352–3, 358, 364, 370, 372, 442, 761
    power desired by, 352
    preoccupation with procreation by, 297–9, 533–4
    psychic problems of, 342–3, 345
    puberty in, 39, 44, 172, 311, 320–1, 342–3, 345, 369, 623, 667, 762
    raised like boys, 295, 734, 761
    religion and, 659
    rescue myth and, 305–6, 734
    response to penis by, 287–8, 301; *see also* penis envy
    rivalry among, 380–1, 588
    self-admiration and narcissism in, 349–51
    sexual freedom for, 457
    sexuality as intriguing and disturbing to, 312–40, 397, 419
    shame in, 349, 363–4
    spontaneity repressed by, 347, 348
    sports and, 343
    surrender and rebellion in, 308–9, 337, 364–9, 377–8
    vanity in, 349
    victim roles of, 305–6, 311
Gnosticism, 196, 245, 252
God, 198, 200, 303–5, 659, 687, 709, 709–11, 713–17
goddesses, fertility, 163–4
Goethe, Johann Wolfgang von, 164, 195, 197, 562–3
golden mean, 645
gonads, 22, 23, 30–1
gonochorism, 22–3, 30, 32
gonorrhea, 168, 169, 187, 602, 606n, 610
Good, 163, 197–8, 206, 209, 237, 476, 658
Gouges, Olympe de, 127, 148
Gourmont, Rémy de, 178, 251
Gournay, Mlle de, 119, 123
Graaf's follicle, 25, 40
grandchildren, 630, 632–3
grandfathers, as sexual predators, 332–3
grandmothers, 192, 627, 630, 632–3
Grasset, Bernard, 513
Great Mother Goddess, 79, 82, 85, 94, 148, 163, 188, 189, 210, 233, 267, 303
Greece, 9, 80, 85, 88, 95–9, 103n, 161, 168, 170, 171, 185, 188, 205, 302, 386, 442, 458, 521, 611, 638
Gregory VI, Pope, 105
Grey, Sir Edward, 143
Gribiche (Colette), 530
Griselda, 206, 305, 361
Griselid (Malraux), 730
guardianship, of women, 93, 99–101, 106, 107, 109–12, 140, 149, 439, 659, 757
Guibert, Jacques-Antoine-Hippolyte, comte de, 694, 705
Guinevere, 109
Guitry, Sacha, 614
Gusdorf, Georges, 706–7
Guyon, Jeanne-Marie Bouvier de la Motte, 660, 711, 713, 714, 716
gynandromorphism, 30
gynecologists, 345, 590, 736

Hadrian, emperor of Rome, 101
haine maternelle, La (*Maternal Hatred*) (de Tervagne), 557
Haiti, 8
Halbwachs, Maurice, 519, 649n

Halévy, Daniel, 501
Hall, Radclyffe, 433, 436n
Hammurabi's Code, 93
happiness, 16, 658
Hari, Mata, 617
Harvey, William, 25
hatred, maternal, 562–3
Hayworth, Rita, 614
heat, 36, 37, 136
Hebrews, 91, 97
Hecuba, 80
Hegel, G. W. F., 7, 12, 23–4, 25, 29, 37, 181,
    260, 449–50, 453, 540, 651–2
    on marriage, 449–50
    on slavery, 74
Heidegger, Martin, 7n, 24, 46, 639, 698
Helen of Hungary, 715
Helen of Troy, 200
Héloïse, 115, 706
Helvétius, Claude Adrien, 124
Hemingway, Ernest, 273
Henry I, king of England, 108
Henry II, king of France, 138
Hercules, 9, 162, 302–3
heredity, laws of, 29
hermaphrodites, 15, 30, 38, 417
hermaphroditic species, 22–3, 24, 32
Hermenches, David Louis de Constant d',
    516
Herodotus, 71, 96–7
Héroët, Antoine, 122
heroism, 214, 216, 224, 228, 262, 306, 661
Hervieu, Paul, 456
Hesiod, 98
hetaeras, 95, 97, 103n, 188, 593, 599, 610–18
    dependence among, 614–15
    erotic liberation of, 613
    freedom of, 612–13, 615–16
    frigidity in, 613–14
    individualism of, 618
    masculine protectors of, 612, 614, 615, 617
    qualities of, 610–11
    servility and, 614
heterosexuality, 420
    absence or failure of, 431
    in masculine or autonomous women,
        417–18, 420, 434
High Wind in Jamaica, A (Hughes), 318–19
Hinduism, 166n, 231
Hippocrates, 25, 163
Hirschfeld, Magnus, 525
historical materialism, 62–8
history, 71–156
    prominence of men vs. women in, 302–3
    as written by men, 148–9
Hitler, Adolf, 146, 161

Hollywood, 611, 614, 616
    "bad woman" in, 207
home, 469–72, 505, 643, 654, 674–5, 685, 700,
    725, 741, 757
Homer, 80
Homo faber, 73, 84
homosexuality, 52, 175, 188, 213, 286, 359, 724,
    737
    male, 418, 419, 572n, 587
    see also lesbians, lesbianism
honeymoon, 459, 485
hormones, 30–1, 763
    female, 417, 761
    imbalances in, 342
    male, 417
    menopause and reduction in, 625
Horney, Karen, 287n, 288, 289
hospitality prostitution, 96
hostility, of mothers to daughters, 631
Hottentots, 177
House in Dormer Forest, The (Webb), 375–6,
    688n
housekeepers, 596
housewife or courtesan dilemma, 131, 142
housewives, 521, 579, 581, 644–5, 657, 663, 667,
    671
    women as workers and, 147–8, 722–3
Hughes, Richard, 318–19
Hugo, Adèle, 494, 594, 597
Hugo, Léopoldine, 691
Hugo, Victor, 131, 594, 597, 691, 694, 701,
    703
humanism, 151, 263, 457–8
Humanité, L', 641
hunting, 72, 73, 83, 108, 179
Hurst, Fanny, 702n
husbands, 663, 685, 701, 722, 738, 741, 757
    attitude toward housework of, 483
    autonomy of, 520, 522
    catching of, 342, 505
    children and, 559
    as cuckolds, 593
    as demigods, 650
    devotion seen as tyranny by, 520
    impossible desires of, 704
    intellectual dominance of, 498–501
    and interests not shared by wives, 512–13
    keeping of, 505–6, 620, 654
    as liberators, 595
    lovers vs., 593–6
    as masters, 468, 596, 597
    as not being deceived, 454
    obligations of, 441
    outside life of, 650
    parents irreplaceable by, 486
    pregnancy and, 536–8

husbands *(continued)*
  prestige and superiority of, 493–4, 497,
    588–9, 591, 654
  privileges of, 647
  in profit by marriage, 637
  repugnance for, 622
  as secondary identity, 485
  as slaves, 522
  subjugation of, 522
  as victims, 647
  on wives' appearance, 579–80
hygiene, 73
hymen, 172, 174, 385, 401
hyperactive hypophysis, 625
hypocrisy, 59, 336, 370, 454, 506, 596, 613, 614,
  652
  love and, 704
hysteria, 345, 371, 405, 712
  culture of, 542
hysterical paralysis, 368

Ibsen, Henrik, 371, 498, 500, 520*n*, 654
identity, affirmation of, 284
illnesses
  imaginary, 345
  prostitution and, 603
immanence, 16–17, 73, 84, 92, 149, 152, 165,
  176, 180, 182, 194, 225, 232, 246, 262, 267,
  269, 270, 271, 310, 335, 360, 383, 392, 411,
  423, 443, 486, 538, 617, 635, 643, 649, 657,
  659, 664, 669, 671, 684, 690, 697, 754
  in infanthood, 284
  marriage as anchor in, 484
  repetition and, 468
Imperia, 118, 119, 611, 613
impotence, 460–1, 733
incest, 55, 93, 94, 170
  marriage as a form of, 451, 467
  unacknowleged feelings of, 623, 628
India, 78*n*, 89, 93, 97, 135, 164, 187–8, 201, 408,
  747
individualism, 117, 124, 452, 457
individuality, 31, 44, 46–7, 106, 421, 449, 458
  as biological fact, 77
  reproduction and, 33–4, 36–8, 46
Indochina, 8, 195*n*, 747
industrial civilization, 140
Industrial Revolution, 11, 128
infanticide, 72, 73, 91, 137, 138, 223, 530
infantile women, 417, 432, 547
infant mortality, 136
infants, 284
  hostility towards, 551–4
  newborn, 549–51
  sexual response to, 555

inferiority complex, 53, 54, 216*n*, 310, 346, 367,
  393, 406–7, 435, 500, 613, 725, 726,
  738–40, 762
infertility, 93
infidelity, 63, 91, 141, 205–6, 407, 450, 468, 501,
  506, 592–8, 595, 596, 702, 705
  as protest, 649
ingénue libertine, L' (*The Innocent Libertine*)
  (Colette), 456, 593
inheritance, 90, 93, 94, 95, 96, 101–2, 105, 107,
  111, 127, 173, 440
inhibitions, 398, 462, 726
insects, 35
intelligence, brain weight vs., 45
intercourse, 179, 397, 424, 460
  frequency of, 462
  woman's position in, 396–7
International Congress of Women's Rights, 141
International Labor Office, 134
International Women's Day, 146–7, 151
intersexuality, 30–1
In the Eyes of Memory (Audry), 324–5
In the Prison of Her Skin (asphyxie, L')
  (Leduc), 308*n*, 332, 556–7, 562
intimacy
  in friendship, 587
  in marriage, 510–11
intuition, 199
invertebrates, as hermaphroditic, 22
Invitation to the Waltz (Lehmann), 349–50, 373
Iroquois, 170
Isabella, queen of Spain, 118, 150
Isabella d'Este, 117
Ishtar, 79, 85, 166*n*, 171, 189
Isis, 79, 85, 164*n*, 188, 302
Islam, 92, 164, 184–5, 193, 449, 479, 659
isolation, 352, 749
Italian Renaissance, 117–19, 151
Italy, 109, 122, 195, 304*n*, 390, 715
  Fascist, 146, 176
  Renaissance in, 117–18

Janet, Pierre, 321–3, 460–1, 491, 594, 686
jealousy, 501, 579, 581, 587–8, 607, 702–3
  maternal, 563
  pathological, 625
Jean de Meung, 11, 116–17
Jean of Aragon, 117
Jefferson, Thomas, 751
Je hais les dormeurs (*I Hate Sleepers*) (Leduc),
  697
Jerome, Saint, 105, 186
Jesus Christ, 116, 185, 188–9, 198, 210, 304, 686,
  713–16
  virgin birth of, 186

jeune fille Violaine, La (*The Young Violaine*) (Claudel), 239*n*, 245*n*
jeunes filles, Les (*The Girls*) (Montherlant), 215, 216*n*, 220*n*, 222, 227*n*
Jews, 4, 6, 10, 12, 92, 113, 148, 228, 237, 647, 659
  antifeminism in tradition of, 104
  as minority, 7–8
Joan of Arc, 109, 115, 151, 172*n*, 303, 377, 659–60, 716
Joan of Naples, 117
Joan of the Cross, 715
John Chrysostom, Saint, 104–5
John of the Cross, Saint, 713, 750
Johnson, Samuel, 121
John the Baptist, Saint, 118
Joinville, Jean de, 113
Jones, Ernest, 287*n*, 420
Jouhandeau, Élise, 477–8, 502–4, 510, 512, 755
Jouhandeau, Marcel, 467, 477–8, 502–4, 510, 755
Judith, 150, 162, 303
Jukes family, 603
Jules Michelet (Halévy), 501*n*
Julius Caesar, 93
June Solstice (Montherlant), 225*n*, 227*n*
Jung, Carl Gustav, 166, 195, 297–9
Jupiter, 85, 99, 303
Justice (Proudhon), 131
Justinian, emperor of Rome, 105
Juvenal, 103, 409*n*, 410

Kafka, Franz, 285, 634, 662, 750
Kali, 166*n*, 192
Kant, Immanuel, 636, 739
Kapital, Das (Marx), 133
Kennedy, Margaret, 319, 373–4, 377, 745
Kessel, Joseph, 597
Khan, Aly, 614
Kierkegaard, Søren, 162, 203, 269, 277, 455–6, 756
Kinsey, Alfred, 385*n*
Kinsey Report, 5*n*, 384–5, 408, 457*n*, 462
kisses, 317, 333, 383, 402, 403, 405, 448, 459, 464, 608
Klein, Melanie, 324
kleptomania, 367–8
Koran, 89, 92
Krafft-Ebing, Richard von, 425–7, 572*n*
Krüdener, Barbara Juliane, Baronness von, 624, 670, 676, 713, 716–17

labor, division by sex of, 62–3, 65–6
labor unions, 133–4
Labour Party, British, 143

La Bruyère, Jean de, 123
Lacan, Jacques, 284*n*
Laclos, Pierre Choderlos de, 273
Lacombe, Rose, 127
Ladies' Champion (Martin Le Franc), 117
Lady Chatterley's Lover (Lawrence), 231*n*, 689*n*
Laforgue, Jules, 203–4, 272–3, 274, 653*n*, 753
Lagache, Daniel, 377, 467, 702
Lake, Veronica, 178
Lalaing, Antione de, 113–14
Lamartine, Alphonse de, 195
Lamentations of Matheolus, The, 116
Lamiel (Stendhal), 265
Lancelot, 109, 303
Landau, Rom, 622
La Rochefoucauld, François de, 667
Last of the Mohicans, The (Cooper), 347
lateness, 649–50
laughter, 365–6, 405, 564
Laura, 196, 252
law, 88, 367–8, 497, 636, 686
  abortion and, 137–9, 524–5, 531, 532, 533, 652
  in ancient Greece, 89, 95–96
  canon, *see* canon law
  civil, 124
  common, 110
  divorce, *see* divorce
  feudal, 110
  first appearance of, 76
  French, 443, 721
  French Salic, 115
  Germanic, 107, 112
  labor, 134
  Napoleonic Code, *see* Napoleonic Code
  property, 107
  prostitutes and, 113
  Roman, 11, 89, 100–3, 104, 111, 112, 137, 148, 149, 443
  unmarried women and, 28, 109, 114, 149, 154, 442–3
  wives under, 117, 128, 140, 442–3
  women and, 81, 86, 88–9, 92, 93, 94, 100–3, 106, 125, 141, 149, 152, 159, 168, 440, 642, 721
Law of the Twelve Tables, 100
Lawrence, D. H., 50*n*, 214, 229–37, 243, 262–5, 410*n*, 443*n*, 499*n*, 501–2, 507–8, 520, 536, 655, 677–8, 689*n*, 696, 755
Lawrence, Frieda, 263, 501–2, 658*n*
Lawrence, T. E., 749
Laws of Manu, 89, 93, 170, 171, 188
Leblanc, Georgette, 513, 573, 676, 678, 691, 741
le Chapelain, André, 115
Lecky, William Edward Hartpole, 113
Lecouvreur, Adrienne, 120
Leduc, Violette, 308*n*, 332, 478, 556–7, 697

Legouvé, Ernest, 131
Le Hardouin, Maria, 306, 308n, 362, 412
Lehmann, Rosamond, 349–50, 355, 373, 702n, 745n
Leibniz, Gottfried, 658
Leiris, Michel, 186–7, 191n, 268, 391
Lenin, V. I., 147, 151
Leonardo da Vinci, 190
Leplae, Claire, 445–6
Le Play, Frederic, 128
Leroux, Pierre, 130, 131
Leroy-Beaulieu, Pierre Paul, 132
lesbians, lesbianism, 234, 388–9, 416, 417–36, 532, 567, 654
  in adolescent girls, 355–9, 389, 420, 428, 587, 762
  artists and writers as, 424
  athletes as, 423
  confusion between virago and, 417
  feminine object of desire for, 419
  intimacy of, 432
  as latent tendency in most women, 622–3
  male domination rejected by, 431–2
  marriage to, 459
  masculine dress of, 572
  men and, 434–45
  as narcissists, 428–30
  outside view of, 419–20, 434
  passivity and, 420
  prostitutes as, 605, 607–8, 616
  responsibility and independence of, 433–4
  as solution to problems of feminine condition, 436
  tendency towards, 416
Lespinasse, Julie de, 120, 685, 694, 696, 698, 704–5
Letters of Two Brides (Balzac), 454
Letters to a Mother (Stekel), 324
Lettres à Françoise mariée (Letters to Françoise, Married) (Prévost), 490–1
Lévi-Strauss, Claude, 6–7, 80–1, 83n, 167n, 169n
Leviticus, 89, 91, 165, 167, 169, 179
Lewes, George Henry, 733–4
libido, 50, 51, 56, 418
  feminine, 52, 58
  male, 58
  passive, 59
Liebknecht, Karl, 146
Liepmann, W., 315–17, 327–9, 333, 346n, 395, 528–9
Life of a Prostitute (Marie-Thérèse), 604, 606, 607–8
Light in August (Faulkner), 186
Lincoln, Abraham, 144
Linnaeus, 186

Liszt, Franz, 695–6, 705
literature, 303, 677, 742–51
  feminine myth in, 214–65, 271–2, 312
Little Infanta of Castile, The (Montherlant), 219n, 221n
Little Senate, The (Erasmus), 122
Little Women (Alcott), 303, 347–8, 362
livre de ma vie, Le (de Noailles), 668, 672
Lloyd George, David, 143
Locke, John, 517
logic
  masculine, 660, 662
  women not trained to, 497–8, 640, 650–1, 654
Lombroso, Cesare, 600
Longueville, duchess de, 119
Lorca, Federico Garcia, 207
Lorenzo in Taos (Luhan), 502n, 677n
Lorris, Guillaume de, 115
lost girls, 210–11
Loti, Pierre, 195
Louis, Saint, king of France, 113
Louis XIII, king of France, 286
Louis XV, king of France, 120
Louis XVI, king of France, 126n
love, 657, 671, 721, 732
  abstract, 360
  boredom vs., 260
  death and, 183
  as duty, 455
  ecstatic union and, 691
  equality and, 261
  eternal, 507
  exclusive, 591
  fear and, 704
  friendship and, 588, 703
  hypertrophic, 495
  hypocrisy and, 704
  idolatrous, 684, 691–5, 708, 709–10
  lack of tranquillity in, 700–1
  and loss of self, 692
  marriage vs., 204–5, 448–9, 451, 454, 455–6, 466–9, 494, 496–7, 510n, 592
  maternal, 556, 569–70
  men and, 683, 684, 699, 708
  mysticism and, 709–17
  necessity of, 690
  passionate, 685
  Platonic theory of, 611
  as refuge, 735
  sexual desire and, 685, 699
  sexuality and, 690
  subject-object duality in, 667
  waiting in, 702
  women and, 592, 664, 683–708
"Lovely Leave, The" (Parker), 581n

lovers, 593–8, 603, 650, 654, 663, 675, 703–8,
    722, 728, 733, 754, 757, 758, 759
  class and, 729
  as demigods, 693, 694, 697, 698, 706, 709,
    710–11
  great women, 685
  impossible desires of, 704
  older women with, 625–6, 633, 643, 685, 729,
    732
Lucretia, 100, 150, 162
Luhan, Mabel Dodge, 501–2, 658n, 677–8, 755
Luna, Isabella da, 118
Luquet, Pierre, 287n, 291
lustfulness, of women, 115
Luther, Martin, 117
Luxemburg, Rosa, 146, 151, 377, 749
lying, 654, 699
Lyon, 133, 195
lys dans la vallée, Le (The Lily in the Valley)
    (Balzac), 455, 672
Lysistrata (Aristophanes), 9, 98

madams, 605–6
Mädchen in Uniform (Girls in Uniform), 355,
    358
maenads, 171
Maeterlinck, Maurice, 269, 513, 678
magic, 84, 182, 183, 187, 190, 192, 193, 205, 206,
    207, 262, 303, 352–3, 639, 645, 654, 656,
    702, 729
  miracles vs., 650–1
Maintenon, Mme de, 119, 124, 150, 199
maison, La (Bordeaux), 469
Maistre, Joseph de, 128
male principle, 47, 163, 170
  woman as weakening to, 179
Malinowski, Bronislaw, 172, 179, 181, 444
Mallarmé, Stéphane, 196, 200, 751
Malraux, André, 202, 231, 707
Malraux, Clara, 730
Malthusian movement, 136–7
mammals, 30, 41, 44
  gender difference in, 36
  individuality in, 34–5
mammary glands, 40, 42
mana, 65, 77, 83, 87, 169, 172
Manichaeism, 88, 185, 208, 214, 658
  housework and, 476, 646–7
Mansfield, Katherine, 351, 494–5, 519, 552, 658,
    687, 747–8
manu, 99–100, 101
Marañón Posadillo, Gregorio, 50, 418
Marat, Jean-Paul, 127
Marcus Aurelius, 101
Margaret of Cortona, 660–1

Margaret of Navarre, 118, 658
Margot, queen of France, 118
Marie B (psychoanalytic subject), 353–5
Marie of France, 109
Marie Thérèse, empress of Austria, 113
Marie-Thérèse (prostitute), 604, 606, 607–8,
    609–10
Marie-Yvonne (case history), 679–80
Marivaux, Pierre de, 261
marriage, 11, 14, 77, 81–3, 90–1, 93, 94, 99, 104,
    107, 109, 111, 120, 179, 187, 321, 340, 358,
    380, 391, 407, 519, 537, 587, 604, 671, 733,
    760
  adultery in, 63, 149–50
  age and other differences in, 492–3, 497
  arranged, 123, 445, 447
  assymetrical situations in, 441–3
  autonomy in, 439, 520
  boredom in, 508
  burdens for women in, 152–3, 519–20
  under canon law, 105
  career and, 154, 381, 443–4, 733
  children's aversion to, 318
  choice in, 445–6
  clergy's attacks on, 115–17, 149
  comic and lewd side of, 458
  continued prestige of, 155–6
  contractual, 79, 440
  contrast between men and women in,
    439–43
  economics of, see economics
  equality in, 94, 110, 114, 140, 521, 733–4
  freedom in, 733–4
  husband's authority in, 112
  indissolubility of, 112
  intimacy in, 510–11
  lovers' fear of, 595
  love vs., 204–5, 448–9, 451, 454, 455–6,
    466–9, 494, 496–7, 510n, 592
  for men vs. women, 439–40, 443–5
  motherhood and, 569, 735
  oppression in, 521
  as paradox, 455
  as partnership, 105–6, 188
  phallic, 230–3
  postponement of, 136
  problems with principle of, 465, 466–8, 484,
    521–3, 625
  prostitution and, 599
  quarrels in, 501–3
  reciprocity in, 520
  repudiations of, 107, 216
  Roman types of, 99–100
  servile, 94
  sexuality in, 342, 440, 466–8, 505, 520, 569,
    587, 596, 604

marriage *(continued)*
  structure of system in, 386
  subordination of women in, 110, 114–15,
    243, 432
  traditional form of, 443, 457
  in transition, 439
  without consent, 106
  as women's destiny, 279, 312, 342, 361,
    381–2, 439, 440–2, 445, 485, 506, 523
marriage counselors, 457
Marro, A., 599–600
Martial, 103
Marx, Karl, 132, 133, 161, 765
Marxism, 49, 62–8, 141, 147
Mary Magdalene, 116, 210, 304, 686, 715
masculine protest, 53, 60, 68, 419, 423, 427
masculine universe, 638, 639
masculine women, 357, 359, 433, 435
  heterosexuality of many, 417–18
  pregnancy of, 543, 545, 547
masculinity, 5, 420
masochism, 290, 304*n*, 305–6, 308*n*, 361, 367,
    368, 411–14, 423, 432, 468, 515, 538, 548*n*,
    660, 690–3, 731–2, 737
  maternal, 559, 561, 565, 647
Master of Santiago, The (Montherlant), 227
masturbation, 179–80, 187, 332, 338, 388, 418,
    504–5, 622
  marital sex as, 467
  vaginal, 385
mater dolorosa, 166*n*, 559, 673
materialism, 44
maternal authority, 379–80
maternal circle, 301, 308, 355
Maternal Hatred (de Tervagne), 308*n*, 332
maternal instinct, 296–7, 548*n*, 761
  nonexistence of, 554
maternal love, 556, 569–70
maternal right, 63, 88, 107
maternity, 35, 36, 46, 48, 66–7, 72, 73, 74, 96,
    105, 126, 127–30, 147, 194, 261, 348, 420,
    440, 443, 621, 630*n*, 744, 757
  autonomy in, 47, 62–3, 273
  as destiny, 312, 532
  as freely chosen, 439, 735, 760
  honor of, 190–2, 526, 532
  as limitation, 75, 136, 143, 149, 568
  matrilineal cultures and, 77–8
  power lacking in, 189–90
  refusal of, 72, 103, 398, 534–5, 735
  as repetition of Life, 73–4
  as reward, 54, 60, 419
  as sacred function, 76
  as slavery, 139
  see also motherhood
maternity leave, 134, 147, 439, 760

matriarchy, 80, 296, 348
matrilineal filiation, 24–5, 81, 85, 99, 105
matrilineal societies, 58, 77–8, 83, 91, 99, 168,
    179, 303, 457
matrons, 506, 515, 543, 547, 612, 617
Matthew, 116, 123
Mauriac, Claude, 13
Mauriac, François, 377, 463–4, 494*n*, 515, 561,
    652*n*
Maurice, Martin, 456
Maurras, Charles, 286
Maya, 209, 210
Mazzetti, Mrs. (case study), 557–8, 562
McCullers, Carson, 314, 319–20
Medea, 9, 80
Medici, Catherine de, 118
Mediterranean, 85, 108, 185, 478
melancholia, 566, 594
Melville, Herman, 751
Member of the Wedding, The (McCullers), 314,
    319–20
men, 740
  on abortion, 529, 531–2
  as active, 25–6, 38, 468
  as admirers, 591–2
  advantages of, 422, 723
  aggressiveness in, 48, 159, 389, 763
  aging of, 178–9, 619, 619–20
  "anatomical destiny" in, 386
  authority of, 640, 651, 696
  autonomy of, 391, 440, 724
  brain weight of, 44–5
  casual sex and, 727–8
  class solidarity in, 737
  clothing and appearance of, 572
  coherent universe of, 656
  conformity by, 724
  as creator, 73–5, 86
  definitions set by, 21, 29, 31, 45–6
  as demigod, 655–6, 685, 735, 762
  despotism of, 758
  diversity of temperament in, 343
  domesticity and, 484, 650–1
  as dominant, 86, 88, 682, 763
  economic privilege of, 156
  entrapment of, 754–5
  equality and, 732, 760, 763, 764–5
  ethical dignity of, 651–2
  as fallen god, 164–6
  familiarity and lost prestige of, 684–5
  fear vs. desire in, 172
  female orgasm and, 689
  feminized, 389, 425
  freedom in, 643
  friendships with, 434–5, 588–92
  history as written by, 148–9

hostility between women and, 753–60
ideologies of, 149
inconstancy of, 211, 507
individuality of, 730
as initiator, 391–2
loftiest attributes absent in many, 661
love and, 359–60, 386, 683, 684, 699, 708
marital choice by, 449
marriage as crisis for, 491–2
marriage as servitude for, 204–5
as master, 74, 173, 387, 462, 659, 752
as nurturer, 34
passage to sexual maturity of, 383–4
passion inspired by, 688
passive role refused by, 389
perversions of, 608–9
possession by, 683
power of, 37, 264
pregnancy and, 536–8
prestige of, 279, 560, 723, 731
as prey, 734
privilege of, 44, 47, 564
as producer and citizen, 571
reasoning learned by, 497–8
religion and, 709
role in procreation of, 77, 83, 87
seduction of, 370
sovereignty of, 387, 522, 684, 754, 756
stigmatas in, 715
subjugation of, 696
submission by, 733–4
superiority of, 53, 76, 142, 290, 292, 301–4,
    341, 347, 563, 628, 684, 731, 732, 754
supremacy of, 310, 650, 657
terror of, 326
triumph of, 84
woman as invention of, 212–13
woman as pleasure to, 563
as women's guardians, 81
as work vs. home, 567–8
young, 626, 732
Menander, 98–9
Mendel, Gregor, 27, 30
Mendousse, Pierre, 356
menopause, 43, 44, 610, 619–25, 630n, 632, 726
menstruation, 39, 40, 41, 43, 72, 167–70, 172,
    268, 269, 316, 323–32, 339, 340, 342,
    344–5, 353, 366, 369, 397, 426, 486, 519,
    532, 540, 657, 736, 762
Mercier, Louis-Sébastien, 124
Méricourt, Théroigne de, 127
Merleau-Ponty, Maurice, 24, 41n, 45, 46,
    49–50, 56
Mes apprentissages (My Apprenticeships)
    (Colette), 414, 584, 694
Messalina, 386, 594

Metternich, Princess Pauline von, 625
Michael, Saint, 303
Michakova, Olga, 148n
Michaux, Henri, 459
Michel, Louise, 141, 643
Michelangelo Buonarroti, 118
Michelet, Jules, 5, 164, 295, 480, 584
Middle Ages, 106–17, 113, 136, 138, 149, 154,
    186, 189, 192, 205n, 208, 442, 626
Middlemarch (Eliot), 746
Middleton Murry, John, 687
Miletus, 98
Mill, John Stuart, 11, 140, 152
Miller, Henry, 210
Mill on the Floss, The (Eliot), 347, 372–3
Minerva, 189
mirror, 668–70, 675
    woman's body as, 657
mirror stage, 284
miscarriage, 529, 530, 531, 535, 542, 632
misogyny, 98, 532, 649, 723, 750
mistresses, 441, 506, 613, 722, 728, 733, 758
    as benefactress, 626
    older, 625–6, 633, 643, 685, 729, 732
    sexual frustration of, 727
Mitra-Varuna (Dumézil), 187–8
Mitsein, 7, 9, 17, 47, 57, 80n, 86
Moby-Dick (Melville), 748
Moi qui ne suis qu'amour (Rolin), 704n
Molière (Jean-Baptiste Poquelin), 123
Molly (psychoanalytic subject), 330–1
Monnier, Thyde, 326, 334
monogamy, 77, 105, 113, 232, 233, 593, 733
Monsieur Vénus (Rachilde), 389
Montaigne, Michel de, 11, 408–9, 449, 451–2,
    592, 595, 599, 625, 755
Montesquieu, Charles de Secondat, baron de,
    120, 124, 567
Montevideo Treaties of 1933, 145
Montgomerie, Mabel de, 108
Montgomerie, Roger de, 108
Montherlant, Henry de, 11, 13, 165n, 214–28,
    229, 233, 243, 262, 264, 289n, 506, 561,
    696
Montpensier, Mlle de, 119
Mora, marquis de, 705
moral codes, male vs. female, 585
morality, 532, 601
    bourgeois, 530–1
    of bourgeois wives, 120
    ersatz, 59
    existentialism and, 16–17
    masculine, 662
    sexual, 148
moral license, 113
Morand, Paul, 195

Mordecai, 303
Morgan, Lewis Henry, 599
Morocco, 92, 177n
Moses and Monotheism (Freud), 55
mother-daughter relationship, 561–4
Mother Earth, 166
motherhood, 59, 233, 283, 321, 342, 444,
    524–70, 531, 532, 537, 653, 701, 735–6
  associated with equality, 569
  desire for, 534
  as emancipation, 35
  forced, 525
  generational conflict over, 632
  joys of, 454
  and relationship with own mother, 551
  and work, 523, 735–6
  see also maternity
Mother-in-Law, 192, 630, 631–2
mothers, 53, 176, 209, 486–7, 657, 667, 671,
    754, 761
  adolescents girls' relationship with, 336,
    369
  aging, 564–5
  anxious, 427
  authority of, 296
  bad, 567–8
  carnality refused in, 212
  child care duties passed to older children by,
    300
  children and, 101, 556–69
  children disliked by, 556–8
  children's response towards, 283, 301
  child's attachment to, 165, 211, 284, 388,
    427
  cities compared with, 195
  daughters' marriage sought by, 441–2,
    446
  daughters' pregnancy, motherhood and,
    535–6, 551
  destiny of repetition of, 309
  domination by, 560
  as enemy, 214–15
  fixation on, 428
  girls integrated into feminine world by,
    295–6
  good vs. bad, 427
  Hitler on, 146
  housework passed along by, 346
  little girls and, 286
  lovers and, 685–6
  masochistic devotion to children by, 559
  as mutilated people, 568
  Oedipus complex and, 211–12
  purification rites for, 165
  rebellion against, 308–9
  as rival, 379–80

  saintly, 267
  son doomed by, 183
  subjugation by, 309
  unwed, 111–12, 128, 398, 444, 529, 533, 569,
    735
  wife vs., 171
  work and, 523, 568–9
mother-son relationships, 560–1, 564
Motion de la pauvre Javotte (Poor Javotte's
    Motion), 127
Mott, Lucretia, 144
Mouloudji, Marcel, 556–7
Mrs. Dalloway (Woolf), 582–3, 634, 658
murder
  abortion as, 137–8
  of women vs. men, 91, 128
Muses, 199, 208, 267
Musset, Alfred, 211
Mussolini, Benito, 161
mutilation, 292, 308
  menopause seen as, 619–20
  self-, 366–7, 714–15
My Life (Duncan), 387, 396n, 546, 675, 680–1,
    688n
Myrdal, Gunnar, 148n
mysticism, 664
  love and, 709–17
myth of woman, 33, 160–213, 279, 303
  in literature, 214–65, 271–2, 312
  on pregnancy, 545–6
  reality related to, 266–74
  as substitute for authentic relationship,
    272–3
myths, mythology, 88
  of male sexual prowess, 655
  mirror double in, 668
  Self-Other division in, 6, 105
  sexual, 162

Nadia (psychoanalytic subject), 321–3
naissance du jour, La (*Break of Day*) (Colette),
    743
Nana (Zola), 615–17
Nancy (psychoanalytic subject), 331
Napoleon I, emperor of France, 112, 127–8,
    161, 229, 303, 702
Napoleonic Code, 91, 112, 127–8, 140
narcissism, 429, 430, 515, 556, 587, 618, 620,
    645, 664, 667–82, 691, 713, 716, 717, 721,
    725, 741
  adolescent, 345–55, 349–51, 360–3, 373, 388,
    397, 411–14, 681, 734, 762
  alienation in, 667, 681–2
  audience and, 675–6, 680
  childhood, 294, 310

clothing and feminine, 571–2, 579
dependency and, 681–2
Narcissus, 202–3
National American Woman Suffrage
  Association, 144
naturalism, 658
Nature, 165, 185, 187, 190, 194, 374, 376–7, 566,
  765
  imagery in descriptions of women, 174–6
  laws of, 683–4
  mother and, 212
  as rebel, 206
  subjugation of, 75, 86, 148, 159, 175, 178, 188,
    189, 294, 656
  woman and, 160, 161, 163, 176, 178, 188, 207,
    208, 213, 250, 262, 264, 268, 470–1, 548,
    572, 657–8
  women writers on, 747–8
Navarre, Margaret of, 122
Nazi Germany, 66–7, 139, 146, 161, 176, 223–4,
  417, 440
Neoplatonism, 658
Nerval, Gérard de, 199, 248, 745
nervous system, 41, 42, 345, 647, 657
  vaginal pleasure and, 385
nesting instinct, 725
Netherlands, 135
Neumann, Therese, 716
neurasthenia, 483
neuroses, 51, 54, 211, 368, 393, 447–8, 566, 623,
  750, 762
newborns, death of, 73
Newcastle, Duchess of, 121
Niboyet, Eugénie, 131
Nietzsche, Friedrich, 166, 201, 203n, 214, 228,
  485, 618, 683, 698, 707
nightmares, adolescent sexuality and, 335
nihilism, 224, 618
nineteenth century, 128–33, 209, 451, 642–3
Ninon de Lenclos, 119, 433, 612–13
Niobe, 80
Noailles, Anna de, 301n, 306, 376, 576, 668,
  669, 672–3, 674, 675–6, 677
nobility, 118, 119, 121
  marriage inequality in, 110
Nogarola, Isotta, 118
nomadic peoples, 73, 76, 77, 78
normality, as ersatz morality, 59
Novalis, 197
"Nuit de noces" ("Bridal Night") (Michaux),
  459
nuit kurde, La (A Night in Kurdistan) (Bloch),
  183–4
nursing, 550, 551, 555
nutrition, 30
nymphomaniacs, 589

object, 349, 416, 419, 428, 653
  self as, 667–8
objectivity, 690
  false, 272
obsessions et la psychasthénie, Les (Obsessions
  and Psychasthenia) (Janet), 460–1,
  686n
obstetrics, 139
Occupation, of France, 222, 224, 226, 228,
  344
odalisques, 417
Oedipus complex, 51, 52, 170, 211, 427, 761
  inversion of, 54
Old Mortality (Porter), 369
Olivier, Jacques, 123
Olympiques, Les (Montherlant), 214
one-celled animals, 21–2
ontology, 56
oogenesis, 30
Ophelia, 204, 649
Oppian Law, 102, 148
oral phase, Freudian, 50
orange bleue, L' (The Blue Orange) (Gauclère),
  285n, 304n, 318n, 332
Orestes, 88, 370
orgasm, 50, 383, 384, 395, 406–11, 425, 465, 467,
  504–5, 590, 595, 689n
  simulated, 608, 614, 654
Origen, 186
Origin of the Family, The (Engels), 63–4, 68
Orpheus, 200
Osanna of Mantua, 715
Osiris, 85, 166, 188
otage, L' (The Hostage) (Claudel), 242n,
  243n
Other, the, 360, 373, 663, 725, 744, 756
  autonomy vs., 294–5
  child as, 555
  clothing and, 575, 579
  eroticism and, 415, 467–8
  love and absorption in, 692
  self as, 668
  Self vs., 348
  in sexuality, 415
  as threat, 88
  woman as, 6–10, 12–14, 17, 44, 48, 58, 60–1,
    66, 67, 75, 79, 80, 82, 83, 86, 88–9, 149,
    159, 160, 161–3, 176, 181–3, 186–7,
    199–200, 203, 206, 209, 213, 237, 245, 246,
    252, 262–5, 266, 270–1, 273–4, 283–4, 348,
    357, 411, 653, 755
Otto, Louise, 146
ova, see eggs
ovaries, 25, 30, 31, 39, 40, 43, 55
ovogenesis, 31, 37
ovulation, 31, 32

pagan gods, 89
Pan, 84
Pandora, 11, 89, 162, 303
Pankhurst family, 143
Papin, Christine and Lea, 477
paranoia, love and, 699–700
Parent-Duchâtelet, A.J.B., 600–1, 603
Paris, 331, 346–7
    gender balance of statues in, 151
    prostitutes in, 601
Parker, Dorothy, 4, 481–2, 508–9, 519, 580–1,
    671–2, 747
Parsifal, 162
Partage de midi (*Break of Noon*) (Claudel),
    237n, 238, 240n
part du diable, La (*The Devil's Share*) (de
    Rougemont), 421
parthenogenesis, 22, 26, 30
Parthenos adamatos, 386
Pascal, Blaise, 504, 634
Pasiphaé (Montherlant), 216
passions, imaginary, 590–1
passivity, 283, 294
paterfamilias, Roman, 100, 101
paternal instinct, 37
paternalism, 76, 267, 457, 526
    capitalist, 64
paternal right, 63
patriarchal society, 86, 187, 267, 386, 448–9, 627
patriarchy, 25, 63, 67, 79–80, 88, 90, 105, 110,
    148, 152, 159, 167, 171, 173, 484
    radical, 93
patrilineal filiation, 81, 91
patrimony, 91, 95, 96, 99, 107, 140, 267
Paul, Alice, 145
Paul, Saint, 104, 123, 127, 443n
peasants, 126, 135, 153–4, 270, 288, 325, 394,
    458, 574
    menopause and, 619
    sexuality and, 601
pederasty, 609
penetration, 35, 335, 396, 399, 415, 419
    as violation, 395
penis, 50–2, 318, 332, 334, 335, 339, 383, 392,
    395, 397, 402, 403, 415, 418, 425, 459, 462,
    467, 560, 667, 761
    child as substitute for, 60, 554, 569, 761
    children and, 283, 289, 291, 292, 301
    as privilege, 286–7, 291–3, 294, 329
    as symbol of autonomy, 293
    value given to, 57, 58, 180, 421, 753
penis envy, 52, 53, 58, 287–8, 291–2, 337, 340,
    753
Penthesilea, 201
père humilié, Le (*The Humiliation of the Father*)
    (Claudel), 241n, 242n

Pericles, 98
peripheral nervous system, 41
Perrault, Charles, 123
persecution complex, 680
Perseus, 200, 302
Pétain, Henri Philippe, 526, 641
Petrarch, 196, 252
phallic marriage, 230–3
phallus, 53, 57, 58, 68, 72, 85n, 87n, 171n, 179,
    181, 229, 233, 237, 262, 286, 421, 655, 723,
    725
    definitions of, 49
    Priapus, 173
    see also penis
Phenomenology of Spirit (Hegel), 449–50
phobias, 401, 589
Phryne, 98, 118, 119, 392, 611
Physiology of Marriage, The (Balzac), 453–5
Piaget, Jean, 287n, 292
Picture of Dorian Gray, The (Wilde), 631
pimps, 604n, 605–7, 614, 728
Pindar, 97
Pitié pour les femmes (*Pity for Women*)
    (Montherlant), 214n, 216n
pituitary gland, 41, 43
placenta, 165
Plato, 10–11, 88, 98, 130, 250, 310
    gender myth in, 23, 180
    Republic of, 130
Platonism, 122, 217, 266, 611
Pliny the Younger, 103, 168
Plumed Serpent, The (Lawrence), 235n, 236,
    410n
Poe, Edgar Allan, 196, 197, 631, 745
poetry, 374
    courtly, 7, 108–9, 115, 117, 123, 200
    woman as, 247–52, 262
political economy, 758
politics, 80, 129, 140, 146, 199
    eighteenth-century women and, 120
    medieval women and, 111
    Russian women in, 147
    seventeenth-century women and, 119,
        124–5
    women in trade unions and, 722
Polo, Marco, 172
polyandry, 77, 93
polygamy, 63, 77, 91, 92, 93, 94, 95, 106, 441
Pompadour, Mme de, 120, 267, 506, 597
Pompeii, 642
Pomponius Labeus, 103
Ponge, Francis, 473–4
population growth, 652
pornotropos, 97
Porter, Katherine Anne, 369
Porto-Riche, Georges de, 205, 456

Positions et propositions (*Positions and Propositions*) (Claudel), 238n, 240n, 242n
possession, 160, 225
Pot-Bouille (Zola), 441–2
potlatch, 65, 575, 583
Poulain de la Barre, François, 10–11, 123–4, 152
"poussière, La" ("Dust") (Audry), 475–6, 672n
power, 293
    will for, 216n
Pradon, Jacques, 123
praying mantis myth, 33, 187n, 216, 267, 272, 523, 651
preagricultural society, 71–5
pregnancy, 72, 138, 152–3, 165, 297–9, 316, 326, 386, 407, 439, 465, 533–48, 558, 568, 569, 602, 603, 619, 630, 648, 728
    "breeders" and enjoyment of, 539, 543, 554
    control of, 524, 533
    cravings in, 542–3, 544
    dependency and, 547–8
    as diminishment of self, 546
    fantasies of, 369
    fear of, 398–9, 401, 533
    fulfillment in, 544
    girls' discovery of, 312–13, 323, 330–1
    last state of, 547
    pains of, 450
    physical manifestations of, 540–1
    as play, 299
    of prostitutes, 610
    relationship with mother and, 535–6
"Prelude" (Mansfield), 351, 494–5
Prévost, Marcel, 456, 490–1, 518
Prie, Mme de, 120
priests, 589, 590, 710–11
primitive society, 71–80, 85, 129, 167, 172, 178, 206, 310, 386, 440
Prince Charming, 155, 200, 201, 208, 341, 359–60, 381, 612, 628, 695
privileged wife, 93–4
procreation, 77–8, 83, 87, 167, 297–9, 384, 650
professions, 154, 300, 760n
    men in, 522
    women in, 144, 345, 357, 381, 444, 723, 739
progesterone, 40, 42
proletariat, 6, 8, 9, 12, 64, 66, 68, 129, 132, 135, 141, 751
    see also working class
Prometheus, 162, 303
property, 65, 454, 469
    collective, 76, 77
    community, 96
    feudalism and, 107, 109
    landed, 140, 468
    marriage and, 442
    personal, 140

private, 12, 63, 64, 65, 87, 90, 91, 94, 110, 112, 130, 149
    and subordination, 110
    woman as, 87, 129, 173, 176, 204
    women's, 94, 95, 99, 102, 107
prostitutes, prostitution, 95, 96–8, 103, 112–14, 121, 142, 149, 155, 201, 257, 386, 396, 432, 441, 574, 577, 599–612, 652–3
    art and, 611–12
    clients of, 608–9
    fantasies of, 368, 491, 603, 623
    gender double-standard for, 652–3
    homosexuality among, 605, 607–8, 616
    as morally adapted to their condition, 609–10
    motives for, 600–5
    pimps and, 604n, 605–7, 614, 728
    poor material conditions for, 610
    sacred, 96–7, 171
    solidarity among, 608
Protestants, 713
Proudhon, Mme, 132, 519
Proudhon, Pierre-Joseph, 131–2, 142, 233, 443n, 451, 519
Proust, Marcel, 332, 696, 704–5, 750
psychasthenia, 369, 491, 674, 686
Psyche, 195–6
psychiatry, 333–4, 566
psychoanalysis, 49–61, 67–8, 211, 291, 324, 421, 541, 602, 753, 762
psychoanalysts, 187, 287, 411, 419, 420, 427, 457, 476, 552, 569, 675, 685
Psychoanalytical Journal, 327
psychophysiological parallelism, 44–5
psychophysiology, 49, 750
psychoses, 216, 321, 425, 491, 678
Ptolemy Philopator, 95
puberty, 311, 623
    in boys, 320, 329
    in girls, 39, 44, 172, 311, 320–1, 342–3, 345, 369, 623, 667, 762
Pure, abbé de, 136
Pyrrhus et Cinéas (de Beauvoir), 699n
Pythagoras, 89, 185, 208, 214
Pythia, 170, 262

Qi (psychoanalytic subject), 491
Quakers, 144, 145
queens, 115, 118, 150
querelle des femmes, 115–17, 149, 208

Ra, 85, 302
Rabelais, François, 123, 171n, 286
Rachel, 616, 677, 742

Racine, Jean, 504, 751
racism, 751
Radegunda, Saint, 115
Rambouillet, Mme de, 119
Rank, Otto, 668
rape, 412
   fantasies of, 468, 590, 623
   fear of, 330, 331, 335–6, 359
   marital, 459
   sexual initiation and, 384, 394, 395–6
rationalism, 4, 67, 171, 185
real woman, 131–2, 142, 237, 273, 725, 734, 761
Récamier, Juliette, 694
Regiment of Women (Dane), 357
regimine principium, De (Thomas Aquinas),
   112–13
Regnard, Jean-François, 123
Régnier, Mathurin, 123
reine morte, La (*Dead Queen, The*)
   (Montherlant), 224, 227
religion, 76, 82, 84, 85, 91, 94, 139, 142, 500,
   687, 699, 721
   chastity and, 206
   love and, 709–17
   male dominance of, 303–5
   marriage and, 95, 100
   mysticism of women in, 108–9, 150, 304–5
   nature of, 49
   older women and, 624–5
   positivist, 129
   women's role in, 10–11, 86, 89, 104, 151, 182,
      185, 189, 640–1, 659–61
Renaissance, 121–2, 149, 612
   Italian, 117–19
Renard, Jules, 557
repopulation, 147
reproduction, 440, 524
   in animals vs. women, 76
   as burden, 72–3
   individuality and, 33–4, 38, 46
   ontological grounding of, 24
   social importance of, 66
Restoration, 128
Reweliotty, Irène, 378, 684, 686
Rhea, 79, 85
Riario, Girolamo, 117
Richard, Marthe, 636
Richardson, Samuel, 251
Richelieu, Cardinal, 119, 151
Richepin, Jean, 209
Richer, Léon, 141
rights, 100
   public v. private, 107
   women's, 75
Rig-Veda, 80
Rilke, Rainer Maria, 470

Rimbaud, Arthur, 248n, 251, 751, 764
Rodin, Auguste, 470
Rogers, Ginger, 578
Rohan, Duchess of, 118
Roland, Marie-Jeanne, 127, 151, 377
Rollin, Charles, 124
Roman Catholic Church, 138–9, 139n, 142, 146,
   189, 195, 237, 246, 262, 304–5, 456, 524,
   661, 715, 741
   on abortion, 525–6
Roman de la Rose, 115–17
Roman Republic, 101, 103
Romanticism, 453
Rome, 85, 89, 99–103, 105, 114, 136, 149, 171,
   173, 187–8, 195, 205, 208, 302, 386, 409,
   440n, 458, 521
Romulus, 188
Room of One's Own, A (Woolf), 120–1
rouge et le noir, Le (*The Red and the Black*)
   (Stendahl), 273
Rougemont, Denis de, 421
Rousseau, Jean-Jacques, 124, 233, 427, 443n,
   707, 748
Roy, Jean-Edouard, 526
Rueling, Anna, 607
Russia, 8, 81
   see also Soviet Union
Russian Revolution, 151
Russian Union for Women's rights, 146
Russo-Japanese War, 146

Sabina, 102–3
Sabine women, 100, 188
Sacher-Masoch, Leopold von, 211
Sachs, Maurice, 286
sacred prostitution, 96–7, 171
sacrifices, 72
Sade, Donatien-Alphonse-François, marquis
   de, 211, 413
sadism, 288, 308, 367, 412, 413, 425, 432, 450,
   606–7, 660, 732
   in mothers, 557, 558, 596
   towards women, 526
sadomasochism, 366–7, 476, 478
Sainte-Beuve, Charles-Augustin, 594, 713
Saint-Evremond, Charles de Marguetel de
   Saint-Denis de, 123
saints, 115, 189, 210, 304, 352, 361
Saint-Simon, Henri, Saint-Simonians, 122, 130,
   131, 139, 141, 245, 251, 453
Salome, 204
salons, 583–4, 634, 638, 675
Samivel (Paul Gayet-Tancrède), 176n
San Celso, Caterina di, 118
Sand, George, 131, 146, 151n, 423, 434, 453

Sandor (case study), 425–7, 428, 434, 572n
Sappho, 98, 148
Sartre, Jean-Paul, 24, 46, 49–50, 55, 148n, 277, 289, 413, 641n, 690n
Satan, 211
satire, 103, 117, 127, 136, 442
Saussure, Ferdinand de, 287n, 291–2
Sauvage, Cécile, 519, 545–6, 549, 554, 683, 687, 701
Scandinavia, 304n, 390, 746
Schiller, Johann Christoph Friedrich von, 338
Schopenhauer, Arthur, 113, 180, 229
Schumann, Clara, 733n
Schumann, Robert, 733n
Schurman, Mlle de, 229
Schwob, Marcel, 210n, 631
Scott, Geoffrey, 516–17
Scudéry, Madeleine de, 119
seduction, 155, 381, 592, 593, 601, 654, 726, 729, 741
  arousal and, 349
  by children, 284, 285, 286
  by man, 729
  man's ambivalence towards, 370
  new, 704
  refusal of, 365
  by woman, 729
Ségur, Mme de, 192, 303, 362, 557
self, cult of the, 351
self-adoration, 355, 688, 741
self-control, women's, 347
self-effacement, 690
self-indulgence, 568
self-mutilation, 366–7
  in mystics, 714–15
self-punishment, 411, 413, 538
self-sufficiency, 737
  limits on, 347
semen, 31
Semitic peoples, 79, 85
Seneca, 103
Seneca Falls Convention, 144
Senghor, Leopold Sédar, 176n
sensuality, 388, 389, 431, 471, 621, 643, 661, 765
sentimentality, 161, 267
separation, 441
  children's response to, 284–5
seraglios, 95
serfs, 110
Serreau, Geneviève, 527, 530
Sertillanges, Père, 142
servants, prostitution and, 601
servant wife, 93–4
Seven Pillars of Wisdom (Lawrence), 748
seventeenth century, 119, 121, 123–4, 151
Sévigné, Mme de, 119, 136, 561

Sèvres, 346, 432, 738–9
sex-brain opposition, 180
sex determination, 30–1
sexes
  differentiation of, 21, 22–4, 37, 43–4
  hierarchy of, 71, 301–4
  in primitive society, 71–5
  separation of, 35
sexual attraction, 569
  aging and, 619
sexual bipotentiality, 30
sexual desire, 59, 182, 390, 451, 458, 505, 653
  aggressive male, 392, 413
  anxiety and, 368
  caution and, 398–9
  children's, 283
  disgust and, 368–9, 389, 398
  love and, 685, 699
  of lovers, 593
  male, 386, 390, 405, 423, 650, 652, 654
  by others, 704–5
  positive, 391
  prostitution and, 600
  women's, 592
sexual differentiation, 76
  in children, 283
sexual freedom, 81, 404, 444, 457, 596, 730, 741, 760
sexual initiation, 383–416, 425, 456, 457–66, 459, 461, 464, 485n, 486, 593, 601–2, 603, 762
  and distaste for married life, 485–91
  healthy, 404
  traumas resulting from, 399–404
sexual initiative, 35, 36, 48
sexuality, 21–2, 23, 37, 68, 273, 519, 685, 688, 766
  awakening of, 369
  as basis of Freudianism, 53
  beauty and, 611
  class and, 601
  destiny and, 363, 754
  disavowing of, 364–6
  equality in, 763
  excitement and desire in, 317
  female dependence in, 385–6
  freedom and, 511
  gender double standard regarding, 652–3
  girls' reactions to emerging, 313–40, 603
  in human life, 55–6
  innocence and, 167
  love and, 690
  in mystic ecstasies, 711–13
  myths of, 162
  passivity and, 389, 411–15
  in pathological and normal behavior, 212

sexuality *(continued)*
  reciprocity and, 415
  unsatisfied, 556, 667
  woman's consciousness and, 62
  working woman and, 726–7
sexual maturity, 405
sexual pleasure, 171, 268, 269, 307, 383–4, 385,
    390, 410, 411, 413, 450–1, 458, 644, 654,
    733
  feigning of, 501, 608, 614, 654
  male and female assymetry in, 415
  moral inhibitions vs., 405–7, 620
  pain and, 411–12
  reproductive function and, 450
  of wives, 457, 462
  woman as insatiable, 408–9, 451n, 626
  woman's peak of, 415, 620, 625
sexual reproduction, 26
sexual sublimation, 367
sexual subordination, 601
Shakespeare, William, 193
Shaw, George Bernard, 12, 130
shrews, 506, 515, 596
shyness, 321, 347
Sibyl, 170
Sido, 477, 490, 561, 584, 706
Sido (Colette), 375n, 477n
Siena, 115, 118
Sieyès, Emmanuel-Joseph, 667
Silesius, Angelus, 691
Simon, Jules, 132
Simonides of Amorgos, 98
sin, 185–6, 765
Sismondi, Jean-Charles Leonard Simonde de,
    133
sisters, older, 300, 348
sixteenth century, 118–19
slavery, 9, 63, 66, 97, 104, 159, 267, 271
  abolition of, 130, 764
  domestic, 601
  of husband, 522
  of man, 661
  master and, 74, 86–7
  opposition to, 144, 150
  polygamy and, 441
  of prostitutes, 605–6
  to reproduction in lower organisms, 32–3
  in U.S., 8, 150, 599, 641
  of women, 46, 62, 63, 64, 66, 86, 89, 91, 94,
    98–9, 107, 125, 129, 131, 146, 147, 149, 156,
    160, 201, 231, 274, 414, 440, 506, 513, 515,
    569, 592, 600, 614, 627, 651, 653n, 657,
    684, 696, 700–1, 726, 730, 733, 753, 756,
    757
sleep, 696–8
Sleeping Beauty, 200, 201, 208, 305, 306

Snow White, 192, 305, 306
social contexts, 48, 61, 62, 341, 415
socialism, 64, 66, 67, 146, 161, 721
  feminism and, 131, 141
  utopian, 130
Socialist Congress of 1879, 141
social life, 570, 572–98, 684
  calls and obligations of, 581–2
  clothing and appearance in, 571–81
  communication lacking in, 584
  of couples, 571
  entertaining in, 582–3
  of men, 153
  representation in, 571, 584
  woman as organizer of, 571
Society of Republican and Revolutionary
    Women, 127
solitude, 352, 444, 662, 681, 703, 733
  social life unable to alleviate, 584
Solomon, 95
Solon, 97
songe, Le (*The Dream*) (Montherlant), 215n,
    217n, 220n, 225
Songe du verger, 111
Song of Songs, 175, 356, 389
"Sonnet to Happiness," 468
sons
  mothers and, 560–1, 564
  older women and, 627–30
Sons and Lovers (Lawrence), 230n, 234n, 236n,
    536
sons-in-law, 631–2
Sophia, 196, 252
Sophocles, 164
Sorel, Cécile, 669, 672, 675, 681
soulier de satin, Le (*The Satin Slipper*)
    (Claudel), 238n, 239n, 241n, 242n, 244n,
    245
Souvenirs (Leblanc), 513
Soviet Union, 66, 146–8, 155, 760
  marriage in, 439
  women in, 64, 67, 761
  see also Russia
Spain, 119, 195, 304n, 390, 611, 715
Spanish Inquisition, 164
Sparta, 66–7, 96, 130, 146, 161, 176, 440, 628
sperm, 23, 25, 26, 27–9, 30, 31, 33, 35, 38, 72,
    387, 398, 399, 730
spermatogenesis, 30, 31, 34, 37
sphinx, woman as, 209, 264, 270
spiders, 33
Spinoza, Baruch, 658
spontaneity, 663, 743–4
sports, 345, 381, 390, 521, 761
  lesbians and, 423
  limitations on girls and, 343

Staël, Mme (Anne-Louise-Germaine) de, 131, 423, 435*n*, 517, 543, 597, 626, 676–8, 680, 726, 729

Stampa, Gaspara, 118

Stein, Gertrude, 435

Steinbeck, John, 175, 470

Stekel, Wilhelm, 58–9, 288, 289, 323, 324, 332–3, 337, 340, 363, 387–8, 393, 398–408, 421–2, 424, 435, 448, 451*n*, 459, 460, 461*n*, 464–8, 494, 495, 504–5, 533, 537, 541, 555, 562–3, 566, 589–90, 623, 673–4, 688–9

Stendhal, Marie-Henri Beyle, 152, 200, 212*n*, 252–61, 263–5, 273, 364, 414, 454, 500, 518, 640, 662, 694, 707, 732, 745, 746, 761

Steno, Nicolas, 25

stepmother, 192, 267

sterility, 78*n*, 170, 178, 736

Stern, Daniel, 131

Stevens, Doris, 145

stigmata, 715–16

stoicism, 642, 658

Stowe, Harriet Beecher, 144, 150

subjectivity, 37, 176, 206, 230, 260, 262–3, 270, 271, 284, 293, 334, 344, 411, 413, 419, 428, 504, 538, 653, 669, 684, 726
   in children, 283, 311
   renunciation of, 723
   women lacking in, 639

sublimation, 212, 709

suicide, 649

Sulpicia, 103

superego, 51, 55, 68

Susa, 79

süsse Mädel (sweet Viennese girl) (psychoanalytic subject), 337–40, 402–4

Swift, Jonathan, 178, 222

Switzerland, 109, 152

Sylvie (Breton), 247

sympathetic nervous system, 647, 657

syphilis, 602, 610

taboos, 91, 167, 170, 187, 192, 325, 367, 391, 398, 404, 762

Talma, Julie, 120

Taming of the Shrew, The (Shakespeare), 193

Tarquinius, 99

technology, 62–6, 68, 84, 639, 650

Temps Modernes, Les, 527, 604

Tencin, Mme de, 120

Tenderness (Bataille), 597

Teresa of Avila, Saint, 118, 120, 150, 304–5, 377, 659, 711–13, 716, 750

termites, 30, 32, 33

terre et les rêveries de la volonté, La (*Earth and Reveries of Will*) (Bachelard), 480*n*

Terres étrangères (*Foreign Lands*) (Arland), 698

Tertullian, 104, 186, 198

Tervagne, Simone de, 308*n*, 332, 557

testicles, 30, 31, 40, 55

theater, 676–7

Thérèse Desqueyroux (Mauriac), 463–4, 494*n*, 515, 652*n*

Thomas Aquinas, Saint, 3–4, 5, 11, 23, 105, 112–13, 127, 138, 185*n*, 217

Thousand and One Nights, The, 95, 181, 185, 206, 218

thyades, 171

thyroid deficiency, 349

thyroid gland, 41, 43

Tiamat, 88

Tiberius, emperor of Rome, 103

Tibet, 172

Tilly, comte de, 419–20

Tirolien, Guy, 195*n*

Tito, Josip Broz, 641

To a God Unknown (Steinbeck), 175

Toklas, Alice, 435

Tolstoy, Leo, 309, 350–1, 352, 487–9, 496–7, 506–8, 511, 513, 518, 519, 520, 521, 538, 547, 552, 570, 579, 587*n*, 648–9, 746

Tolstoy, Sophia, 214, 216, 487–9, 493, 496–7, 506, 508, 513, 518–19, 520, 537–8, 552, 565, 579, 584, 648–9

tomboys, 310, 344, 347, 348, 422, 435

"Too Bad" (Parker), 481–2, 508–9, 671–2

tools, 62–6, 68, 72, 75, 84, 86, 148

Tornabuoni, Lucrezia, 118

totalitarian regimes, 161

totems, 65, 76, 77, 82, 764

To the Lighthouse (Woolf), 471*n*, 658

toutouier, Le (Colette), 586–7

Trajan, emperor of Rome, 102

transcendence, 16–17, 66, 68, 73–4, 83, 84, 159, 180, 181, 182, 205, 211, 225, 232–3, 259–60, 262–3, 265, 267, 287, 301, 310, 311, 334, 344, 359, 374, 383, 387, 443, 468–9, 476, 503, 512, 522, 538, 539, 612, 616, 635, 652, 659, 661, 664, 668–9, 684, 690, 697, 702, 709, 713, 721, 723, 748
   clothing and, 722
   customs and fashions vs., 177–8
   erotic, 349
   between lovers, 467
   phallus and, 655, 753–4
   of woman, 416, 656, 698
   women's desire for, 152, 658

transvestism, 422, 424–5, 435, 724

Trepov, Fyodor, 146

Trial, The (Kafka), 748

Tristan, Flora, 131, 151, 643

Tristan legend, 183, 205, 698

troubadours, 115
Troy, 200
Troyes, Chrétien de, 109
true womanhood, 12–13, 15, 295–6
Truquin, Norbert, 133
Tunisia, 92, 177n
twentieth century, 134–5

Uganda, 78n
"Ulalume" (Poe), 196
Ulysses (Joyce), 748
United Nations, equality of women in, 15
United Nations Commission on the Status of
    Women, 148
United States, 4, 136, 139, 140, 155n, 208, 271,
    324, 342, 474, 522, 548, 603, 617, 634, 636,
    681, 726, 735, 746, 757, 761, 851
  alimony in, 441
  birth control in, 399
  blacks in, 6, 7–8, 12, 13, 135, 144, 148, 223,
    311–12, 343–4, 386, 654, 736
  bridge in, 582
  burlesque in, 611
  "catching" a husband in, 447
  Cinderella myth in, 201
  Civil War in, 144, 150, 641
  divorce in, 521
  housework in, 154
  sexual freedom in, 404, 444, 730
  sexuality and marriage in, 404–5, 456–7,
    462
  slavery in, 8, 150, 599
  women's rights and suffragism in, 143–5
  women's wages in, 135
  working women in, 577, 740
unmarried women, 11, 153, 155, 439
  doctors and, 589–90
  domestic expectations of, 725
  legal rights of, 109, 114, 128, 149, 154,
    442–3
  sexuality of, 444
  voting rights for, 141
urination, 313, 334, 337, 398
  position for, 286–7, 288–93, 299, 668n
Ursins, princesse des, 119, 150, 678
usus, 99
uterus, 31, 36, 40, 42, 72, 399, 408
  as central to womanhood, 3, 5, 284
  see also womb

Vagabond, The (Colette), 431, 687, 694, 733
vagina, 172, 210, 384, 397, 401, 402, 403, 464,
    730
  eroticism and, 50, 51, 52, 54, 68

vaginal pleasure, 405–6, 409–10, 418, 451n
vaginismus, 385, 424
Valentino, Rudolph, 591
Valentinois, Béatrice de, 109
Valérie (Krüdener), 676
Valéry, Paul, 196
Valkyries, 172n
Valle-Inclán, Ramón de, 207
Valois, Marguerite de, 122
values
  masculine, 755
  natural hierarchy of, 45
  women and, 61
vampire, woman as, 187, 523
van Gogh, Vincent, 750
Varuna, 188
vases communicants, Les (*Communicating
    Vessels*) (Breton), 247, 248
vassals, 108, 190, 270
  wives as, 485, 515
  woman as, 341–2, 423, 432, 440, 442, 657,
    721, 726–7, 733
vaudeville, 192
Vautel, Clément, 233
Vaux, Clotilde de, 129
Vé, Mlle, 713
Velleian Senate decree, 105, 111
venereal disease, 727–8
Venus, 171, 179
Verlaine, Paul, 192
vertebrates, 30–1, 35
vestal virgins, 102
Vesuvians movement, 131
victimhood, 305–6, 311, 362, 515, 660
Vigée-Lebrun, Elisabeth-Louise, 744
Vignes, H., 42n, 169n
Vigny, Alfred de, 169
ville, La (*The City*) (Claudel), 238n, 239n,
    230n
Villon, François, 179
violence
  in boys, 343, 367, 394
  fear of, 358–9
  in girls, 367
  girls lacking in, 345, 639
  among lesbians, 433
  logic as, 498
  of male desire, 405
  by pimps, 607
  reason as, 651
  in sex, 390–1
  sexual initiation and, 384, 394
  of women's temper, 648
Viollis, Andrée, 747
Vipère au poing (*Viper in the Fist*) (Bazin),
    557

viragoes, 108, 737
Virginia, 100, 103
virginity, 89, 91, 92, 189, 209–10, 217, 267, 318, 359, 390, 393, 395, 399, 400, 401, 404, 442, 457, 460, 516, 590, 593, 601
  agitation and, 388
  in ancient Greece, 386
  female, 56
  loss of, 401, 448, 528
  male, 391
  myths of, 172–4
  in older women, 174
  valuation of, 391
Virgin Mary, 116, 118, 162, 186, 189, 197–8, 203, 304, 338, 465, 539, 690, 715
  cult of, 108, 189
virility, 415, 419, 421, 423, 425, 461, 607, 656, 667, 724, 731, 756
  of boys, 286–7, 329, 334
  girls' envy of, 300–1, 684, 753
  humiliation of, 501
  testing of, 294
  valorization of, 52
  woman's lack of, 217
  in women, 119, 347, 419–20, 424, 425–7, 432–3
viriloid women, 50, 54, 417–18
Vittorini, Elio, 161–2, 185, 190
Viviani, René, 141
Vivien, Renée, 358, 388–9, 429–30, 432
voile noire, La (Le Hardouin), 306
Voix des Femmes, La, 131
Volland, Sophie, 377
Voltaire (François-Marie Arouet), 124
vomiting, in pregnancy, 541–2
voting rights, women's, 140–5, 152, 721
voyeurism, 468
vrilles de la vigne, Les (The Tender Shoot) (Colette), 429
vulvas, 85n

wages
  equal, 147
  women's, 134–5, 154
war, 71–2, 83, 96, 106, 179, 227, 262, 525–6, 615, 645
  prostitution and, 604
  sexual metaphors of, 386
War and Peace (Tolstoy), 309, 350–1, 506–8, 547, 570, 587n, 746
Warens, Françoise-Louise de, 427, 633, 707, 729
warriors, 73–4, 92, 98, 108, 185
  women as, 71–72, 109
water, 163, 166, 202–3

watering hoses, 289
Waves, The (Woolf), 379, 471n
weaning, 284, 287
Weather in the Streets, The (Lehmann), 702
Webb, Mary, 375–6, 380n, 688n, 748
wedding night, 391, 393–4, 454, 457–9, 460–1, 593
weight loss, at puberty, 321, 322–3
Weldon, Mrs., 674
Welles, Orson, 201, 614
Well of Loneliness, The (Hall), 433, 436n
wet dreams, 398
Wharton, Edith, 492–3, 575, 747
white slave trade, 605
Whitman, Walt, 751
Whole, child's desire to return to, 284
widows, 93, 94, 96, 106, 107, 115, 129, 154, 440, 637
  legal rights of, 109
  unexpected possibilities discovered by, 499
Wilde, Oscar, 631
will for power, 216
Wilson, Woodrow, 145
Winchilsea, Lady, 121
wives, 89, 129, 179, 456, 600, 667, 671, 673, 754
  attitudes towards pregnancy in, 533
  autonomy denied to, 484, 511–12
  autonomy of, 513, 520, 521
  boredom of, 514–15, 516, 522, 532
  as burden, 492
  daily routine for, 513–15
  as dependent, 515, 544
  duties of, 441
  erotic attraction and, 505
  eroticism lacking in, 204–5
  frustrations of, 515–20
  "good," 193–4
  husbands defied by, 500–5
  husbands' dominance of, 498–500
  husbands' interests not shared by, 512–13
  independence feigned by, 654
  individuality of, 511–12, 570
  indulgence by, 505–6
  love and neglect of duties in, 700–1
  morality of bourgeois, 120
  as mothers, 192
  as parasites, 127, 130, 149, 382, 443–4, 446, 448, 484, 521, 522, 599–600, 615, 618, 636, 637, 650, 653, 721, 734, 737, 755
  as passive, 654
  pathological attachments by, 495–7
  precarious activities of, 484
  as primary identity, 485
  as property, 596

wives *(continued)*
restrictions on, 95
right to sexual pleasure of, 457, 486
servitude of, 114, 439, 481, 570, 671
sexual double-standard and, 653
sexual frustration of, 726–7
sexuality as service in, 441, 444, 449
sexual pleasure absent in, 462–5, 487–90,
496
stoic pride in, 515–16
subordination of, 110, 128, 492, 493, 513,
569
work and, 147, 154, 513, 523
Wollstonecraft, Mary, 139, 148
woman
active personality of, 424
adulthood in, 300
aging of, 43, 178–9, 415, 427–8, 577–8,
619–37, 706, 726
alienation of, 91–2
altruism in, 264–5, 267–8
ambiguity in condition of, 662
ambivalence towards men by, 655–6
arousal in, 390
autonomy of, 130, 387, 416, 419, 420, 431,
621, 663, 723, 735, 765
autonomy vs. Otherness of, 294–5
as Beauty, 249, 252
becoming of, 283
blind faith in, 642
boredom of, 758
brain weight of, 44–5
as burdensome, 759–60
as chained to the household, 111
chances not given to, 152
childhood memories and, 671
"childless," 567
children as pleasure to, 563
Christianity and oppression of, 103–4
complaint by, 646
complicity by, 663
as confined in her sex, 21
contrariness of, 650
"counter-universe" not constructed by,
638–9, 655
couplehood necessary to, 584
as deadly, 183
defeatist attitude of, 647–8, 738–9
defiance by, 726
defining of, 3–5, 21, 29, 31, 45–6, 49, 61, 62,
267–8
dependence of, 130, 131, 159, 321, 411, 412,
522, 596, 639, 650, 654, 663, 681–2, 684,
746, 765
devotion demanded by, 696
dignity of, 728–9

divinization of, 161
as domestic animal, 222
domination of, 188, 193
domineering, 424, 468, 731
as double, 765
easy, 730
emancipation of, 131, 261, 723, 754, 764
emotions in, 432, 558
equality of, 14, 36, 45, 62, 63–4, 72, 96,
101–2, 140, 141, 144, 145, 147, 261, 264,
273, 440, 569, 659, 722, 723, 732, 755, 760,
761, 763–6
as erotic object, 572, 577, 579–80
erotic peak of, 415
as eternal child, 639, 686
family life and profession balanced by, 156
as flesh, 261, 268
freedom of, 737, 757, 766
free movement and, 748–9
function of, 14n
"good," 254–5
as hero's amusement, 228
hostility between men and, 753–60
as hypocrite, 271
impurity of, 167–8
incompleteness of, 105
independence of, 547, 637, 685, 723, 727,
734, 738–9
indictments against, 638
individuality of, 38, 44, 46, 458
inequality of, 95, 152, 758
as "inessential," 23
inferiority complex in, 53–4
inferiority of, 10–12, 14, 21, 220, 568, 659,
639, 734, 737, 754, 765
infidelity condemned in, 598
initiative taken by, 729
intellectual, 633, 725–6, 738–9
irresponsibility of, 575
lateness by, 649–50
law and, 134, 154
liberation of, 274, 530–1, 575, 664, 746,
756
literary identifications of, 672
logical reasoning not learned by, 497–8,
640, 650–1, 654
as "lost sex," 274
in love, 683–708, 757–8
lying and dissimulation by, 271, 585, 653–4
magic reality of, 656
male judgment of, 392–3
as man's invention, 212–13
man's own reflection in, 263, 264
man's reciprocal relations with, 263–4
masculine, 357, 359
masculine authority accepted by, 640

as mediator, 213, 262
mediocrity of, 749
men's dreams dreamed by, 162
misunderstood feeling of, 674
as monogamous, 733
mystery of, 222, 253, 263, 268–71, 311, 591
mysticism and, 170–1, 377, 709–17
myth of, 80, 160–213
nature and, 83
as negative of man, 5, 6
obedience owed by, 639
as object, 416, 671, 723
as Other, 6–10, 12–14, 17, 44, 48, 60–1, 67,
     75, 79, 80, 82, 83, 86, 88–9, 149, 159, 160,
     161–3, 176, 181, 182, 183, 186–7, 199, 200,
     203, 206, 209, 213, 237, 245, 246, 252,
     262–5, 266, 270–1, 273–4, 283–4, 348, 357,
     411, 653, 755
passivity of, 25–6, 38, 262, 304n, 389–91,
     414, 418, 419, 424, 428, 431, 433, 639, 648,
     653, 662, 664, 668, 669, 685, 689, 729–30,
     754, 763
as perfidious, 209
as physical being, 643–4
physical limitations of, 46, 62, 65–6, 68,
     71–2, 86, 231, 342, 344, 647, 728
physiological destiny of, 619
pleasing of men by, 156, 620, 722, 726
pleasure as binding to, 733
as poetry, 247–52, 262
as possession, 160, 335, 440
power and, 47–8
powerlessness of, 649
as prey, 363–4, 383, 419, 423, 554, 688, 690,
     723, 729, 754, 755
as prisoners, 257
privileges of, 111
as property, 90–1, 106, 129, 204, 206
protection of, 758
protest by, 649–51
as regenerator, 245, 251
religious feeling towards man by, 305
renunciation by, 469, 620
repetition by, 73, 568, 640, 644, 657, 661
repressed, 596
rescuing of, 200
resignation in, 642, 757
respect for, 105
rights of, 152
rivalry and jealousy among, 587–8, 616
roles played by, 432
scorn for, 108
self-assurance lacking in, 740
self-expression by, 742
self-forgetfulness needed by, 740–1
servility of, 726

servitude of, 205
as sex object, 572, 574, 577, 579–80, 621
sexual initiation of, 383–5, 391–416
sexuality as service by, 386, 597, 653, 721,
     722, 760
as sexually unsatisfied, 450, 643
as sexual prey, 416
sexual satisfaction sought by, 727–31
situation and character of, 638–64
slavery and, 74–5
social life organized by, 571
solidarity lacking among, 130, 141
spiritualization of, 194–5
subjection of, 156, 270
subjugation of, 44, 75, 83, 86, 88, 105, 129,
     201, 377, 397, 413
submission and subservience of, 54, 74, 99,
     124, 161, 189, 193, 262, 263, 264, 415, 423,
     462, 643, 651, 658, 693, 722, 729, 731, 763
subordination of, 43–4, 75, 89, 104, 105, 110,
     233, 237, 279
suffering and, 268, 516, 528, 548n, 642
sympathetic nature of, 663
temptations to, 685
as thing, 89
timidity of, 745
traditional destiny of, 279
as trained to center on love, 592
treachery of, 205
veneration of, 82, 262
virile characteristics in, 40
virility lacking in, 217
vocation of, 757
waiting by, 305–6, 649–50
worry by, 645–6
young, 732
womb, 164–5, 181, 194, 261, 284, 544, 657, 730
Women in Love (Lawrence), 229n, 230n, 234n
Women's Party, 145
Women's Social and Political Union, 143
Women's Suffrage, 141
Woolf, Virginia, 120–1, 379, 380, 470–1, 519,
     582–3, 634, 658, 746, 748
work
     appearance and elegance for women
          required at, 154
     freedom not found in, 721
     marriage and, 733
     by men, 519
     motherhood and, 523, 568–9
     by women, 63–4, 66, 132–6, 144–9, 153–6,
          274, 346, 439, 519, 523, 577, 603, 604,
          610n, 615, 619, 620 643, 685, 721–2, 725–7,
          733–42, 757, 760, 761
workers, 84, 86, 87, 147, 639
     exploitation of, 721–72

workers (continued)
  political action and heroism in, 661
  women as, 11–12, 132–6, 144–9, 153–6, 274,
    643
working class, 757
  bourgeois women lacking in solidarity with,
    130, 141, 663
  economic power of, 127
  emancipation of, 130, 131, 643
  independence of women in, 126, 127, 149,
    643n
  marriage equality in, 110, 114–15, 126
  menopause and, 619
  sexuality and, 601
  see also proletariat
World War I, 143, 418
World War II, 147, 346
Wright, Richard, 736
writers, 120–1, 545, 742–51
  lesbian, 424
  in Sweden, 145

Wuthering Heights (Brontë), 693, 746, 747
Wylie, Philip, 155n, 191, 201, 635
Wyoming, 144

Xanthippe, 99, 205, 521
Xenophon, 98

Yver, Colette, 733

Zasulich, Vera, 146, 150
Zetkin, Clara, 146
Zeus, 85, 163
Zola, Emile, 313, 441–2, 615–17
Zuckerman, Solly, Baron, 47
Zuylen, Belle de (Isabelle de Charrière),
    377, 427, 516–18, 597, 633, 636,
    642
zygotes, 22

THE PHILOSOPHY OF JEAN-PAUL SARTRE
edited by Robert Denoon Cumming

Here in one volume is a unique, essential overview of the philosophy of Jean-Paul Sartre. Extensive excerpts from Sartre's major philosophical and literary writings—*Being and Nothingness, The Critique of Dialectical Reason, Nausea, No Exit, The Flies, St. Genet,* as well as lesser-known works—are organized systematically, illustrating the key elements of his thinking.

Philosophy

NO EXIT AND THREE OTHER PLAYS
by Jean-Paul Sartre

No Exit, Sartre's most well-known existentialist play, shows the great novelist and philosopher's mastery over drama. *No Exit* is his unforgettable portrayal of hell; *The Flies,* a modern reworking of the Electra-Orestes story. *Dirty Hands* depicts a young intellectual torn between theory and praxis, and *The Respectful Prostitute* is a scathing attack on American racism.

Drama

RESISTANCE, REBELLION, AND DEATH
by Albert Camus

In the speech he gave upon accepting the Nobel Prize in Literature in 1957, Albert Camus said that a writer "cannot serve today those who make history; he must serve those who are subject to it." And in these twenty-three political essays, he demonstrates his commitment to history's victims, from the fallen *maquis* of the French Revolution to the casualties of the Cold War. *Resistance, Rebellion, and Death* displays Camus' rigorous moral intelligence addressing issues that range from colonial warfare in Algeria to the social cancer of capital punishment.

Essays

THE MYTH OF SISYPHUS
by Albert Camus

One of the most influential works of the twentieth century, *The Myth of Sisyphus and Other Essays* is a crucial exposition of existentialist thought. Influenced by works such as *Don Juan* and the novels of Kafka, these essays begin with a meditation of suicide; the question of living or not living in a universe devoid of order or meaning. With lyric eloquence, Albert Camus brilliantly posits a way out of despair, reaffirming the value of personal existence, and the possibility of life lived with dignity and authenticity.

Philosophy

THE HISTORY OF SEXUALITY
by Michel Foucault

Why has there been such a veritable explosion of discussion about sex in the West since the seventeenth century? How did we ever come to believe that our increasing talk about it would make us feel less repressed? In *The History of Sexuality,* his ambitious multipart study, Michel Foucault offers a dazzling, iconoclastic exploration of why we feel compelled to continually analyze and discuss sex, and of the social and mental mechanisms of power that cause us to direct the question of what we are to what our sexuality is.

Philosophy

VINTAGE BOOKS
Available wherever books are sold.
www.randomhouse.com

val = 1

8 bytes

yis   sun . yo